Step by Step

MICROSOFT®

ADO.NET

STEP BY STEP

PUBLISHED BY
Microsoft Press
A Division of Microsoft Corporation
One Microsoft Way
Redmond, Washington 98052-6399

Library of Congress Cataloging-in-Publication Data
Riordan, Rebecca.
Microsoft ADO.NET Step by Step / Rebecca M. Riordan.
p. cm.
Includes index.
ISBN 0-7356-1236-6
1. Database design. 2. Object oriented programming (Computer science) 3. ActiveX. I. Title.

QA76.9.D26 R56 2002
005.75'85--dc21 2001054641

Printed and bound in the United States of America.

3 4 5 6 7 8 9 QWT 8 7 6 5 4 3

Distributed in Canada by H.B. Fenn and Company Ltd.

A CIP catalogue record for this book is available from the British Library.

Microsoft Press books are available through booksellers and distributors worldwide. For further information about international editions, contact your local Microsoft Corporation office or contact Microsoft Press International directly at fax (425) 936-7329. Visit our Web site at www.microsoft.com/mspress. Send comments to *mspinput@microsoft.com.*

Acquisitions Editor: Danielle Bird
Project Editor: Rebecca McKay

Body Part No. X08-05018

To my very dear friend, Stephen Jeffries

Contents

Introduction

ADO.NET is the data access component of Microsoft's new .NET Framework. Microsoft bills ADO.NET as "an evolutionary improvement" over previous versions of ADO, a claim that has been hotly debated since its announcement. It is certainly true that the ADO.NET object model bears very little relationship to earlier versions of ADO.

In fact, whether you decide to love it or hate it, one fact about the .NET Framework seems undeniable: it levels the playing ground. Whether you've been at this computer game longer than you care to talk about or you're still sorting out your heaps and stacks, learning the .NET Framework will require a major investment. We're *all* beginners now.

So welcome to *Microsoft ADO.NET Step by Step*. Through the exercises in this book, I will introduce you to the ADO.NET object model, and you'll learn how to use that model in developing data-bound Windows Forms and Web Forms. In later topics, we'll look at how ADO.NET interacts with XML and how to access older versions of ADO from the .NET environment.

Since we're all beginners, an exhaustive treatment would be, well, exhausting, so this book is necessarily limited in scope. My goal is to provide you with an understanding of the ADO.NET objects—what they are and how they work together. So fair warning: this book will *not* make you an expert in ADO.NET. (How I wish it were that simple!)

What this book *will* give you is a road map, a fundamental understanding of the environment, from which you will be able to build expertise. You'll know what you need to do to start building data applications. The rest will come with time and experience. This book is a place to start.

Although I've pointed out language differences where they might be confusing, in order to keep the book within manageable proportions I've assumed that you are already familiar with Visual Basic .NET or Visual C# .NET. If you're completely new to the .NET environment, you might want to start with *Microsoft Visual Basic .NET Step by Step* by Michael Halvorson (Microsoft Press, 2002) or *Microsoft Visual C# .NET Step by Step* by John Sharp and Jon Jagger (Microsoft Press, 2002), depending on your language of choice.

The exercises that include programming are provided in both Microsoft Visual Basic and Microsoft C#. The two versions are identical (except for the difference between the languages), so simply choose the exercise in the language of your choice and skip the other version.

Conventions and Features in This Book

You'll save time by understanding, before you start the lessons, how this book displays instructions, keys to press, and so on. In addition, the book provides helpful features that you might want to use.

- Numbered lists of steps (1, 2, and so on) indicate hands-on exercises. A rounded bullet indicates an exercise that has only one step.
- Text that you are to type appears in **bold**.
- Terms are displayed in *italic* the first time they are defined.
- A plus sign (+) between two key names means that you must press those keys at the same time. For example, "Press Alt+Tab" means that you hold down the Alt key while you press Tab.
- Notes labeled "tip" provide additional information or alternative methods for a step.
- Notes labeled "important" alert you to essential information that you should check before continuing with the lesson.
- Notes labeled "ADO" point out similarities and differences between ADO and ADO.NET.
- Notes labeled "Roadmap" refer to places where topics are discussed in depth.
- You can learn special techniques, background information, or features related to the information being discussed by reading the shaded sidebars that appear throughout the lessons. These sidebars often highlight difficult terminology or suggest future areas for exploration.
- You can get a quick reminder of how to perform the tasks you learned by reading the Quick Reference at the end of a lesson.

Using the ADO.NET Step by Step CD-ROM

The *Microsoft ADO.NET Step by Step* CD-ROM inside the back cover contains practice files that you'll use as you complete the exercises in the book. By using the files, you won't need to waste time creating databases and entering sample data. Instead, you can concentrate on how to use ADO.NET. With the files and the step-by-step instructions in the lessons, you'll also learn by doing, which is an easy and effective way to acquire and remember new skills.

System Requirements

In order to complete the exercises in this book, you will need the following software:

- Microsoft Windows 2000 or Microsoft Windows XP
- Microsoft Visual Studio .NET
- Microsoft SQL Server Desktop Engine (included with Visual Studio .NET) or Microsoft SQL Server 2000

This book and practice files were tested primarily using Windows 2000 and Visual Studio .NET Professional; however, other editions of Visual Studio .NET, such as Visual Basic .NET Standard and Visual C# .NET Standard, should also work.

Since Windows XP Home Edition does not include Internet Information Services (IIS), you won't be able to create **local** ASP.NET Web applications (discussed in chapters 12 and 13) using Windows XP Home Edition. Windows 2000 and Windows XP Professional do include IIS.

Installing the Practice Files

Follow these steps to install the practice files on your computer so that you can use them with the exercises in this book.

1. Insert the CD in your CD-ROM drive.

   A Start menu should appear automatically. If this menu does not appear, double-click StartCD.exe at the root of the CD.
2. Click the Getting Started option.
3. Follow the instructions in the Getting Started document to install the practice files and setup SQL Server 2000 or the Microsoft SQL Server Desktop Engine (MSDE).

Using the Practice Files

The practice files contain the projects and completed solutions for the ADO.NET Step by Step book. Folders marked "Finish" contain working solutions. Folders marked "Start" contain the files needed to perform the exercises in the book.

Uninstalling the Practice Files

Follow these steps to remove the practice files from your computer.

1. Insert the CD in your CD-ROM drive.

   A Start menu should appear automatically. If this menu does not appear, double-click StartCD.exe at the root of the CD.
2. Click the Uninstall Practice Files option.
3. Follow the steps in the Uninstall Practice Files document to remove the practice files.

Need Help with the Practice Files?

Every effort has been made to ensure the accuracy of the book and the contents of this CD-ROM. As corrections or changes are collected for this book, they will be placed on a Web page and any errata will also be integrated into the Microsoft online Help tool known as the Knowledge Base. To view the list of known corrections for this book, visit the following page:

http://support.microsoft.com/support/misc/kblookup.asp?id=Q314759

To search the Knowledge Base and review your support options for the book or CD-ROM, visit the Microsoft Press Support site:

http://www.microsoft.com/mspress/support/

If you have comments, questions, or ideas regarding the book or this CD-ROM, or questions that are not answered by searching the Knowledge Base, please send them to Microsoft Press via e-mail to:

mspinput@microsoft.com

or by postal mail to:

Microsoft Press
Attn: Microsoft ADO.NET Step by Step Editor
One Microsoft Way
Redmond, WA 98052-6399

Please note that product support is not offered through the above addresses.

PART 1

Getting Started with ADO.NET

CHAPTER

1

Getting Started with ADO.NET

In this chapter, you'll learn how to:

- ✔ *Identify the primary objects that make up Microsoft ADO.NET are and how they interact*
- ✔ *Create Connection and DataAdapter objects by using the DataAdapter Configuration Wizard*
- ✔ *Automatically generate a DataSet*
- ✔ *Bind control properties to a DataSet*
- ✔ *Load data into a DataSet at run time*

Like other components of the .NET Framework, ADO.NET consists of a set of objects that interact to provide the required functionality. Unfortunately, this can make learning to use the object model frustrating—you feel like you need to learn all of it before you can understand any of it.

The solution to this problem is to start by building a conceptual framework. In other words, before you try to learn the details of how any particular object functions, you need to have a general understanding of what each object does and how the objects interact.

That's what we'll do in this chapter. We'll start by looking at the main ADO.NET objects and how they work together to get data from a physical data store, to the user, and back again. Then, just to whet your appetite, we'll work through building a set of objects and binding them to a simple data form.

On the Fundamental Interconnectedness of All Things

In later chapters in this section, we'll examine each object in the ADO.NET object model in turn. At least in theory. In reality, because the objects are so closely interlinked, it's impossible to look at any single object in isolation.

Roadmap

A roadmap note like this will point you to the discussion of a property or method that hasn't yet been introduced.

Where it's necessary to use a method or property that we haven't yet examined, I'll use roadmap notes, like the one in the margin next to this paragraph, to point you to the chapter where they are discussed.

The ADO.NET Object Model

The figure below shows a simplified view of the primary objects in the ADO.NET object model. Of course, the reality of the class library is more complicated, but we'll deal with the intricacies later. For now, it's enough to understand what the primary objects are and how they typically interact.

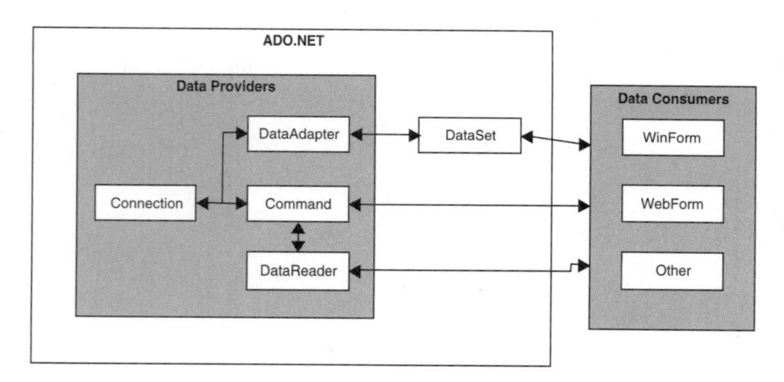

The ADO.NET classes are divided into two components: the Data Providers (sometimes called Managed Providers), which handle communication with a physical data store, and the DataSet, which represents the actual data. Either component can communicate with data consumers such as WebForms and WinForms.

Data Providers

The Data Provider components are specific to a data source. The .NET Framework includes two Data Providers: a generic provider that can communicate with any OLE DB data source, and a SQL Server provider that has been optimized for Microsoft SQL Server versions 7.0 and later. Data Providers for other databases such as Oracle and DB2 are expected to become available, or you can write your own. (You may be relieved to know that we won't be covering the creation of Data Providers in this book.)

The two Data Providers included in the .NET Framework contain the same objects, although their names and some of their properties and methods are different. To illustrate, the SQL Server provider objects begin with SQL (for example, SQLConnection), while the OLE DB objects begin with OleDB (for example, OleDbConnection).

The Connection object represents the physical connection to a data source. Its properties determine the data provider (in the case of the OLE DB Data Provider), the data source and database to which it will connect, and the string to be used during connecting. Its methods are fairly simple: You can open and close the connection, change the database, and manage transactions.

The Command object represents a SQL statement or stored procedure to be executed at the data source. Command objects can be created and executed independently against a Connection object, and they are used by DataAdapter objects to handle communications from a DataSet back to a data source. Command objects can support SQL statements and stored procedures that return single values, one or more sets of rows, or no values at all.

A DataReader is a fast, low-overhead object for obtaining a forward-only, read-only stream of data from a data source. They cannot be created directly in code; they are created only by calling the *ExecuteReader* method of a Command.

The DataAdapter is functionally the most complex object in a Data Provider. It provides the bridge between a Connection and a DataSet. The DataAdapter contains four Command objects: the SelectCommand, UpdateCommand, InsertCommand, and DeleteCommand. The DataAdapter uses the SelectCommand to fill a DataSet and uses the remaining three commands to transmit changes back to the data source, as required.

Microsoft ActiveX Data Objects (ADO)

In functional terms, the Connection and Command objects are roughly equivalent to their ADO counterparts (the major difference being the lack of support for server-side cursors), while the DataReader functions like a firehose cursor. The DataAdapter and DataSet have no real equivalent in ADO.

DataSets

The DataSet is a memory-resident representation of data. Its structure is shown in the figure below. The DataSet can be considered a somewhat simplified relational database, consisting of tables and their relations. It's important to understand, however, that the DataSet is always disconnected from the data source—it doesn't "know" where the data it contains came from, and in fact, it can contain data from multiple sources.

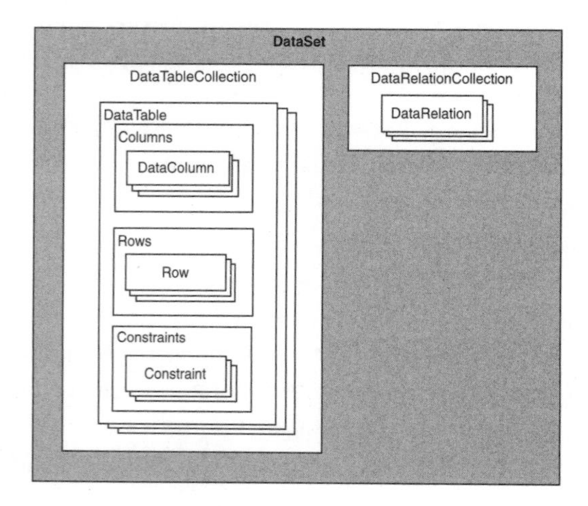

The DataSet is composed of two primary objects: the DataTableCollection and the DataRelationCollection. The DataTableCollection contains zero or more DataTable objects, which are in turn made up of three collections: Columns, Rows, and Constraints. The DataRelationCollection contains zero or more DataRelations.

The DataTable's Columns collection defines the columns that compose the DataTable. In addition to ColumnName and DataType properties, a DataColumn's properties allow you to define such things as whether or not it allows nulls (AllowDBNull), its maximum length (MaxLength), and even an expression that is used to calculate its value (Expression).

The DataTable's Rows collection, which may be empty, contains the actual data as defined by the Columns collection. For each Row, the DataTable maintains its original, current, and proposed values. As we'll see, this ability greatly simplifies certain kinds of programming tasks.

ADO

The ADO.NET DataTable provides essentially the same functionality as the ADO Recordset object, although it obviously plays a very different role in the object model.

The DataTable's Constraints collection contains zero or more Constraints. Just as in a relational database, Constraints are used to maintain the integrity of the data. ADO.NET supports two types of constraints: ForeignKeyConstraints, which maintain relational integrity (that is, they ensure that a child row cannot be orphaned), and UniqueConstraints, which maintain data integrity (that is, they ensure that duplicate rows cannot be added to the table). In addition, the PrimaryKey property of the DataTable ensures entity integrity (that is, it enforces the uniqueness of each row).

Finally, the DataSet's DataRelationCollection contains zero or more DataRelations. DataRelations provide a simple programmatic interface for navigating from a master row in one table to the related rows in another. For example, given an Order, a DataRelation allows you to easily extract the related OrderDetails rows. (Note, however, that the DataRelation itself doesn't enforce relational integrity. A Constraint is used for that.)

Binding Data to a Simple Windows Form

The process of connecting data to a form is called *data binding*. Data binding can be performed in code, but the Microsoft Visual Studio .NET designers make the process very simple. In this chapter, we'll use the designers and the wizards to quickly create a simple data bound Windows form.

important

If you have not yet installed this book's practice files, work through "Installing and Using the Practice Files" in the Introduction, and then return to this chapter.

Adding a Connection and DataAdapter to a Form

Roadmap

We'll examine the Connection object in Chapter 2 and the DataAdapter in Chapter 4.

The first step in binding data is to create the Data Provider objects. Visual Studio provides a DataAdapter Configuration Wizard to make this process simple. Once the DataAdapter has been added, you can check that its configuration is correct by using the DataAdapter Preview window within Visual Studio.

Add a Connection to a Windows Form

1 Open the EmployeesForm project from the Visual Studio Start Page.

2 Double-click Employees.vb (or Employees.cs if you're using C#) in the Solution Explorer to open the form.

Visual Studio displays the form in the form designer.

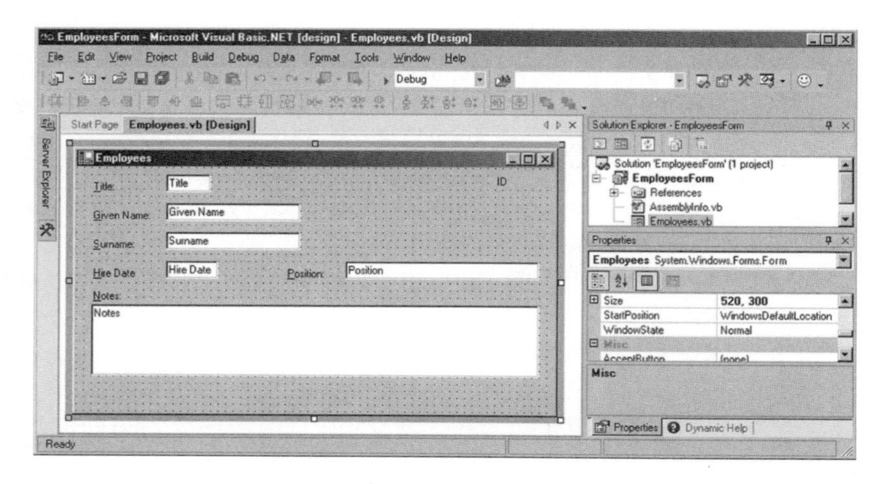

3 Drag a SQLDataAdapter onto the form from the Data tab of the Toolbox.

Visual Studio displays the first page of the DataAdapter Configuration Wizard.

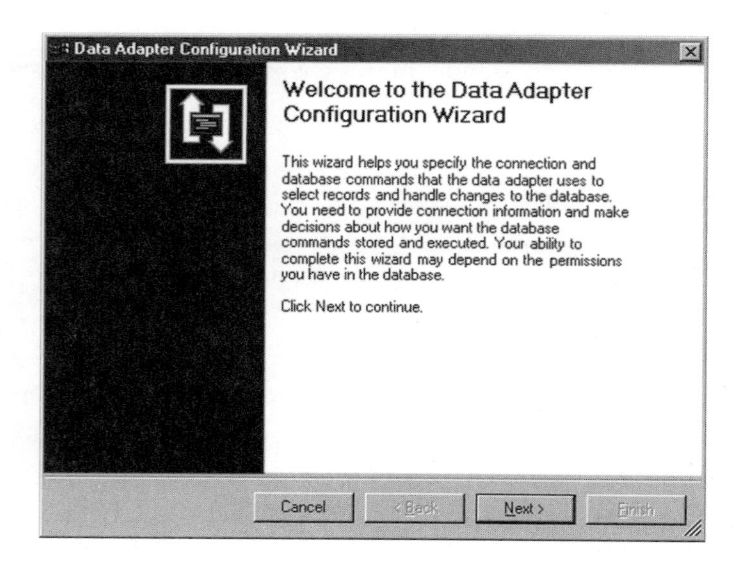

4 Click Next.

The DataAdapter Configuration Wizard displays a page asking you to choose a connection.

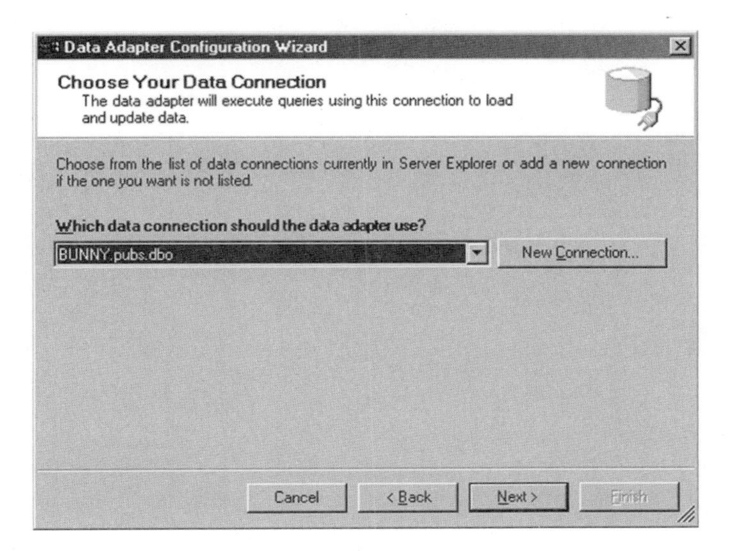

5 Click New Connection.

The Data Link Properties dialog box opens.

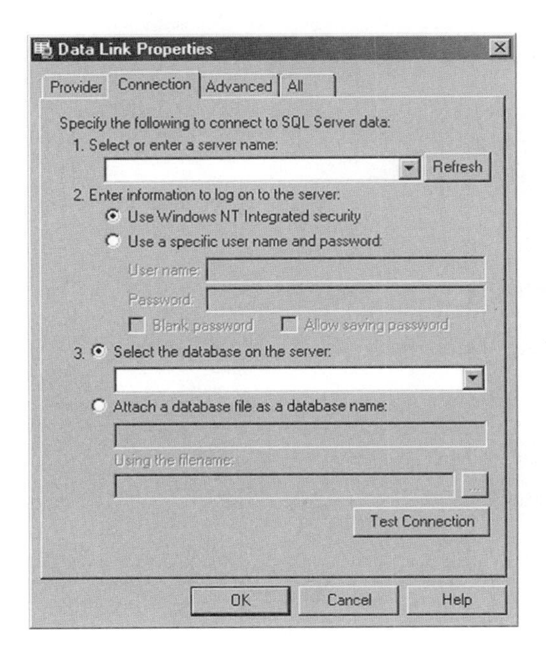

6 Specify the name of your server, the appropriate logon information, select the Northwind database, and then click Test Connection.

The DataAdapter Configuration Wizard displays a message indicating that the connection was successful.

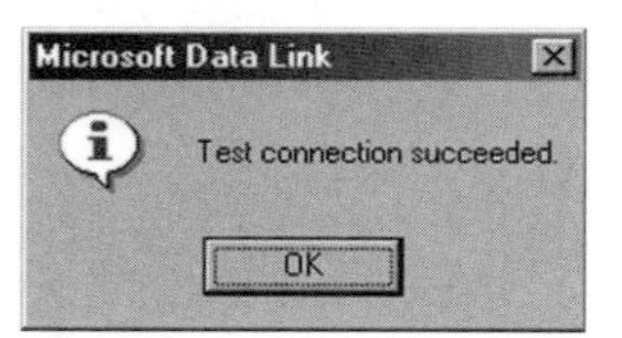

tip

If you're unsure how to complete step 6, check with your system administrator.

7 Click OK to close the message, click OK to close the Data Link Properties dialog box, and then click Next to display the next page of the DataAdapter Configuration Wizard.

The DataAdapter Configuration Wizard displays a page requesting that you choose a query type.

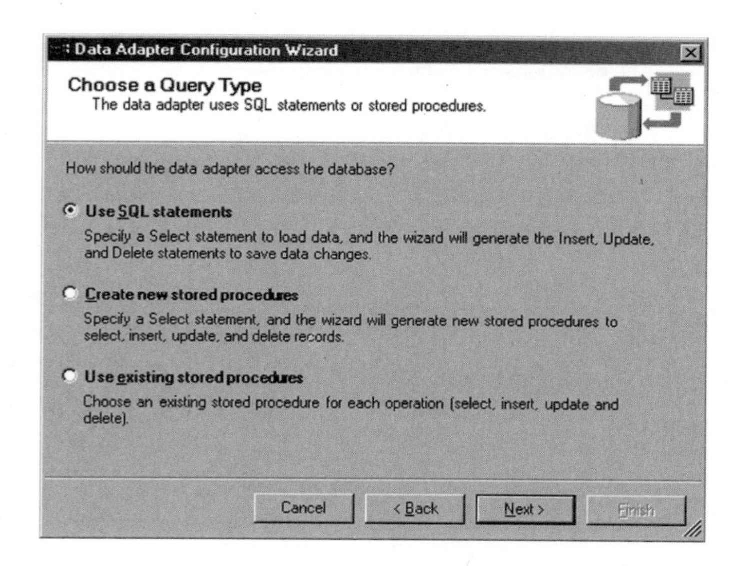

8 Verify that the Use SQL statements option is selected, and then click Next.

The DataAdapter Configuration Wizard displays a page requesting the SQL statement(s) to be used.

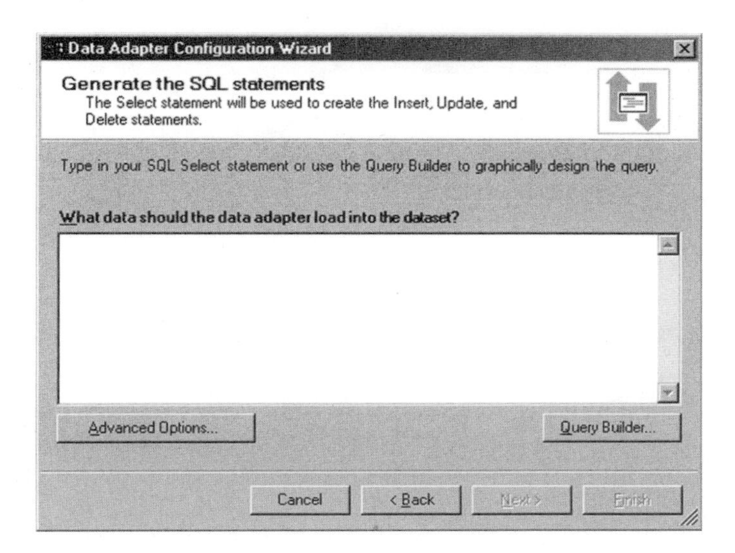

9 Click Query Builder.

The DataAdapter Configuration Wizard opens the Query Builder and displays the Add Table dialog box.

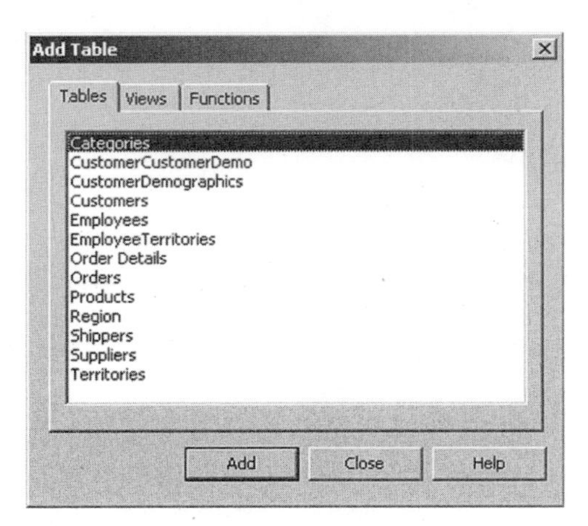

10 Select the Employees table, click Add, and then click Close.

The Add Table dialog box closes, and the Employees table is added to the Query Builder.

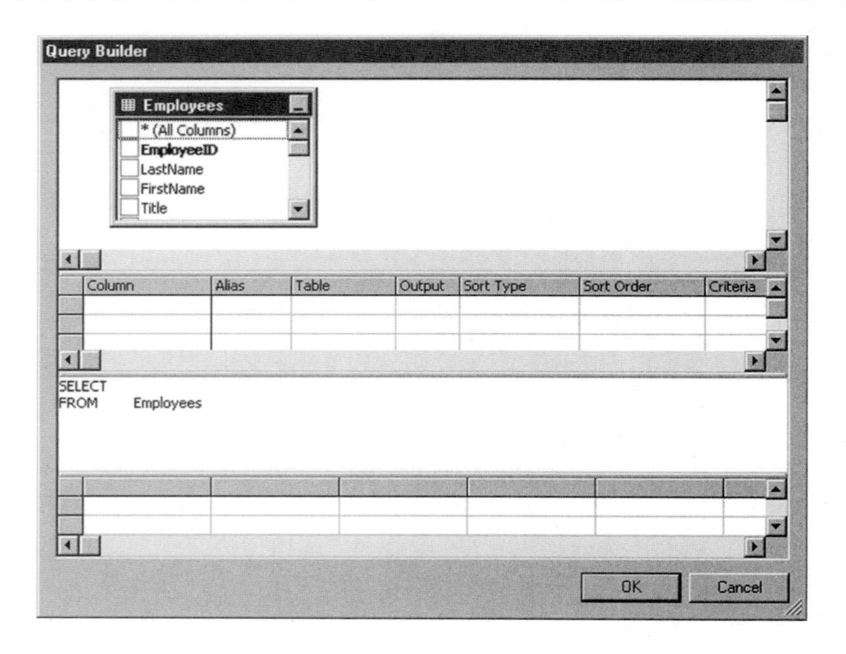

11 Add the following fields to the query by selecting the check box next to the field name in the top pane: *EmployeeID, LastName, FirstName, Title, TitleOfCourtesy, HireDate, Notes.*

The Query Builder creates the SQL command.

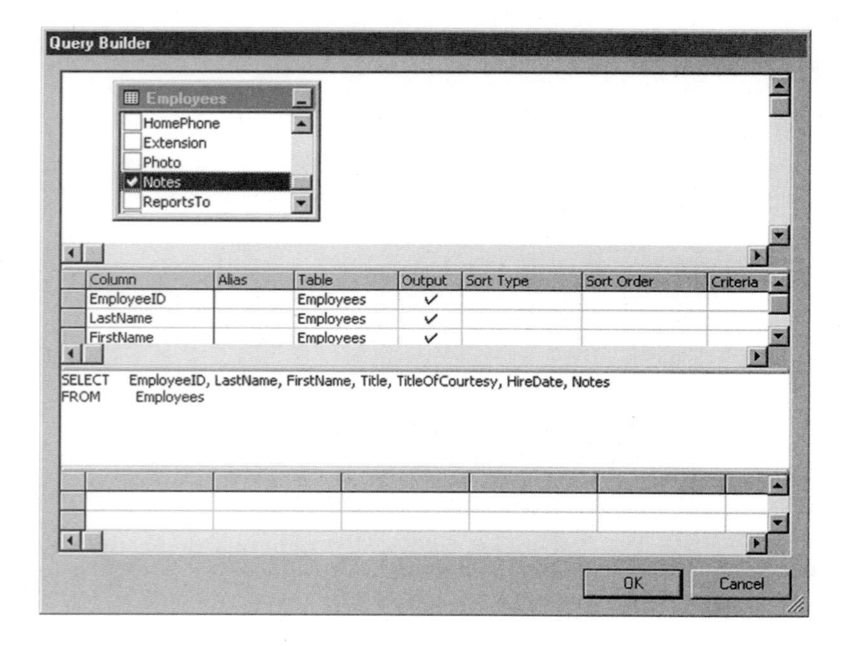

12 Click OK to close the Query Builder, and then click Next.

The DataAdapter Configuration Wizard displays a page showing the results of adding the Connection and DataAdapter objects to the form.

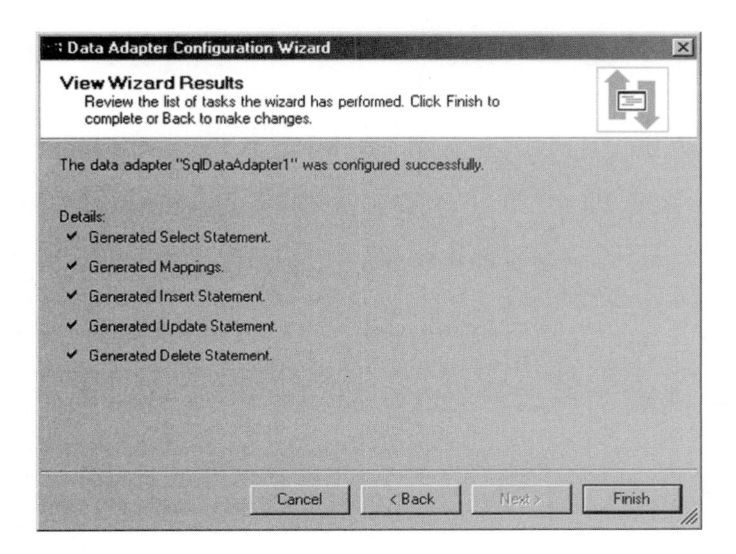

13 Click Finish to close the DataAdapter Configuration Wizard.

The DataAdapter Configuration Wizard creates and configures a SQLDataAdapter and a SQLConnection, and then adds them to the Component Designer.

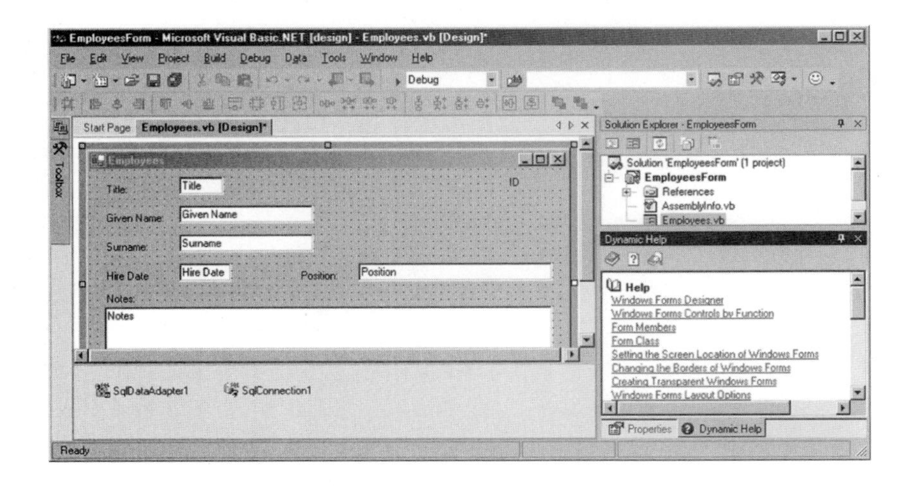

Creating DataSets

Roadmap
We'll examine the DataSet in Chapter 6.

The Connection and DataAdapter objects handle the physical communication with the data store, but you must also create a memory-resident representation of the actual data that will be bound to the form. You can bind a control to almost any structure that contains data, including arrays and collections, but you'll typically use a DataSet.

As with the Data Provider objects, Visual Studio provides a mechanism for automating this process. In fact, it can be done with a simple menu choice, although because Visual Studio exposes the code it creates, you can further modify the basic DataSet functionality that Visual Studio provides.

Create a DataSet

1 On the Data menu, choose Generate Dataset.

The Generate Dataset dialog box opens.

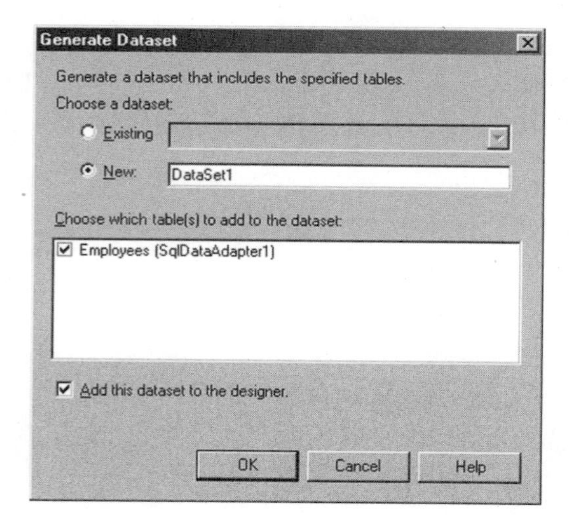

2 In the New text box, type **dsEmployees**.

Generate Dataset

Generate a dataset that includes the specified tables.

Choose a dataset:

Existing

New: dsEmployees

Choose which table(s) to add to the dataset:

Employees (SqlDataAdapter1)

Add this dataset to the designer.

OK Cancel Help

3 Click OK.

Visual Studio creates the DataSet class and adds an instance of it to the bottom pane of the forms designer.

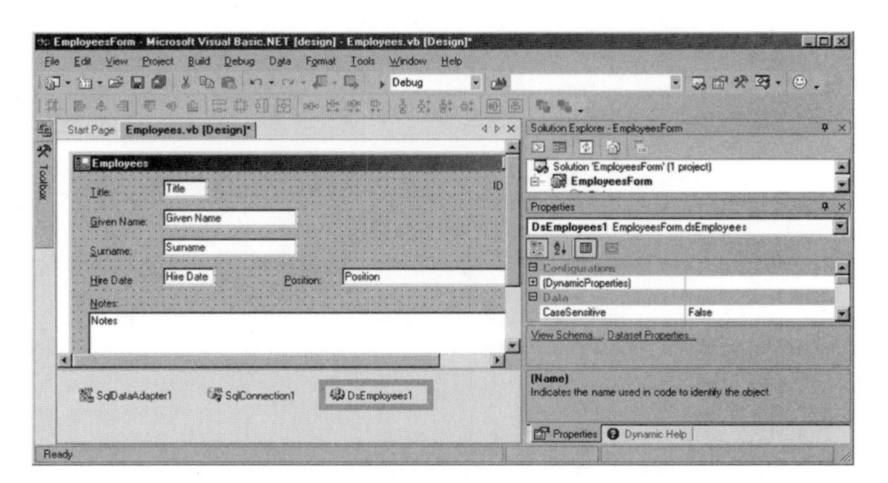

Simple Binding Controls to a DataSet

The .NET Framework supports two kinds of binding: simple and complex. *Simple binding* occurs when a single data element, such as a date, is bound to a control. *Complex binding* occurs when a control is bound to multiple data values, for example, binding a list box to a DataSet that contains a list of Order Numbers.

Roadmap

We'll examine simple and complex data binding in more detail in Chapters 10 and 11.

Almost any property of a control can support simple binding, but only a subset of Windows and WebForms controls (such as DataGrids and ListBoxes) can support complex binding.

Bind the Text Property of a Control to a DataSet

1. Click the txtTitle text box in the forms designer to select it.
2. Click the plus sign next to DataBindings to expand the DataBindings properties.
3. Click the drop-down arrow for the Text property.

   Visual Studio displays a list of available data sources.
4. In the list of available data sources for the Text property, click the plus sign next to the DsEmployees1 data source, and then click the plus sign next to the Employees DataTable.

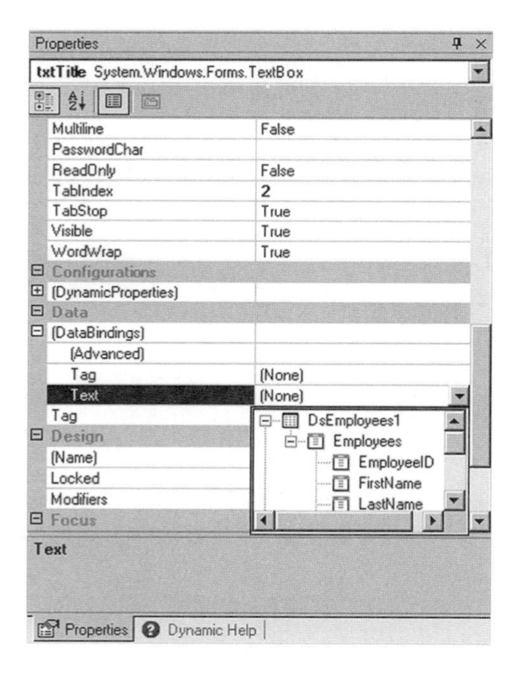

5. Click the TitleOfCourtesy column to select it.
6. Repeat steps 1 through 5 to bind the Text property of the remaining controls to the columns of the Employees DataTable, as shown in the following table.

Control	DataTable Column
lblEmployeeID	EmployeeID
txtGivenName	FirstName
txtSurname	LastName
txtHireDate	HireDate
txtPosition	Title
txtNotes	Notes

Loading Data into the DataSet

We now have all the components in place for manipulating the data from our data source, but we have one task remaining: We must actually load the data into the DataSet.

If you're used to working with data bound forms in environments such as Microsoft Access, it may come as a surprise that you need to do this manually. Remember, however, that the ADO.NET architecture has been designed to operate without a permanent connection to the database. In a disconnected environment, it's appropriate, and indeed necessary, that the management of the connection be under programmatic control.

Roadmap
We'll examine the Fill *method in Chapter 4.*

The DataAdapter's *Fill* method is used to load data into the DataSet. The DataAdapter provides several versions of the *Fill* method. The simplest version takes the name of a DataSet as a parameter, and that's the one we'll use in the exercise below.

Load Data into the DataSet

Visual Basic .NET

1. Press F7 to view the code for the form.
2. Expand the region labeled "Windows Form Designer generated code" and navigate to the New Sub.
3. Add the following line of code just before the end of the procedure:

```
SqlDataAdapter1.Fill(DsEmployees1)
```

Roadmap
The DataAdapter's Fill *method is discussed in Chapter 4.*

This line calls the DataAdapter's *Fill* method, passing the name of the DataSet to be filled.

4. Press F5 to build and run the program.

Visual Studio displays the form with the first row displayed.

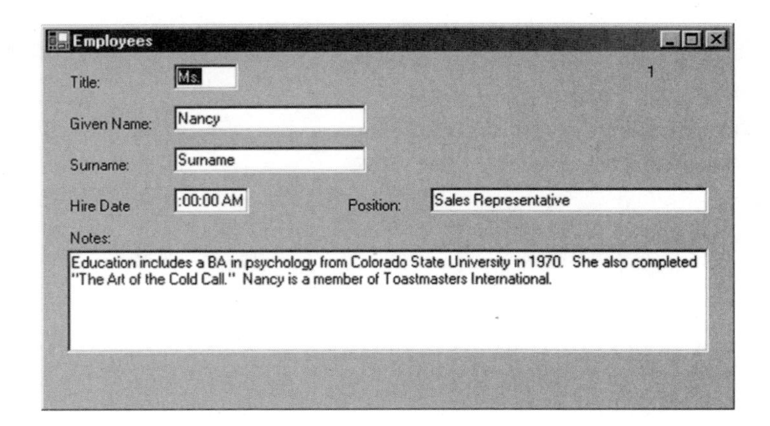

5 Admire your data bound form for a few minutes (see, that wasn't so hard!), and then close the form.

Visual C# .NET

1 Press F7 to view the code for the form.

2 Add the following line of code to the end of the Employees procedure:

```
sqlDataAdapter1.Fill(dsEmployees1);
```

This line calls the DataAdapter's *Fill* method, passing the name of the DataSet to be filled.

Roadmap
The DataAdapter's Fill *method is discussed in Chapter 4.*

3 Press F5 to build and run the program.

Visual Studio displays the form with the first row displayed.

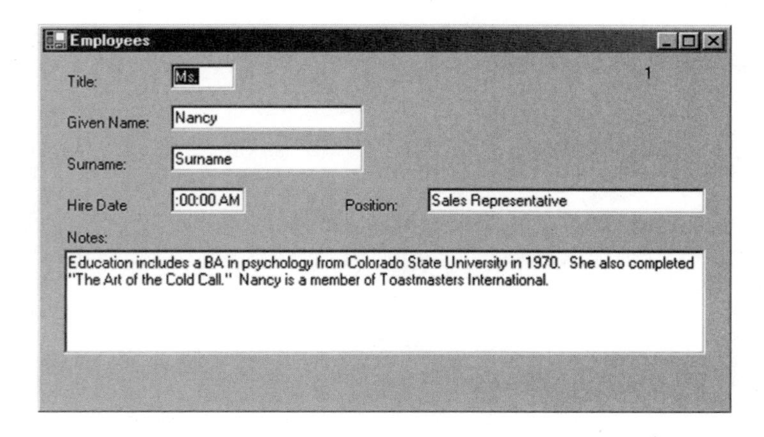

4 Admire your data bound form for a few minutes (see, that wasn't so hard!), and then close the form.

Chapter 1 Quick Reference

To	Do this
Add a Connection and DataAdapter to a form by using the DataAdapter Configuration Wizard	Drag a DataAdapter object onto the form and follow the wizard instructions
Use Visual Studio to automatically generate a typed DataSet	Select Create DataSet from the Data menu, complete the Generate Dataset dialog box as required, and then click OK
Simple bind properties of a control to a data source	In the Properties window DataBindings section, select the data source, DataTable, and column
Load data into a DataSet	Use the *Fill* method of the DataAdapter. For example: `myDataAdapter.Fill(myDataSet)`

PART 2

Data Providers

CHAPTER

2

Creating Connections

In this chapter, you'll learn how to:

- ✔ *Add an instance of a Server Explorer Connection to a form*
- ✔ *Create a Connection using code*
- ✔ *Use Connection properties*
- ✔ *Use an intermediary variable to reference multiple types of Connections*
- ✔ *Bind Connection properties to form controls*
- ✔ *Open and close Connections*
- ✔ *Respond to a Connection.StateChange event*

In the previous chapter, we took a brief tour through the ADO.NET object model. In this chapter, we'll begin to examine the objects in detail, starting with the lowest level object, the Connection.

Understanding Connections

Connections are responsible for handling the physical communication between a data store and a .NET application. Because the Connection object is part of a Data Provider, each Data Provider implements its own version. The two Data Providers supported by the .NET Framework implement the OleDbConnection in the System.Data.OleDB namespace and the SqlConnection in the System.Data.SqlClient namespace, respectively.

note

It's important to understand that if you're using a Connection object implemented by another Data Provider, the details of the implementation may vary from those described here.

The OleDbConnection, not surprisingly, uses OLE DB and can be used with any OLE DB provider, including Microsoft SQL Server. The SqlConnection goes directly to SQL Server without going through the OLE DB provider and so is more efficient.

Microsoft ActiveX Data Objects (ADO)

Since ADO.NET merges the ADO object model with OLE DB, it is rarely necessary to go directly to OLE DB for performance reasons. You might still need to use OLE DB directly if you need specific functionality that isn't exposed by ADO.NET, but again, these situations are likely to be rarer than when using ADO.

Creating Connections

In the previous chapter, we created a Connection object by using the DataAdapter Configuration Wizard. The Data Form Wizard, accessed by clicking Add Windows Form on the Project menu, also creates a Connection automatically. In this chapter, we'll look at several other methods for creating Connections in Microsoft Visual Studio .NET.

Design Time Connections

Visual Studio's Server Explorer provides the ability, at design time, to view and maintain connections to a number of different system services, including event logs, message queues, and, most important for our purposes, data connections.

important

If you have not yet installed this book's practice files, work through "Installing and Using the Practice Files" in the Introduction and then return to this chapter.

Add a Design Time Connection to the Server Explorer

1. Open the Connection project from the Visual Studio start page or from the Project menu.
2. Double-click ConnectionProperties.vb (or ConnectionProperties.cs, if you're using C#) in the Solution Explorer to open the form.

   Visual Studio displays the form in the form designer.

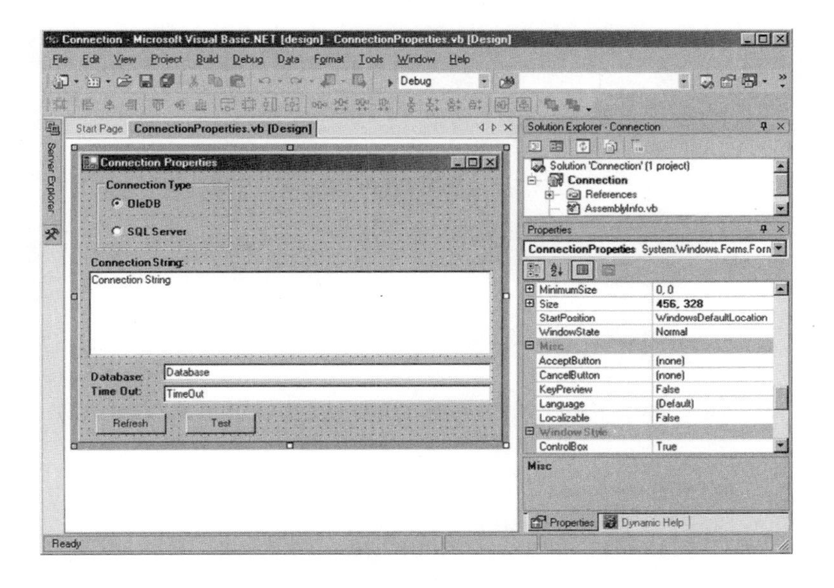

3. Open the Server Explorer.
4. Click the Connect to Database button.

   Visual Studio displays the Data Link Properties dialog box.

> **tip**
>
> You can also display the Data Link Properties dialog box by choosing Connect to Database on the Tools menu.

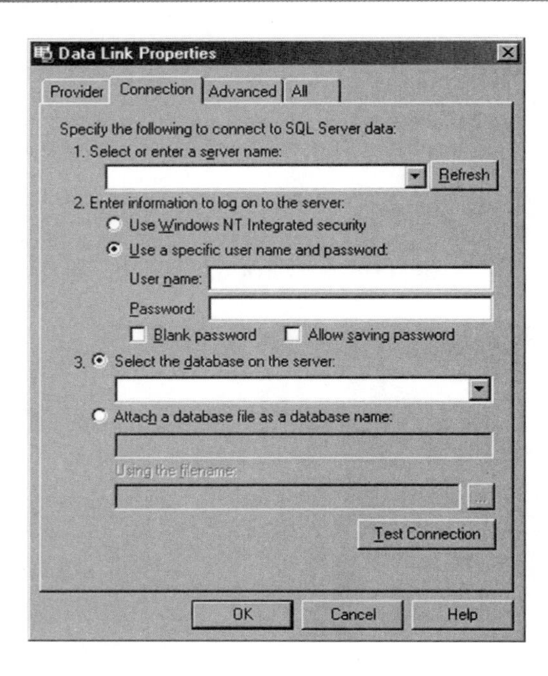

5 Click the Provider tab and then select Microsoft Jet 4.0 OLE DB Provider.

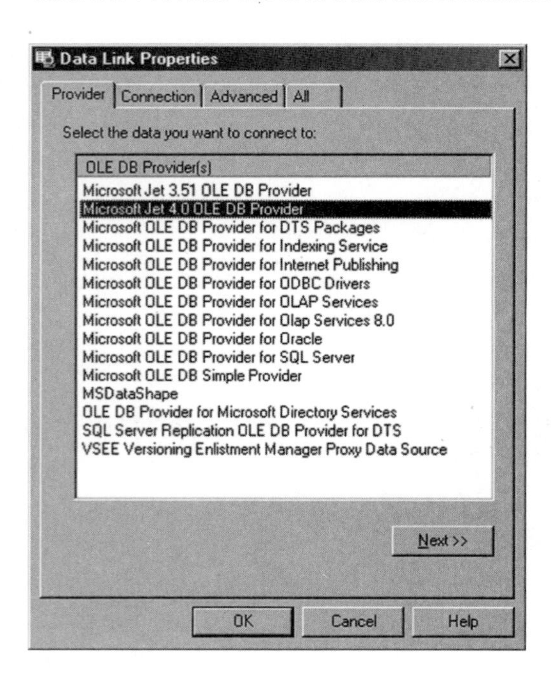

6 Click Next.

Visual Studio displays the Connection tab of the dialog box.

7 Click the ellipsis button after Select or enter a database name, navigate to the folder containing the sample files, and then select the nwind sample database.

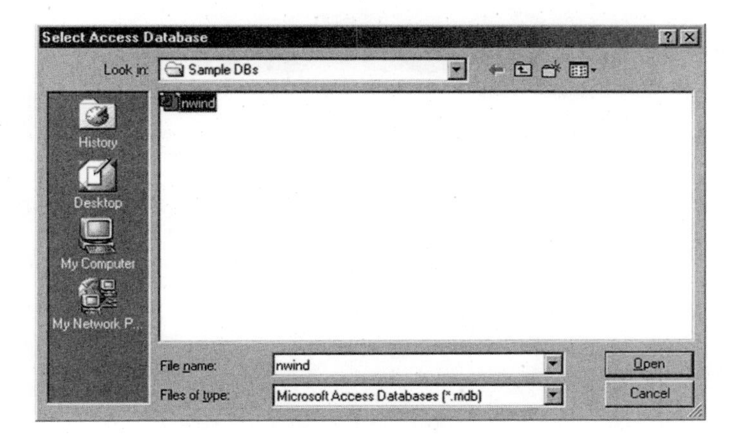

8 Click Open.

Visual Studio creates a Connection string for the database.

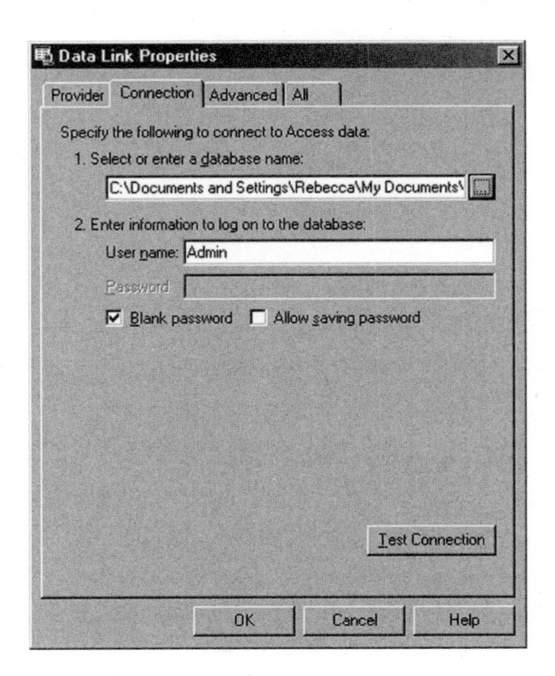

9 Click OK.

Visual Studio adds the Connection to the Server Explorer.

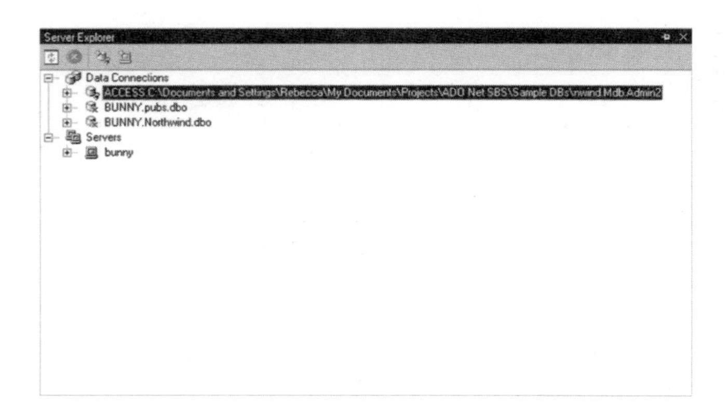

10 Right-click the Connection in the Server Explorer, click Rename from the context menu, and then rename the Connection *Access nwind.*

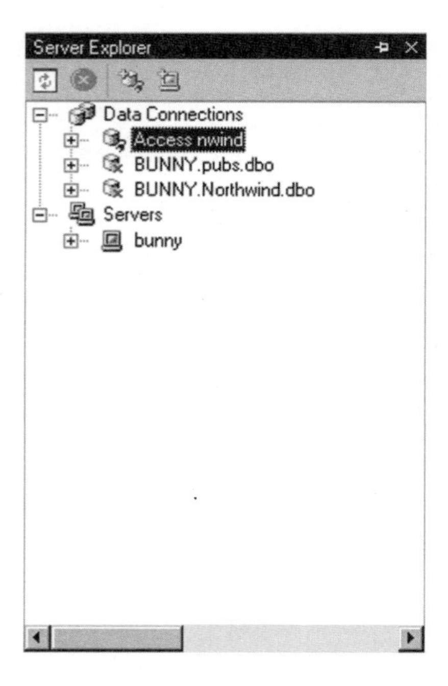

Database References

In addition to Database Connections in the Server Explorer, Visual Studio also supports *Database References*. Database References are set as part of a *Database Project*, which is a special type of project used to store SQL scripts, Data Commands, and Data Connections.

Database References are created in the Solution Explorer (rather than the Server Explorer) and, unlike Database Connections defined in the Server Explorer, they are stored along with the project.

Data connections defined through the Server Explorer become part of your Visual Studio environment—they will persist as you open and close projects. Database references, on the other hand, exist as part of a specific project and are only available as part of the project.

Design time connections aren't automatically included in any project, but you can drag a design time connection from the Server Explorer to a form, and Visual Studio will create a pre-configured Connection object for you.

Add an Instance of a Design Time Connection to a Form

- Select the Access nwind Connection in the Server Explorer and drag it onto the Connection Properties form.

  Visual Studio adds a pre-configured OleDbConnection to the Component Designer.

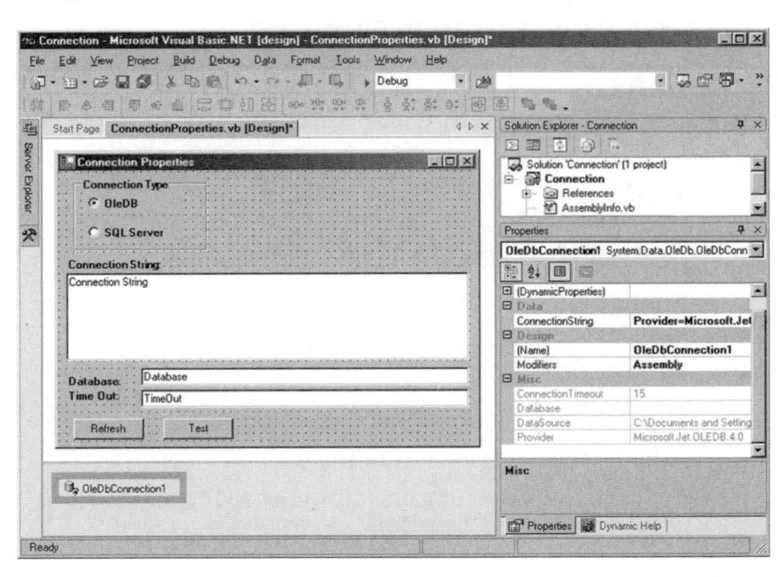

Creating a Connection at Run Time

Using Visual Studio to create form-level Connections is by far the easiest method, but if you need a Connection that isn't attached to a form, you can create one at run time in code.

> **note**
>
> You wouldn't ordinarily create a form-level Connection object in code because the Visual Studio designers are easier and just as effective.

The Connection object provides two overloaded versions of its constructor, giving you the option of passing in the ConnectionString, as shown in Table 2-1.

Method	Description
New()	Creates a Connection with the ConnectionString property set to an empty string
New(ConnectionString)	Creates a Connection with the ConnectionString property specified

Table 2-1 Connection Constructors

The ConnectionString is used by the Connection object to connect to the data source. We'll explore it in detail in the next section of this chapter.

Create a Connection in Code

Visual Basic .NET

1. Display the code for the ConnectionProperties form by pressing F7.
2. Add the following lines after the Inherits statement:

   ```
   Friend WithEvents SqlDbConnection1 As New _
   System.Data.SqlClient.SqlConnection()
   ```

   This code creates the new Connection object using the default values.

Visual C# .NET

1. Display the code for the ConnectionProperties form by pressing F7.
2. Add the following lines after the opening bracket of the class declaration:

   ```
   internal System.Data.SqlClient.SqlConnection SqlDbConnection1;
   ```

This code creates the new Connection object. (For the time being, ignore the warning that the variable is never assigned to.)

Using Connection Properties

The significant properties of the OleDbConnection and SqlDbConnection objects are shown in Table 2-2 and Table 2-3, respectively.

Property	Meaning	Default
ConnectionString	The string used to connect to the data source when the *Open* method is executed	Empty
ConnectionTimeout	The maximum time the Connection object will continue attempting to make the connection before throwing an exception	15 seconds
Database	The name of the database to be opened once a connection is opened	Empty
DataSource	The location and file containing the database	Empty
Provider	The name of the OLE DB Data Provider	Empty
ServerVersion	The version of the server, as provided by the OLE DB Data Provider	Empty
State	A ConnectionState value indicating the current state of the Connection	Closed

Table 2-2 OleDbConnection Properties

Property	Meaning	Default
ConnectionString	The string used to connect to the data source when the *Open* method is executed	Empty
ConnectionTimeout	The maximum time the Connection object will continue attempting to make the connection before throwing an exception	15 seconds
Database	The name of the database to be opened once a connection is opened	Empty
DataSource	The location and file containing the database	Empty

(continued)

(continued)

PacketSize	The size of network packets used to communicate with SQL Server	8192 bytes
ServerVersion	The version of SQL Server being used	Empty
State	A ConnectionState value indicating the current state of the Connection	Closed
WorkStationID	A string identifying the database client, or, if that is not specified, the name of the workstation	Empty

Table 2-3 SqlConnection Properties

As you can see, the two versions of the Connection object expose a slightly different set of properties: The SqlDbConnection doesn't have a Provider property, and the OleDbConnection doesn't expose PacketSize or WorkStationID. To make matters worse, not all OLE DB Data Providers support all of the OleDbConnection properties, and if you're working with a custom Data Provider, all bets are off.

What this means in real terms is that we still can't quite write code that is completely data source-independent unless we're prepared to give up the optimization of specific Data Providers. However, as we'll see, the problem isn't as bad as it might at first seem, since the .NET Framework provides a number of ways to accommodate run-time configuration.

Rather more tedious to deal with are the different names of the objects, but using an intermediate variable can minimize the impact, as we'll see later in this chapter.

The ConnectionString Property

The ConnectionString is the most important property of any Connection object. In fact, the remaining properties are read-only and set by the Connection based on the value provided for the ConnectionString.

All ConnectionStrings have the same format. They consist of a set of keywords and values, with the pairs separated by semicolons, and the whole thing is delimited by either single or double quotes:

```
"keyword = value;keyword = value;keyword = value"
```

Keyword names are case-insensitive, but the values may not be, depending on the data source. The use of single or double quotes follows the normal rules for strings. For example, if the database name is Becca's Data, then the

ConnectionString must be delimited by double quotes: "Database=Becca's Data". 'Database = Becca's Data' would cause an error.

If you use the same keyword multiple times, the last instance will be used. For example, given the ConnectionString "database=Becca's Data; database=Northwind", the initial database will be set to Northwind. The use of multiple instances is perfectly legal; no syntax error will be generated.

ADO

Unlike ADO, the ConnectionString returned by the .NET Framework is the same as the user-set string, with the exception that the user name and password are returned only if Persist Security Info is set to true (it is false by default).

Unfortunately, the format of the ConnectionString is the easy part. It's determining the contents that can be difficult because it will always be unique to the Data Provider. You can always cheat (a little) by creating a design time connection using the Data Link Properties dialog box, and then copying the values.

The ConnectionString can only be set when the Connection is closed. When it is set, the Connection object will check the syntax of the string and then set the remaining properties (which, you'll remember, are read-only). The ConnectionString is fully validated when the Connection is opened. If the Connection detects an invalid or unsupported property, it will generate an exception (either an OleDbException or a SqlDbException, depending on the object being used).

Setting a ConnectionString Property

In this exercise, we'll set the ConnectionString for the SqlDbConnection that we created in the previous exercise. The ConnectionString that your system requires will be different from the one in my installation. (I have SQL Server installed locally, and my machine name is BUNNY, for example.)

Fortunately, the DataAdapter Configuration Wizard in Chapter 1 created a design time Connection for you. If you select that connection in the Server Explorer, you can see the values in the Properties window. In fact, you can copy and paste the entire ConnectionString from the Properties window if you want. (If you didn't do the exercise in Chapter 1, you can create a design time connection by using the technique described in the Add a Design Time Connection exercise in this chapter.)

Set a ConnectionString Property

Visual Basic .NET

1. Expand the region labeled "Windows Form Designer generated code" and navigate to the New Sub.
2. Add the following line to the procedure after the InitializeComponent call, filling in the ConnectionString values required for your implementation:

```
Me.SqlDbConnection1.ConnectionString = "<<add your
ConnectionString here>>"
```

Visual C# .NET

1. Scroll down to the ConnectionProperties Sub.
2. Add the following lines to the procedure after the InitializeComponent call, filling in the ConnectionString values required for your implementation:

```
this.SqlDbConnection1 = new
   System.Data.SqlClient.SqlConnection();
this.SqlDbConnection1.ConnectionString =
   "<<add your ConnectionString here>>";
```

Using Other Connection Properties

With the Connection objects in place, we can now add the code to display the Connection properties on the sample form. But first, we need to use a little bit of object-oriented sleight of hand in order to accommodate the two different types of objects.

One method would be to write conditional code. In Visual Basic, this would look like:

```
If Me.rbOleChecked then
 Me.txtConnectionString.Text = Me.OleDbConnection1.ConnectionString
 Me.txtDatabase.Text = Me.OleDbConnection1.Database.String
 Me.txtTimeOut.Text = Me.OleDbConnection1.ConnectionTimeout
Else
 Me.txtConnectionString.Text = Me.SqlDbConnection1.ConnectionString
 Me.txtDatabase.Text = Me.SqlDbConnection1.Database.String
 Me.txtTimeOut.Text = Me.SqlDbConnection1.ConnectionTimeout
End If
```

Another option would be to use compiler constants to conditionally compile code. Again, in Visual Basic:

```
#Const SqlVersion

#If SqlVersion Then
 Me.txtConnectionString.Text = Me.OleDbConnection1.ConnectionString
 Me.txtDatabase.Text = Me.OleDbConnection1.Database.String
 Me.txtTimeOut.Text = Me.OleDbConnection1.ConnectionTimeout
#Else
 Me.txtConnectionString.Text = Me.SqlDbConnection1.ConnectionString
 Me.txtDatabase.Text = Me.SqlDbConnection1.Database.String
 Me.txtTimeOut.Text = Me.SqlDbConnection1.ConnectionTimeout
#End If
```

But either option requires a lot of typing, in a lot of places, and can become a maintenance nightmare. If you only need to access the ConnectionString, Database, and TimeOut properties (and these are the most common), there's an easier way.

Connection objects, no matter the Data Provider to which they belong, must implement the IDbConnection interface, so by declaring a variable as an IDbConnection, we can use it as an intermediary to access a few of the shared properties.

Create an Intermediary Variable

Visual Basic .NET

1. Declare the variable by adding the following line of code at the beginning of the class module, under the Connection declarations we added previously:

   ```
   Dim myConnection As System.Data.IDbConnection
   ```

2. Add procedures to set the value of the myConnection variable when the user changes their choice in the Connection Type group box. Do that by using the CheckedChanged event of the two Radio Buttons.

   Select the rbOleDB control in the Class Name box of the editor and the CheckedChanged event in the Method Name box.

   Visual Studio adds the CheckedChanged event handler template to the class.

3. Add the following assignment statement to the procedure:

   ```
   myConnection = Me.OleDbConnection1
   ```

4. Repeat steps 2 and 3 for the rbSql radio button, substituting the SqlDbConnection object:

   ```
   myConnection = Me.SqlDbConnection1
   ```

Visual C# .NET

1. Declare the variable by adding the following line of code at the beginning of the class module, under the Connection declaration we added previously:

```
private System.Data.IDbConnection myConnection;
```

2. Add procedures to set the value of the myConnection variable when the user changes their choice in the Connection Type group box. Do that by using the CheckedChanged event of the two radio buttons.

   Add the following event handlers to the code window below the Dispose procedure:

```
private void rbOleDB_CheckChanged(object sender, EventArgs e)
{
   myConnection = this.oleDbConnection1;
}

private void rbSQL_CheckChanged (object sender, EventArgs e)
{
   myConnection = this.SqlDbConnection1;
}
```

3. Connect the event handlers to the actual radio button events. Add the following code to the end of the ConnectionProperties sub:

```
this.rbOleDB.CheckedChanged += new
   EventHandler(this.rbOleDB_CheckChanged);
this.rbSQL.CheckedChanged += new
   EventHandler(this.rbSQL_CheckChanged);
```

Binding Connection Properties to Form Controls

Now that we have the intermediary variable in place, we can add the code to display the Connection (or rather, the IDbConnection properties) in the control:

Bind Connection Properties to Form Controls

Visual Basic .NET

1. Add the following procedure to the class module:

```
Private Sub RefreshValues()
     Me.txtConnectionString.Text = Me.myConnection.ConnectionString
     Me.txtDatabase.Text = Me.myConnection.Database
     Me.txtTimeOut.Text = Me.myConnection.ConnectionTimeout
End Sub
```

2 Add a call to the RefreshValues procedure to the end of each of the CheckedChanged event handlers.

3 Save and run the program by pressing F5. Choose each of the Connections in turn to confirm that their properties are displayed in the text boxes.

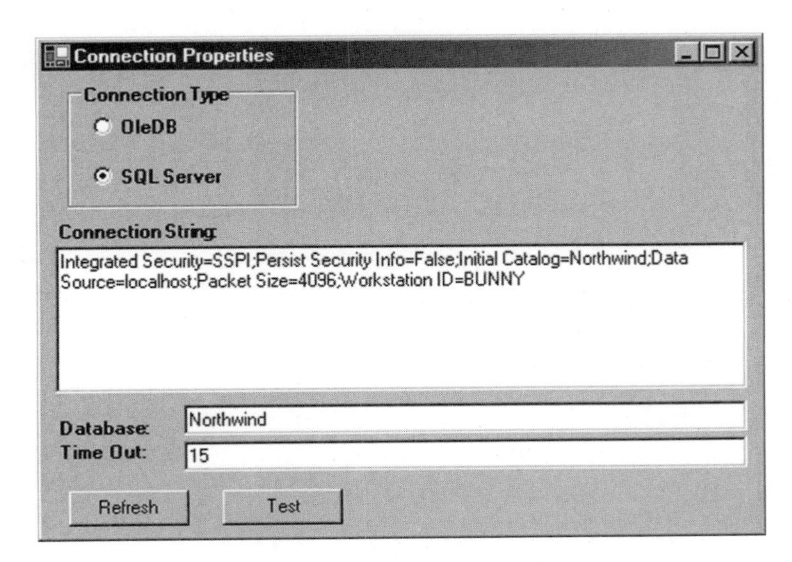

4 Close the application.

Visual C# .NET

1 Add the following procedure to the class module below the CheckChanged event handlers:

```
private void RefreshValues()
{
    this.txtConectionString.Text = this.myConnection.ConnectionString;
    this.txtDatabase.Text = this.myConnection.Database;
    this.txtTimeOut.Text = this.myConnection.ConnectionTimeout.ToString();
}
```

2 Add a call to the RefreshValues procedure to the end of each of the CheckedChanged event handlers.

3 Save and run the program by pressing F5. Choose each of the Connections in turn to confirm that their properties are displayed in the text boxes.

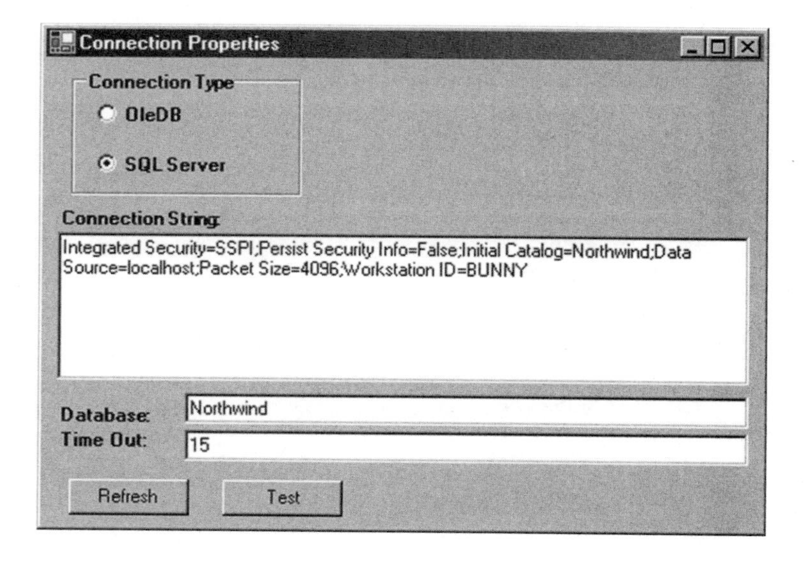

4 Close the application.

Using Dynamic Properties

Another way to handle ConnectionString configurations is to use .NET Framework dynamic properties. When an application is deployed, dynamic properties are stored in an external configuration file, allowing them to be easily changed.

Connection Methods

Both the SqlConnection and OleDbConnection objects expose the same set of methods, as shown in Table 2-4.

Method	Description
BeginTransaction	Begins a database transaction
ChangeDatabase	Changes the current database on an open Connection
Close	Closes the connection to the data source
CreateCommand	Creates and returns a Data Command associated with the Connection
Open	Establishes a connection to the data source

Table 2-4 Connection Methods

Roadmap

We'll examine transaction processing in Chapter 5.

The Connection methods that you will use most often are *Open* and *Close*, which do exactly what you would expect them to—they open and close the connection. The *BeginTransaction* method begins transaction processing for a Connection, as we'll see in Chapter 5.

Roadmap

We'll examine Data Commands in Chapter 3.

The *CreateCommand* method can be used to create an ADO.NET Data Command object. We'll examine this method in Chapter 3.

Opening and Closing Connections

The *Open* and *Close* methods are invoked automatically by the two objects that use a Connection, the DataAdapter and Data Command. You can also invoke them explicitly in code, if required.

Roadmap

We'll examine the DataAdapter in Chapter 4.

If the *Open* method is invoked on a Connection by the DataAdapter or a Data Command, these objects will leave the Connection in the state in which they found it. If the Connection was open when a *DataAdapter.Fill* method is invoked, for example, it will remain open when the Fill operation is complete. On the other hand, if the Connection is closed when the *Fill* method is invoked, the DataAdapter will close it upon completion.

If you invoke the *Open* method explicitly, the data source connection will remain open until it is explicitly closed. It will not be closed automatically, even if the Connection object goes out of scope.

important

You must *always* explicitly invoke a *Close* method when you have finished using a Connection object, and for scalability and performance purposes, you should call *Close* as soon as possible after you've completed the operations on the Connection.

Connection Pooling

Although it's easiest to think of *Open* and *Close* methods as discrete operations, in fact the .NET Framework pools connections to improve performance. The specifics of the connection pooling are determined by the Data Provider.

The OLE DB Data Provider automatically uses OLE DB connection pooling. You have no programmatic control over the process. The SQL Server Data Provider uses implicit pooling by default, based on an exact match in the connection string, but the OLE DB Data Provider supports some additional keywords in the ConnectionString to control pooling. See online help for more details.

Open and Close a Connection

Visual Basic .NET

1 Select the btnTest control in the Class Name combo box of the editor and the Click event in the Method Name combo box.

Visual Studio adds the click event handler template.

2 Add the following lines to the procedure to open the connection, display its status in a message box, and then close the connection:

```
myConnection.Open()
MessageBox.Show(Me.myConnection.State.ToString)
myConnection.Close()
```

3 Press F5 to save and run the application.

4 Change the Connection Type, and then click the Test button.

The application displays the Connection state.

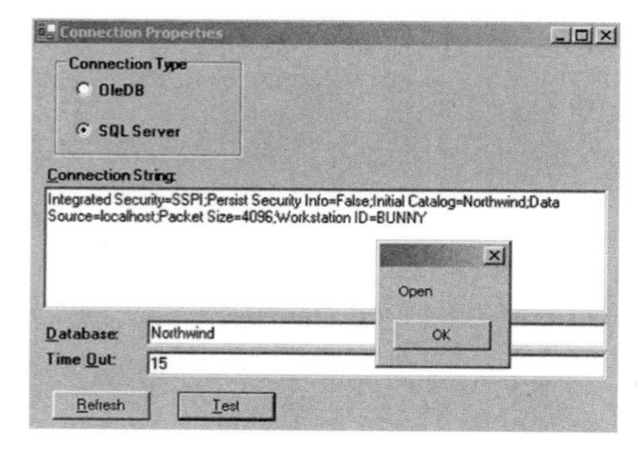

5 Close the application.

Visual C# .NET

1. Add the following procedure to the code window to open the connection, display its status in a message box, and then close the connection:

```
private void btnTest_Click(object sender, System.EventArgs e)
{
    this.myConnection.Open();
    MessageBox.Show(this.myConnection.State.ToString());
    this.myConnection.Close();
}
```

2. Add the following code, which connects the event handler to the btnTest.Click event, to the end of the ConnectionProperties sub:

```
this.btnTest.Click += new EventHandler(this.btnTest_Click);
```

3. Press F5 to save and run the application.
4. Change the Connection Type and then click the Test button.

   The application displays the Connection state.

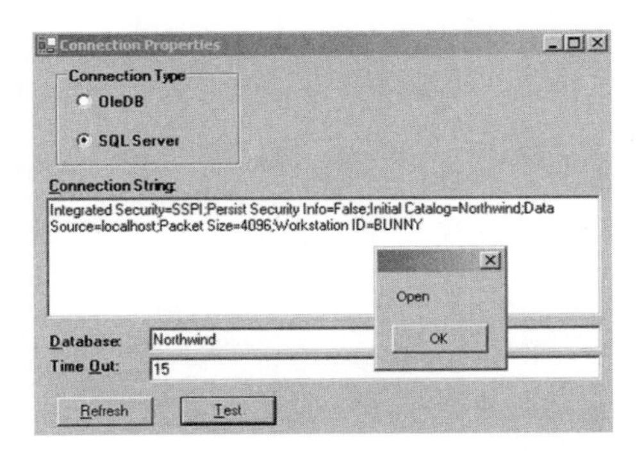

5. Close the application.

Handling Connection Events

Both the OLE DB and the SQL Server Connection objects provide two events: StateChange and InfoMessage.

StateChange Events

Not surprisingly, the StateChange event fires whenever the state of the Connection object changes. The event passes a StateChangeEventArgs to its handler, which, in turn, has two properties: OriginalState and CurrentState. The possible values for OriginalState and CurrentState are shown in Table 2-5.

State	Meaning
Broken	The Connection is open, but not functional. It may be closed and re-opened
Closed	The Connection is closed
Connecting	The Connection is in the process of connecting, but has not yet been opened
Executing	The Connection is executing a command
Fetching	The Connection is retrieving data
Open	The Connection is open

Table 2-5 Connection States

Respond to a StateChange Event

Visual Basic .NET

1. Select OleDbConnection1 in the Class Name combobox of the editor and the StateChange event in the Method Name combobox.

   Visual Studio adds the event declaration to the class.

2. Add the following code to display the previous and current Connection states:

```
Dim theMessage As String
theMessage = "The Connection is changing from " & _
             e.OriginalState.ToString & _
             " to " & e.CurrentState.ToString
MessageBox.Show(theMessage)
```

3. Repeat steps 1 and 2 for SqlDbConnection1.
4. Save and run the program.
5. Click the Test button.

   The application displays MessageBoxes as the Connection is opened and closed.

Visual C# .NET

1 Add the following procedure code to display the previous and current Connection states for each of the two Connection objects:

```
private void oleDbConnection1_StateChange (object sender,
StateChangeEventArgs e)
{
   string theMessage;
   theMessage = "The Connection State is changing from " +
          e.OriginalState.ToString() +
          " to " + e.CurrentState.ToString();
   MessageBox.Show(theMessage);
}
private void SqlDbConnection1_StateChange (object sender,
StateChangeEventArgs e)
{
   string theMessage;
   theMessage = "The Connection State is changing from " +
          e.OriginalState.ToString() +
          " to " + e.CurrentState.ToString();
   MessageBox.Show(theMessage);
}
```

2 Add the code to connect the event handlers to the ConnectionProperties sub:

```
this.oleDbConnection1.StateChange += new
  System.Data.StateChangeEventHandler(this.oleDbConnection1_StateChange);
this.SqlDbConnection1.StateChange += new
  System.Data.StateChangeEventHandler(this.SqlDbConnection1_StateChange);
```

3 Save and run the program.

4 Change the Connection Type and then click the Test button.

The application displays two MessageBoxes as the Connection is opened and closed.

InfoMessage Events

The InfoMessage event is triggered when the data source returns warnings. The information passed to the event handler depends on the Data Provider.

Chapter 2 Quick Reference

To	Do this
Create a Server Explorer Connection	Click the Connect to Database button in the Server Explorer, or choose Connect to Database on the Tools menu
Add an instance of a Server Explorer Connection to a form	Drag the Connection from the Server Explorer to the form
Create a Connection using code	Use the New constructor. For example: `Dim myConn as New OleDbConnection()`
Use an intermediary variable to reference multiple types of	Declare the variable as an IDbConnection. For example: `Dim myConn As System.Data.IDbConnection Connections`
Open a Connection	Use the Open method. For example: `myConn.Open`
Close a Connection	Use the Close method. For example: `myConn.Close`

CHAPTER

3

Data Commands and the DataReader

In this chapter, you'll learn how to:

- ✔ *Add a Data Command to a form*
- ✔ *Create a Data Command at run time*
- ✔ *Set Command properties at run time*
- ✔ *Configure the Parameters collection in Microsoft Visual Studio .NET*
- ✔ *Add and configure Parameters at run time*
- ✔ *Set Parameter values*
- ✔ *Execute a Command*
- ✔ *Create a DataReader to return Command results*

The Connection object that we examined in Chapter 2 represents the physical connection to a data source; the conduit for exchanging information between an application and the data source. The mechanism for this exchange is the Data Command.

Understanding Data Commands and DataReaders

Essentially, an ADO.NET data command is simply a SQL command or a reference to a stored procedure that is executed against a Connection object. In addition to retrieving and updating data, the Data Command can be used to execute certain types of queries on the data source that do not return a result set and to execute data definition (DDL) commands that change the structure of the data source.

When a Data Command does return a result set, a DataReader is used to retrieve the data. The DataReader object returns a read-only, forward-only stream of data from a Data Command. Because only a single row of data is in memory at a time (unlike a DataSet, which, as we'll see in Chapter 6, stores the entire result set), a DataReader requires very little overhead. The *Read* method of the DataReader is used to retrieve a row, and the *GetType* methods (where *Type* is a system data type, such as *GetString* to return a data string) return each column within the current row.

As part of the Data Provider, Data Commands and DataReaders are specific to a data source. Each of the .NET Framework Data Providers implements a Command and a DataReader object: OleDbCommand and OleDbDataReader in the System.Data.OleDb namespace; and SqlCommand and SqlDataReader in the System.Data.SqlClient namespace.

Creating Data Commands

Like most of the objects that can exist at the form level, Data Commands can either be created and configured at design time in Visual Studio or at run time in code. DataReaders can be created only at run time, using the *ExecuteReader* method of the Data Command, as we'll see later in this chapter.

Creating Data Commands in Visual Studio

A Command object is created in Visual Studio just like any other control—simply drag the control off of the Data tab of the Toolbox and drop it on the form. Since the Data Command has no user interface, like most of the objects we've covered, Visual Studio will add the control to the Component Designer.

Add a Data Command to a Form at Design Time

In this exercise we'll create and name a Data Command. We'll configure its properties in later lessons.

1 Open the DataCommands project from the Visual Studio start page or from the Project menu.

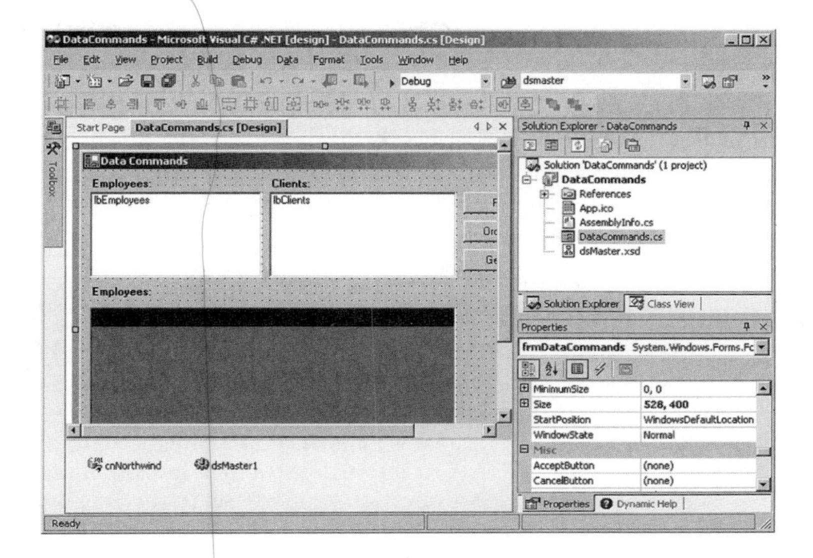

2 Double-click DataCommands.vb (or DataCommands.cs, if you're using C#) in the Solution Explorer to open the form.

Visual Studio displays the form in the form designer.

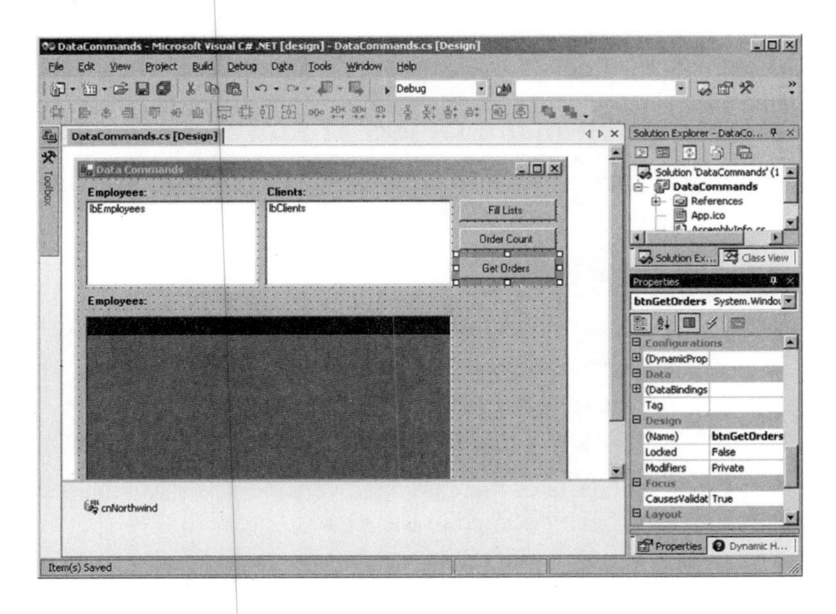

3 Drag a SqlCommand control from the Data tab of the Toolbox to the form.

Visual Studio adds the command to the form.

4 In the Properties window, change the name of the Command to cmdGetEmployees.

Creating Data Commands at Run Time

ROADMAP
We'll discuss the version of the Command constructor that supports transactions in Chapter 5.

The Data Command supports four versions of its constructor, as shown in Table 3-1. The New() version sets all the properties to their default values, while the other versions allow you to set properties of the Command object during creation. Whichever version you choose, of course, you can set or change property values after the Command is created.

Property	Description
New()	Creates a new, default instance of the Data Command
New(Command)	Creates a new Data Command with the CommandText set to the string specified in *Command*
New(Command, Connection)	Creates a new Data Command with the CommandText set to the string specified in *Command* and the Connection property set to the SqlConnection specified in *Connection*
New(Command, Connection, Transaction)	Creates a new Data Command with the CommandText set to the string specified in *Command*, the Connection property set to the Connection specified in *Connection,* and the Transaction property set to the Transaction specified in *Transaction*

Table 3-1 Command Constructors

Create a Command Object at Run Time

Once again, we will create the Command object in this exercise and set its properties later in the chapter.

Visual Basic .NET

1. Press F7 to display the code editor window.
2. Add the following line after the Inherits statement:

```
Friend WithEvents cmdGetCustomers As
System.Data.SqlClient.SqlCommand
```

   This line declares the command variable. (One variable, cmdGetOrders, has already been declared in the exercise project.)
3. Expand the region labeled "Windows Form Designer generated code".
4. Add the following line to end of the New Sub:

```
Me.cmdGetCustomers = New System.Data.SqlClient.SqlCommand()
```

   This command instantiates the Command object using the default constructor. (cmdGetOrders has already been instantiated.)

Visual C# .NET

1. Press F7 to display the code editor window.
2. Add the following line after the opening bracket of the class declaration:

```
internal System.Data.SqlClient.SqlCommand cmdGetCustomers;
```

   This line declares the command variable.
3. Scroll down to the frmDataCmds Sub.
4. Add the following line to the procedure after the InitializeComponent call:

```
this.cmdGetCustomers = new System.Data.SqlClient.SqlCommand();
```

   This command instantiates the Command object using the default constructor. (cmdGetOrders has already been declared and instantiated.)

Command Properties

The properties exposed by the Data Command object are shown in Table 3-2. These properties will only be checked for syntax errors when they are set. Final validation occurs only when the Command is executed by a data source.

Property	Description
CommandText	The SQL statement or stored procedure to execute
CommandTimeout	The time (in seconds) to wait for a response from the data source
CommandType	Indicates how the CommandText property is to be interpreted, defaults to Text
Connection	The Connection object on which the Data Command is to be executed
Parameters	The Parameters Collection
Transaction	The Transaction in which the command will execute
UpdatedRowSource	Determines how results are applied to a DataRow when the Command is used by the *Update* method of a DataAdapter

Table 3-2 Data Command Properties

The CommandText property, which is a string, contains either the actual text of the command to be executed against the connection or the name of a stored procedure in the data source.

The CommandTimeout property determines the time that the Command will wait for a response from the server before it generates an error. Note that this is the wait time before the Command begins receiving results, *not* the time it takes the command to execute. The data source might take ten or fifteen minutes to return all the rows of a huge table, but provided the first row is received within the specified CommandTimeout period, no error will be generated.

The CommandType property tells the command object how to interpret the contents of the CommandText property. The possible values are shown in Table 3-3. TableDirect is only supported by the OleDbCommand, not the SqlCommand, and is equivalent to SELECT * FROM <tablename>, where the <tablename> is specified in the CommandText property.

Property	Description
StoredProcedure	The name of a stored procedure
TableDirect	A table name
Text	A SQL text command

Table 3-3 CommandType Values

The Connection property contains a reference to the Connection object on which the Command will be executed. The Connection object must belong to the same namespace as the Command object, that is, a SqlCommand must contain a reference to a SqlConnection and an OleDbCommand must contain a reference to an OleDbConnection.

The Command object's Parameters property contains a collection of Parameters for the SQL command or stored procedure specified in CommandText. We'll examine this collection in detail later in this exercise.

ROADMAP

We'll examine the Transaction property in Chapter 5.

The Transaction property contains a reference to a Transaction object and serves to enroll the Command in that transaction. We'll examine this property in detail in Chapter 5.

ROADMAP

We'll examine the DataAdapter in Chapter 4 and the DataRow in Chapter 7.

The UpdatedRowSource property determines how results are applied to a DataRow when the Command is executed by the *Update* method of the DataAdapter. The possible values for the UpdatedRowSource property are shown in Table 3-4.

Property	Description
Both	Both the output parameters and the first row returned by the Command will be mapped to the changed row
FirstReturnedRecord	The first row returned by the Command will be mapped to the changed row
None	Any returned parameters or rows are discarded
OutputParameters	Output parameters of the Command will be mapped to the changed row

Table 3-4 UpdatedRowSource Values

If the Data Command is generated automatically by Visual Studio, the default value of the UpdatedRowSource property is None. If the Command is generated at run time or created by the user at design time, the default value is Both.

Setting Command Properties at Design Time

As might be expected, the properties of a Command control created in Visual Studio are set using the Properties window. In specifying the CommandText property, you can either type the value directly or use the Query Builder to generate the required SQL statement. You must specify the Connection property before you can set the CommandText property.

Set Command Properties in Visual Studio

1 In the form designer, select cmdGetEmployees in the Component Designer.

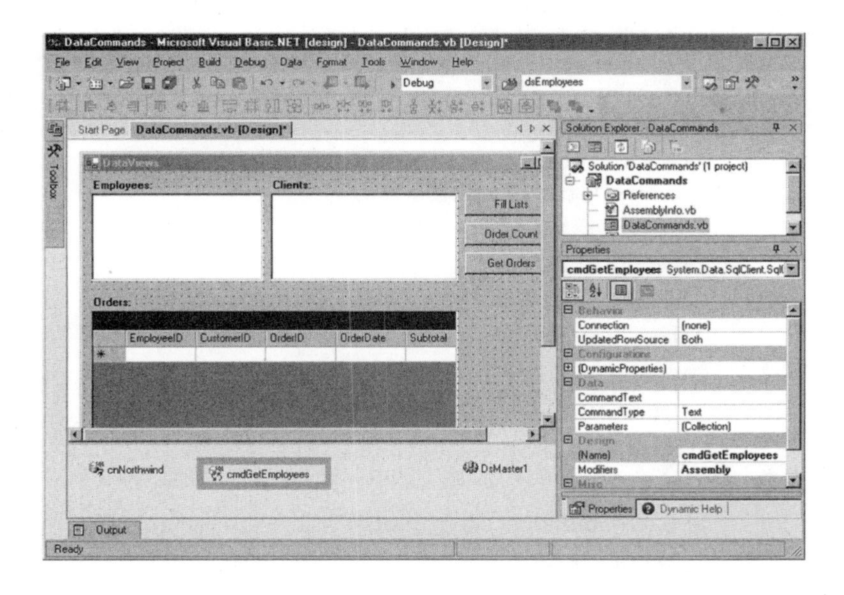

2 In the Properties window, select the Connection property, expand the Existing node in the drop-down list, and then click cnNorthwind.

3 Select the CommandText property, and then click the ellipsis button.

Visual Studio displays the Query Builder's Add Table dialog box.

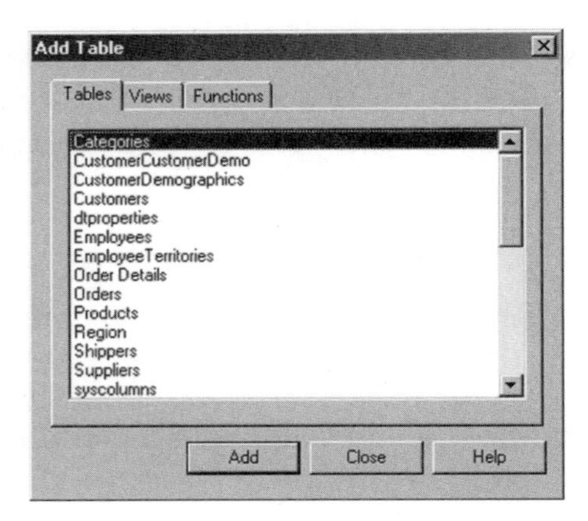

4 Click the Views tab in the Add Table dialog box, and then click EmployeeList.

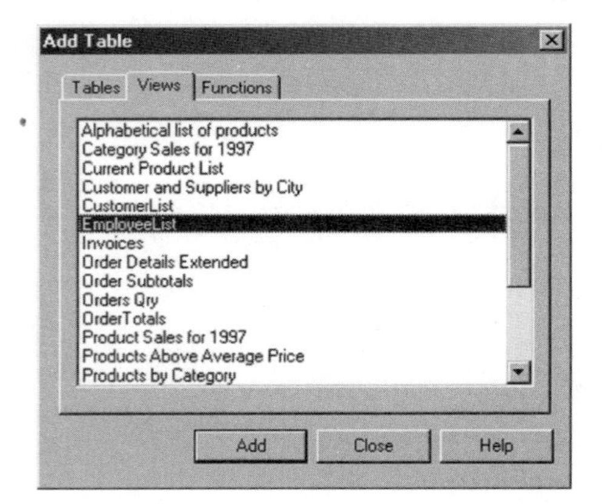

5 Click Add, and then click Close.

Visual Studio adds EmployeeList to the Query Builder.

6 Select the check box next to (All Columns) in the Diagram pane of the Query Builder to select all columns.

Visual Studio updates the SQL text in the SQL pane.

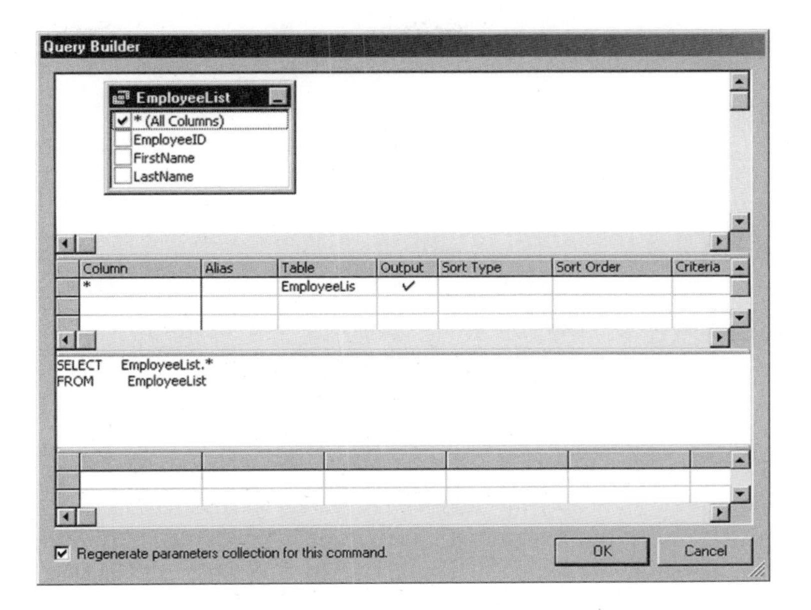

7 Click OK.

Visual Studio generates the SQL command and sets the CommandText property in the Properties window.

Setting Command Properties at Run Time

The majority of the properties of the Command object are set by using simple assignment statements. The exception is the Parameters collection, which because it is a collection, uses the *Add* method.

Set Command Properties at Run Time

Visual Basic .NET

1 In the Code window, add the following lines below the variable instantiations of the New Sub:

```
Me.cmdGetCustomers.CommandText = "SELECT * FROM CustomerList"
Me.cmdGetCustomers.CommandType = CommandType.Text
Me.cmdGetCustomers.Connection = Me.cnNorthwind
```

2 The first line specifies the command to be executed on the Connection—it simply returns all rows from the CustomerList view. The second line specifies that the CommandText property is to be treated as a SQL command, and the third line sets the Connection on which the command is to be executed.

Visual C# .NET

1 In the Code window, add the following lines below the variable instantiation:

```
this.cmdGetCustomers.CommandText = "SELECT * FROM CustomerList";
this.cmdGetCustomers.CommandType = CommandType.Text;
this.cmdGetCustomers.Connection = this.cnNorthwind;
```

2 The first line specifies the command to be executed on the Connection—it simply returns all rows from the CustomerList view. The second line specifies that the CommandText property is to be treated as a SQL command, and the third line sets the Connection on which the command is to be executed.

Using the Parameters Collection

There are three steps to using parameters in queries and stored procedures—you must specify the parameters in the query or stored procedure, you must specify the parameters in the Parameters collection, and finally you must set the parameter values.

If you're using a stored procedure, the syntax for specifying parameters will be determined by the data source when the stored procedure is created. If you are using parameters in a SQL command specified in the CommandText property of the Command object, the syntax requirement is determined by the .NET Data Provider.

Unfortunately, the two Data Providers supplied in the .NET Framework use different syntax. OleDbCommand objects use a question mark (?) as a placeholder for a parameter:

```
SELECT * FROM Customers WHERE CustomerID = ?
```

SqlDbCommand objects use named parameters, prefixed with the @ character:

```
SELECT * FROM Customers WHERE CustomerID = @custID
```

Having created the stored procedure or SQL command, you must then add each of the parameters to the Parameters collection of the Command object. Again, if you are using Visual Studio, it will configure the collection for you, but if you are creating or re-configuring the Command object at run time, you must use the *Add* method of the Parameters collection to create a Parameter object for each parameter in the query or stored procedure.

The Parameters collection provides a number of methods for configuring the collection at run time. The most useful of these are shown in Table 3-5. Note that because the OleDbCommand doesn't support named parameters, the parameters will be substituted in the order they are found in the Parameters collection. Because of this, it is important that you configure the items in the collection correctly. (This can be a very difficult bug to track, and yes, that *is* the voice of experience.)

Property	Description
Add(Value)	Adds a new parameter at the end of the collection with the specified *Value*
Add(Parameter)	Adds a Parameter to the end of the collection
Add(Name, Value)	Adds a Parameter with the name specified in the *Name* string and the specified *Value* to the end of the collection
Add(Name, Type)	Adds a Parameter of the specified *Type* with the name specified in the *Name* string to the end of the collection
Add(Name, Type, Size)	Adds a Parameter of the specified *Type* and *Size* with the name specified in the *Name* string to the end of the collection
Add(Name, Type, Size, SourceColumn)	Adds a Parameter of the specified *Type* and *Size* with the name specified in the *Name* string to the end of the collection, and maps it to the DataTable column specified in the *SourceColumn* string
Clear	Removes all Parameters from the collection
Insert(Index, Value)	Inserts a new Parameter with the *Value* specified at the position specified by the zero-based *Index* into the collection
Remove(Value)	Removes the parameter with the specified *Value* from the collection
RemoveAt(Index)	Removes the parameter at the position specified by the zero-based *Index* into the collection
RemoveAt(Name)	Removes the parameter with the name specified by the *Name* string from the collection

Table 3-5 Parameters Collection Methods

Configure the Parameters Collection in Visual Studio

1. In the form designer, drag a SqlCommand object onto the form.

   Visual Studio adds a new command to the Component Designer.

2. In the Properties window, change the new Command's name to cmdOrderCount.

3. In the Properties window, expand the Existing node in the Connection property's drop-down list, and then click cnNorthwind.

4. Select the CommandText property, and then click the ellipsis button.

   Visual Studio opens the Query Builder and the Add Table dialog box.

5. Click the Views tab in the Add Table dialog box, and then click OrderTotals.
6. Click Add, and then click Close.

   Visual Studio adds OrderTotals to the Query Builder.
7. Change the SQL statement in the SQL pane to read as follows:

```
SELECT Count(*) AS OrderCount
FROM OrderTotals
WHERE (EmployeeID = @empID) AND (CustomerID = @custID)
```

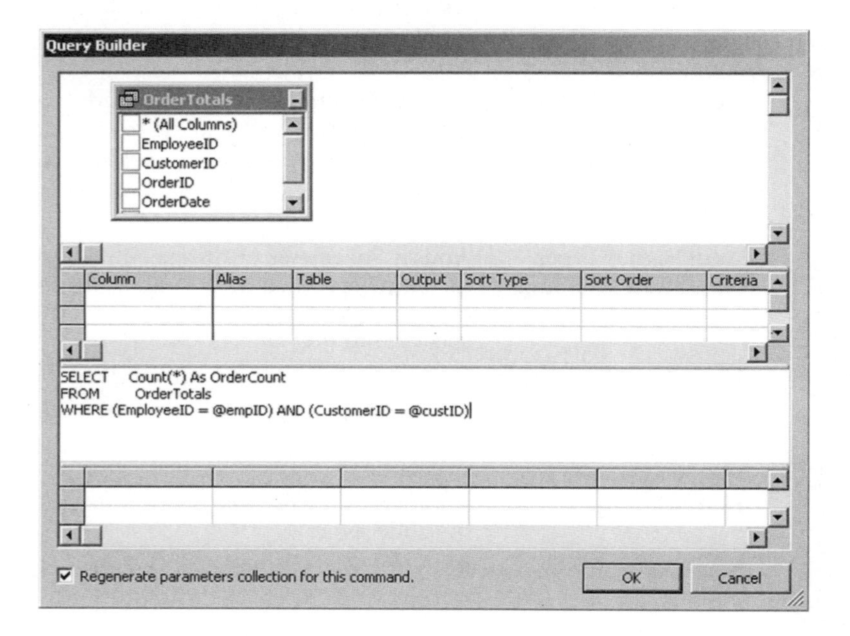

8. Verify that the Regenerate parameters collection for this command check box is selected, and then click OK.

   Visual Studio displays a warning message.

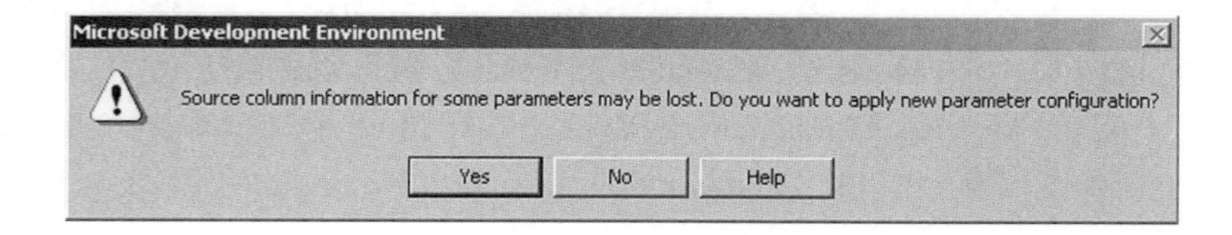

9. Click Yes.

   Visual Studio generates the CommandText property and the Parameters collection.

10 In the Properties window, select the Parameters property, and then click the ellipsis button.

Visual Studio displays the SqlParameter Collection Editor. Because the Query Builder generated the parameters for us, there is nothing to do here. However, you could add, change, or remove parameters as necessary.

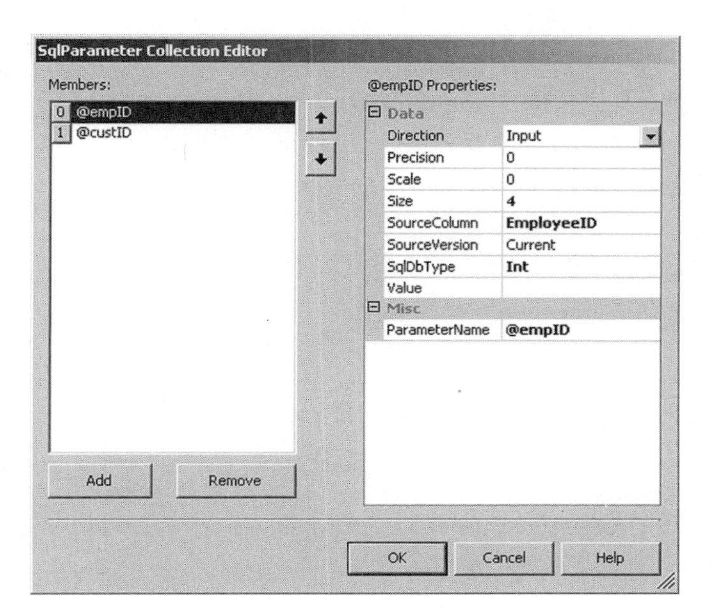

11 Click OK.

Add and Configure Parameters at Run Time

Visual Basic .NET

1 Press F7 to display the code editor.

2 Add the following lines to the end of the New Sub:

```
Me.cmdGetOrders.Parameters.Add("@custID", SqlDbType.VarChar)
Me.cmdGetOrders.Parameters.Add("@empID", SqlDbType.Int)
```

Visual C# .NET

1 Press F7 to display the code editor.

2 Add the following lines after the property instantiations:

```
this.cmdGetOrders.Parameters.Add("@custID", SqlDbType.VarChar);
this.cmdGetOrders.Parameters.Add("@empID", SqlDbType.Int);
```

Set Parameter Values

After you have established the Parameters collection and before you execute the command, you must set the values for each of the Parameters. This can be done only at run time with a simple assignment statement.

Visual Basic .NET

1. In the Code Editor window, select btnOrderCount in the Object Name list, and Click in the Method Name box.

   Visual Studio adds the click event handler for the button.

2. Add the following code to the event handler:

```
Dim cnt As Integer
Dim strMsg As String

Me.cmdOrderCount.Parameters("@empID").Value = _
   Me.lbEmployees.SelectedItem("EmployeeID")
Me.cmdOrderCount.Parameters("@custID").Value = _
   Me.lbClients.SelectedItem("CustomerID")
```

   The code first declares a couple of variables that will be used in the next exercise, and then sets the value of each of the parameters in the cmdOrderCount.Parameters collection to the value of the Employees and Clients list boxes, respectively.

Visual C# .NET

1. Add the following event handler to the code below the existing btnGetOrders_Click procedure:

```
private void btnOrderCount_Click(object sender,
System.EventArgs e)
{
   int cnt;
   string strMsg;
   System.Data.DataRowView drv;

   drv = (System.Data.DataRowView)
          this.lbEmployees.SelectedItem;
   this.cmdOrderCount.Parameters["@empID"].Value =
          drv["EmployeeID"];
   drv = (System.Data.DataRowView)
          this.lbClients.SelectedItem;
   this.cmdOrderCount.Parameters["@custID"].Value =
          drv["CustomerID"];
}
```

The code first declares a couple of variables that will be used in the next exercise, and then sets the value of each of the parameters in the cmdOrderCount.Parameters collection to the value of the Employees and Clients list boxes, respectively.

2 Connect the event handler to the click event by adding the following line to the end of the frmDataCmds sub:

```
this.btnOrderCount.Click += new
   EventHandler(this.btnOrderCount_Click);
```


Command Methods

The methods exposed by the Command object are shown in Table 3-6. Of these, the most important are the four *Execute* methods: *ExecuteNonQuery*, *ExecuteReader*, *ExecuteScalar*, and *ExecuteXmlReader*.

ExecuteNonQuery is used when the SQL command or stored procedure to be executed returns no rows. An Update query, for example, would use the *ExecuteNonQuery* method.

ExecuteScalar is used for SQL commands and stored procedures that return a single value. The most common example of this sort of command is one that returns a count of rows:

```
SELECT Count(*) from OrderTotals
```

Method	Description
Cancel	Cancels execution of a Data Command
CreateParameter	Creates a new parameter
ExecuteNonQuery	Executes a command against the Connection and returns the number of rows affected
ExecuteReader	Sends the CommandText to the Connection and builds a DataReader
ExecuteScalar	Executes the query and returns the first column of the first row of the result set
ExecuteXmlReader	Sends the CommandText to the Connection and builds an XMLReader
Prepare	Creates a prepared (compiled) version of the command on the data source
ResetCommandTimeout	Resets the CommandTimeout property to its default value

Table 3-6 Command Methods

The *ExecuteReader* method is used for SQL Commands and stored procedures that return multiple rows. The method creates a DataReader object. We'll discuss DataReaders in detail in the next section.

The *ExecuteReader* method may be executed with no parameters, or you can supply a CommandBehavior value that allows you to control precisely how the Command will perform. The values for CommandBehavior are shown in Table 3-7.

Property	Description
CloseConnection	Closes the associated Connection when the DataReader is closed
KeyInfo	Indicates that the query returns column and primary key information
SchemaOnly	Returns the database schema only, without affecting any rows in the data source
SequentialAccess	The results of each column of each row will be accessed sequentially
SingleResult	Returns only a single value
SingleRow	Returns only a single row

Table 3-7 CommandBehavior Values

Most of the CommandBehavior values are self-explanatory. Both KeyInfo and SchemaOnly are useful if you cannot determine the structure of the command's result set prior to run time.

The SequentialAccess behavior allows the application to read large binary column values using the *GetBytes* or *GetChars* methods of the DataReader, while the SingleResult and SingleRow behaviors can be optimized by the Data Provider.

Execute a Command

Visual Basic .NET

- Add the following code to the btnOrderCount_Click event handler that we began in the last exercise:

```
Me.cnNorthwind.Open()
cnt = Me.cmdOrderCount.ExecuteScalar
Me.cnNorthwind.Close()

strMsg = "There are " & cnt.ToString & " Orders for this "
strMsg &= "Employee/Customer combination."
MessageBox.Show(strMsg)
```

The first three lines of code open the cnNorthwind Connection, call the *ExecuteScalar* method to return a single value from the cmdOrderCount Command, and then close the Connection. The last three lines simply display the results in a message box.

Visual C# .NET

- Add the following code to the btnOrderCount_Click event handler that we began in the last exercise:

```
this.cnNorthwind.Open();
cnt = (Int) this.cmdOrderCount.ExecuteScalar();
this.cnNorthwind.Close();

strMsg = "There are " + cnt.ToString() + " Orders for this ";
strMsg += "Employee/Customer combination.";
MessageBox.Show(strMsg);
```

The first three lines of code open the cnNorthwind Connection, call the *ExecuteScalar* method to return a single value from the cmdOrderCount Command, and then close the Connection. The last three lines simply display the results in a message box.

DataReaders

The DataReader's properties are shown in Table 3-8. The Item property supports two versions: Item(Name), which takes a string specifying the name of the column as a parameter, and Item(Index), which takes an Int32 as an index into the columns collection. (As with all collections in the .NET Framework, the collection index is zero-based.)

Property	Description
Depth	The depth of nesting for the current row in hierarchical result sets. SQL Server always returns zero.
FieldCount	The number of columns in the current row.
IsClosed	Indicates whether the DataReader is closed.
Item	The value of a column.
RecordsAffected	The number of rows changed, inserted, or deleted.

Table 3-8 DataReader Properties

The methods exposed by the DataReader are shown in Table 3-9. The *Close* method, as we've seen, closes the DataReader and, if the CloseConnection behavior has been specified, closes the Connection as well. The

GetDataTypeName, *GetFieldType*, *GetName*, *GetOrdinal* and *IsDbNull* methods allow you to determine, at run time, the properties of a specified column.

Note that *IsDbNull* is the only way to check for a null value, since the .NET Framework doesn't have an intrinsic Null data type.

Method	Description
Close	Closes the DataReader
GetType	Gets the value of the specified column as the specified type
GetDataTypeName	Gets the name of the data source type
GetFieldType	Returns the system type of the specified column
GetName	Gets the name of the specified column
GetOrdinal	Gets the ordinal position of the column specified
GetSchemaTable	Returns a DataTable that describes the structure of the DataReader
GetValue	Gets the value of the specified column as its native type
GetValues	Gets all the columns in the current row
IsDbNull	Indicates whether the column contains a nonexistent value
NextResult	Advances the DataReader to the next result
Read	Advances the DataReader to the next row

Table 3-9 DataReader Methods

The *Read* method retrieves the next row of the result set. When the DataReader is first opened, it is positioned at the beginning of file, *before* the first row, not *at* the first row. You must call *Read* before the first row of the result set will be returned.

The *NextResult* method is used when a SQL command or stored procedure returns multiple result sets. It positions the DataReader at the beginning of the next result set. Again, the DataReader will be positioned *before* the first row, and you must call *Read* before accessing any results.

The *GetValues* method returns all of the columns in the current row as an object array, while the *GetValue* method returns a single value as one of the .NET Framework types. However, if you know the data type of the value to be returned in advance, it is more efficient to use one of the *GetType* methods shown in Table 3-10.

note

The SqlDataReader object supports additional *GetType* methods for values of System.Data.SqlType. They are detailed in online help.

Method Name	Method Name	Method Name
GetBoolean	*GetFloat*	*GetInt16*
GetByte	*GetGuid*	*GetInt32*
GetBytes	*GetDateTime*	*GetInt64*
GetChar	*GetDecimal*	*GetString*
GetChars	*GetDouble*	*GetTimeSpan*

Table 3-10 GetType Methods

Create a DataReader to Return Command Results

Visual Basic .NET

1. In the code editor window, select btnFillLists in the Object Name list, and Click in the Method Name box.

   Visual Studio adds the click event handler to the code.

2. Add the following variable declarations to the event handler:

```
Dim dr As System.Data.DataRow
Dim rdrEmployees As System.Data.SqlClient.SqlDataReader
Dim rdrCustomers As System.Data.SqlClient.SqlDataReader
```

3. Add the following code to fill the EmployeeList table:

```
Me.cnNorthwind.Open()
rdrEmployees = Me.cmdGetEmployees.ExecuteReader()

With rdrEmployees
    While .Read
        dr = Me.dsMaster1.EmployeeList.NewRow
        dr(0) = .GetInt32(0)
        dr(1) = .GetString(1)
        dr(2) = .GetString(2)
        Me.dsMaster1.EmployeeList.Rows.Add(dr)
    End While
End With
rdrEmployees.Close()
Me.cnNorthwind.Close()
```

Roadmap
We'll examine the DataSet in Chapter 6.

The code first opens the Connection, and then creates the DataReader with the *ExecuteReader* method. The *While .Read* loop first creates a new DataRow, retrieves each column from the DataRow and assigns its value to a column, and then adds the new row to the EmployeeList table. Finally, the DataReader and the Connection are closed.

4 Add the final code to the procedure:

```
Me.cnNorthwind.Open()
rdrCustomers = Me.cmdGetCustomers.ExecuteReader()
With rdrCustomers
   While .Read
      dr = Me.dsMaster1.CustomerList.NewRow
      dr(0) = .GetString(0)
      dr(1) = .GetString(1)
      Me.dsMaster1.CustomerList.Rows.Add(dr)
   End While
End With
rdrCustomers.Close()
Me.cnNorthwind.Close()
```

This code is almost identical to the previous section, except that it uses the cmdGetCustomers command to fill the CustomerList table. Note that the Connection is closed and re-opened between calls to the *ExecuteReader* method. This is necessary because the Connection will return a status of Busy until either it or the DataReader are explicitly closed.

5 Press F5 to run the application.

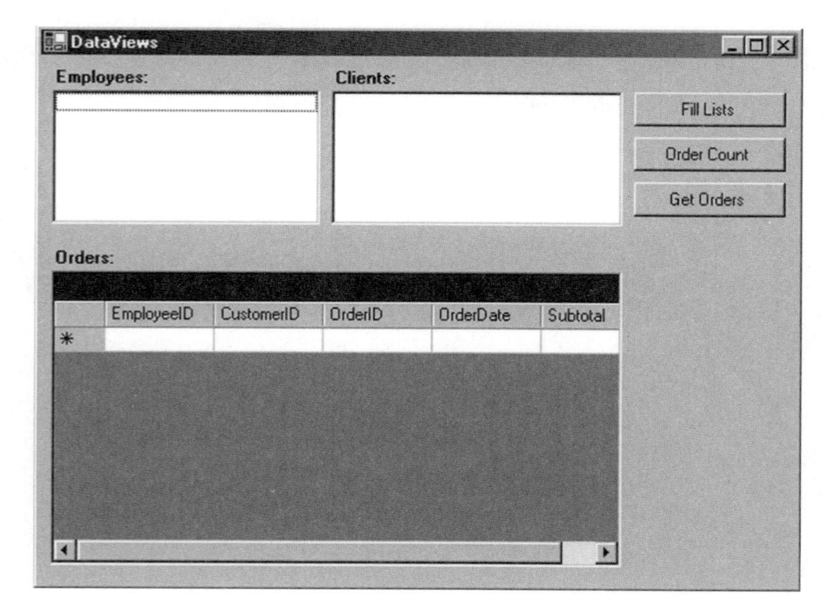

6 Click Fill Lists.

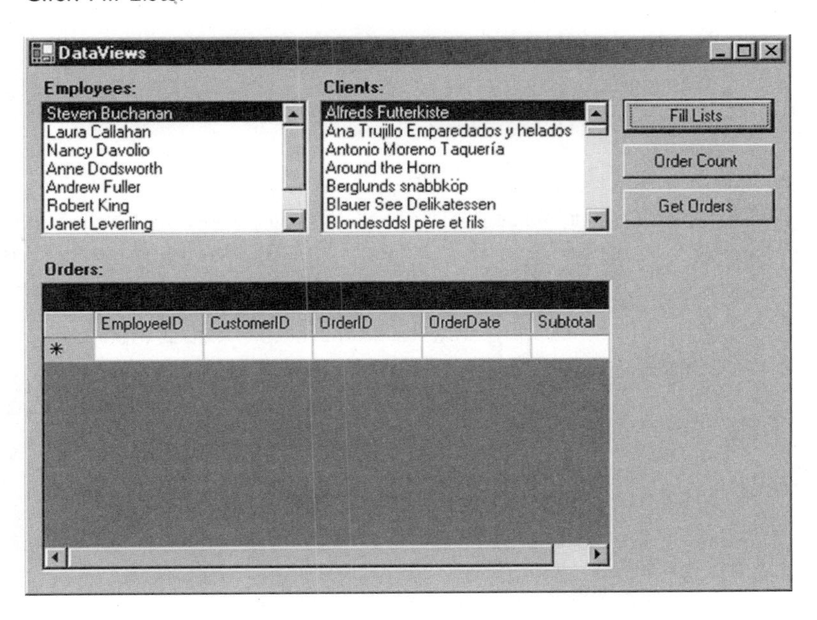

7 Select different combinations of Employee and Customer, and then click Order Count, and, if you like, click Get Orders.

The Get Orders button click event handler, which is provided for you, also calls the *ExecuteReader* method, but this time against the cmdGetOrders object.

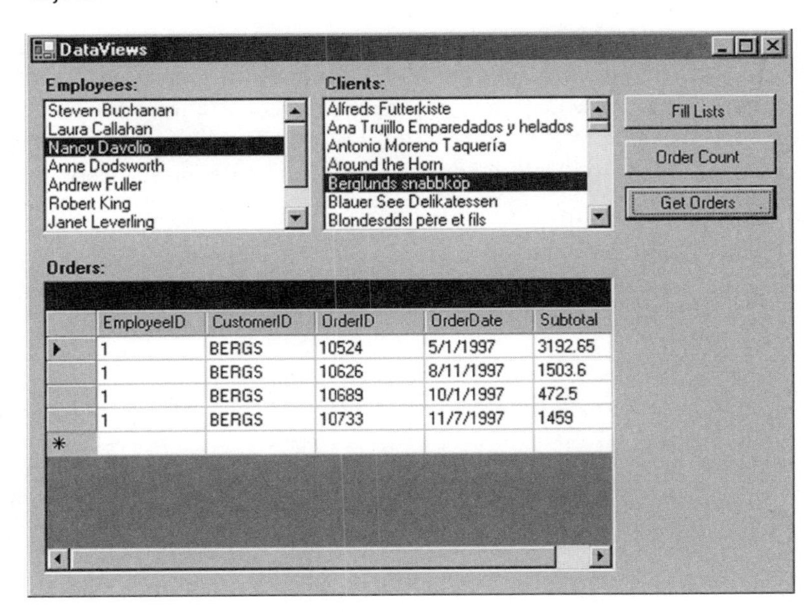

Visual C# .NET

1 Create the following event handler in the code editor window:

```
private void btnFillLists_Click(object sender,
System.EventArgs e)
{
   System.Data.DataRow dr;
   System.Data.SqlClient.SqlDataReader rdrEmployees;
   System.Data.SqlClient.SqlDataReader rdrCustomers;
}
```

2 Add the following code to fill the EmployeeList table:

```
this.cnNorthwind.Open();
rdrEmployees = this.cmdGetEmployees.ExecuteReader();

while (rdrEmployees.Read())
{
   dr = this.dsMaster1.EmployeeList.NewRow();
   dr[0] = rdrEmployees.GetInt32(0);
   dr[1] = rdrEmployees.GetString(1);
   dr[2] = rdrEmployees.GetString(2);
   this.dsMaster1.EmployeeList.Rows.Add(dr);
}

rdrEmployees.Close();
this.cnNorthwind.Close();
```

Roadmap

We'll examine the DataSet in Chapter 6.

The code first opens the Connection, and then creates the DataReader with the *ExecuteReader* method. The while (rdrEmployees.Read()) loop first creates a new DataRow, retrieves each column from the DataRow and assigns its value to a column, and then adds the new row to the EmployeeList table. Finally, the DataReader and the Connection are closed.

3 Add the final code to the procedure:

```
this.cnNorthwind.Open();
rdrCustomers = this.cmdGetCustomers.ExecuteReader();
```

```
while (rdrCustomers.Read())
{
   dr = this.dsMaster1.CustomerList.NewRow();
   dr[0] = rdrCustomers.GetString(0);
   dr[1] = rdrCustomers.GetString(1);
   this.dsMaster1.CustomerList.Rows.Add(dr);
}

rdrCustomers.Close();
this.cnNorthwind.Close();
```

This code is almost identical to the previous section, except that it uses the cmdGetCustomers command to fill the CustomerList table. Note that the Connection is closed and re-opened between calls to the *ExecuteReader* method. This is necessary because the Connection will return a status of Busy until either it or the DataReader are explicitly closed.

4 Link the event handler to the event by adding the following line to the frmDataCmds sub:

```
this.btnFillLists.Click += New
   EventHandler(this.btnFillLists_Click);
```

5 Press F5 to run the application.

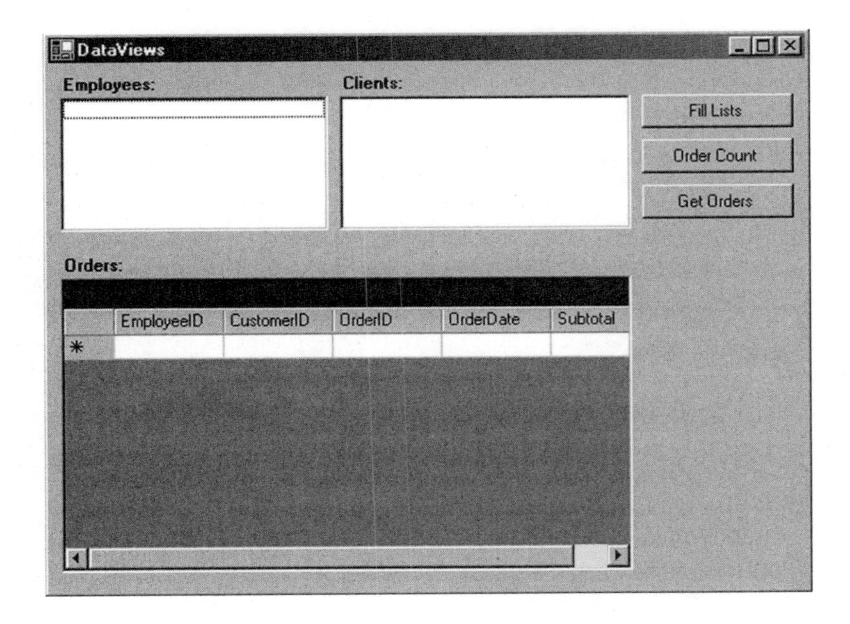

6 Click Fill Lists.

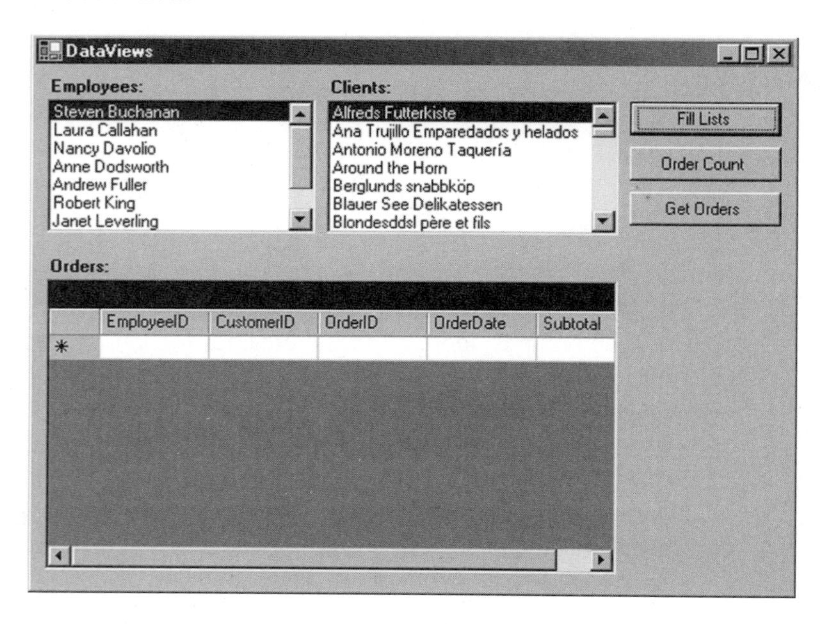

7 Select different combinations of Employee and Customer, and then click Order Count, and, if you like, click Get Orders.

The Get Orders button click event handler, which is provided for you, also calls the *ExecuteReader* method, but this time against the cmdGetOrders object.

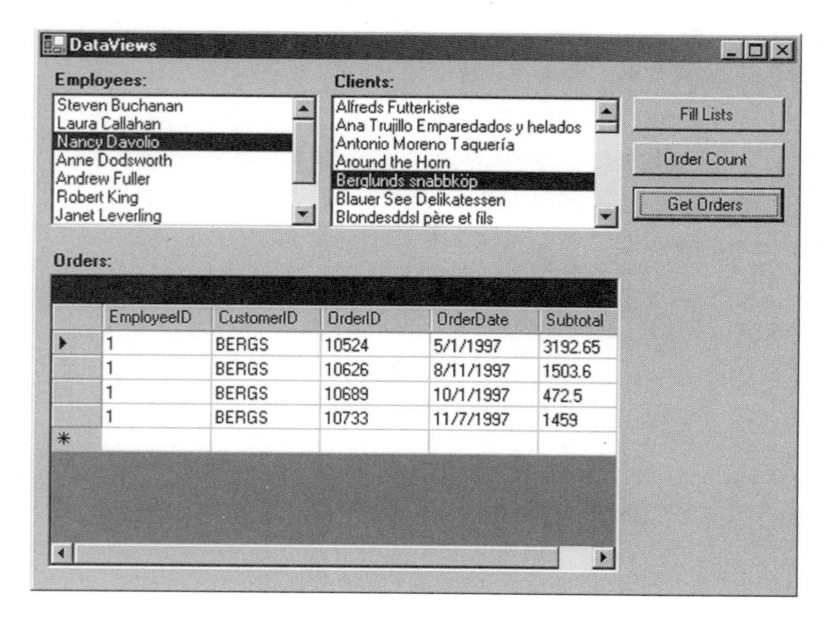

Chapter 3 Quick Reference

To	Do this
Add a Data Command to a form	Drag an OleDbCommand or SqlCommand from the Data tab of the Toolbox to the form.
Create a Data Command at run time	Use one of the New constructors. For example: Dim myCmd as New System.Data.SqlClient.SqlCommand()
Configure the Parameters collection in Visual Studio	Click the ellipsis button in the Parameters property of the Property window.
Add and configure Parameters at run time	Use one of the *Add* methods of the Parameters collection. For example: mySqlCmd.Parameters.Add ("@myParam", SqlDbType.Type)
Execute a Command that doesn't return a result	Use the *ExecuteNonQuery* method. For example: intResults = myCmd.ExecuteNonQuery()
Execute a Command that returns a single value	Use the *ExecuteScalar* method. For example: myResult = myCmd.ExecuteScalar()
Create a DataReader to return Command results	Use the *ExecuteReader* method. For example: myReader = myCmd.ExecuteReader()

CHAPTER

4

The DataAdapter

In this chapter, you'll learn how to:

- ✔ *Create a DataAdapter*
- ✔ *Preview the results of a DataAdapter*
- ✔ *Set a DataAdapter's properties*
- ✔ *Use the Table Mappings dialog box*
- ✔ *Use the DataAdapter's methods*
- ✔ *Respond to DataAdapter events*

In this chapter, we'll examine the DataAdapter, which sits between the Connection object we looked at in the previous chapter and the DataSet, which we'll examine in Chapter 5.

Understanding the DataAdapter

Like the Connection and Command objects, the DataAdapter is part of the Data Provider, and there is a version of the DataAdapter specific to each Data Provider. In the release version of the .NET Framework, this means the OleDbDataAdapter in the System.Data.OleDb namespace and the SqlDataAdapter in the System.Data.SqlClient namespace. Both of these objects inherit from the System.Data.DbDataAdapter, which in turn inherits from the System.Data.DataAdapter.

DataAdapters act as the "glue" between a data source and the DataSet object. In very abstract terms, the DataAdapter receives the data from the Connection object and passes it to the DataSet. It then passes changes back from the DataSet to the Connection to update the data in the data source. (Remember that the data source can be any kind of data, not just a database.)

tip

Typically, there is a one-to-one relationship between a DataAdapter and a DataTable within a DataSet, but a SelectCommand that returns multiple result sets may link to multiple tables in the DataSet.

To perform updates on the data source, DataAdapters contain references to four Data Commands, one for each possible action: SelectCommand, UpdateCommand, InsertCommand, and DeleteCommand.

note

With the exception of some minor differences in the *Fill* method, which we'll look at later, the SqlDataAdapter and OleDbDataAdapter have identical properties, methods, and events. For the sake of simplicity, we'll only use the SqlDataAdapter in this chapter, but all of the code samples will work equally well with OleDb if you change the class names of the objects.

Creating DataAdapters

Microsoft Visual Studio .NET provides several different methods for creating DataAdapters interactively. We saw one in Chapter 1, when we used the Data Adapter Configuration Wizard, and we'll explore a couple more in this section. Of course, if you need to, you can create a DataAdapter manually in code, and we'll look at that in this section, as well.

Using the Server Explorer

If you have created a design time connection to a data source in the Server Explorer, you can automatically create a DataAdapter by dragging the appropriate table, query, or stored procedure onto your form. If you don't already have a connection on the form, Visual Studio will create a preconfigured connection as well.

Create a DataAdapter from the Server Explorer

1. Open the DataAdapters project from the Visual Studio start page or by using the Open menu.
2. In the Solution Explorer, double-click DataAdapters.vb (or DataAdapters.cs, if you're using C#) to open the form.

   Visual Studio displays the form in the form designer.

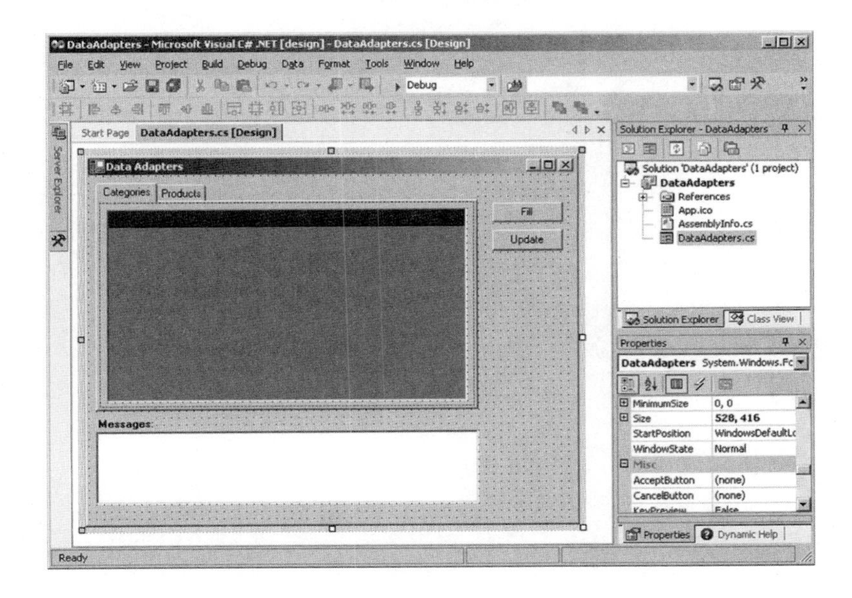

3. In the Server Explorer, expand the SQL Northwind connection (the name of the Connection will depend on your system configuration), and then expand its Tables collection.

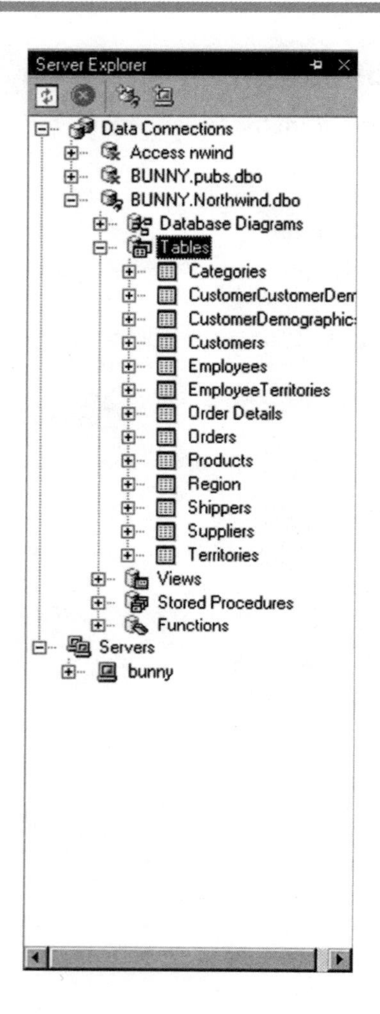

4 Drag the Categories table onto the form.

Visual Studio adds an instance of the SqlDataAdapter and because it didn't already exist, an instance of the SqlConnection to the component designer.

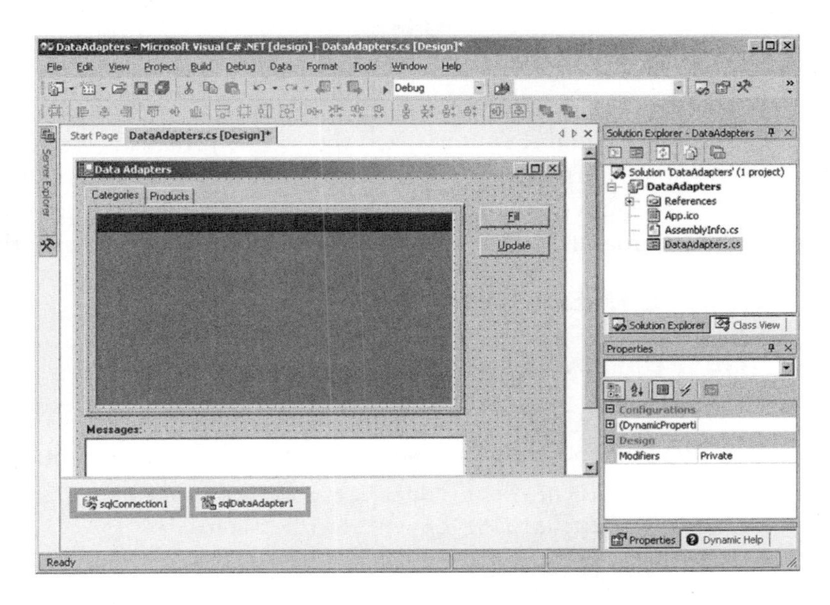

5 Select the SqlDataAdapter1 on the form, and then in the Properties window, change its name to daCategories.

Using the Toolbox

As we saw in Chapter 1, if you drag a DataAdapter from the Toolbox (either an SqlDataAdapter or an OleDbDataAdapter), Visual Studio will start the Data Adapter Configuration Wizard. If you want to configure the DataAdapter manually, you can simply cancel the wizard and set the DataAdapter's properties using code or the Properties window.

Create a DataAdapter Using the Toolbox

In this exercise, we'll only create the DataAdapter. We'll set its properties later in the chapter.

1 In the Toolbox, drag a SqlDataAdapter from the Data tab onto the form.

Visual Studio starts the Data Adapter Configuration Wizard.

2 Click Cancel.

Visual Studio creates an instance of the SqlDataAdapter in the component designer.

3 In the Properties window, change the name of the DataAdapter to daProducts.

Creating DataAdapters at Run Time

When we created ADO.NET objects in code in previous chapters, we first declared them and then initialized them. The process is essentially the same to create a DataAdapter, but it has a little twist—because a DataAdapter references four command objects, you must also declare and instantiate each of the commands, and then set the DataAdapter to reference them.

Create a DataAdapter in Code

Visual Basic .NET

1. Press F7 to display the code for the DataAdapters form.
2. Type the following statements after the Inherits statement:

```
Friend WithEvents cmdSelectSuppliers As New _
   System.Data.SqlClient.SqlCommand()
Friend WithEvents cmdInsertSuppliers As New _
   System.Data.SqlClient.SqlCommand()
Friend WithEvents cmdUpdateSuppliers As New _
   System.Data.SqlClient.SqlCommand()
Friend WithEvents cmdDeleteSuppliers As New _
   System.Data.SqlClient.SqlCommand()
Friend WithEvents daSuppliers As New _
   System.Data.SqlClient.SqlDataAdapter()
```

   These lines declare the four command objects and the DataAdapter, and initialize each object with its default constructor.

3. Open the region labeled "Windows Form Designer generated code" and add the following lines to the New Sub after the call to *InitializeComponent*:

```
Me.daSuppliers.DeleteCommand = Me.cmdDeleteSuppliers
Me.daSuppliers.InsertCommand = Me.cmdInsertSuppliers
Me.daSuppliers.SelectCommand = Me.cmdSelectSuppliers
Me.daSuppliers.UpdateCommand = Me.cmdUpdateSuppliers
```

   These lines assign the four Command objects to the daSuppliers DataAdapter.

Visual C# .NET

1. Press F7 to display the code for the DataAdapters form.
2. Type the following statements at the beginning of the class definition:

```
private System.Data.SqlClient.SqlCommand cmdSelectSuppliers;
private System.Data.SqlClient.SqlCommand cmdInsertSuppliers;
```

```
private System.Data.SqlClient.SqlCommand cmdUpdateSuppliers;
private System.Data.SqlClient.SqlCommand cmdDeleteSuppliers;
private System.Data.SqlClient.SqlDataAdapter daSuppliers;
```

These lines declare the four Command objects and the DataAdapter.

3 Scroll down to the DataAdapters function and add the following lines after the call to *InitializeComponent*:

```
this.cmdDeleteSuppliers = new
   System.Data.SqlClient.SqlCommand();
this.cmdInsertSuppliers = new
   System.Data.SqlClient.SqlCommand();
this.cmdSelectSuppliers = new
   System.Data.SqlClient.SqlCommand();
this.cmdUpdateSuppliers = new
   System.Data.SqlClient.SqlCommand();
this.daSuppliers = new
   System.Data.SqlClient.SqlDataAdapter();
```

These lines instantiate each object using the default constructor.

4 Add the following lines to assign the four command objects to the daSuppliers DataAdapter:

```
this.daSuppliers.DeleteCommand = this.cmdDeleteSuppliers;
this.daSuppliers.InsertCommand = this.cmdInsertSuppliers;
this.daSuppliers.SelectCommand = this.cmdSelectSuppliers;
this.daSuppliers.UpdateCommand = this.cmdUpdateSuppliers;
```


Previewing Results

Visual Studio provides a quick and easy method to check the configuration of a form-level DataAdapter: the DataAdapter Preview dialog box.

Preview the Results of a DataAdapter

1 Make sure that daCategories is selected in the component designer.

2 Select Preview Data in the bottom portion of the Properties window.

Visual Studio opens the DataAdapter Preview window.

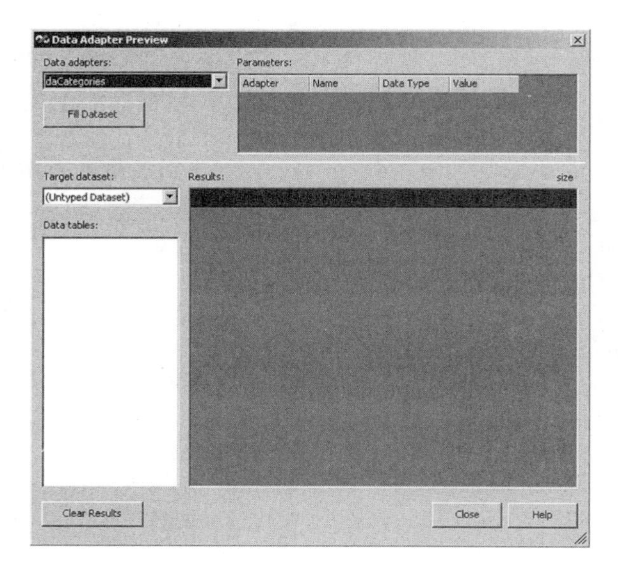

3 Click Fill Dataset.

Visual Studio displays the rows returned by the DataAdapter.

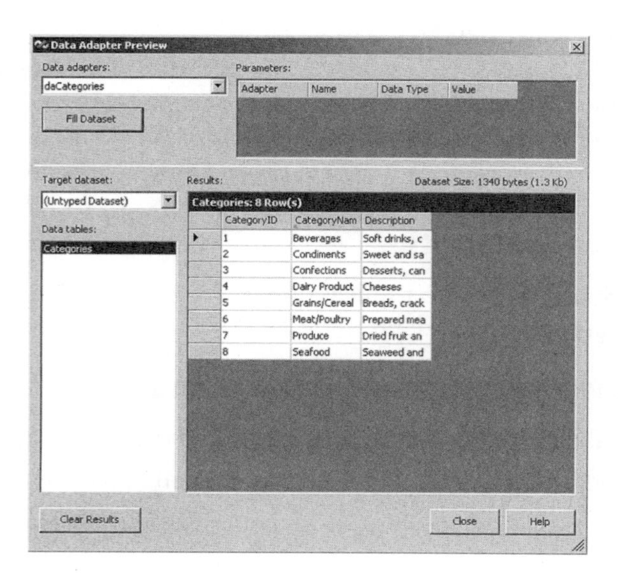

4 Click Close.

Visual Studio closes the DataAdapter Preview window.

DataAdapter Properties

The properties exposed by the DataAdapter are shown in Table 4-1. The SqlDataAdapter and OleDbDataAdapter objects expose the same set of properties.

Property	Description
AcceptChangesDuringFill	Determines whether *AcceptChanges* is called on a DataRow after it is added to the DataTable
DeleteCommand	The Data Command used to delete rows in the data source
InsertCommand	The Data Command used to insert rows in the data source
MissingMappingAction	Determines the action that will be taken when incoming data cannot be matched to an existing table or column
MissingSchemaAction	Determines the action that will be taken when incoming data does not match the schema of an existing DataSet
SelectCommand	The Data Command used to retrieve rows from the data source
TableMappings	A collection of DataTableMapping objects that determine the relationship between the columns in a DataSet and the data source
UpdateCommand	The Data Command used to update rows in the data source

Table 4-1 DataAdapter Properties

Roadmap
We'll examine AcceptChanges *in Chapter 9.*

The AcceptChangesDuringFill property determines whether the *AcceptChanges* method is called for each row that is added to a DataSet. The default value is *true*.

The MissingMappingAction property determines how the system reacts when a SelectCommand returns columns or tables that are not found in the DataSet. The possible values are shown in Table 4-2. The default value is *Passthrough*.

Value	Description
Error	Throws a SystemException
Ignore	Ignores any columns or tables not found in the DataSet
Passthrough	The column or table that is not found is added to the DataSet, using its name in the data source

Table 4-2 MissingMappingAction Values

Similarly, the MissingSchemaAction property determines how the system will respond if a column is missing in the DataSet. The MissingSchemaAction property will be called only if the MissingMappingAction is set to *Passthrough*. The possible values are shown in Table 4-3. The default value is *Add*.

Value	Description
Add	Adds the necessary columns to the DataSet
AddWithKey	Adds both the necessary columns and tables and PrimaryKey constraints
Error	Throws a SystemException
Ignore	Ignores the extra columns

Table 4-3 MissingSchemaAction Values

In addition, the DataAdapter has two sets of properties that we'll examine in detail: the set of Command objects that tell it how to update the data source to reflect changes made to the DataSet and a TableMappings property that maintains the relationship between columns in a DataSet and columns in the data source.

DataAdapter Commands

As we've seen, each DataAdapter contains references to four Command objects, each of which has a CommandText property that contains the actual SQL command to be executed.

If you create a DataAdapter by using the Data Adapter Configuration Wizard or by dragging a table, view, or stored procedure from the Server Explorer, Visual Studio will attempt to automatically generate the CommandText property for each command. You can also edit the SQL command in the Properties window, although you must first associate the command with a Connection object.

> **note**
>
> Every DataAdapter command must be associated with a Connection. In most cases, you will use a single Connection for all of the commands, but this isn't a requirement. You can associate a different Connection with each command, if necessary.

You must specify the CommandText property for the SelectCommand object, but the .NET Framework can generate the commands for update, insert, and delete if they are not specified.

Internally, Visual Studio uses the CommandBuilder object to generate commands. You can instantiate a CommandBuilder object in code and use it to generate commands as required. However, you must be aware of the CommandBuilder's limitations. It cannot handle parameterized stored procedures, for example.

Set CommandText in the Properties Window

1 Select the daProducts object in the form designer, and then in the Properties window, expand the Select Command properties.

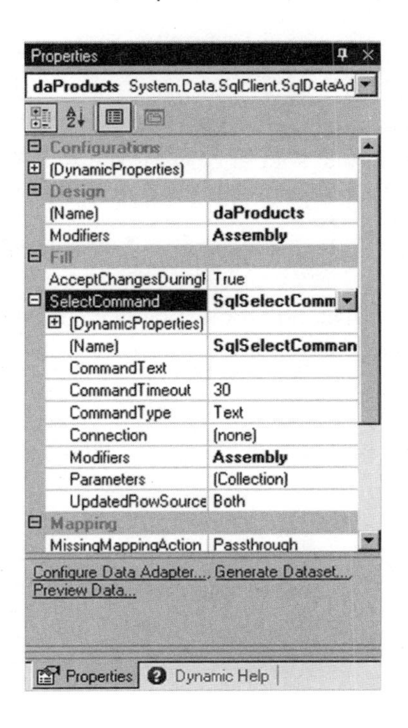

2 Select the SelectCommand's Connection property, expand the Existing node in the list, and then choose SqlConnection1.

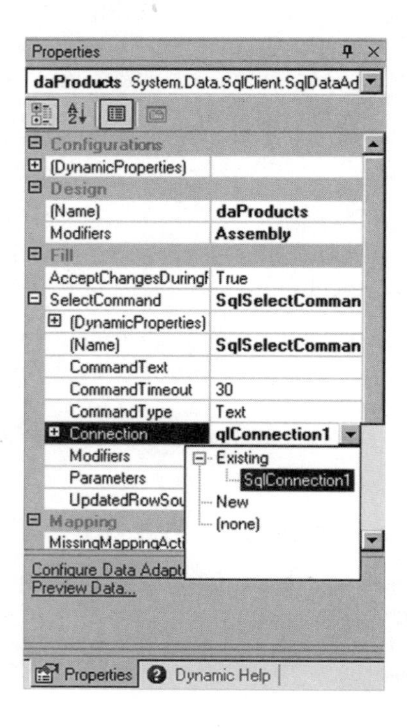

3 Select the CommandText property, and then click the ellipsis button. Visual Studio opens the Query Builder and opens the Add Table dialog box.

4 Select the Products table, click Add, and then click Close.

Visual Studio closes the Add Table dialog box and adds the table to the Query Builder.

5 Add the CategoryID, ProductID, and ProductName columns to the query by selecting each column's check box.

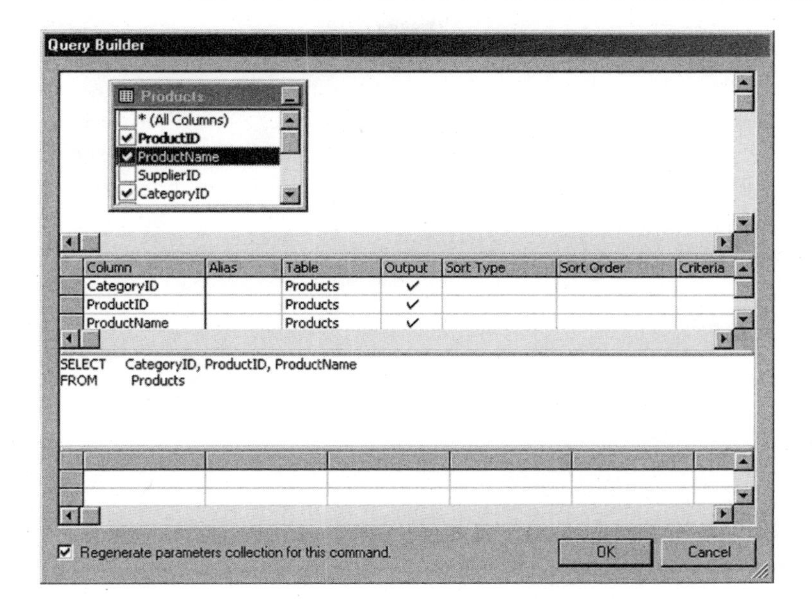

6 Click OK.

Visual Studio generates the CommandText property.

Set CommandText in Code

Visual Basic .NET

- In the code editor, add the following lines of code to the bottom of the New Sub:

```
Me.cmdSelectSuppliers.CommandText = "SELECT * FROM Suppliers"
Me.cmdSelectSuppliers.Connection = Me.SqlConnection1
```

Visual C# .NET

- In the code editor, add the following lines to the bottom of the DataAdapters Sub:

```
this.cmdSelectSuppliers.CommandText = "SELECT * FROM Suppliers";
this.cmdSelectSuppliers.Connection = this.sqlConnection1;
```

The TableMappings Collection

A DataSet has no knowledge of where the data it contains comes from, and a Connection has no knowledge of what happens to the data it retrieves. The DataAdapter maintains the connection between the two. It does this by using the TableMappings collection.

The structure of the TableMappings collection is shown in the following figure. At the highest level, the TableMappings collection contains one or more DataTableMapping objects. Typically, there is only one DataTableMapping object because most DataAdapters return only a single record set. However, if a DataAdapter manages multiple record sets, as might be the case with a stored procedure that returns multiple result sets, there will be a DataTableMapping object for each record set.

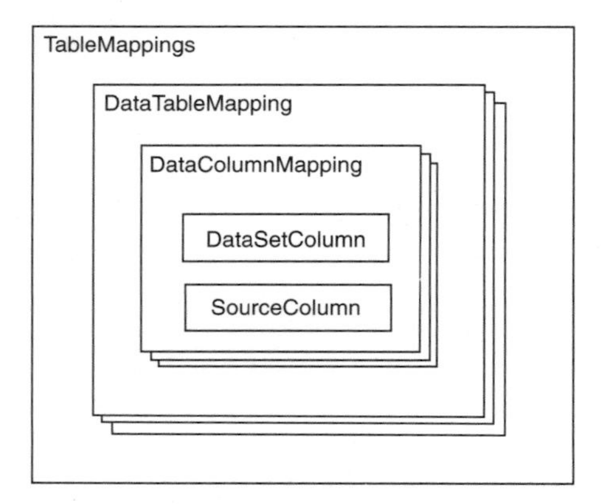

The DataTableMapping object is another collection, which contains one or more DataColumnMapping objects. The DataColumnMapping object consists of two properties: the SourceColumn, which is the case-sensitive name of the column within the data source, and the DataSetColumn, which is the case-*in*sensitive name of the column within the DataSet. There is a DataColumnMapping object for each column managed by the DataAdapter.

By default, the .NET Framework will create a TableMappings collection (and all of the objects it contains) with the DataSetColumn name set to the SourceColumn name. There are times, however, when this isn't what you want. For example, you might want to change the mappings for reasons of convenience or because you're working with a pre-existing DataSet with difference column names.

Change a DataSet Column Name Using the Table Mappings Dialog Box

1. Select the daCategories DataAdapter in the form designer.
2. In the Properties window, expand the Mapping properties.

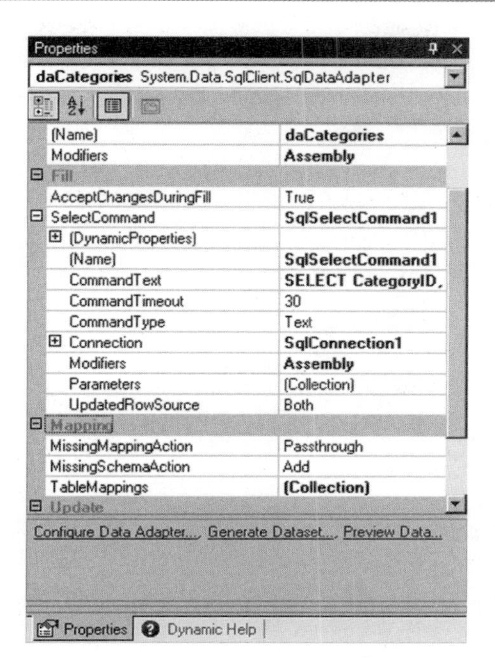

3 Select the TableMappings property and click the ellipsis button. Visual Studio displays the Table Mappings dialog box.

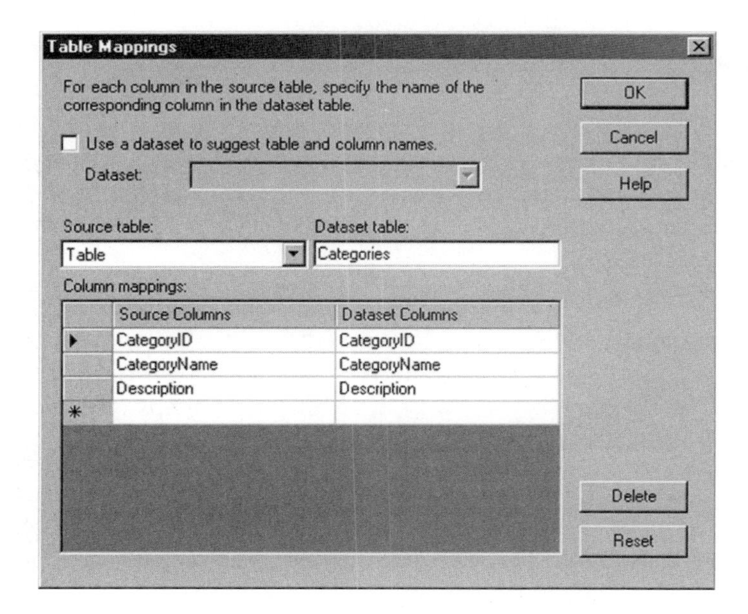

4 Change the name of the Dataset column from CategoryName to Name.

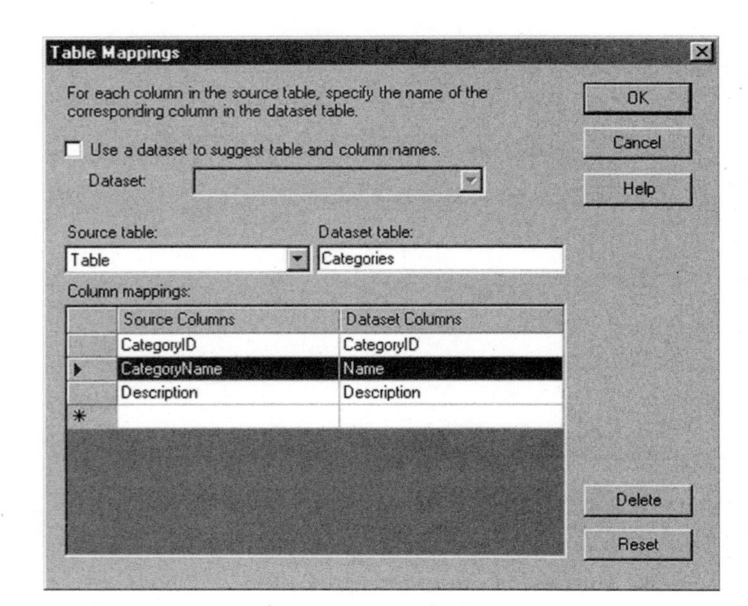

5 Click OK.

Visual Studio updates the collection.

DataAdapter Methods

The DataAdapter supports two important methods: *Fill*, which loads data from the data source into the DataSet, and *Update*, which transfers data the other direction—loading it from the DataSet into the data source. We'll examine both in this set of exercises.

Generating DataSets and Binding Data

Roadmap
We'll examine DataSets in Chapter 6.

Before we can examine the *Fill* and *Update* methods, we must create and link the DataSets to be used to store the data. We haven't examined DataSets yet (we'll do that in Chapter 6), so just follow the steps outlined and try not to worry about them.

Generate and Bind DataSets

1 Select the daCategories DataAdapter in the form designer.

2 On the Data menu, choose Generate Dataset.

Visual Studio displays the Generate Dataset dialog box.

3 In the New text box, change the name of the new DataSet to dsCategories.

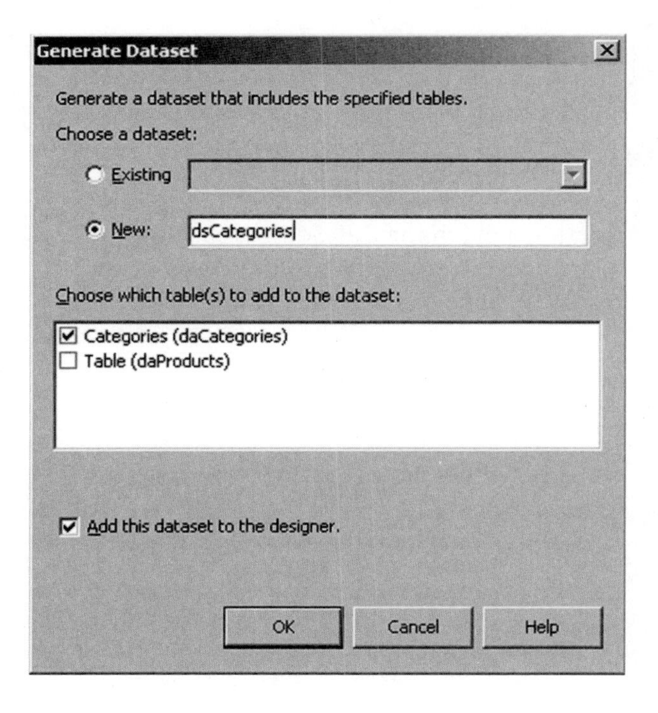

4. Click OK.

   Visual Studio creates the dsCategories DataSet and adds an instance of it to the form designer.

5. Repeat steps 1 through 4 for the daProducts DataAdapter. Name the new DataSet dsProducts.

6. Select the dgCategories object in the drop-down list box of the Properties window.

7. In the Properties window, expand the DataBindings section.

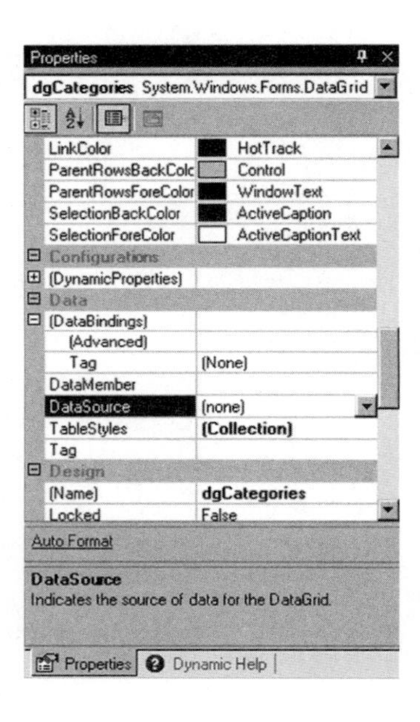

8. Select dsCategories1 in the DataSource list.

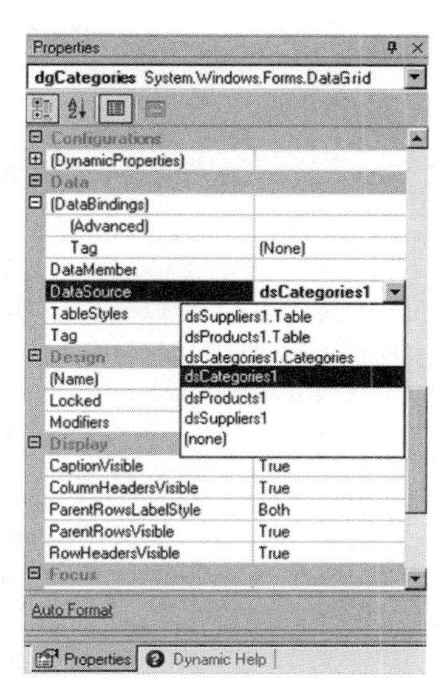

9 Select Categories in the DataMember list.

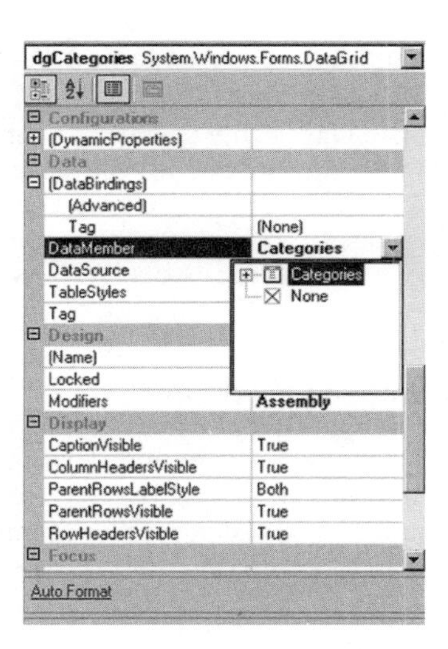

10 Repeat steps 6 through 9 for the dgProducts control, binding it to the dsProducts1 DataSource and Table DataMember.

The *Fill* Method

The *Fill* method loads data from a data source into one or more tables of a DataSet by using the command specified in the DataAdapter's SelectCommand. The DbDataAdapter object, from which both the

OleDbDataAdapter and the SqlDataAdapter are inherited, supports several variations of the *Fill* method, as shown in Table 4-4.

Method	Description
Fill(DataSet)	Creates a DataTable named Table and populates it with the rows returned from the data source
Fill(DataTable)	Fills the specified DataTable with the rows returned from the data source
Fill(DataSet, tableName)	Fills the DataTable named in the *tableName* string, within the DataSet specified, with the rows returned from the data source
Fill(DataTable, DataReader)	Fills the DataTable using the specified DataReader (Because DataReader is declared as an IDataReader, either an OleDbDataReader or a SQLDataReader can be used)
Fill(DataTable, command, CommandBehavior)	Fills the DataTable using the SQL string passed in command and the specified CommandBehavior
Fill(DataSet, startRecord, maxRecords, tableName)	Fills the DataTable specified in the tableName string, beginning at the zero-based startRecord and continuing for maxRecords or until the end of the result set
Fill(DataSet, tableName, DataReader, startRecord, maxRecords)	Fills the DataTable specified in the tableName string, beginning at the zero-based startRecord and continuing for maxRecords or until the end of the result set, using the specified DataReader (Since DataReader is declared as an IDataReader, either an OleDbDataReader or a SQLDataReader can be used)
Fill(DataSet, startRecord, maxRecords, tableName, command, CommandBehavior)	Fills the DataTable specified in the tableName string, beginning at the zero-based startRecord and continuing for maxRecords or until the end of the result set, using the SQL text contained in command and the specified CommandBehavior

Table 4-4 DbDataAdapter *Fill* Methods

In addition, the OleDbDataAdapter supports the two additional versions of the *Fill* method shown in Table 4-5, which are used to load data from Microsoft ActiveX Data Objects (ADO).

Method	Description
Fill(DataTable, adoObject)	Fills the specified DataTable with rows from the ADO Recordset or Record object specified in adoObject
Fill(DataSet, adoObject, tableName)	Fills the specified DataTable with rows from the ADO Recordset or Record object specified in adoObject, using the DataTable specified in the tableName string to determine the TableMappings

Table 4-5 OleDbDataAdapter *Fill* Methods

The SqlDataAdapter supports only the methods provided by the DbDataAdapter. DataAdapters included in other Data Providers can, of course, support additional versions of the *Fill* method.

important

The Microsoft SQL Server decimal data type allows a maximum of 38 significant digits, while the .NET Framework decimal type only allows a maximum of 28. If a row in a SQL table contains a decimal field with more than 28 significant digits, the row will not be added to the DataSet and a FillError will be raised.

Use the *Fill* Method

Visual Basic .NET

1. Press F7 to display the code editor for the DataAdapters form.
2. Select btnFill in the ClassName list, and then select Click in the MethodName list.

   Visual Studio displays the Click event handler template.
3. Add the following lines of code to clear each dataset to the sub:

```
Me.dsCategories1.Clear()
Me.dsProducts1.Clear()
```

4. Add the following code to fill each DataSet from the DataAdapters:

```
Me.daCategories.Fill(Me.dsCategories1.Categories)
Me.daProducts.Fill(Me.dsProducts1._Table)
```

5 Press F5 to run the program.

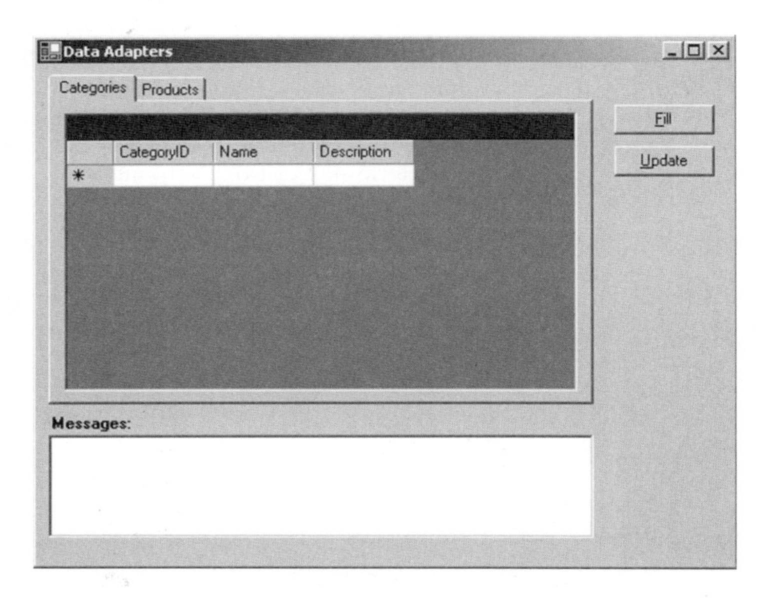

6 Click Fill.

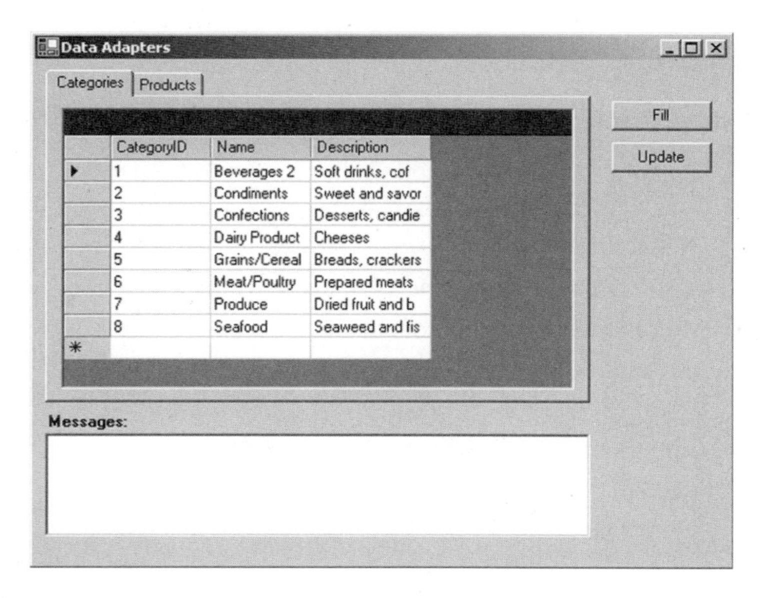

7 Verify that each of the data grids has been filled correctly, and then close the application.

Visual C# .NET

1. Double-click the Fill button.

   Visual Studio adds a Click event handler to the code window.

2. Add the following code to the event handler:

```
private void btnFill_Click(object sender, System.EventArgs e)
{
   this.dsCategories1.Clear();
   this.dsProducts1.Clear();
}
```

   These lines clear the contents of each DataSet.

3. Add the following code to fill each DataSet from the DataAdapters:

```
this.daCategories.Fill(this.dsCategories1.Categories);
this.daProducts.Fill(this.dsProducts1._Table);
```

4. Press F5 to run the program.

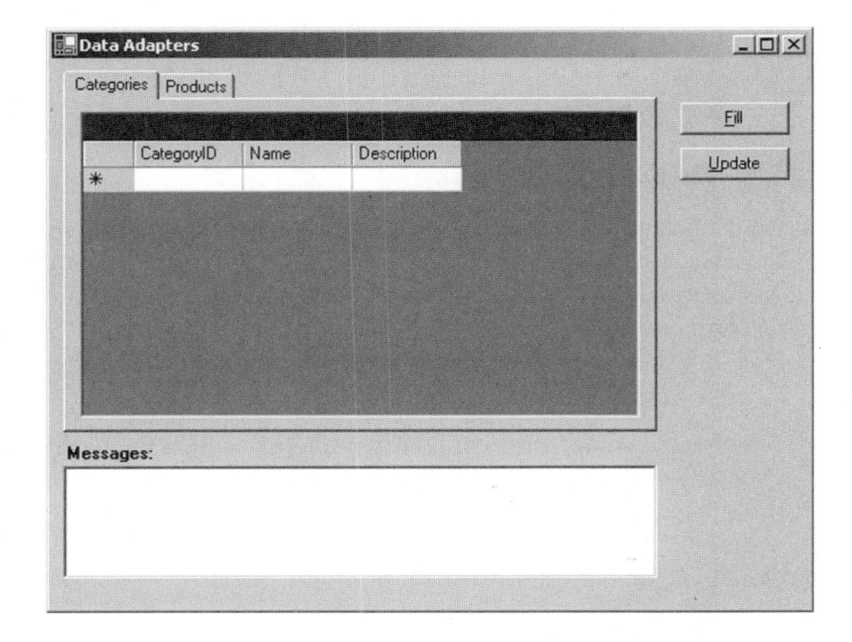

5. Click Fill.

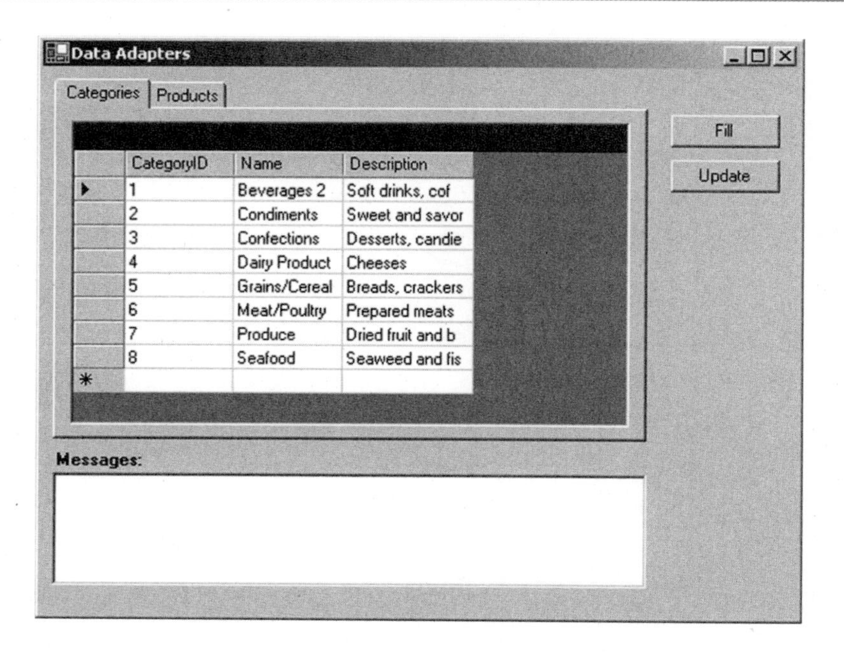

6 Verify that each of the data grids has been filled correctly, and then close the application.

The *Update* Method

Remember that the DataSet doesn't retain any knowledge about the source of the data it contains, and that the changes you make to DataSet rows aren't automatically propagated back to the data source. You must use the DataAdapter's *Update* method to do this. The *Update* method calls the DataAdapter's InsertCommand, DeleteCommand, or UpdateCommand, as appropriate, for each row in a DataSet that has changed.

The System.Data.Common.DbDataAdapter, which you will recall is the DataAdapter class from which relational database Data Providers inherit their DataAdapters, supports a number of versions of the *Update* method, as shown in Table 4-6. Neither the SqlDataAdapter nor the OleDbDataAdapter add any additional versions.

Method	Description
Update(DataSet)	Updates the data source from a DataTable named Table in the specified DataSet
Update(dataRows)	Updates the data source from the specified array of dataRows
Update(DataTable)	Updates the data source from the specified DataTable
Update(dataRows, DataTableMapping)	Updates the data source from the specified array of dataRows, using the specified DataTableMapping
Update(DataSet, sourceTable)	Updates the data source from the DataTable specified in sourceTable in the specified DataSet

Table 4-6 DbDataAdapter *Update* Methods

Update a Data Source Using the *Update* Method

Visual Basic .NET

1. In the code editor, select the btnUpdate control in the ControlName list, and then select the Click event in the MethodName list.

   Visual Studio displays the Click event handler template.

2. Add the following code to call the *Update* method:

```
Me.daCategories.Update(Me.dsCategories1.Categories)
```

3. Press F5 to run the application.
4. Click Fill.

   The application fills the data grids.

> **tip**
> You can drag the data grid's column headings to widen them.

5. Click the CategoryName of the first row, and then change its value from Beverages to Old Beverages.

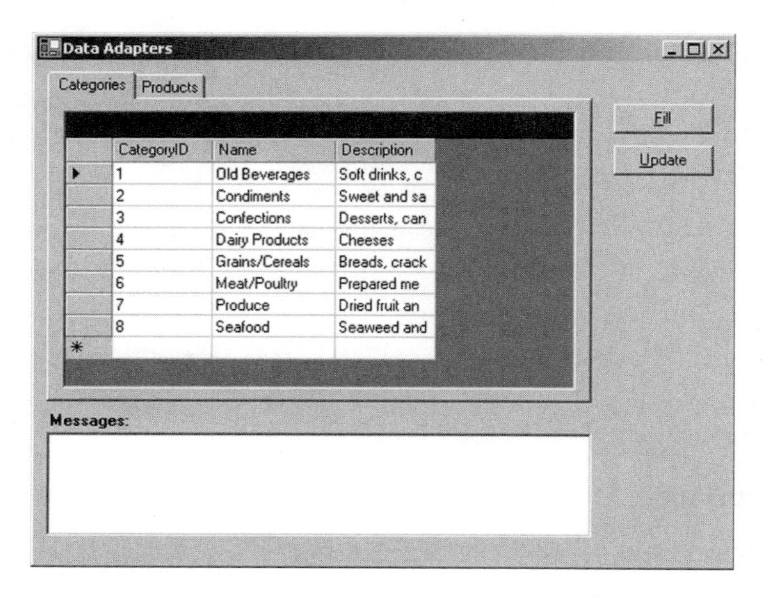

6. Click Update.

   The application updates the data source.
7. Click Fill to ensure that the change has been propagated to the data source.
8. Close the application.

Visual C# .NET

1. Add the following event handler in the code editor, below the btnFill_Click handler we added in the previous exercise:

```
private void btnUpdate_Click (object sender, System.EventArgs e)
{
   this.daCategories.Update(this.dsCategories1.Categories);
}
```

2. Add the following code to connect the event handler in the class definition:

```
this.btnUpdate.Click += new
   EventHandler(this.btnUpdate_Click);
```

3. Press F5 to run the application.
4. Click Fill.

   The application fills the data grids.

> **tip**
>
> You can drag the data grid's column headings to widen them.

5 Click the CategoryName of the first row, and then change its value from Beverages to Old Beverages.

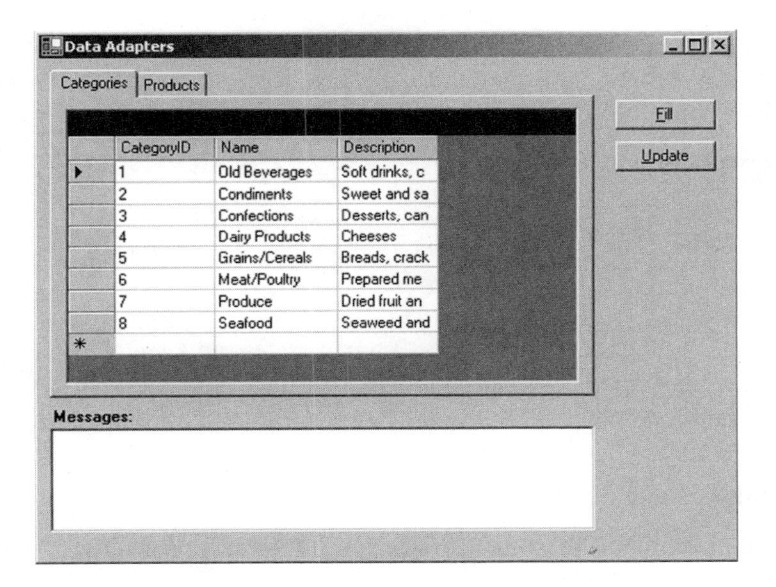

6 Click Update.

The application updates the data source.

7 Click Fill to ensure that the change has been propagated to the data source.

8 Close the application.

Handling DataAdapter Events

Other than the events caused by errors, the DataAdapter supports only two events: OnRowUpdating and OnRowUpdated. These two events occur on either side of the actual dataset update, providing fine control of the process.

OnRowUpdating Event

The OnRowUpdating event is raised after the *Update* method has set the parameter values of the command to be executed but before the command is executed. The event handler for this event receives an argument whose properties provide essential information about the command that is about to be executed.

The class of the event arguments is defined by the Data Provider, so it will be either OleDbRowUpdatingEventArgs or SqlRowUpdatingEventArgs if one of the .NET Framework Data Providers is used. The properties of RowUpdatingEventArgs are shown in Table 4-7.

Properties	Description
Command	The Data Command to be executed
Errors	The errors generated by the .NET Data Provider
Row	The DataReader to be updated
StatementType	The type of Command to be executed. The possible values are *Select, Insert, Delete,* and *Update*
Status	The UpdateStatus of the Command
TableMapping	The DataTableMapping used by the update

Table 4-7 RowUpdatingEventArgs Properties

The Command property contains a reference to the actual Command object that will be used to update the data source. Using this reference, you can, for example, examine the Command's CommandText property to determine the SQL that will be executed and change it if necessary.

The StatementType property of the event argument defines the action that is to be performed. The property is an enumeration that can evaluate to *Select, Insert, Update,* or *Delete.* The StatementType property is read-only, so you cannot use it to change the type of action to be performed.

The Row property contains a read-only reference to the DataRow to be propagated to the data source, while the TableMapping property contains a reference to the DataTableMapping that is being used for the update.

When the event handler is first called, the Status property, which is an UpdateStatus enumeration, defines the status of the event. If it is ErrorsOccurred, the Errors property will contain a collection of Errors.

You can set the Status property within the event handler to determine what action the system is to take. In addition to ErrorsOccured, which causes an exception to be thrown, the possible exit status values are *Continue,*

SkipAllRemainingRows, and *SkipCurrentRow. Continue,* which is the default value, does exactly what you would expect—it instructs the system to continue processing. *SkipAllRemainingRows* actually discards the update to the current row, as well as any remaining unprocessed rows, while *SkipCurrentRow* only cancels processing for the current row.

Respond to an OnRowUpdating Event

Visual Basic .NET

1. In the code editor, select daCategories in the ControlName list and then select RowUpdating in the MethodName list.

   Visual Studio displays the RowUpdating event handler template.

2. Add the following text to the Messages control to indicate that the event has been triggered:

```
Me.txtMessages.Text &= vbCrLf & "Beginning Update…"
```

3. Press F5 to run the application, and then click Fill to fill the data grids.
4. Change the CategoryName for Category 1, which we changed to Old Beverages in the previous exercise, back to Beverages.

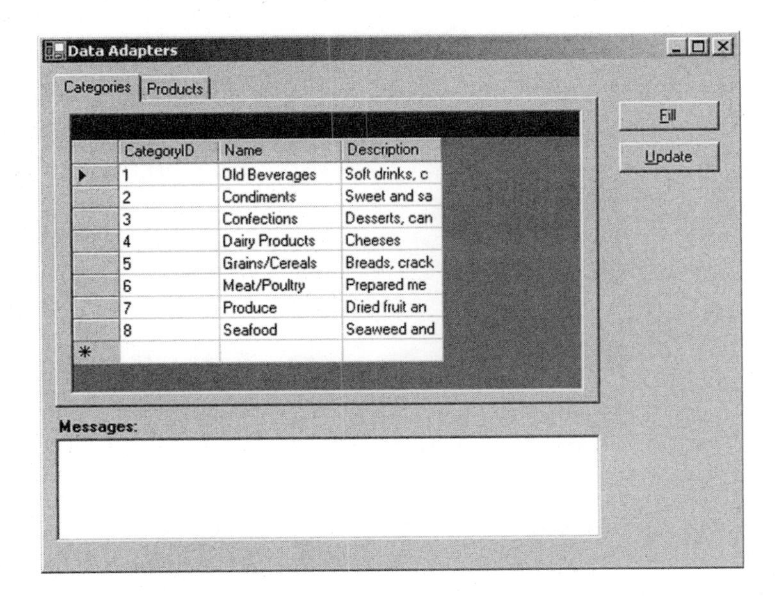

5. Click Update.

   The application updates the text in the Messages control.

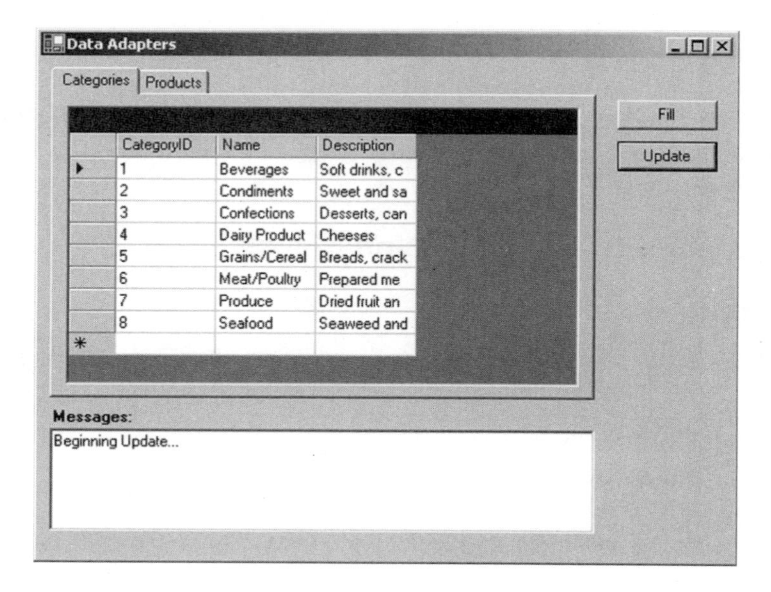

6 Close the application.

Visual C# .NET

1 Add the following event handler in the code editor:

```
private void daCategories_RowUpdate(object sender,
   System.Data.SqlClient.SqlRowUpdatedEventArgs e)
{
   string strMsg;

   strMsg = "Beginning update...";
   this.txtMessages.Text += strMsg;
}
```

The code adds text to the Messages control to indicate that the event has been triggered.

2 Add the following code to connect the event handler in the class description:

```
this.daCategories.RowUpdating += new
   System.Data.SqlClient.SqlRowUpdatingEventHandler
   (this.daCategories_RowUpdating);
```

3 Press F5 to run the application, and then click Fill to fill the data grids.

4 Change the CategoryName for Category 1, which we changed to Old Beverages in the previous exercise, back to Beverages.

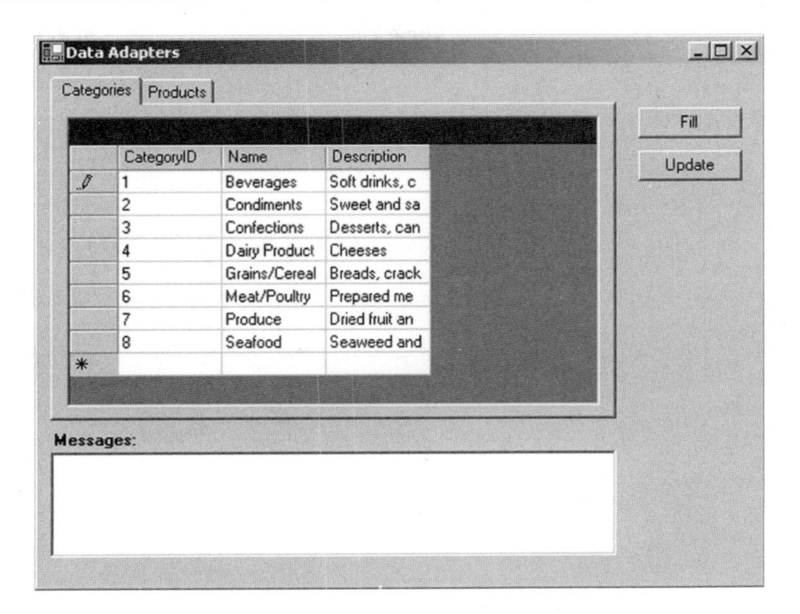

5 Click Update.

The application updates the text in the Messages control.

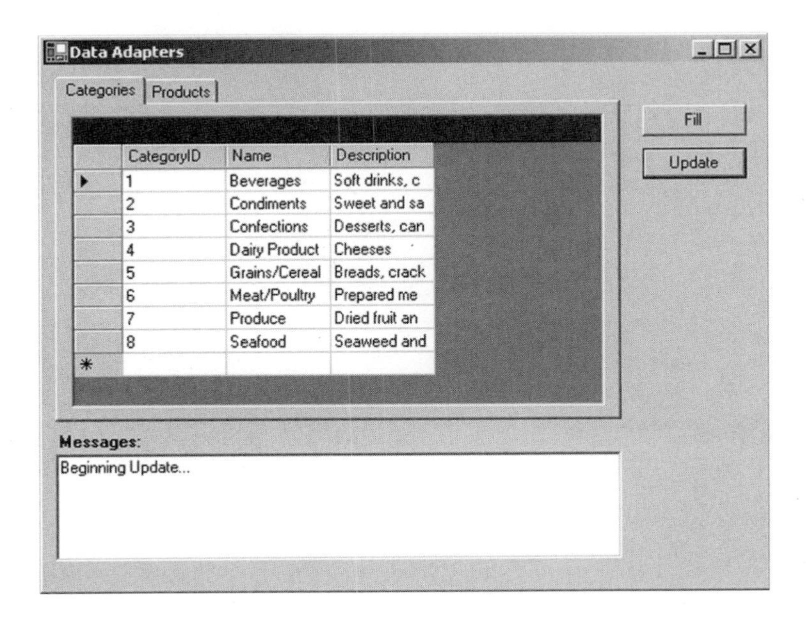

6 Close the application.

Examine the RowUpdatingEventArgs Properties

Visual Basic .NET

1. Add the following lines to the daCategories_RowUpdating event handler that you created in the previous exercise:

```
this.txtMessages.Text += "\r\n Executing a command of type";
this.txtMessages.Text +=args.StatementType.ToString();
```

2. Press F5 to run the application, and then click Fill.
3. Change the CategoryName of Category 1 to New Beverages, and then click Update.

   The application updates the text in the Messages control.

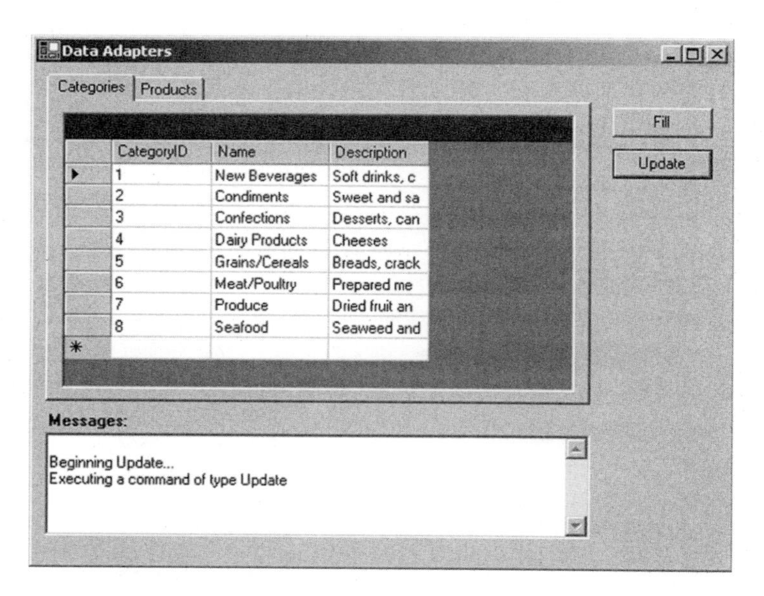

4. Close the application.

Visual C# .NET

1. Change the da_Categories_RowUpdated event handler that you created in the previous exercise to read:

```
string strMsg;

strMsg = "\r\nUpdate Completed.";
strMsg += ", " + e.RecordsAffected.ToString();
strMsg += " records(s) updated.";
this.txtMessages.Text += strMsg;
```

2 Press F5 to run the application, and then click Fill.

3 Change the CategoryName of Category 1 to New Beverages, and then click Update.

The application updates the text in the Messages control.

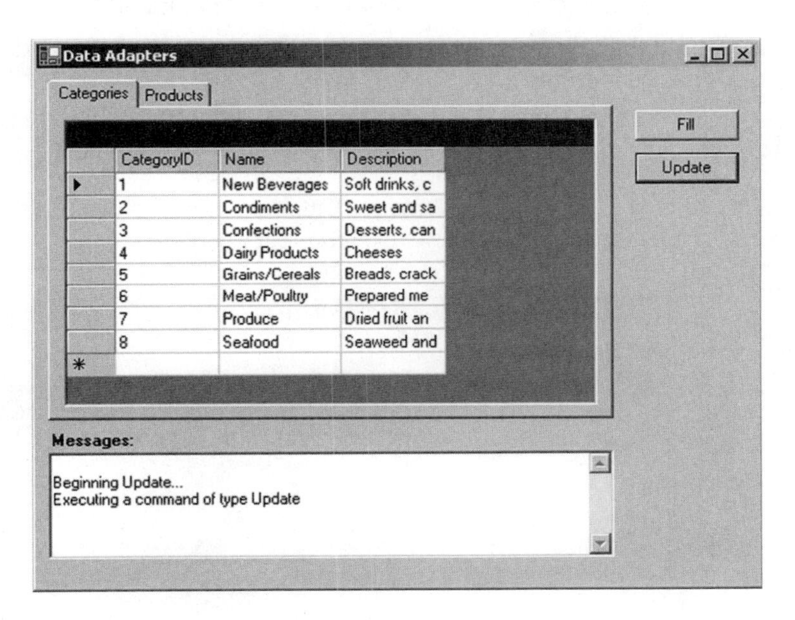

4 Close the application.

OnRowUpdated Event

The OnRowUpdated event is raised after the *Update* method executes the appropriate command against the data source. The event handler for this event is either passed an *SqlRowUpdatedEventArgs* or an *OleDbRowUpdatedEventArgs* argument, depending on the Data Provider.

Either way, the event argument contains all of the same properties as the *RowUpdatingEvent* argument, plus an additional property, a read-only *RecordsEffected* argument that indicates the number of rows that were changed, inserted, or deleted by the SQL command that was executed.

Respond to an OnRowUpdated Event

Visual Basic .NET

1. Select daCategories in the ControlName list and then select RowUpdated in the MethodName list.

   Visual Studio displays the RowUpdated event handler template.

2. Add the following text to the Messages control to indicate that the event has been triggered:

```
Me.txtMessages.Text &= vbCrLf & "Update completed"
```

3. Press F5 to run the application, and then click Fill to fill the data grids.
4. Change the CategoryName for Category 1, which we changed to New Beverages in the previous exercise, back to Beverages.

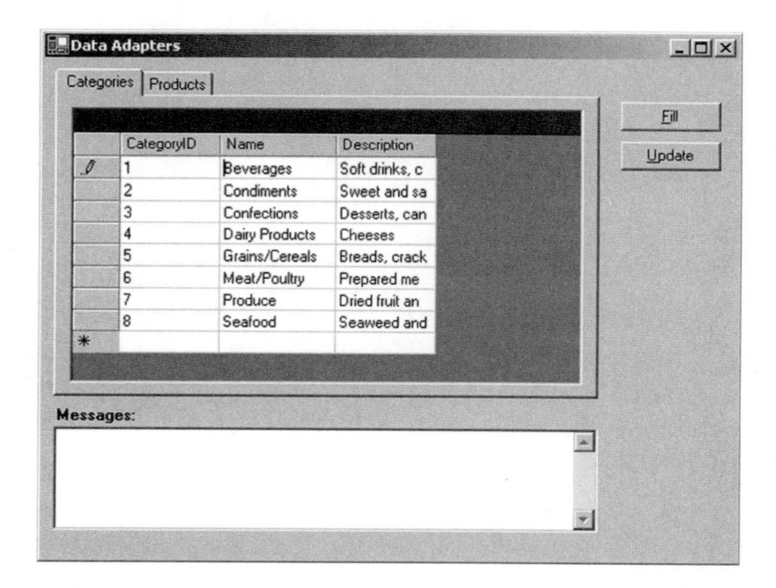

5. Click Update.

   The application updates the text in the Messages control.

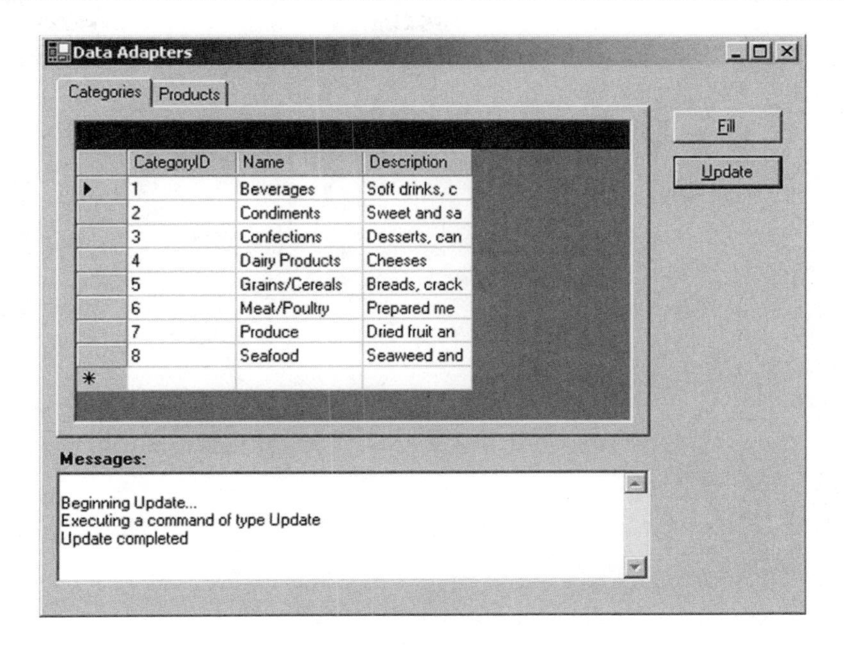

6 Close the application.

Visual C# .NET

1 Add the following code to add the RowUpdated event template to the code editor:

```
private void daCategories_RowUpdate(object sender,
   System.Data.SqlClient.SqlRowUpdatedEventArgs e)
{
   string strMsg;

   strMsg = "\r\nUpdate Completed.";
   this.txtMessages.Text += strMsg;
}
```

2 Add the following code to connect the event handler in the class description:

```
this.daCategories.RowUpdated +=
   new System.Data.SqlClient.SqlRowUpdatedEventHandler
   (this.daCategories_RowUpdated);
```

3 Press F5 to run the application, and then click Fill to fill the data grids.

4 Change the CategoryName for Category 1, which we changed to New Beverages in the previous exercise, back to Beverages.

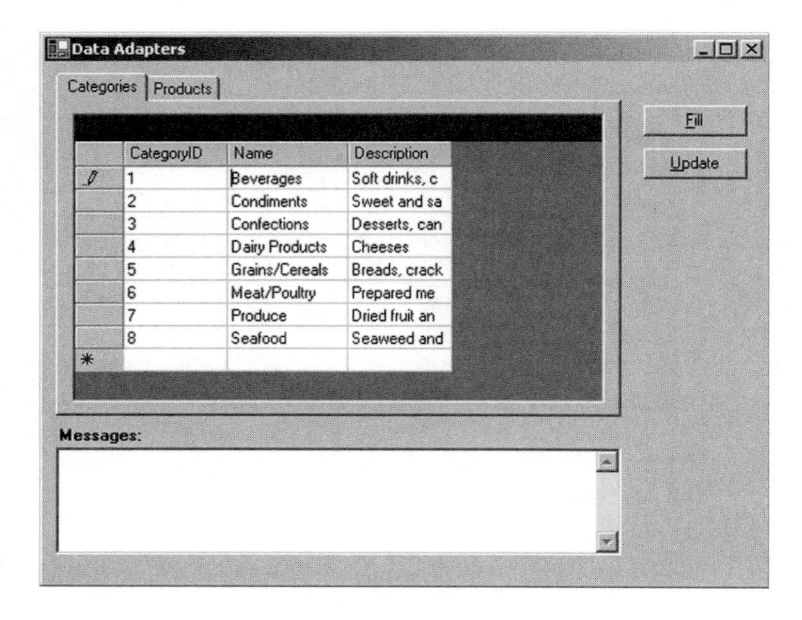

5 Click Update.

The application updates the text in the Messages control.

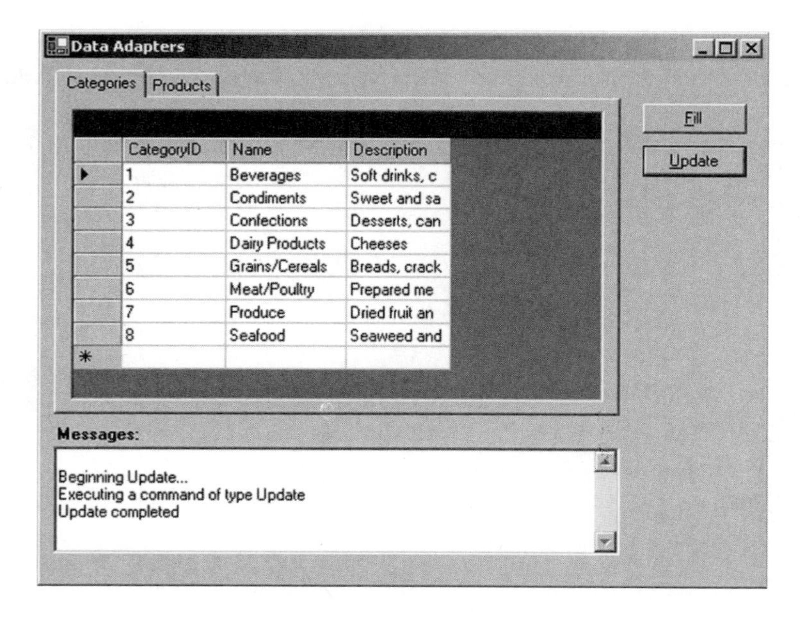

6 Close the application.

Examine the RowUpdatedEventArgs Properties

Visual Basic .NET

1. Add the following lines to the daCategories_RowUpdated event handler that you created in the previous exercise:

```
Me.txtMessages.Text &= ", " & e.RecordsAffected.ToString & "
    record(s) updated."
```

2. Press F5 to run the application, and then click Fill.
3. Change the CategoryName of Category 1 to Beverages 2, and then click Update.

   The application updates the text in the Messages control.

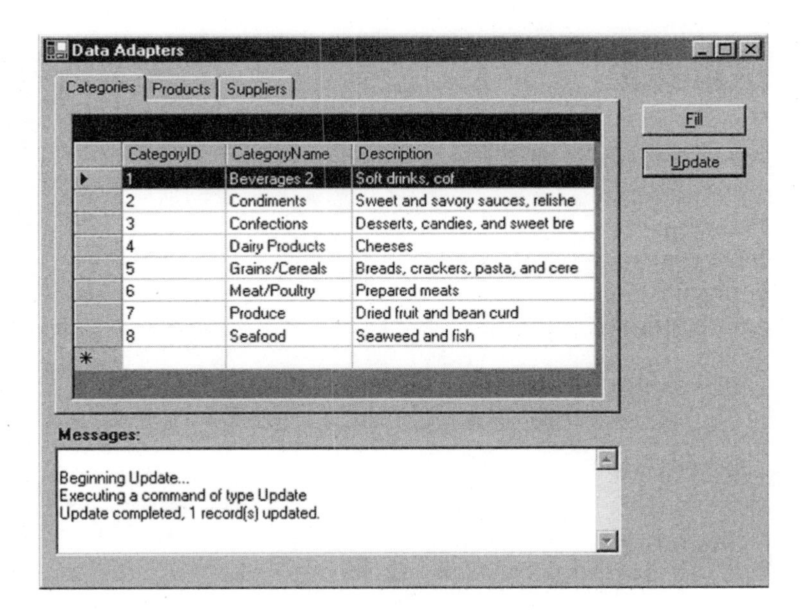

4. Close the application.

Visual C# .NET

1. Change the daCategories_RowUpdated event handler that you created in the previous exercise to read:

```
string strMsg;

strMsg = "\r\nUpdate Completed.";
strMsg += ", " + e.RecordsAffected.ToString();
strMsg += " records(s) updated.";
this.txtMessages.Text += strMsg;
```

2 Press F5 to run the application, and then click Fill.

3 Change the CategoryName of Category 1 to Beverages 2, and then click Update.

The application updates the text in the Messages control.

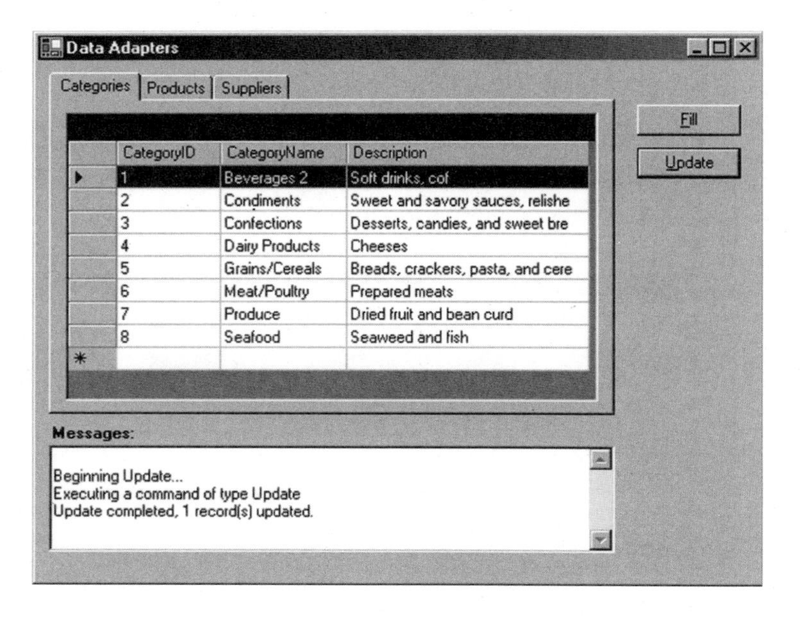

4 Close the application.

Chapter 4 Quick Reference

To	Do this
Create a DataAdapter in the Server Explorer	Drag a table into the form designer.
Create a DataAdapter using the Toolbox	Drag an OleDbDataAdapter or an SqlDataAdapter onto the form designer. Cancel the Data Adapter Configuration Wizard if you wish to configure the DataAdapter manually.
Create a DataAdapter in code	Declare the DataAdapter variable and the four Command object variables, and then instantiate them and assign the Command objects to the DataAdapter.
Preview the results of a DataAdapter	Select the DataAdapter in the form designer, and then click Preview Dataset in the Properties window.

Transaction Processing in ADO.NET

In this chapter, you'll learn how to:

- ✔ *Create a transaction*
- ✔ *Create a nested transaction*
- ✔ *Commit a transaction*
- ✔ *Rollback a transaction*

In the last few chapters, we've seen how ADO.NET data provider objects interact in the process of editing and updating. In this chapter, we'll complete our examination of data providers in ADO.NET with an exploration of transaction processing.

Understanding Transactions

A *transaction* is a series of actions that must be treated as a single unit of work—either they must all succeed, or they must all fail. The classic example of a transaction is the transfer of funds from one bank account to another. To transfer the funds, an amount, say $100, is withdrawn from one account and deposited in the other. If the withdrawal were to succeed while the deposit failed, money would be lost into cyberspace. If the withdrawal were to fail and the deposit succeed, money would be invented. Clearly, if either action fails, they must both fail.

ADO.NET supports transactions through the Transaction object, which is created against an open connection. Commands that are executed against the connection while the transaction is pending must be enrolled in the transaction by assigning a reference to the Transaction object to their Transaction property. Commands cannot be executed against the Connection outside the transaction while it is pending.

If the transaction is committed, all of the commands that form a part of that transaction will be permanently written to the data source. If the transaction is rolled back, all of the commands will be discarded at the data source.

Creating Transactions

The Transaction object is implemented as part of the data provider. There is a version for each of the intrinsic data providers: OleDbTransaction in the System.Data.OleDb namespace and SqlTransaction in the System.Data.SqlClient namespace.

The SqlTransaction object is implemented using Microsoft SQL Server transactions—creating a SqlTransaction maps directly to the *BeginTransaction* statement. The OleDbTransaction is implemented within OLE DB. No matter which data provider you use, you shouldn't explicitly issue *BeginTransaction* commands on the database.

Creating New Transactions

Transactions are created by calling the *BeginTransaction* method of the Connection object, which returns a reference to a Transaction object. *BeginTransaction* is overloaded, allowing an IsolationLevel to optionally be specified, as shown in Table 5-1. The Connection must be valid and open when *BeginTransaction* is called.

Method	Description
BeginTransaction()	Begins a transaction
BeginTransaction (IsolationLevel)	Begins a transaction at the specified IsolationLevel

Table 5-1 Connection *BeginTransaction* Methods

Because SQL Server supports named transactions, the SqlClient data provider exposes two additional versions of *BeginTransaction*, as shown in Table 5-2.

Method	Description
BeginTransaction (TransactionName)	Begins a transaction with the name specified in the TransactionName string
BeginTransaction (IsolationLevel, TransactionName)	Begins a transaction at the specified IsolationLevel with the name specified in the TransactionName string

Table 5-2 Additional SQL *BeginTransaction* Methods

ADO

Unlike ADO, the ADO.NET *Commit* and *Rollback* methods are exposed on the Transaction object, not the Command object.

The optional IsolationLevel parameter to the *BeginTransaction* method specifies the connection's locking behavior. The possible values for IsolationLevel are shown in Table 5-3.

Value	Meaning
Chaos	Pending changes from more highly ranked transactions cannot be overwritten
ReadCommitted	Shared locks are held while the data is being read, but data can be changed before the end of the transaction
ReadUncommitted	No shared locks are issued and no exclusive locks are honored
RepeatableRead	Exclusive locks are placed on all data used in the query
Serializable	A range lock is placed on the DataSet
Unspecified	An existing isolation level cannot be determined

Table 5-3 Isolation Levels

Create a New Transaction

Visual Basic .NET

1. Open the Transactions project from the Microsoft Visual Studio .NET Start Page or by using the File menu.
2. Double-click Transactions.vb to display the form in the form designer.

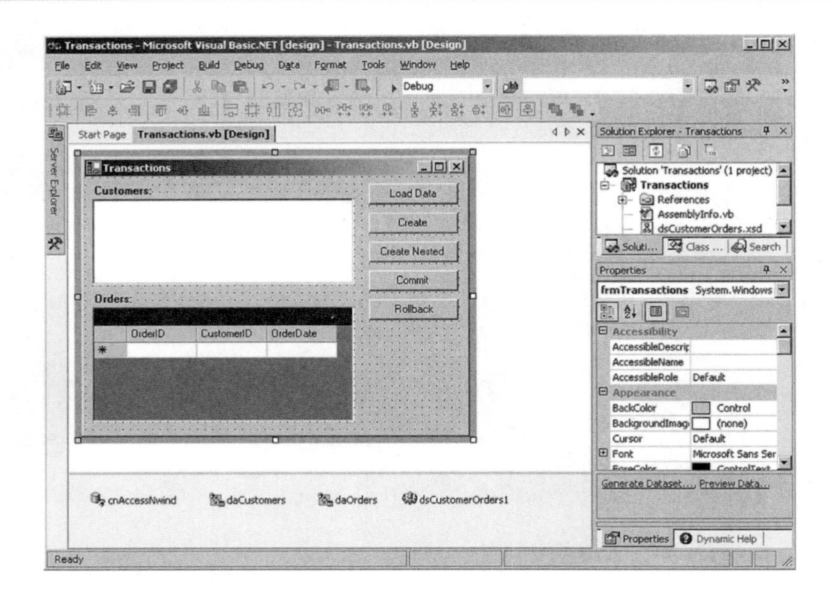

3. Double-click Create.

   Visual Studio opens the code editor window and adds the Click event handler.

4. Add the following code to the procedure:

```
Dim strMsg As String
Dim trnNew As System.Data.OleDb.OleDbTransaction

Me.cnAccessNwind.Open()
trnNew = Me.cnAccessNwind.BeginTransaction()
strMsg = "Isolation Level: "
strMsg &= trnNew.IsolationLevel.ToString
MessageBox.Show(strMsg)
Me.cnAccessNwind.Close()
```

   The code creates a new Transaction using the default method, and then displays its IsolationLevel in a message box.

5 Press F5 to run the application.

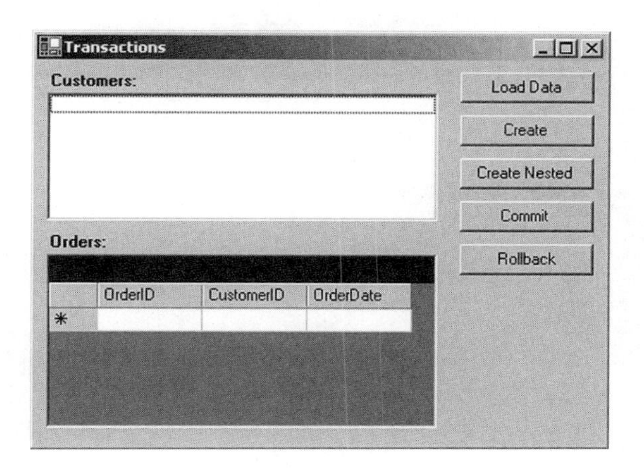

6 Click Load Data.

The application fills the DataSet and displays the Customers and Orders lists.

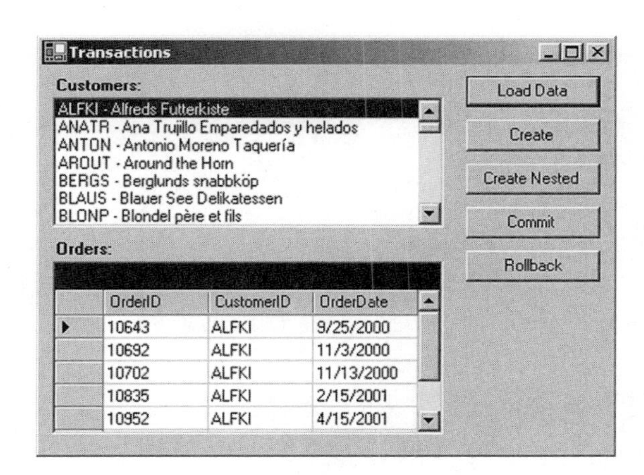

7 Click Create.

The application displays the transaction's IsolationLevel in a message box.

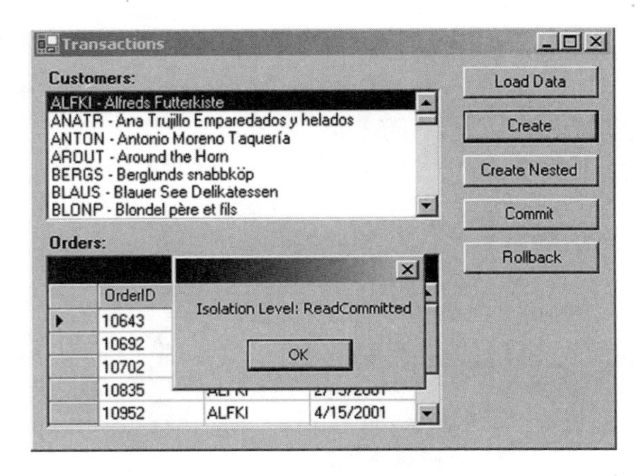

8 Click OK in the message box, and then close the application.

Visual C# .NET

1 Open the Transactions project from the Visual Studio Start Page or by using the File menu.

2 Double-click Transactions.cs to display the form in the form designer.

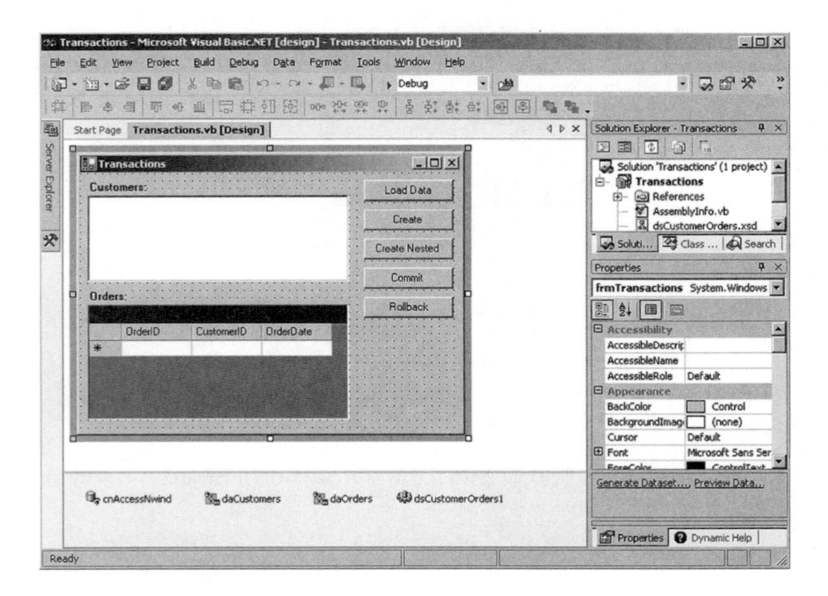

3 Double-click Create.

Visual Studio opens the code editor window and adds the Click event handler.

4 Add the following code to the procedure:

```
string strMsg;
System.Data.OleDb.OleDbTransaction trnNew;

this.cnAccessNwind.Open();
trnNew = this.cnAccessNwind.BeginTransaction();
strMsg = "Isolation Level: ";
strMsg += trnNew.IsolationLevel.ToString();
MessageBox.Show(strMsg);
this.cnAccessNwind.Close();
```

The code creates a new Transaction using the default method, and then displays its IsolationLevel in a message box.

5 Press F5 to run the application.

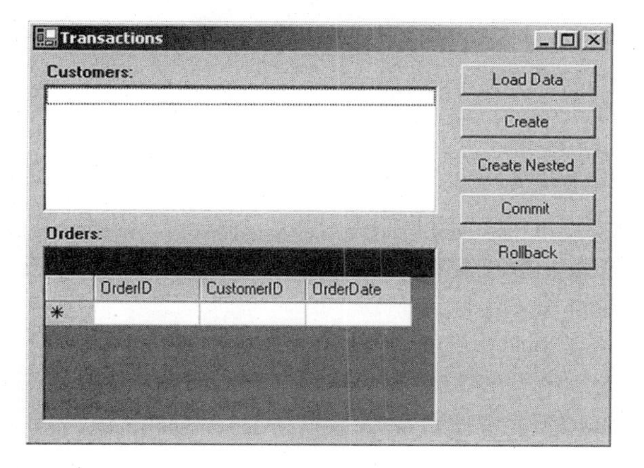

6 Click Load Data.

The application fills the DataSet and displays the Customers and Orders lists.

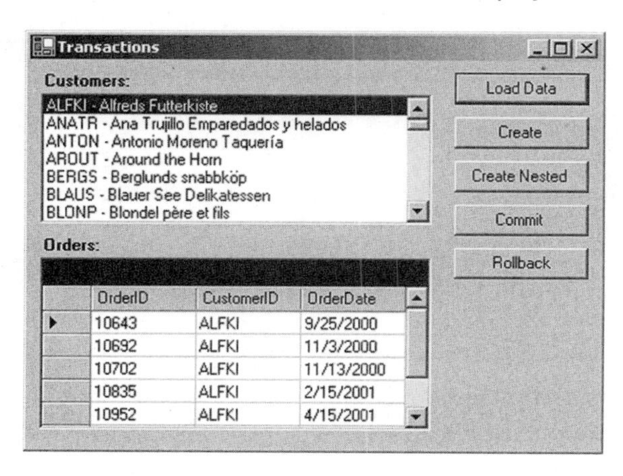

7 Click Create.

The application displays the transaction's IsolationLevel in a message box.

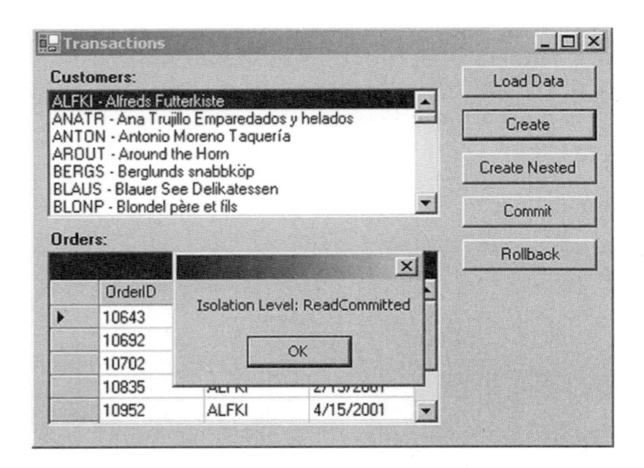

8 Click OK in the message box, and then close the application.

Creating Nested Transactions

Although it isn't possible to have two transactions on a single Connection, the OleDbTransaction object supports nested transactions. (They aren't supported on SQL Server.)

> **ADO**
>
> Multiple transactions on a single Connection, which were supported in ADO, are no longer supported in ADO.NET.

The syntax for creating a nested transaction is the same as that for creating a first-level transaction, as shown in Table 5-4. The difference is that nested transactions are created by calling the *BeginTransaction* method on the Transaction object itself, not on the Connection.

All nested transactions must be committed or rolled back before the transaction containing them is committed; however, if the parent (containing) transaction is rolled back, the nested transactions will also be rolled back, even if they have previously been committed.

Method	Description
BeginTransaction()	Begins a transaction
BeginTransaction (IsolationLevel)	Begins a transaction at the specified IsolationLevel

Table 5-4 Transaction *BeginTransaction* Methods

Create a Nested Transaction

Visual Basic .NET

1 Select btnNested in the code editor's ControlName list, and then select Click in the MethodName list.

 Visual Studio adds the Click event handler to the code.

2 Add the following code to the procedure:

```
Dim strMsg As String
Dim trnMaster As System.Data.OleDb.OleDbTransaction
Dim trnChild As System.Data.OleDb.OleDbTransaction

Me.cnAccessNwind.Open()

trnMaster = Me.cnAccessNwind.BeginTransaction

trnChild = trnMaster.Begin
strMsg = "Child Isolation Level: "
strMsg &= trnChild.IsolationLevel.ToString
MessageBox.Show(strMsg)

Me.cnAccessNwind.Close()
```

 The code first creates a transaction, trnMaster, on the Connection object. It then creates a second, nested transaction, trnChild, on the trnMaster transaction, and displays its IsolationLevel in a message box.

3 Press F5 to run the application.

4 Click Load Data.

5 Click Create Nested.

 The application displays the child transaction's IsolationLevel in a message box.

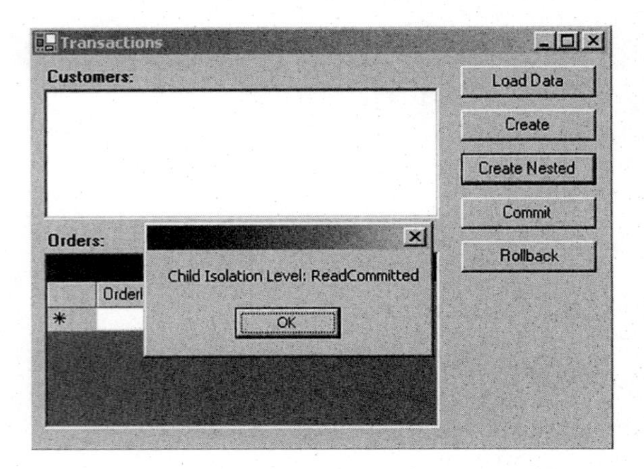

6 Click OK in the message box, and then close the application.

Visual C# .NET

1 Add the following procedure to the code:

```
private void btnNested_Click(object sender, System.EventArgs e)
{
    string strMsg;
    System.Data.OleDb.OleDbTransaction trnMaster;
    System.Data.OleDb.OleDbTransaction trnChild;

    this.cnAccessNwind.Open();

    trnMaster = this.cnAccessNwind.BeginTransaction();

    trnChild = trnMaster.Begin();
    strMsg = "Child Isolation Level: ";
    strMsg += trnChild.IsolationLevel.ToString();
    MessageBox.Show(strMsg);

    this.cnAccessNwind.Close();
}
```

The code first creates a transaction, trnMaster, on the Connection object. It then creates a second, nested transaction, trnChild, on the trnMaster transaction, and displays its IsolationLevel in a message box.

2 Add the code to bind the click handler to the top of the frmTransactions() sub:

```
this.btnNested.Click += new EventHandler(this.btnNested_Click);
```

3 Press F5 to run the application.

4 Click Load Data.

5 Click Create Nested.

The application displays the child transaction's IsolationLevel in a message box.

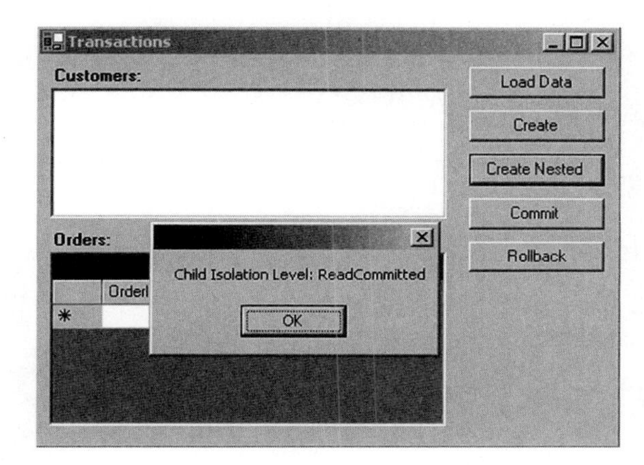

6 Click OK in the message box, and then close the application.

Using Transactions

There are three steps to using transactions after they are created. First they are assigned to the commands that will participate in them, then the commands are executed, and finally the transaction is closed by either committing it or rolling it back.

Assigning Transactions to a Command

Once a transaction has been begun on a connection, all commands executed against that connection must participate in that transaction. Unfortunately, this doesn't happen automatically—you must set the Transaction property of the command to reference the transaction.

However, once the transaction is committed or rolled back, the transaction reference in any commands that participated in the transaction will be reset to Nothing, so it isn't necessary to do this step manually.

Committing and Rolling Back Transactions

The final step in transaction processing is to commit or roll back the changes that were made by the commands participating in the transaction. If the transaction is committed, all of the changes will be accepted in the data source. If it is rolled back, all of the changes will be discarded, and the data source will be returned to the state it was in before the transaction began.

Transactions are committed using the transaction's *Commit* method and rolled back using the transaction's *Rollback* method, neither of which takes any parameters. The actions are typically wrapped in a Try...Catch block.

Commit a Transaction

Visual Basic .NET

1. Select btnCommit in the ControlName list, and then select Click in the MethodName list.

   Visual Studio adds the Click event handler to the code.

2. Add the following lines to the procedure:

```
Dim trnNew As System.Data.OleDb.OleDbTransaction

AddRows("AAAA1")

Me.cnAccessNwind.Open()
trnNew = Me.cnAccessNwind.BeginTransaction()
Me.daCustomers.InsertCommand.Transaction = trnNew
Me.daOrders.InsertCommand.Transaction = trnNew
Try
    Me.daCustomers.Update(Me.dsCustomerOrders1.CustomerList)
    Me.daOrders.Update(Me.dsCustomerOrders1.Orders)
    trnNew.Commit()
    MessageBox.Show("Transaction Committed")
Catch err As System.Data.OleDb.OleDbException
    trnNew.Rollback()
    MessageBox.Show(err.Message.ToString)
Finally
    Me.cnAccessNwind.Close()
End Try
```

   The AddRows procedure, which is provided in Chapter 1, adds a Customer row and an Order for that Customer.

   Within a Try...Catch block, the code commits the two Update commands if they succeed, and then displays a message confirming that the transaction has completed without errors.

3 Press F5 to run the application.

4 Click Load Data.

The application fills the DataSet, and then displays the Customers and Orders lists.

5 Click Commit.

The application displays a message box confirming the updates.

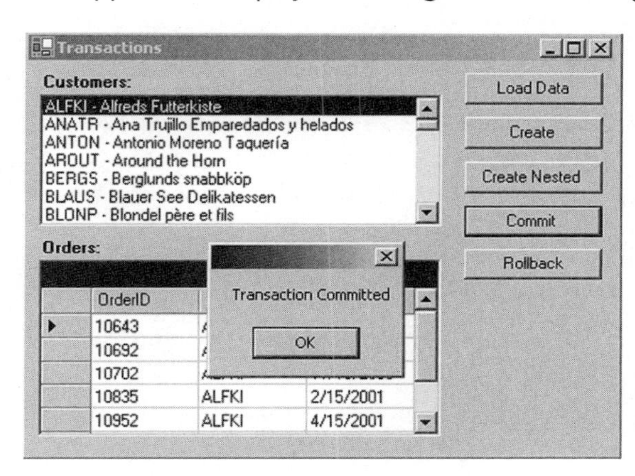

6 Click OK in the message box, and then click Load Data to confirm that the rows have been added.

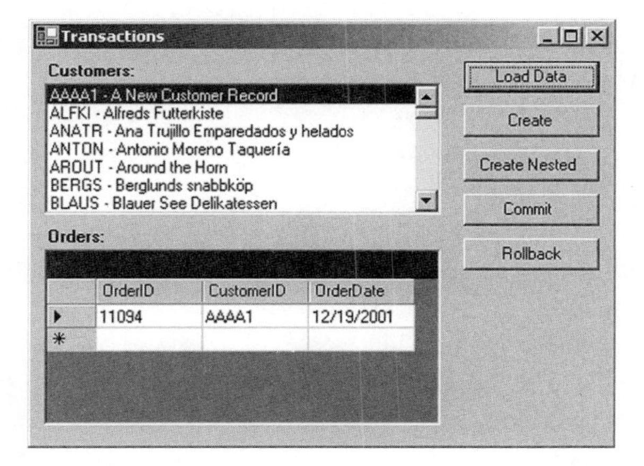

7 Close the application.

Visual C# .NET

1. Add the following procedure to the code:

```
private void btnCommit_Click(object sender, System.EventArgs e)
{
   System.Data.OleDb.OleDbTransaction trnNew;

   AddRows("AAAA1");

   this.cnAccessNwind.Open();
   trnNew = this.cnAccessNwind.BeginTransaction();
   this.daCustomers.InsertCommand.Transaction = trnNew;
   this.daOrders.InsertCommand.Transaction = trnNew;
   try
   {
         this.daCustomers.Update(this.dsCustomerOrders1.CustomerList);
         this.daOrders.Update(this.dsCustomerOrders1.Orders);
         trnNew.Commit();
         MessageBox.Show("Transaction Committed");
   }
   catch (System.Data.OleDb.OleDbException err)
   {
         trnNew.Rollback();
         MessageBox.Show(err.Message.ToString());
   }
   finally
   {
         this.cnAccessNwind.Close();
   }
}
```

   The AddRows procedure, which is provided in Chapter 1, adds a Customer row and an Order for that Customer.

   Within a Try…Catch block, the code commits the two Update commands if they succeed, and then displays a message confirming that the transaction has completed without errors.

2. Add the code to bind the click handler to the top of the frmTransactions() sub:

```
this.btnCommit.Click += new EventHandler(this.btnCommit_Click);
```

3. Press F5 to run the application.

4 Click Load Data.

The application fills the DataSet, and then displays the Customers and Orders lists.

5 Click Commit.

The application displays a message box confirming the updates.

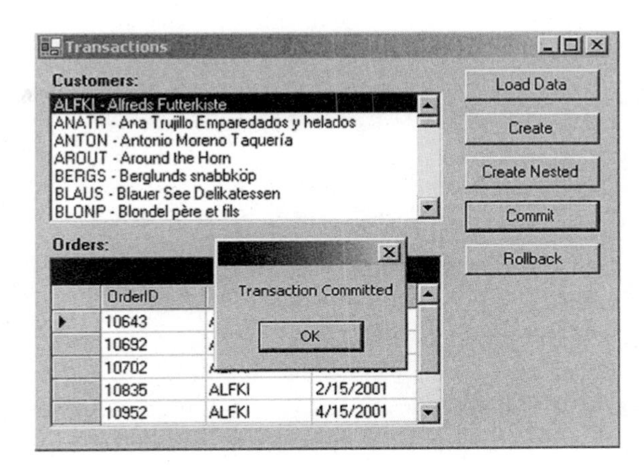

6 Click OK in the message box, and then click Load Data to confirm that the rows have been added.

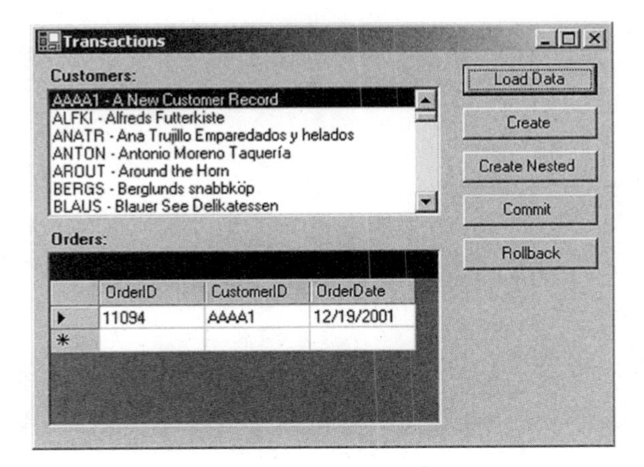

7 Close the application.

Rollback a Transaction

Visual Basic .NET

1. Select btnRollback in the ControlName list, and then select Click in the MethodName list.

   Visual Studio adds the Click event handler to the code.

2. Add the following lines to the procedure:

```
Dim trnNew As System.Data.OleDb.OleDbTransaction

AddRows("AAAA2")

Me.cnAccessNwind.Open()
trnNew = Me.cnAccessNwind.BeginTransaction()
Me.daCustomers.InsertCommand.Transaction = trnNew
Me.daOrders.InsertCommand.Transaction = trnNew
Try
    Me.daOrders.Update(Me.dsCustomerOrders1.Orders)
    Me.daCustomers.Update(Me.dsCustomerOrders1.CustomerList)
    trnNew.Commit()
    MessageBox.Show("Transaction Committed")
Catch err As System.Data.OleDb.OleDbException
    trnNew.Rollback()
    MessageBox.Show(err.Message.ToString)
Finally
    Me.cnAccessNwind.Close()
End Try
```

   This procedure is almost identical to the Commit procedure in the previous exercise. However, because the order of the Updates is reversed so that the Order is added before the Customer, the first Update will fail and a message box will display the error.

3. Press F5 to run the application.

4. Click Load Data.

   The application fills the DataSet, and then displays the Customers and Orders lists.

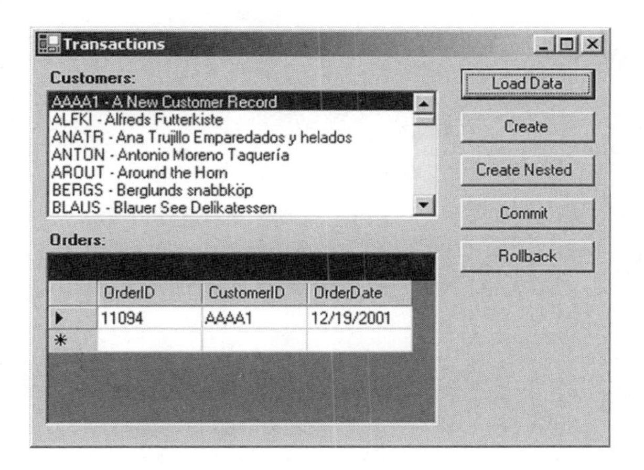

5 Click Rollback.
The application displays a message box explaining the error.

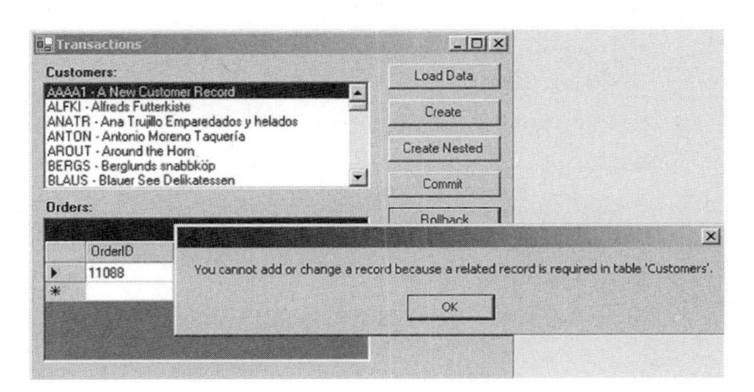

6 Click OK to close the message box, and then click Load Data to confirm that the rows have not been added.

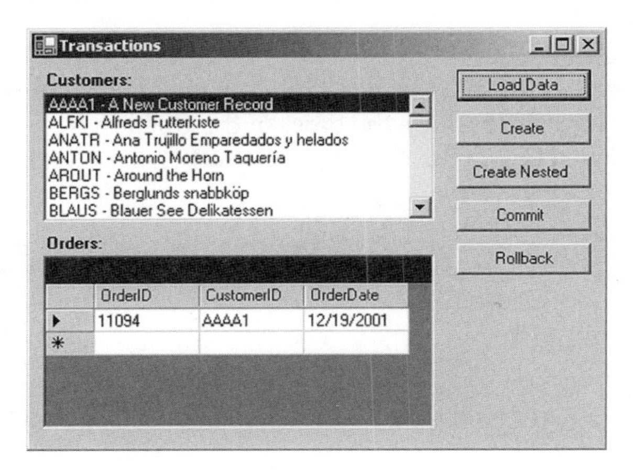

7 Close the application.

Visual C# .NET

1. Add the following procedure to the code:

```
private void btnRollback_Click(object sender, System.EventArgs e)
{
   System.Data.OleDb.OleDbTransaction trnNew;

   AddRows("AAAA2");

   this.cnAccessNwind.Open();
   trnNew = this.cnAccessNwind.BeginTransaction();
   this.daCustomers.InsertCommand.Transaction = trnNew;
   this.daOrders.InsertCommand.Transaction = trnNew;
   try
   {
          this.daOrders.Update(this.dsCustomerOrders1.Orders);
          this.daCustomers.Update(this.dsCustomerOrders1.CustomerList);
          trnNew.Commit();
          MessageBox.Show("Transaction Committed");
   }
   catch (System.Data.OleDb.OleDbException err)
   {
          trnNew.Rollback();
          MessageBox.Show(err.Message.ToString());
   }
   finally
   {
          this.cnAccessNwind.Close();
   }
}
```

   This procedure is almost identical to the Commit procedure in the previous exercise. However, because the order of the Updates is reversed so that the Order is added before the Customer, the first Update will fail and a message box will display the error.

2. Add the code to bind the click handler to the top of the frmDataSets() sub:

```
this.btnRollback.Click += new EventHandler(this.btnRollback_Click);
```

3. Press F5 to run the application.
4. Click Load Data.

   The application fills the DataSet, and then displays the Customers and Orders lists.

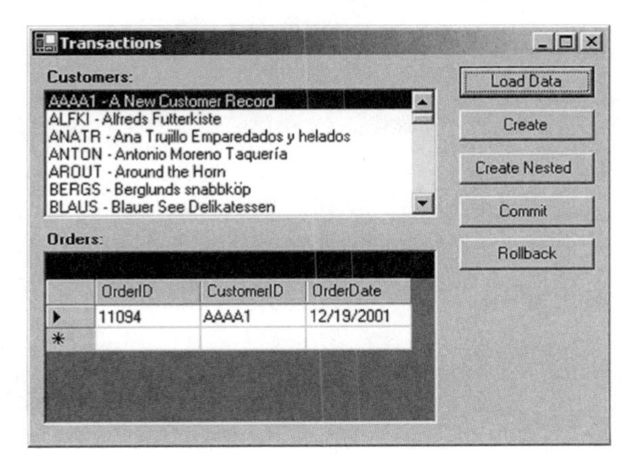

5 Click Rollback.

The application displays a message box explaining the error.

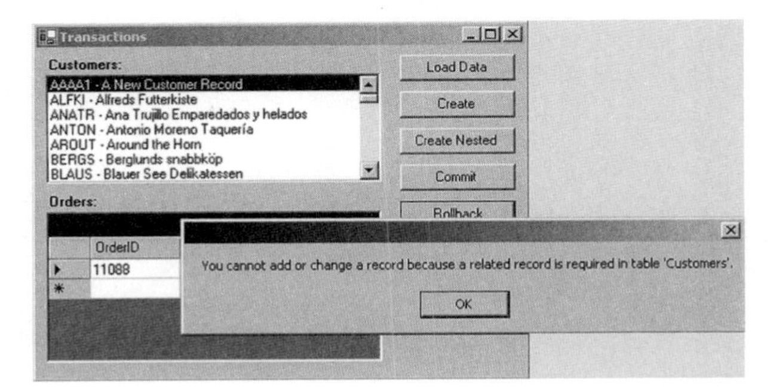

6 Click OK to close the message box, and then click Load Data to confirm that the rows have not been added.

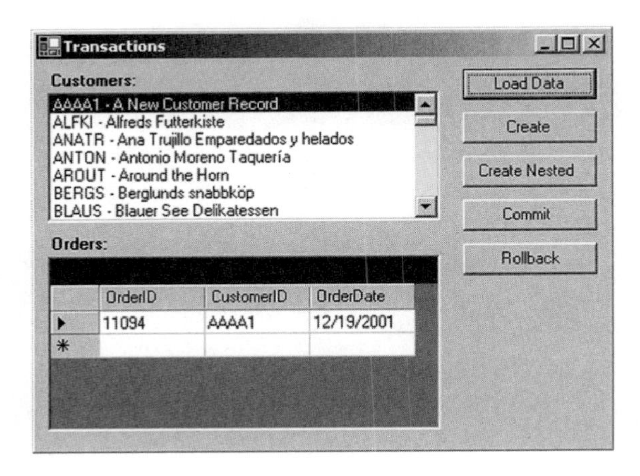

7 Close the application.

Chapter 5 Quick Reference

To	Do this
Create a transaction	Call the *BeginTransaction* method of the Connection object: `myTrans = myConn.BeginTransaction`
Create a nested transaction	Call the *BeginTransaction* method of the Transaction object: `nestedTrans = myTrans.BeginTransaction()`
Commit a transaction	Call the *Commit* method of the Transaction: `myTrans.Commit()`
Rollback a transaction	Call the *Rollback* method of the Transaction: `myTrans.Rollback()`

PART 3

Manipulating Data

The DataSet

In this chapter, you'll learn how to:

- ✔ *Create Typed and Untyped DataSets*
- ✔ *Add DataTables to DataSets*
- ✔ *Add DataRelations to DataSets*
- ✔ *Clone and copy DataSets*

Beginning with this chapter, we'll move away from the ADO.NET Data Providers to examine the objects that support the manipulation of data in your applications. We'll start with the DataSet, the memory-resident structure that represents relational data.

note

In this chapter, we'll begin an application that we'll continue to work with in subsequent chapters.

Understanding DataSets

The structure of the DataSet is shown in the following figure.

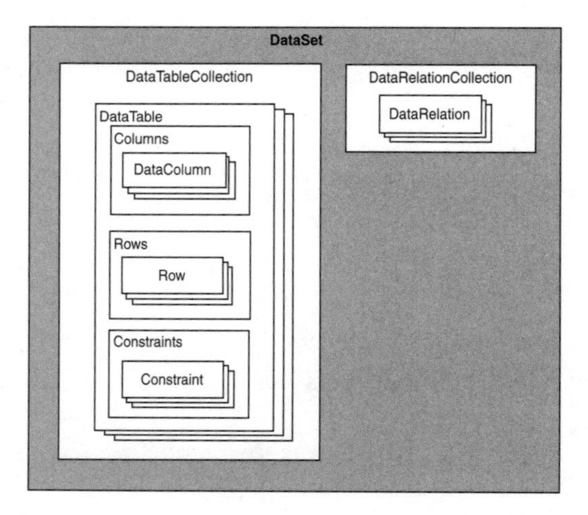

ADO.NET supports two distinct kinds of DataSets: Typed and Untyped. Architecturally, an Untyped DataSet is a direct instantiation of the *System.Data.DataSet* object, while a Typed DataSet is a distinct class that inherits from *System.Data.DataSet*.

In functional terms, a Typed DataSet exposes its tables, and the columns within them, as object properties. This makes manipulating the DataSet far simpler syntactically because you can reference tables and columns directly by their names.

For example, given a Typed DataSet called *dsOrders* that contains a DataTable called *OrderHeaders*, you can reference the value of the *OrderID* column in the first row as:

```
Me.dsOrders.OrderHeaders(0).OrderID
```

If you were working with an Untyped DataSet with the same structure, however, you would need to reference the *OrderHeaders* DataTable and *OrderID* Column through the Tables and Item collections, respectively:

```
Me.dsOrders.Tables("OrderHeader").Rows(0).Item("OrderID")
```

If you're working in Microsoft Visual Studio, the Visual Studio code editor supports a Typed DataSet's tables and columns through IntelliSense, which makes the reference even easier.

The Typed DataSet provides another important benefit: it allows compile-time type checking of data values, which is referred to as *strong typing*. For example, assuming that *OrderTotal* is numeric, the compiler would generate an error in the following line:

```
Me.dsOrders.OrderHeader.Rows(0).OrderTotal = "Hello, world"
```

But if you were working with an Untyped DataSet, the following line would compile without error:

```
Me.dsOrders.Tables("OrderHeader").Rows(0).Item("OrderTotal") = "Hello, world"
```

Despite the advantages of the Typed DataSet, there are times when you'll need an Untyped DataSet. For example, your application may receive a DataSet from a middle-tier component or a Web service, and you won't know the structure of the DataSet until run time. Or you may need to reconfigure a DataSet's schema at run time, in which case regenerating a Typed DataSet would be an unnecessary overhead.

Creating DataSets

As always, Visual Studio provides several different methods for creating DataSets, both interactively and programmatically.

Creating Typed DataSets

Roadmap

We'll explore the XML Schema Designer in Chapter 13.

In previous chapters, we created Typed DataSets from DataAdapters by using the Generate Dataset command. In this chapter, we'll use the Component Designer. You can also create them programmatically and by using the XML Schema Designer. We'll examine both of those techniques in detail in Part V. We will, however, use the Schema Designer in this chapter to confirm our changes.

Create a Typed DataSet Using the Component Designer

1. Open the DataSets project from the Start page or the Project menu.
2. Double-click DataSets.vb (or DataSets.cs, if you're using C#) in the Solution Explorer.

   Visual Studio opens the form in the form designer.

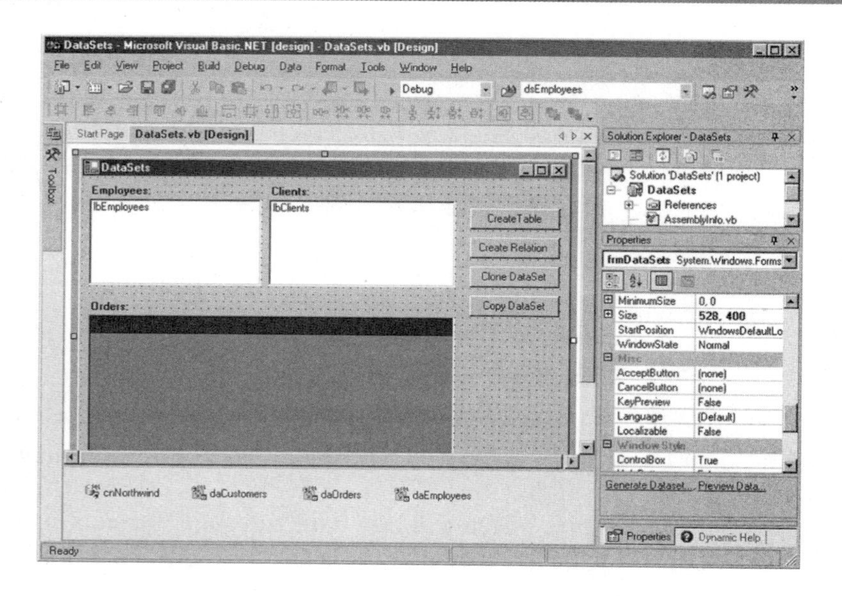

3 Select the daCustomers DataAdapter in the Component Designer.

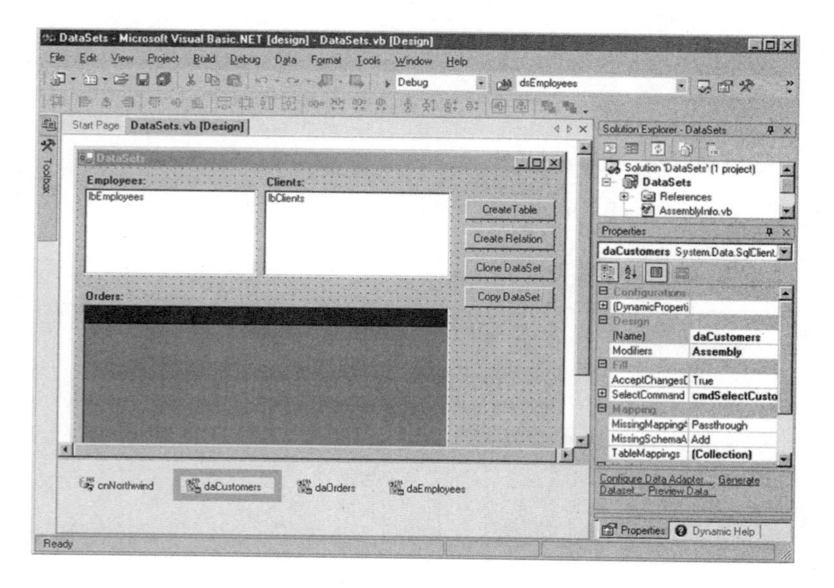

4 Choose Generate Dataset from the Data menu.

The Generate Dataset dialog box opens.

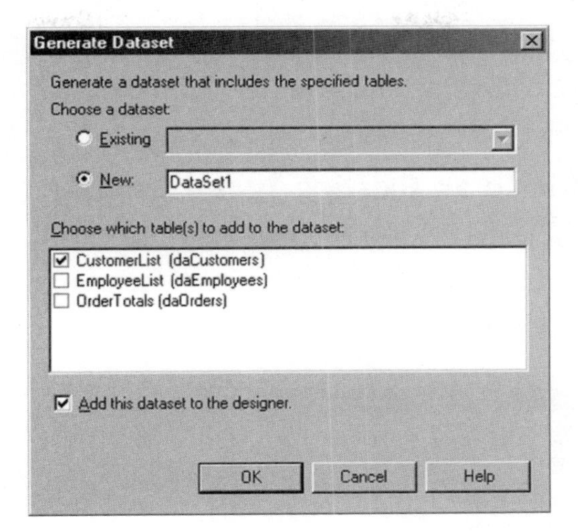

5 In the New text box, change the name of the new DataSet to **dsMaster**.

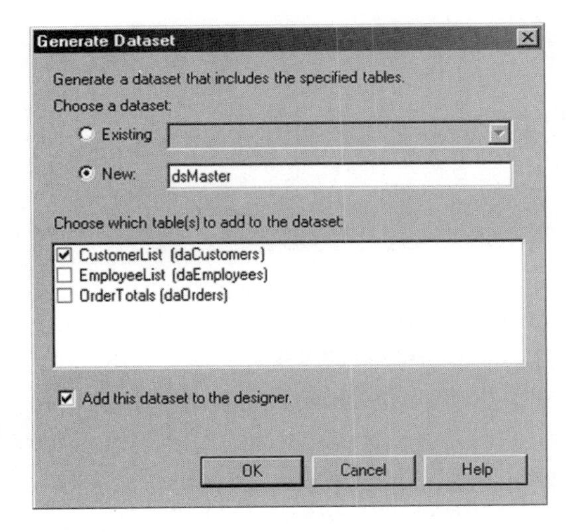

6 Click OK.

Visual Studio creates a Typed DataSet and adds an instance of it to the Component Designer.

The DataSet object's Tables collection, being a collection, can contain multiple DataTables, and the Visual Studio Generate Dataset dialog box allows you to add the result sets returned by a DataAdapter to an existing DataSet.

Because all of the result sets returned by the defined DataAdapters are displayed in the Generate Dataset dialog box, you can add them all in a single operation by selecting the check boxes next to their names.

Add a DataTable to an Existing Typed DataSet

1. Select daOrders in the Component Designer.
2. Choose Generate dataset from the Data Menu.

   Visual Studio displays the Generate dataset dialog.

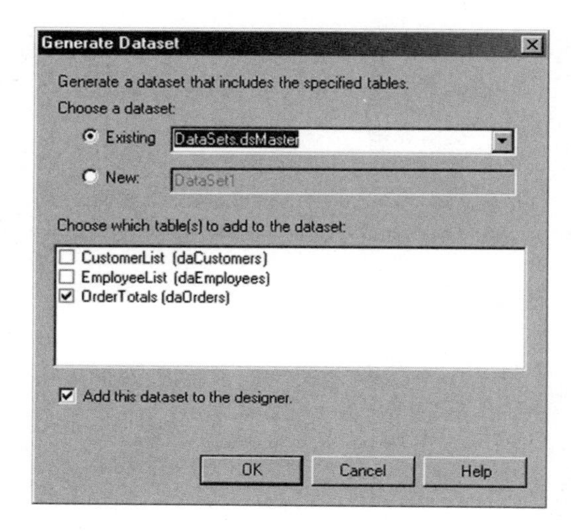

3. Verify that the default option to add the DataTable to the existing dsMaster DataSet is selected, and then click OK.

   Visual Studio adds the DataTable to dsMaster.
4. Select dsMaster in the Component Designer, and then click View Schema at the bottom of the Properties window.

   Visual Studio opens the XML Schema Designer.

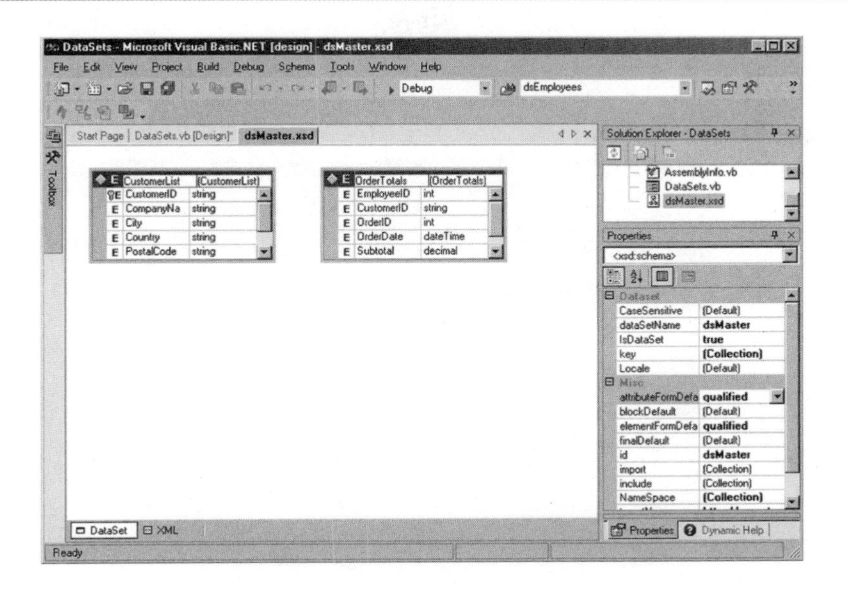

5 Verify that the DataSet contains both DataTables, and then close the XML Schema Designer.

Creating Untyped DataSets

You can create Untyped DataSets both interactively in Visual Studio and programmatically at run time. Within Visual Studio, you can create both Typed and Untyped DataSets by dragging the DataSet control from the Toolbox.

Create an Untyped DataSet Using Visual Studio

1 Drag a DataSet control from the Data tab of the Toolbox onto the form.

Visual Studio displays the Add Dataset dialog.

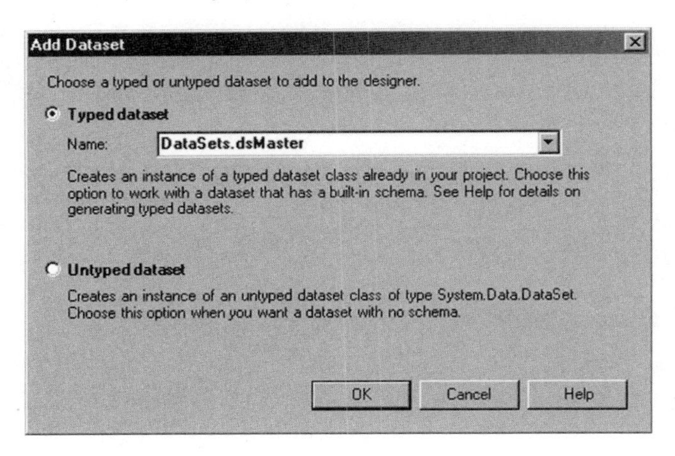

2 Select the Untyped dataset option, and then click OK.

Visual Studio adds the DataSet to the Component Designer.

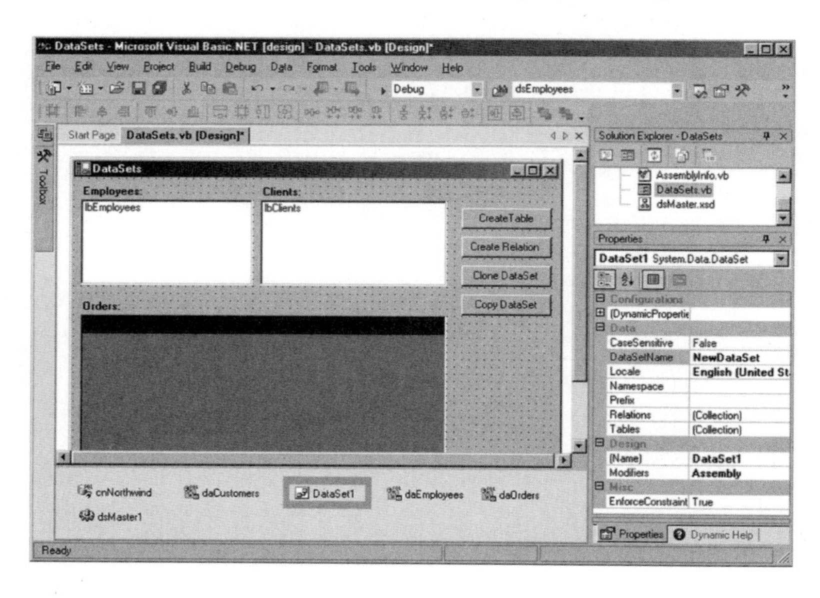

3 In the Properties window, change both the DataSetName property and the Name property to **dsUntyped**.

The DataSet object supports three versions of the usual *New* constructor to create an Untyped DataSet in code, as shown in Table 6-1. Only the first two are typically used in application programs.

Method	Description
New()	Creates an Untyped DataSet with the default name NewDataSet
New(dsName)	Creates an Untyped DataSet with the name passed in the *dsName* string
New(SerializationInfo, StreamingContext)	Used internally by the .NET Framework

Table 6-1 DataSet Constructors

Create an Untyped DataSet at Run Time

Visual Basic .NET

1 Press F7 to open the code editor.

2 Expand the region labeled Windows Form Designer generated code, and then scroll to the bottom of the class-level declarations.

3 Add the following declaration to the end of the section:

```
Dim dsEmployees As New System.Data.DataSet("dsEmployees")
```

Visual C# .NET

1 Press F7 to open the code editor.

2 Add the following declaration to the beginning of the class declaration:

```
private System.Data.DataSet dsEmployees;
```

3 Add the following instantiation to the frmDataSets sub, after the call to InitializeComponent:

```
dsEmployees = new System.Data.DataSet("dsEmployees");
```


DataSet Properties

The properties exposed by the DataSet object are shown in Table 6-2.

Property	Value
CaseSensitive	Determines whether comparisons are case-sensitive
DataSetName	The name used to reference the DataSet in code
DefaultViewManager	Defines the default filtering and sorting order of the DataSet
EnforceConstraints	Determines whether constraint rules are followed during changes
ExtendedProperties	Custom user information
HasErrors	Indicates whether any of the DataRows in the DataSet contain errors
Locale	The locale information to be used when comparing strings
Namespace	The namespace used when reading or writing an XML document
Prefix	An XML prefix used as an alias for the namespace
Relations	A collection of DataRelation objects that define the relationship of the DataTables within the DataSet
Tables	The collection of DataTables contained in the DataSet

Table 6-2 DataSet Properties

Roadmap
We'll examine the DataSet's XML-related methods in Chapter 14.

The majority of properties supported by the DataSet are related to its interaction with XML. We'll examine these properties in Chapter 14. Of the non-XML properties, the two most important are the Tables and Relations collections, which contain and define the data maintained within the DataSet.

The DataSet Tables Collection

Roadmap
We'll examine the properties and methods of DataTables in detail in Chapter 5.

For Typed DataSets, the contents of the DataSet's Tables collection are defined by the DataSet schema. For Untyped DataSets, you can create the tables and their columns either programmatically or through the Visual Studio designers.

Add a DataTable to an Untyped DataSet Using Visual Studio

1 Select the dsUntyped DataSet in the form designer.

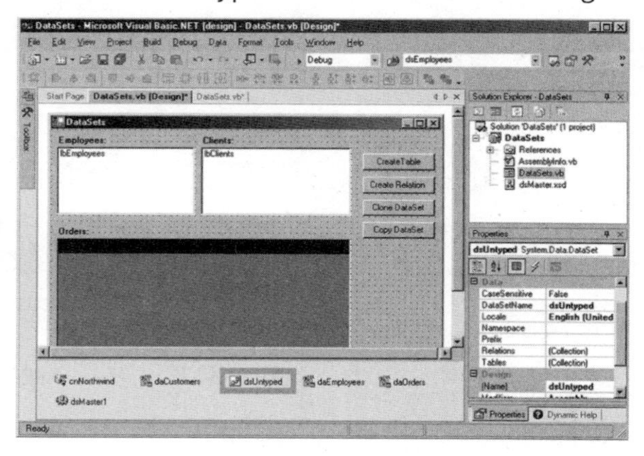

2 In the Properties window, select the Tables property, and then click the ellipsis button.

The Tables Collection Editor opens.

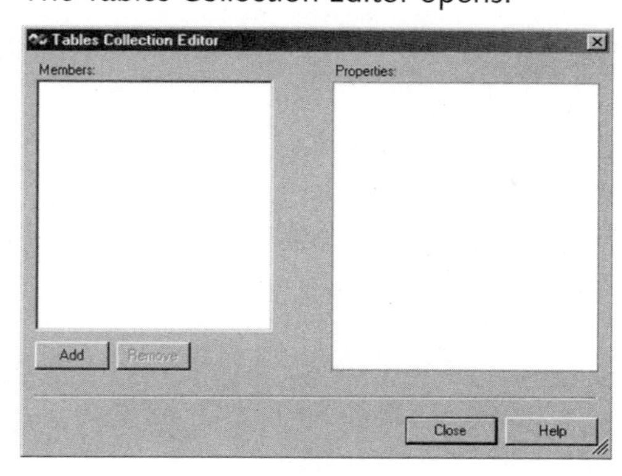

3 Click Add.

Visual Studio adds a new table called Table1 to the DataSet.

4 Change both the Name and TableName properties to **dtMaster**.

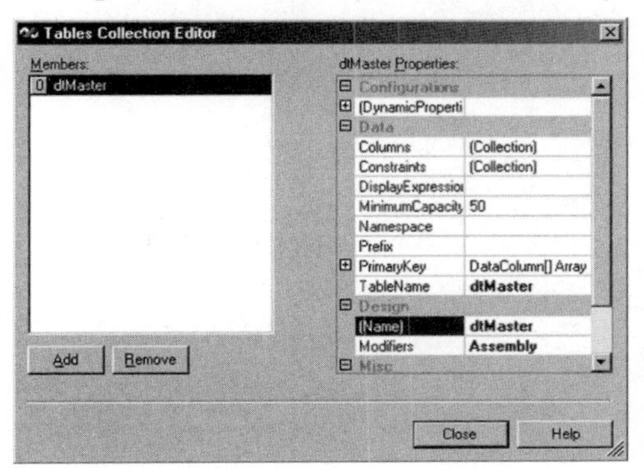

5 Select the Columns property, and then click the ellipsis button.

The Columns Collection Editor opens.

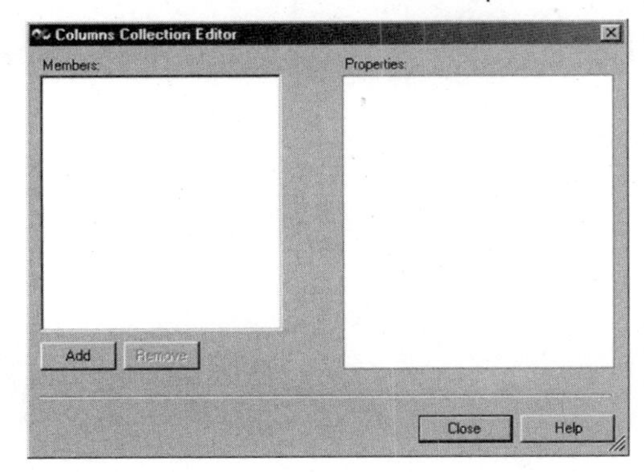

6 Click Add.

Visual Studio adds a column named Column1 to the DataTable.

7 Set the column's properties to the values shown in the following table.

Property	Value
AllowDbNull	*False*
AutoIncrement	*True*
Caption	*MasterID*
ColumnName	*MasterID*
DataType	*System.Int32*
Name	*MasterID*

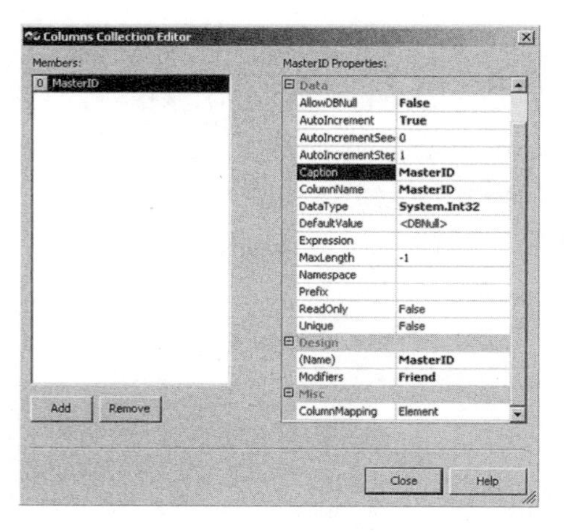

8 Click Add again, and then set the new column's properties to the values shown in the following table.

Property	Value
Caption	*MasterValue*
ColumnName	*MasterValue*
Name	*MasterValue*

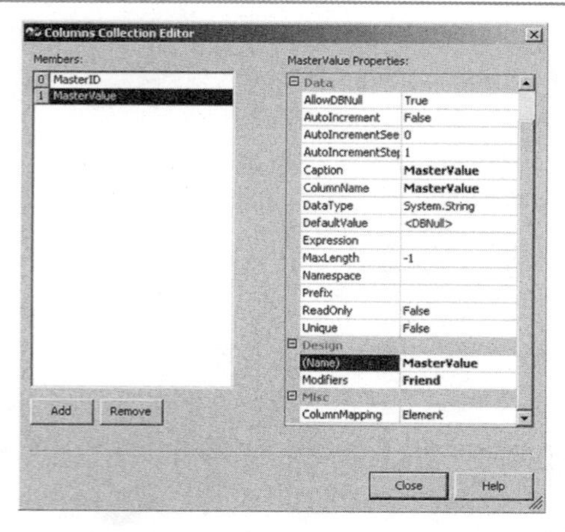

9 Click Close.

The Columns Collection Editor closes.

10 In the Tables Collection Editor, click Add to add a second table to the DataSet.

11 Change both the Name and TableName properties to **dtChild**.

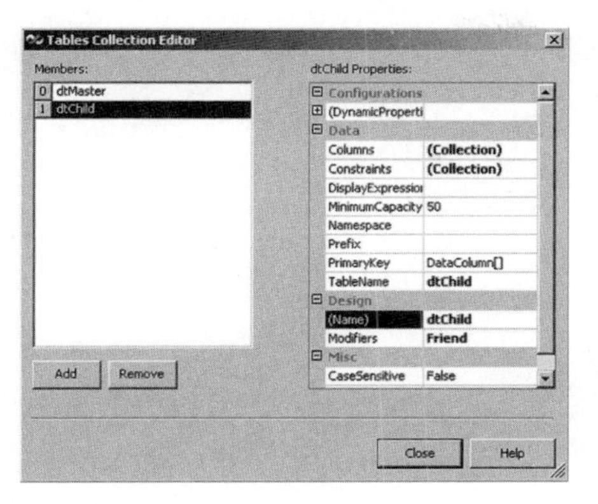

...

12 Click the Columns property, and then click the ellipsis button.

The Columns Collection Editor opens.

13 Click Add.

Visual Studio adds a column named Column1 to the DataTable.

14 Set the column's properties to the values shown in the following table.

Property	Value
AllowDbNull	*False*
AutoIncrement	*True*
Caption	*ChildID*
ColumnName	*ChildID*
DataType	*System.Int32*
Name	*ChildID*

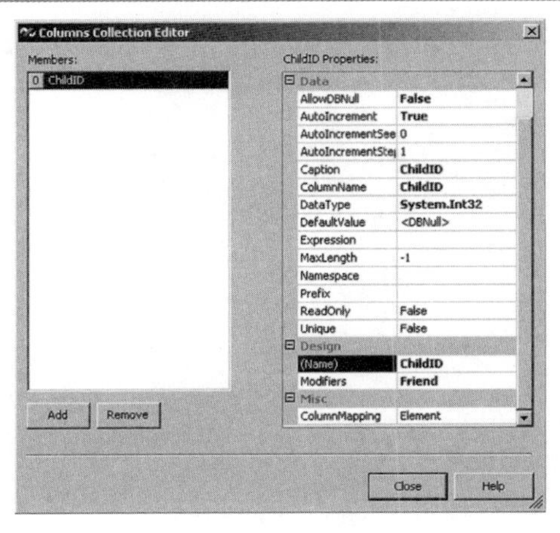

15 Click Add again, and then set the column's properties to the values shown in the following table.

Property	Value
AllowDbNull	*False*
Caption	*MasterLink*
ColumnName	*MasterLink*
DataType	*System.Int32*
Name	*MasterLink*

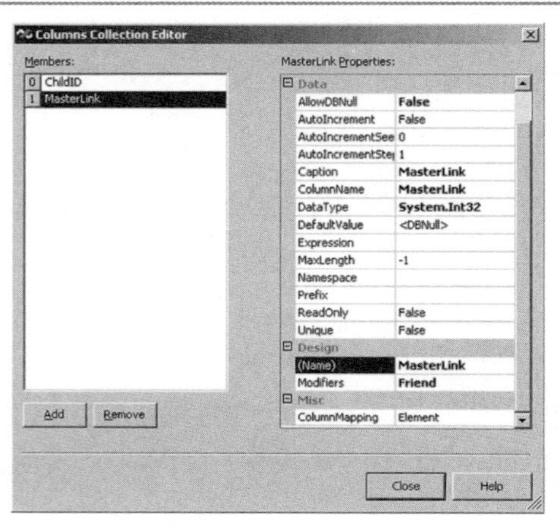

16 Click Add again, and then set the new column's properties to the values shown in the following table.

Property	Value
Caption	*ChildValue*
ColumnName	*ChildValue*
Name	*ChildValue*

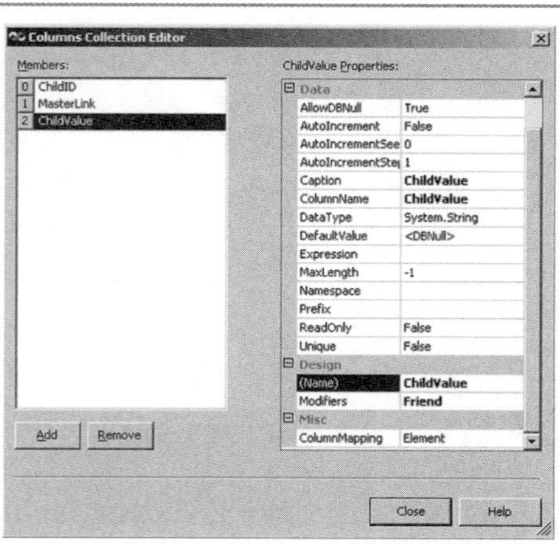

17 Click Close.

The Columns Collection Editor closes.

18 Click Close on the Tables Collection Editor.

Add a DataTable to an Untyped DataSet at Run Time

Visual Basic .NET

1 In the code editor window, select btnTable in the ControlName list, and then select Click in the MethodName list.

Visual Studio adds the Click event handler template to the code.

2 Add the following code to create the Employees table and its columns:

```
Dim strMessage as String

'Create the table
Dim dtEmployees As System.Data.DataTable
dtEmployees = Me.dsEmployees.Tables.Add("Employees")

'Add the columns
dtEmployees.Columns.Add("EmployeeID", _
   Type.GetType("System.Int32"))
dtEmployees.Columns.Add("FirstName", _
   Type.GetType("System.String"))
dtEmployees.Columns.Add("LastName", _
   Type.GetType("System.String"))

'Fill the DataSet
Me.daEmployees.Fill(Me.dsEmployees.Tables("Employees"))
strMessage = "The first employee is "
strMessage &= _
   Me.dsEmployees.Tables("Employees").Rows(0).Item("LastName")
MessageBox.Show(strMessage)
```

3 Press F5 to run the application.

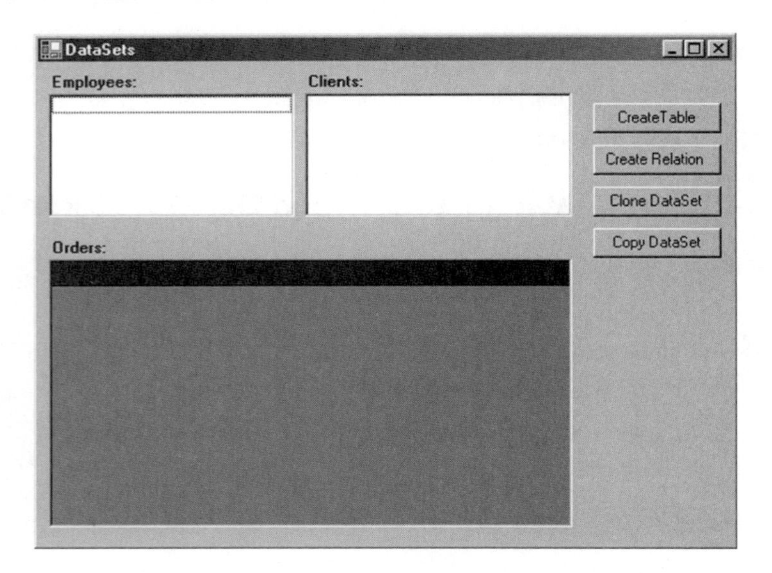

4 Click CreateTable.

The application displays a message box containing the last name of the first employee.

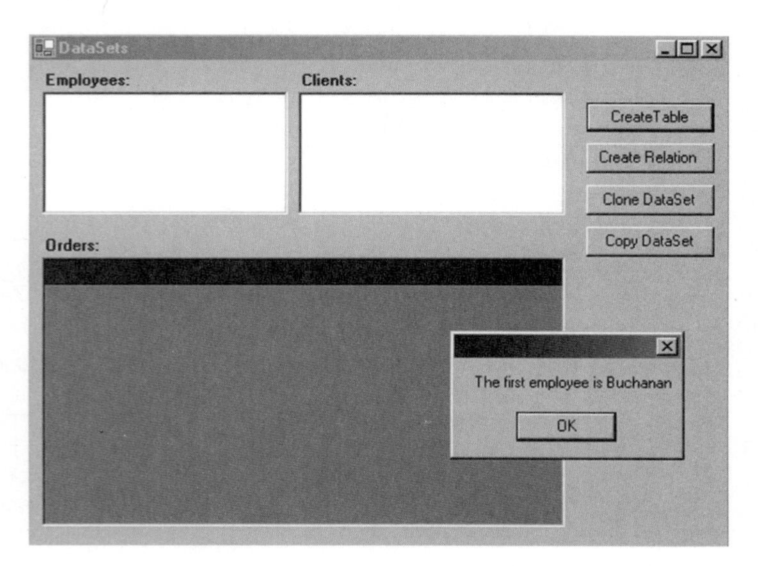

5 Click OK to close the message box, and then close the application.

Visual C# .NET

1 In the form designer, double-click the Create Table button.

   Visual Studio adds the Click event handler to the code.

2 Add the following code to create the Employees table and its columns:

```
string strMessage;

// Create the table
System.Data.DataTable dtEmployees;
dtEmployees = this.dsEmployees.Tables.Add("Employees");

//Add the columns
dtEmployees.Columns.Add("EmployeeID", Type.GetType("System.Int32"));
dtEmployees.Columns.Add("FirstName", Type.GetType("System.String"));
dtEmployees.Columns.Add("LastName", Type.GetType("System.String"));

//Fill the dataset
this.daEmployees.Fill(this.dsEmployees.Tables["Employees"]);

strMessage = "The first employee is ";
strMessage +=
this.dsEmployees.Tables["Employees"].Rows[0]["LastName"];
MessageBox.Show(strMessage);
```

3 Press F5 to run the application.

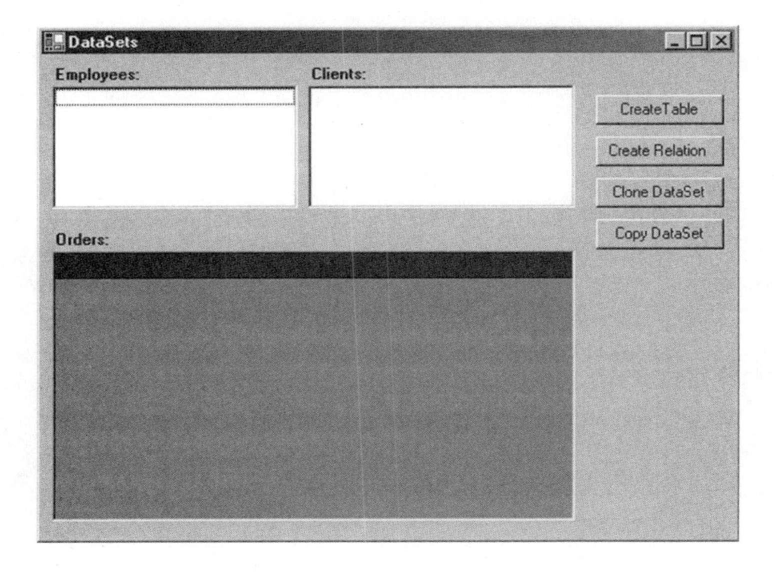

4 Click CreateTable.

The application displays a message box containing the last name of the first employee.

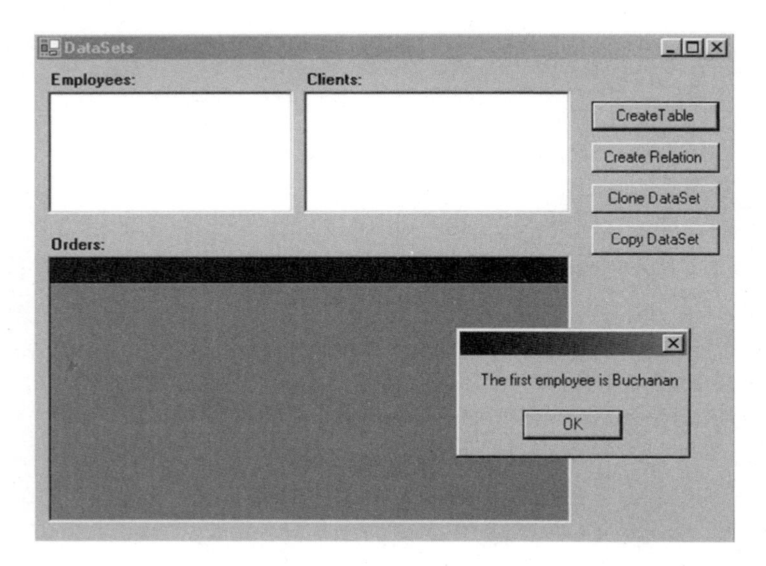

5 Click OK to close the message box, and then close the application.

DataSet Relations

While the DataSet's Tables collection defines the structure of the data stored in a DataSet, the Relations collection defines the relationships between the DataTables. The Relations collection contains zero or more DataRelation objects, each one representing the relationship between two tables.

As we'll see in the next chapter, the DataRelation object allows you to easily move between parent and child rows—given a parent, you can find all the related children, or given a child, you can find its parent row. DataRelation objects also provide a mechanism for enforcing relational integrity through their ChildKeyConstraint and ParentKeyConstraint properties.

important

Even if constraints are established in the DataRelation object, they will be enforced only if the DataSet's EnforceConstraints property is *True*.

Add a DataRelation to an Untyped DataSet Using Visual Studio

1. Select the dsUntyped DataSet in the Component Designer.
2. In the Properties window, select the Relations property, and then click the ellipsis button.

   The Relations Collection Editor opens.

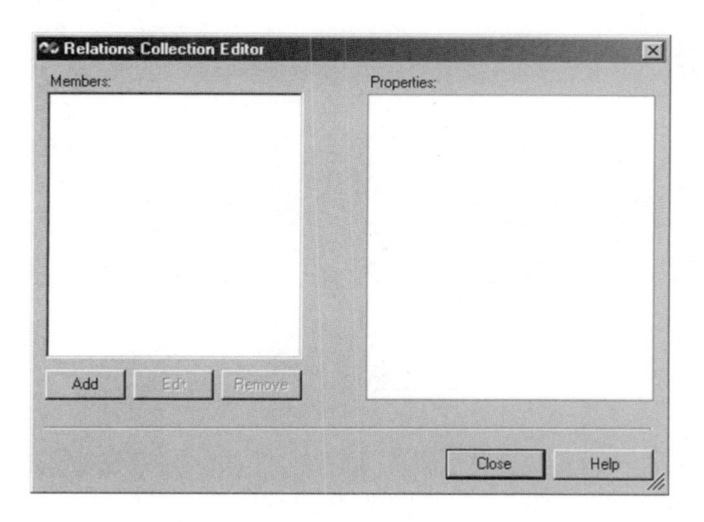

3. Click Add.

   The Relation dialog box opens.

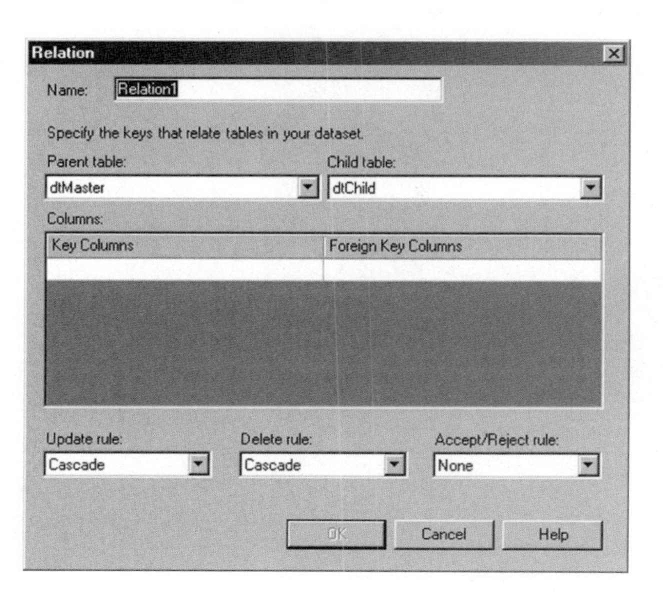

4 Change the name of the relation to **MasterChild**, the Key Column to **MasterID,** and the Foreign Key Column to **MasterLink**.

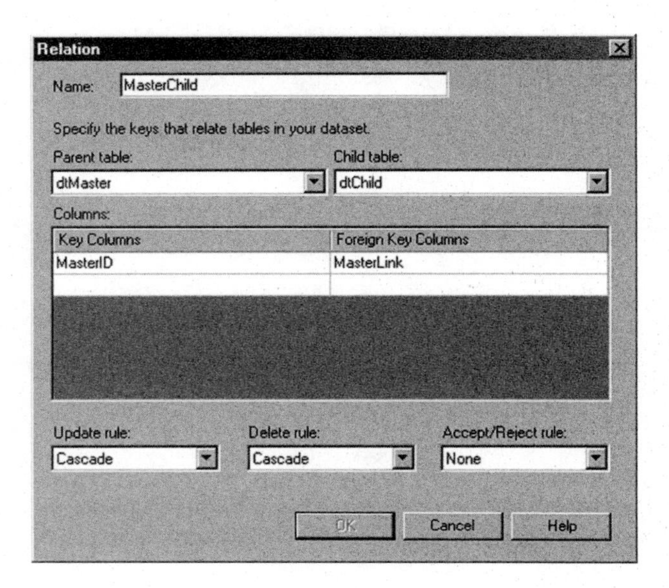

5 Click OK.

Visual Studio adds the DataRelation to the DataSet.

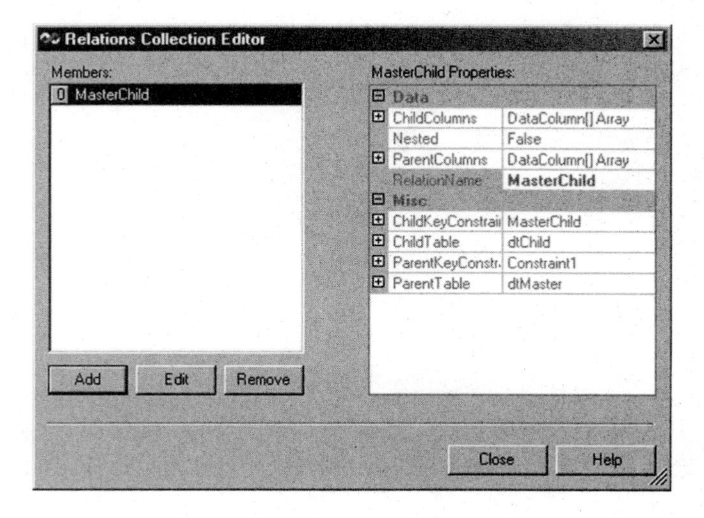

6 Click Close.

> ***Roadmap***
> *We'll discuss the XML Schema Designer in Chapter 13.*

The Visual Studio Relations Collection Editor is available for only Untyped DataSets. For Typed DataSets, you can use the XML Schema Designer, which we'll examine in Chapter 13, or you can add DataRelations programmatically. You can, of course, also add DataRelations to Untyped DataSets at run time.

Add a DataRelation to a Dataset at Run Time

Visual Basic .NET

1. In the code editor, select btnRelation in the ControlName list, and then select Click in the MethodName list.

   Visual Studio adds the Click event handler template to the code.

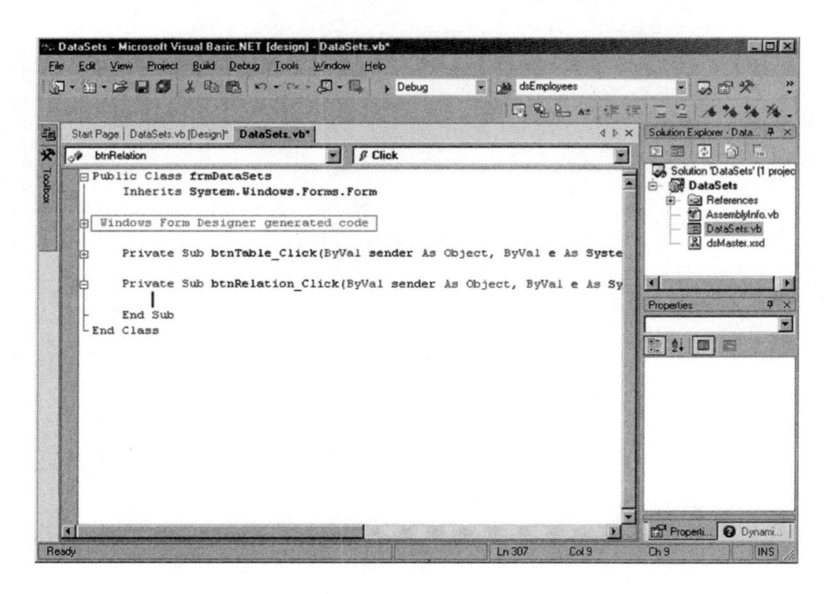

2. Add the following code to create the DataRelation:

```
Dim strMessage As String

'Add a new relation
Me.dsMaster1.Relations.Add("CustomerOrders", _
   Me.dsMaster1.CustomerList.CustomerIDColumn, _
   Me.dsMaster1.OrderTotals.CustomerIDColumn)

strMessage = "The name of the DataRelation is "
strMessage &= Me.dsMaster1.Relations(0).RelationName.ToString
MessageBox.Show(strMessage)
```

3. Press F5 to run the application.
4. Click Create Relation.

   The application adds the DataRelation, and then displays a message box containing the name of the DataRelation.

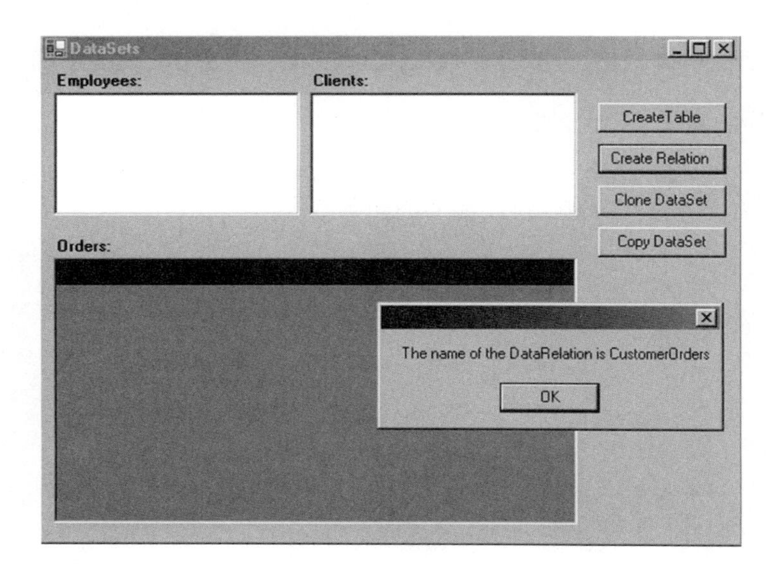

5. Click OK to close the message box, and then close the application.

Visual C# .NET

1. In the form designer, double-click the Create Relation button.

   Visual Studio adds the Click event handler to the code.
2. Add the following code to create the DataRelation:

```
string strMessage;

//Add a new relation
this.dsMaster1.Relations.Add("CustomerOrders",
   this.dsMaster1.CustomerList.CustomerIDColumn,
   this.dsMaster1.OrderTotals.CustomerIDColumn);

strMessage = "The name of the DataRelation is ";
strMessage+=
   this.dsMaster1.Relations[0].RelationName.ToString();
MessageBox.Show(strMessage);
```

3. Press F5 to run the application.

4 Click Create Relation.

The application adds the DataRelation, and then displays a message box containing the name of the DataRelation.

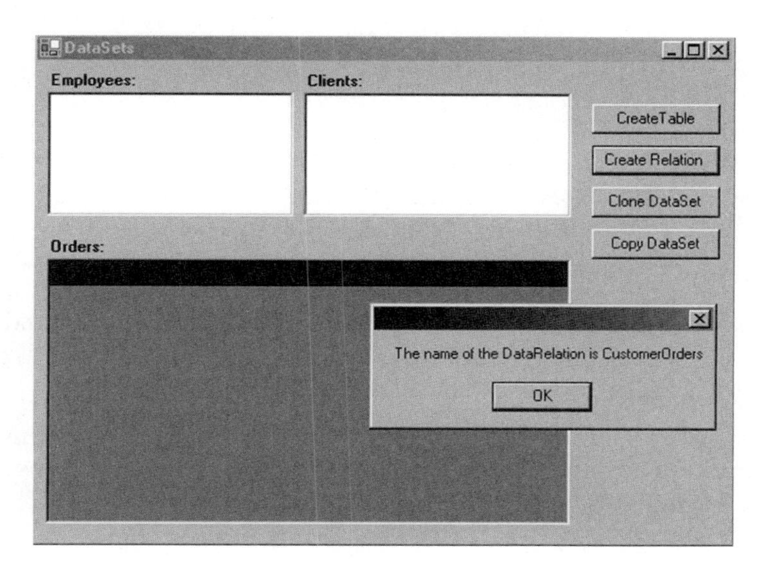

5 Click OK to close the message box, and then close the application.

DataSet Methods

Roadmap
We'll examine the relationship between ADO.NET and XML in Part V.

The primary methods supported by the DataSet object are listed in Table6-3. Like the DataSet's properties, the majority of its methods are related to its interaction with XML and will be examined in Part V.

Method	Description
AcceptChanges	Commits all pending changes to the DataSet
Clear	Empties all the tables in the DataSet
Clone	Copies the structure of a DataSet
Copy	Copies the structure and contents of a DataSet
GetChanges	Returns a DataSet containing only the changed rows in each of its tables
GetXml	Returns an XML representation of the DataSet
GetXmlSchema	Returns an XSD representation of the DataSet's schema
HasChanges	Returns a Boolean value indicating whether the DataSet has pending changes

(continued)

(continued)

InferXmlSchema	Infers a schema from an XML TextReader or file
Merge	Combines two DataSets
ReadXml	Reads an XML schema and data into the DataSet
ReadXmlSchema	Reads an XML schema into the DataSet
RejectChanges	Rolls back all changes pending in the DataSet
Reset	Returns the DataSet to its original state
WriteXml	Writes an XML schema and data from the DataSet
WriteXmlSchema	Writes the DataSet structure as an XML schema

Table 6-3 Primary DataSet Methods

Roadmap
We'll examine the HasChanges, GetChanges, AcceptChanges *and* RejectChanges *methods in Chapter 9.*

HasChanges, GetChanges, AcceptChanges, RejectChanges, and *Merge* are used when updating the DataSet's Tables collection, and we'll examine those in the Chapter 9.

That leaves only three methods: *Clear*, which we've used extensively already; *Clone*, which creates an empty copy of the DataSet; and *Copy*, which creates a complete copy of the DataSet and its data.

Cloning a DataSet

The *Clone* method creates an exact duplicate of a DataSet, including its Tables, Relations, and constraints.

Clone a DataSet

Visual Basic .NET

1. In the code editor, select btnClone in the ControlName list, and then select Click in the MethodName list.

   Visual Studio adds the Click event handler template.

2. Add the following code to clone the record set:

```
Dim strMessage As String
Dim dsClone As System.Data.DataSet

dsClone = Me.dsMaster1.Clone()
strMessage = "The cloned dataset has "
strMessage &= dsClone.Tables.Count.ToString
strMessage &= " Tables."
MessageBox.Show(strMessage)
```

3 Press F5 to run the application.

4 Click Clone DataSet.

The application displays a message box containing the number of tables in the new DataSet.

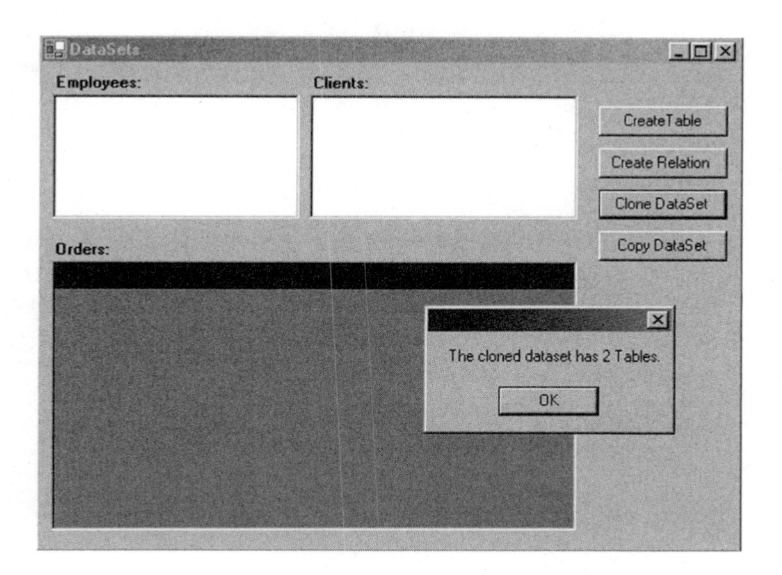

5 Close the application.

Visual C# .NET

1 In the form designer, double-click the Clone DataSet button.

Visual Studio adds the Click event handler to the code.

2 Add the following code to clone the record set:

```
string strMessage;
System.Data.DataSet dsClone;

dsClone = this.dsMaster1.Clone();

strMessage = "The cloned dataset has ";
strMessage += dsClone.Tables.Count.ToString();
strMessage += " tables.";
MessageBox.Show(strMessage);
```

3 Press F5 to run the application.

4 Click Clone DataSet.

The application displays a message box containing the number of tables in the new DataSet.

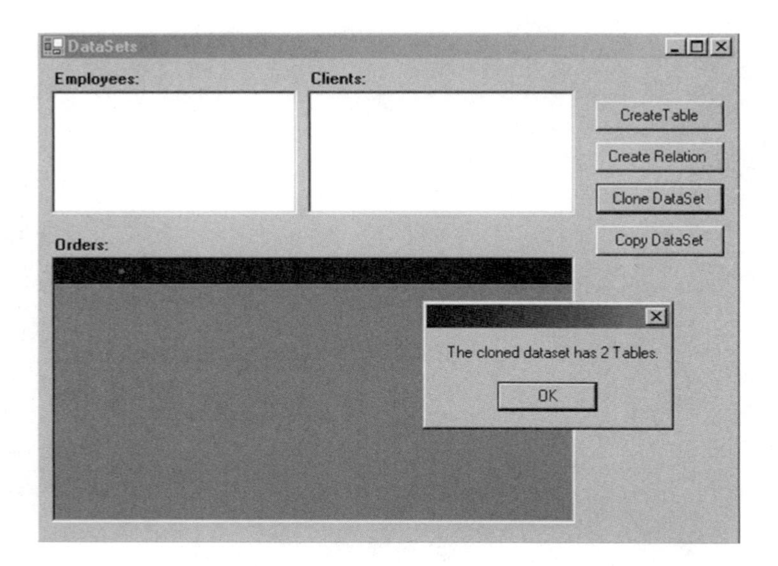

5 Close the application.

Copying a DataSet

Unlike the *Clone* method, which duplicates only the structure of a DataSet, the *Copy* method copies both its structure and its data.

Copy a DataSet

Visual Basic .NET

1 In the code editor, select btnCopy in the ControlName list, and then select Click in the MethodName list.

Visual Studio adds the Click event handler template.

2 Add the following code to copy the DataSet:

```
Dim strMessage As String
Dim dsCopy As System.Data.DataSet
```

```
'Fill the original dataset
Me.daCustomers.Fill(Me.dsMaster1.CustomerList)

dsCopy = Me.dsMaster1.Copy
strMessage = "The copied dataset has "
strMessage &= _
   dsCopy.Tables("CustomerList").Rows.Count.ToString
strMessage &= " rows in the CustomerList."
```

3 Press F5 to run the application.

4 Click Copy DataSet.

Visual Studio displays a message box containing the number of rows in the CustomerList table.

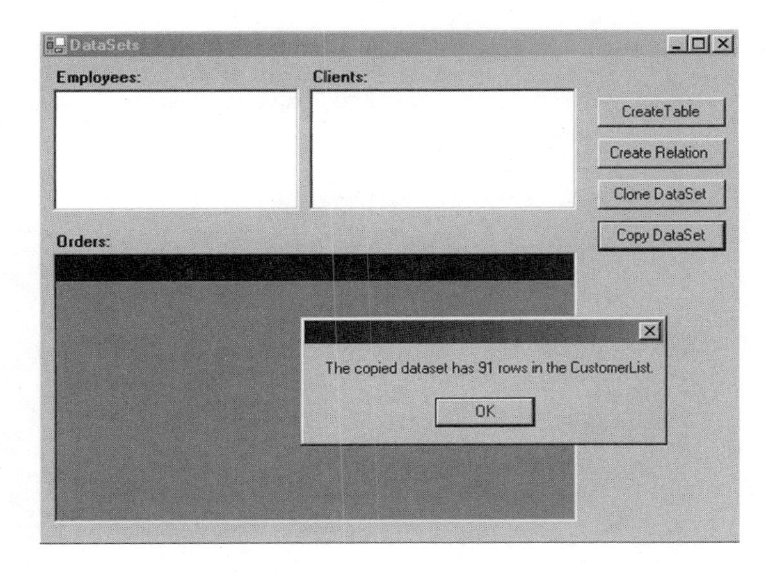

5 Click OK to close the message box, and then close the application.

Visual C# .NET

1 In the form designer, double-click the Copy DataSet button.

Visual Studio adds the Click event handler to the code.

2 Add the following code to copy the DataSet:

```
string strMessage;
System.Data.DataSet dsCopy;

//Fill the original dataset
this.daCustomers.Fill(this.dsMaster1.CustomerList);

dsCopy = this.dsMaster1.Copy();
strMessage = "The copied dataset has ";
strMessage +=
   dsCopy.Tables["CustomerList"].Rows.Count.ToString();
strMessage += " rows in the CustomerList.";
MessageBox.Show(strMessage);
```

3 Press F5 to run the application.

4 Click Copy DataSet.

Visual Studio displays a message box containing the number of rows in the CustomerList table.

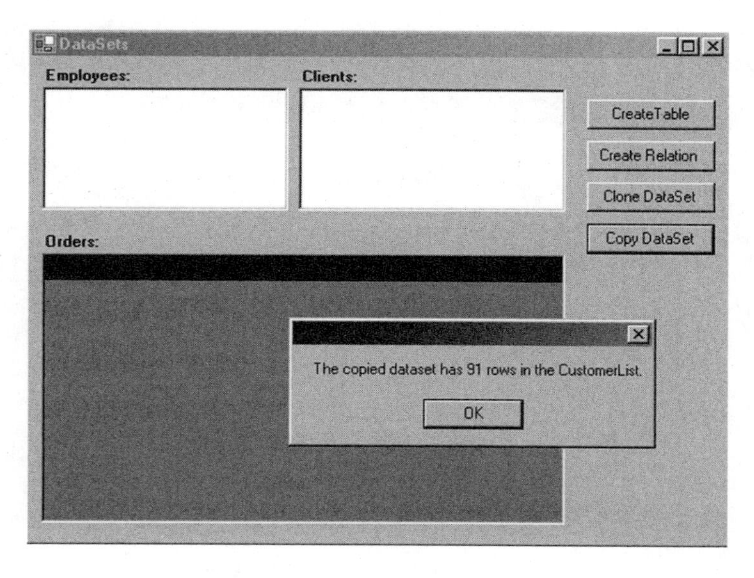

5 Click OK to close the message box, and then close the application.

Chapter 6 Quick Reference

To	Do this
Create a Typed DataSet using the Component Designer	Select a DataAdapter, and then choose Generate Dataset From the Data menu.
Create an Untyped DataSet using Visual Studio	Drag a DataSet control from the Data tab of the Toolbox onto the form.
Create an Untyped DataSet at run time	Use the *New* method of the DataSet object: `myDs = New System.Data.DataSet()`
Add a DataTable to an Untyped DataSet using Visual Studio	In the Property window for the DataSet, click the Tables property, and then click the ellipsis button.
Add a DataTable to an Untyped DataSet at run time	Use the *Add* method of the DataTable's Columns collection: `myTable.Columns.Add("Name",Type.GetType("type")`
Add a DataRelation to an Untyped DataSet using Visual Studio	In the Properties window, click the Relations property, and then click the ellipsis button.
Add a DataRelation to a DataSet at run time	Use the *Add* method of the DataSet's Relations collection: `myDS.Relations.Add("Name", ParentCol, ChildCol)`
Clone a DataSet	Use the *Clone* method: `newDS =myDS.Clone()`
Copy a DataSet	Use the *Copy* method: `newDS = myDS.Copy()`

The DataTable

In this chapter, you'll learn how to:

- ✔ *Create an independent DataTable at run time*
- ✔ *Add a DataTable to an existing DataSet*
- ✔ *Add a PrimaryKey constraint by using the* FillSchema *method*
- ✔ *Create a calculated column in a DataTable*
- ✔ *Add a new row to the Rows collection*
- ✔ *Display the RowState of a DataRow*
- ✔ *Add a ForeignKey constraint to a DataTable*
- ✔ *Add a UniqueConstraint to a DataTable*
- ✔ *Display a subset of rows within a DataTable*
- ✔ *Retrieve data related to the current DataRow*

We've been working with DataTables in the previous several chapters, but in this chapter, we'll take a detailed look at their structure, properties, and methods.

Understanding DataTables

Remember that we defined DataSets as an in-memory representation of relational data. DataTables contain the actual data. They can exist as part of the DataSet's Tables collection or can be created independently.

As we'll see, although the DataTable has properties of its own, it functions primarily as a container for three collections: the Columns collection, which defines the structure of the table; the Rows collection, which contains the data itself; and the Constraints collection, which works in conjunction with the DataTable's PrimaryKey property to enforce integrity rules on the data.

Creating DataTables

In previous chapters, we used a number of techniques to create DataTables as part of a DataSet—we used the *Fill* method of the DataAdapter, the *Add* method of the DataSet, and the Table Collection Editor that's part of Microsoft Visual Studio .NET. Tables can also be created for Typed DataSets by using the XML Schema Designer in Visual Studio, as we'll see in Part V.

Roadmap
Run-time DataTables can also be created by using the DataSet's ReadXML, ReadXMLSchema, *and* InferXmlSchema *methods. We'll examine those in Chapter 14.*

In this chapter, we'll concentrate on creating DataTables at run time, using the DataSet's *Add* method and the DataTable's *New* constructor.

Creating Independent DataTables

Although DataTables are most often used as part of a DataSet, they can be created independently. You might want to create an independent DataTable to provide data for a bound control, for example, or simply so that it can be configured before being added to the DataSet.

The three forms of the DataTable's *New* constructor are shown in Table 7-1. Of these, only the first two are typically used in application programs.

Method	Description
New()	Creates a new DataTable
New(TableName)	Creates a new DataTable with the name specified in the *TableName* string
New(SerializableInfo, StreamingContext)	Used internally by the .NET Framework

Table 7-1 DataTable Constructors

Create an Independent DataTable Object at Run Time

Visual Basic .NET

1. Open the DataTables project on the Start Page or from the Project menu.
2. Double-click DataTables.vb in the Server Explorer.

   Visual Studio opens the form designer.

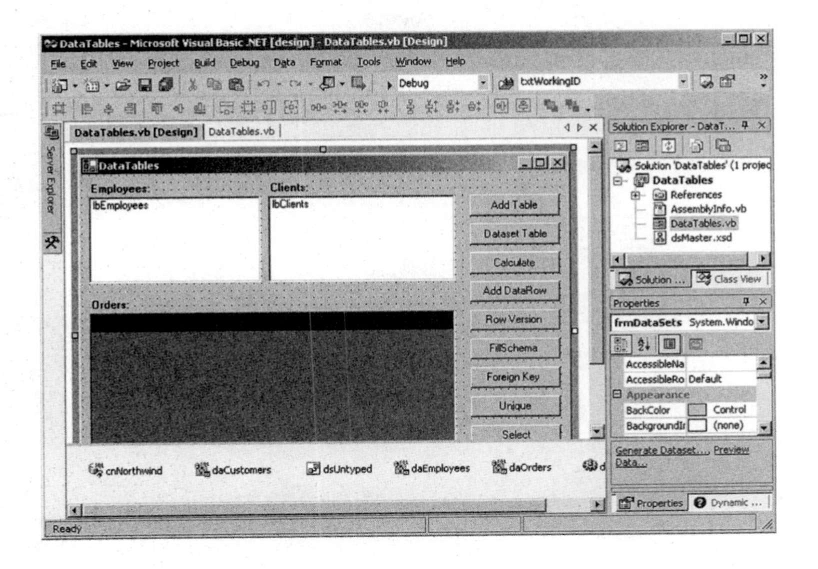

3. On the form, double-click Add Table.

   Visual Studio adds the Click event handler template to the code.

4. Add the following code to create a DataTable, and then set its name to Employees:

```
Dim strMessage As String

'Create the table
Dim dtEmployees As New System.Data.DataTable("Employees")

strMessage = "The table name is "
strMessage &= dtEmployees.TableName.ToString
MessageBox.Show(strMessage)
```

   This code uses the *New(tableName)* version of the constructor to create a DataTable named dtEmployees, and then displays the table name in a message box.

5. Press F5 to run the application.

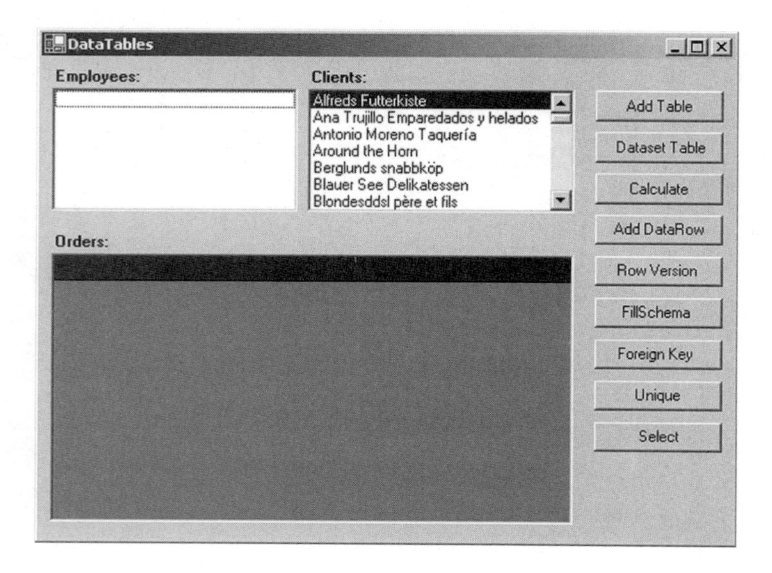

6 Click Add Table.

The application displays a message box containing the name of the table.

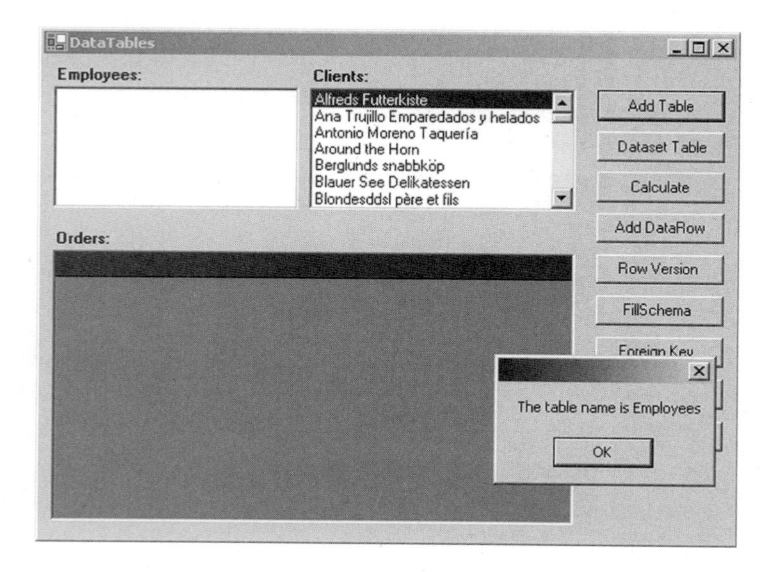

7 Close the application.

Visual C# .NET

1. Open the DataTables project on the Start Page or from the Project menu.
2. Double-click DataTables.cs in the Server Explorer.

   Visual Studio opens the form designer.

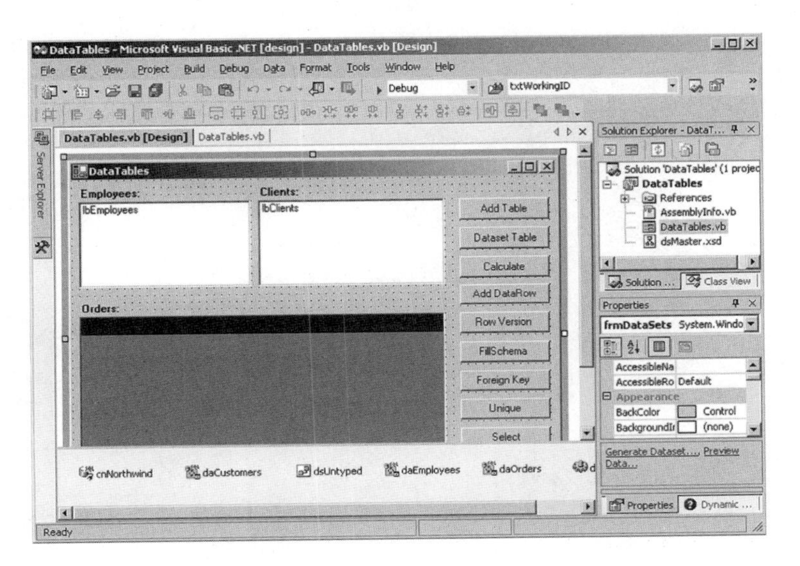

3. In the form designer, double-click Add Table.

   Visual Studio adds the Click event handler template to the code.
4. Add the following code to create a DataTable, and then set its name to Employees:

```
string strMessage;

//Create the table
System.Data.DataTable dtEmployees;
dtEmployees = new System.Data.DataTable("Employees");

strMessage = "The table name is ";
strMessage += dtEmployees.TableName.ToString();

MessageBox.Show(strMessage);
```

   This code uses the *New(tableName)* version of the constructor to create a DataTable named dtEmployees, and then displays the table name in a message box.

5 Press F5 to run the application.

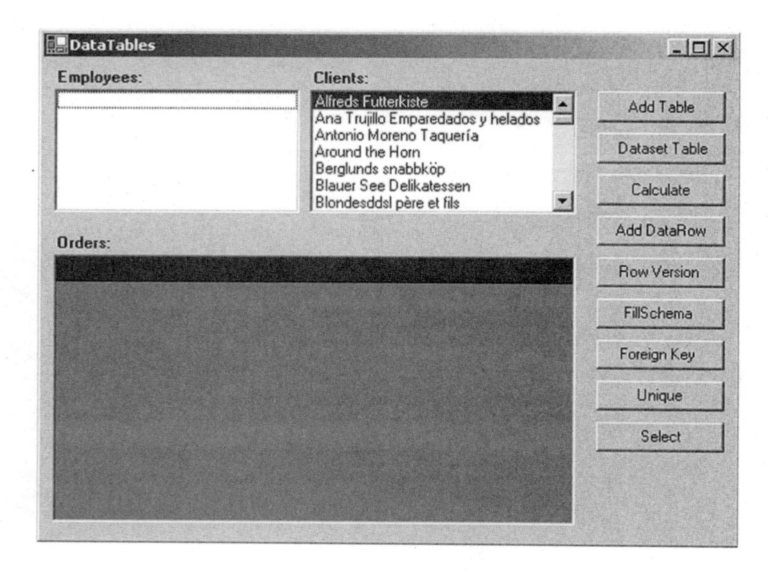

6 Click Add Table.

The application displays a message box containing the name of the table.

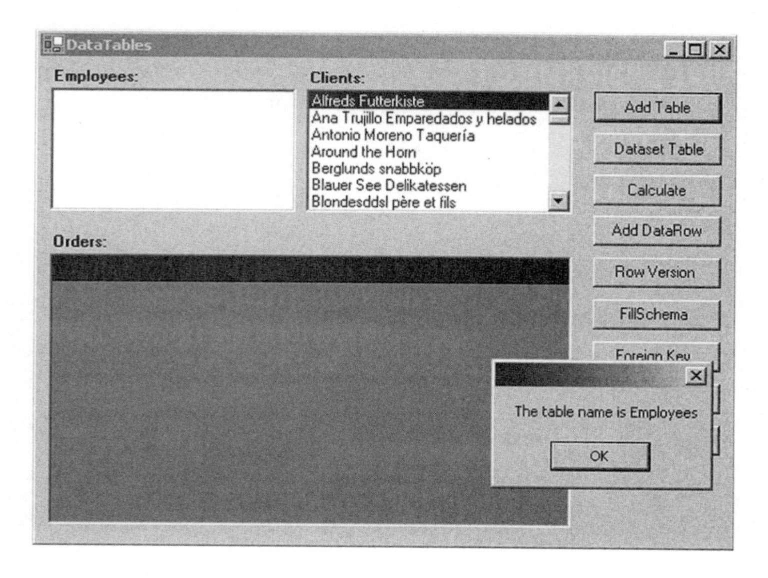

7 Close the application.

Creating DataSet Tables

Table 7-2 shows the four methods that can be used to add a table to the DataSet's Tables collection. These methods are called on the Tables collection, not the DataSet itself, for example, *myDataSet.Tables.Add()*, not *myDataSet.Add()*.

Method	Description
Tables.Add()	Creates a new DataTable within the DataSet with the name Table*N*, where *N* is a sequential number
Tables.Add (TableName)	Creates a new DataTable with the name specified in the *TableName* string
Tables.Add (DataTable)	Adds the specified *DataTable* to the DataSet
Tables.AddRange (TableArray)	Adds the DataTables included in the *TableArray* array to the DataSet

Table 7-2 DataSet Add Table Methods

The first version of the *Add* method creates a DataTable with the name Table*N*, where *N* is a sequential number. Note that this behavior is different from creating an independent DataTable without passing a table name to the constructor. In the latter case, the TableName property will be an empty string.

We used the second version of the *Add* method, *Add(TableName)*, in the previous chapter. This version creates the new table and sets its TableName property to the string supplied as a parameter.

You can add an independent DataTable that you've created at run time, or add a DataTable that exists in another DataSet, by using the *Add(DataTable)* version, while the *AddRange* method allows you to add an array of DataTables (again, either DataTables that you've created at run time or DataTables belonging to another DataSet).

Create a DataTable Using the *Tables.Add* Method

Visual Basic .NET

1 In the code editor, select btnDataSet in the ControlName list, and then select Click in the MethodName list.

 Visual Studio adds the Click event handler template to the code.

2 Add the following code to add a DataTable with a default name to the DataSet:

```
Dim strMessage As String

'Create the table
Me.dsEmployees.Tables.Add()

strMessage = "The table name is "
strMessage &= Me.dsEmployees.Tables(0).TableName.ToString
MessageBox.Show(strMessage)
```

 The code uses the version of the *Add* method that creates a new table with the default name of Table*N*.

3 Press F5 to run the application.

4 Click DataSet Table.

 The application displays a message box containing the name of the table.

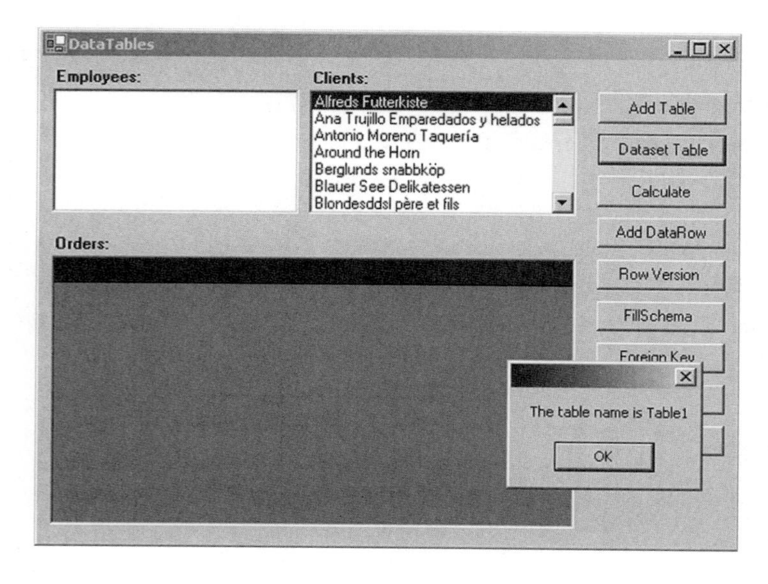

5 Close the application.

Visual C# .NET

1. In the form designer, double-click the Dataset Table button.

   Visual Studio adds the Click event handler to the code window.

2. Add the following code to add a DataTable with a default name to the DataSet:

```
string strMessage;

//Create the table
this.dsEmployees.Tables.Add();

strMessage = "The table name is ";
strMessage += this.dsEmployees.Tables[0].TableName.ToString();
MessageBox.Show(strMessage);
```

   The code uses the version of the *Add* method that creates a new table with the default name of Table*N*.

3. Press F5 to run the application.

4. Click DataSet Table.

   The application displays a message box containing the name of the table.

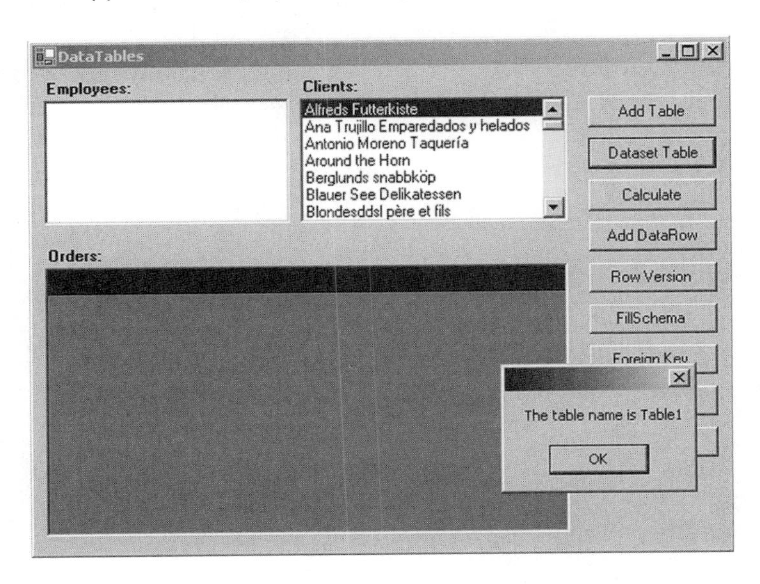

5. Close the application.

DataTable Properties

The primary properties of the DataTable are shown in Table 7-3. The most important of these are the three collections that control the data—Columns, Rows, and Constraints. We'll look at each of these in detail later in this chapter.

Property	Description
CaseSensitive	Determines how string comparisons will be performed.
ChildRelations	A collection of DataRelation objects that have this DataTable as the Parent table.
Columns	The collection of DataColumn objects within the DataTable.
Constraints	The collection of constraints maintained by the DataTable.
DataSet	The DataSet of which this DataTable is a member.
DisplayExpression	An expression used to represent the table name in the user interface (UI).
HasErrors	Indicates whether there are errors in any of the rows belonging to the DataTable.
ParentRelations	A collection of DataRelation objects that have this DataTable as the Child table.
PrimaryKey	An array of columns that function as the primary key of the table.
Rows	The collection of rows belonging to the table.
TableName	The name of the DataTable in the DataSet. This is the name by which the DataTable is referenced in code.

Table 7-3 DataTable Properties

If the DataTable belongs to a DataSet, the CaseSensitive property will default to the value of the corresponding DataSet.CaseSensitive property. Otherwise, the default value will be *False*.

The ChildRelations and ParentRelations collections contain references to the DataRelations that reference the table as a child or parent, respectively. For most independent DataTables, these collections will be *Null*, but it is theoretically possible to add a relation to the ChildRelations and ParentRelations collections if, for example, the DataTable is related to itself.

The DisplayExpression property is similar to the Caption property of a column in that it determines how the name of the table will be displayed to the user at run time, but unlike the Caption property, DisplayExpression uses an expression to determine the value at run time. One of the uses of the DataExpression property is to calculate the way the table is displayed based on the contents of the table.

Using DataTable Properties

Most DataTable properties are set just like the properties of any other object—by a simple assignment, or if the property is a collection, by calling the collection's *Add* method. Additionally, the structure of a DataTable based on a table in a data source can be established using the *FillSchema* method of the DataAdapter. In Chapter 6, we used *FillSchema* to load the entire structure of a DataTable. It can also be used to load DataTable constraints such as the primary key.

Add a PrimaryKey Constraint Using the DataAdapter's *FillSchema* Method

Visual Basic .NET

1. In the code editor, select btnSchema in the ControlName list, and then select Click in the MethodName list.

   Visual Studio adds the Click event handler template.

2. Add the following code to create the table and its PrimaryKey constraint by using *FillSchema*:

```
Dim strMessage As String

Me.dsEmployees.Tables.Add("Employees")
Me.daEmployees.FillSchema(Me.dsEmployees.Tables("Employees"), _
    SchemaType.Source)

With Me.dsEmployees.Tables("Employees")
    strMessage = "Primary Key:  "
    strMessage &= .PrimaryKey(0).ColumnName.ToString
    strMessage &= vbCrLf & "Constraint Count:  "
    strMessage &= .Constraints(0).ConstraintName.ToString
    MessageBox.Show(strMessage)
End With
```

3. Press F5 to run the application.

4 Click FillSchema.

The application displays a message box showing the column of the primary key and the number of constraints.

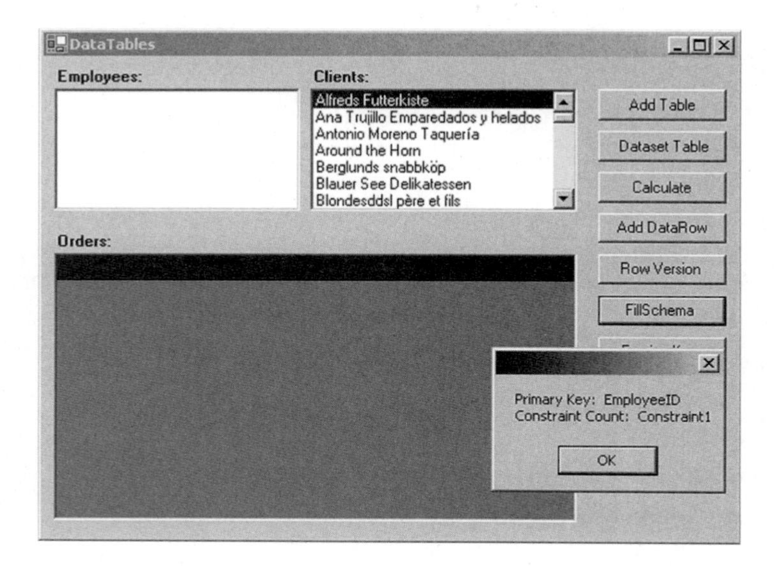

5 Close the application.

Visual C# .NET

1 In the form designer, double-click the FillSchema button.

Visual Studio adds the Click event handler to the code window.

2 Add the following code to create the table and its PrimaryKey constraint by using *FillSchema*:

```
string strMessage;
System.Data.DataTable dt;

dt = this.dsEmployees.Tables.Add("Employees");

this.daEmployees.FillSchema(dt,
   SchemaType.Source);
```

```
strMessage = "Primary Key:  ";
strMessage += dt.PrimaryKey[0].ColumnName.ToString();
strMessage += "\nConstraint Count: ";
strMessage += dt.Constraints[0].ConstraintName.ToString();
MessageBox.Show(strMessage);
```

3. Press F5 to run the application.
4. Click FillSchema.

   The application displays a message box showing the column of the primary key and the number of constraints.

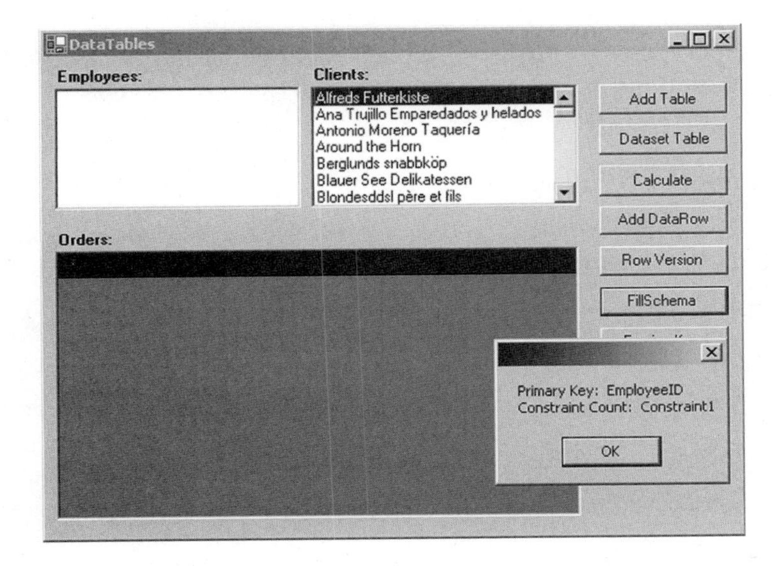

5. Close the application.

The Columns Collection

The DataTable's Columns collection contains zero or more DataColumn objects that define the structure of the table. If the DataTable is created by a DataAdapter's *Fill* or *FillSchema* method, the Columns collection will be generated automatically.

If you're creating a DataColumn in code, you can use one of the *New* constructors shown in Table 7-4.

Method	Description
New()	Creates a new DataColumn with no ColumnName or Caption
New(columnName)	Creates a new DataColumn with the name specified in the *columnName* string
New(columnName, dataType)	Creates a new DataColumn with the name specified in the *columnName* string and the data type specified by the *dataType* parameter
New(columnName, DataType, Expression)	Creates a new DataColumn with the name specified in the *columnName* string and the specified *DataType* and *Expression*
New(columnName, DataType, Expression, ColumnMapping)	Creates a new DataColumn with the name specified in the *columnName* string and the specified *DataType*, *Expression*, and *ColumnMapping*

Table 7-4 DataColumn Constructors

The primary properties of the DataColumn are shown in Table 7-5. They correspond closely to the properties of data columns in most relational databases.

Property	Description
AllowDbNull	Determines whether the column can be left empty
AutoIncrement	Determines whether the system will automatically increment the value of the column
AutoIncrementSeed	The starting value for an AutoIncrement column
AutoIncrementStep	The increment by which an AutoIncrement column will be increased. For example, if the AutoIncrementSeed is 1, and the AutoIncrementStep is 3, the first value will be 1, the second 4, the third 7, and so on
Caption	The name of the column displayed in some controls, such as the *DataGrid*. The default value is the ColumnName
ColumnName	The name of the table in the DataSet's Tables collection. This is the name by which the column can be referenced in code
DataType	The .NET Framework data type of the column
DefaultValue	The value of the column provided by the system if no other value is provided
Expression	The expression used to calculate the value of the column
MaxLength	The maximum length of a text column

ReadOnly	Determines whether the value of the column can be changed after the row containing it has been added to the table
Unique	Determines whether each row in the table must have a unique value for this column

Table 7-5 DataColumn Properties

important

There is an incompatibility between the .NET Framework decimal data type and the Microsoft SQL Server decimal data type. The .NET Framework decimal data type allows a maximum of 28 significant digits, while the SQL Server decimal data type allows 38 significant digits. If a DataColumn is defined as *System.Decimal* and it is filled from a SQL Server table, any rows containing more than 28 significant digits will cause an exception.

Create a Calculated Column

Visual Basic .NET

1. Select btnCalculate in the ControlName list, and then select Click in the MethodName list.

   Visual Studio adds the Click event handler template to the code.

2. Add the following code, which first adds an Employees table to the dsEmployees DataSet and then uses the daEmployees DataAdapter to create the pre-existing columns and fill them with data:

```
Dim dcName As System.Data.DataColumn

'Create the table
Me.dsEmployees.Tables.Add("Employees")

'Fill the table from daEmployees
Me.daEmployees.Fill(Me.dsEmployees.Tables(0))
```

3. Add the following code to create the column and then add it to the table:

```
'Create the column
dcName = New System.Data.DataColumn("Name")
dcName.DataType = System.Type.GetType("System.String")
dcName.Expression = "FirstName + ' ' + LastName"

'Add the calculated column
Me.dsEmployees.Tables("Employees").Columns.Add(dcName)
```

4 Add the following code to bind the lbEmployees list box to the calculated column so that we can see the results:

> **important**
> Make sure that you choose the lbEmployees list box, not the lblEmployees label.

```
'Bind to the listbox
Me.lbEmployees.DataSource = Me.dsEmployees.Tables("Employees")
Me.lbEmployees.DisplayMember = "Name"
```

5 Press F5 to run the application.

6 Click Calculate.

The application displays the full name of the employees in the list box.

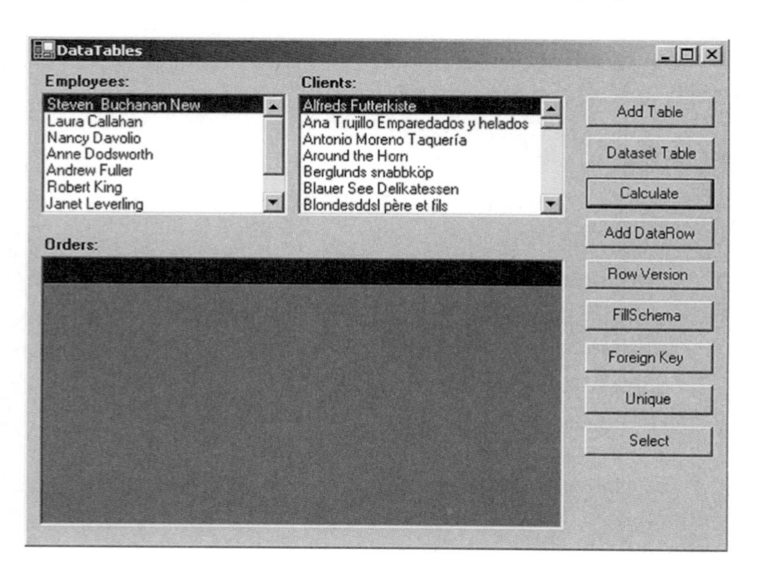

7 Close the application.

Visual C# .NET

1 In the form designer, double-click the Calculate button.

Visual Studio adds the Click event handler to the code window.

2 Add the following procedure, which first adds an Employees table to the dsEmployees DataSet, and then uses the daEmployees DataAdapter to create the pre-existing columns and fill them with data:

```
System.Data.DataColumn dcName;

//Create the table
this.dsEmployees.Tables.Add("Employees");

//Fill the data from the dataset
this.daEmployees.Fill(this.dsEmployees.Tables[0]);
```

3 Add the following code to create the column and then add it to the table:

```
//Create the column
dcName = new System.Data.DataColumn("Name");
dcName.DataType = System.Type.GetType("System.String");
dcName.Expression = "FirstName + ' ' + LastName";

//Add the calculated column
this.dsEmployees.Tables["Employees"].Columns.Add(dcName);
```

4 Add the following code to bind the lbEmployees list box to the calculated column so that we can see the results:

important

Make sure that you choose the lbEmployees list box, not the lblEmployees label.

```
//Bind to the listbox
this.lbEmployees.DataSource =
this.dsEmployees.Tables["Employees"];
this.lbEmployees.DisplayMember = "Name";
```

5 Press F5 to run the application.

6 Click Calculate.

The application displays the full name of the employees in the list box.

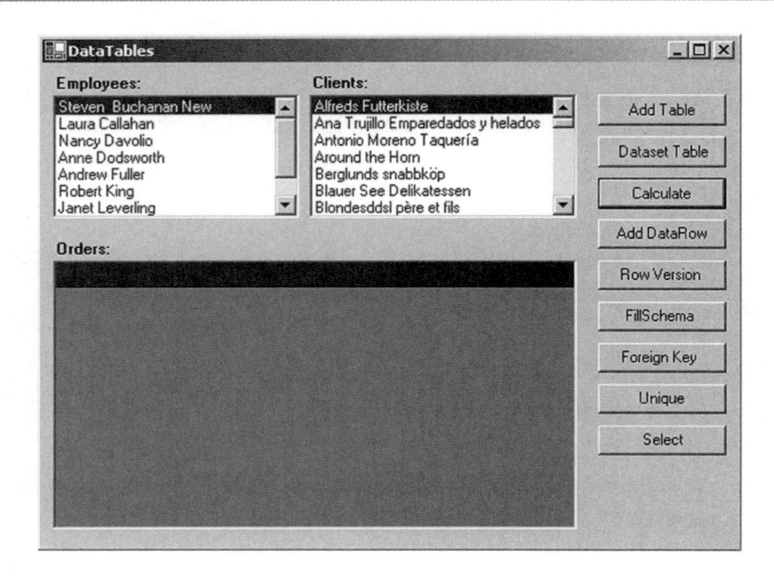

7 Close the application.

Rows

As we've seen previously, the DataTable's Rows collection contains the actual data that is contained in the DataTable, in the form of zero or more DataRow objects. The structure of the DataRow is shown in Table 7-6.

Property	Description
HasErrors	Indicates whether there are any errors in the row
Item	The value of a column in the DataRow
ItemArray	The value of all columns in the DataRow represented as an array
RowError	The custom error description for a row
RowState	The DataRowState of a row
Table	The DataTable to which the DataRow belongs

Table 7-6 DataRow Properties

Because the Rows property is a collection, you can add new data to the DataTable by using the *Add* method, which is available in two forms, as shown in Table 7-7.

Method	Description
Add(DataRow)	Adds the specified *DataRow* to the table
Add(dataValues())	Creates a new DataRow in the table and sets its Item values as specified in the *dataValues* object array

Table 7-7 Rows.Add Methods

Add a New Row to the Rows Collection

Visual Basic .NET

1. Select btnAddRow in the ControlName list, and then select Click in the MethodName list.

   Visual Studio adds the Click event handler template to the code.

2. Add the following code to create a new DataRow, and add it to the Customers table:

```
Dim drNew As System.Data.DataRow

'Create the new row
drNew = Me.dsMaster1.CustomerList.NewRow
drNew.Item("CustomerID") = "ANEWR"
drNew.Item("CompanyName") = "A New Row"

'Add row to table
Me.dsMaster1.CustomerList.Rows.Add(drNew)

'Refresh the display
Me.lbClients.Refresh()
```

3. Press F5 to run the application.
4. Click Add DataRow.

   The application adds the new row to the table.

5. Scroll to the bottom of the Clients list box to confirm the addition.

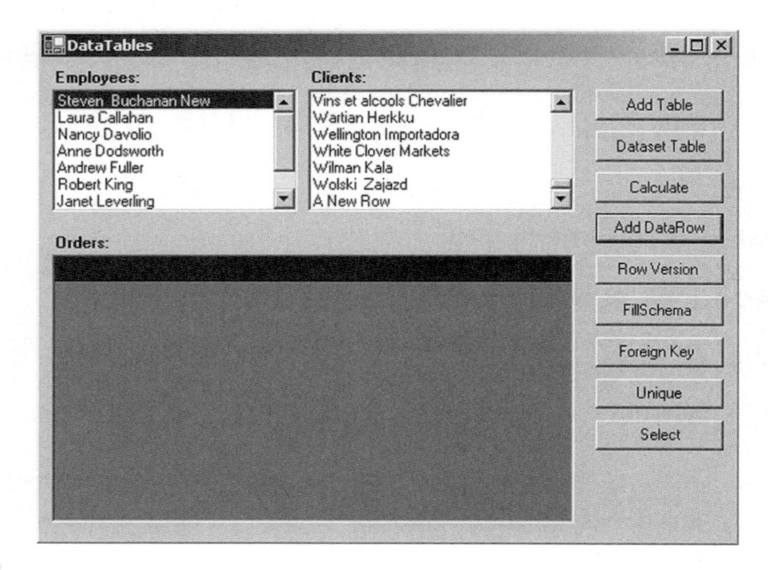

6 Close the application.

Visual C# .NET

1 In the form designer, double-click the Add DataRow button.

Visual Studio adds the Click event handler to the code window.

2 Add the following procedure to create a new DataRow, and add it to the Customers table:

```
System.Data.DataRow drNew;

//Create the new row
drNew = this.dsMaster1.CustomerList.NewRow();
drNew["CustomerID"] = "ANEWR";
drNew["CompanyName"] = "A New Row";

//Add row to table
this.dsMaster1.CustomerList.Rows.Add(drNew);

//Refresh the display
this.lbClients.Refresh();
```

3 Press F5 to run the application.

4 Click Add DataRow.

The application adds the new row to the table.

5 Scroll to the bottom of the Clients list box to confirm the addition.

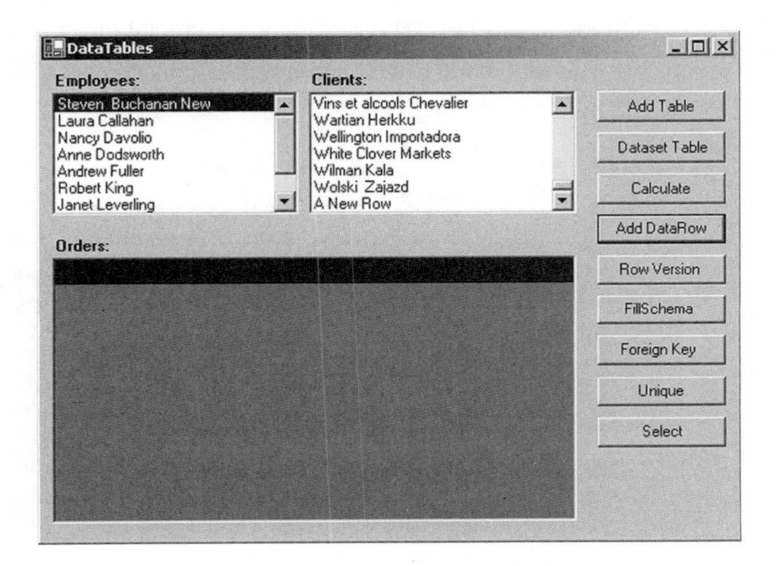

6 Close the application.

The RowState property of the DataRow reflects the actions that have been taken since the DataTable was created or since the last time the *AcceptChanges* method was called. The possible values for the RowState property are shown in Table 7-8.

Property	Description
Added	The DataRow is new.
Deleted	The DataRow has been deleted from the table.
Detached	The DataRow has not yet been added to a table.
Modified	The contents of the DataRow have been changed.
Unchanged	The DataRow has not been modified.

Table 7-8 DataRowState Values

Display the Row State

Visual Basic .NET

1. Select btnVersion in the ControlName list, and then select Click in the MethodName list.

   Visual Studio adds the Click event handler template to the code.

2. Add the following code to edit a row and display its properties:

```
Dim strMessage As String

With Me.dsMaster1.CustomerList.Rows(0)
    .Item("CustomerID") = "NEWVAL"
    strMessage = "The RowState is " & .RowState.ToString
    strMessage &= vbCrLf & "The original value was "
    strMessage &= .Item("CustomerID", DataRowVersion.Original)
    strMessage &= vbCrLf & "The new value is "
    strMessage &= .Item("CustomerID", DataRowVersion.Current)
End With

MessageBox.Show(strMessage)
```

3. Press F5 to run the application.
4. Click Row Version.

   The application displays a message box indicating the changes.

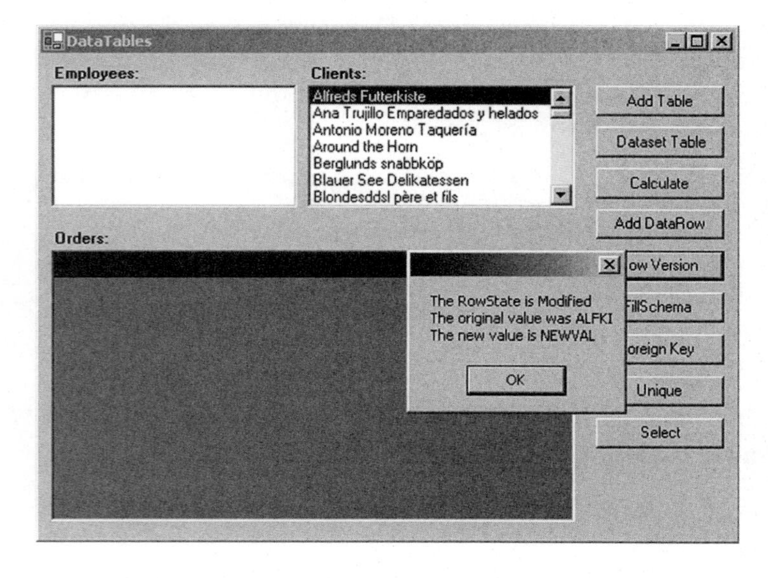

5. Close the application.

Visual C# .NET

1. In the form designer, double-click the Row Version button.

   Visual Studio adds the Click event handler to the code window.

2. Add the following procedure to edit a row and display its properties:

```
string strMessage;
System.Data.DataRow dr;

dr = this.dsMaster1.CustomerList.Rows[0];
dr["CustomerID"] = "NEWVAL";

strMessage = "The RowState is " + dr.RowState.ToString();
strMessage += "\nThe original value was ";
strMessage += dr["CustomerID", DataRowVersion.Original];
strMessage += "\nThe new value is ";
strMessage += dr["CustomerID", DataRowVersion.Current];

MessageBox.Show(strMessage);
```

3. Press F5 to run the application.
4. Click Row Version.

   The application displays a message box indicating the changes.

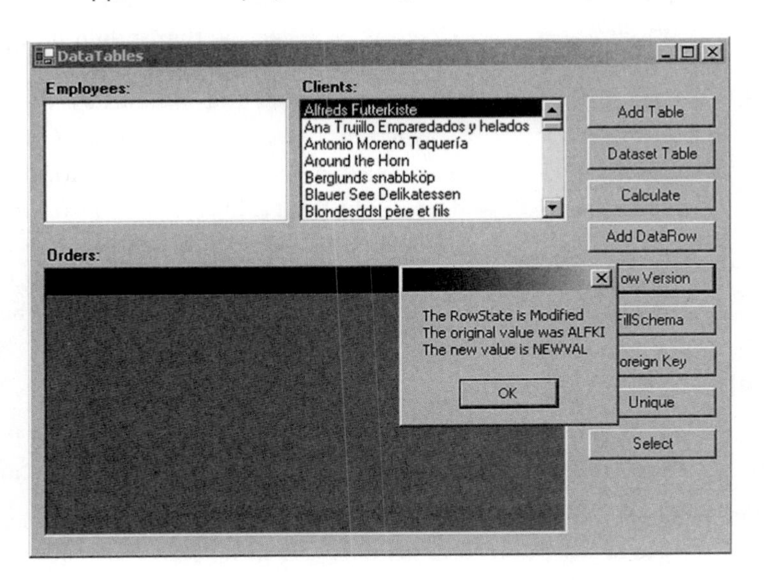

5. Close the application.

Constraints

Along with the DataTable's PrimaryKey property, the Constraints collection is used to maintain the integrity of the data within a DataTable. The *System.Data.Constraint* object has only the two properties, which are shown in Table 7-9.

Property	Description
ConstraintName	The name of the constraint. This property is used to reference the Constraint in code.
Table	The DataTable to which the constraint belongs.

Table 7-9 Constraint Properties

Obviously, an object that has only a name and a container is of little use when it comes to enforcing integrity. In real applications, you will instantiate one of the objects that inherits from Constraint, ForeignKeyConstraint, or UniqueConstraint.

The properties of the ForeignKeyConstraint object are shown in Table 7-10. This constraint represents the rules that are enforced when a parent-child relationship exists between tables (or between rows within a single table).

Property	Description
AcceptRejectRule	Determines the action that should take place when the *AcceptChanges* method is called
Columns	The collection of child columns for the constraint
DeleteRule	The action that will take place when the row is deleted
RelatedColumns	The collection of parent columns for the constraint
RelatedTable	The parent DataTable for the constraint
Table	Overrides the Constraint.Table property to return the child DataTable for the constraint
UpdateRule	The action that will take place when the row is updated

Table 7-10 ForeignKeyConstraint Properties

The actions to take place to enforce integrity are maintained by three properties of the ForeignKeyConstraint: AcceptRejectRule, DeleteRule, and UpdateRule.

The possible values of the AcceptRejectRule property are Cascade or None. The DeleteRule and UpdateRule properties can be set to any of the values shown in Table 7-11. Both properties have a default value of Cascade.

Property	Description
Cascade	Delete or update the related rows
None	Take no action on the related rules
SetDefault	Set values in the related rows to their default values
SetNull	Set values in the related rows to *Null*

Table 7-11 Action Rules

Add a ForeignKeyConstraint

Visual Basic .NET

1. In the code editor, select btnForeign in the ControlName list, and then select Click in the MethodName list.

   Visual Studio adds the Click event handler template to the code.

2. Add the following code to create the ForeignKeyConstraint:

```
Dim strMessage As String
Dim fkNew As System.Data.ForeignKeyConstraint

With Me.dsUntyped
    fkNew = New System.Data.ForeignKeyConstraint("NewFK", _
            .Tables("dtMaster").Columns("MasterID"), _
            .Tables("dtChild").Columns("MasterLink"))
    .Tables("dtChild").Constraints.Add(fkNew)

    strMessage = "The new constraint is called "
    strMessage &=
      .Tables("dtChild").Constraints(0).ConstraintName.ToString
End With

MessageBox.Show(strMessage)
```

3. Press F5 to run the application.

4. Click Foreign Key.

   The application adds the ForeignKeyConstraint and displays its name in a message box.

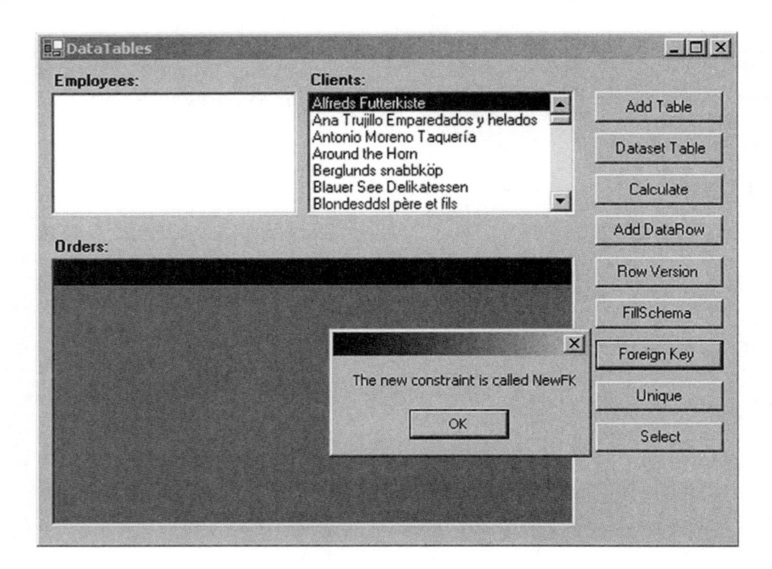

5 Close the application.

Visual C# .NET

1 In the form designer, double-click the Foreign Key button.

Visual Studio adds the Click event handler to the code window.

2 Add the following code to create the ForeignKeyConstraint:

```
string strMessage;
System.Data.ForeignKeyConstraint fkNew;
System.Data.DataSet ds = this.dsUntyped;

fkNew = new System.Data.ForeignKeyConstraint("NewFK",
   ds.Tables["dtMaster"].Columns["MasterID"],
   ds.Tables["dtChild"].Columns["MasterLink"]);
ds.Tables["dtChild"].Constraints.Add(fkNew);

strMessage = "The new constraint is called ";
strMessage +=
   ds.Tables["dtChild"].Constraints[0].ConstraintName.ToString();
MessageBox.Show(strMessage);
```

3 Press F5 to run the application.

4 Click Foreign Key.

The application adds the ForeignKeyConstraint and displays its name in a message box.

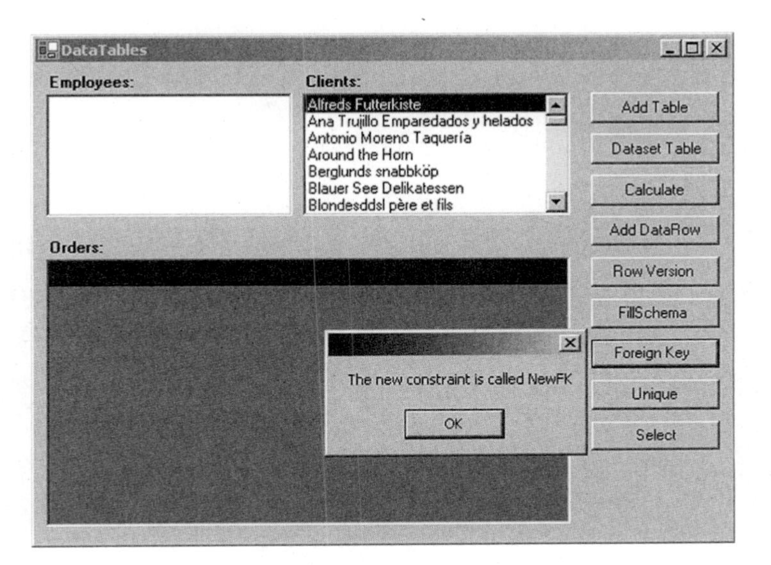

5 Close the application.

The UniqueConstraint ensures that the column or columns specified in its Columns property are unique within the table. Its structure is much simpler than a ForeignKeyConstraint, as shown in Table 7-12.

Property	Description
Columns	The array of columns affected by the constraint
IsPrimaryKey	Indicates whether the constraint is on the primary key

Table 7-12 UniqueConstraint Properties

Add a UniqueConstraint

Visual Basic .NET

1 In the code editor, select btnUnique in the ControlName list, and then select Click in the MethodName list.

Visual Studio adds the Click event handler template to the code.

2 Add the following code to create the UniqueConstraint:

```
Dim strMessage As String
Dim ucNew As System.Data.UniqueConstraint

With Me.dsUntyped.Tables("dtMaster")
    ucNew = New System.Data.UniqueConstraint("NewUnique", _
            .Columns("MasterValue"))
    .Constraints.Add(ucNew)

    strMessage = "The new constraint is called "
    strMessage &= .Constraints("NewUnique").ConstraintName.ToString
End With

MessageBox.Show(strMessage)
```

3 Press F5 to run the application.

4 Click Unique.

The application adds the UniqueConstraint and displays its name in a message box.

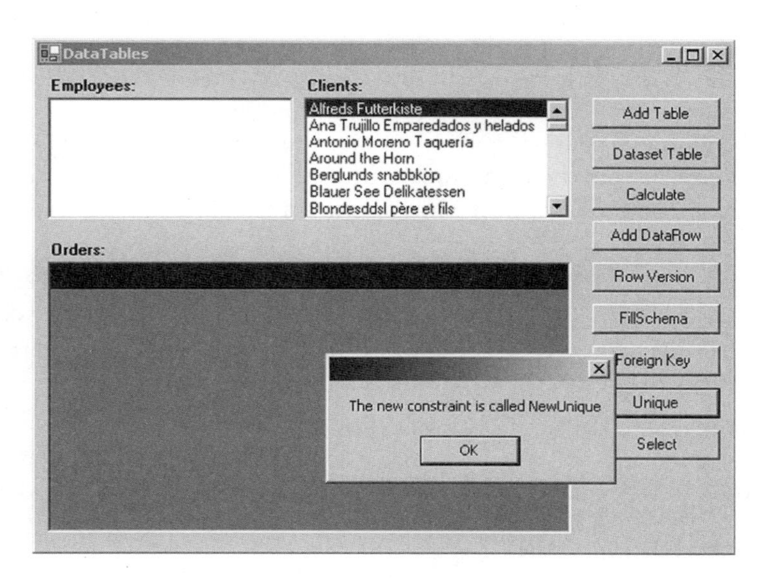

5 Close the application.

Visual C# .NET

1. In the form designer, double-click the Unique button.

   Visual Studio adds the Click event handler to the code window.

2. Add the following code to create the UniqueConstraint:

```
string strMessage;
System.Data.UniqueConstraint ucNew;
System.Data.DataTable dt = this.dsUntyped.Tables["dtMaster"];

ucNew = new System.Data.UniqueConstraint("NewUnique",
   dt.Columns["MasterValue"]);
dt.Constraints.Add(ucNew);

strMessage = "The new constraint is called ";
strMessage += dt.Constraints["NewUnique"].ConstraintName.ToString();
MessageBox.Show(strMessage);
```

3. Press F5 to run the application.
4. Click Unique.

   The application adds the UniqueConstraint and displays its name in a message box.

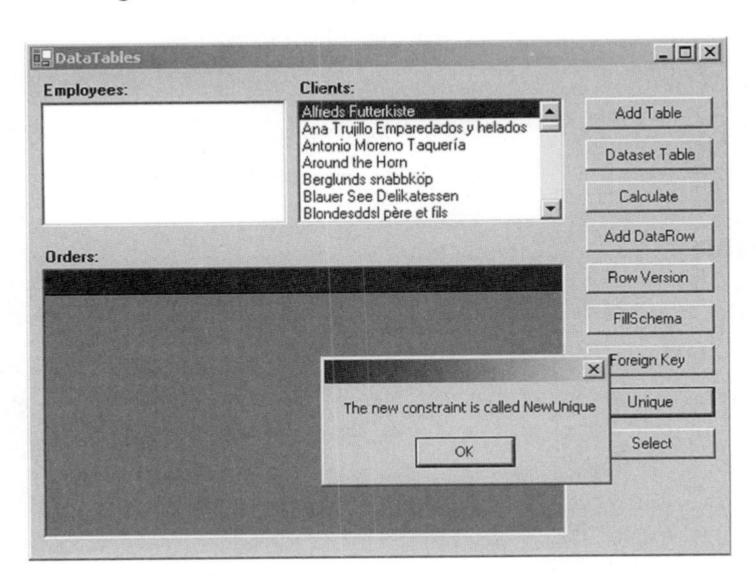

5. Close the application.

DataTable Methods

The methods supported by the DataTable are shown in Table 7-13. We've already used some of these, such as the *Clear* method, in previous exercises. We'll examine most of the others in Chapter 9.

Method	Description
AcceptChanges	Commits the pending changes to all DataRows
BeginLoadData	Turns off notifications, index maintenance, and constraint enforcement while a bulk data load is being performed. Used in conjunction with the *LoadDataRow* and *EndLoadData* methods
Clear	Removes all DataRows from the DataTable
Clone	Copies the structure of a DataTable
Compute	Performs an aggregate operation on the DataTable
Copy	Copies the structure and data of a DataTable
EndLoadData	Reinstates notifications, index maintenance, and constraint enforcement after a bulk data load has been performed
ImportRow	Copies a DataRow, including all row values and the row state, into a DataTable
LoadDataRow	Used during bulk updating of a DataTable to update or add a new DataRow
NewRow	Creates a new DataRow that matches the DataTable schema
RejectChanges	Rolls back all pending changes on the DataTable
Select	Gets an array of DataRow objects

Table 7-13 DataTable Methods

The *Select* Method

The *Select* method is used to filter and sort the rows of a DataTable at run time. The *Select* method doesn't affect the contents of the table. Instead, the method returns an array of DataRows that match the criteria you specify.

note

The DataView, which we'll examine in the following chapter, also allows you to filter and sort data rows.

Use the *Select* Method to Display a Subset of Rows

Visual Basic .NET

1 In the code editor, select btnSelect in the ControlName list, and then select Click in the MethodName list.

   Visual Studio adds the Click event handler template to the code.

2 Add the following code to select only those Customers whose CustomerID begins with A, and rebind the lbCustomers list box to the array of selected rows:

```
Dim drFound() As System.Data.DataRow
Dim dr As System.Data.DataRow

drFound = Me.dsMaster1.CustomerList.Select("CustomerID LIKE" _
& " 'A*'")

Me.lbClients.DataSource = Nothing
Me.lbClients.Items.Clear()

For Each dr In drFound
   Me.lbClients.Items.Add(dr("CompanyName"))
Next

Me.lbClients.Refresh()
```

3 Press F5 to run the application.

4 Click Select.

   The application displays a subset of rows in the lbCustomers list box.

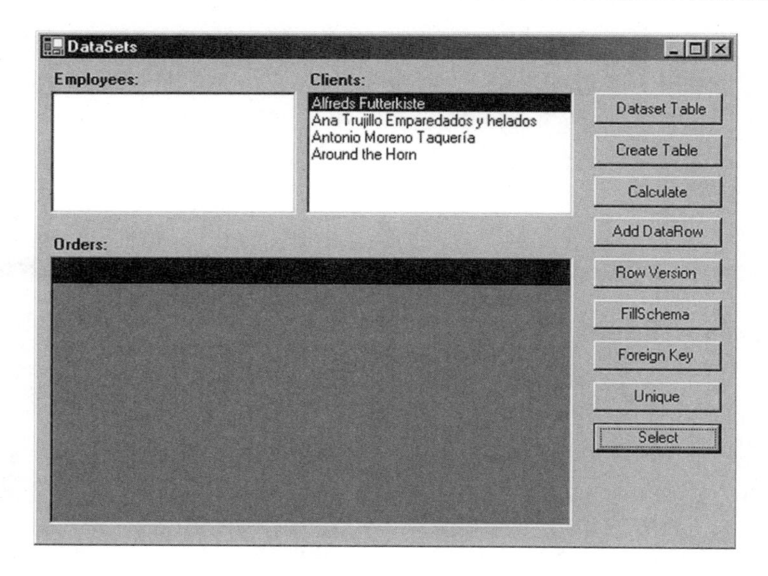

5 Close the application.

Visual C# .NET

1 In the form designer, double-click the Select button.

   Visual Studio adds the Click event handler to the code window.

2 Add the following code to select only those Customers whose CustomerID begins with A, and rebind the lbCustomers list box to the array of selected rows:

```
System.Data.DataRow[] drFound;

drFound = this.dsMaster1.CustomerList.Select("CustomerID LIKE"
+ " 'A*'");

this.lbClients.DataSource = null;
this.lbClients.Items.Clear();

foreach (System.Data.DataRow dr in drFound)
{
   this.lbClients.Items.Add(dr["CompanyName"]);
}

this.lbClients.Refresh();
```

3 Press F5 to run the application.

4 Click Select.

   The application displays a subset of rows in the lbCustomers list box.

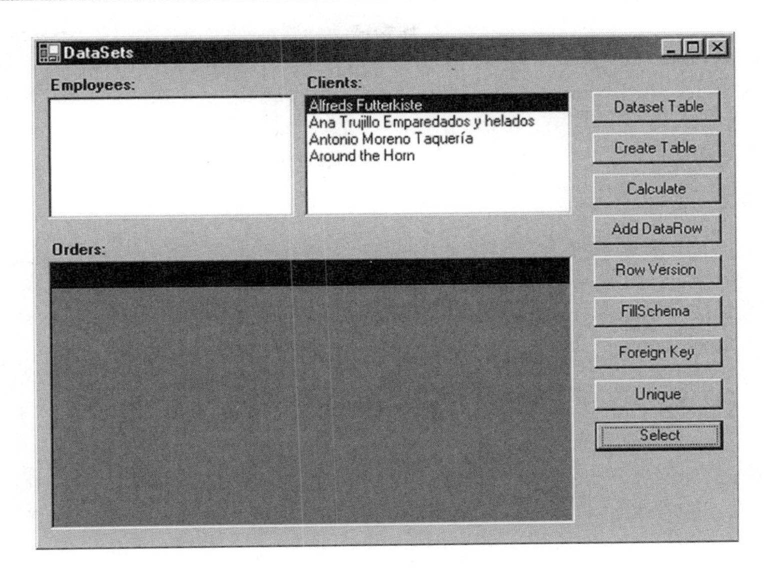

5 Close the application.

DataRow Methods

The methods supported by the DataRow object are shown in Table 7-14. The majority of the methods are used when editing data and we'll look at them in detail in Chapter 9.

Method	Description
AcceptChanges	Commits all pending changes to a DataRow
BeginEdit	Begins an edit operation
CancelEdit	Cancels an edit operation
Delete	Deletes the row
End Edit	Ends an edit operation
GetChildRows	Gets all the child rows of a DataRow
GetParentRow	Gets the parent row of a DataRow based on the specified DataRelation
GetParentRows	Gets the parent rows of a DataRow based on the specified DataRelation
HasVersion	Indicates whether a specified version of a DataRow exists
IsNull	Indicates whether the specified Column is *Null*
RejectChanges	Rolls back all pending changes to the DataRow
SetParentRow	Sets the parent row of a DataRow

Table 7-14 DataRow Methods

The *GetChildRows* and *GetParentRows* methods of the DataRow are used to navigate the relationships you set up using the DataSet's Relations collection. Both methods are overloaded, allowing you to pass either a DataRelation or a string representing the name of the DataRelation, and, optionally, a RowState value.

Use the *GetChildRows* Method to Retrieve Data

Visual Basic .NET

1. In the code editor, select lbClients in the ControlName list, and then select SelectedIndexChanged in the MethodName list.

   Visual Studio adds the Click event handler template to the code.

2. Add the following code to create a relation in dsMaster1, retrieve the child rows of the current list box selection, and then display them in the dgOrders data grid:

```
Dim drCurrent As System.Data.DataRow
Dim dsCustOrders As New System.Data.DataSet()
Dim drCustOrders() As System.Data.DataRow

'Create the relation if necessary
If Me.dsMaster1.Relations.Count = 0 Then
    Me.dsMaster1.Relations.Add("CustomerOrders", _
        Me.dsMaster1.CustomerList.CustomerIDColumn, _
        Me.dsMaster1.OrderTotals.CustomerIDColumn)
End If

drCurrent = Me.lbClients.SelectedItem.Row
dsCustOrders.Merge(drCurrent.GetChildRows("CustomerOrders"))

Me.dgOrders.SetDataBinding(dsCustOrders, "OrderTotals")
Me.dgOrders.Refresh()
```

3. Press F5 to run the application.

4. Select different items in the Clients list.

   The application displays the Client's rows in the Orders data grid.

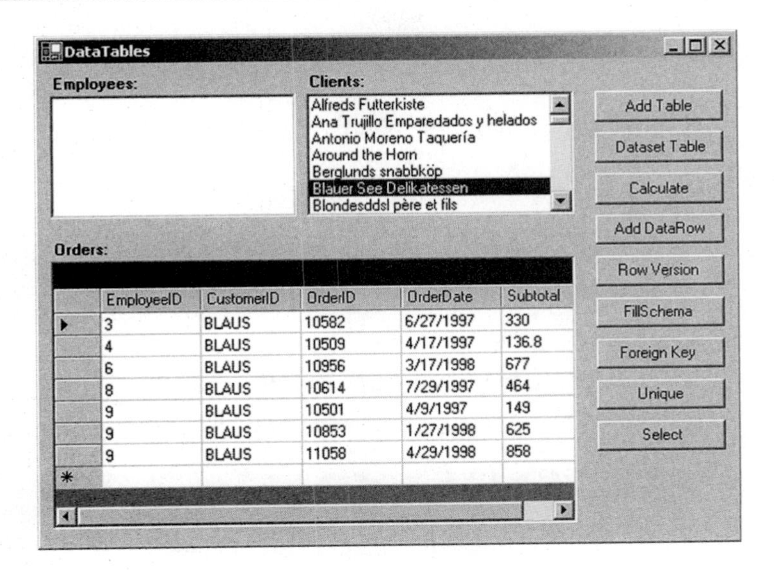

5 Close the application.

Visual C# .NET

1 In the form designer, double-click the Select button.

Visual Studio adds the Click event handler to the code window.

2 Add the following code to create a relation in dsMaster1, retrieve the child rows of the current list box selection, and then display them in the dgOrders data grid:

```
System.Data.DataRowView drCurrent;
System.Data.DataSet dsCustOrders;

dsCustOrders = new System.Data.DataSet();
//Create the relation if necessary
if (this.dsMaster1.Relations.Count == 0)
{
   this.dsMaster1.Relations.Add("CustomerOrders",
           this.dsMaster1.CustomerList.CustomerIDColumn,
           this.dsMaster1.OrderTotals.CustomerIDColumn);
}
```

(continued)

(continued)

```
drCurrent = (System.Data.DataRowView) this.lbClients.SelectedItem;

dsCustOrders.Merge(drCurrent.Row.GetChildRows("CustomerOrders"));

this.dgOrders.SetDataBinding(dsCustOrders, "OrderTotals");
this.dgOrders.Refresh();
```

3 Press F5 to run the application.

4 Select different items in the Clients list.

The application displays the Client's rows in the Orders data grid.

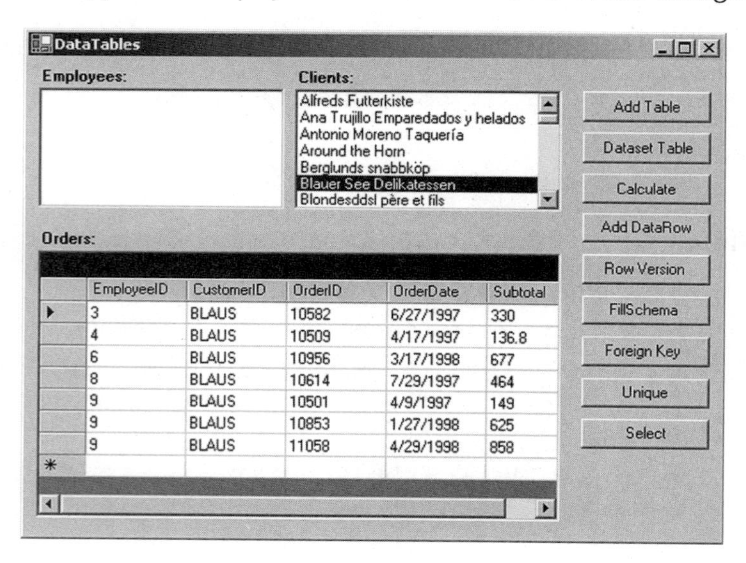

5 Close the application.

DataTable Events

The events supported by the DataTable are shown in Table 7-15. All of the events are used as part of data validation, and we'll examine them in more detail in Chapter 10.

Event	Description
ColumnChanged	Raised after a DataRow item has been changed
ColumnChanging	Raised before a DataRow item has been changed
RowChanged	Called after a DataRow has been changed
RowChanging	Called before a DataRow has been changed
RowDeleted	Called after a DataRow has been deleted
RowDeleting	Called before a DataRow is deleted

Table 7-15 DataTable Events

Chapter 7 Quick Reference

To	Do this
Create an independent DataTable at run time	Use the *New* method: `myTable = New.System.Data.DataTable()`
Add a DataTable to an existing DataSet	Use the *Add* method of the DataSet's Tables collection: `myDataSet.Tables.Add(TableName)`
Add a PrimaryKey constraint based on a table in the data source	Use the DataAdapter's *FillSchema* method: `myDA.FillSchema(mytable. SchemaType.Source)`
Create a calculated column	Set the Expression property of the column: `MyColumn.Expression = "New " & "Value"`

Add a new DataRow	Create the DataRow by using the *NewRow* method, and then add it to the DataTable:
	`myRow = myTable.NewRow`
	`myTable.Rows.Add(myRow)`

Display a subset of rows	Use the DataTable's *Select* method: `DataRowArray = myTable.Select("Criteria")`
Retrieve data related to the current DataRow	Use the *GetChildRows* method: `myRow.GetChildRows("RelationName")`

The DataView

In this chapter, you'll learn how to:

- ✔ *Add a DataView to a form*
- ✔ *Create a DataView at run time*
- ✔ *Create calculated columns in a DataView*
- ✔ *Sort DataView rows*
- ✔ *Filter DataView rows*
- ✔ *Search a DataView based on a primary key value*

In the previous chapter, we looked at the *Select* method of the DataTable, which provides a mechanism for filtering and sorting DataRows. The DataView provides another mechanism for performing the same actions. Unlike the *Select* method, a DataView is a separate object that sits on top of a DataTable.

Understanding DataViews

A DataView provides a filtered and sorted view of a single DataTable. Although the DataView provides the same functionality as the DataTable's *Select* method, it has a number of advantages. Because they are distinct objects, DataViews can be created and configured at both design time and run time, making them easier to implement in many situations.

Furthermore, unlike the array of DataRows returned from a *Select* method, DataViews can be used as the data source for bound controls. (Remember that in the previous chapter we had to load the DataRow array returned by the *Select* method into a DataSet before we could display its contents in the data grid.)

You can create multiple DataViews for any given DataTable. In fact, every DataTable contains at least one DataView in its DefaultDataView property. The properties of the DefaultDataView can be set at run time, but not at design time.

The rows of a DataView, although very much like DataRows, are actually DataRowView objects that reference DataRows. The DataRowView properties are shown in Table 8-1. Only the Item property is also exposed by the DataRow; the other properties are unique.

Property	Description
DataView	The DataView to which this DataRowView belongs
IsEdit	Indicates whether the DataRowView is currently being edited
IsNew	Indicates whether the DataRowView is new
Item	The value of a column in the DataRowView
Row	The DataRow that is being viewed
RowVersion	The current version of the DataRowView

Table 8-1 DataRowView Properties

DataViewManagers

Functionally, a DataViewManager is similar to a DataSet. Just as a DataSet acts as a container for DataTables, the DataViewManager acts as a container for DataViews, one for each DataTable in a DataSet.

The DataViews within the DataViewManager are accessed through the DataViewSettings collection of the DataViewManager. It's convenient to think of a DataViewSetting existing for each DataTable in a DataSet. In reality, the DataViewSetting isn't physically created until (and unless) it is referenced in code.

DataViewManagers are most often used when the DataSet contains related tables because they allow you to persist sorting and filtering criteria across calls to *GetChildRows*. If you were to use individual DataViews on the child table, the sorting and filtering criteria would need to be reset after each call. With a DataViewManager, after the criteria have been established, the rows returned by *GetChildRows* will be sorted and filtered automatically.

In Chapter 7, we saw that the DataSet has a DefaultViewManager property. In reality, you're actually binding to the default DataViewManager when you bind a control to a DataSet. Under most circumstances, you can ignore this technicality, but it can be useful for setting default sorting and filtering criteria.

> Note, however, that the DataSet's DefaultViewManager property is read-only—you can set its properties, but you cannot create a new DataViewManager and assign it to the DataSet as the default DataViewManager.

Creating DataViews

Because DataViews are independent objects, you can create and configure them at design time using Microsoft Visual Studio. You can, of course, also create and configure DataViews at run time in code.

Using Visual Studio

Visual Studio supports the design-time creation of DataViews through the DataView control on the Data tab of the Toolbox. Like any other control with design-time support, you simply drag the control onto a form and set its properties in the Properties window.

Create and Bind a DataView Using Visual Studio

1. Open the DataViews project from the Start menu or the Project menu.
2. Double-click DataViews.vb (or DataViews.cs if you're using C#) in the Solution Explorer.

   Visual Studio .NET opens the form designer.

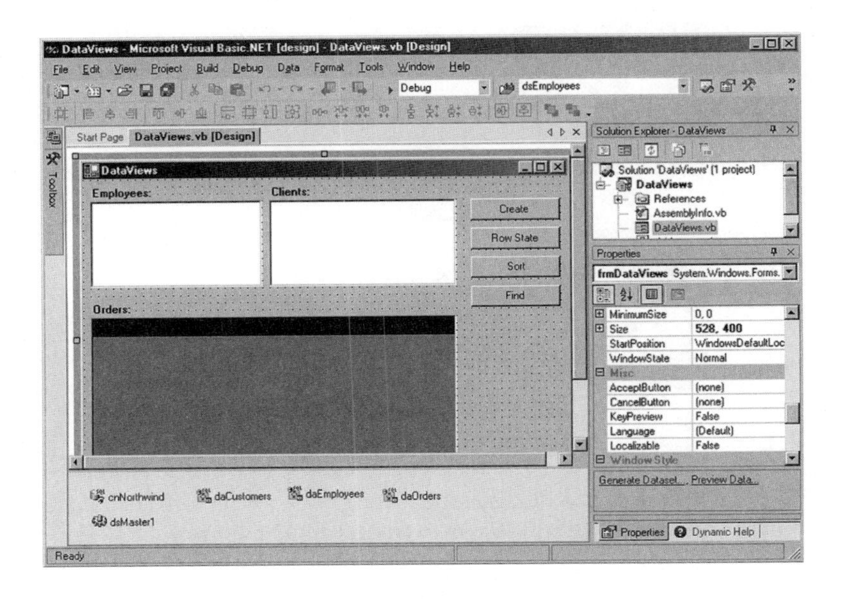

3. Drag a DataView control from the Data tab of the Toolbox to the form.

   Visual Studio adds the control to the component designer.

4. In the Properties window, change the DataView's name to dvOrders.

5. Change the Table property to dsMaster1.OrderTotals, and then change the Sort property to OrderID.

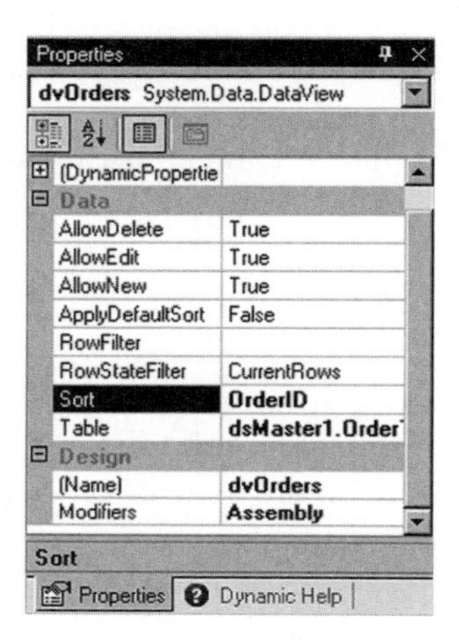

6. Select the dgOrders data grid, and then change the DataSource property to dvOrders.

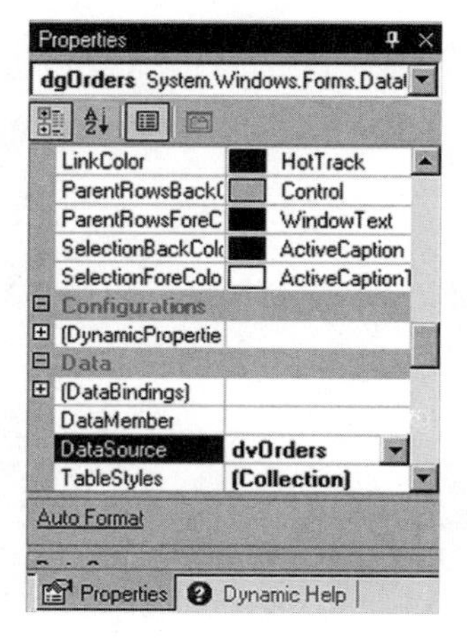

7. Press F5 to run the application.

   Visual Studio displays the information in the Orders data grid arranged according to the values in the OrderID column.

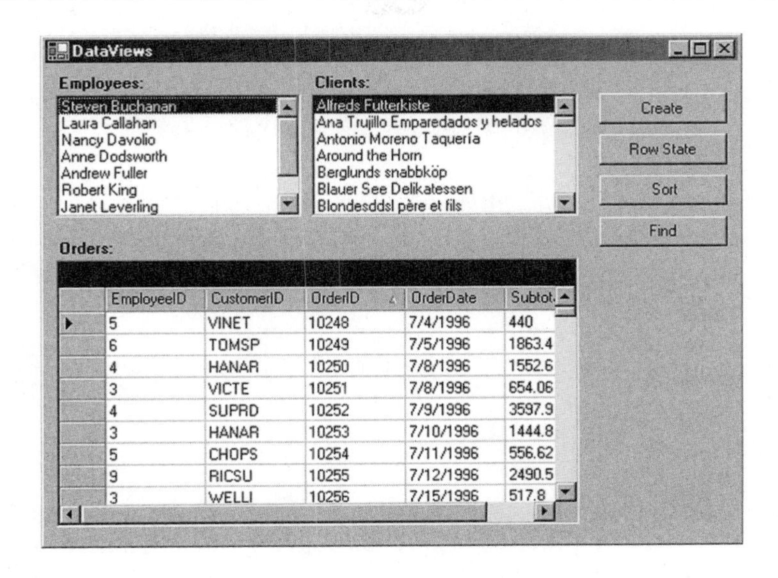

8 Close the application.

Creating DataViews at Run Time

Like most of the objects in the .NET Framework Class Library, the DataView supports a *New* constructor, which allows the DataView to be created in code at run time. The DataView supports the two versions of the *New* constructor, which are shown in Table 8-2.

Method	Description
New()	Creates a new DataView
New(DataTable)	Creates a new DataView and sets its Table property to the specified *DataTable*

Table 8-2 DataView Constructors

Create a DataView at Run Time

Visual Basic .NET

1 Double-click Create.

Visual Studio opens the code editor and adds the Click event handler template.

2 Add the following code to the method:

```
Dim drCurrent As System.Data.DataRow
Dim dvNew As New System.Data.DataView()

'retrieve the selected row in lbOrders
drCurrent = Me.lbClients.SelectedItem.Row

'configure the dataview
dvNew.Table = Me.dsMaster1.OrderTotals
dvNew.RowFilter = "CustomerID = '" & drCurrent(0) & "'"

'rebind the datagrid
Me.dgOrders.DataSource = dvNew
```

The code first declares a DataRow variable that will contain the item selected in the lbClients list box, and then creates a new DataView using the default constructor. Next drCurrent is assigned to the current selection in the list box.

The Table property of the dvNew DataView is set to the OrderTotals table, and the RowFilter property is set to show only the orders for the selected client. Finally the dgOrders data grid is bound to the new DataView.

3 Press F5 to run the application, click in the Clients list box, and then click Create.

The data grid displays the orders for only the selected client.

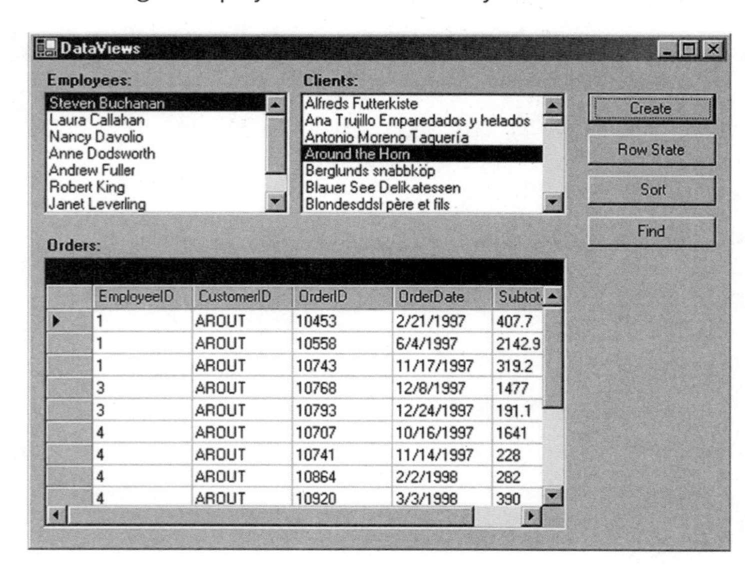

4 Close the application.

Visual C# .NET

1 Double-click Create.

Visual Studio opens the code editor and adds the Click event handler template and the Click event delegate.

2 Add the following code to the method:

```
System.Data.DataRowView drCurrent;
System.Data.DataView dvNew;
dvNew = new System.Data.DataView();

//retrieve the selected row in lbOrders
drCurrent = (System.Data.DataRowView)this.lbClients.SelectedItem;

//configure the dataview
dvNew.Table = this.dsMaster1.OrderTotals;
dvNew.RowFilter = "CustomerID = '" + drCurrent[0] + "'";

//rebind the datagrid
this.dgOrders.DataSource = dvNew;
```

The code first declares a DataRowView variable that will contain the item selected in the lbClients list, and then creates a new DataView using the default constructor. Next drCurrent is assigned to the current selection in the list.

The Table property of the dvNew DataView is set to the OrderTotals table, and the RowFilter property is set to show only the orders for the selected client. Finally the dgOrders data grid is bound to the new DataView.

3 Press F5 to run the application, click in the Clients list, and then click Create.

The data grid displays the orders for only the selected client.

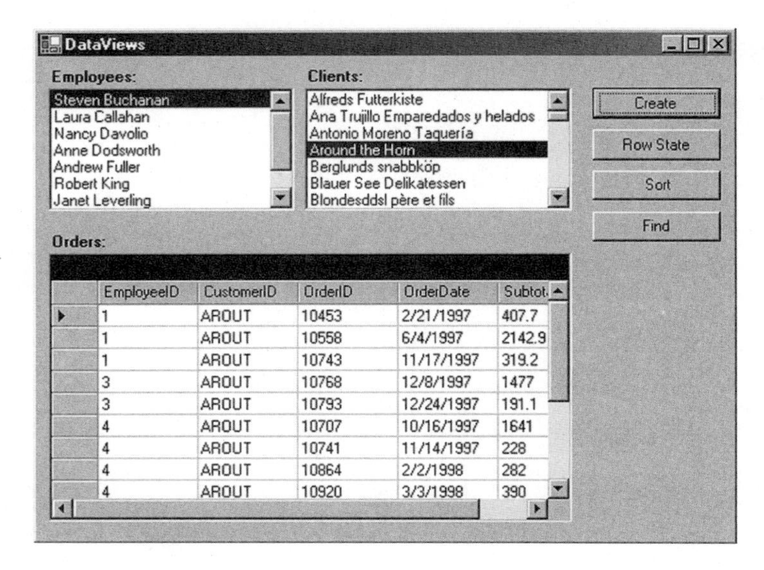

4 Close the application.

DataView Properties

The properties exposed by the DataView object are shown in Table 8-3. The AllowDelete, AllowEdit, and AllowNew properties determine whether the data reflected by the DataView can be changed through the DataView. (Data can always be changed by referencing the row in the underlying DataTable.)

Property	Description
AllowDelete	Determines whether rows in the DataView can be deleted
AllowEdit	Determines whether rows in the DataView can be changed
AllowNew	Determines whether rows can be added to the DataView
Apply DefaultSort	Determines whether the default sort order, determined by the underlying data source, will be used
Count	The number of DataRowViews in the DataView
DataViewManager	The DataViewManager to which this DataView belongs
Item(Index)	The DataRowView at the specified *Index* in the DataView
RowFilter	The expression used to filter the rows contained in the DataView
RowStateFilter	The DataViewRowState used to filter the rows contained in the DataView
Sort	The expression used to sort the rows contained in the DataView
Table	The DataTable that is the source of rows for the DataView

Table 8-3 DataView Properties

The Count property does exactly what one might expect—it returns the number of DataRows reflected in the DataView, while the DataViewManager and Table properties serve to connect the DataView to other objects within an application.

Finally the RowFilter, RowStateFilter, and Sort properties control the DataRows that are reflected in the DataView and how those rows are ordered. We'll examine each of these properties later in this chapter.

DataColumn Expressions

Expressions, technically DataColumn Expressions, are used by the RowFilter and Sort properties of the DataView. We've used DataColumn Expressions in previous chapters when we created a calculated column in a DataTable and when we set the sort and filter expressions for the DataTable *Select* method. Now it's time to examine them more closely.

A DataColumn Expression is a string, and you can use all the normal string handling functions to build one. For example, you can use the & concatenation operator to join two strings into a single Expression:

```
myExpression = "CustomerID = '" & strCustID & "'"
```

Note that the value of strCustID will be surrounded by single quotation marks in the resulting text. In building DataColumn Expressions, columns may be referred to directly by using the ColumnName property, but any actual text values must be quoted.

In addition, certain special characters must be "escaped," that is, wrapped in square brackets. For example, if you had a column named Miles/Gallon, you would have to surround the column name with brackets:

```
MyExpression = "[Miles/Gallon] > 10"
```

tip

You can find the complete list of special characters in the online Help for the DataColumn.Expression property.

Numeric values in DataColumn Expressions require no special handling, as shown in the previous example, but date values must be surrounded by hash marks:

```
MyExpression = "OrderDate > #01/01/2001#"
```

important

Dates in code must conform to US usage, that is, month/day/year.

As we've seen, DataRow columns are referred to by the ColumnName property. You can reference a column in a Child DataRow by adding "Child" before the ColumnName in the Child row:

```
MyExpression = "Child.OrderTotal > 3000"
```

The syntax for referencing a Parent row is identical:

```
MyExpression = "Parent.CustomerID = 'AFLKI'"
```

Parent and Child references are frequently used along with one of the aggregate functions shown in Table 8-4. The aggregate functions can also be used directly, without reference to Child or Parent rows.

Function	Result
Sum	Sum
Avg	Average
Min	Minimum
Max	Maximum
Count	Count
StDev	Statistical standard deviation
Var	Statistical variance

Table 8-4 Aggregate Functions

When setting the expressions for DataViews, you will frequently be comparing values. The .NET Framework handles the usual range of operators, as shown in Table 8-5.

Operator	Action
AND	Logical AND
OR	Logical OR
NOT	Logical NOT
<	Less than
>	Greater than
<=	Less than or equal to
>=	Greater than or equal to
<>	Not equal

IN	Determines whether the value specified is contained in a set
LIKE	Inexact match using a wildcard character

Table 8-5 Comparison Operators

The IN operator requires that the set of values to be searched be separated by commas and surrounded by parentheses:

```
MyExpression = "myColumn IN ('A','B','C')
```

The LIKE operator treats the characters * or % as interchangeable wildcards—both replace zero or more characters. The wildcard characters can be used at the beginning or end of a string, or at both ends, but cannot be contained within a string.

DataColumn Expressions also support the arithmetic operators shown in Table 8-6.

Operator	Action
+	Addition
-	Subtraction
*	Multiplication
/	Division
%	Modulus (integer division)

Table 8-6 Arithmetic Operators

The arithmetic + operator is also used for string concatenation within a DataColumn Expression rather than the more usual & operator.

Finally DataColumn Expressions support a number of special functions, as shown in Table 8-7.

Function	Result
Convert(Expression, Type)	Converts the value returned by *Expression* to the specified .NET Framework *Type*
Len(String)	The number of characters in the *String*
ISNULL(Expression, ReplacementValue)	Determines whether *Expression* evaluates to *Null*, and if so, it returns *ReplacementValue*
IF(Expression, ValueIfTrue, ValueIfFalse)	Returns *ValueIfTrue* if *Expression* evaluates to *True*; otherwise returns *ValueIfFalse*
SUBSTRING(Expression, Start, Length)	Returns *Length* characters of the string returned by *Expression*, beginning at the zero-based position specified by *Start*

Table 8-7 Special Functions

Sort Expressions

Although the DataColumn Expressions used in the Sort property can be arbitrarily complex, in most cases they will take the form of one or more ColumnNames separated by commas:

```
myDataView.Sort = "CustomerID, OrderID"
```

Optionally, the ColumnNames may be followed by *ASC* or *DESC* to cause the values to be sorted in ascending or descending order, respectively. The default sort is ascending, so the *ASC* keyword isn't strictly necessary, but it can sometimes be useful to include it for clarity.

Change the Sorting Method

Visual Basic .NET

1. In the code editor, select btnSort in the ControlName list, and then select Click in the MethodName list.

   Visual Studio adds the Click event handler template to the code.

2. Add the following code to the method:

   ```
   'Change the sort order
   Me.dvOrders.Sort = "EmployeeID, CustomerID, OrderID DESC"

   'Refresh the datagrid
   Me.dgOrders.Refresh()
   ```

   The code sets the sort order of the dvOrders DataView to sort first by EmployeeID, then by CustomerID, and finally by OrderID in descending order.

3. Press F5 to run the application.

4. Click Sort.

   The application displays the sorted contents of the data grid.

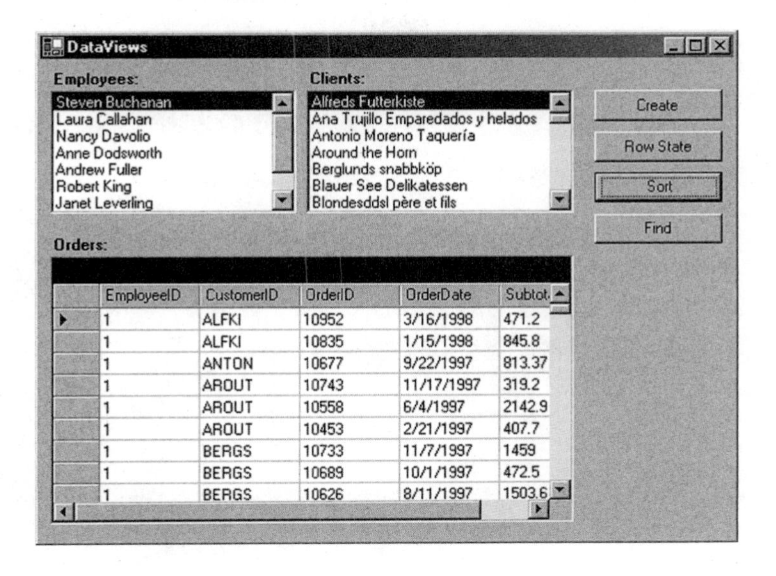

5 Close the application.

Visual C# .NET

1 In the form designer, double-click the Create button.

Visual Studio adds the Click event handler to the code window.

2 In the code editor, add a Click event handler for the btnSort button after the btnCreate_Click event handler that we created in the previous exercise:

```
private void btnSort_Click (object sender, System.EventArgs e)
{

}
```

3 Add the following code to the method:

```
//Change the sort order
this.dvOrders.Sort = "EmployeeID, CustomerID, OrderID DESC";

//Refresh the datagrid
this.dgOrders.Refresh();
```

The code sets the sort order of the dvOrders DataView to sort first by EmployeeID, then by CustomerID, and finally by OrderID in descending order.

4 Press F5 to run the application.

5 Click Sort.

The application displays the sorted contents of the data grid.

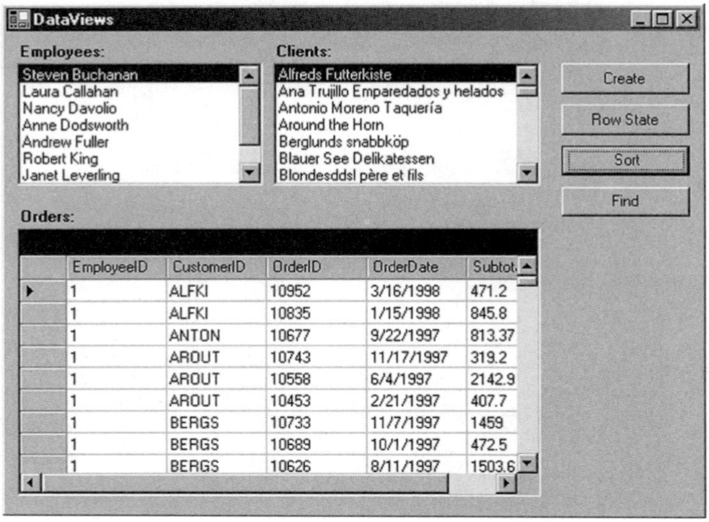

6 Close the application.

RowStateFilter

In the previous chapter, we saw that each DataRow maintains its status in its RowState property. The DataView's RowStateFilter property can be used to limit the DataRowViews within the DataView to those with a certain RowState or to return values of a given state. The possible values for the RowStateFilter property are shown in Table 8-8.

Member Name	Description
Added	Only those rows that have been added
CurrentRows	All current row values
Deleted	Only those rows that have been deleted
ModifiedCurrent	Current row values for rows that have been modified
ModifiedOriginal	Original values of rows that have been modified
None	No rows
OriginalRows	Original values of all rows
Unchanged	Only those rows that haven't been modified

Table 8-8 DataViewRowState Values

Display Only New Rows

Visual Basic .NET

1. In the code editor, select btnRowState in the ControlName list, and then select Click in the MethodName list.

   Visual Studio adds the Click event handler template.

2. Add the following code to the method:

```
Dim drNew As System.Data.DataRowView

'Add a new order
drNew = Me.dvOrders.AddNew()
drNew("CustomerID") = "ALFKI"
drNew("EmployeeID") = 1
drNew("OrderID") = 0

'Set the RowStateFilter
Me.dvOrders.RowStateFilter = DataViewRowState.Added

'Refresh the datagrid
Me.dgOrders.Refresh()
```

   The code first creates a new DataRowView (we'll examine the *AddNew* method in the following section), and then sets the RowStateFilter to display only new (or added) rows. Finally the dgOrders data grid is refreshed to display the changes.

3. Press F5 to run the application, and then click Row State.

   The data grid shows only the new order.

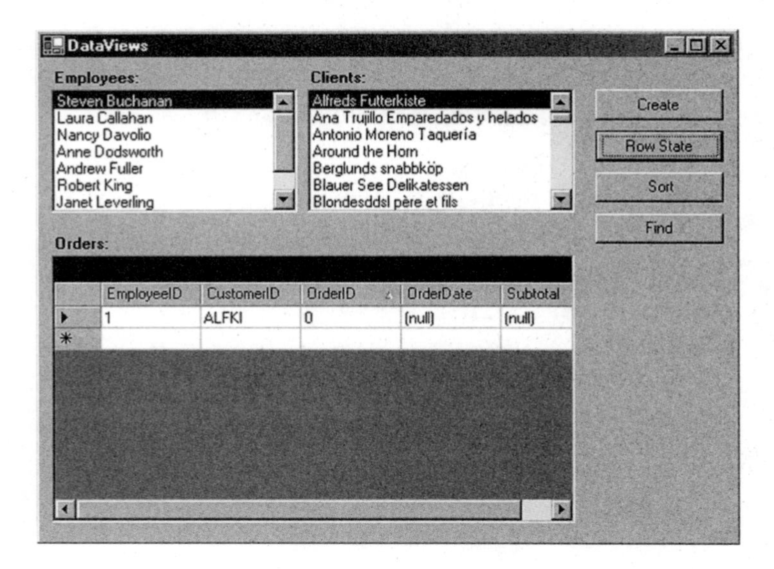

4 Close the application.

Visual C# .NET

1 In the Form Designer, double-click the Row State button.

Visual Studio adds the Click event handler to the code window.

2 In the code editor, add a Click event handler for the btnRowState button after the btnSort event handler that we created in the previous exercise:

```
private void btnRowState_Click (object sender, System.EventArgs e)
{

}
```

3 Add the following code to the method:

```
System.Data.DataRowView drNew;

//Add a new row
drNew = this.dvOrders.AddNew();
drNew["CustomerID"] = "AFLKI";
drNew["EmployeeID"] = 1;
drNew["OrderID"] = 0;

//Set the RowStateFilter
this.dvOrders.RowStateFilter = DataViewRowState.Added;

//Refresh the datagrid
this.dgOrders.Refresh();
```

The code first creates a new DataRowView (we'll examine the *AddNew* method in the following section), and then sets the RowStateFilter to display only new (or added) rows. Finally the dgOrders data grid is refreshed to display the changes.

4 Press F5 to run the application, and then click Row State.

The data grid shows only the new order.

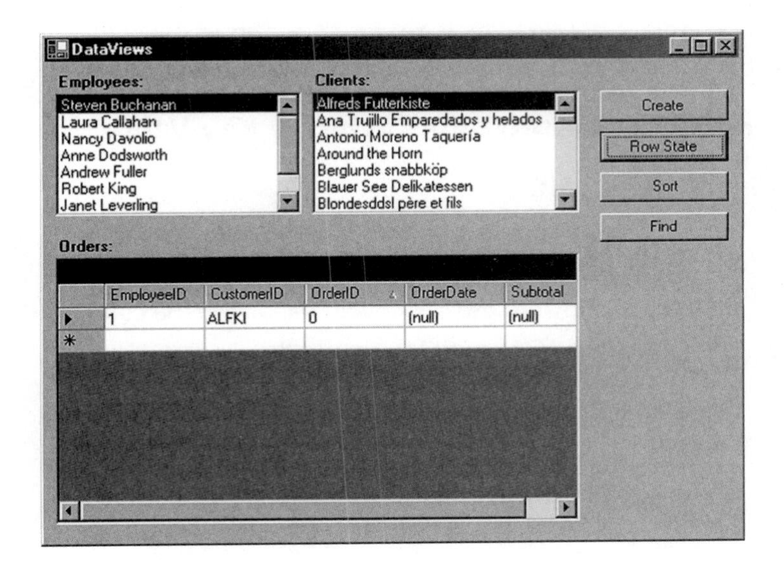

5 Close the application.

DataView Methods

The primary methods supported by the DataView are shown in Table 8-9. The *AddNew* method adds a new DataRowView to the DataView, while the *Delete* method deletes the row at the specified index.

Method	Description
AddNew	Adds a new DataRowView to the DataView
Delete	Removes a DataRowView from a DataView
Find	Finds one or more DataRowViews containing the primary key value(s) that are specified

Table 8-9 DataView Methods

The *Find* Method

The DataView's *Find* method finds one or more rows based on primary key values. If you want to find a row based on some other column value, you must use the RowFilter property of the DataView.

There are two versions of the *Find* method, allowing you to pass either a single value or an array of values. The *Find* method returns the index of the row that was found (or an array of rows if an array of primary keys is provided) or *Null* if the value is not found in the DataView.

Find a Row Based on Its Primary Key Value

Visual Basic .NET

1. In the code editor, select btnFind in the ControlName list, and then select Click in the MethodName list.

   Visual Studio adds the Click event handler to the code.

2. Add the following code to the method:

```
Dim idxFound As Integer
Dim strMessage As String

idxFound = Me.dvOrders.Find(10255)

strMessage = "The OrderID is " & _
   Me.dvOrders(idxFound).Item("OrderID")
strMessage &= vbCrLf & "The CustomerID is " & _
   Me.dvOrders(idxFound).Item("CustomerID")
strMessage &= vbCrLf & "The EmployeeID is " & _
   Me.dvOrders(idxFound).Item("EmployeeID")
MessageBox.Show(strMessage)
```

   The code uses the *Find* method to find Order 10255 and then displays the results in a message box.

3. Press F5 to run the application, and then click Find.

   The application displays the results.

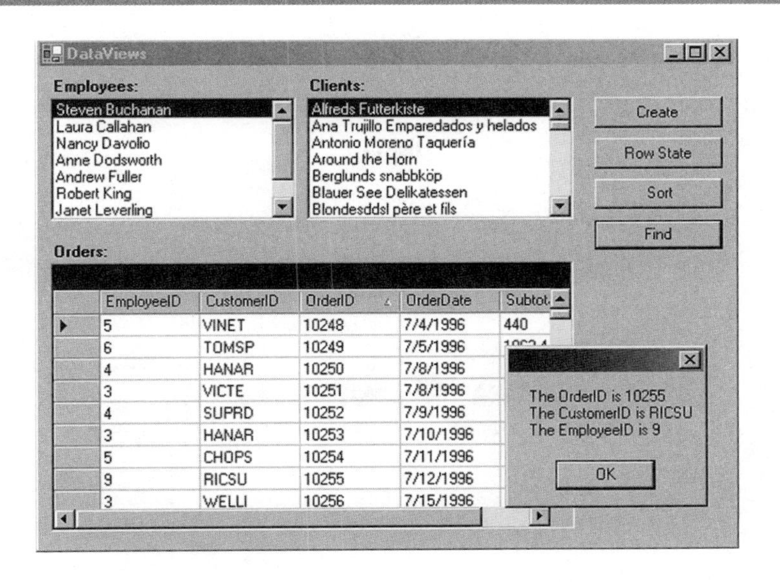

4 Close the application.

Visual C# .NET

1 In the form designer, double-click the Find button.

Visual Studio adds the Click event handler to the code window.

2 In the code editor, add a Click event handler for the btnFind button after the btnRowState event handler that we created in the previous exercise:

```
private void btnFind_Click (object sender, System.EventArgs e)
{

}
```

3 Add the following code to the method:

```
int idxFound;
string strMessage;

idxFound = this.dvOrders.Find(10255);

strMessage = "The OrderID is " +
   this.dvOrders[idxFound]["OrderID"];
strMessage += "\nThe CustomerID is " +
   this.dvOrders[idxFound]["CustomerID"];
strMessage += "\nThe EmployeeID is " +
   this.dvOrders[idxFound]["EmployeeID"];
MessageBox.Show(strMessage);
```

The code uses the *Find* method to find Order 10255 and then displays the results in a message box.

4. Press F5 to run the application, and then click Find.

   The application displays the results.

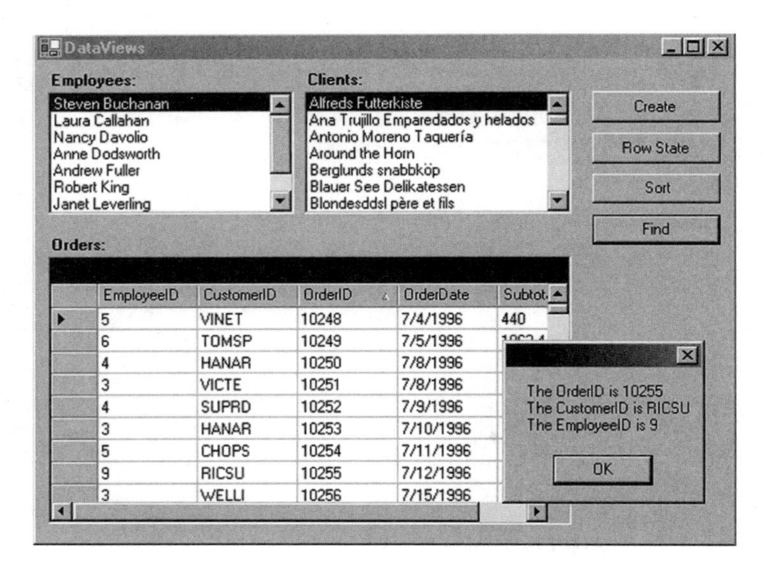

5. Close the application.

Chapter 8 Quick Reference

To	Do this
Add a DataView to a form	Drag a DataView control from the Data tab of the Toolbox onto the form
Create a DataView at run time	Use one of the *New* constructors. For example: `Dim myDataView as New System.Data.DataView()`
Sort DataView rows	Set the Sort property of the DataView. For example: `myDataView.Sort = "CustomerID"`
Filter DataView rows	Set the RowFilter or RowStateFilter property. For example: `myDataView.RowStateFilter = DataViewRowState.Added`
Find a row in a DataView	Pass the primary key value to the DataView's *Find* method. For example: `idxFound = myDataView.Find(1011)`

PART 4

Using the ADO.NET Objects

Editing and Updating Data

In this chapter, you'll learn how to:

- ✔ *Use the RowState property of a DataRow*
- ✔ *Retrieve a specific version of a DataRow*
- ✔ *Add a row to a DataTable*
- ✔ *Delete a row from a DataTable*
- ✔ *Edit a DataRow*
- ✔ *Temporarily suspend enforcement of constraints during updates*
- ✔ *Accept changes to data*
- ✔ *Reject changes to data*

In the previous few chapters, we've examined each of the Microsoft ADO.NET objects in turn. Starting with this chapter, we'll look at how these objects work together to perform specific tasks. Specifically, in this chapter, we'll examine the process of editing and updating data.

Understanding Editing and Updating Data

Given the disconnected architecture of ADO.NET, there are four distinct phases to the process of editing and updating data from a data source: data retrieval, editing, updating the data source, and finally, updating the DataSet.

First, the data is retrieved from the data source, stored in memory, and possibly displayed to the user. This is typically done using the *Fill* method of a

DataAdapter to fill the tables of a DataSet, but as we've seen, data may also be retrieved using a Command and a DataReader.

Next, the data is modified as required. Values can be changed, new rows can be added, and existing rows can be deleted. Data modification can be done under programmatic control or by the data binding mechanisms of Windows Forms and Web Forms.

Roadmap
We'll examine the data binding mechanisms of Windows Forms and Web Forms in Chapters 10 and 11.

We'll be exploring how to make changes to data under programmatic control in this chapter. In Windows Forms, the data binding architecture handles transmitting changes from data-bound controls to the dataset. No other action is required. In Web Forms, any data changes must of course be submitted to the server.

If the changes made to the in-memory copy of the data are to be persisted, they must be propagated to the data source. If a DataSet is used for managing the in-memory data, the data source propagation can be done by using the *Update* method of the DataAdapter. Alternatively, Command objects may be used directly to submit the changes. (Of course, as we saw in Chapter 3, the DataAdapter uses Command objects to submit the changes, as well.)

Finally the DataSet can be updated to reflect the new state of the data source. This is done by using the *AcceptChanges* method of the DataSet or DataTable. Both the *Fill* method and the *Update* method of the DataAdapter call *AcceptChanges* automatically. If you execute Data Commands directly, you must call *AcceptChanges* explicitly to update the status of the DataSet.

Concurrency

With the disconnected methodology used by ADO.NET, there is always a chance that a row in the data source may have been changed since the time it was loaded into the DataSet. This is a *concurrency violation*.

The *Update* method supports a DBConcurrencyException, which one might expect to be thrown if a concurrency violation occurs. In fact, the DBConcurrencyException is thrown whenever the number of rows updated by a Data Command is zero. This is typically due to a concurrency violation, but it's important to understand that this is not necessarily the case.

DataRow States and Versions

As we saw in Chapter 7, the DataRow maintains a RowState property that indicates whether the row has been added, deleted, or modified. In addition, the DataTable maintains multiple copies of each row, each reflecting a different version of the DataRow. We'll explore both the RowState property and row versions in this section.

RowState Properties

The RowState property of the DataRow reflects the actions that have been taken since the DataTable was created or since the last time the *AcceptChanges* method was called. The possible values for RowState, as defined by the DataRowState enumeration, are shown in Table 9-1.

Property	Description
Added	The DataRow is new
Deleted	The DataRow has been deleted from the table
Detached	The DataRow has not yet been added to a table
Modified	The contents of the DataRow have been changed
Unchanged	The DataRow has not been modified

Table 9-1 DataRowStates

The baseline values of the rows in a DataSet are established when the *AcceptChanges* method is called, either by the *Fill* or *Update* methods of the DataAdapter or explicitly by program code. At that time, all of the DataRows have their RowState set to Unchanged.

Not surprisingly, if the value of any column of a DataRow is changed after *AcceptChanges* is called, its RowState is set to Modified. If new DataRows are added to the DataSet by using the *Add* method of the DataSet's Row collection, their RowState will be Added. The new rows will maintain the status of Added even if their contents are changed before the next call to *AcceptChanges*.

If a DataRow is deleted by using the *Delete* method, it isn't actually removed from the DataSet until the *AcceptChanges* method is called. Instead, their RowState is set to Deleted and, as we'll see, its Current values are set to *Null*.

DataRows don't necessarily belong to a DataTable. These independent rows will have a RowState of Detached until they are added to the Rows collection of a table.

Row Versions

A DataTable may maintain multiple versions of any given DataRow, depending on the actions that have been performed on it since the last time *AcceptChanges* was called. The possible DataRowVersions are shown in Table 9-2.

Version	Meaning
Current	The current values of each column
Default	The default values used for new rows
Original	The values set when the row was created, either by a *Fill* operation or by adding the row manually
Proposed	The values assigned to the columns in a row after a *BeginEdit* method has been called

Table 9-2 DataRowVersions

There will always be a Current version of every row in the DataSet. The Current version of the DataRow reflects any changes that have been made to its values since the row was created.

Rows that existed in the DataSet when *AcceptChanges* was last called will have an Original version, which contains the initial data values. Rows that are added to the DataSet will not contain an Original version until *AcceptChanges* is called again.

If any of the columns of a DataTable have values assigned to its DefaultValue property, all the DataRows in the table will have a Default version, with the values determined by the DefaultValues of each column.

DataRows will have a Proposed version after a call to *DataRow.BeginEdit* and before either *EndEdit* or *CancelEdit* is called. We'll examine these methods, which are used to temporarily suspend data constraints, in the next section.

Exploring DataRow States and Versions

The example application for this chapter displays the Original and Current values of a DataSet based on the EmployeeList view in the Northwind sample database. Because the display is based on the Windows Form BindingContext object, which we won't be examining until Part V, the code to display these values is already in place.

1. Open the Editing project from the Start page or from the File menu.
2. Double-click Editing.vb (or Editing.cs, if you're using C#) in the Solution Explorer.

   Microsoft Visual Studio displays the Editing form in the form designer.

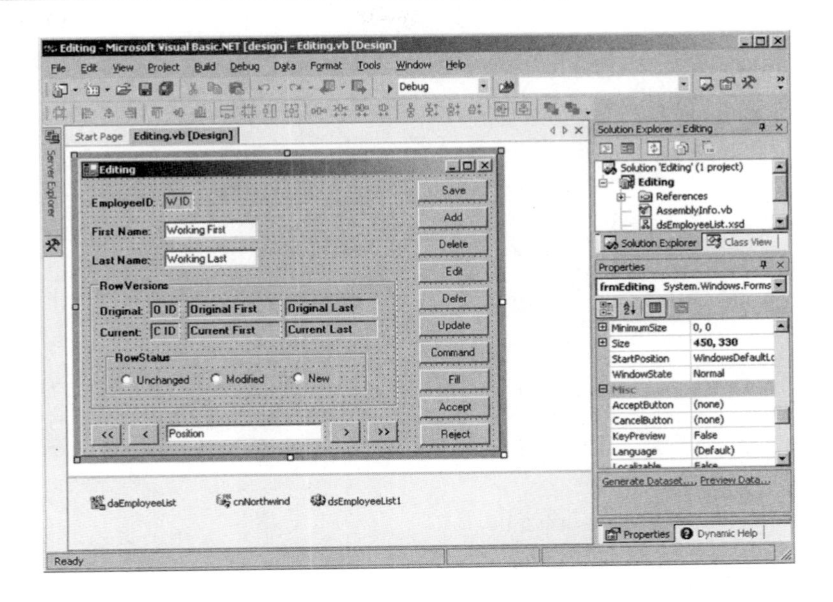

3 Press F5 to run the application.

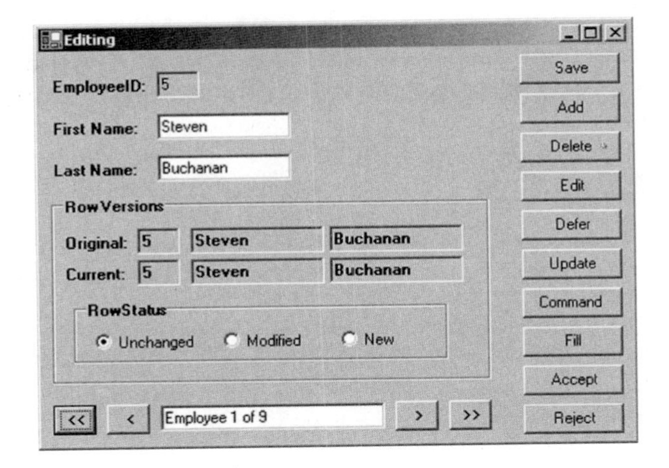

4 Use the navigation buttons at the bottom of the form to move through the DataSet.

Note that all the rows have identical Current and Original versions and that the RowStatus is Unchanged.

5 Change the value of the First Name or Last Name text box of one of the rows, and then click Save.

The Current version of the row is updated to reflect the name, and the RowStatus changes to Modified.

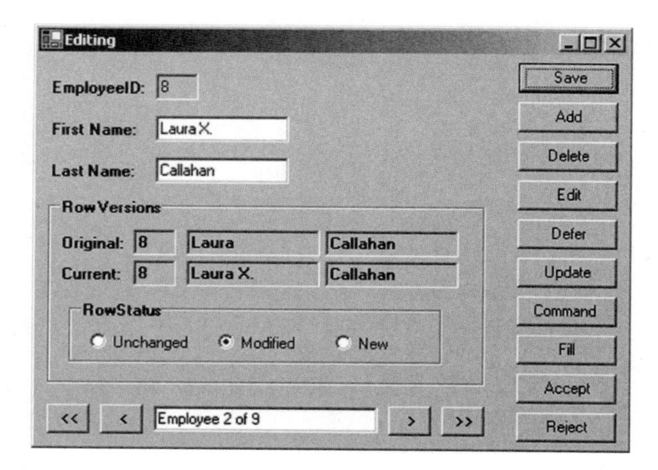

6 Close the application.

Editing Data in a DataSet

Roadmap
We'll examine editing using data-bound controls in Parts V and VI.

Editing data after it has been loaded into a DataSet is a straightforward process of calling methods and setting property values. In this chapter, we'll concentrate on manipulating the contents of the DataSet programmatically, leaving the discussion of using Windows and Web Form controls to Parts V and VI, respectively.

Adding a DataRow

There is no way to create a new row directly in a DataTable. Instead, a DataRow object must be created independently and then added to the DataTable's Rows collection.

The DataTable's *NewRow* method returns a detached row with the same schema as the table on which it is called. The values of the row can then be set, and the new row appended to the DataTable.

Add a Row to a DataTable

Visual Basic .NET

1 Double-click Add in the form designer.

Visual Studio opens the code editor and adds the Click event handler.

2 Add the following code to the procedure:

```
Dim drNew As System.Data.DataRow

drNew = Me.dsEmployeeList1.EmployeeList.NewRow()
drNew.Item("FirstName") = "New First"
drNew.Item("LastName") = "New Last"
Me.dsEmployeeList1.EmployeeList.Rows.Add(drNew)
```

The first line declares the DataRow variable that will contain the new row. Then the *NewRow* method is called, instantiating the variable; its fields are set; and it is added to the Rows collection of the EmployeeList table.

3 Press F5 to run the application.

4 Click Add.

The application adds a new row.

5 Move to the last row in the DataSet by clicking the >> button.

The application displays the new row.

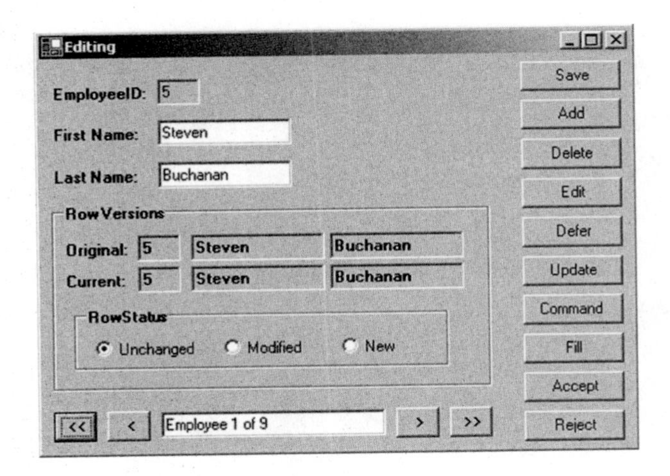

6 Close the application.

Visual C# .NET

1 Double-click Add in the form designer.

Visual Studio opens the code editor and adds the Click event handler.

2. Add the following code to the procedure:

```
dsEmployeeList.EmployeesRow drNew;

drNew = (dsEmployeeList.EmployeesRow)
   this.dsEmployeeList1.Employees.NewRow();
drNew["FirstName"] = "New First";
drNew["LastName"] = "New Last";
this.dsEmployeeList1.Employees.AddEmployeesRow(drNew);
```

   The first line declares the DataRow variable that will contain the new row. Then the *NewRow* method is called, instantiating the variable; its fields are set; and it is added to the Rows collection of the EmployeeList table.

3. Press F5 to run the application.
4. Click Add.

   The application adds a new row.

5. Move to the last row in the DataSet by clicking the >> button.

   The application displays the new row.

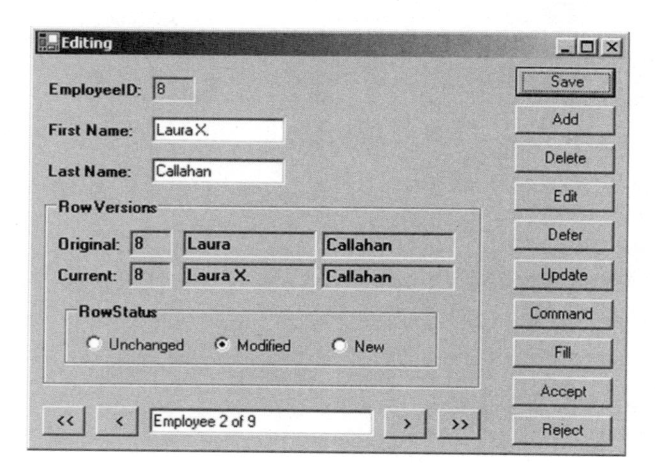

6. Close the application.

Deleting a DataRow

The DataTable's Rows collection supports three methods to remove DataRows, as shown in Table 9-3. Each of these methods physically removes the DataRow from the collection.

Method	Description
Clear()	Removes all rows from the DataTable
Remove(DataRow)	Removes the specified *DataRow*
RemoveAt(Index)	Removes the DataRow at the position specified by the integer *Index*

Table 9-3 Remove Methods

However, a row that has been physically removed by using one of these methods won't be deleted from the data source. If you need to delete the row from the data source as well, you must use the *Delete* method of the DataRow object instead.

The *Delete* method physically removes the DataRow only if it was added to the DataTable since the last time *AcceptChanges* was called. Otherwise, it sets the RowState to Deleted and sets the current values to *Null*.

Delete a DataRow Using the *Delete* method

Visual Basic .NET

1. In the code editor, select btnDelete in the ControlName list, and then select Click from the MethodName list.

   Visual Studio adds the Click event handler to the code.

2. Add the following code to the procedure:

```
Dim dr As System.Data.DataRow

'Get row currently displayed in the form
dr = GetRow()

'Delete the row
dr.Delete()

'Move to the next record & display
Me.BindingContext(Me.dsEmployeeList1, "EmployeeList").Position += 1
UpdateDisplay()
```

   The *GetRow* and *UpdateDisplay* procedures, which are not intrinsic to the .NET Framework, are contained in the Utility Functions region of the code.

3. Press F5 to run the application.
4. Use the navigation buttons to display the row for Nancy Davolio.
5. Click Delete.

   The application deletes the row, displays the next row, and changes the number of employees to 8.

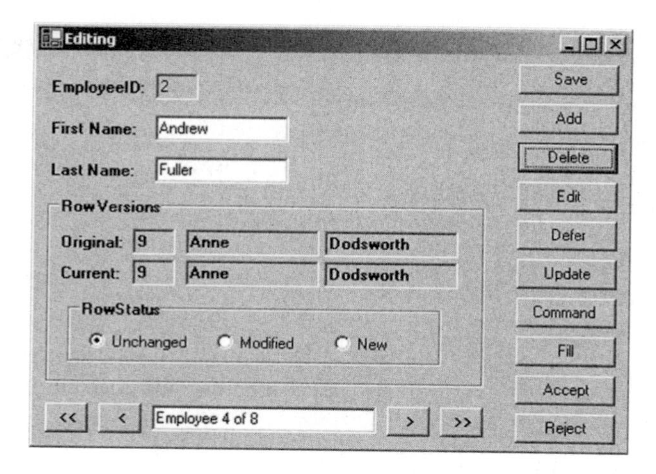

6 Close the application.

Visual C# .NET

1 In the form designer, double-click the Delete button.

Visual Studio adds the Click event handler to the code window.

2 Add the following event handler to the code window:

```
System.Data.DataRow dr;

//Get row currently displayed in the form
dr = GetRow();

//Delete the row
dr.Delete();

//Move to the next record & display
this.BindingContext[this.dsEmployeeList1, "Employees"].Position += 1;
UpdateDisplay();
```

The *GetRow* and *UpdateDisplay* procedures, which are not intrinsic to the .NET Framework, are contained in the Utility Functions region of the code.

3 Press F5 to run the application.

4 Use the navigation buttons to display the row for Nancy Davolio.

5 Click Delete.

The application deletes the row, displays the next row, and changes the number of employees to 8.

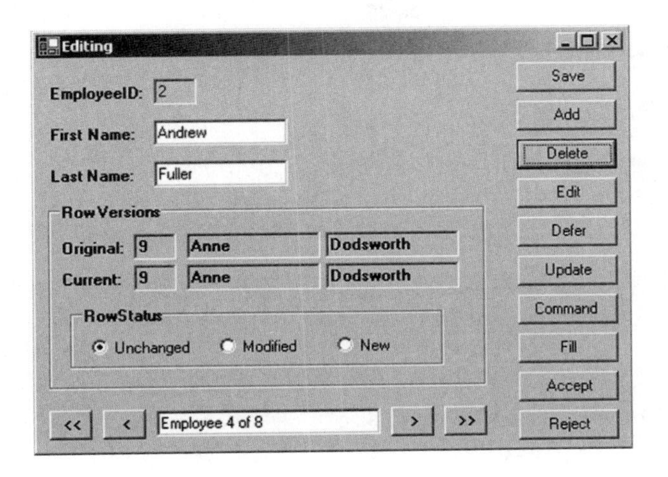

6 Close the application.

Changing DataRow Values

Changing the value of a column in a DataRow couldn't be simpler—just reference the column using the Item property of the DataRow, and assign the new value to it by using a simple assignment operator.

The Item property is overloaded, supporting the forms shown in Table 9-4. However, the three forms of the property that specify a DataRowVersion are read-only and cannot be used to change the values. The other three forms return the Current version of the value and may be changed.

Method	Description
Item(columnName)	Returns the value of the column with the ColumnName property identified by the *columnName* string
Item(dataColumn)	Returns the value of the specified *dataColumn*
Item(columnIndex)	Returns the value of the column specified by the *columnIndex* integer value (the Columns collection is zero-based)
Item(columnName, rowVersion)	Returns the value of the *rowVersion* version of the column with the ColumnName property identified by the *columnName* string
Item(dataColumn, rowVersion)	Returns the value of the *rowVersion* version of the specified *dataColumn*
Item(columnIndex, rowVersion)	Returns the value of the *rowVersion* version of the column specified by the *columnIndex* integer value

Table 9-4 DataRow Item Properties

Edit a DataRow

Visual Basic .NET

1. In the code editor, select btnEdit in ControlName list, and then select Click in the MethodName list.

   Visual Studio adds the Click event handler to the code.

2. Add the following code to the procedure:

```
Dim drCurrent As System.Data.DataRow

drCurrent = GetRow()
drCurrent.Item("FirstName") = "Changed "
UpdateDisplay()
```

   Again, the *GetRow* and *UpdateDisplay* procedures, which reference the Windows Form data binding architecture, are not intrinsic to the .NET Framework. They are in the Utility Functions region of the code.

3. Press F5 to run the application.
4. Click Edit.

   The application changes the Current version of the FirstName column to Changed and changes the RowStatus to Modified.

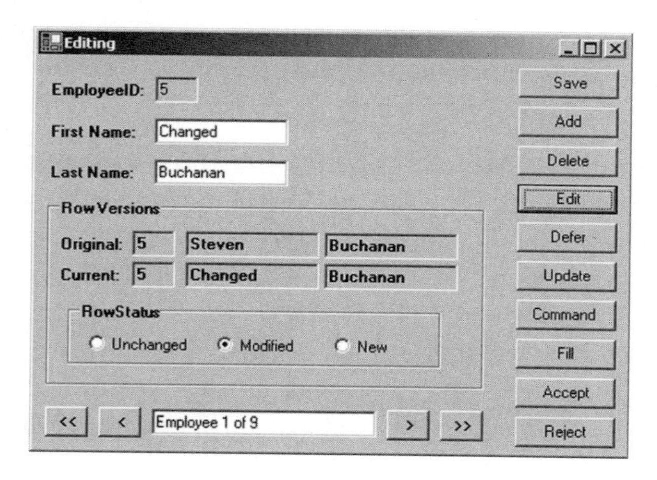

5. Close the application.

Visual C# .NET

1. In the form designer, double-click the Edit button.

   Visual Studio adds the Click event handler to the code window.

2 Add the following procedure to the code window:

```
System.Data.DataRow drCurrent;

drCurrent = GetRow();
drCurrent["FirstName"] = "Changed ";
UpdateDisplay();
```

Again, the *GetRow* and *UpdateDisplay* procedures, which reference the Windows Form data binding architecture, are not intrinsic to the .NET Framework. They are in the Utility Functions region of the code.

3 Press F5 to run the application.

4 Click Edit.

The application changes the Current version of the FirstName column to Changed and changes the RowStatus to Modified.

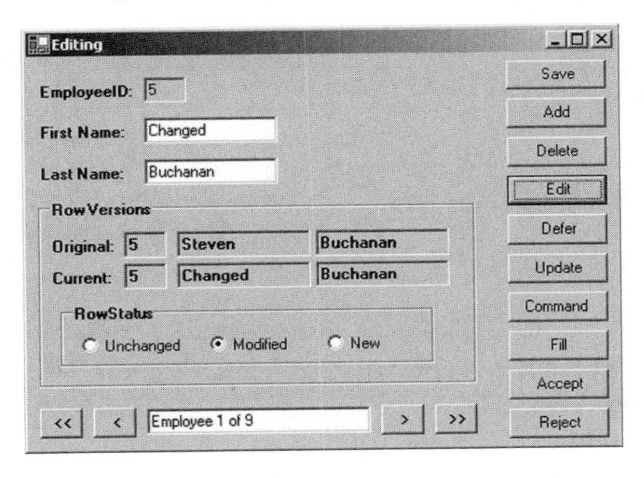

5 Close the application.

Deferring Changes to DataRow Values

Sometimes it's necessary to temporarily suspend validation of data until a series of edits have been performed, either for performance reasons or because rows will temporarily be in violation of business or integrity constraints.

BeginEdit does just that—it suspends the Column and Row change events until either *EndEdit* or *CancelEdit* are called. During the editing process, assignments are made to the Proposed version of the DataRow instead of to the Current version. This is the only time the Proposed version exists.

If the edit is completed by calling *EndEdit*, the Proposed column values are copied to the Current version and the Proposed version of the DataRow is removed. If the edit is completed by calling *CancelEdit*, the Proposed version of the DataRow is removed, leaving the Current column values unchanged. In effect, *EndEdit* and *CancelEdit* commit and rollback the changes, respectively.

Use BeginEdit to Defer Column Changes

Visual Basic .NET

1. In the code editor, select btnDefer in the ControlName list, and then select Click in the MethodName list.

   Visual Studio adds the Click event handler template to the code.

2. Add the following code to the procedure:

```
Dim drCurrent As System.Data.DataRow

drCurrent = GetRow()
With drCurrent
    .BeginEdit()
    .Item("FirstName") = "Proposed Name"
    MessageBox.Show(drCurrent.Item("FirstName", DataRowVersion.Proposed))
    .CancelEdit()
End With
```

3. Press F5 to run the application.
4. Click Defer.

   The application displays Proposed Name in a message box.

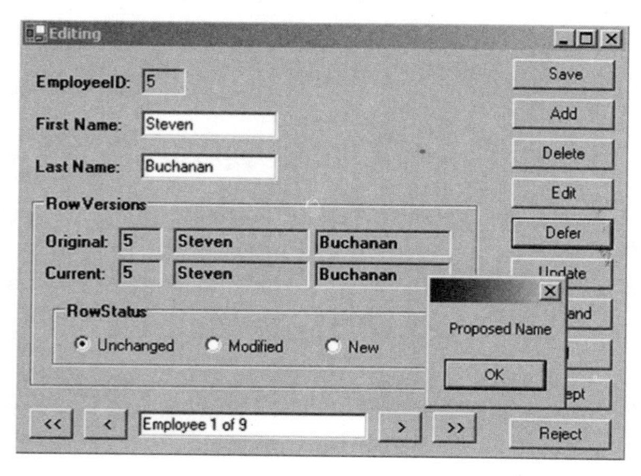

5 Click OK to close the message box.

Because the edit was canceled, the Current value of the column and the RowStatus remain unchanged.

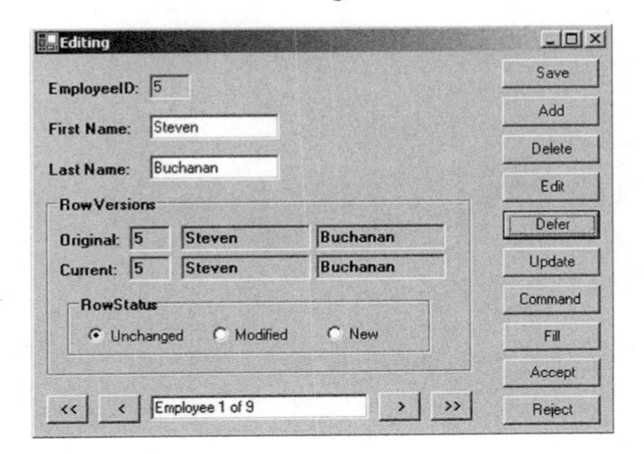

6 Close the application.

Visual C# .NET

1 In the form designer, double-click the Defer button.

Visual Studio adds the Click event handler to the code window.

2 Add the following procedure to the code window:

```
System.Data.DataRow drCurrent;

drCurrent = GetRow();

drCurrent.BeginEdit();
drCurrent["FirstName"]= "Proposed Name";
MessageBox.Show(drCurrent["First Name",
   System.Data.DataRowVersion.Proposed].ToString());
drCurrent.CancelEdit();
```

3 Press F5 to run the application.

4 Click Defer.

The application displays Proposed Name in a message box.

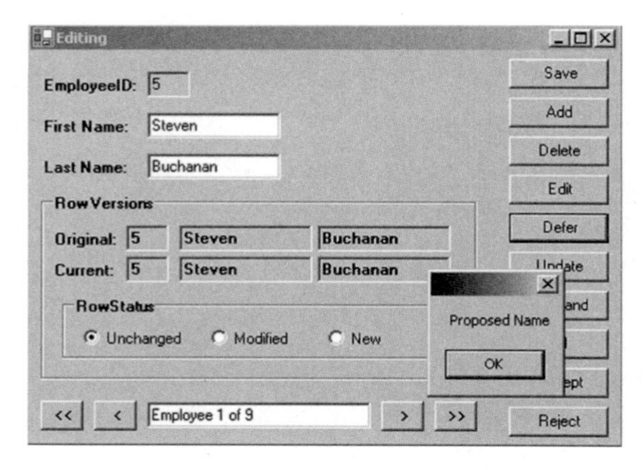

5 Click OK to close the message box.

Because the edit was canceled, the Current value of the column and the RowStatus remain unchanged.

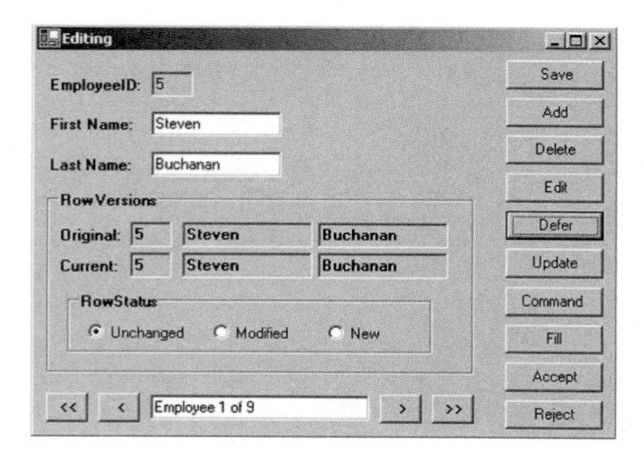

6 Close the application.

Updating Data Sources

After changes have been made to the in-memory copy of the data represented by the DataSet, they can be propagated to the data source either by executing the appropriate Command objects against a connection or by calling the *Update* method of the DataAdapter (which, of course, executes the Command objects that it references).

Using the DataAdapter's *Update* Method

The *System.Data.Common.DbDataAdapter*, which you will recall is the DataAdapter class from which relational database Data Providers inherit their DataAdapters, supports a number of versions of the *Update* method, as shown in Table 9-5. Neither the SqlDataAdapter nor the OleDbDataAdapter add any additional versions.

Update Method	Description
Update(DataSet)	Updates the data source from a DataTable named Table in the specified *DataSet*
Update(dataRows)	Updates the data source from the specified array of *dataRows*
Update(DataTable)	Updates the data source from the specified *DataTable*
Update(dataRows, DataTableMapping)	Updates the data source from the specified array of *dataRows*, using the specified *DataTableMapping*
Update(DataSet, sourceTable)	Updates the data source from the DataTable specified in *sourceTable* in the specified *DataSet*

Table 9-5 DbDataAdapter Update Methods

The Command object exposes a property called RowUpdated that controls whether the DataSet will be updated using any results from executing the SQL command on the data source. The possible values for the OnRowUpdated property are shown in Table 9-6.

Value	Description
Both	Maps both the output parameters and the first returned row to the changed row in the DataSet
FirstReturnedRecord	Maps the values in the first returned row to the changed row in the DataSet
None	Ignores any output parameters or returned rows
OutputParameters	Maps output parameters to the changed row in the DataSet

Table 9-6 UpdateRowSource Values

By default, commands that are automatically generated for a DataAdapter will have their UpdatedRowSource values set to *None*. Commands that are created by setting the CommandText property, either in code or by using the Query Builder, will default to *Both*.

When the *Update* method is called, the following actions occur:

1. The DataAdapter examines the RowState of each row in the specified DataSet or DataTable and executes the appropriate command—insert, update, or delete.
2. The Parameters collection of the appropriate Command object will be filled based on the SourceColumn and SourceVersion properties.
3. The RowUpdating event is raised.
4. The command is executed.
5. Depending on the value of the OnRowUpdated property, the DataAdapter may update the row values in the DataSet.
6. The RowUpdated event is raised.
7. *AcceptChanges* is called on the DataSet or DataTable.

Update a Data Source

Visual Basic .NET

1. In the code editor, select btnUpdate in the ControlName list, and then select Click in the MethodName list.

   Visual Studio adds the Click event handler.
2. Add the following code to the procedure:

```
Me.daEmployeeList.Update(Me.dsEmployeeList1.EmployeeList)
UpdateDisplay()
```

3. Press F5 to run the application.
4. Type **Changed** after Steven in the First Name text box, and then click Save.

   The application sets the Current value of the column to Steven Changed.

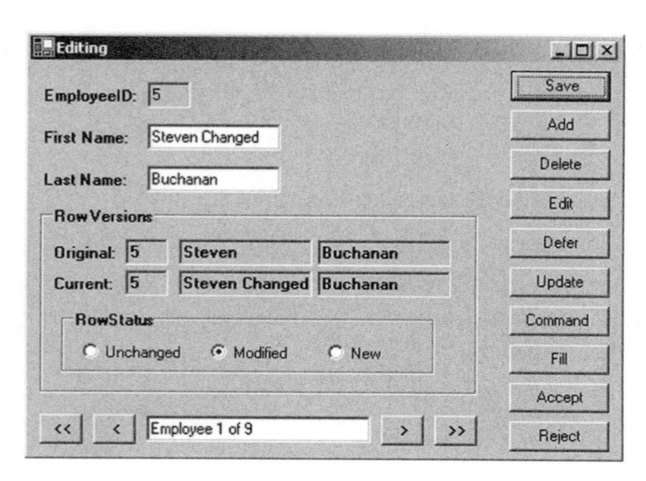

5 Click Update.

The application updates the data source and then resets the contents of the DataSet.

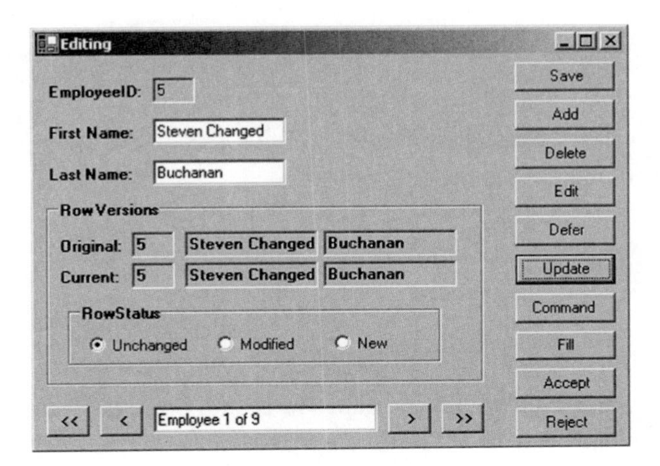

6 Close the application.

Visual C# .NET

1 In the form designer, double-click the Update button.

Visual Studio adds the Click event handler to the code window.

2 Add the following procedure to the code window:

```
this.daEmployeeList.Update(this.dsEmployeeList1.Employees);
UpdateDisplay();
```

3 Press F5 to run the application.

4 Type **Changed** after Steven in the First Name text box, and then click Save.

The application sets the Current value of the column to Steven Changed.

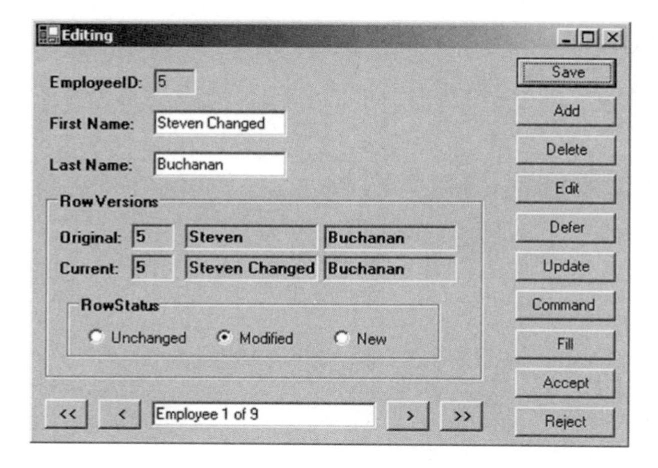

5 Click Update.

The application updates the data source and then resets the contents of the DataSet.

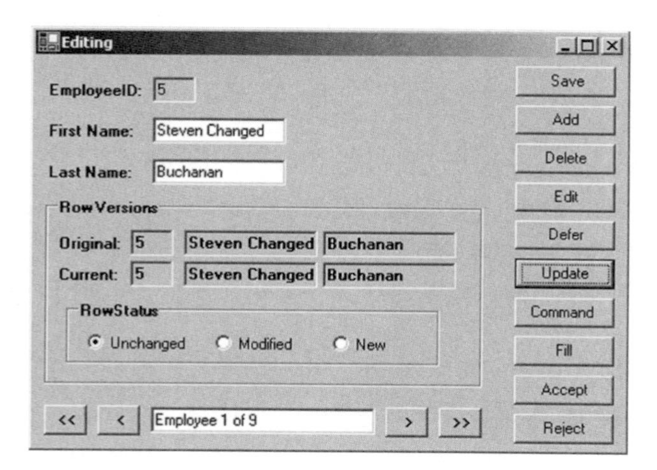

6 Close the application.

Executing Command Objects

The DataAdapter's *Update* method, although very convenient, isn't always the best choice for persisting changes to a data source. Sometimes, of course, you won't be using a DataAdapter. Sometimes you'll be using a structure other than a DataSet to store the data. And sometimes, in order to maintain data integrity, it will be necessary to perform operations in a particular order. In any of these situations, you can use Command objects to control the order in which the updates are performed.

When the DataAdapter's *Update* method is used to propagate changes to a data source, it will use the SourceColumn and SourceVersion properties to fill the Parameters collection. As we saw in Chapter 8, when executing a Command object directly, you must explicitly set the Parameter values.

Update a Data Source Using a Data Command

Visual Basic .NET

1. In the code editor, select btnCmd in the ControlName list, and then select Click in the MethodName list.

   Visual Studio adds the Click event handler to the code.

2. Add the following code to the procedure:

```
Dim cmdUpdate As System.Data.SqlClient.SqlCommand
Dim drCurrent As System.Data.DataRow

cmdUpdate = Me.daEmployeeList.UpdateCommand
drCurrent = GetRow()

cmdUpdate.Parameters("@first").Value = drCurrent("FirstName")
cmdUpdate.Parameters("@last").Value = drCurrent("LastName")
cmdUpdate.Parameters("@empID").Value = drCurrent("EmployeeID")

Me.cnNorthwind.Open()
cmdUpdate.ExecuteNonQuery()
Me.cnNorthwind.Close()
```

   This code first creates two temporary variables, and then it sets them to the Update command of the daEmployeeList DataAdapter and the row currently being displayed on the form, respectively. It then sets the three parameters in the Update command to the values of the row. Finally the connection is opened, the command executed, and the connection closed.

3. In the code editor, select btnFill in the ControlName list, and then select Click in the MethodName list.

   Visual Studio adds the Click event handler to the code.

4. Add the following code to the procedure:

```
Me.dsEmployeeList1.EmployeeList.Clear()
Me.daEmployeeList.Fill(Me.dsEmployeeList1.EmployeeList)
UpdateDisplay()
```

   This code reloads the data into the DataSet from the data source, and then it updates the version and row status information of the form.

5 Press F5 to run the application.

6 In the First Name text box, change Steven Changed to Steven, and then click Save.

The application updates the Current value of the DataRow.

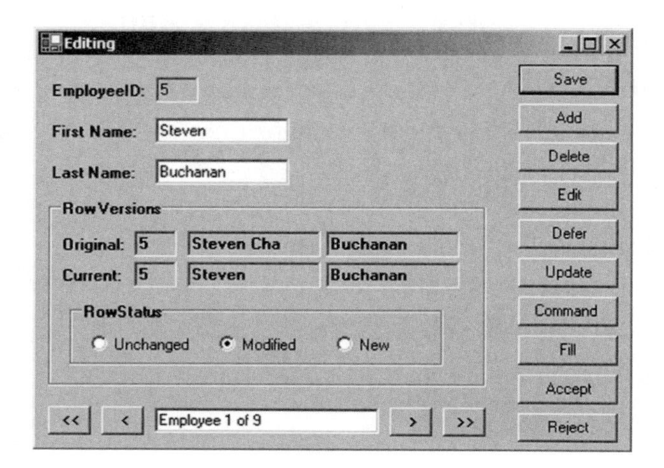

7 Click Command.

The application updates the data source, but because executing the command directly does not update the DataSet, the change isn't reflected.

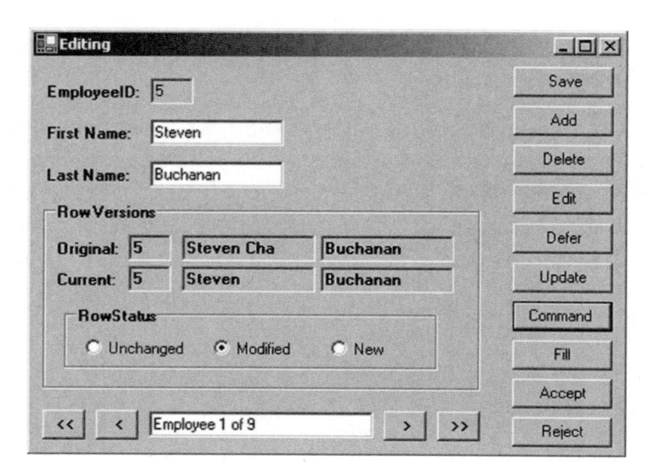

8 Click Fill.

The application reloads the data. Note that the First Name text box has been changed.

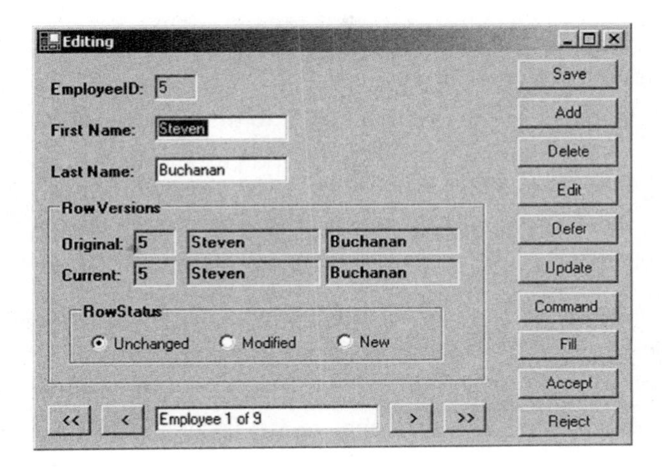

9 Close the application.

Visual C# .NET

1 In the form designer, double-click the Command button.

Visual Studio adds the Click event handler to the code window.

2 Add the following procedure to the code editor:

```
System.Data.SqlClient.SqlCommand cmdUpdate;
System.Data.DataRow drCurrent;

cmdUpdate = this.daEmployeeList.UpdateCommand;
drCurrent = GetRow();

cmdUpdate.Parameters["@FirstName"].Value = drCurrent["FirstName"];
cmdUpdate.Parameters["@LastName"].Value = drCurrent["LastName"];
cmdUpdate.Parameters["@empID"].Value = drCurrent["EmployeeID"];

this.cnNorthwind.Open();
cmdUpdate.ExecuteNonQuery();
this.cnNorthwind.Close();

this.dsEmployeeList1.AcceptChanges();
UpdateDisplay();
```

This code first creates two temporary variables, and then it sets them to the Update command of the daEmployeeList DataAdapter and the row currently being displayed on the form, respectively. It then sets the three parameters in the Update command to the values of the row. Finally the connection is opened, the command executed, and the connection closed.

3. In the form designer, double-click the Fill button.

   Visual Studio adds the event handler to the code window.

4. Add the following procedure to the code window:

```
this.dsEmployeeList1.Employees.Clear();
this.daEmployeeList.Fill(this.dsEmployeeList1.Employees);
UpdateDisplay();
```

   This code reloads the data into the DataSet from the data source and then updates the version and row status information of the form.

5. Press F5 to run the application.

6. In the First Name text box, change Steven Changed to Steven, and then click Save.

   The application updates the Current value of the DataRow.

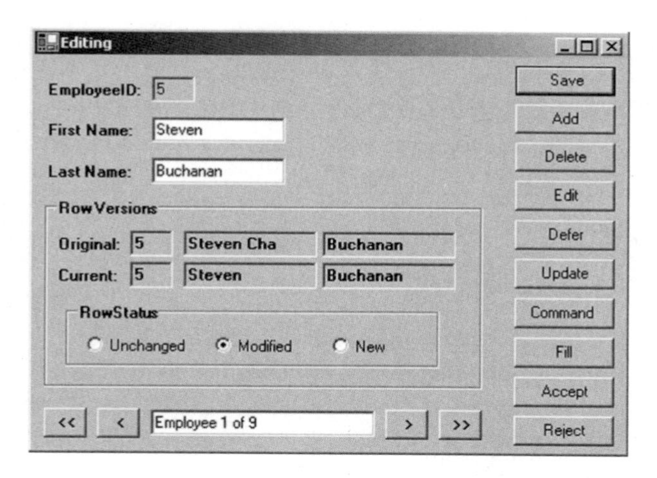

7. Click Command.

   The application updates the data source, but because executing the command directly does not update the DataSet, the change isn't reflected.

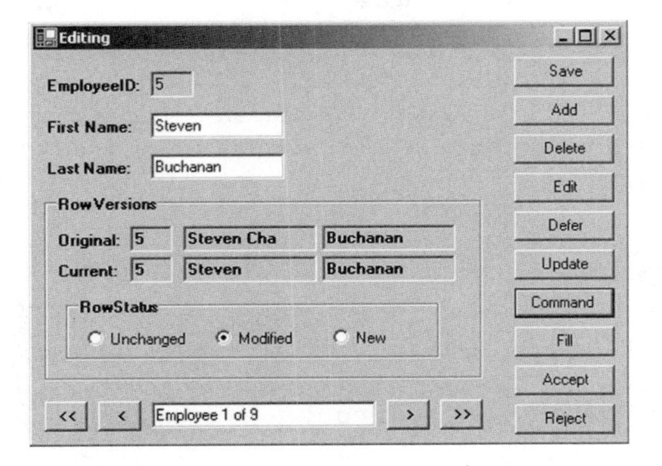

8 Click Fill.

The application reloads the data. Note that the First Name text box has been changed.

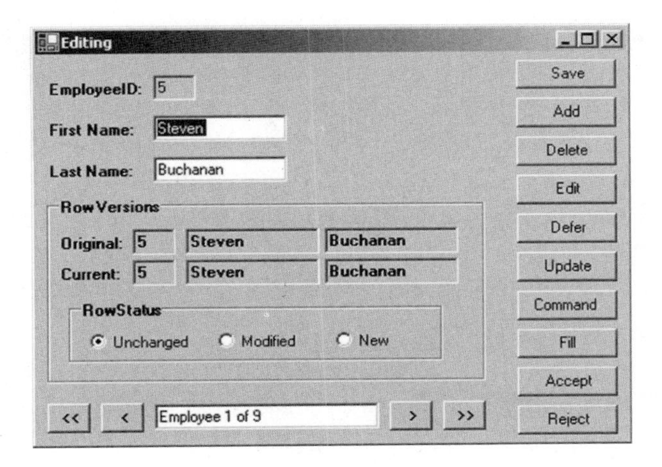

9 Close the application.

Accepting and Rejecting DataSet Changes

The final step in the process of updating data is to set a new baseline for the DataRows. This is done by using the *AcceptChanges* method. The DataAdapter's *Update* method calls *AcceptChanges* automatically. If you execute a command directly, you must call *AcceptChanges* to update the row state values.

If instead of accepting the changes made to the DataSet, you want to discard them, you can call the *RejectChanges* method. *RejectChanges* returns the DataSet to the state it was in the last time *AcceptChanges* was called, discarding all new rows, restoring deleted rows, and returning all columns to their original values.

> **important**
>
> If you call *AcceptChanges* or *RejectChanges* prior to updating the data source, you will lose the ability to persist the changes made since the last time *AcceptChanges* was called using the *Update* method. The DataAdapter's *Update* method uses the RowStatus property to determine which rows to persist, and both *AcceptChanges* and *RejectChanges* set the RowStatus of every row to Unchanged.

Using AcceptChanges

The *AcceptChanges* method is supported by the DataSet, the DataTable, and the DataRow. Under most circumstances, you need only call *AcceptChanges* on the DataSet because it calls *AcceptChanges* for each DataTable that it contains, and the DataTable, in turn, calls *AcceptChanges* for each DataRow.

When the *AcceptChanges* call reaches the DataRow, rows with a RowStatus of either Added or Modified will have the Original values of each column changed to the Current values, and their RowStatus will be set to Unchanged. Deleted rows will be removed from the Rows collection.

Accept Changes to a DataSet

Visual Basic .NET

1. Add the following code to the end of the *btnCmd_Click* procedure that you created in the previous exercise:

   ```
   Me.dsEmployeeList1.AcceptChanges()
   UpdateDisplay()
   ```

2. Press F5 to run the application.

3 In the Last Name text box, type **New** after Buchanan, and then click Save. The application updates the Current value.

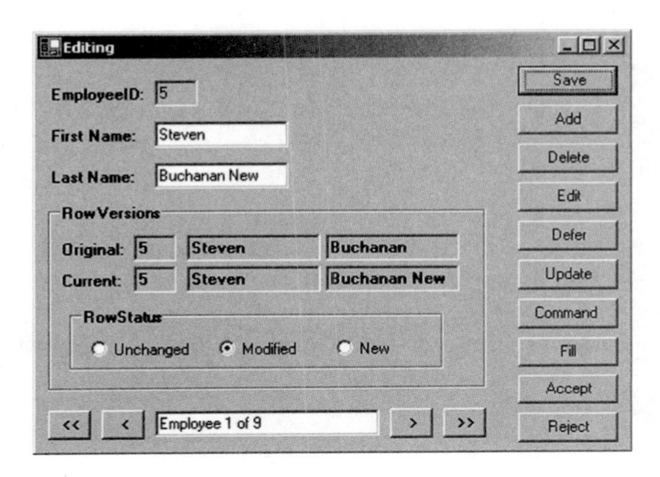

4 Click Command.

Because the *AcceptChanges* method is called, the Version and RowStatus information is updated.

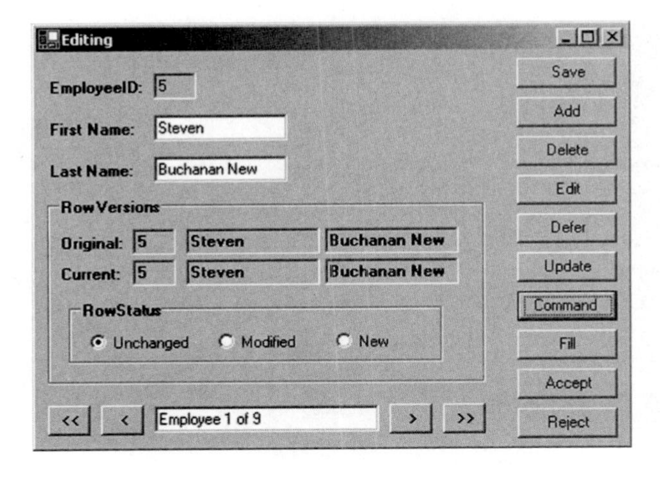

5 In the Last Name text box, change Buchanan New back to Buchanan, and then click Save.

The application updates the Current value and RowStatus.

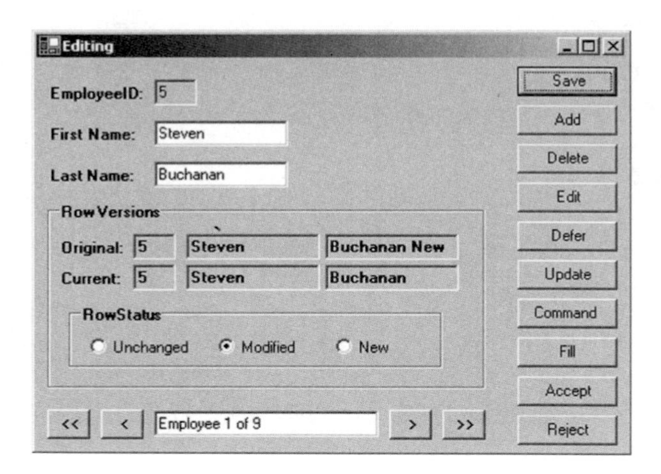

6 Click Accept.

The application updates the Original value and RowStatus.

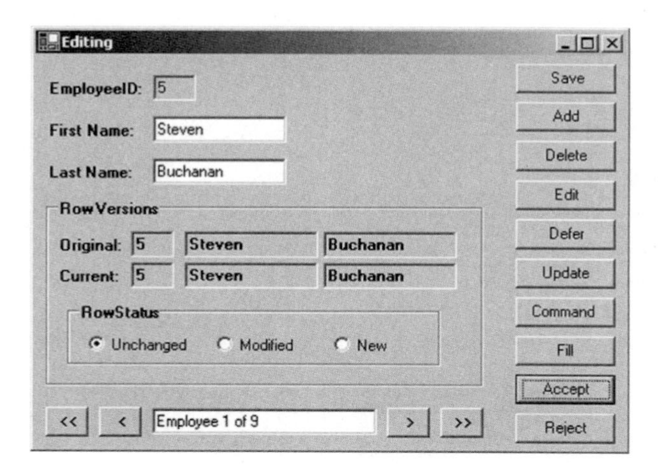

7 Click Update, and then click Fill.

Because the RowStatus of the DataRow had been reset to Unchanged, no changes were persisted to the data source.

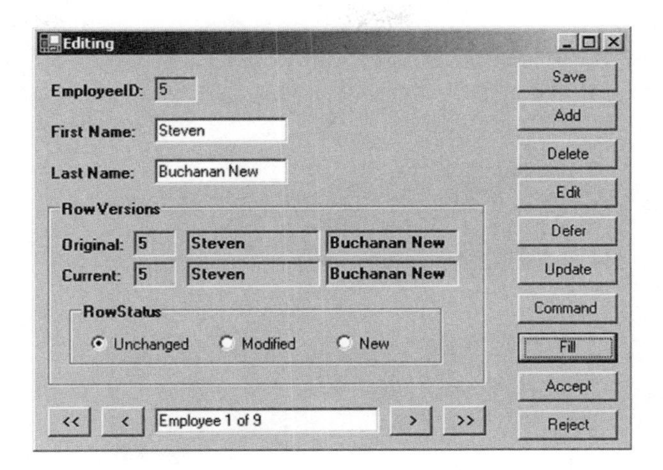

8 Close the application.

Visual C# .NET

1 Add the following code to the end of the *btnCmd_Click* procedure that you created in the previous exercise:

```
this.dsEmployeeList1.AcceptChanges();
UpdateDisplay();
```

2 Press F5 to run the application.

3 In the Last Name text box, type **New** after Buchanan, and then click Save.

The application updates the Current value.

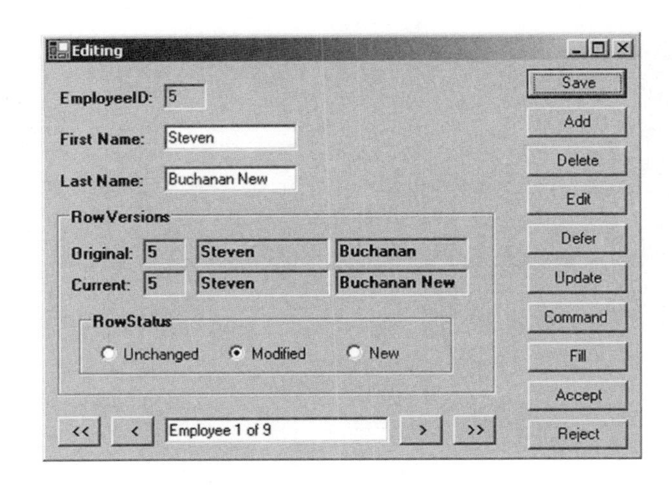

4 Click Command.

Because the *AcceptChanges* method is called, the Version and RowStatus information is updated.

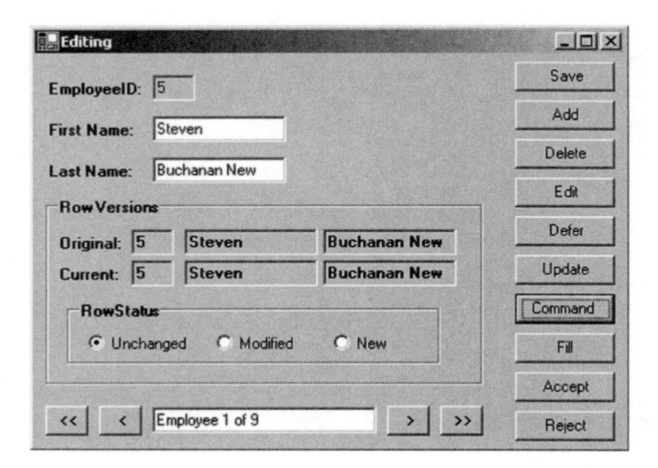

5 In the Last Name text box, change Buchanan New back to Buchanan, and then click Save.

The application updates the Current value and RowStatus.

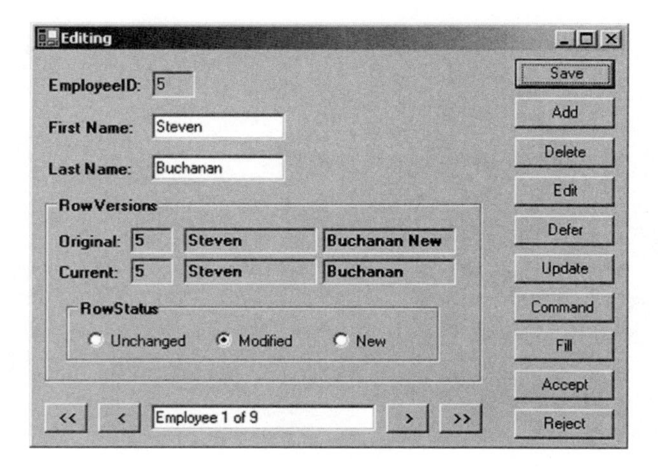

6 Click Accept.

The application updates the Original value and RowStatus.

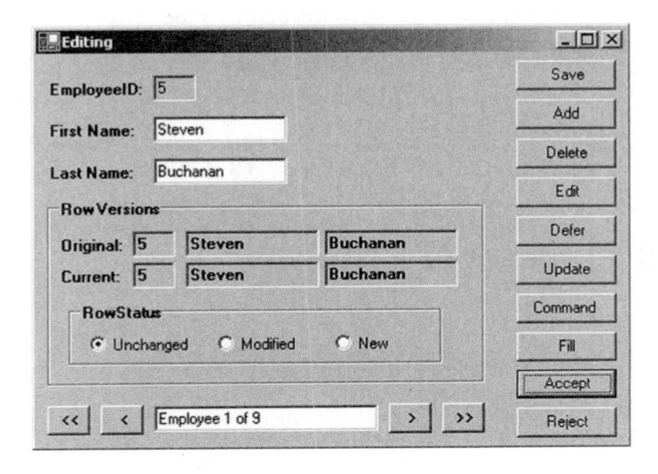

7 Click Update, and then click Fill.

Because the RowStatus of the DataRow had been reset to Unchanged, no changes were persisted to the data source.

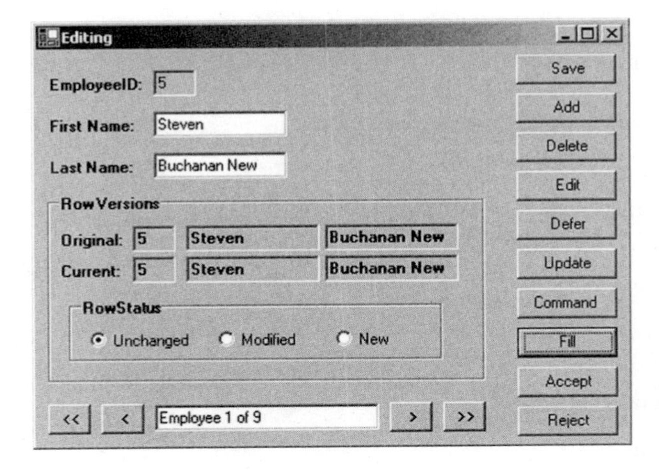

8 Close the application.

Using *RejectChanges*

Like *AcceptChanges*, the *RejectChanges* method is supported by the DataSet, DataTable, and DataRow objects, and each object cascades the call to the objects below it in the hierarchy.

When the *RejectChanges* call reaches the DataRow, rows with a RowStatus of either Deleted or Modified will have the Current values of each column changed to the Original values, and their RowStatus will be set to Unchanged. Added rows will be removed from the Rows collection.

Reject the Changes to a DataRow

Visual Basic .NET

1. In the code editor, select btnReject in the ControlName list, and then select Click in the MethodName list.

   Visual Studio adds the Click event handler to the code.

2. Add the following code to the procedure:

   ```
   Me.dsEmployeeList1.RejectChanges()
   UpdateDisplay()
   ```

3. Press F5 to run the application.
4. In the First Name text box, change Stephen to Reject, and then click Save.

   The application updates the Current value and RowStatus.

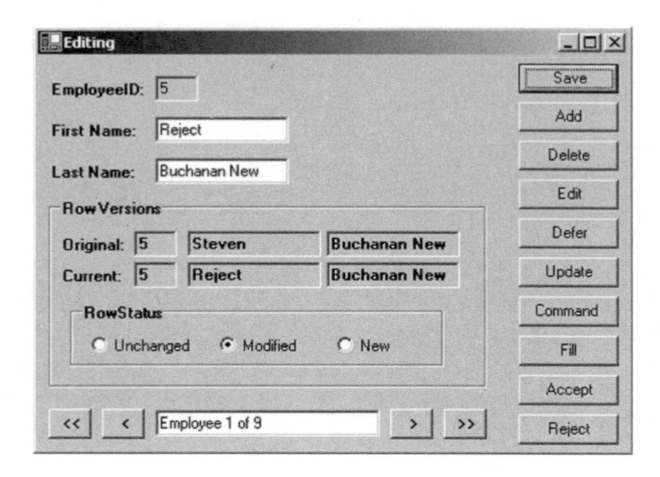

5 Click Reject.

The application returns the Current version of the row to its Original values and then resets the RowStatus to Unchanged.

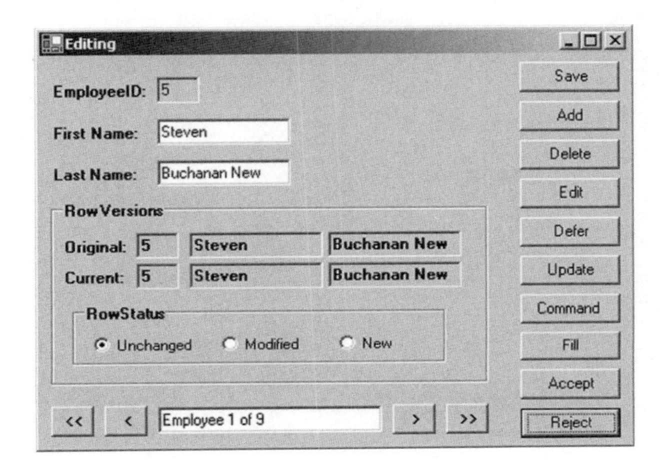

6 Close the application.

Visual C# .NET

1 In the form designer, double-click the Reject button.

Visual Studio adds the Click event handler to the code window.

2 Add the following procedure to the code editor:

```
this.dsEmployeeList1.RejectChanges();
UpdateDisplay();
```

3 Press F5 to run the application.

4 In the First Name text box, change Stephen to Reject, and then click Save.

The application updates the Current value and RowStatus.

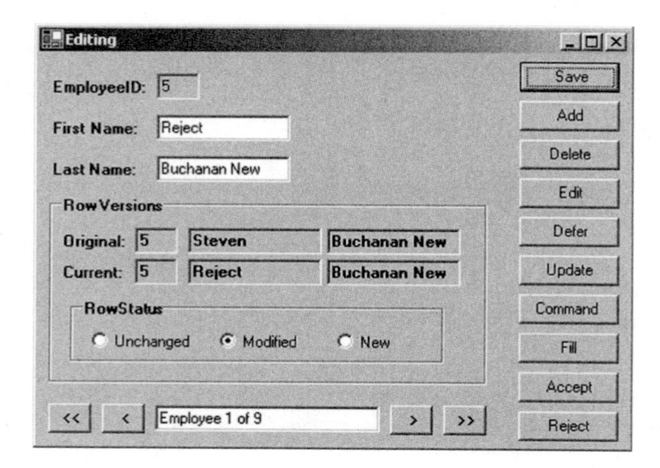

5 Click Reject.

The application returns the Current version of the row to its Original values and then resets the RowStatus to Unchanged.

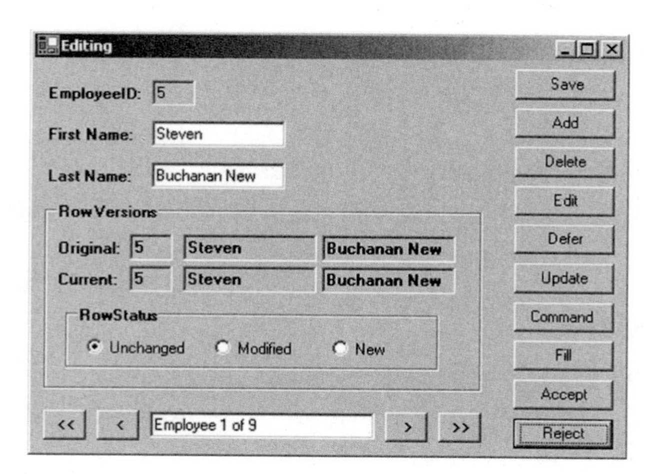

6 Close the application.

Chapter 9 Quick Reference

To	Do this

Add a row to a DataTable	Use the *NewRow* method of the DataTable to create the row, and then use the *Add* method of the Rows collection:
	`newRow = myTable.NewRow()`
	`myTable.Rows.Add(newRow)`

Delete a row from a DataTable	Use the *Delete* method of the DataRow: `myRow.Delete()`
Change the values in a DataReader	Use the DataRow's Item property: `myRow.Item("Row Name") = newValue`

Suspend constraint enforcement	Use *BeginEdit* combined with either *EndEdit* or *CancelEdit*:
	`myRow.BeginEdit()`
	`myRow.Item("Row Name") = newValue`
	`myRow.EndEdit()`
	Or:
	`myRow.BeginEdit()`
	`myRow.Item("Row Name") = newValue`
	`myRow.CancelEdit()`

Accept changes to data	Use the *AcceptChanges* method of the DataSet, DataTable, or DataRow: `myDataSet.AcceptChanges()`
Reject changes to data	Use the *RejectChanges* method of the DataSet, DataTable, or DataRow: `myDataSet.RejectChanges()`

ADO.NET Data-Binding in Windows Forms

In this chapter, you'll learn how to:

- *Simple-bind control properties using the Properties window*
- *Simple-bind control properties using the Advanced Binding dialog box*
- *Simple-bind control properties at run time*
- *Complex-bind control properties using the Properties window*
- *Complex-bind control properties at run time*
- *Use CurrencyManager properties*
- *Respond to CurrencyManager events*
- *Use the Binding object's properties*

In previous chapters, we have, of course, been binding data to controls on Windows Forms, but we haven't really looked at the process in any detail. We'll begin to do that in this chapter. We'll start by examining the underlying mechanisms used to bind Windows Forms controls to Microsoft ADO.NET data sources. In Chapter 11, we'll examine the techniques used to perform some common data-binding tasks.

Understanding Data-Binding in Windows Forms

The Microsoft .NET Framework provides an extremely powerful and flexible mechanism for binding data to properties of controls. Although in the majority of cases you will bind to the displayed value of a control—for example, the DisplayMember property of a ListBox control or the Text property of a TextBox control—you can bind *any* property of a control to a data source.

This makes it possible, for example, to bind the background and foreground colors of a form and the font characteristics of its controls to a row in a database table. By using this technique, you could allow users to customize an application's user interface without requiring any changes to the code base.

Data Sources

Windows Forms controls can be bound to any data source, not just traditional database tables. Technically, to qualify as a data source, an object must implement the IList, IBindingList, or IEditableObject interface.

The IList interface, the simplest of the three, is implemented by arrays and collections. This means that it's possible, for example, to bind the Text property of a label to the contents of a ListBox control's ObjectCollection (although it's difficult to think of a situation in which doing so might be useful). Any object that implements both the IList and the IComponent interfaces can be bound at design time as well as at run time.

The IBindingList interface, which is implemented by the DataView and DataViewManager objects, supports change notification. Objects that implement this interface raise ListChanged events to notify the application when either an item in the list or the list itself has been changed.

Finally, the IEditableObject interface, which is implemented by the DataRowView object, exposes the *BeginEdit*, *EndEdit*, and *CancelEdit* methods.

Fortunately, when you're working within ADO.NET, you can largely ignore the details of interface implementation. They're really only important if you are building your own data source objects.

Within the .NET Framework, the actual binding of data in a Windows form is handled by a number of objects working in conjunction, as shown below.

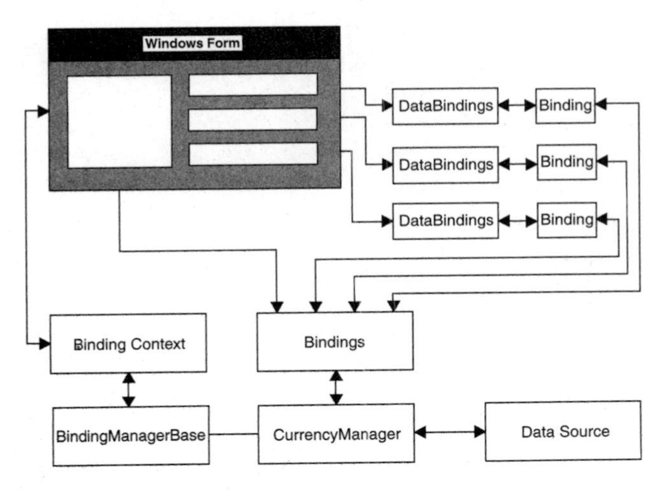

At the highest level in the logical architecture is the BindingContext object. Any object that inherits from the Control class can contain a BindingContext object. In most cases, you'll use the form's BindingContext object, but if your form includes a container control, such as a Panel or a GroupBox, that contains data-bound controls, it may be easier to create a separate BindingContext object for the container control because it saves a level of indirection when referencing the contained controls.

The BindingContext object manages one or more BindingManagerBase objects, one for each data source that is referenced by the form. The BindingManagerBase is an abstract class, so instances of this object cannot be directly instantiated. Instead, the objects managed by the BindingContext object will actually be instances of either the PropertyManager class or the CurrencyManager class. All of these objects are implemented in the System.Windows.Forms namespace.

If the data source can return only a single value, the BindingManagerBase object will be an instance of the PropertyManager class. If the data source returns (or *can* return) a collection of objects, the BindingManagerBase object will be an instance of the CurrencyManager class. ADO.NET objects will always instantiate CurrencyManagers.

The CurrencyManager object keeps track of position in the list and manages the bindings to that data source. Note that the data source itself doesn't know which item is being displayed.

ADO

The CurrencyManager's Position property maintains the current row in a data source. ADO.NET data sources don't support cursors and therefore have no knowledge of the "current" row. This may at first seem awkward, but is actually a more powerful architecture because it's now possible to maintain multiple "cursors" in a single data source.

There is a separate instance of the CurrencyManager object for each discrete data source. If all of the controls on a form bind to a single data source, there will be a single CurrencyManager. For example, a form that contains text boxes displaying fields from a single table will contain a single CurrencyManager object. However, if there are multiple data sources, as in a form that displays master/detail information, there will be separate CurrencyManager objects for each data source.

Windows Forms controls contain a DataBindings collection that contains the Binding objects for that control. The Binding object, as we'll see, specifies the data source, the control that is being bound, and the property of the control that will display the data for simple-bound properties.

The CurrencyManager inherits a BindingsCollection property from the BindingManagerBase class. The BindingsCollection contains references to the Binding objects for each control.

Binding Controls to an ADO.NET Data Source

Windows Forms controls in the .NET Framework support two different types of data binding: simple and complex. The distinction is really quite simple. Control properties that contain a single value are simple-bound, while properties that contain multiple values, such as the displayed contents of list boxes and data grids, are complex-bound.

Any given control can contain both simple-bound and complex-bound attributes. For example, the MonthCalendar control's MaxDate property, which determines the maximum allowable selected date, is a simple-bound property containing a single *DateTime* value, while its BoldedDates property, which contains an array of dates that are to be displayed in bold formatting, would be complex-bound.

Simple-Binding Control Properties

In the .NET Framework, any property of a control that contains a single value can be simple-bound to a single value in a data source.

Binding can take place either at design time or at run time. In either situation, you must specify three values: the name of property to be bound, the data source, and a navigation path within the data source that resolves to a single value.

The navigation path consists of a period-delimited hierarchy of names. For example, to reference the ProductID column of the Products table, the navigation path would be Products.ProductID.

The Microsoft Visual Studio .NET Properties window contains a Data Bindings section that displays the properties that are most commonly data-bound. Other properties are available through the (Advanced) section, which opens the Advanced Data Binding dialog box. The Advanced Data Binding dialog box provides design time access to all the simple-bound properties of the selected control.

Bind a Property Using the Properties Window

1. Open the Binding project from the Start page or by using the File menu.
2. In the Solution Explorer, double-click Binding.vb (or Binding.cs, if you're using C#) to open the form.

   Visual Studio displays the form in the form designer.

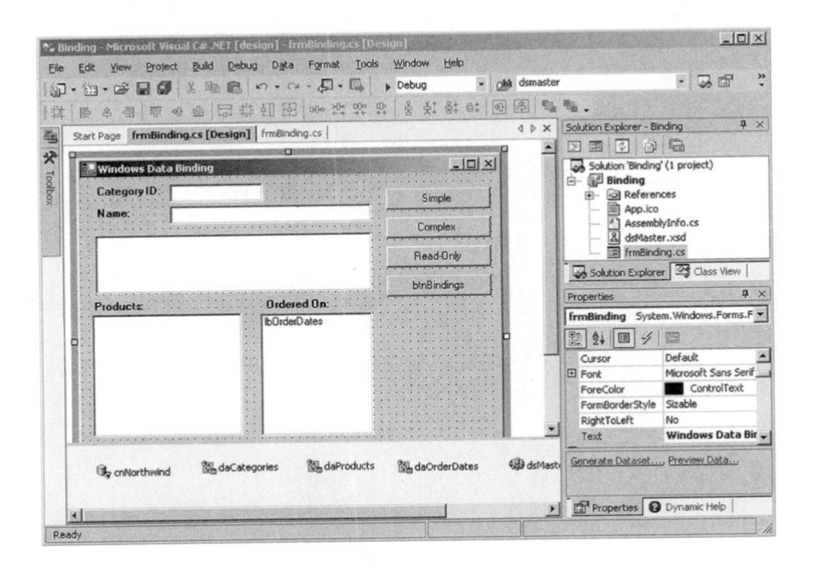

3 Select the tbCategoryID text box (after the Category ID label).

4 In the Properties window, expand the Data Bindings section, and then open the drop-down list for the Text property.

5 Expand dsMaster1, expand Categories, and then select CategoryID.

Bind a Property Using the Advanced Binding Dialog Box

1 In the form designer, select the tbCategoryName text box (after the Name label).

2 In the Properties window, expand the DataBindings section (if necessary), and then click the Ellipsis button after the (Advanced) property.

Visual Studio opens the Advanced Data Binding dialog box with the Text property selected.

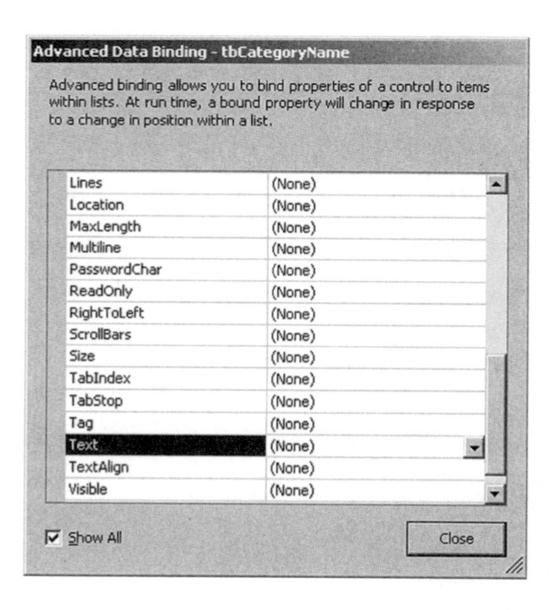

3 Open the drop-down list for the Text property, expand dsMaster, expand Categories, and then select CategoryName.

4 Click Close.

Visual Studio sets the data binding. Because Text is one of the default data-bound properties, its value is shown in the Properties window.

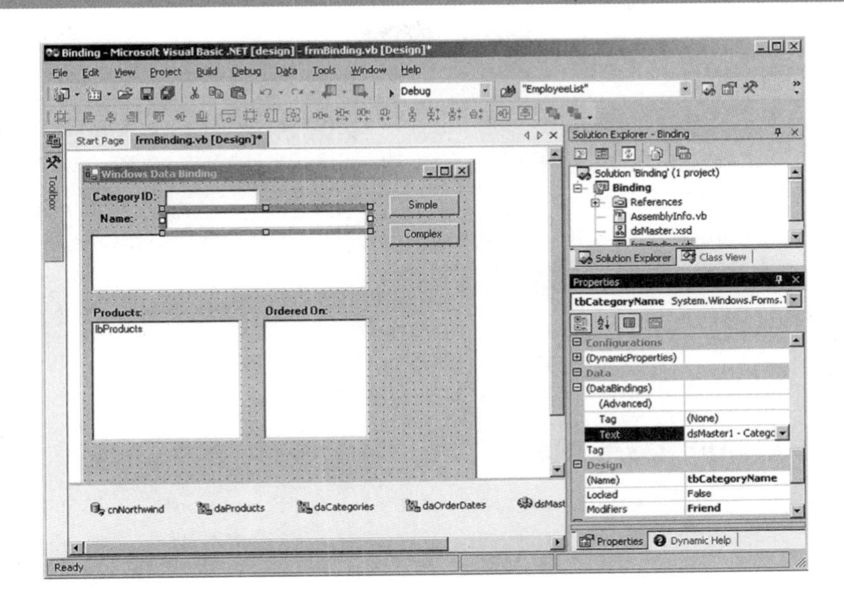

When you bind a control at design time, you simply select the appropriate column from the drop-down list in the Properties window or the Advanced Data Binding dialog box. When you're binding at run time, you must specify two values separately.

The .NET Framework provides a lot of flexibility in how you specify the data source and navigation path values when creating a binding at run time. For example, both of the following Binding objects will refer to the ProductID column of the Products table:

```
bndFirst = New System.Windows.Forms.Binding("Text", Me.dsMaster1, _
    "Products.ProductID")
bndSecond = New System.Windows.Forms.Binding("Text", _
    Me.dsMaster.Products, "ProductID")
```

However, because the data source properties are different, the .NET Framework will create different CurrencyManagers to manage them, and the controls on the form will not be synchronized.

In some situations, this might be useful. For example, you might need to display two different rows of a table on a single form, and this technique makes it easy to do so. However, in the majority of cases, you'll want all the controls on a form that are bound to the same table to display information from the same row, and in order to achieve this, you must be consistent in the way you specify the data source and navigation path values.

tip

If you're creating a binding at run time that you want synchronized with design-time bindings, specify only the top-level of the hierarchy as the data source:

```
bndFirst = New System.Windows.Forms.Binding("Text",
   Me.dsMaster1, "Products.ProductID")
```

Bind a Property at Run Time

Visual Basic .NET

1. In the form designer, double-click the Simple button.

   Visual Studio opens the code editor and adds the btnSimple Click event handler.

2. Add the following lines to bind the tbCategoryDescription text box to the Categories.Description column:

   ```
   Dim newBinding As System.Windows.Forms.Binding

   newBinding = New System.Windows.Forms.Binding("Text", _
      Me.dsMaster1, "Categories.Description")
   Me.tbCategoryDescription.DataBindings.Add(newBinding)
   ```

   This code first declares a new Binding object, and then instantiates it by passing the property name ("Text"), data source (Me.dsMaster1), and navigation path ("Categories.Description") to the constructor. Finally, the new Binding object is added to the DataBindings collection of the tbCategoryDescription control by using the *Add* method.

3. Press F5 to run the application.

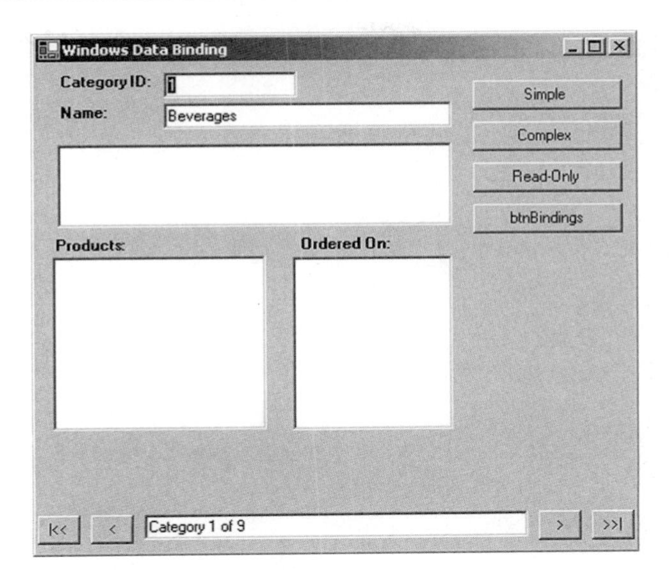

4 Click the Simple button.

The application adds the binding and displays the value in the text box.

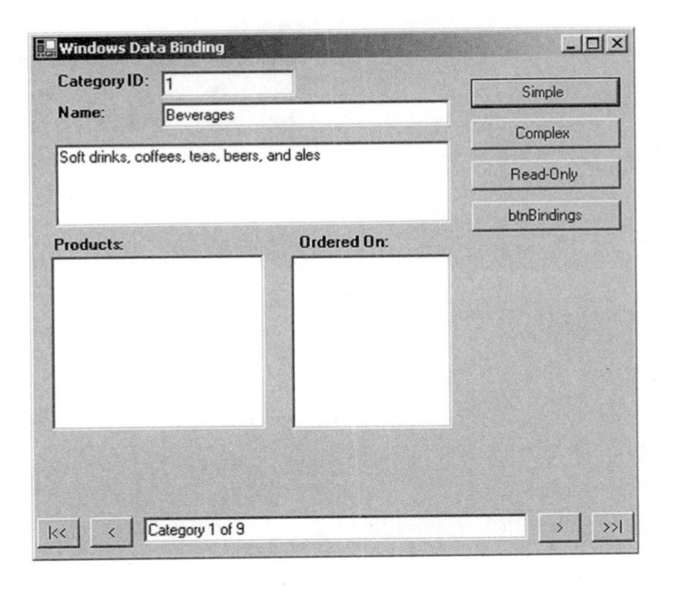

5 Click the Next button (">") at the bottom of the form.

The application displays the next category, along with its description.

Roadmap

We'll examine the code that implements these buttons later in this chapter.

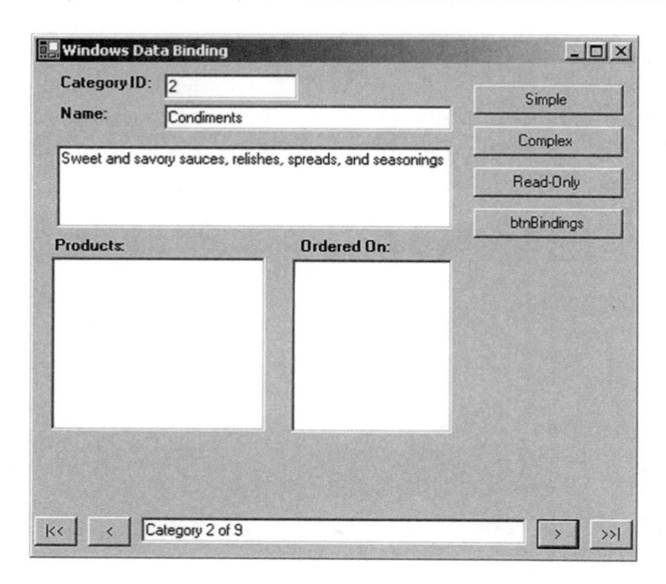

> **important**
>
> If we had passed dsMaster1.Categories as the data source and "Description" as the navigation path to the Binding's constructor, the *Description* field would not display data from the current row because Visual Studio would have created a second CurrencyManager. When creating bindings that are to be synchronized with design-time bindings, be sure to specify only the DataSet as the data source.

6. Close the application.

Visual C# .NET

1. In the form designer, double-click the Simple button.

   Visual Studio opens the code editor and adds the btnSimple Click event handler.

2. Add the following lines to bind the tbCategoryDescription text box to the Categories.Description column:

```
System.Windows.Forms.Binding newBinding;

newBinding = new System.Windows.Forms.Binding("Text",
   this.dsMaster1, "Categories.Description");
this.tbCategoryDescription.DataBindings.Add(newBinding);
```

This code first declares a new Binding object, and then instantiates it by passing the property name ("Text"), data source (Me.dsMaster1), and navigation path ("Categories.Description") to the constructor. Finally, the new Binding object is added to the DataBindings collection of the tbCategoryDescription control by using the *Add* method.

3 Press F5 to run the application.

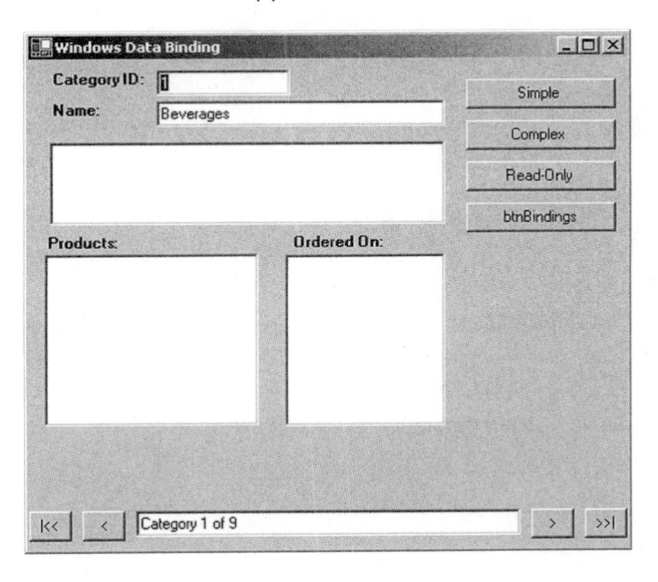

4 Click the Simple button.

The application adds the binding and displays the value in the text box.

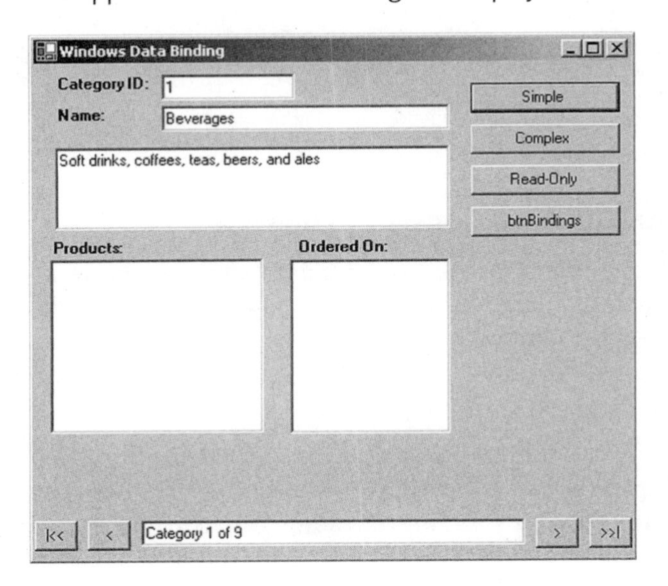

Roadmap
We'll examine the code that implements these buttons later in this chapter.

5 Click the Next button (">") at the bottom of the form.

The application displays the next category, along with its description.

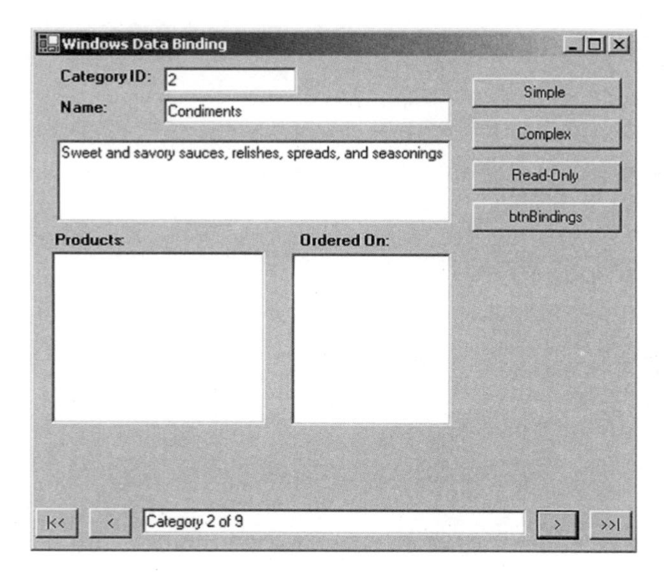

important

If we had passed dsMaster1.Categories as the data source and "Description" as the navigation path to the Binding's constructor, the *Description* field would not display data from the current row because Visual Studio would have created a second CurrencyManager. When creating bindings that are to be synchronized with design-time bindings, be sure to specify only the DataSet as the data source.

6 Close the application.

Complex-Binding Control Properties

Unlike simple-bound properties, which must be bound to a single value, complex-bound control properties contain (and possibly display) multiple items. The most common examples of complex-bound controls are, of course, the ListBox and ComboBox, but any control property that accepts multiple values can be complex-bound.

Although the techniques can vary somewhat depending on the specific control, most complex-bound controls are bound by setting the DataSource property directly rather than by adding a Binding object to the DataBindings collection.

The most common complex-bound controls, the ListBox, ComboBox, and DataGrid, also expose a DisplayMember property, which determines what will be displayed by the control. In the case of the ListBox and ComboBox controls, the DisplayMember property must resolve to a single value, while the DataGrid control can display multiple values for each row (for example, all the columns of a DataTable).

Roadmap

We'll examine the use of the ValueMember property to create look-up tables in Chapter 11.

In addition, the ListBox and ComboBox controls expose a ValueMember property, which allows the control to display a user-friendly name while updating an underlying DataSet with the value of a different column.

One particularly convenient possibility when using complex-bound controls is to bind to a relationship rather than to a DataSet, which causes the items displayed in the control to be automatically filtered. We'll see an example of this technique in the following exercise.

Add a Complex Data-Binding Using the Properties Window

1. In the form designer, select the lbProducts ListBox.
2. In the Properties window, select DataSource, and then select dsMaster1 from the drop-down list.
3. In the DisplayMember drop-down list, expand Categories, expand CategoryProducts, and then select the ProductName column.
4. Press F5 to run the application.

   Visual Studio displays the products in the current category.

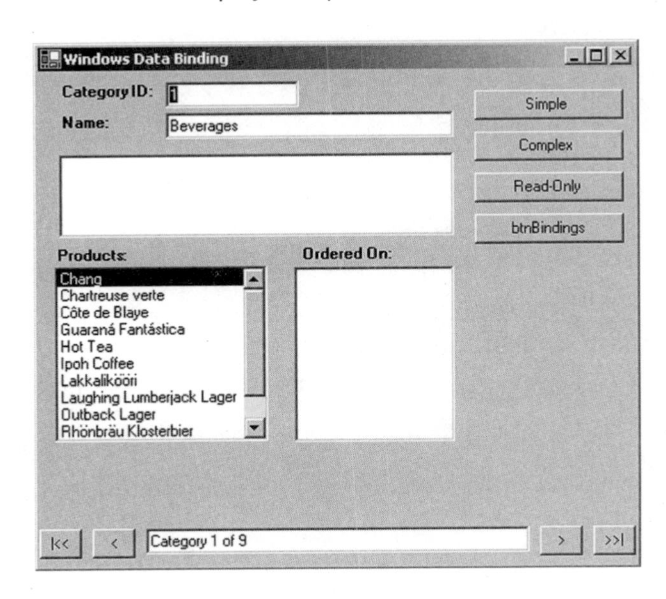

Roadmap

We'll examine the code that implements these buttons later in this chapter.

5 Click the Next button (">") at the bottom of the form.

The application displays the next category, along with its products.

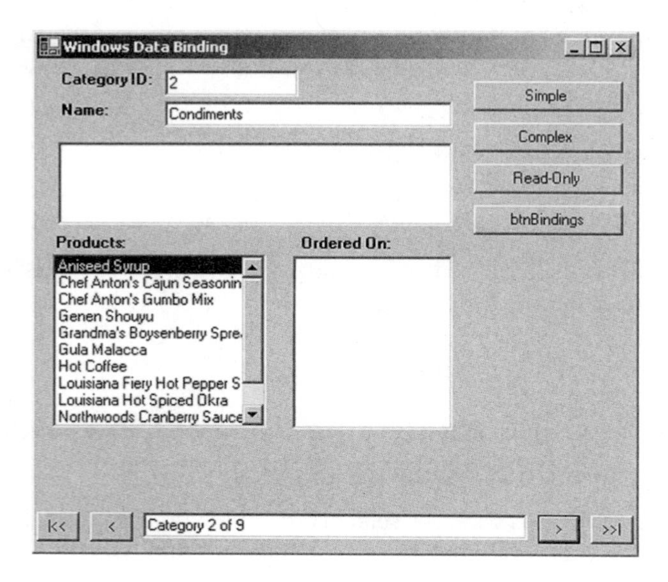

6 Close the application.

Add a Complex Data-Binding at Run Time

Visual Basic .NET

1 In the form designer, double-click the Complex button.

Visual Studio opens the code editor and adds the Click event handler for the btnComplex button.

2 Add the following code to the event handler:

```
Me.lbOrderDates.DataSource = Me.dvOrderDates;
Me.lbOrderDates.DisplayMember = "OrderDate";
```

This code simply sets the DataSource and DisplayMember properties to the OrderDate column of the dvOrderDates DataView.

3 Press F5 to run the application, and then click the Complex button.

The OrderDates list box displays the dates for the product selected in the Products list box.

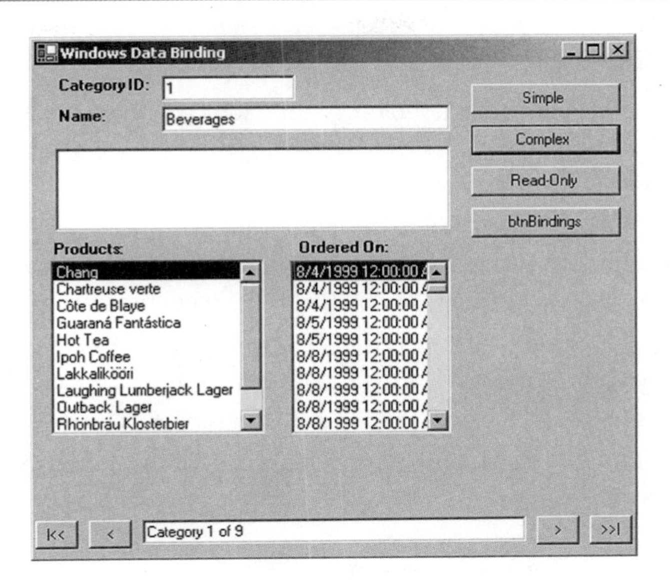

4 Select a different product to confirm that the dates that are displayed change.

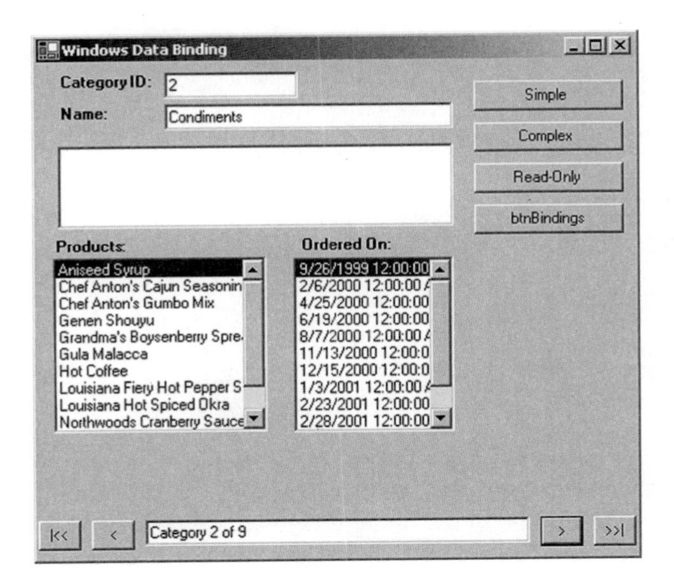

5 Close the application.

Visual C# .NET

1. In the form designer, double-click the Complex button.

   Visual Studio opens the code editor and adds the Click event handler for the btnComplex button.

2. Add the following code to the event handler:

```
Me.lbOrderDates.DataSource = Me.dvOrderDates;
Me.lbOrderDates.DisplayMember = "OrderDate";
```

   This code simply sets the DataSource and DisplayMember properties to the OrderDate column of the dvOrderDates DataView.

3. Press F5 to run the application, and then click the Complex button.

   The OrderDates list box displays the dates for the product selected in the Products list box.

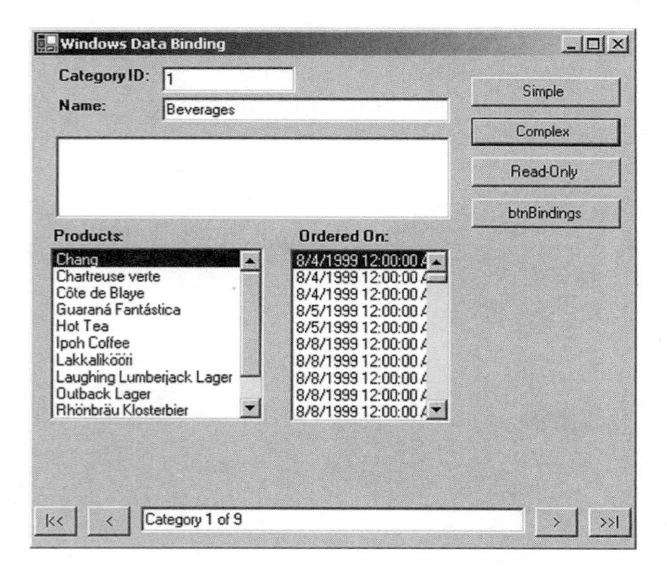

4. Select a different product to confirm that the dates that are displayed change.

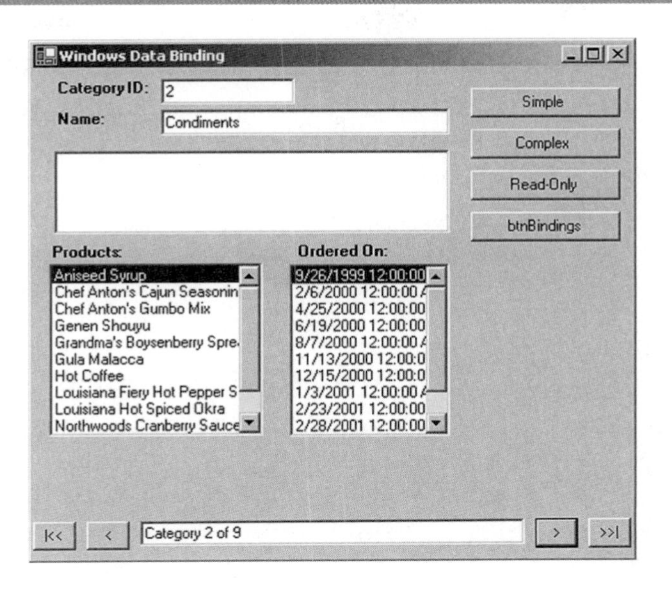

5 Close the application.

Using the BindingContext Object

As we have seen, the BindingContext object is the highest level object in the binding hierarchy and manages the BindingManagerBase objects that control the interaction between a data source and the controls bound to it.

The BindingContext object doesn't expose any useful methods or events, and has only a single property, as shown in Table 10-1. The Item property is used to index into the BindingManagerBase collection contained in the BindingContext object. The first version, which uses only the data source as a parameter, is used if no navigation path is required. For example, if a DataTable is specified as the data source for a DataGrid, you could use the following syntax to retrieve the CurrencyManager that controls that binding:

```
Me.myDG.DataSource = Me.myDataSet.myTable
myCurrencyManager = Me.BindingContext(me.myDataSet.myTable)
```

The second version of the Item property allows the specification of the navigation path. However, the navigation path provided here must resolve to a list, not a single property. For example, if a text box is bound to the Description column of a DataTable, the following syntax would be used to retrieve the CurrencyManager that controls the binding:

```
Me.myText.DataBindings.Add("Text",Me.myDataSet,"myTable.Description")
myCurrencyManager = Me.BindingContext(Me.myDataSet.myTable)
```

Property	Description
Item(*DataSource*)	Returns the BindingManagerBase object associated with the specified *DataSource*
Item(*DataSource, DataMember*)	Returns the BindingManagerBase object associated with the specified *DataSource* and *DataMember*, where the *DataMember* is a table or relation

Table 10-1 BindingContext Properties

Using the CurrencyManager Object

The CurrencyManager object is fundamental to the Windows Forms data-binding architecture. Through its properties, methods, and events, the CurrencyManager object manages the link between a data source and the controls that display data from that source.

CurrencyManager Properties

The properties exposed by the CurrencyManager are shown in Table 10-2. With the exception of the Position property, they are all read-only.

Property	Description
Bindings	The collection of Binding objects being managed by the CurrencyManager
Count	The number of rows managed by the CurrencyManager
Current	The value of the current object in the data source
List	The list managed by the CurrencyManager
Position	Gets or sets the current item in the list managed by the CurrencyManager

Table 10-2 CurrencyManager Properties

The Bindings and List properties define the relationship between the data source and the controls bound to it. The Bindings property, which returns a BindingsCollection object, contains the Binding object for each individual control property that is bound to the data source. We'll examine the Binding object later in this chapter.

The List property returns a reference to the data source that is managed by the CurrencyManager. The List property returns a reference to the IList interface. To treat the data source as its native type in code, you must explicitly cast it to that type.

As might be expected, the Count property returns the number of rows in the list managed by the CurrencyManager. Unlike some other environments, the Count property is immediately available—it is not necessary to move to the end of the list before the Count property is set.

The Current property returns the value of the current row in the data source as an object. Like the List property, if you want to treat the value returned by Current as its native type, you must explicitly cast it.

Remember that the Current property is read-only. To change the current row in the data source, you must use the Position property, which is the only property exposed by the CurrencyManager that is *not* read-only. The Position property is an integer that represents the zero-based index into the List property.

Use CurrencyManager Read-Only Properties

Visual Basic .NET

1. In the code editor, select btnReadOnly in the Control Name combo box, and then select Click in the Method Name combo box.

   Visual Studio adds the Click event handler to the code.

2. Add the following code to the method:

```
Dim strMsg As String
Dim cm As System.Windows.Forms.CurrencyManager
Dim dsrc As System.Data.DataView

cm = Me.BindingContext(Me.dsMaster1, "Categories")
dsrc = CType(cm.List, System.Data.DataView)

strMsg = "There are " & cm.Count.ToString & " rows in "
strMsg += dsrc.Table.TableName.ToString & "."
strMsg += vbCrLf & "There are " & cm.Bindings.Count.ToString
strMsg += " controls bound to it."
MessageBox.Show(strMsg)
```

   The first three lines declare some local variables. The fourth line sets the variable *cm* to the CurrencyManager for the Categories DataTable, while the next line assigns the variable *dsrc* to the data source referenced by the List property.

   Note that the value returned by List is explicitly cast to a DataView. (Remember that although Categories is a DataTable, data binding always occurs to the default view.)

The remaining lines display the Count and Bindings.Count properties in a message box.

3. Press F5 to run the application.
4. Click the Read-Only button.

   The application displays the CurrencyManager properties, showing two bound controls.

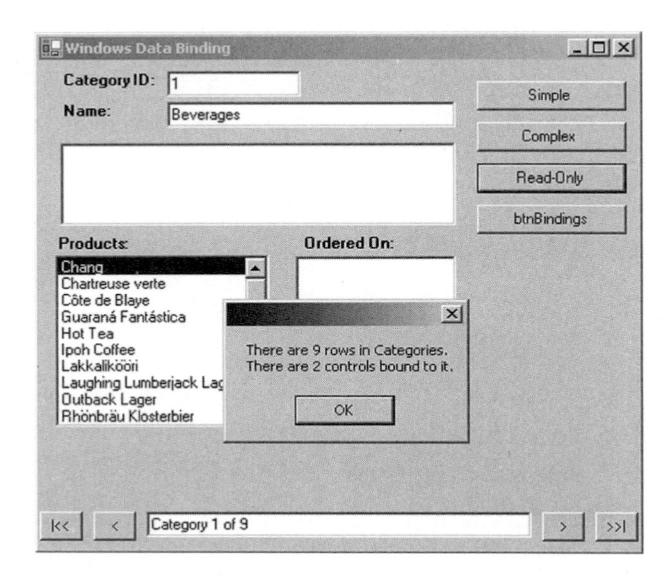

5. Dismiss the dialog box, and then click the Simple button.

   The application adds the binding for the Description control.
6. Click the Read-Only button.

   The application displays the CurrencyManager properties, showing three bound controls.

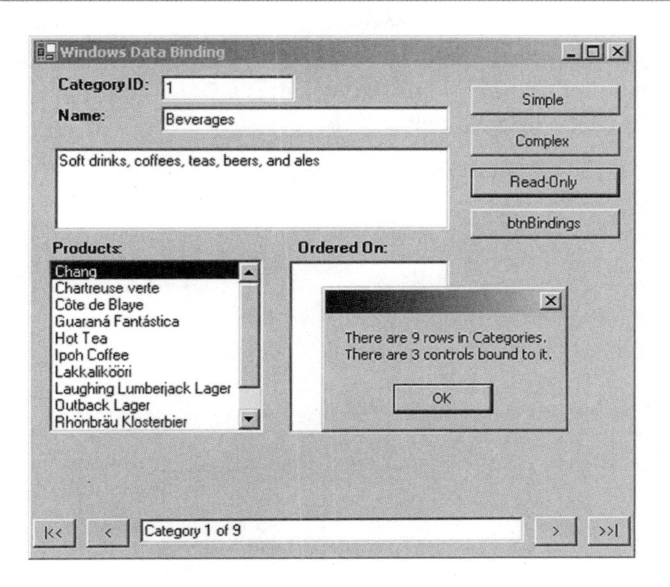

7 Close the application.

Visual C# .NET

1 In the form designer, double-click the Read-Only button.

Visual Studio adds the event handler to the code window.

2 Add the following code to the procedure:

```
string strMsg;
System.Windows.Forms.CurrencyManager cm;
System.Data.DataView dsrc;

cm = (System.Windows.Forms.CurrencyManager)
   this.BindingContext[this.dsMaster1, "Categories"];
dsrc = (System.Data.DataView) cm.List;

strMsg = "There are " + cm.Count.ToString() + " rows in ";
strMsg += dsrc.Table.TableName.ToString() + ".";
strMsg += "\nThere are " + cm.Bindings.Count.ToString();
strMsg += " controls bound to it.";
MessageBox.Show(strMsg);
```

The first three lines declare some local variables. The fourth line sets the variable *cm* to the CurrencyManager for the Categories DataTable, while the next line assigns the variable *dsrc* to the data source referenced by the List property.

Note that the value returned by List is explicitly cast to a DataView. (Remember that although Categories is a DataTable, data binding always occurs to the default view.)

The remaining lines display the Count and Bindings.Count properties in a message box.

3 Press F5 to run the application.

4 Click the Read-Only button.

The application displays the CurrencyManager properties, showing two bound controls.

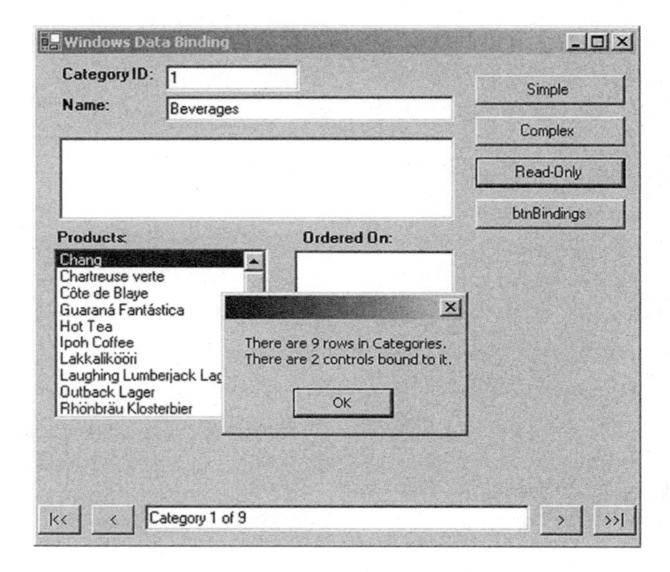

5 Dismiss the dialog box, and then click the Simple button.

The application adds the binding for the Description control.

6 Click the Read-Only button.

The application displays the CurrencyManager properties, showing three bound controls.

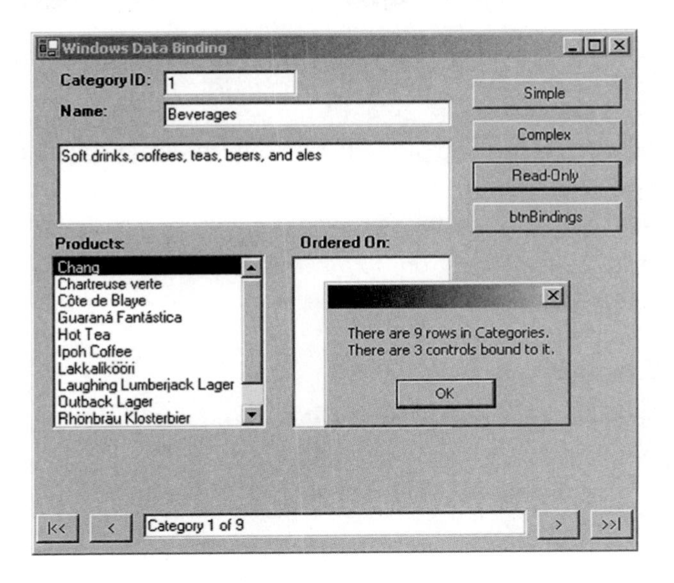

7 Close the application.

Use the Position Property

Visual Basic .NET

1 Open the region labeled "Navigation Buttons."

2 Add the following code to the btnFirst_Click event handler:

```
Me.BindingContext(Me.dsMaster1, "Categories").Position = 0
UpdateDisplay()
```

This code sets the Position property of the CurrencyManager for the Categories DataTable to the beginning (remember that Position is a zero-based index), and then calls the UpdateDisplay function. UpdateDisplay, which is contained in the Utility Functions region, simply displays "Category x of y" in the text box at the bottom of the form.

3 Add the following code to the btnPrevious_Click event handler:

```
With Me.BindingContext(Me.dsMaster1, "Categories")
    If .Position = 0 Then
        Beep()
    Else
        .Position -= 1
        UpdateDisplay()
    End If
End With
```

This code uses Microsoft Visual Basic's With … End With structure to simplify the reference to the CurrencyManager. Note that it checks to see if the Position property is already set at the beginning of the file before decrementing the value. The Position property does not throw an exception if it is set outside the bounds of the list.

4 The remaining navigation code is already there, so press F5 to run the application.

5 Use the navigation buttons to move through the display.

6 Close the application.

Visual C# .NET

1 Open the region labeled "Navigation Buttons."

2 Add the following code to the btnFirst_Click event handler:

```
this.BindingContext[this.dsMaster1, "Categories"].Position = 0;
UpdateDisplay();
```

This code sets the Position property of the CurrencyManager for the Categories DataTable to the beginning (remember that Position is a zero-based index), and then calls the UpdateDisplay function. UpdateDisplay, which is contained in the Utility Functions region, simply displays "Category x of y" in the text box at the bottom of the form.

3 Add the following code to the btnPrevious_Click event handler:

```
System.Windows.Forms.BindingManagerBase bmb;
bmb = (System.Windows.Forms.BindingManagerBase)
  this.BindingContext[this.dsMaster1, "Categories"];

bmb.Position -= 1;
UpdateDisplay();
```

4 The remaining navigation code is already there, so press F5 to run the application.

5 Use the navigation buttons to move through the display.

6 Close the application.

CurrencyManager Methods

The public methods exposed by the CurrencyManager object are shown in Table 10-3.

Method	Description
AddNew	Adds a new item to the underlying list
CancelCurrentEdit	Cancels the current edit operation
EndCurrentEdit	Commits the current edit operation

Refresh	Redisplays the contents of bound controls
RemoveAt(Index)	Removes the item at the position specified by *Index* in the underlying list
ResumeBinding	Resumes data binding and data validation after the *SuspendBinding* method has been called
SuspendBinding	Temporarily suspends data binding and data validation

Table 10-3 CurrencyManager Methods

The data editing methods *AddNew* and *RemoveAt*, which add and remove items from the data source, along with the *CancelCurrentEdit* and *EndCurrentEdit* methods, are for use only within complex-bound controls. Unless you are creating a custom version of a complex-bound control, use the DataView's or DataRowView's equivalent methods.

Roadmap
We'll examine the SuspendBinding *and* ResumeBinding *methods in Chapter 11.*

The *SuspendBinding* and *ResumeBinding* methods allow binding (and hence data validation) to be temporarily suspended. As we'll see in Chapter 11, these methods are typically used when data validation requires that values be entered into multiple fields before they are validated.

The *Refresh* method is used only with data sources that don't support change notification, such as collections and arrays.

CurrencyManager Events

The events exposed by the CurrencyManager are shown in Table 10-4.

Event	Description
CurrentChanged	Occurs when the bound value changes
ItemChanged	Occurs when the current item has changed
PositionChanged	Occurs when the Position property has changed

Table 10-4 CurrencyManager Events

The CurrentChanged and PositionChanged events both occur whenever the current row in the CurrencyManager's list changes. The difference is the event arguments passed into the event—PositionChanged receives the standard *System.EventArgs*, while ItemChanged receives an argument of the type *ItemChangedEventArgs*, which includes an Index property.

The ItemChanged event occurs when the underlying data is changed. Under most circumstances, when working with ADO.NET objects, you will use the DataRow or DataColumn Changed and Changing events because they provide greater flexibility, but there is nothing to prevent responding to the CurrencyManager's ItemChanged event if it is more convenient.

Respond to an ItemChanged Event

Visual Basic .NET

1 Add the following event handler to the code editor:

```
Private Sub Position_Changed(ByVal sender As System.Object, _
   ByVal e As System.EventArgs)
   Dim strMsg As String

   strMsg = "Row " & (Me.BindingContext(Me.dsMaster1, _
      "Categories").Position + 1).ToString
   MessageBox.Show(strMsg)
End Sub
```

The code simply displays the current row number in a message box.

2 Expand the Region labeled Windows Form Designer generated code, and add the following code to the end of the New sub to connect the event handler to the PositionChanged event:

```
AddHandler Me.BindingContext(dsMaster1, Categories").PositionChanged, _
   AddressOf Me.Position_Changed
```

3 Press F5 to run the application, and then click the Next button (">").

The application displays a message box showing the new row number.

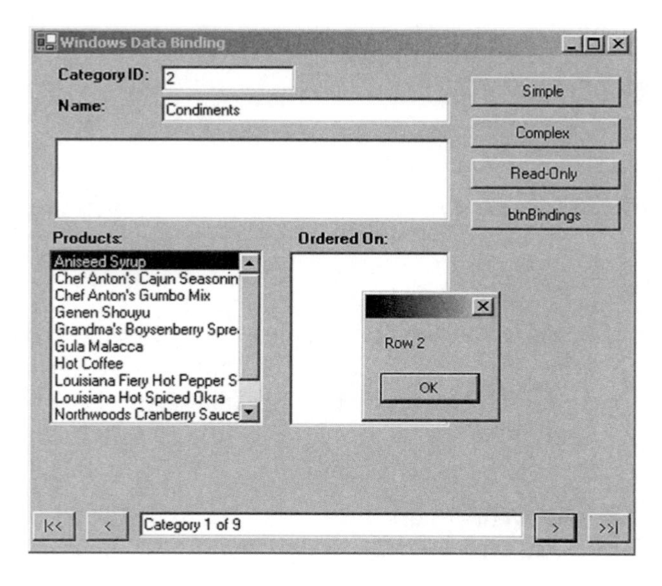

4 Close the application.

Visual C# .NET

1 Add the following event handler to the code editor:

```
private void Position_Changed(object sender, System.EventArgs e)
{
   string strMsg;

   strMsg = "Row " + (this.BindingContext[this.dsMaster1,
      "Categories"].Position + 1).ToString();
   MessageBox.Show(strMsg);
}
```

The code simply displays the current row number in a message box.

2 Add the code to bind the event handler to the bottom of the frmBindings() sub:

```
this.BindingContext[this.dsMaster1, "Categories"].PositionChanged
   += new EventHandler(this.Position_Changed);
```

3 Press F5 to run the application, and then click the Next button (">").

The application displays a message box showing the new row number.

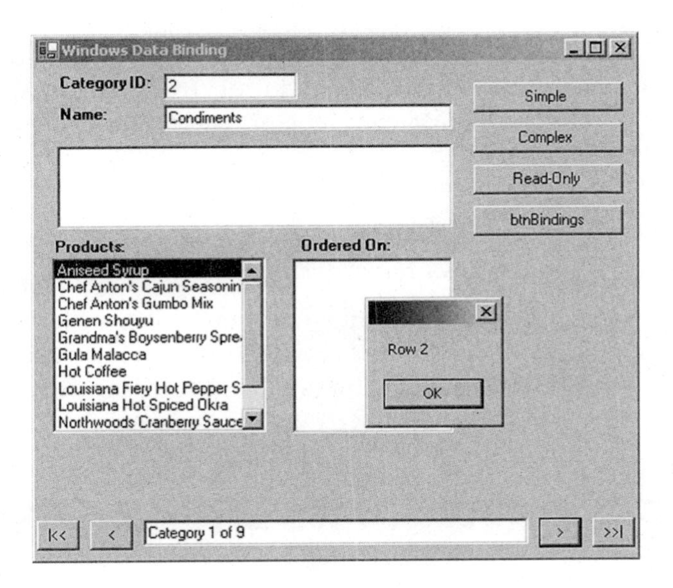

4 Close the application.

Using the Binding Object

The Binding object represents the link between a simple-bound control property and the CurrencyManager. The control's DataBindings collection contains a Binding object for each bound property.

Binding Object Properties

The properties exposed by the Binding object are shown in Table 10-5. All of the properties are read-only.

Property	Description
BindingManagerBase	The BindingManagerBase that manages this Binding object
BindingMemberInfo	Returns information regarding this Binding object based on the *DataMember* specified in its constructor
Control	The control being bound
DataSource	The data source for the binding
IsBinding	Indicates whether the binding is active
PropertyName	The control's data-bound property

Table 10-5 Binding Properties

The BindingManagerBase, Control, and PropertyName properties define the data binding. The BindingManagerBase property returns the CurrencyManager or PropertyManager that manages the Binding object, while the Control and PropertyName properties specify the control property containing the data.

The IsBinding property indicates whether the binding is active. It returns *True* unless SuspendBinding has been evoked.

The DataSource property returns the data source to which the control property is bound as an object. Note that it returns the data source only, not the navigation path. To retrieve the Binding object's navigation path, you must use the BindingMemberInfo property, a complex object whose fields are shown in Table 10-6.

Field	Description
BindingField	The data source property specified by the Binding object's navigation path
BindingMember	The complete navigation path of the Binding object
BindingPath	The navigation path up to, but not including, the data source property, specified by the Binding object's navigation path

Table 10-6 BindingMemberInfo Properties

The *BindingMember* field of the BindingMemberInfo property represents the entire navigation path of the binding, while the *BindingField* field represents only the final field. The *BindingPath* field represents everything up to the *BindingField*. For example, given the navigation path "Categories.CategoryProducts.ProductID," the *BindingField* is "ProductID," while the *BindingPath* is "Categories.CategoryProducts." Note that all three properties return a string value, not an object reference.

Use the BindingMemberInfo Property

Visual Basic .NET

1. In the code editor, select btnBindings in the Control Name combo box, and then select Click in the Method Name combo box.

   Visual Studio adds the event handler template to the code.

2. Add the following code to the method:

```
Dim strMsg As String
Dim bmo As System.Windows.Forms.BindingMemberInfo

bmo = Me.tbCategoryID.DataBindings(0).BindingMemberInfo
strMsg = "BindingMember:  " + bmo.BindingMember.ToString
strMsg += vbCrLf & "BindingPath:  " + _
   bmo.BindingPath.ToString
strMsg += vbCrLf & "BindingField:  " + _
   bmo.BindingField.ToString
MessageBox.Show(strMsg)
```

   The first two lines declare local variables to be used in the method. The third line assigns the BindingMemberInfo property of the first (and only) Binding object in the tbCategoryID DataBindings collection to the *bmo* variable. The remaining lines display the BindingMember, BindingPath, and BindingField properties in a message box.

3. Press F5 to run the application, and then click the BindingMemberInfo button.

   The application displays the BindingMemberInfo fields in a dialog box.

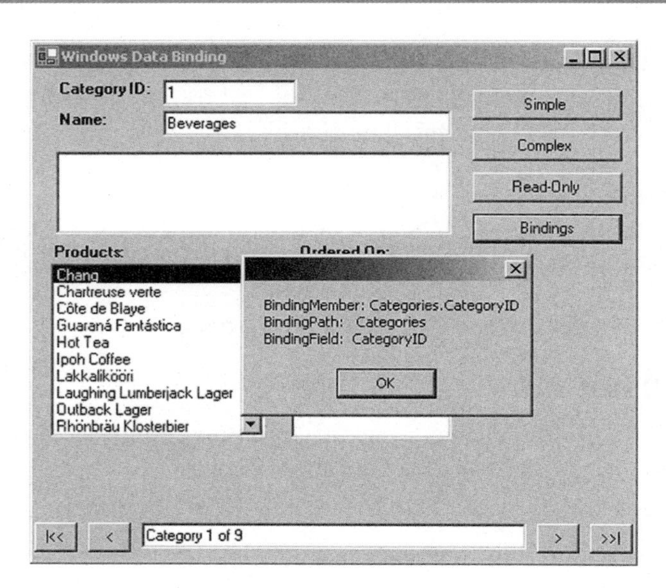

4 Close the application.

Visual C# .NET

1 In the form designer, double-click the Bindings button.

Visual Studio adds the event handler to the code window.

2 Add the following code to the procedure:

```
string strMsg;
System.Windows.Forms.BindingMemberInfo bmo;

bmo = this.tbCategoryID.DataBindings[0].BindingMemberInfo;

strMsg = "BindingMember:  " + bmo.BindingMember.ToString();
strMsg += "\nBindingPath:  " + bmo.BindingPath.ToString();
strMsg += "\nBindingField:  " + bmo.BindingField.ToString();
MessageBox.Show(strMsg);
```

3 Press F5 to run the application, and then click the Bindings button.

The application displays the *BindingMemberInfo* fields in a dialog box.

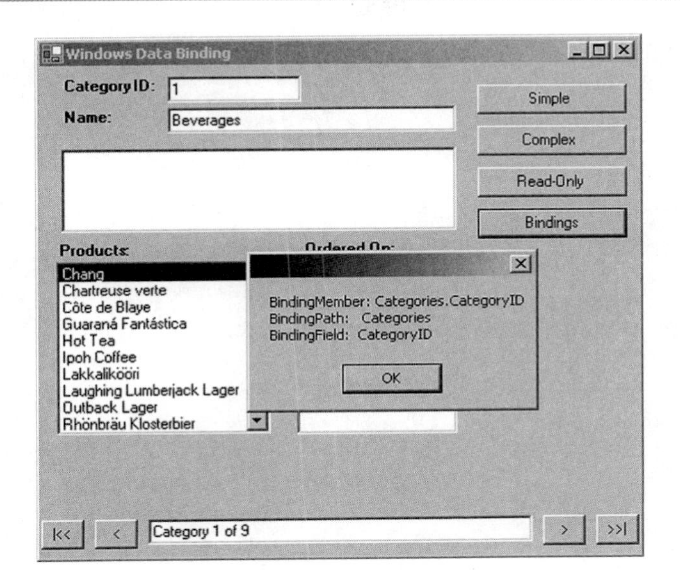

4 Close the application.

Binding Object Events

The events exposed by the Binding object are shown in Table 10-7. The Format and Parse events are used to control the way data is displayed to the user. We'll examine both of these events in detail in Chapter 11.

Roadmap

We'll examine the Format and Parse events in Chapter 11.

Event	Description
Format	Occurs when data is pushed from the data source to the control or pulled from the control to the data source
Parse	Occurs when data is pulled from the control to the data source

Table 10-7 Binding Events

Chapter 10 Quick Reference

To	Do this

Simple-bind control properties at run time	Create a new Binding object, and add it to the control's DataBindings collection:
	`newBinding = New Binding(<propertyString>, <dataSource>, <navigationPath>)`
	`myControl.DataBindings.Add(newBinding)`

Complex-bind control properties at run time	Set the DataSource and DisplayMember properties:
	`myControl.DataSource = myDataSource`
	`myControl.DisplayMember = "field"`

Use CurrencyManager properties	Obtain a reference to the CurrencyManager by specifying the data source and navigation path, and then reference its properties in the usual way:
	`myCM = Me.BindingContext(<dataSource>, <path>)`
	`MessageBox.Show(myCM.Count.ToString())`

CHAPTER

11

Using ADO.NET in Windows Forms

In this chapter, you'll learn how to:

- ✔ *Format data using the Format and Parse events*
- ✔ *Use specialized controls to simplify data entry*
- ✔ *Use data relations to display related data*
- ✔ *Find rows based on a DataSet's Sort column*
- ✔ *Find rows based on other criteria*
- ✔ *Work with data change events*
- ✔ *Work with validation events*
- ✔ *Use the ErrorProvider component*

In the previous chapter, we examined the objects that support Microsoft ADO.NET data binding. In this chapter, we'll explore using ADO.NET and Windows Forms to perform some common tasks.

Formatting Data

The Binding object exposes two events, Format and Parse, which support formatting data for an application. The Format event occurs whenever data is pushed from the data source to the control, and when it is pulled from the control back to the data source, as shown in the figure below.

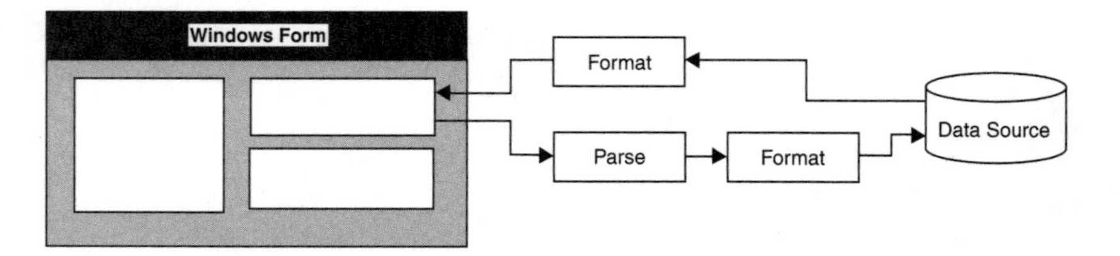

The Format event is used to translate the data from its native format to the format you want to display to the user, while the Parse event is used to translate it back to its original format.

Both events receive a *ConvertEventArgs* argument, which has the properties shown in Table 11-1. The Value property contains the actual data. When the event is triggered, this property will contain the original data in its original format. To change the formatting, you set this value to the new data or format within the event handler. The DesiredType property is used when you are changing the data type of the value.

Property	Description
DesiredType	The data type of the desired value
Value	The data value

Table 11-1 ConvertEventArgs Properties

Using the Format Event

Because the Format event occurs both when data is being pushed from the data source and when it is pulled from the control, you must be sure you know which action is taking place before performing any action. If you change the data type of the value, you can use the DesiredType property to perform this check.

However, if the data type remains the same, you must use a method that is external to the event to determine which way the data is being moved. Setting the Tag property of the control is an easy way to manage this. If you're using the Tag property for another purpose, you can use a form-level variable or determine the direction from the value itself.

Change the Format of Data Using the Format Event

Visual Basic .NET

1. In Microsoft Visual Studio .NET, open the UsingWindows project from the Start page or by using the File menu.

2 Double-click the Master.vb form.

Visual Studio displays the form in the form designer.

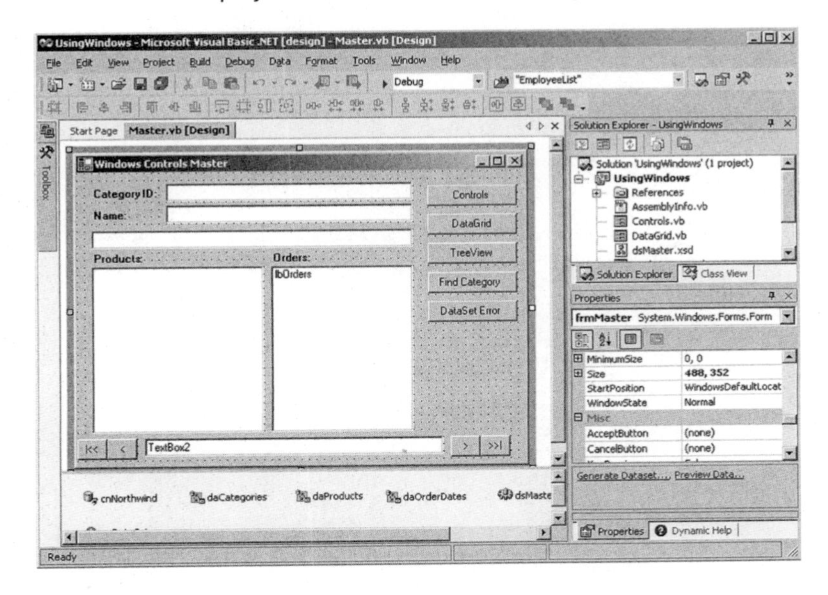

3 Press F7 to display the code editor.

4 Add the following event handler to the code:

```
Private Sub FormatName (ByVal sender As Object, ByVal e As _
   ConvertEventArgs)
   If Me.tbCategoryName.Tag <> "PARSE" Then
        e.Value = CType(e.Value, String).ToUpper
   End If
   Me.tbCategoryName.Tag = "FORMAT"
   MessageBox.Show(e.Value, "Format")
End Sub
```

This code first checks the tbCategoryName text box's Tag property to see if the value is "PARSE." If it isn't "PARSE," it translates the Value property of e to uppercase. It then sets the Tag property to "FORMAT" and displays a message box showing the Value property.

5 Expand the Region labeled Windows Form Designer generated code.

6 In the New sub, after the call to *UpdateDisplay()*, add the code to call the procedure:

```
AddHandler Me.tbCategoryName.DataBindings(0).Format, _
   AddressOf Me.FormatName
```

This line adds the handler to the first (and only) Binding object in the tbCategoryName text box's DataBindings collection.

7 Press F5 to run the application. The message box is displayed twice before the application's form is displayed, once when the control is bound and a second time when the data is first pushed to the control.

8 Close both message boxes.

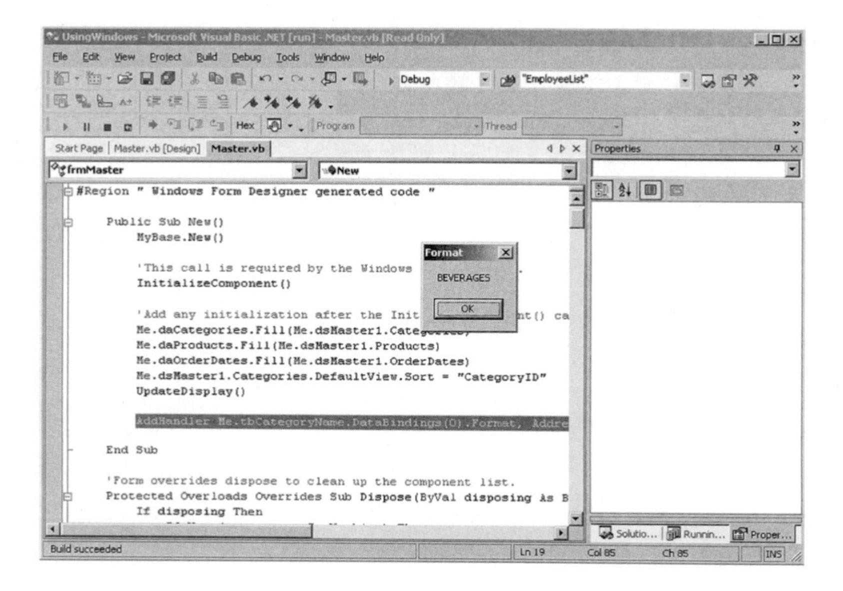

9 Click the Next button (">").

The application displays the formatted CategoryName for the next row.

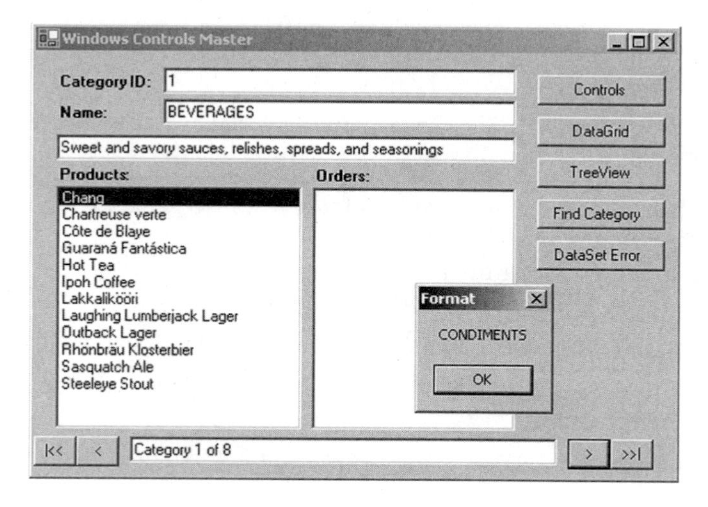

10 Close the message box.

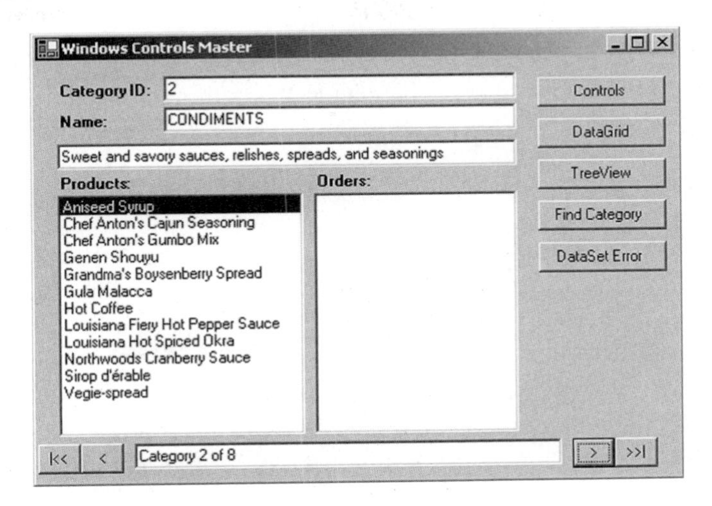

11 Close the application.

Visual C# .NET

1 In Microsoft Visual Studio .NET, open the UsingWindows project from the Start page or by using the File menu.

2 Double-click the Master.cs form.

Visual Studio displays the form in the form designer.

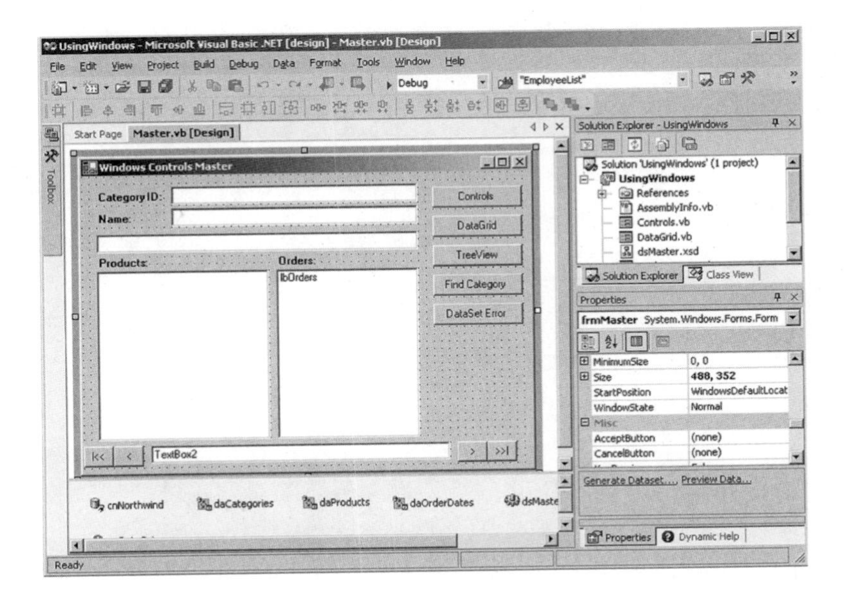

3 Press F7 to display the code editor.

4 Add the following event handler to the bottom of the class definition:

```
private void FormatName(object sender, ConvertEventArgs e)
{
   string eStr = (string) e.Value;

   if ((string) this.tbCategoryName.Tag != "PARSE")
         e.Value = eStr.ToUpper();
   this.tbCategoryName.Tag = "FORMAT";
   MessageBox.Show((string)e.Value, "Format");
}
```

This code first checks the tbCategoryName text box's Tag property to see if the value is "PARSE." If it isn't "PARSE," it translates the Value property of *e* to uppercase. It then sets the Tag property to "FORMAT" and displays a message box showing the Value property.

5 In the frmMaster sub, after the call to *UpdateDisplay()*, add the code to call the procedure:

```
this.tbCategoryName.DataBindings[0].Format +=
   new ConvertEventHandler(this.FormatName);
```

This line adds the handler to the first (and only) Binding object in the tbCategoryName text box's DataBindings collection.

6 Press F5 to run the application. The message box is displayed twice before the application's form is displayed, once when the control is bound and a second time when the data is first pushed to the control.

7 Close both message boxes.

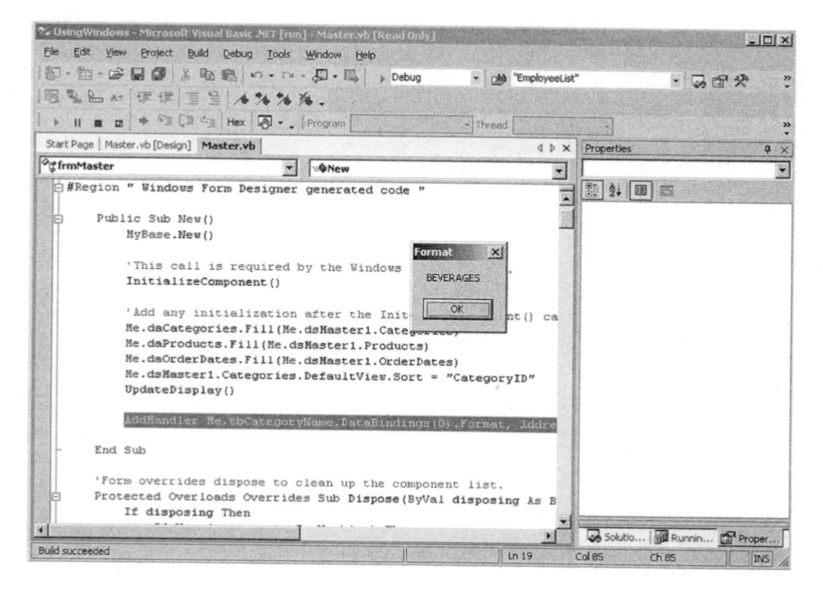

8 Click the Next button (">").

The application displays the formatted CategoryName for the next row.

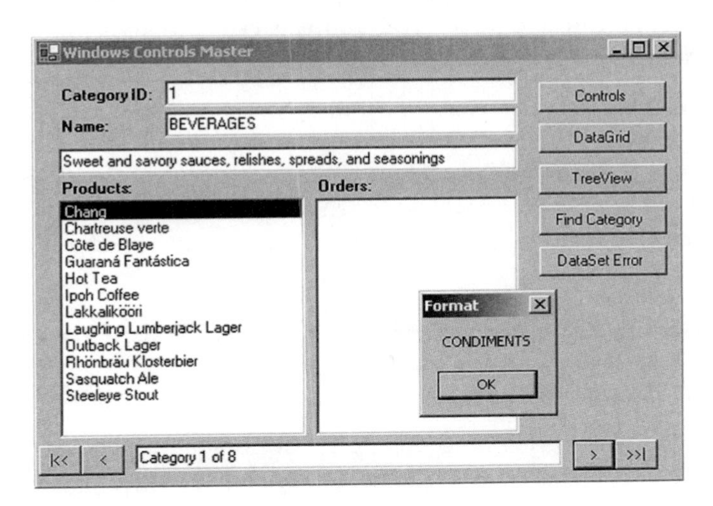

9 Close the message box.

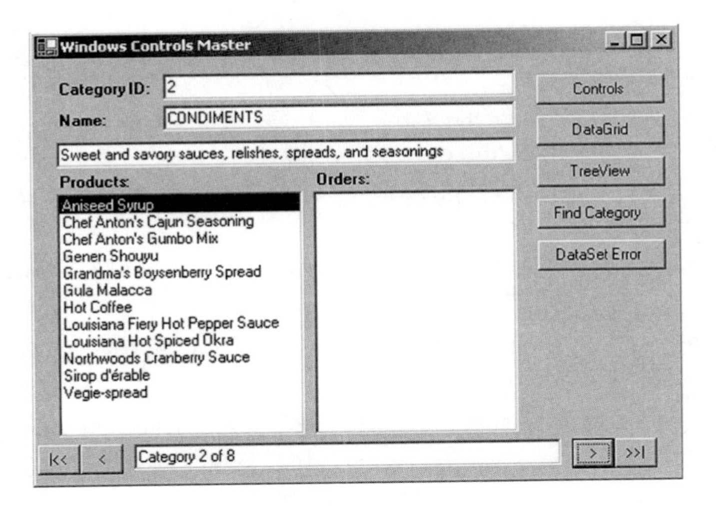

10 Close the application.

Using the Parse Event

As we have seen, the Parse event occurs when data is being pulled from a control back to the data source, and it is typically used to "un-format" data that has been customized for display.

Because Parse is called only once, this "un-formatting" operation should always happen, unlike the Format operation, which should take place only when data is being pushed to the control. However, you do need to be careful to set up any variables or properties required to make sure that the Format event, which will always be called after Parse, doesn't reformat data before it is submitted to the data source.

Restore the Original Format of Data Using the Parse Event

Visual Basic .NET

1 Add the following procedure to the bottom of the code editor:

```
Private Sub ParseName(ByVal sender As Object, ByVal e As _
   ConvertEventArgs)
   Me.tbCategoryName.Tag = "PARSE"
   e.Value = CType(e.Value, String).ToLower
   MessageBox.Show(e.Value, "Parse")
End Sub
```

Note that because the Parse event occurs only when data is being pulled from the control, there is no need to check the Tag property.

2 Add the following handler to the New sub, after the handler from the previous exercise:

```
AddHandler Me.tbCategoryName.DataBindings(0).Parse, _
   AddressOf Me.ParseName
```

3 Press F5 to run the application, and close both of the preliminary Format event message boxes.

4 Add a couple of spaces after "BEVERAGES," and then click the Next button (">").

The application displays the Parse message box.

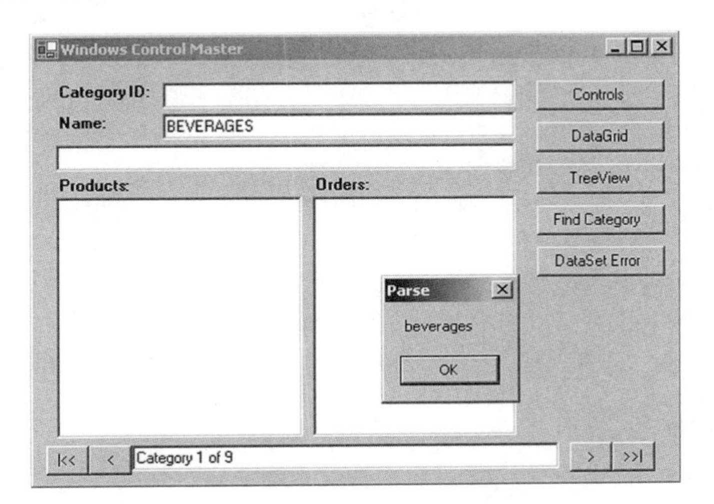

5 Close the Parse message box, and then close the application.

important

The code for this book was checked with a pre-release version of Visual Studio .NET (build 4997). A bug in that build interfered with the click event firing if the project had both a Parse and Format event handler and if either of these displayed a MessageBox.

We fully expect that this will be fixed before Visual Studio .NET is released; however, if the project re-displays the Beverages category, please refer to the Microsoft Press Web site for further information.

6 Comment out the two AddHandler statements in the New sub. (Otherwise, the message boxes will get irritating as we work through the remaining exercises.)

Visual C# .NET

1 Add the following procedure to the bottom of the class file:

```
private void ParseName(object sender, ConvertEventArgs e)
{
   string eStr = (string) e.Value;

   this.tbCategoryName.Tag = "PARSE";
   e.Value = eStr.ToLower();
   MessageBox.Show((string)e.Value, "Parse");
}
```

Note that because the Parse event occurs only when data is being pulled from the control, there is no need to check the Tag property.

2. Add the following handler to the New sub, after the handler from the previous exercise:

```
this.tbCategoryName.DataBindings[0].Parse += new
    ConvertEventHandler(this.ParseName);
```

3. Press F5 to run the application, and close both of the preliminary Format event message boxes.
4. Add a couple of spaces after "BEVERAGES," and then click the Next button (">").

   The application displays the Parse message box.

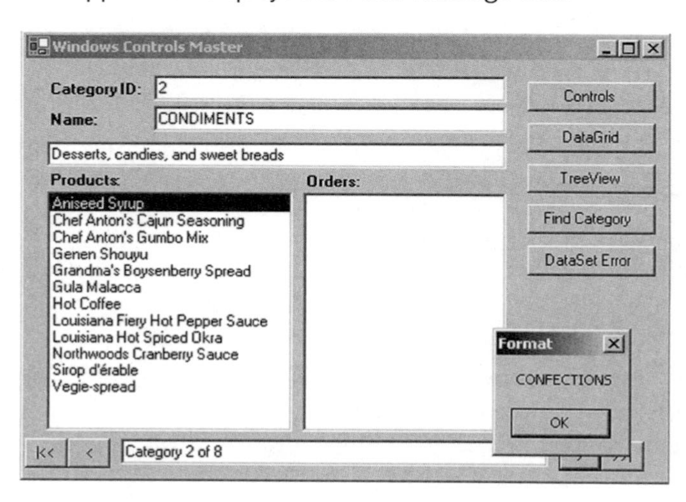

5. Close the Parse message box, and then close the application.

important

When a message box is displayed, it stops code in the application from executing until the user clicks one of the message box buttons. Stopping the execution of code with a message box can cause events to fire incorrectly. For example, the Parse and Format event handlers for this sample include a call to MessageBox.Show. When you run the sample, add a couple of spaces in the Name text box, and click the Next button, you might notice that the Click event for the Next button does not fire. To ensure that the events for this sample fire correctly, you can comment out the calls to MessageBox.Show or replace the calls to MessageBox.Show with Console.WriteLine or Debug.WriteLine. Console.WriteLine or Debug.WriteLine won't stop code from executing and will output specified text to the Visual Studio .NET Output window so that you can see how the events are firing.

6 Comment out the two statements that add the ConvertEventHandlers in the frmMaster sub. (Otherwise, the message boxes will get irritating as we work through the remaining exercises.)

Displaying Data in Windows Controls

The Microsoft .NET Framework supports a wide variety of controls for use on Windows forms, and as we've seen, any form property can be bound, directly or indirectly, to an ADO.NET data source.

The details of each control are unfortunately outside the scope of this book, but in this section, we'll examine some specific techniques for data-binding.

Simplifying Data Entry

One of the reasons that so many controls are provided, of course, is to make data entry simpler and more accurate. TextBox controls are always an easy choice, but the time spent choosing and implementing controls that more closely match the way the user thinks about the data will be richly rewarded.

To take a fairly simple example, it is certainly possible to use a ComboBox containing True and False or Yes and No to represent Boolean values, but in most circumstances, it's far more effective to use the CheckBox control provided by the .NET Framework.

The Checked property of the CheckBox control, which determines whether the box is selected, can be simple-bound either at design time by using the Properties window or at run time in code by using standard techniques.

Use the CheckBox Control for Boolean Values

1 In the Solution Explorer, double-click Controls.vb (or Controls.cs, if you're using C#).

Visual Studio .NET opens the form in the form designer.

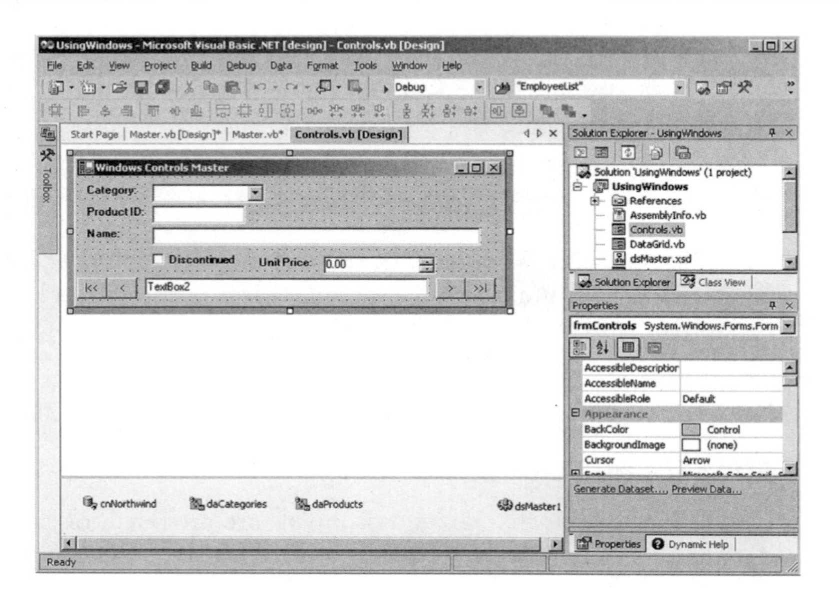

2 Select the Discontinued CheckBox control.

3 In the Properties window, expand the Data Bindings section (if necessary).

4 Select the Checked property. In the drop-down list, expand dsMaster1, and then expand ProductsExtended and select Discontinued.

5 Press F5 to run the application.

6 Click the Controls button.

The application displays the Controls form.

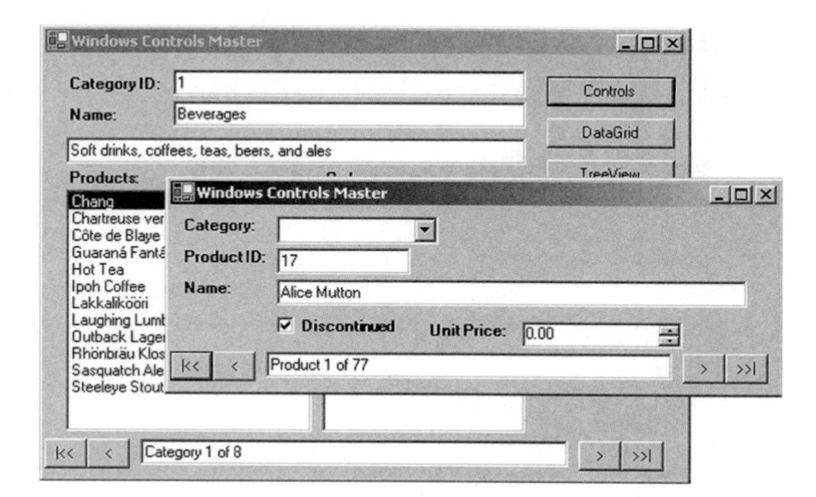

7. Move through the DataTable by pressing the Next button (">"), confirming that only discontinued products have the field checked.
8. Close the Controls window.
9. Close the application.

In order to simplify the database schema, many tables use *artificial keys*—an identity value of some type rather than a key derived from the entity's attributes. These artificial keys are convenient, but they don't typically have any meaning for users. When working with the primary table, the artificial key can often be hidden from users or simply ignored by them. With foreign keys, however, this is rarely the case.

Fortunately, the .NET Framework controls that inherit from the ListControl class, including both ListBox controls and ComboBox controls, make it easy to bind the control to one column while displaying another, even a column in a different table.

The technique is reasonably straightforward. First set the DataSource and DisplayMember properties of the list control to the user-friendly table and column. Under most circumstances, this won't be the table that the form is updating. Then, to set the data binding, set the ValueMember property to the key field in the form being updated, and finally create a Binding object linking the SelectedValue property to the field to be updated.

For example, given the database schema shown in the figure below, if you were creating a form to update the Relatives table, you would typically use a ComboBox control to represent the Relationship type rather than forcing the user to remember that Type 1 means Sister, Type 2 means Father, and so on.

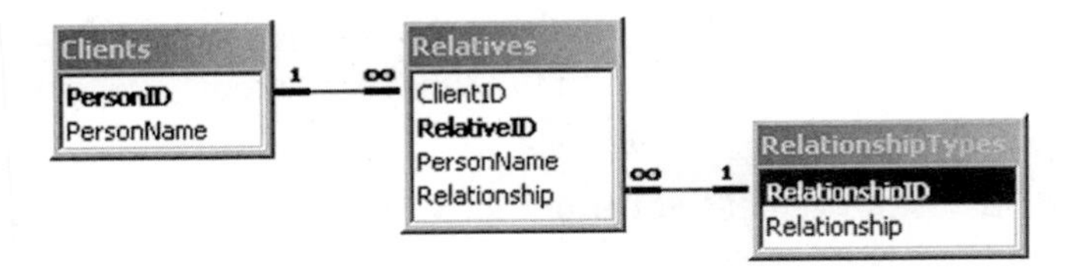

To implement this in the .NET Framework, you would set the ComboBox control's DisplayMember property to *RelationshipTypes.Relationship*, and then set its ValueMember property to *RelationshipTypes.RelationshipID*. With these settings, the ComboBox control will display Sister but return a SelectedValue of 1.

Once the properties have been set, either in the Properties window or in code, you must then add a Binding object to the ComboBox control to link the SelectedValue to the *Relationship* field in the Relatives table. Because SelectedValue isn't available for data-binding at design time, you must do this in code:

```
[VB]
Me.RelationshipType.DataBindings.Add("SelectedValue", myDS, _
    "Relatives.Relationship")
[C#]
this.RelationshipType.DataBindings.Add("SelectedValue", myDS,
    "Relatives.Relationship");
```

Display Full Names in a ComboBox Control

Visual Basic .NET

1. In the form designer, select the Category combo box (cbCategory) on the Controls form.
2. In the Properties window, select the DataSource property.
3. In the drop-down list, select dsMaster1.
4. In the Properties window, select the DisplayMember property.
5. In the drop-down list, expand Categories, and then select CategoryName.
6. In the Properties window, select the ValueMember property.
7. In the drop-down list, expand Categories, and then select CategoryID.
8. Press F7 to open the code editor window.
9. Expand the Region labeled Windows Form Designer generated code.
10. Add the following code after the call to *UpdateDisplay* in the New sub:

    ```
    Me.cbCategory.DataBindings.Add("SelectedValue", Me.dsMaster1, _
        "ProductsExtended.CategoryID")
    ```

    This code binds the ValueMember property of the control to the CategoryID column of the ProductsExtended DataTable.
11. Press F5 to run the application.
12. Click the Controls button.

    The application displays the Controls form and populates the Category combo box.

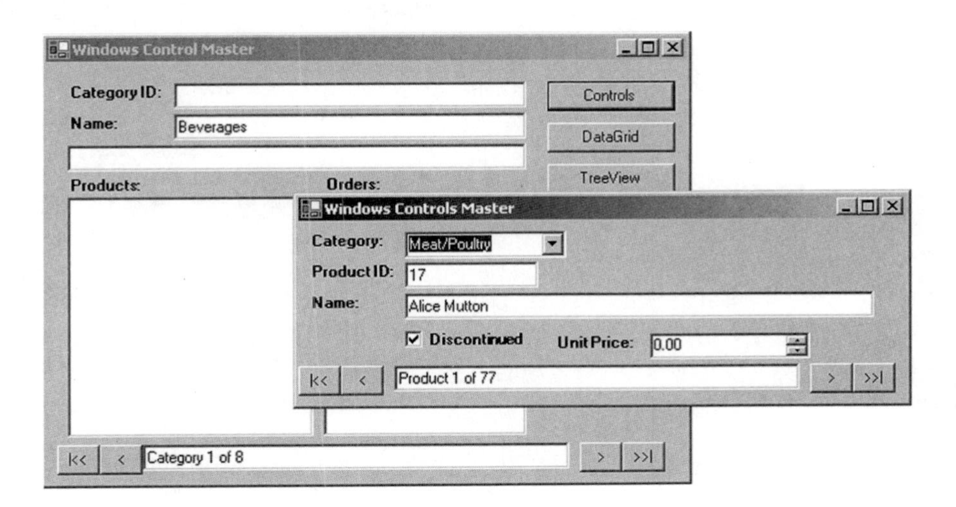

13 Close the Controls form and the application.

Visual C# .NET

1. In the form designer, select the Category combo box (cbCategory) on the Controls form.
2. In the Properties window, select the DataSource property.
3. In the drop-down list, select dsMaster1.
4. In the Properties window, select the DisplayMember property.
5. In the drop-down list, expand Categories, and then select CategoryName.
6. In the Properties window, select the ValueMember property.
7. In the drop-down list, expand Categories, and then select CategoryID.
8. Press F7 to open the code editor window.
9. Add the following code after the call to *UpdateDisplay* in the frmControls sub:

   ```
   this.cbCategory.DataBindings.Add("SelectedValue",
     this.dsMaster1, "ProductsExtended.CategoryID");
   ```

   This code binds the ValueMember property of the control to the CategoryID column of the ProductsExtended DataTable.
10. Press F5 to run the application.
11. Click the Controls button.

    The application displays the Controls form and populates the Category combo box.

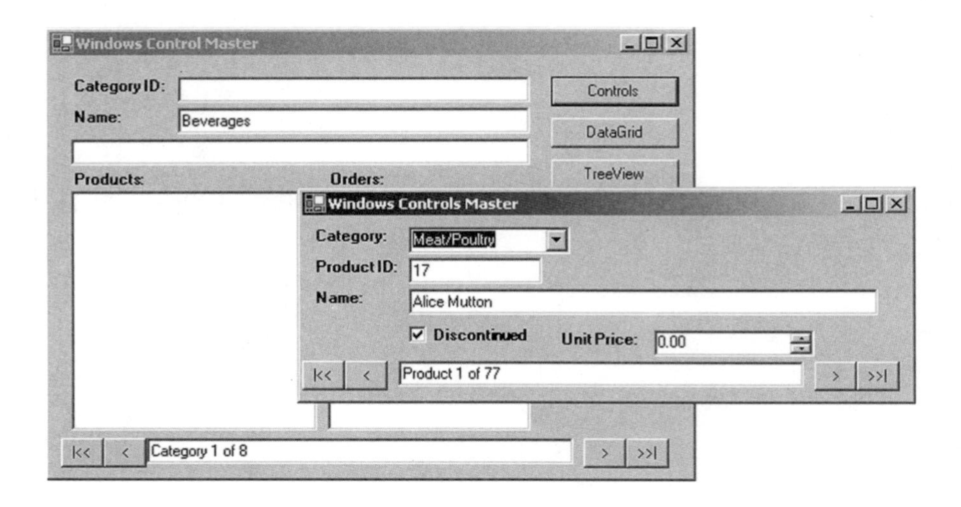

12 Close the Controls form and the application.

Numeric data is presented to the user in a text box. Unfortunately, the .NET Framework version of the control doesn't provide any method to constrain data entry to numeric characters. One option is to use the NumericUpDown control. The user can type directly into this control (numeric characters only) or use the up and down arrows to set the value.

The NumericUpDown control can be simple-bound at design time or at run time by using the standard techniques, and it allows a fine degree of control over the format of the numbers—you can specify the number of decimal places, the increment by which the value changes when the user clicks the up and down arrows, and the minimum and maximum values.

Use NumericUpDown Controls

1. In the form designer, select the UnitPrice NumericUpDown control (udPrice).
2. In the Properties window, expand the Data Bindings section, if necessary, and then select the Value property.
3. In the drop-down list box, expand dsMaster, expand ProductsExtended, and then select UnitPrice.
4. Press F5 to run the application.
5. Click the Controls button.

   The application displays the Controls form and populates the UnitPrice NumericUpDown control.

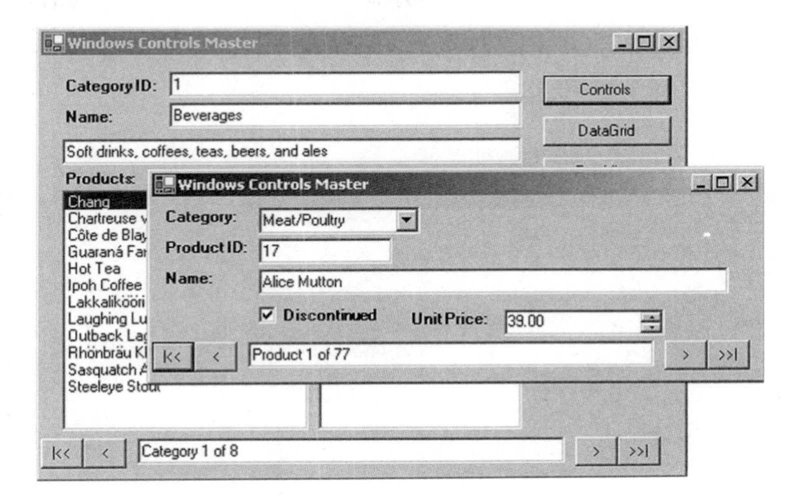

6 Close the Controls form and the application.

7 Close the Controls form designer and code editor.

Working with DataRelations

The data model implemented by ADO.NET, with its ability to specify multiple DataTables and the relationships between them, makes it easy to represent relationships of arbitrary depth on a single form.

By binding the control to a DataRelation rather than to a DataTable, the .NET Framework will automatically handle synchronization of controls on a form.

Create a Nested ListBox

Visual Basic .NET

1 Select the code editor for Master.vb.

2 In the New sub, add the following data bindings below the two commented *AddHandler* calls:

```
Me.lbOrders.DataSource = Me.dsMaster1
Me.lbOrders.DisplayMember = _
   "Categories.CategoriesProducts.ProductOrders.OrderDate"
```

3 Press F5 to run the application.

Visual Studio displays the application's main form and populates the Orders list box.

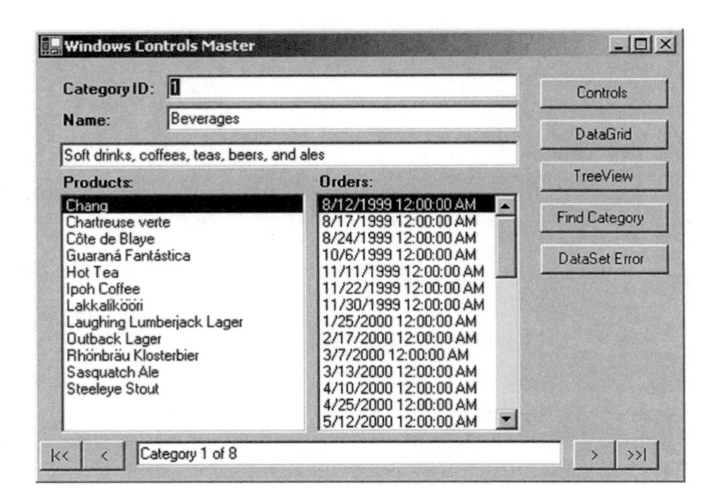

4 Select different products in the Products list box.

The application displays the date on which each Product was ordered.

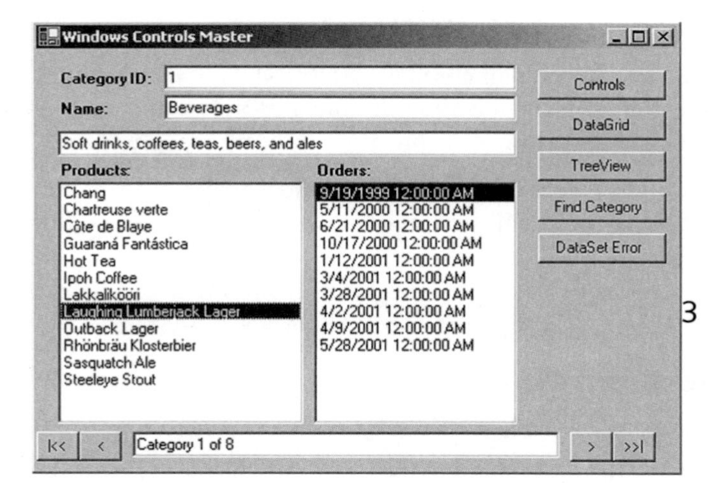

5 Close the application.

Visual C# .NET

1 Select the code editor for Master.cs.

2 In the frmMaster sub, add the following data bindings below the two commented ConvertEventHandlers:

```
this.lbOrders.DataSource = this.dsMaster1;
this.lbOrders.DisplayMember =
   "Categories.CategoriesProducts.ProductOrders.OrderDate";
```

3 Press F5 to run the application.

Visual Studio displays the application's main form and populates the Orders list box.

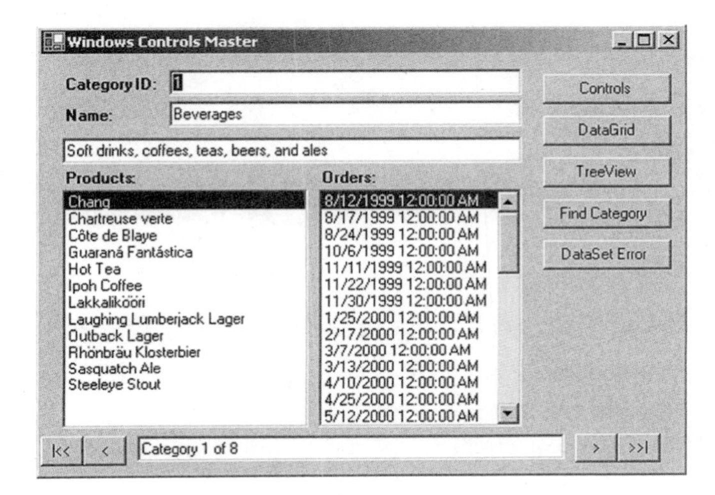

4 Select different products in the Products list box.

The application displays the date on which each Product was ordered.

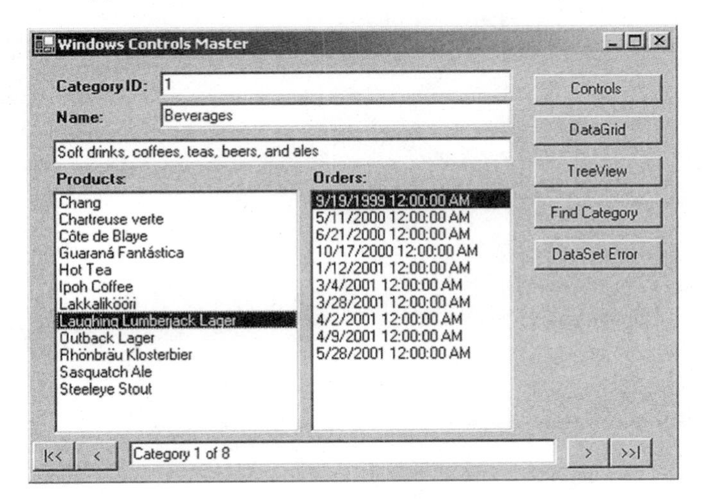

5 Close the application.

In the previous exercise, we used two ListBox controls to represent a hierarchical relationship in the data. The DataGrid control also supports the display of hierarchical data, and it has the advantage of allowing multiple columns from the data source to be displayed simultaneously. Unfortunately, because it can display only a single table at a time, the DataGrid control forces the user to manually navigate the hierarchy and some users find this confusing.

> **note**
>
> The DataGrid is a complex control, and details of its uses are outside the scope of this book. The following exercise walks you through the process of displaying two related DataTables in the DataGrid control. For more information on using this control, refer to the Visual Studio and .NET Framework documentation.

Displaying Hierarchical Data Using the DataGrid

1. In the Solution Explorer, double-click DataGrid.vb (or DataGrid.cs, if you are using C#).

   Visual Studio opens the form in the form designer.

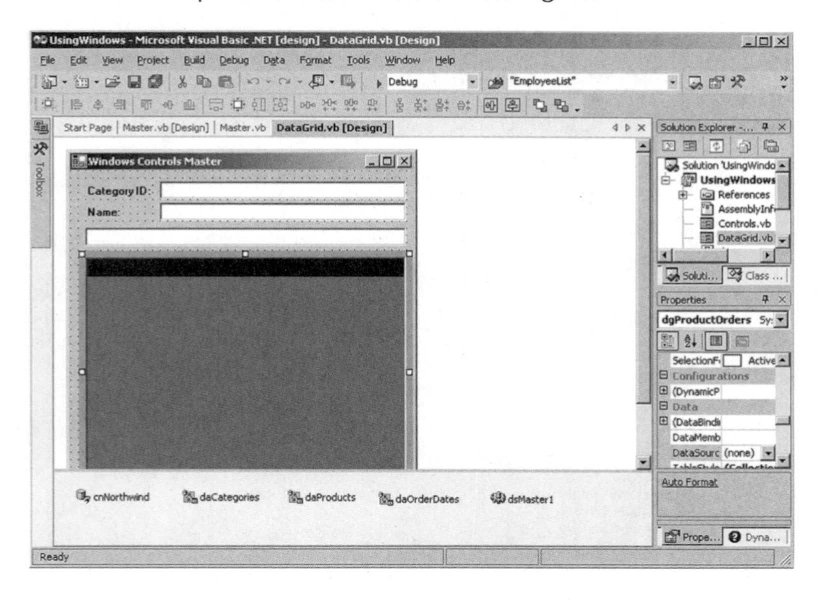

2. Select the dgProductOrders DataGrid.
3. In the Properties window, select the DataSource property, expand the drop-down list, and then select dsMaster1.
4. Select the DataMember property, expand the drop-down list, expand Categories, and then select CategoriesProducts.

5 Click the Ellipsis button after the TableStyles property.

Visual Studio displays the DataGridTableStyle Collection Editor.

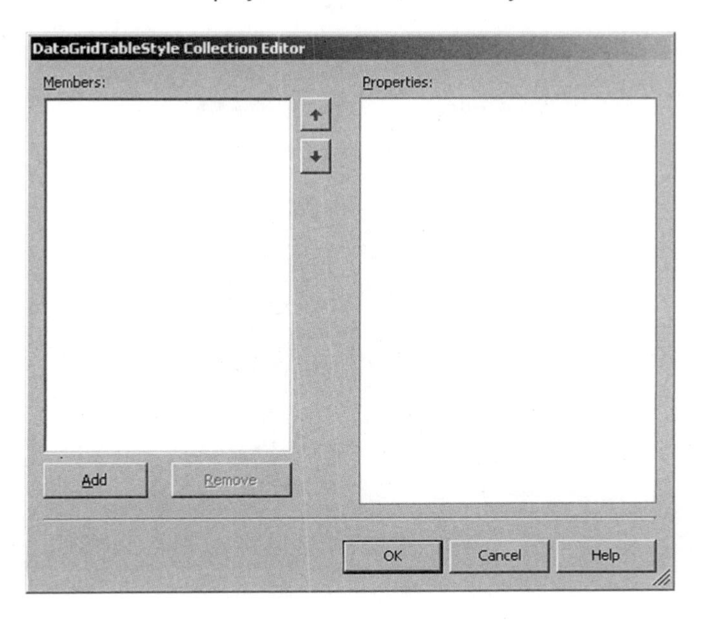

6 Click the Add button.

Visual Studio adds a DataGridTableStyle.

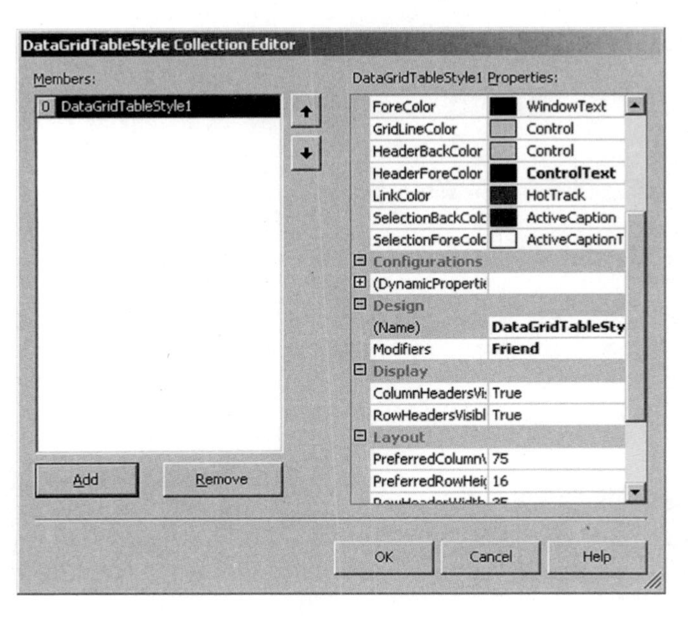

7 Change the Name property of the DataGridTableStyle to tsProducts.

8 Select the MappingName property, expand the drop-down list, expand Categories, and then select CategoriesProducts.

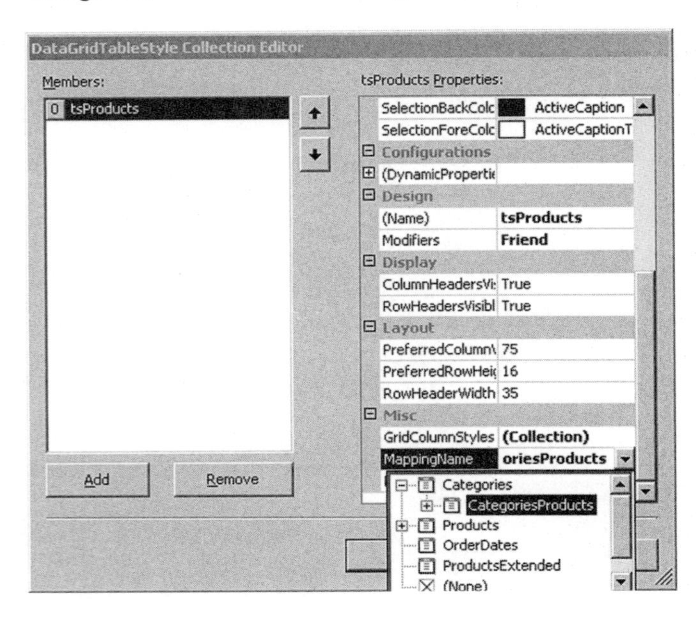

9 Click the Add button again.

Visual Studio adds a second DataGridTableStyle.

10 Change the Name property to tsOrders and the MappingName property to Categories.CategoriesProducts.ProductOrders.

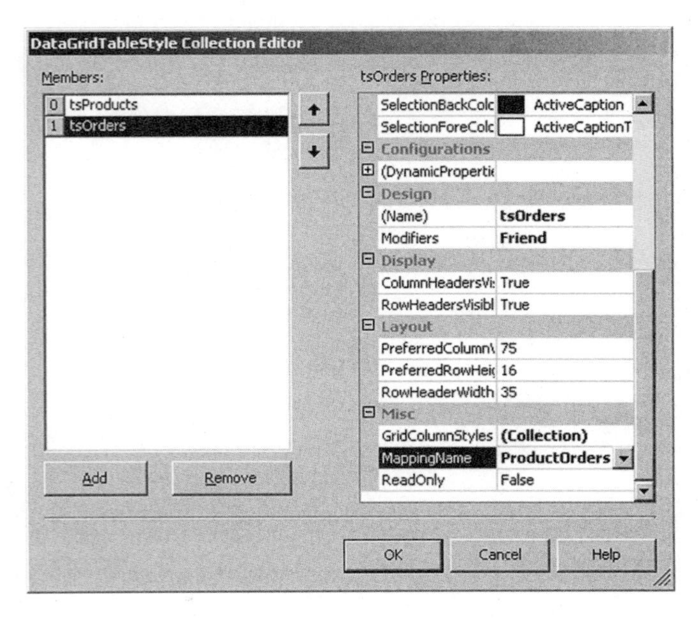

11 Click OK to close the editor.

12 Press F5 to run the application, and then click the DataGrid button.

The application displays the DataGrid form.

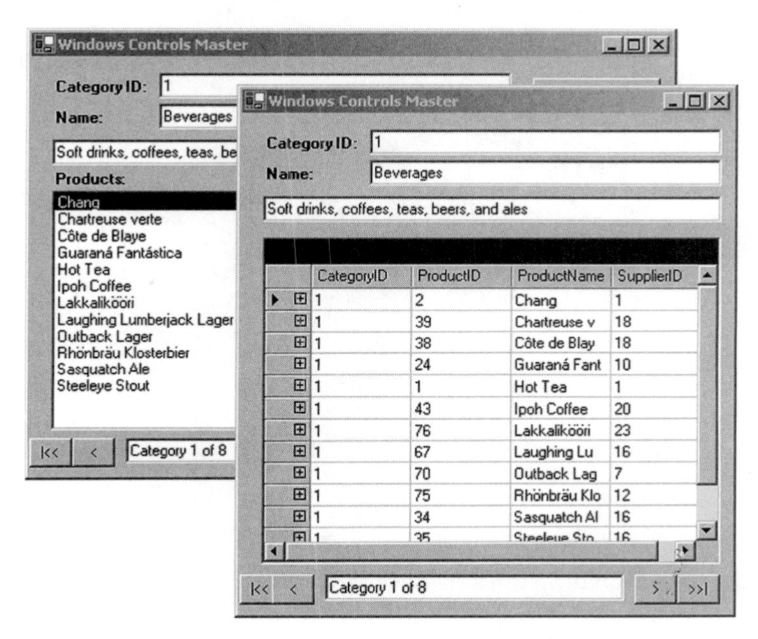

13 Expand one of the rows in the DataGrid.

The application displays the name of the related table.

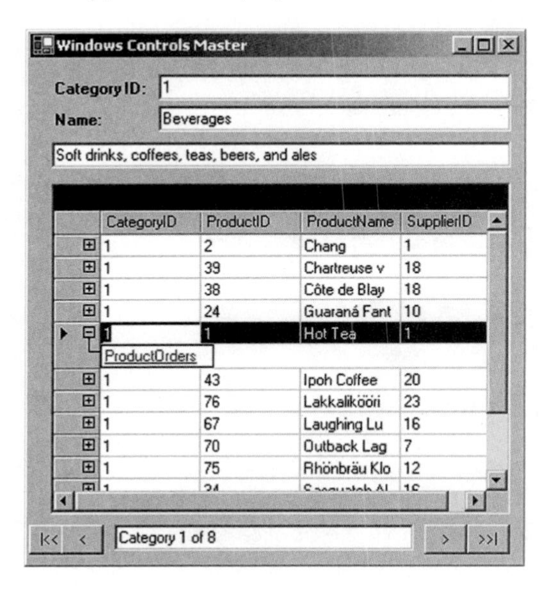

14 Select ProductOrders.

The application displays the selected orders.

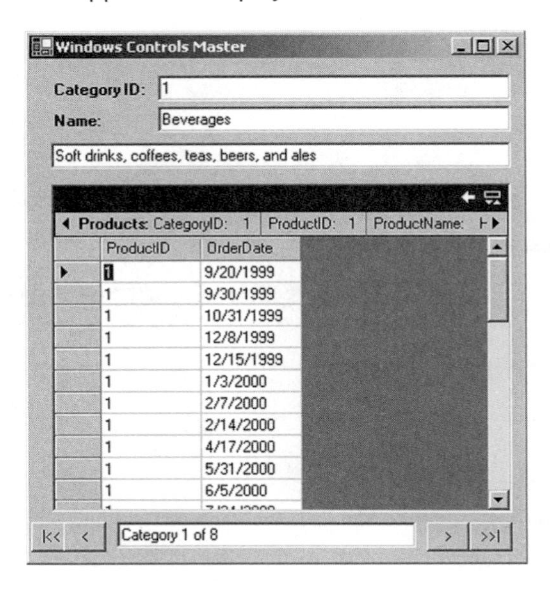

15 Click the Back button.

The application returns to the Products display.

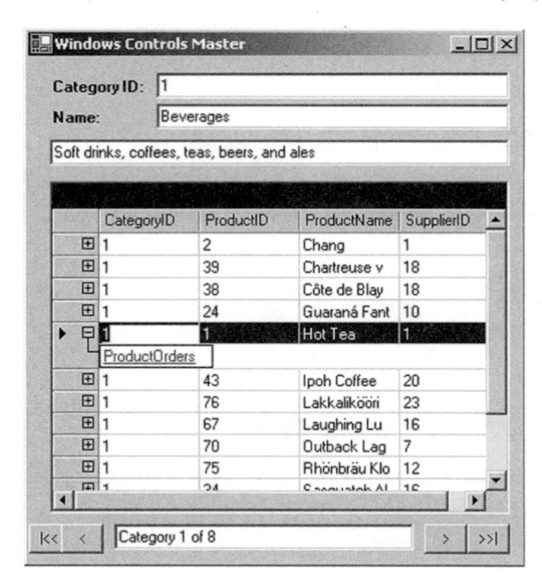

16 Close the window, and close the application.

17 Close the DataGrid.vb (or DataGrid.cs, if you're using C#) form.

The DataGrid control is fairly easy to bind to multiple DataTables, but because it can display only a single table at any time, it can be confusing for the user. The TreeView control can also represent hierarchical data, and it does so in a way that often matches the user's expectations more closely.

Unfortunately, the TreeView control can't be directly bound to a data source. Instead, you must manually add the data by using the *Add* method of its Nodes collections. The following exercise walks you through the process.

Displaying Hierarchical Data Using the TreeView

Visual Basic .NET

1 In the Solution Explorer, double-click TreeView.vb.

Visual Studio displays the form in the form designer.

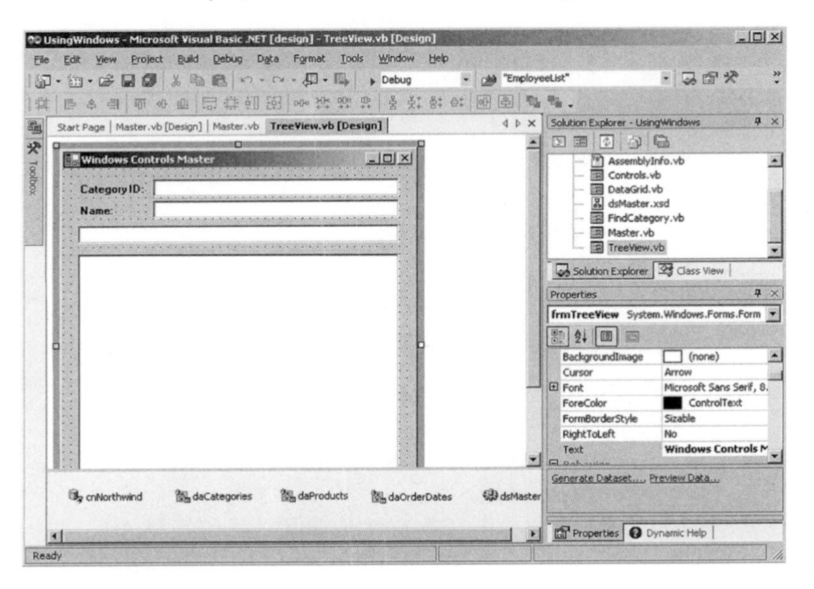

2 Press F7 to display the code editor.

3 Add the following procedure to the bottom of the code editor:

```
Private Sub AddNodes(ByVal sender As Object, ByVal e As EventArgs)
    Dim dvCategory As System.Data.DataRowView
    Dim arrProducts() As System.Data.DataRow
    Dim currProduct As dsMaster.ProductsRow
    Dim arrOrders() As System.Data.DataRow
```

(continued)

(continued)

```
        Dim currOrder As dsMaster.OrderDatesRow
        Dim root As System.Windows.Forms.TreeNode
        With Me.tvProductOrders
            .BeginUpdate()
            .Nodes.Clear()

            dvCategory = _
               Me.BindingContext(Me.dsMaster1, "Categories").Current
            arrProducts = _
               dvCategory.Row.GetChildRows("CategoriesProducts")
            For Each currProduct In arrProducts
               root = .Nodes.Add(currProduct.ProductName)
               arrOrders = currProduct.GetChildRows("ProductOrders")


               For Each currOrder In arrOrders
                   root.Nodes.Add(currOrder.OrderDate)
               Next
            Next currProduct

            .EndUpdate()
        End With
    End Sub
```

4. Expand the Region labeled Windows Form Designer generated code.
5. Add the following code below the call to *UpdateDisplay* in the New sub:

```
AddHandler Me.BindingContext(Me.dsMaster1, _
   "Categories").PositionChanged, AddressOf _
   Me.AddNodes
AddNodes(Me, New System.EventArgs())
```

   The first line links the AddNodes procedure to the PositionChanged event so that it will be called each time the Category changes. The second line calls the procedure directly to set up the initial display.
6. Press F5 to run the application, and then click the TreeView button.

   Visual Studio displays the TreeView form.

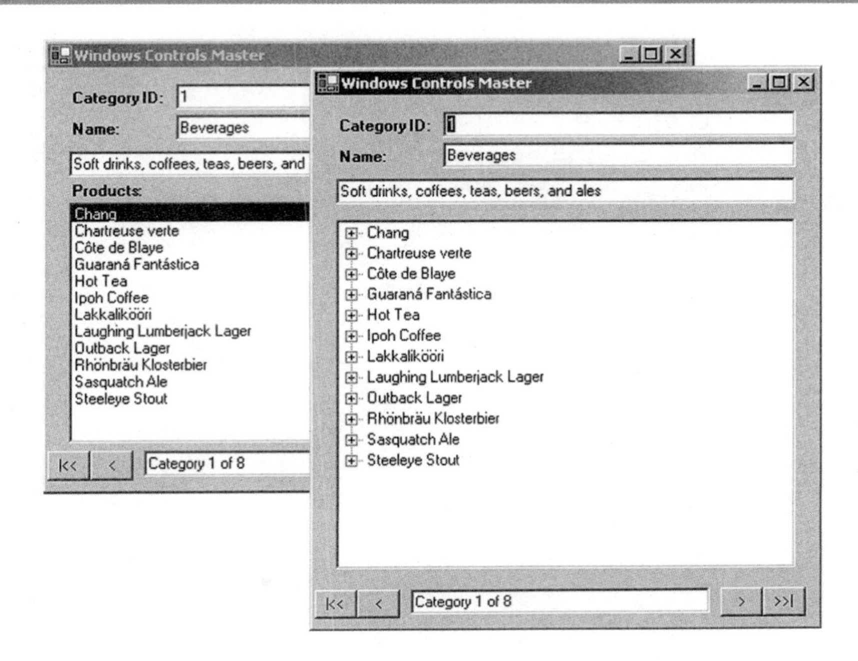

7 Verify that the TreeView is updated correctly by clicking the Next button (">") and expanding nodes.

8 Close the TreeView form and the application.

9 Close the TreeView form designer and code editor.

Visual C# .NET

1 In the Solution Explorer, double-click TreeView.cs.

Visual Studio displays the form in the form designer.

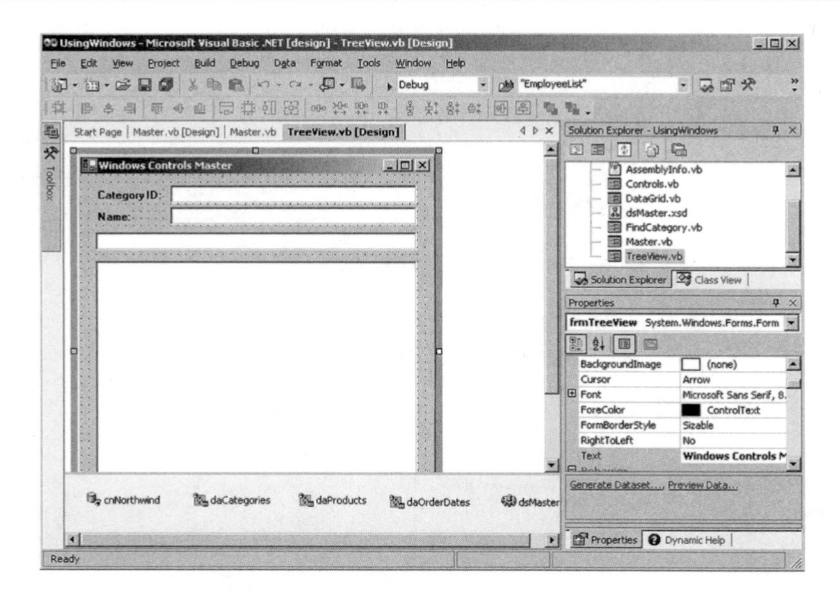

2 Press F7 to display the code editor.

3 Add the following procedure to the bottom of the code editor:

```
private void AddNodes(object sender, System.EventArgs e)
{
   System.Data.DataRowView dvCategory;
   System.Data.DataRow[] arrProducts;
   System.Data.DataRow[] arrOrders;
   System.Windows.Forms.TreeNode root;
   System.Windows.Forms.TreeView tv;

   tv = this.tvProductOrders;

   tv.BeginUpdate();
   tv.Nodes.Clear();

   dvCategory = (System.Data.DataRowView)
      this.BindingContext[this.dsMaster1, "Categories"].Current;
   arrProducts = dvCategory.Row.GetChildRows("CategoriesProducts");
   foreach (dsMaster.ProductsRow currProduct in arrProducts)
   {
         root = tv.Nodes.Add(currProduct.ProductName);
         arrOrders = currProduct.GetChildRows("ProductOrders");
         foreach (dsMaster.OrderDatesRow currOrder in arrOrders)
```

```
            {
                root.Nodes.Add(currOrder.OrderDate.ToString());
            }
        }
        tv.EndUpdate();
    }
```

4. Add the following code below the call to *UpdateDisplay* in the frmTreeView sub:

```
this.BindingContext[this.dsMaster1, "Categories"].PositionChanged +=
    new EventHandler(this.AddNodes);
System.EventArgs ea;
ea = new System.EventArgs();
AddNodes(this, ea);
```

   The first line links the AddNodes procedure to the PositionChanged event so that it will be called each time the Category changes. The remaining lines call the procedure directly to set up the initial display.

5. Press F5 to run the application, and then click the TreeView button.

   Visual Studio displays the TreeView form.

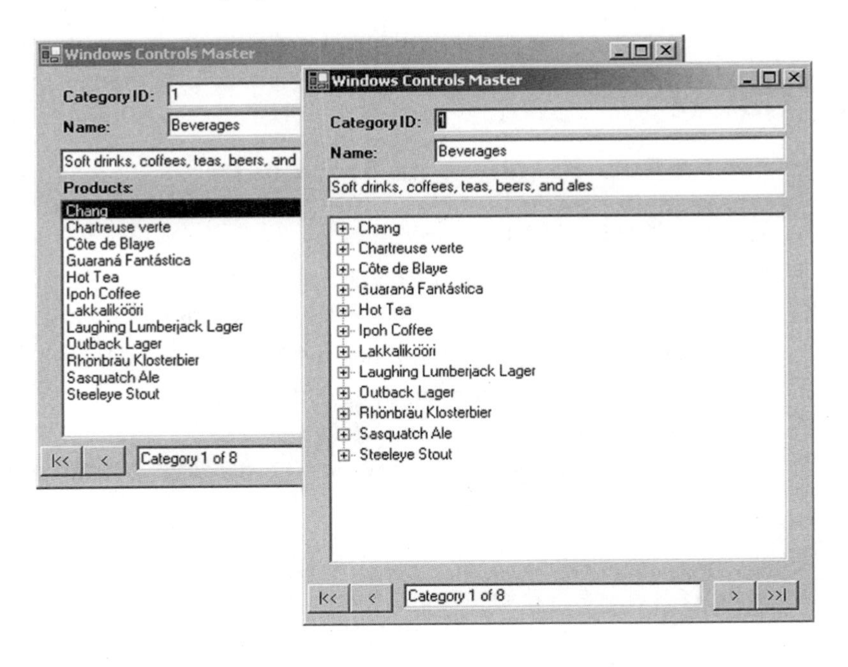

6. Verify that the TreeView is updated correctly by clicking the Next button (">") and expanding nodes.

7 Close the TreeView form and the application.

8 Close the TreeView form designer and code editor.

Finding Data

Finding a specific row in a DataTable is a common application task. Unfortunately, the BindingContext object, which controls the data displayed by the controls on a form, doesn't directly support a *Find* method. Instead, you must use either a DataView object to find a row based on the current Sort key or use a DataTable object to find a row based on more complex criteria.

Finding Sorted Rows

Using the DataView's *Find* method is straightforward, but it can be used only to find a row based on the row(s) currently specified in the Sort property. If your controls are bound to a DataView, you can reference the object directly. If you bound the controls to a DataTable, you can use the DefaultView property to obtain a reference without creating a new object.

Once you have a reference to a DataView, you can use the *Find* method, which returns the index of the row matching the specified criteria or -1 if no matching row is found. The index of the row in the DataView will correspond directly to the same row's index in the BindingContext object, so it's a simple matter of setting the BindingContext.Position property to the value that is returned.

Find a Row Based on Its Sort Column

Visual Basic .NET

1 In the code editor for Master.vb, select btnFindCategory in the Control Name combo box, and then select Click in the Event combo box.

   Visual Studio adds an event handler to the code editor.

2 Add the following code to the event handler:

```
Dim fcForm As New frmFindCategory()
Dim dv As System.Data.DataView = Me.dsMaster1.Categories.DefaultView
Dim id As Integer
Dim idx As Integer

If fcForm.ShowDialog() = DialogResult.OK Then
    If fcForm.GetID = 0 Then
```

```
    Else
        id = fcForm.GetID
        idx = dv.Find(id)
        If idx = -1 Then
          MessageBox.Show("Category " + id.ToString + " not found",
              _ "Error")
        Else
          Me.BindingContext(Me.dsMaster1, _
              "Categories").Position = idx
        End If
    End If
End If
fcForm.Dispose()
```

After declaring some variables and calling fcForm as a dialog box, the code sets up an *if … else* statement to handle the two possible search criteria. (We'll complete the first section of the *if* statement in the following exercise.)

The variable id is set to the value of the *GetID* field on fcForm, and then the code uses the *Find* method to locate the index of the row containing that field. *Find* returns -1 if the row is not found, in which case the code displays an error message. If the row is found, it is displayed in the Master form by setting the BindingContext.Position property.

3 Press F5 to run the application, and click the Find Category button.

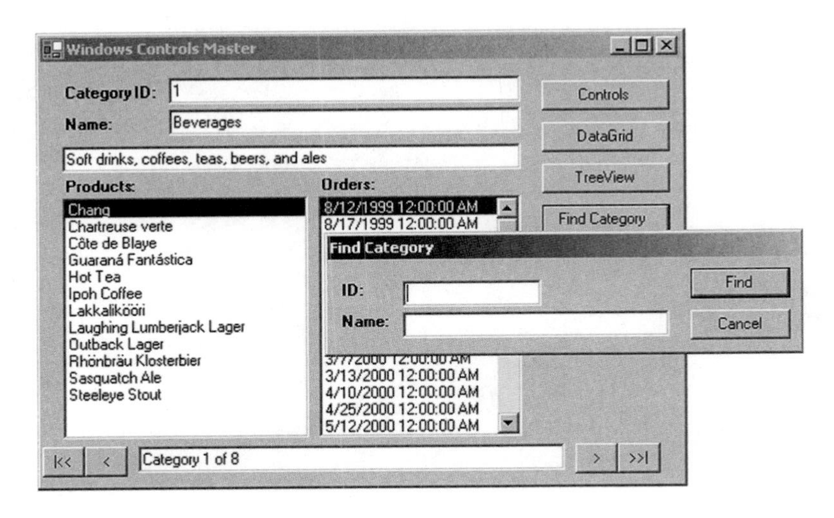

4 Type **3** in the *ID* field, and then click Find.

The application displays Category 3 on the Master form.

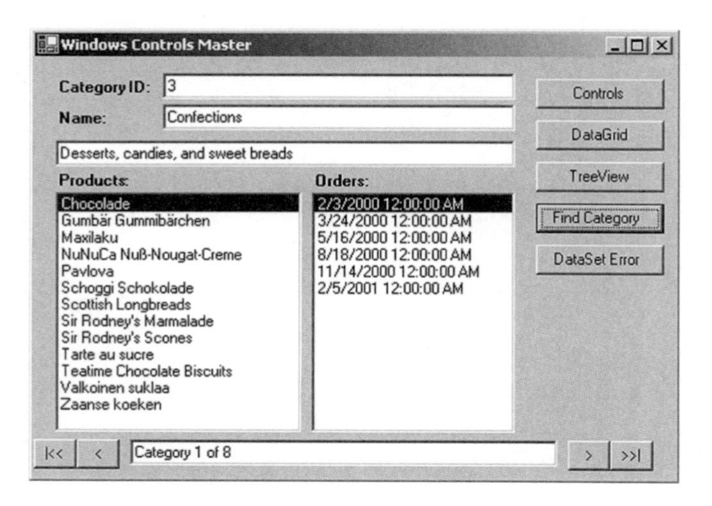

5 Close the application.

Visual C# .NET

1 In the form designer, double-click the btnFindCategory button on the Master form.

Visual Studio adds an event handler to the code editor.

2 Add the following code to the event handler:

```
frmFindCategory fcForm = new frmFindCategory();
System.Data.DataView dv = this.dsMaster1.Categories.DefaultView;
int id;
int idx;

if (fcForm.ShowDialog() == DialogResult.OK)
   if (fcForm.GetID == 0)
   {
   }
   else
   {
          id = fcForm.GetID;
          idx = dv.Find(id);
          if (idx == -1)
             MessageBox.Show("Category " + id.ToString(), "Error");
          else
             this.BindingContext[this.dsMaster1,
                "Categories"].Position = idx;
   }
fcForm.Dispose();
```

After declaring some variables and calling fcForm as a dialog box, the code sets up an *if … else* statement to handle the two possible search criteria. (We'll complete the first section of the *if* statement in the following exercise.)

The variable id is set to the value of the *GetID* field on fcForm, and then the code uses the *Find* method to locate the index of the row containing that field. *Find* returns -1 if the row is not found, in which case the code displays an error message. If the row is found, it is displayed in the Master form by setting the BindingContext.Position property.

3 Press F5 to run the application, and click the Find Category button.

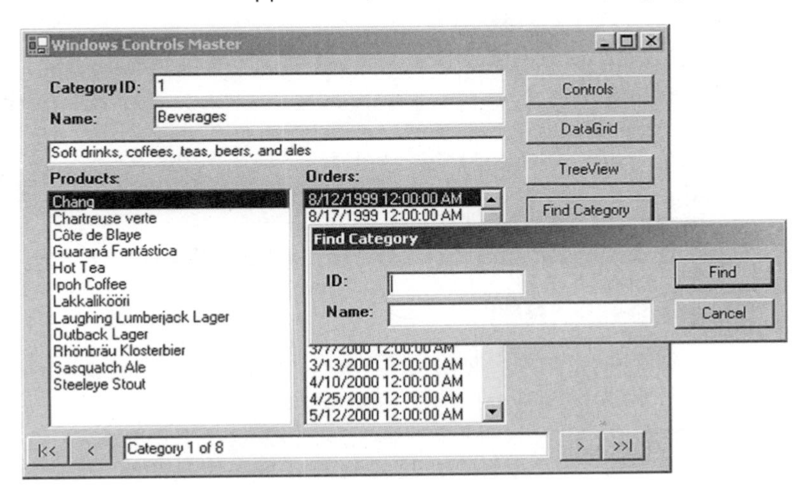

4 Type **3** in the *ID* field, and then click Find.

The application displays Category 3 on the Master form.

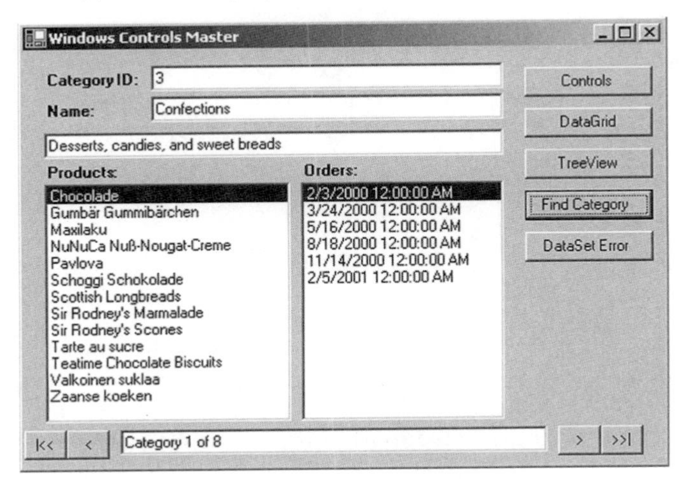

5 Close the application.

Finding Rows Based on Other Criteria

The DataView object's *Find* method is easy to use but limited in scope. If you need to find a row based on complex criteria, or on a single column other than the one on which the data is sorted, you must use the DataTable's *Select* method.

As we saw in Chapter 7, the *Select* method is easy to use, but positioning the CurrencyManager to the correct row requires several steps. The process requires using both the DataView and the DataTable object to perform the search, along with the BindingContext object to display the results. In truth, the whole process is decidedly awkward, but you'll learn the steps by rote soon enough.

First you must execute the *Select* method with the required criteria against the DataTable. Once the appropriate row is found, you obtain the Sort column value from the array returned by the *Select* method and use that to perform a *Find* against the DataView. Finally, you use the Position property of the BindingContext to display the result.

Find a Row Based on an Unsorted Column

Visual Basic .NET

1. Add the following code after the line *If fcForm.GetID = 0* in the *btnFindCategory_Click* procedure we began in the previous exercise:

```
Dim name As String
Dim dt As System.Data.DataTable = Me.dsMaster1.Categories
Dim dr() As System.Data.DataRow

name = fcForm.GetName

Try
   dr = dt.Select("CategoryName = '" & name & "'")
   id = CType(dr(0), dsMaster.CategoriesRow).CategoryID
   idx = dv.Find(id)
   Me.BindingContext(Me.dsMaster1, "Categories").Position = idx
Catch
   MessageBox.Show("Category " + name + " not found", "Error")
End Try
```

This code uses the DataTable's *Select* method to find the specified category name. *Select* returns an array of rows, so the second line uses the CType function to convert the first row of the array3—*dr(0)*—to a CategoriesRow, and sets id to the CategoryID. It then finds the CategoryID in the

DataView and positions the Master form to the row by using the BindingContext.Position property by using the same code from the previous exercise.

2 Press F5 to run the application, and then click the Find Category button.

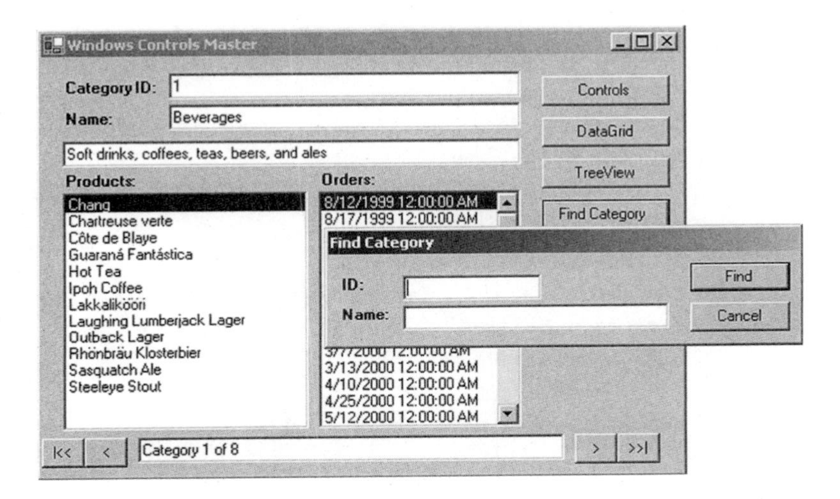

3 Type **Condiments** in the *Name* field, and then click Find.

The application displays the Condiments category in the Master form.

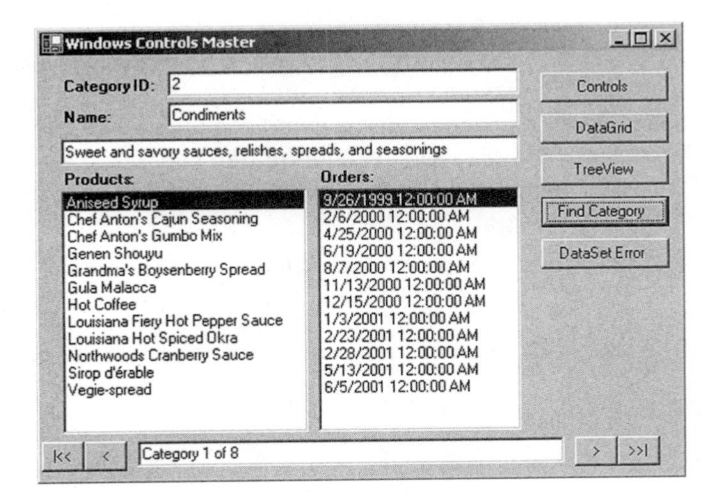

4 Close the application.

Visual C# .NET

1. Add the following code after the line *If (fcForm.GetID == 0)* in the *btnFindCategory_Click* procedure we began in the previous exercise:

```
string name;
System.Data.DataTable dt = this.dsMaster1.Categories;
dsMaster.CategoriesRow cr;
System.Data.DataRow[] dr;

name = fcForm.GetName;

try
{
   dr = dt.Select("CategoryName = '" + name + "'");
   cr = (dsMaster.CategoriesRow) dr[0];
   id = cr.CategoryID;
   idx = dv.Find(id);
   this.BindingContext[this.dsMaster1, "Categories"].Position = idx;
}
catch
{
   MessageBox.Show("Category " + name + " not found", "Error");
}
```

   This code uses the DataTable's *Select* method to find the specified category name. *Select* returns an array of rows, so the second line uses the CType function to convert the first row of the array—*dr(0)*—to a CategoriesRow, and sets id to the CategoryID. It then finds the CategoryID in the DataView and positions the Master form to the row by using the BindingContext.Position property by using the same code from the previous exercise.

2. Press F5 to run the application, and then click the Find Category button.

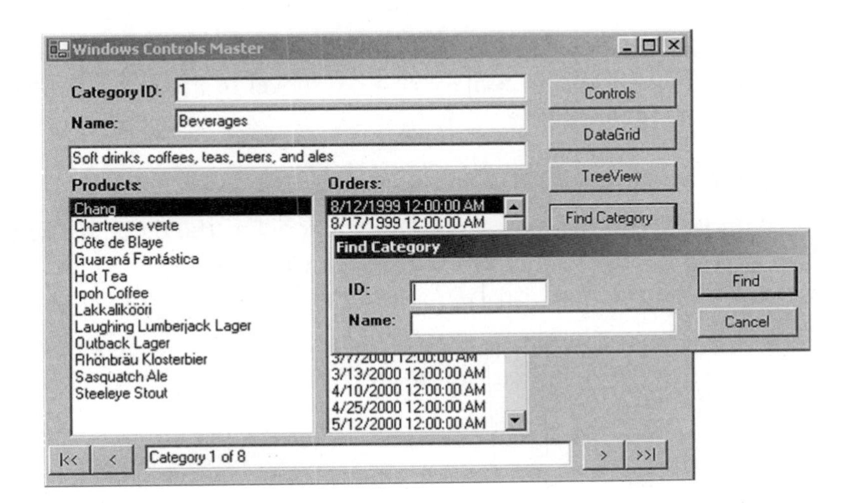

3 Type **Condiments** in the *Name* field, and then click Find.

The application displays the Condiments category in the Master form.

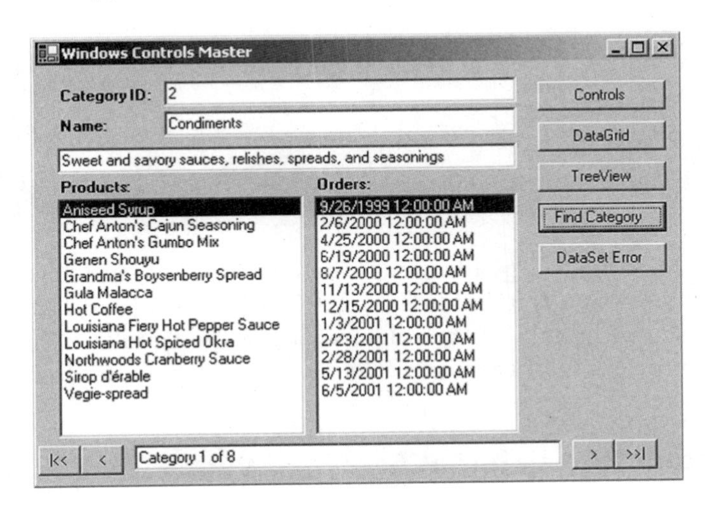

4 Close the application.

Validating Data in Windows Forms

The .NET Framework supports a number of techniques for validating data entry prior to submitting it to a data source. First, as we've already seen, is the use of controls that constrain the data entry to appropriate values.

After the data has been entered, the .NET Framework exposes a series of events at both the control and data level to allow you to trap and manage problems.

Data Change Events

Data validation is most often implemented at the data source level. This tends to be more efficient because the validation will occur regardless of which control or controls are used to change the data.

As we saw in Chapter 7, the DataTable object exposes six events that can be used for data validation. In order of occurrence, they are:

- ColumnChanging
- ColumnChanged
- RowChanging
- RowChanged
- RowDeleting
- RowDeleted

> **note**
> If a row is being deleted, only the RowDeleting and RowDeleted events occur.

If you are using a Typed DataSet, you can create separate event handlers for each column in a DataTable. If you're using an Untyped DataSet, a single event handler must handle all the columns in a single DataRow. You can use the Column property of the *DataColumnChangeArgs* parameter, which is passed to the event to determine which column is being changed.

Respond to a ColumnChanging Event

Visual Basic .NET

1 Add the following procedure to the bottom of the code editor:

```
Private Sub Categories_ColumnChanging(ByVal sender As Object, _
    ByVal e As DataColumnChangeEventArgs)
        Dim str As String

        str = "Column:  " & e.Column.ColumnName.ToString
        str += vbCrLf + "New Value:  " & e.ProposedValue
        MessageBox.Show(str, "Column Changing")
End Sub
```

2 Add the following event handler to the end of the New sub:

```
AddHandler dsMaster1.Categories.ColumnChanging, AddressOf _
   Me.Categories_ColumnChanging
```

3 Press F5 to run the application.

4 Change the Category Name to Beverages New, and then click the Next button (">").

The application displays the column name and new value in a message box.

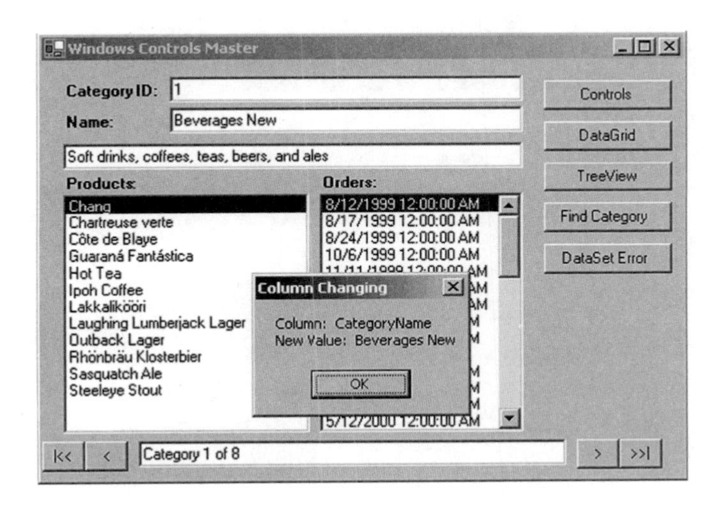

5 Close the message box, and then close the application.

6 Comment out the ColumnChanging event handler in the New sub.

Visual C# .NET

1 Add the following procedure to the class file:

```
private void Categories_ColumnChanging(object
   sender, DataColumnChangeEventArgs e)
{
   string str;

   str = "Column:  " + e.Column.ColumnName.ToString();
   str += "\nNew Value:  " + e.ProposedValue;
   MessageBox.Show(str, "Column Changing");
}
```

2 Add the following event handler to the end of the frmMaster sub:

```
this.dsMaster1.Categories.ColumnChanging +=
   new DataColumnChangeEventHandler(this.Categories_ColumnChanging);
```

3 Press F5 to run the application.

4 Change the Category Name to Beverages New, and then click the Next button (">").

The application displays the column name and new value in a message box.

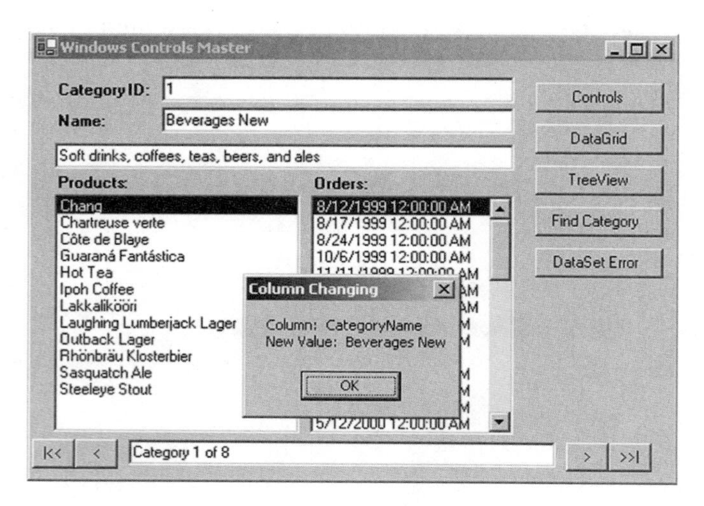

5 Close the message box, and then close the application.

6 Comment out the event handler in the frmMaster sub.

The column change events are typically used for validating discrete values—for example, if the value is within a specified range or has the correct format. For data validation that relies on multiple column values, you can use the row change events.

Respond to a RowChanging Event

Visual Basic .NET

1 Add the following procedure to the code editor:

```
Private Sub Categories_RowChanging(ByVal sender As Object, _
   ByVal e As DataRowChangeEventArgs)
      Dim str As String

      str = "Action:  " & e.Action.ToString
      str += vbCrLf + "ID:  " & e.Row("CategoryID")
      MessageBox.Show(str, "Row Changing")
End Sub
```

2 Add the following code to the end of the New sub:

```
AddHandler dsMaster1.Categories.RowChanging, AddressOf _
    Me.Categories_RowChanging
```

3 Press F5 to run the application.

4 Change the Category Name to New, and then click Next button (">"). Close the Column Changing message.

The application displays the Action and Category ID.

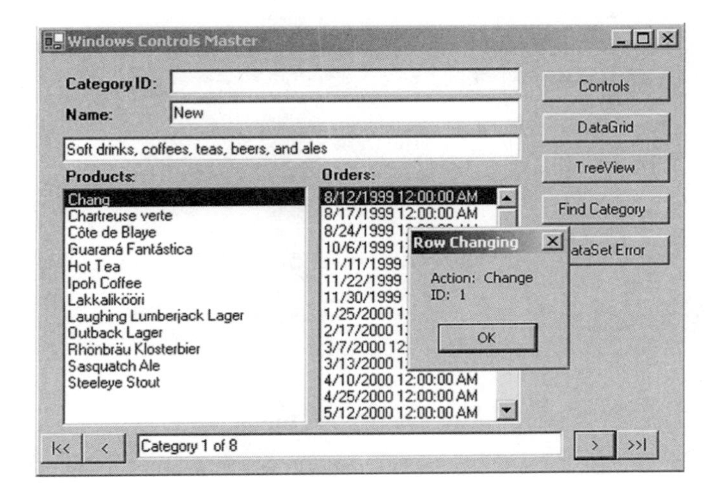

5 Close the message, and then close the application.

6 Comment out the RowChanging event handlers in the New sub.

Visual C# .NET

1 Add the following procedure to the code editor:

```
private void Categories_RowChanging(object sender,
    DataRowChangeEventArgs e)
{
    string str;

    str = "Action:  " + e.Action.ToString();
    str += "\nID:  " + e.Row["CategoryID"];
    MessageBox.Show(str, "Row Changing");
}
```

2 Add the following code to the end of the frmMaster sub:

```
this.dsMaster1.Categories.RowChanging += new
    DataRowChangeEventHandler(this.Categories_RowChanging);
```

3. Press F5 to run the application.
4. Change the Category Name to New, and then click Next button (">"). Close the Column Changing message.

   The application displays the Action and Category ID.

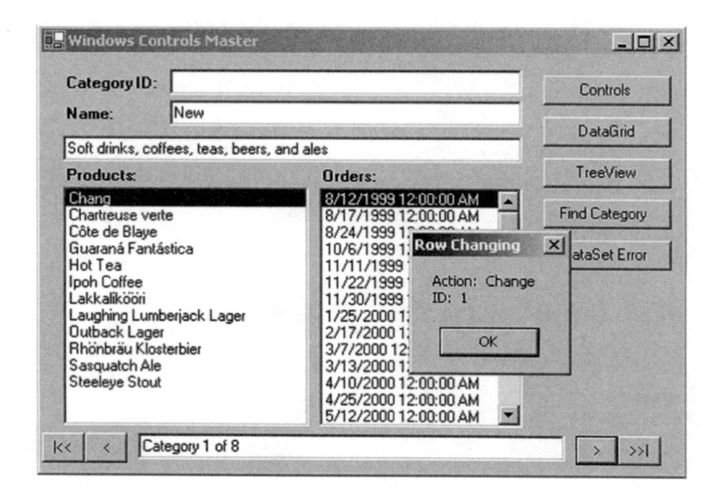

5. Close the message, and then close the application.
6. Comment out the ColumnChanging event handler in the frmMaster sub.

Control Validation Events

In addition to the DataTable events, data validation can also be triggered by individual controls. Every control supports the following events, in order:

- Enter
- GotFocus
- Leave
- Validating
- Validated
- LostFocus

In addition, the CurrencyManager object supports the ItemChanged event, which is triggered before a new row becomes current.

Respond to an ItemChanged Event

Visual Basic .NET

1 Add the following procedure to the code editor:

```
Private Sub Categories_ItemChanged(ByVal sender As Object, _
   ByVal e As ItemChangedEventArgs)
      Dim str As String

      str = "Index into CurrencyManager List:  " & e.Index.ToString
      MessageBox.Show(str, "Item Changed")
End Sub
```

2 Add the following code to the end of the New sub:

```
AddHandler CType(Me.BindingContext(Me.dsMaster1, "Categories"), _
   CurrencyManager).ItemChanged, AddressOf Me.Categories_ItemChanged
```

3 Press F5 to run the application.

4 Delete the category description, and then click the Next button (">").

The application displays the index of the row that has been changed.

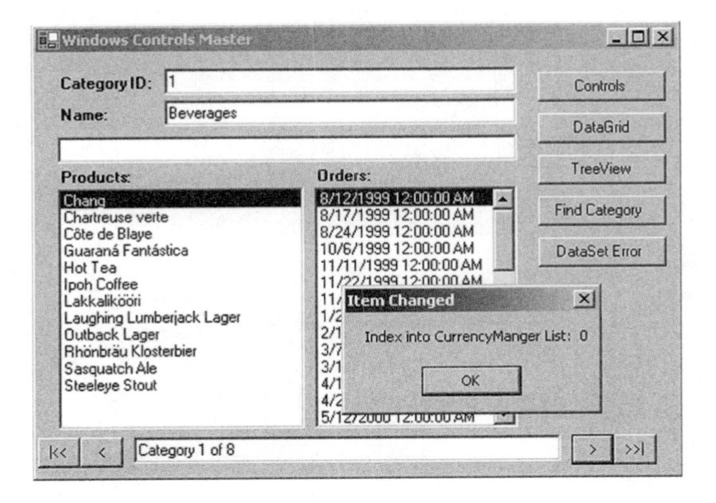

5 Close the message box, and then close the application.

6 Comment out the event handler in the New sub.

Visual C# .NET

1. Add the following procedure to the code editor:

```
private void Categories_ItemChanged(object sender,
   ItemChangedEventArgs e)
{
   string str;

   str = "Index into CurrencyManager List:  " + e.Index.ToString();
   MessageBox.Show(str, "Item Changed");
}
```

2. Add the following lines to the end of the frmMaster sub:

```
CurrencyManager cm = (CurrencyManager)
   this.BindingContext[this.dsMaster1, "Categories"];
cm.ItemChanged += new
   ItemChangedEventHandler(this.Categories_ItemChanged);
```

3. Press F5 to run the application.
4. Delete the category description, and then click the Next button (">").

   The application displays the index of the row that has been changed.

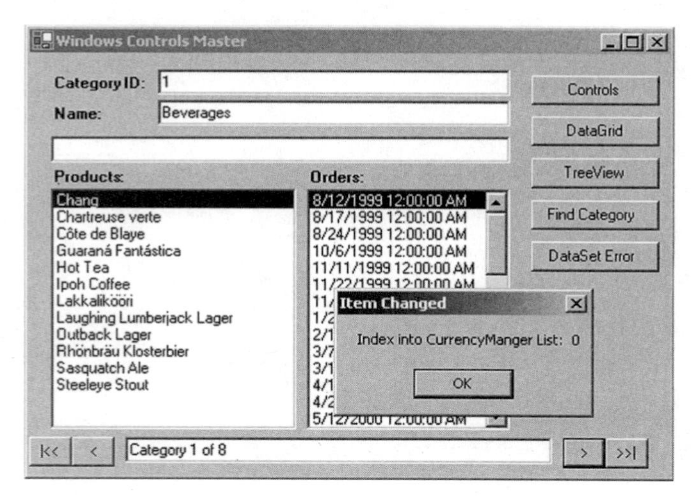

5. Close the message box, and then close the application.
6. Comment out the event handler in the New sub.

For purposes of data validation, the Validating and Validated events roughly correspond to the ColumnChanging and ColumnChanged events, but they have the advantage of occurring as soon as the user leaves the control, rather than when the BindingContext object is repositioned.

Respond to a Validating Event

Visual Basic .NET

1. In the code editor, select tbCategoryName in the Control Name combo box, and then select Validating in the Method combo box.

   Visual Studio adds the event handler template to the code editor.

2. Add the following code to the procedure:

```
If Me.tbCategoryName.Text = "Cancel" Then
   MessageBox.Show("Change the Name from 'Cancel'", "Validating")
   e.Cancel = True
End If
```

3. Press F5 to run the application.
4. Change the Category Name to Cancel, and then click the Next button (">").

   The application cancels the change and redisplays the original row.

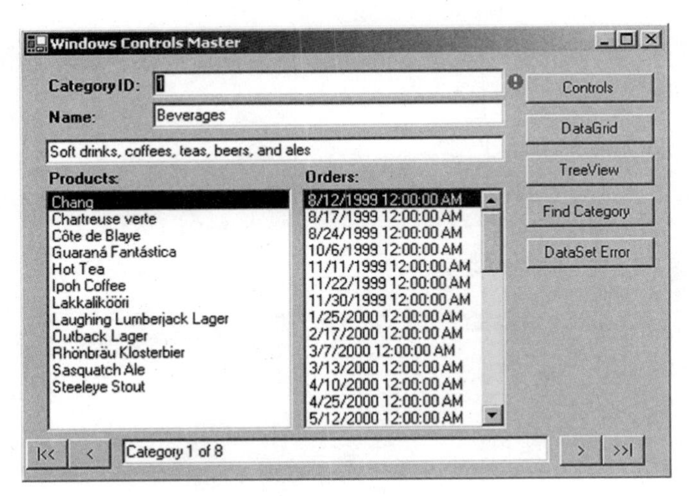

5. Close the application.

Visual C# .NET

1 Add the following procedure to the class file:

```
private void Categories_Validating(object sender, CancelEventArgs e)
{
   if (this.tbCategoryName.Text == "Cancel")
   {
      MessageBox.Show("Change the Name from 'Cancel'",
         "Validating");
      e.Cancel = true;
   }
}
```

2 Add the following lines to the frmMaster sub:

```
this.tbCategoryName.Validating +=
   new CancelEventHandler(this.Categories_Validating);
```

3 Press F5 to run the application.

4 Change the Category Name to Cancel, and then click the Next button (">").

The application cancels the change.

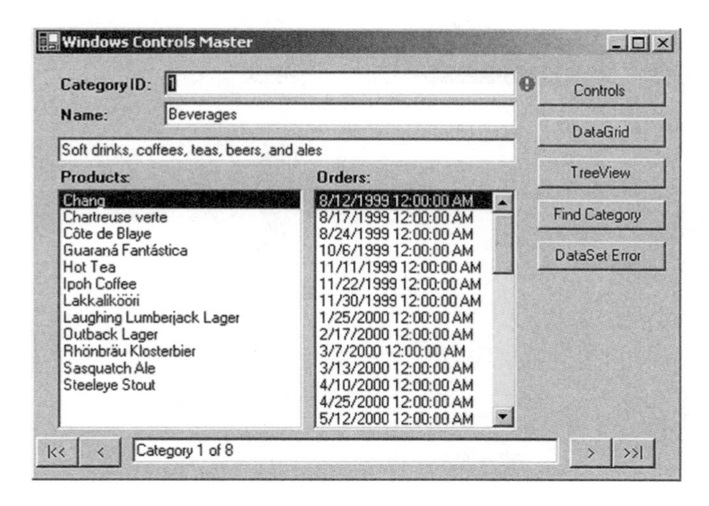

5 Close the application.

Using the ErrorProvider Component

In the previous exercises, we've used MessageBox controls in response to data validation errors. This is a common technique, but it's not a very good one from a usability standpoint. MessageBox controls are disruptive, and after they are dismissed, the error information contained in them also disappears.

Fortunately, the .NET Framework provides a much better mechanism for displaying errors to the user: the ErrorProvider component. The ErrorProvider, which can be bound to either a specific control or a data source object, displays an error icon next to the appropriate control. If the user places the mouse pointer over the icon, a ToolTip will display the specified error message.

Use an ErrorProvider with a Form Control

Visual Basic .NET

1. In the code editor, select tbCategoryID in the Control Name combo box, and then select Validating in the Method Name combo box.

   Visual Studio adds the event handler template to the code editor.

2. Add the following code to the event handler:

```
If Me.tbCategoryID.Text = "Error" Then
   Me.epControl.SetError(Me.tbCategoryID, _
       "Please re-enter the CategoryID")
   e.Cancel = True
Else
   Me.epControl.SetError(Me.tbCategoryID, "")
End If
```

3. Press F5 to run the application.
4. Change the CategoryID to Error, and then click the Next button (">").

   The application displays a blinking error icon after the CategoryID control.

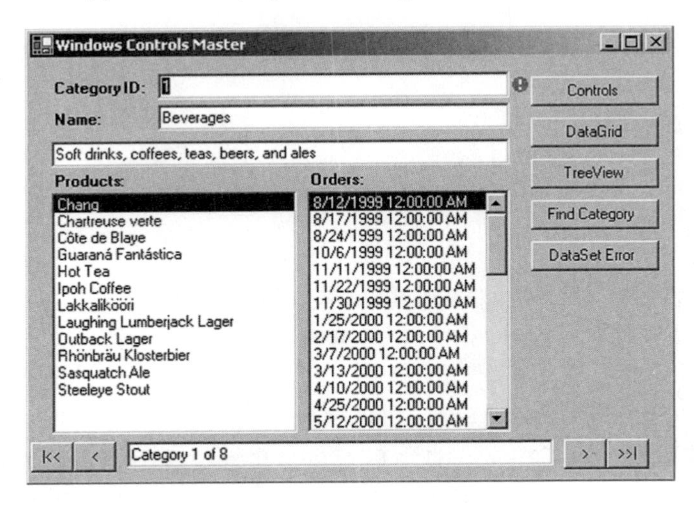

5. Place the mouse pointer over the icon.

   The application displays the ToolTip.

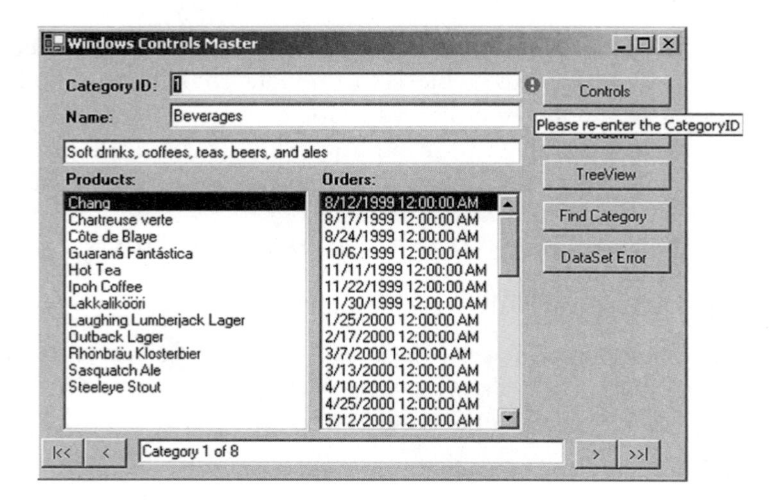

6 Close the application.

Visual C# .NET

1 Add the following procedure to the class module:

```
private void Categories_Error(object sender, CancelEventArgs e)
{
    if (this.tbCategoryID.Text == "Error")
    {
        this.epControl.SetError(this.tbCategoryID, "Please re-
            enter the CategoryID");
        e.Cancel = true;
    }
    else
    {
        this.epControl.SetError(this.tbCategoryID, "");
    }
}
```

2 Add the following line to the end of the frmMaster sub:

```
this.tbCategoryID.Validating +=
    new CancelEventHandler(this.Categories_Error);
```

3 Press F5 to run the application.

4 Change the CategoryID to Error, and then click the Next button (">").

The application displays a blinking error icon after the CategoryID control.

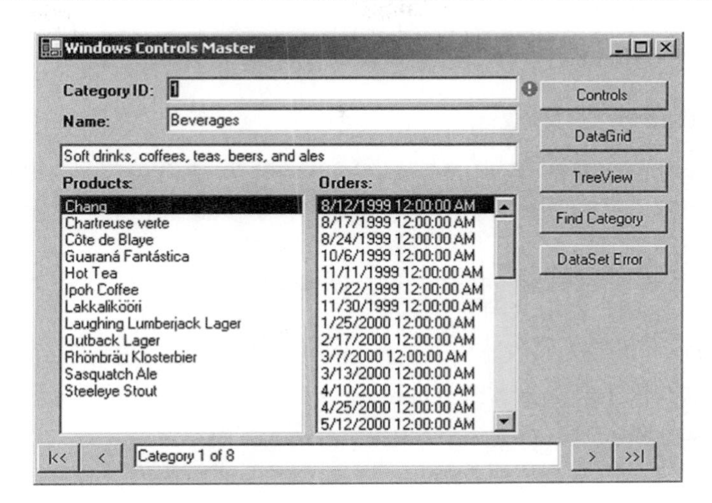

5 Place the mouse pointer over the icon.

The application displays the ToolTip.

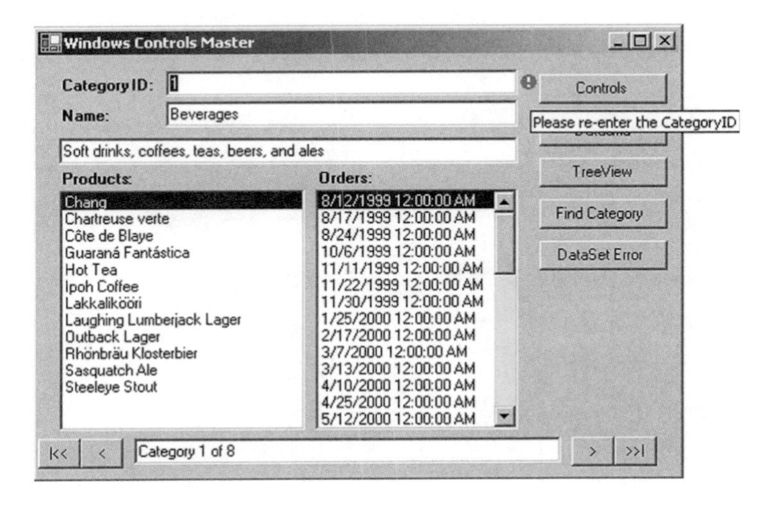

6 Close the application.

The previous exercise demonstrated the use of the ErrorProvider from within the Validating event of a control. But the ErrorProvider component can also be bound to a data source, and it can display errors for any column or row containing errors.

Binding an ErrorProvider to a data source object has the advantage of allowing multiple errors to be displayed simultaneously—a significant improvement in system usability.

Use an ErrorProvider with a DataColumn

Visual Basic .NET

1. In the form designer, select the epDataSet ErrorProvider control.
2. In the Properties window, select the DataSource property, expand the drop-down list, and then select dsMaster1.
3. Select the DataMember property, expand the drop-down list, and then select Categories.
4. Double-click the btnDataSet button.

   Visual Studio adds the event handler template to the code editor.
5. Add the following code to the event handler:

```
Me.dsMaster1.Categories.Rows(0).SetColumnError("Description", _
    "Error Created Here")
```

   This code artificially creates an error condition for the Description column of the second row in the Categories table.
6. Press F5 to run the application, and then click the DataSet Error button.

   Visual Studio displays an error icon after the Description text box.

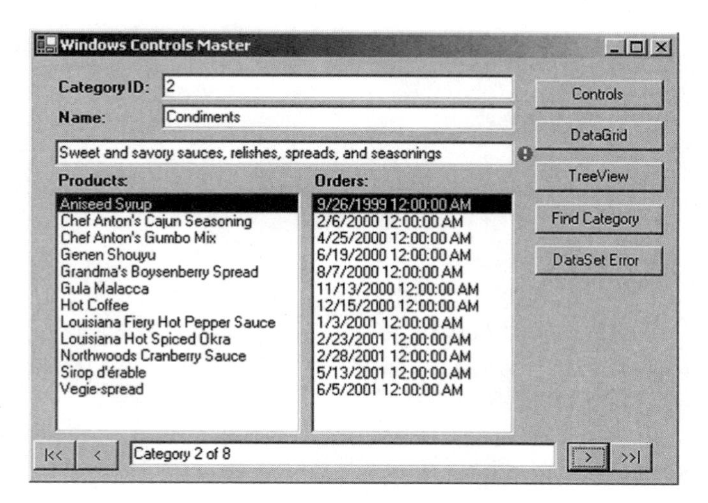

7. Close the application.

Visual C# .NET

1. In the form designer, select the epDataSet ErrorProvider control.
2. In the Properties window, select the DataSource property, expand the drop-down list, and then select dsMaster1.
3. Select the DataMember property, expand the drop-down list, and then select Categories.
4. Double-click the btnDataSet button.

   Visual Studio adds the event handler template to the code editor.
5. Add the following code to the event handler:

```
this.dsMaster1.Categories.Rows[0].SetColumnError("Description",
   "Error Created Here");
```

   This code artificially creates an error condition for the Description column of the second row in the Categories table.
6. Press F5 to run the application, and then click the DataSet Error button.

   Visual Studio displays an error icon after the Description text box.

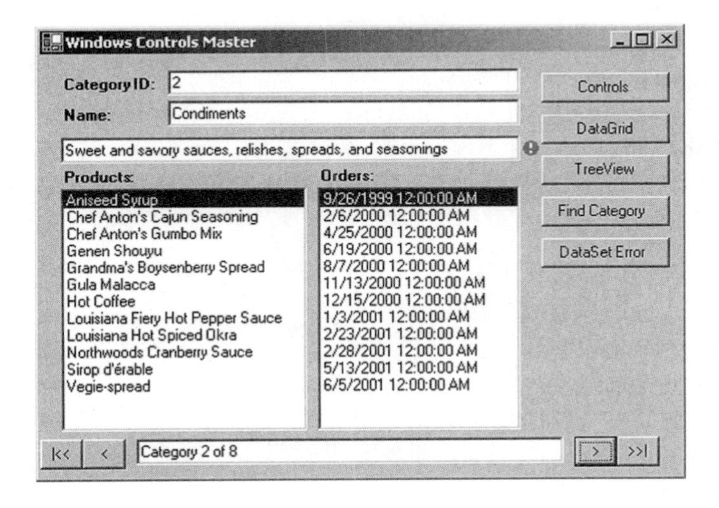

7. Close the application.

Chapter 11 Quick Reference

<table>
<tr><th>To</th><th>Do this</th></tr>
<tr><td>Use the Format event</td><td>Create the event handler, changing the Value property of the ConvertEventArgs parameter, and then bind it to the control's Format event</td></tr>
<tr><td>Use the Parse event</td><td>Create the event handler, changing the Value property of the ConvertEventArgs parameter, and then bind it to the control's Parse event</td></tr>
<tr><td>Use the CheckBox control to display Boolean values in a DataTable</td><td>Bind the value of the control's Checked property</td></tr>
<tr><td>Bind a ComboBox to a key value it doesn't display</td><td>Set the control's DisplayMember property to the column to be displayed, and set the ValueMember property to the key value</td></tr>
<tr><td>Create a nested ListBox</td><td>Set the ListBox's DisplayMember property to the entire hierarchy, including the DataRelation:
<pre><code>myListBox.DisplayMember =
      "tblParent.drRelation.tblChild.Column"</code></pre></td></tr>
<tr><td>Display hierarchical data using the DataGrid control</td><td>In the form designer, use the DataGridTableStyle Collection editor (available from the TableStyles property in the Properties Window) to add the related tables to the DataGrid</td></tr>
<tr><td>Display hierarchical data using the TreeView control</td><td>Use the DataRow's GetChildRows method to manually add the nodes to the TreeView's Nodes array:
<pre><code>for each mainRow in masterTable
    rootNode = _
         myTreeView.Nodes.Add(mainRow.myColumn)
    childArray = _
         mainRow.GetChildRows("myRelation")
    for each childRow in childArray
         rootNote.Nodes.Add(childRow.myColumn)
    next childRow
next mainRow</code></pre></td></tr>
<tr><td>Find rows based on the Sort column</td><td>Use the DataView's Find method to return the position of the row:
<pre><code>rowIndex = myDataView.Find(theKey)
myBindingContext.Position = rowIndex</code></pre></td></tr>
</table>

Find Rows based on an Unsorted Column	Use the DataTable's *Select* method to return the row, and then use the DataView's *Find* method to find its position:
	`drFound = myTable.Select(strCriteria)`
	`rowSortKey = drFound(0).myColumn`
	`rowIndex = myDataView.Find(rowSortKey)`
	`myBindingContext.Position = rowIndex`

Validate Data at the DataTable level	Respond to one of the DataTable change events: ColumnChanging, ColumnChanged, RowChanging, RowChanged, RowDeleting, or RowDeleted
Validate Data at the Control level	Respond to one of the Control validation events: Enter, GotFocus, Leave, Validating, Validated, LostFocus
Use an ErrorProvider with a Form Control	Set the ErrorProvider's ContainerControl property to the control, and then, if necessary, call the *SetError* method to display an error condition from within the control's Validating event

CHAPTER

12

Data-Binding in Web Forms

In this chapter, you'll learn how to:

- ✔ *Simple-bind controls at design time*
- ✔ *Simple-bind controls at run time*
- ✔ *Display bound data on a page*
- ✔ *Complex-bind controls at design time*
- ✔ *Complex-bind controls at run time*
- ✔ *Use the DataBinder object*
- ✔ *Store a DataSet in the session state*
- ✔ *Store a DataSet in the ViewState*
- ✔ *Update a data source using a Command object*

In the previous eleven chapters, we've examined the ADO.NET object model, using examples in Windows forms. In this chapter, we'll examine the way that Microsoft ADO.NET interacts with Microsoft ASP.NET and Web forms.

Understanding Data-Binding in Web Forms

As part of the Microsoft .NET Framework, ADO.NET is independent of any application in which it is deployed, whether it's a Windows form, like the exercises in the previous chapters, a Web form, or a middle-level business object. But the way that data is pushed to and pulled from controls is a function of the control itself, not of ADO.NET, and the Web form data-binding architecture is very different from anything we've seen so far.

The Web form data-binding architecture is based on two assumptions. The first assumption is that the majority of data access is read-only—data is displayed to users, but in most cases, it is not updated by them. The second assumption is that performance and scalability, while not insignificant in the Microsoft Windows operating system, are of critical importance when applications are deployed on the Internet.

To optimize performance for read-only data access, the .NET Framework Web form data-binding architecture is also read-only—when you bind a control to a data source, the data will only be pushed to the bound property; it will not be pulled back from the control.

This doesn't mean that it's impossible, or even particularly difficult, to edit data by using Web forms, but it has to be done manually. As a simple example, if you have a Windows Form TextBox control bound to a column in a DataSet, and the user changes the value of that TextBox, the new value will be automatically propagated to the DataSet by the .NET Framework, and the Item, DataColumn, and DataRow change events will be triggered.

If a TextBox control on a Web form is bound to a column in a DataSet, however, the user must explicitly submit any changes to the server, and you must write the code to handle the submission, both on the client and the server. After the changes reach the DataSet, of course, the DataColumn and DataRow change events will still be triggered.

Most of this arises from the nature of the Internet itself. In a traditional Web programming environment, a page is created, sent to the user's browser, and then the user, the page, and any information the page contains are forgotten. In other words, the Internet is, by default, *stateless*—the state of a page is not maintained between round-trips to the server.

ASP.NET, the part of the .NET Framework that supports Web development, supports a number of mechanisms for maintaining state, where appropriate, on both the client and server. We'll examine some of these as they relate to data access later in this chapter.

In addition to being stateless, traditional Internet applications are also disconnected. When working with older data object models, this can sometimes be a problem, but as we've seen, ADO.NET itself uses a disconnected data model, so this poses no problem.

Data Sources

Like controls on Windows forms, Web form controls can be bound to any data source, not only traditional database tables. Technically, to qualify as a Web form data source, an object must implement the IEnumerable interface. Arrays, Collections, DataReaders, DataSets, DataViews, and DataRows all implement the IEnumerable interface, and any of them can be used as the data source for a Web form control.

Because the management of server resources and the resulting scalability issues are critical in the Internet environment, the choice of data access methods must be given careful consideration. In most cases, when data is read into the page and then discarded, it's better to use an ADO.NET DataReader rather than a DataSet because a DataReader provides better performance and conserves server memory. However, this isn't always the case, and there are situations in which using the DataSet is both easier and more efficient.

If, for example, you're working with related data, the DataSet object, with its support for DataRelations and its *GetChildRows* and *GetParentRows* methods, is both easier to implement and more efficient because it requires fewer round-trips to the data source. Also, as we'll see in Chapter 15, the DataSet provides the mechanism for reading data from and writing data to an XML stream.

Finally if the data will be accessed multiple times, as it is when you're paging through data, it can be more efficient to store a DataSet than to re-create it each time. This isn't always the case, however. In some situations, the memory that is required to store a large DataSet outweighs the performance gains from maintaining the data. Also, if the data being stored is at all volatile, you run the risk of the stored data becoming out of sync with the primary data store.

Roadmap

We'll examine binding to DataRelations in Chapter 13.

There is one other major difference in the data-binding architectures of Windows and Web forms: Web forms do not directly support data-binding to an ADO.NET DataRelation object. As we saw in Chapter 11, binding to a DataRelation provides a simple and efficient method for displaying master/detail relationships. To perform the same function in a Web form, you must use the DataBinder property. We'll examine binding to DataRelations in Chapter 13.

Binding Controls to an ADO.NET Data Source

Like controls on Windows forms, Web form controls support simple-binding virtually any property to a single value in data source and complex-binding control properties that display multiple values. However, the binding mechanisms for Web forms are somewhat different from those that we've seen and used with Windows forms.

> **note**
> In the Web form documentation, simple- and complex-binding are referred to as single-value and multirecord binding.

Simple-Binding Control Properties

Web form controls can always be bound at run time. They can also be bound at design time if the data source is available. (Because Web Forms applications tend to use Data commands more often than DataSets, the data source is less often available at design time.)

Unlike Windows forms, simple-bound Web form control properties don't expose data-binding properties. Instead, the value is explicitly retrieved and assigned to the property at run time by using a data-binding expression.

In Microsoft Visual Studio .NET, the Properties window supports a tool for creating data-binding expressions, or you can create them at run time. The run time data-binding expression is delimited by <%# and %>:

```
propName = (<%# dataExpression %>)
```

The *dataExpression* can be any expression that resolves to a single data item—a column of a DataRow, a property of another control on the page, or even an expression.

Note, however, that Web forms don't support a BindingContext object or anything similar to it, so there is no concept of a current row. You must specifically indicate which row of a data source, such as a DataTable, will be displayed in the bound property. So, for example, to refer to a DataColumn within a DataSet, you would need to use the following syntax:

```
<%# myDataSet.myTable.DefaultView(0).myColumn %>
```

You can use a data-binding expression almost anywhere in a Web form page, as long as the expression evaluates at run time to the correct data type. You can, of course, use type-casting to coerce the value to the correct type. For example:

```
myTextbox.Text = <%# myDataSet.myTable.Rows.Count.ToString() %>
```

Simple-Bind a Control Property at Design Time

1. Open the WebForms project from the Start page or the File menu.
2. In the Solution Explorer, double-click WebForm1.aspx.

   Visual Studio displays the page in the form designer.

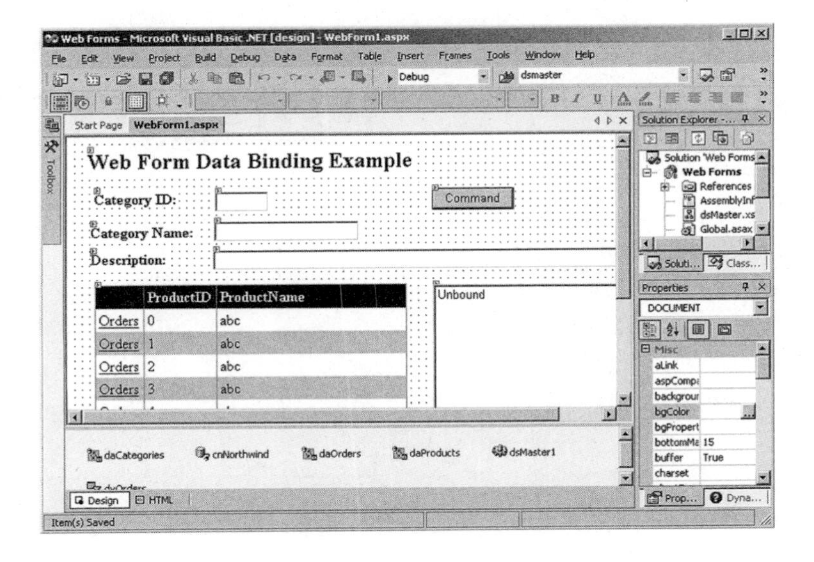

3. Select the tbCategoryName text box.
4. In the Properties window, select (DataBindings) and click the Ellipsis button.

   Visual Studio opens the DataBindings dialog box.

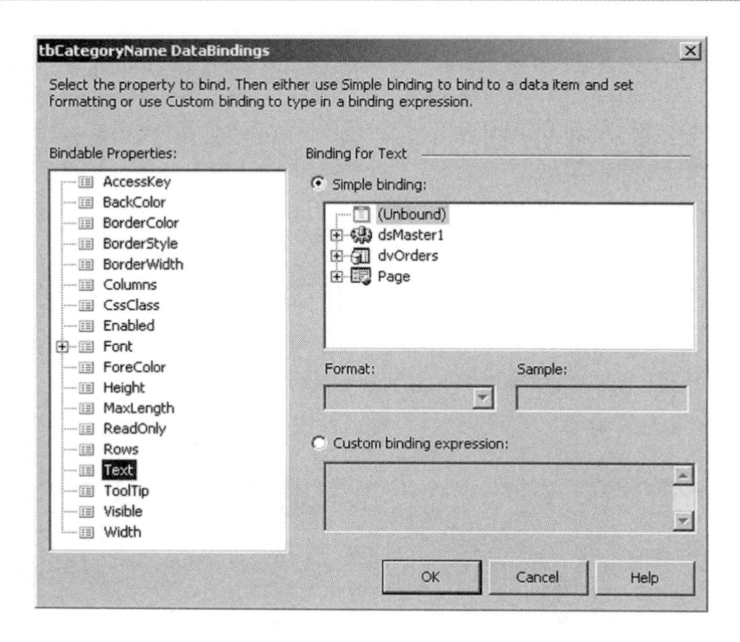

5 In the Simple Binding pane, expand dsMaster1/Categories/DefaultView/DefaultView.[0], and select CategoryName.

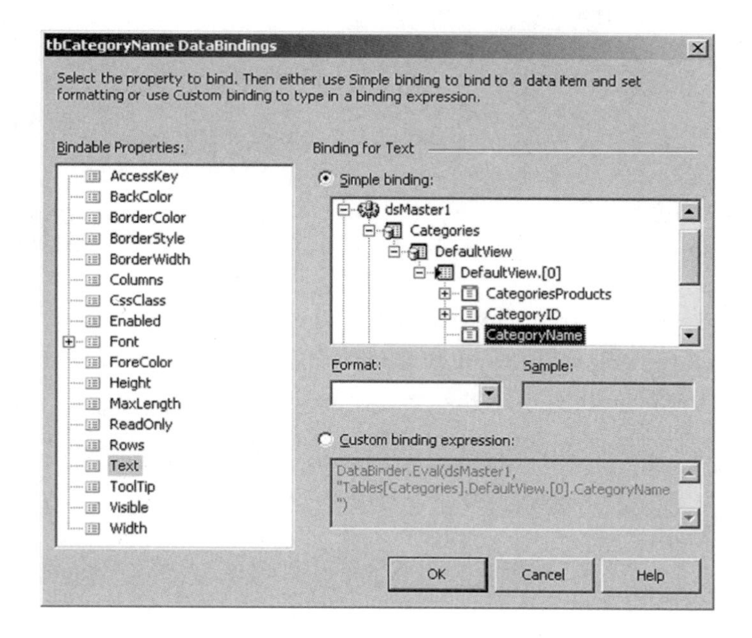

6 Click OK.

Visual Studio creates the binding.

note

You can examine the syntax of the data-binding attribute on the HTML tab of the project. Find the tag that defines the tbCategoryName text box.

If the data source isn't available at design time, you can bind a control property at run time. Although it's possible to do this in the control tag, it's much easier to do so by using the DataBinding event that is raised when the *DataBind* method is called for the control.

Simple-Bind a Control Property at Run Time

Visual Basic .NET

1. Press F7 to display WebForm1.aspx.vb.
2. Select tbCategoryDescription in the Control Name combo box, and then select DataBinding in the Method Name combo box.

   Visual Studio adds the event handler.
3. Add the following code to the procedure:

```
Me.tbCategoryDescription.Text = Me.dsMaster1.Categories(0).Description
```

Visual C# .NET

1. Select tbCategoryDescription in the form designer.
2. In the Properties Window, click the Events button, and then double-click DataBinding.

   Visual Studio opens the code window and adds the event handler.
3. Add the following code to the procedure:

```
this.tbCategoryDescription.Text =
   this.dsMaster1.Categories[0].Description;
```

Just as with Windows forms, before you can display the data on your Web form, you must explicitly load it from the data source by filling a DataAdapter or executing a Data command. But Web forms require an additional step: You must push the data into the control properties.

This is done by calling the *DataBind* method, which is implemented by all controls that inherit from *System.Web.UI.Control*. A call to the *DataBind* method cascades to its child controls. Thus, calling *DataBind* for the Page class will call the *DataBind* method for all the controls contained by the Page class.

When the *DataBind* method is invoked for a control, either directly or by cascading, the data expressions embedded in control tags will be resolved and the DataBinding events for the controls will be triggered.

If you're using a Web form to update data, you must be careful when you call the *DataBind* method. Much like a DataSet's *AcceptChanges* method, *DataBind* replaces the values currently contained in the bound properties.

Display Bound Data in the Page

Visual Basic .NET

1 In the code editor, add the following code to the Page_Load event:

```
Me.daCategories.Fill(Me.dsMaster1.Categories)
Me.daProducts.Fill(Me.dsMaster1.Products)
Me.daOrders.Fill(Me.dsMaster1.Orders)
Me.DataBind()
```

This code fills the three tables in the DataSet, and then calls the DataBind event for the page, which will push the data into each of the bound controls that it contains.

2 Press F5 to run the application.

Visual Studio displays the page in the default browser.

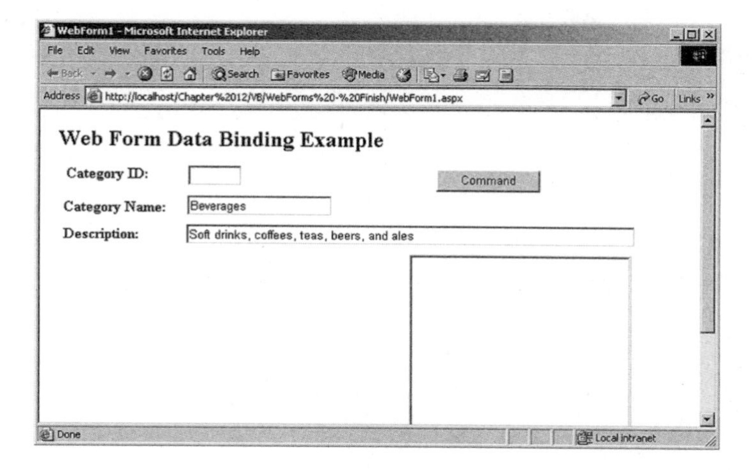

3 Close the browser.

Visual C# .NET

1. In the code editor, add the following code to the Page_Load event:

```
this.daCategories.Fill(this.dsMaster1.Categories);
this.daProducts.Fill(this.dsMaster1.Products);
this.daOrders.Fill(this.dsMaster1.Orders);
this.DataBind();
```

2. Press F5 to run the application.

   Visual Studio displays the page in the default browser.

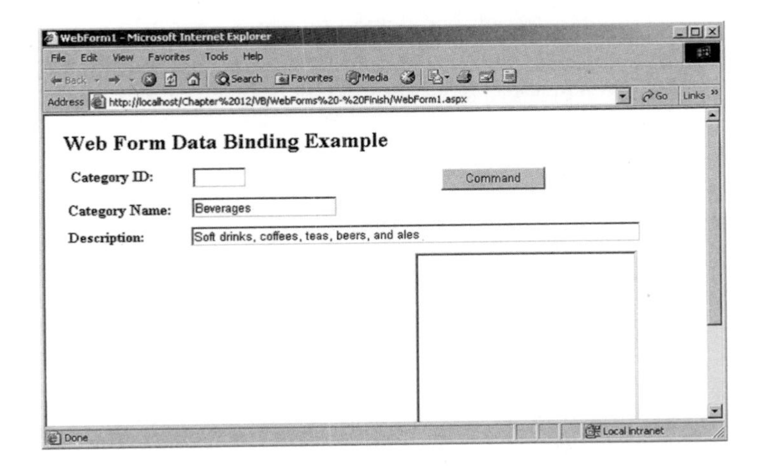

3. Close the browser.

Complex-Binding Control Properties

The process of complex-binding Web form controls closely resembles the process for complex-binding Windows form controls. Complex-bound controls in both environments expose the DataSource and DataMember properties for defining the source of the data, and Web form controls expose a DataValueField property that is equivalent to the ValueMember property of a Windows form control.

The DataList and DataGrid controls also expose a DataKeyField property that stores the primary key information within the data source. The DataKeyField, which populates a DataKeyFields collection, allows you to store the primary key information without necessarily displaying it in the control.

In addition, the ListBox, DropDownList, CheckBoxList, RadioButtonList, and HtmlSelect controls expose a DataTextField property that defines the column to be displayed. The DataTextField property is equivalent to the DisplayMember property of a Windows form control.

Roadmap
We'll examine binding to DataRelations in Chapter 13.

If the DataSource property is being set to a DataSet and the DataMember property is being set to a DataTable, you can simply set the properties directly. As we'll see in Chapter 13, it is also possible to bind to DataRelations, but the process is somewhat less than straightforward.

Complex-Bind a Control at Design Time

1. Display the form designer.
2. Select the dgProducts DataGrid.
3. In the Properties window, expand the Data section (if necessary), select the DataSource property, and then select dsMaster1 in the drop-down list.

> **note**
> Clear the Events button if you're working in C#.

4. Select the DataMember property, and then select Products.
5. Press F5 to run the application.

   Visual Studio displays the page in the default browser, showing all the products in the data grid.

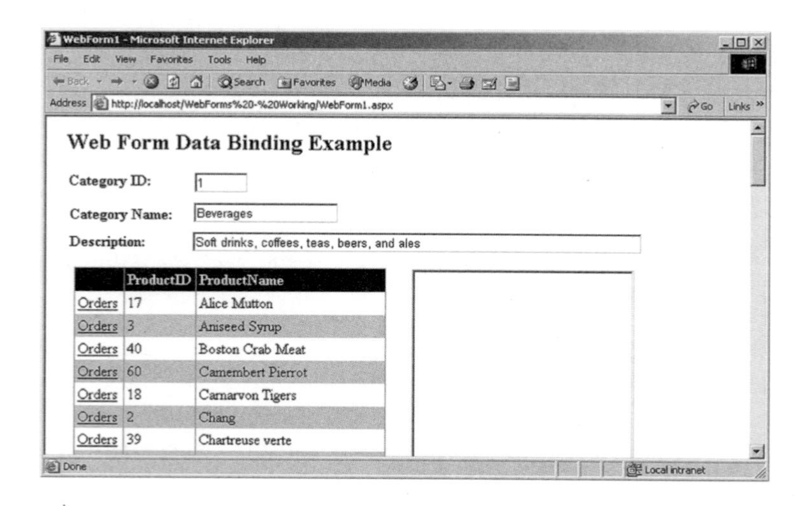

6. Close the browser.

In this exercise, we'll bind the lbOrders ListBox control in response to the SelectedItemChanged event of the dgProducts DataGrid control. The SelectedItemChanged event occurs when the user clicks one of the Orders buttons in the DataGrid because its CommandName property has been set to Select.

Complex-Bind a Control at Run Time

Visual Basic .NET

1. In the form designer, double-click the dgProducts DataGrid control.

   Visual Studio adds a SelectedIndexChanged event handler to the code editor.

2. Add the following code to the procedure:

```
Me.dvOrders.Table = Me.dsMaster1.Orders
Me.dvOrders.RowFilter = "ProductID = " & _
   Me.dgProducts.SelectedItem.Cells(1).Text
Me.lbOrders.DataSource = Me.dvOrders
Me.lbOrders.DataTextField = "OrderDate"
Me.lbOrders.DataBind()
```

   The code sets the RowFilter property of the dvOrders DataView to the ProductID of the row selected in the DataGrid. It then sets the DataSource and DataMember properties of the ListBox, and then calls the *DataBind* method to push the data to the control.

3. Press F5 to run the application.

   Visual Studio displays the page in the default browser.

4. Click the Orders button in one of the rows in the data grid.

   The page displays the order dates in the list box. Note that the browser made a round-trip to the server to retrieve the data.

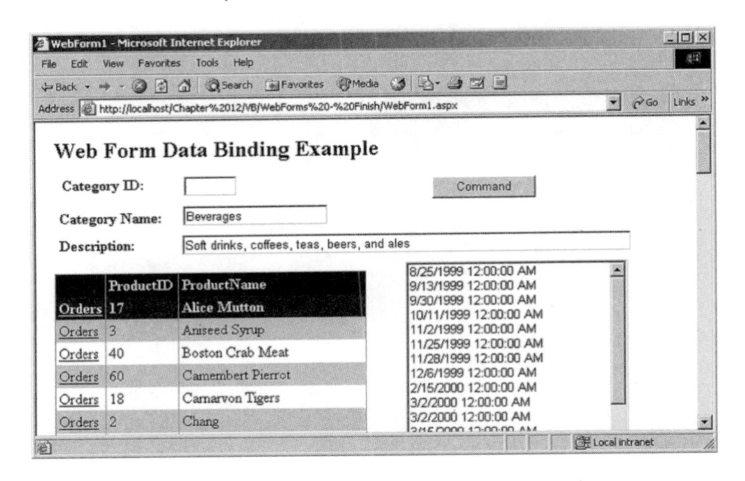

5 Close the browser.

Visual C# .NET

1 In the form designer, double-click the dgProducts DataGrid control.

Visual Studio adds a Select Click handler to the code editor.

2 Add the following code to the procedure:

```
this.dvOrders.Table = this.dsMaster1.Orders;
this.dvOrders.RowFilter = "ProductID = " +
   this.dgProducts.SelectedItem.Cells[1].Text;
this.lbOrders.DataSource = this.dvOrders;
this.lbOrders.DataTextField = "OrderDate";
this.lbOrders.DataBind();
```

The code sets the RowFilter property of the dvOrders DataView to the ProductID of the row selected in the DataGrid. It then sets the DataSource and DataMember properties of the ListBox, and then calls the *DataBind* method to push the data to the control.

3 Press F5 to run the application.

Visual Studio displays the page in the default browser.

4 Click the Orders button in one of the rows in the data grid.

The page displays the order dates in the list box. Note that the browser made a round-trip to the server to retrieve the data.

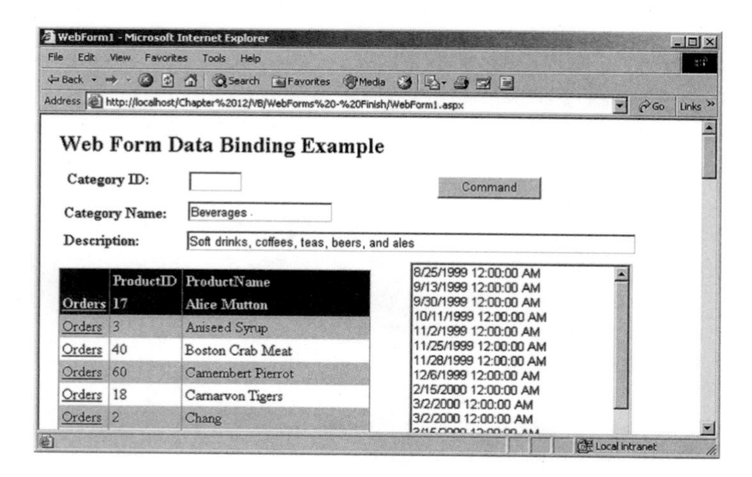

5 Close the browser.

Using the DataBinder Object

In addition to embedding data-binding expressions directly in the HTML stream, the .NET Framework also exposes the DataBinder object, which evaluates data-binding expressions and optionally formats the result as a string.

The DataBinder syntax is straightforward, and it can perform type conversion automatically, which greatly simplifies coding in some circumstances. This is particularly true when working with an ADO.NET object—multiple castings are required, and the syntax is complex. However, the DataBinder object is late-bound, and like all late-bound objects, it does incur a performance penalty, primarily due to its type conversion.

The DataBinder object is a static object, which means that it can be used without instantiation. It can be called either from within the HTML for the page (surrounded by <%# and %> brackets) or in code.

The DataBinder object exposes no properties or events, and only a single method, *Eval*. The *Eval* method is overloaded to accept an optional format string, as shown in Table 12-1.

Method	Description
Eval(dataSource, dataExpression)	Returns the value of *dataExpression* in the *dataSource* at run time
Eval(dataSource, dataExpression, formatStr)	Returns the value of *dataExpression* in the *dataSource* at run time, and then formats it according to the *formatStr*

Table 12-1 *Eval* Methods

The *Eval* method expects a data container object as the first parameter. When working with ADO.NET objects, this is usually a DataSet, DataTable, or DataView object. It can also be the Container object if the expression runs from within a List control in a template, such as a DataList, DataGrid, or Repeater, in which case the first parameter should always be *Container.DataItem*.

The second parameter of the *Eval* method is a string that represents the specific data item to be returned. When working with ADO.NET objects, this parameter would typically be the name of a DataColumn, but it can be any valid data expression.

The final, optional parameter is a format specifier identical in format to those used by the *String.Format* method. If the format specifier is omitted, the *Eval* method returns an object, which must be explicitly cast to the correct type.

Use the DataBinder to Bind a Control Property

Visual Basic .NET

1. In the code editor, select tbCategoryID in the Control Name combo box, and then select DataBinding in the Method Name combo box.

   Visual Studio adds the event handler to the code.

2. Add the following line to the procedure:

```
Me.tbCategoryID.Text = _
   DataBinder.Eval(Me.dsMaster1.Categories.DefaultView(0), _
   "CategoryID")
```

   Notice that you must explicitly record the first row of the DataTable's DefaultView. This is because Web forms have no CurrencyManager to handle retrieving a current row from the DataSet.

3. Press F5 to run the application.

   Visual Studio displays the page in the default browser with the CategoryID value.

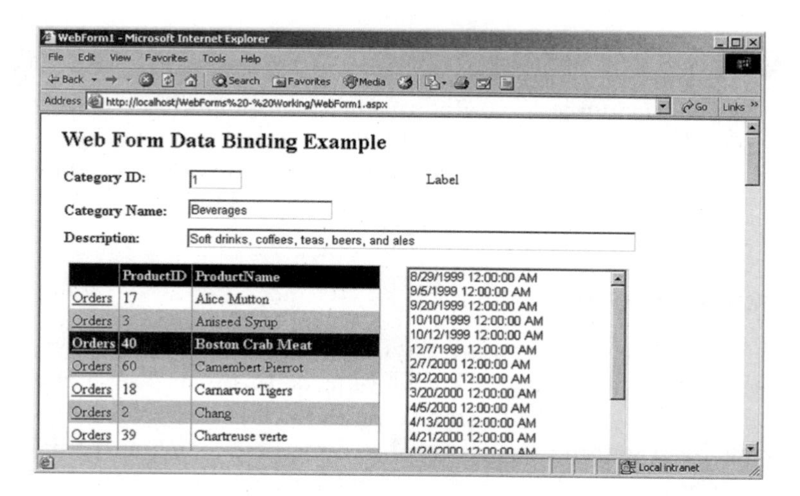

4. Close the browser.

Visual C# .NET

1. In the form designer, select tbCategoryID, display the events in the Properties Window, and double-click DataBinding.

   Visual Studio adds the event handler to the code editor window.

2 Add the following line to the procedure:

```
this.tbCategoryID.Text =
   DataBinder.Eval(this.dsMaster1.Categories.DefaultView[0],
   "CategoryID").ToString();
```

Notice that you must explicitly record the first row of the DataTable's DefaultView. This is because Web forms have no CurrencyManager to handle retrieving a current row from the DataSet.

3 Press F5 to run the application.

Visual Studio displays the page in the default browser with the CategoryID value.

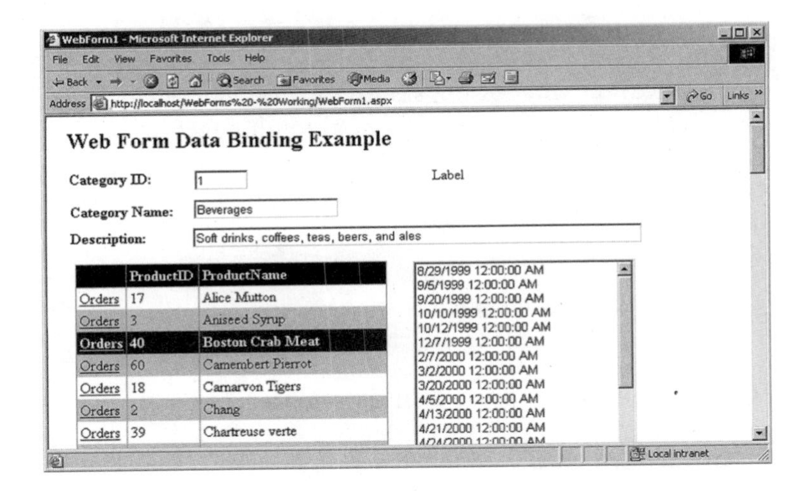

4 Close the browser.

Maintaining ADO.NET Object State

Because the Web form doesn't maintain state between round-trips to the server, if you want to maintain a DataSet between the time that the page is first created and the time that it takes the user to send it back with changes, you must do so explicitly.

You can maintain a DataSet on the server by storing it in either the Application or Session state, or you can maintain it on the client by storing it in the Page class's ViewState. You can also store the DataSet in a hidden field on the page, although because this is how the Page class implements ViewState, there's rarely any advantage to doing so.

Whether you maintain the data on the server or the page, you must always be aware of concurrency issues. You're saving round-trips to the data source, and the performance gains can be significant, particularly if the data requires calculations. However, changes to the data source won't be reflected in the stored data. If the data is volatile, you must re-create the ADO.NET objects each time in order to ensure that they reflect the most recent changes.

Maintaining ADO.NET Objects on the Server

ASP.NET provides a number of mechanisms for maintaining state within an Internet application. On the server side, the two easiest mechanisms to use are the Application state and the Session state. Both state structures are dictionaries that store data as name/value pairs. The value is stored and retrieved as an object, so you must cast it to the correct type when you restore it.

The Application and Session states are used identically; the difference is scope. The Application state is global to all pages and all users within the application. The Session state is specific to a single browser session. (Please refer to the ASP.NET documentation for additional information about Application and Session states.)

The IsPostBack property of the Page class, which is False the first time a Page is loaded for a specific browser session and True thereafter, can be used in the Page_Load event to control when the data is created and loaded.

Store the DataSet in the Session State

Visual Basic .NET

1 Change the Page_Load event to store the DataSet in the Session state:

```
If Me.IsPostBack Then
   Me.dsMaster1 = CType(Session("dsMaster"), DataSet)
Else
   Me.daCategories.Fill(Me.dsMaster1.Categories)
   Me.daProducts.Fill(Me.dsMaster1.Products)
   Me.daOrders.Fill(Me.dsMaster1.Orders)
   Session("dsMaster") = Me.dsMaster1
End If
Me.DataBind()
```

2 Press F5 to run the application.

Visual Studio displays the page in the default browser.

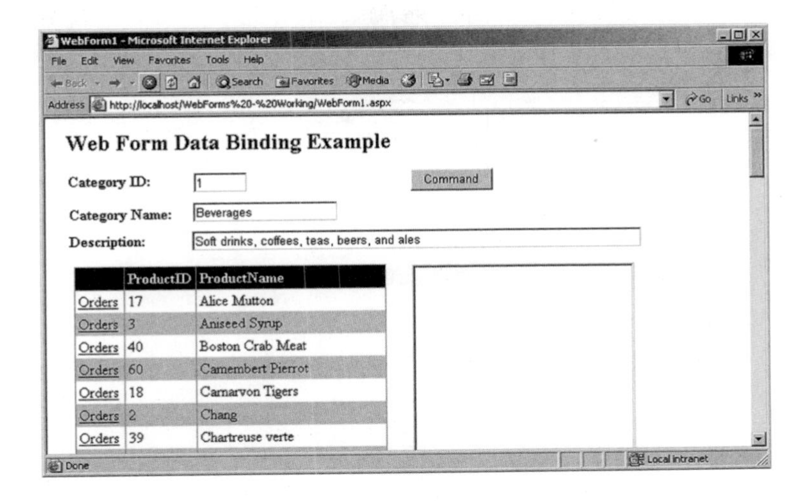

3. Click several items in the dgProducts data grid.

   You might be able to notice a slight increase in performance.

4. Close the browser.

Visual C# .NET

1. Change the Page_Load event to store the DataSet in the Session state:

```
if (this.IsPostBack)
    this.dsMaster1 = (dsMaster) Session["dsMaster"];
else
{
    this.daCategories.Fill(this.dsMaster1.Categories);
    this.daProducts.Fill(this.dsMaster1.Products);
    this.daOrders.Fill(this.dsMaster1.Orders);
    this.Session["dsMaster"] = this.dsMaster1;
}
this.DataBind();
```

2. Press F5 to run the application.

   Visual Studio displays the page in the default browser.

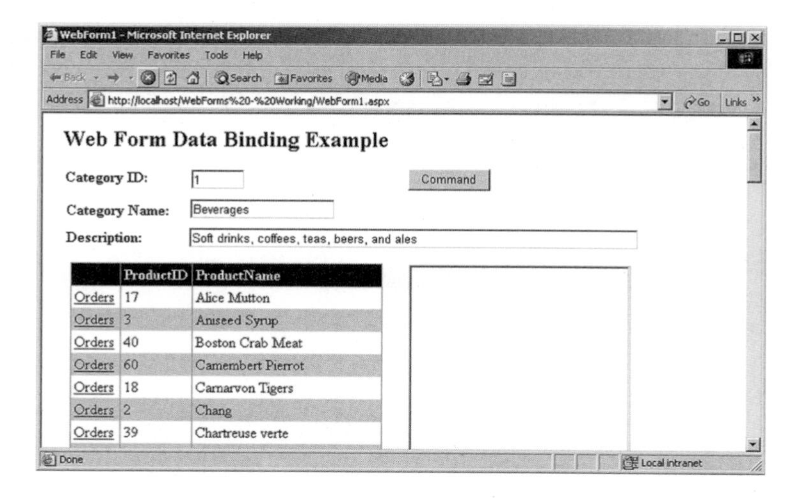

3 Click several items in the dgProducts data grid.

You may be able to notice a slight increase in performance.

4 Close the browser.

Maintaining ADO.NET Objects on the Page

Storing data on the server can be convenient, but it does consume server resources which, in turn, negatively impacts application scalability. An alternative is to store the data on the page itself. This relieves the pressure on the server, but because the data is passed as part of the data stream, it can increase the time it requires to load and post the page.

Data is stored on the page either in a custom hidden field or in the ViewState property of a control. In theory, any ViewState property can be used, but the Page class's ViewState is the most common property.

Store the DataSet in the ViewState

Visual Basic .NET

1 Change the Page_Load event handler to store the data in the Page class ViewState:

```
If Me.IsPostBack Then
   Me.dsMaster1 = CType(ViewState("dsMaster"), DataSet)
```

```
Else
  Me.daCategories.Fill(Me.dsMaster1.Categories)
  Me.daProducts.Fill(Me.dsMaster1.Products)
  Me.daOrders.Fill(Me.dsMaster1.Orders)
  ViewState("dsMaster") = Me.dsMaster1
End If
Me.DataBind()
```

2 Press F5 to run the application.

Visual Studio displays the page in the default browser.

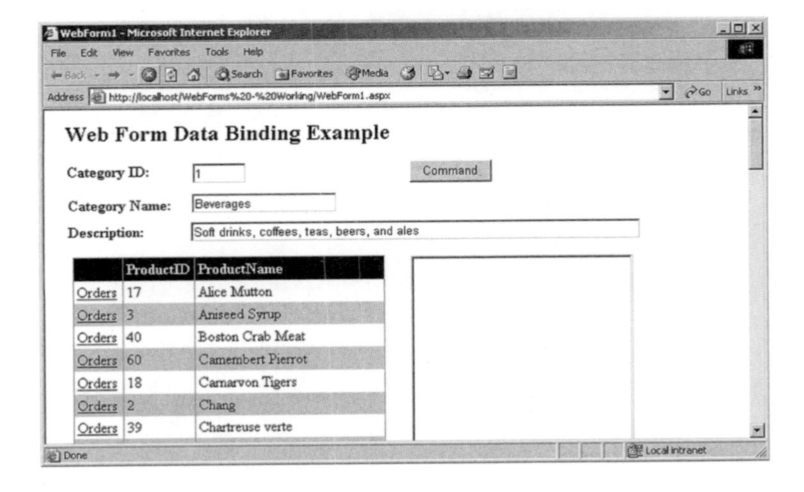

3 Click several items in the dgProducts data grid.

4 Close the browser.

Visual C# .NET

1 Change the Page_Load event handler to store the data in the Page class ViewState:

```
if (this.IsPostBack)
   this.dsMaster1 = (dsMaster) ViewState["dsMaster"];
else
{
   this.daCategories.Fill(this.dsMaster1.Categories);
   this.daProducts.Fill(this.dsMaster1.Products);
   this.daOrders.Fill(this.dsMaster1.Orders);
   this.ViewState["dsMaster"] = this.dsMaster1;
}
this.DataBind();
```

2 Press F5 to run the application.

Visual Studio displays the page in the default browser.

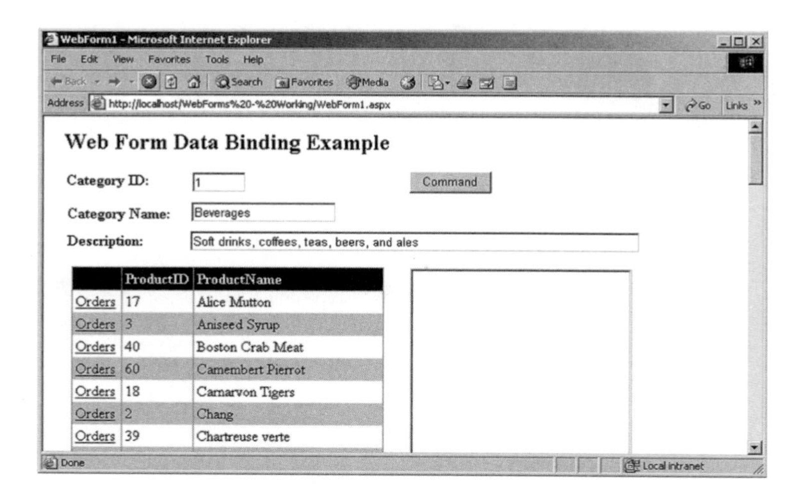

3 Click several items in the dgProducts data grid.

4 Close the browser.

Updating a Data Source from a Web Form

Remember that ADO.NET objects behave in exactly the same manner when they're instantiated in a Web form page as when they're used in a Windows form. Because of this, in theory, the processes of updating a data source should be identical.

On one level, this is true. The actual update is performed by directly running a Data command or by calling the *Update* method of a DataAdapter. But remember that a Web form page doesn't maintain its state and that data-binding architecture is one-way.

Because the Web form data-binding architecture is one-way, you must explicitly push the values returned by the page into the appropriate object. With a Windows form, after a control property has been bound to a column in a DataTable, any changes that the user makes to the value will be immediately and automatically reflected in the DataTable.

On a Web form, on the other hand, you must explicitly retrieve the value from the control and update the ADO.NET object. You might, for example, use the control values to set the parameters of a Data command or update a row in a DataTable.

Update a Data Source Using a Command Object

Visual Basic .NET

1. Change the Page_Load event code to read:

   ```
   If Not IsPostBack Then
     Me.daCategories.Fill(Me.dsMaster1.Categories)
     Me.daProducts.Fill(Me.dsMaster1.Products)
     Me.daOrders.Fill(Me.dsMaster1.Orders)
     Me.DataBind()
   End If
   ```

   The IsPostBack property prevents the *Fill* and *DataBind* methods from being called when the page is posted back. Remember that *DataBind* replaces existing values.

2. In the code editor, select btnCommand in the Control Name combo box, and then select Click in the Method Name combo box.

   Visual Studio adds the event handler to the code.

3. Add the following code to the event handler:

   ```
   Dim cmdUpdate As System.Data.OleDb.OleDbCommand
   cmdUpdate = Me.daCategories.UpdateCommand

   With cmdUpdate
      .Parameters(0).Value = Me.tbCategoryName.Text
      .Parameters(1).Value = Me.tbCategoryDescription.Text
      .Parameters(2).Value = Me.tbCategoryID.Text
   End With

   Me.cnNorthwind.Open()
   cmdUpdate.ExecuteNonQuery()
   Me.cnNorthwind.Close()
   ```

   The code uses the *UpdateCommand* of the daCategories DataAdapter to perform the update. (This is a shortcut that wouldn't ordinarily be available.) The three parameters are set to the values of the relevant fields on the page, and then the Connection is opened, the Command is executed, and the Connection is closed.

4. Press F5 to run the application.

   Visual Studio displays the page in the default browser.

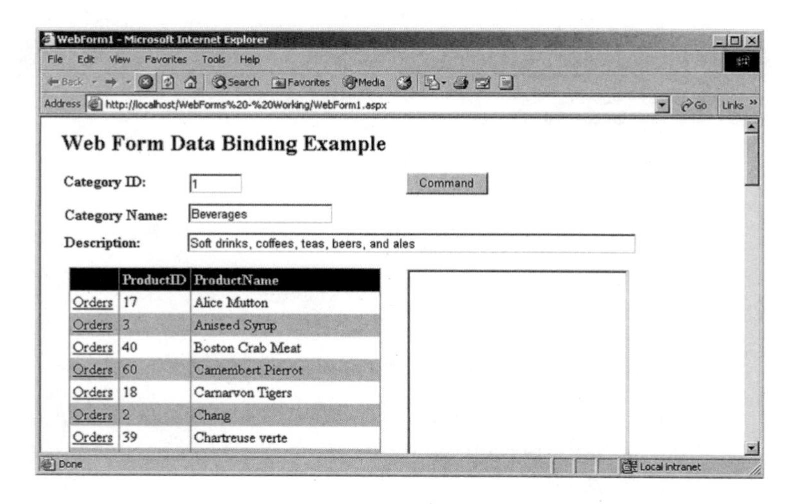

5 Change the Category Name to Categories New.

6 Click Command.

The page updates the database.

7 Close the browser.

Visual C# .NET

1 Change the Page_Load event code to read:

```
if (IsPostBack == false)
{
   this.daCategories.Fill(this.dsMaster1.Categories);
   this.daProducts.Fill(this.dsMaster1.Products);
   this.daOrders.Fill(this.dsMaster1.Orders);
   this.DataBind();
}
```

The IsPostBack property prevents the *Fill* and *DataBind* methods from being called when the page is posted back. Remember that *DataBind* replaces existing values.

2 In the form designer, double-click btnCommand.

Visual Studio adds the event handler to the code.

3 Add the following code to the event handler:

```
System.Data.OleDb.OleDbCommand cmdUpdate;
cmdUpdate = this.daCategories.UpdateCommand;
```

```
cmdUpdate.Parameters[0].Value = this.tbCategoryName.Text;
cmdUpdate.Parameters[1].Value =
this.tbCategoryDescription.Text;
cmdUpdate.Parameters[2].Value = this.tbCategoryID.Text;

this.cnNorthwind.Open();
cmdUpdate.ExecuteNonQuery();
this.cnNorthwind.Close();
```

The code uses the *UpdateCommand* of the daCategories DataAdapter to perform the update. (This is a shortcut that wouldn't ordinarily be available.) The three parameters are set to the values of the relevant fields on the page, and then the Connection is opened, the Command is executed, and the Connection is closed.

4 Press F5 to run the application.

Visual Studio displays the page in the default browser.

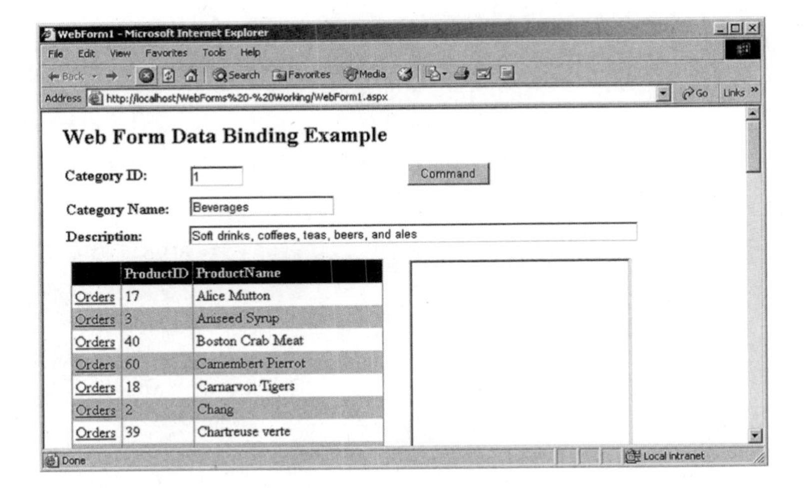

5 Change the Category Name to Categories New.

6 Click Command.

The page updates the database.

7 Close the browser.

Chapter 12 Quick Reference

To	Do this
Simple-bind a control at design time	Use the dialog displayed when you click the Ellipsis button in the DataBindings property in the Properties Window
Simple-bind a control at run time	Push the data into the control in the control's DataBinding event: `myControl.Text = myTable[0].myColumn`
Display bound data on a page	Call the *DataBind* method for the Page, or individual controls: `Me.DataBind()`
Complex-bind controls at design time	Set the DataSource and DataMember properties in the Properties Window
Complex-bind controls at run time	Set the DataSource, DataMember and, if applicable, the DataTextField properties of the control, and call its *DataBind* method
Use the DataBinder object	Call its *Eval* method, passing in the container and column values: `myControl.Text = DataBinder.Eval(myTable[0], "myColumn")`

Store data in the Session state	Set or retrieve the DataSet based on the IsPostBack property:
	`If Me.IsPostBack Then`
	`    myTable = CType(Session("myTable"), DataTable)`
	`Else`
	`    myDA.Fill(myTable)`
	`    Session("myTable") = myTable`
	`EndIf`

Store data in the ViewState	Set or retrieve the DataSet based on the IsPostBack property:
	`If Me.IsPostBack Then`
	`  myTable = CType(ViewState("myTable"), DataTable)`
	`Else`
	`    myDA.Fill(myTable)`
	`    ViewState("myTable") = myTable`
	`EndIf`

Using ADO.NET in Web Forms

In this chapter, you'll learn how to:

- ✔ *Display data in a DataGrid control*
- ✔ *Implement sorting in a DataGrid control*
- ✔ *Display data in a DataList control*
- ✔ *Display a DataList control as flowed text*
- ✔ *Implement paging in a DataGrid control*
- ✔ *Implement manual navigation in a Web form*
- ✔ *Use validation controls to control user entry*

In the previous chapter, we examined the basic data-binding architecture for Web forms. In this chapter, we'll examine a few common data-binding tasks in more detail.

Using Template-Based Web Controls

Microsoft ASP.NET Web Forms expose two controls that are specifically designed to display data: the DataGrid and DataList. Both controls display the rows of a data source, but vary in their capabilities.

Like its Windows forms equivalent, the DataGrid control displays data in a tabular format. It provides intrinsic support for in-place editing and paging data, but it has relatively limited formatting capabilities. The DataList control also provides intrinsic support for in-place editing, and allows for more flexible formatting.

The Microsoft .NET Framework also supports a Repeater control that allows almost unlimited formatting capability, but it has limited support in the Design View of the Page Designer—the majority of the formatting must be done directly in the HTML View of the Page Designer.

All three of these controls support *templates*, which are sets of controls that define the content of each section of the control. (A template is not the same as a style, which defines appearance, rather than content.) The template sections that are available, as well as the precise behavior of each section, differ between controls.

The DataGrid control, for example, doesn't support an AlternatingItemTemplate, and its ItemTemplates define the contents of a column, while the ItemTemplate for a DataList defines the contents of a row. We'll examine the specific templates supported by each control later in this chapter.

All three template-based controls can contain buttons that raise events on the server. As we'll see, the DataGrid and DataList controls have intrinsic support for in-place editing, and all three controls also support user-defined buttons. When a user clicks a user-defined button, an ItemCommand event is sent to the control that contains the template.

The ItemCommand's event argument parameter exposes the properties required to determine which button and which item within the control triggered the event. The three controls expose different classes of event arguments, but all three expose the same properties, as shown in Table 13-1.

Property	Description
CommandArgument	String used as an argument for the command
CommandName	String used to determine the command to be performed
CommandSource	The button that generated the event
Item	The selected item in the containing control

Table 13-1 ItemCommand Event Arguments

The CommandArgument and CommandName properties are defined when the button is added to the control. The CommandSource property refers to the button itself, while the Item is the selected row in the control.

Using the DataGrid Control

As with Windows forms, the DataGrid control is bound to a data source by using the DataSource and DataMember properties. One row will be displayed in the DataGrid for every row in the data source. By default, a column will be displayed for each column in the data source, but as we'll see, this can be configured through the Property Builder.

In addition to the DataSource and DataMember properties, the DataGrid control exposes a DataKeyField, which is roughly equivalent to the ValueMember property of the Windows form version and can be set to the name of a column in the data source that uniquely identifies each row. The column specified as the DataKeyField doesn't need to be displayed in the DataGrid. Note, however, that the DataKeyField doesn't support multicolumn keys.

Add a DataGrid to a Web Form

1 Open the UsingWebForms project from the Start page or the File menu.

2 In the Solution Explorer, double-click the DataGrid.aspx file.

Microsoft Visual Studio .NET opens the page in the form designer.

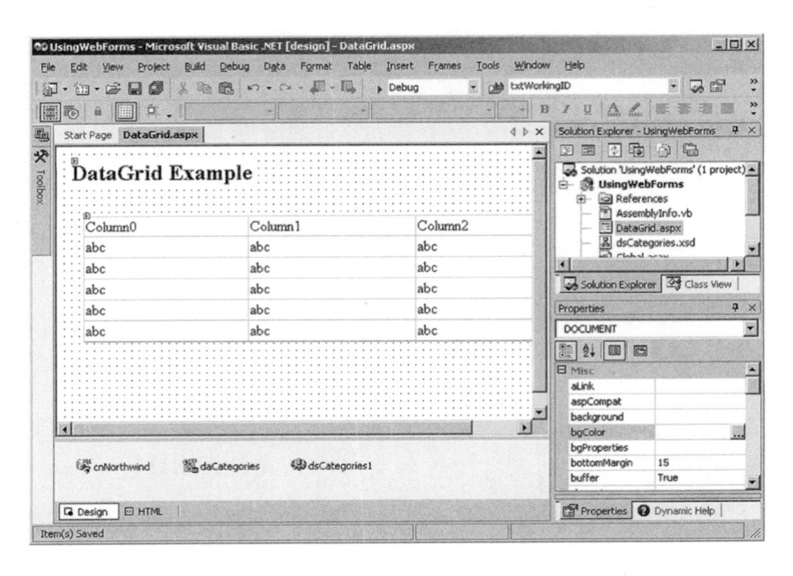

3 Select the DataGrid, and then click Property Builder in the bottom pane of the Properties window.

Visual Studio displays the dgCategories Property Builder.

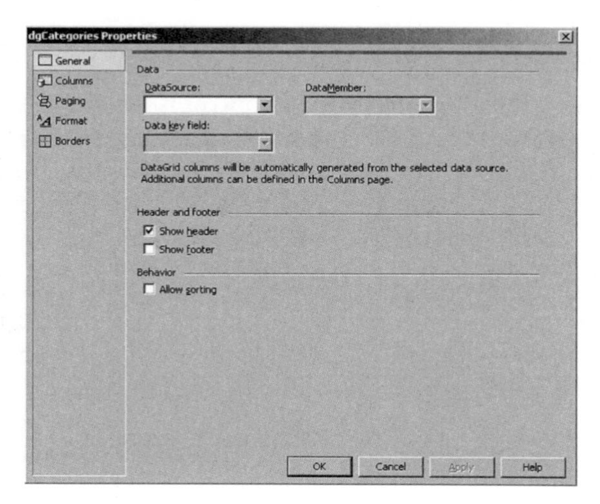

4 Set dvCategories as the DataSource and CategoryID as the DataKeyField.

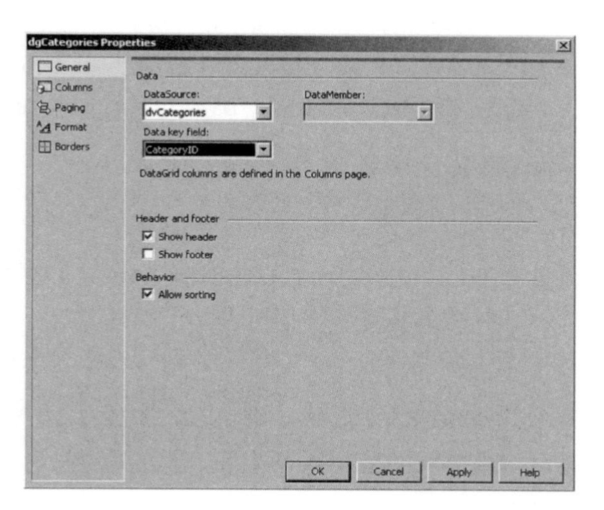

The columns displayed in the DataGrid are defined on the Columns tab of the Property Builder. Five types of columns are available, as shown in Table 13-2.

Column Type	Description
Bound	A column from the data source
Button	A button with custom functionality
Select	An intrinsic button that allows a row to be selected
Edit, Update, Cancel	Intrinsic buttons that support in-place editing
Delete	An intrinsic button that allows a row to be deleted
Hyperlink	Displays the data as a hyperlink

Template	Custom combinations of controls, which may be data-bound

Table 13-2 DataGrid Column Types

A Bound column displays a column from the data source. You can determine whether the column is visible and whether it is read-only in the Property Builder. The Property Builder also allows you to specify a data formatting expression to control the way the data is displayed.

A Button column is a user-defined control. You specify fixed text for the button or bind the text to a column in the data source by setting its TextField property.

In addition to the generic Button column, the DataGrid exposes a set of intrinsic buttons to support in-place editing: Edit, Update, and Cancel (which work as a set), Select, and Delete. As we'll see, these intrinsic buttons trigger custom server-side events rather than the generic ItemCommand. The Select and Delete buttons can be data-bound by setting their TextField properties.

A Hyperlink column embeds an <HREF> tag in the text, allowing the user to navigate to a different page by selecting a value in the column.

Finally the Template column allows a fine degree of formatting control by using the Template editor. Any of the other column types can also converted to Template columns by clicking the Link button in the Properties window. We'll examine the use of Template columns later in this chapter.

Add Data-Bound Columns to a DataGrid

1 Select Columns in the left pane of the Property Builder.

Visual Studio displays the Columns tab.

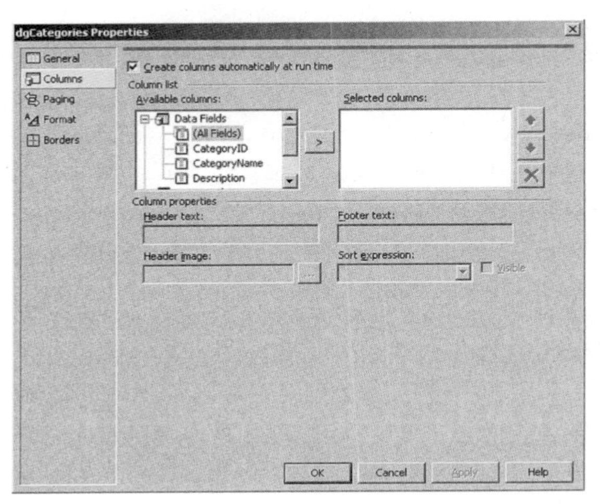

2. Clear the Create Column Automatically At Run Time check box.
3. In the Available Columns list, expand the Button column node, choose the Select Column type, and then click the Add button (">") to move it to the Selected Columns list.

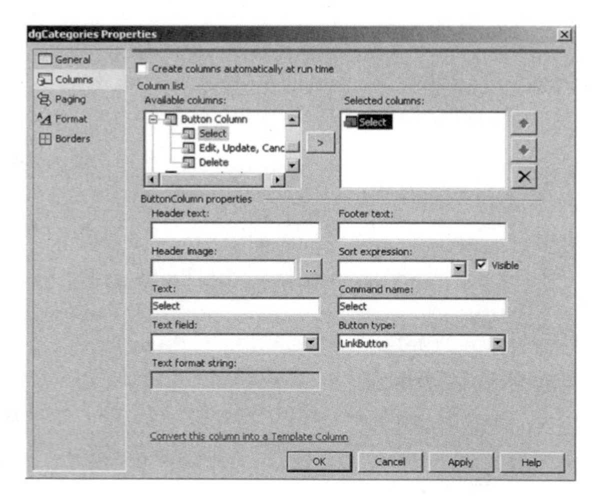

4. Delete the Text property, and then set the TextField property to *CategoryID*.

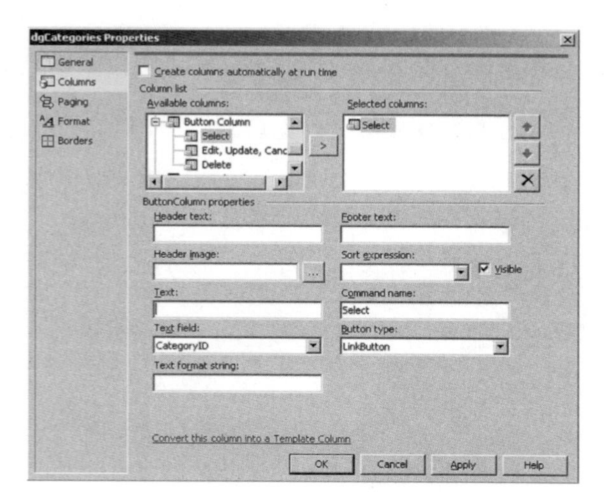

5. In the Available Columns list, expand the Data Fields node (if necessary), and then move CategoryName and Description to the Selected Columns list.

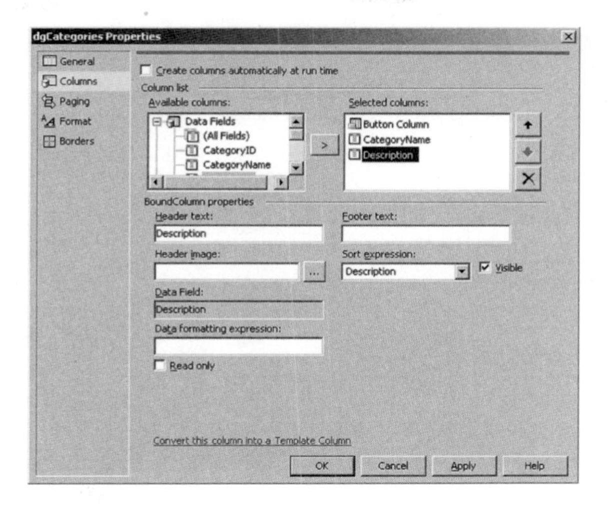

6 Click OK.

Visual Studio configures the DataGrid columns.

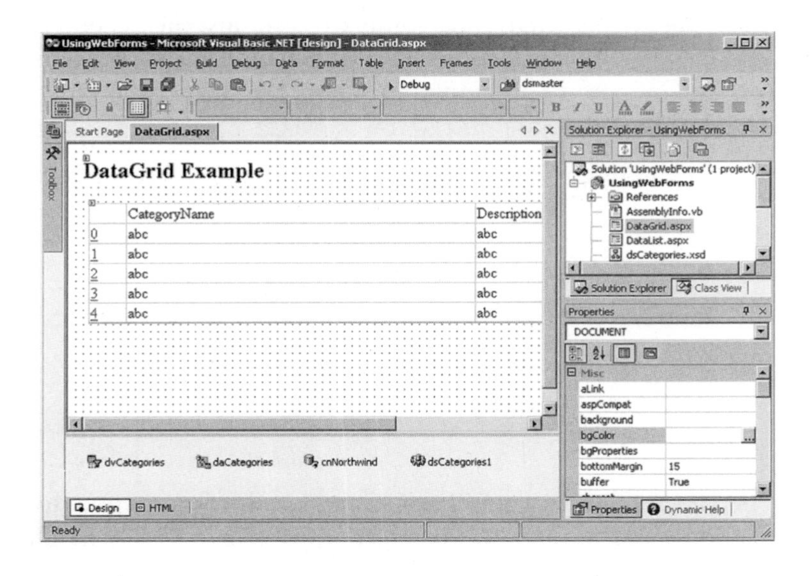

7 Press F5.

Visual Studio displays the page in the default browser.

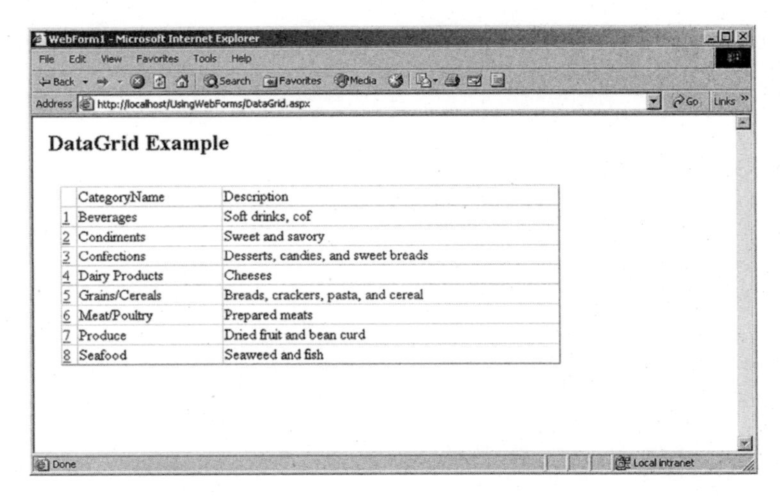

	CategoryName	Description
1	Beverages	Soft drinks, cof
2	Condiments	Sweet and savory
3	Confections	Desserts, candies, and sweet breads
4	Dairy Products	Cheeses
5	Grains/Cereals	Breads, crackers, pasta, and cereal
6	Meat/Poultry	Prepared meats
7	Produce	Dried fruit and bean curd
8	Seafood	Seaweed and fish

8 Close the browser.

Unlike the other two template-based controls, the DataGrid control doesn't require you to specify the contents of each template. Except for columns that are explicitly declared to be Template columns, the general formatting of the DataGrid controls the contents and the layout of each section. You can convert any column to a Template column by clicking the Link button in the Property Builder.

Template columns in the DataGrid expose the following sections:

- HeaderTemplate
- FooterTemplate
- ItemTemplate
- AlternatingItemTemplate
- EditItemTemplate
- Pager

The HeaderTemplate and FooterTemplate sections define the layout of the fixed top and bottom sections of the DataGrid. The ItemTemplate and AlternatingItemTemplate sections define the controls used to display values, while the EditItemTemplate section defines the controls that are used to edit the values. The Pager section is used for automatic data paging, which we'll discuss later in this chapter.

Add a Template Column to the DataGrid

1 Select the DataGrid in the form designer, and then click Property Builder in the bottom pane of the Properties window.

Visual Studio displays the Property Builder.

2 Select Columns in the left pane of the Property Builder.

Visual Studio displays the Columns tab.

3 In the Available Columns list, expand the Data Fields node (if necessary), and then add Current to the Selected Columns list. Use the up and down arrows to position the Current column between the Button column and CategoryName.

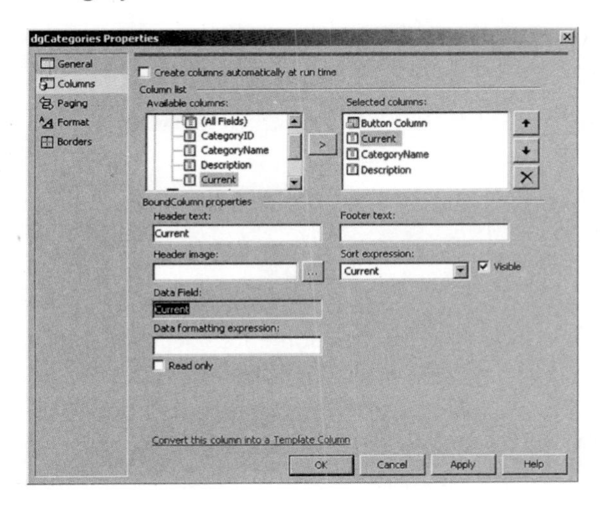

4 Click the link labeled Convert This Column Into a Template Column.

Visual Studio displays the Template column properties.

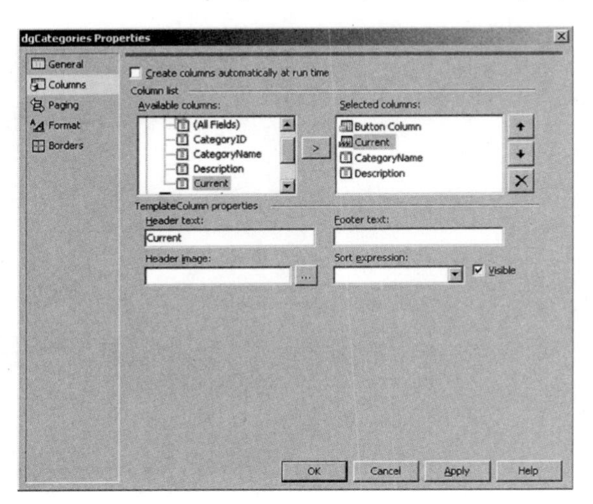

5 Click OK.

Visual Studio adds the column to the DataGrid in the form designer.

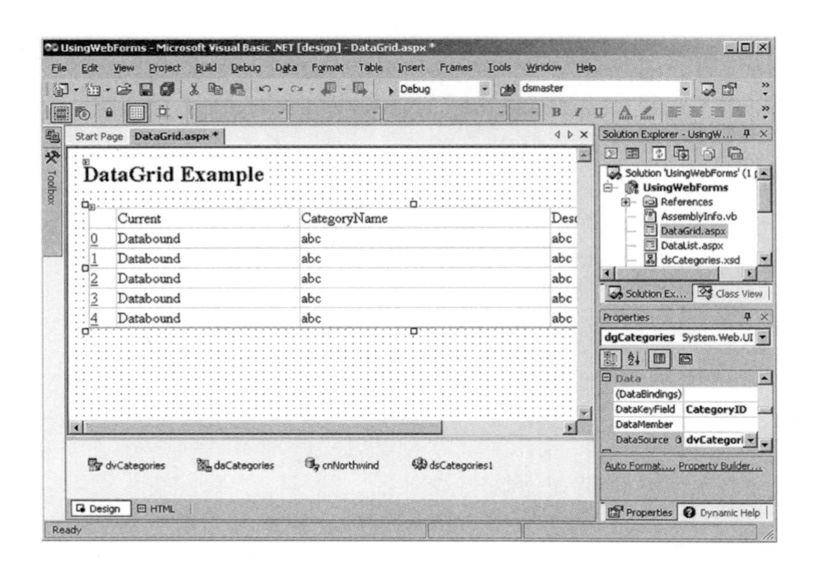

6 Right-click the DataGrid in the form designer. On the context menu, choose Edit Template, and then on the submenu, select Columns[1] – Current.

Visual Studio displays the Template editor.

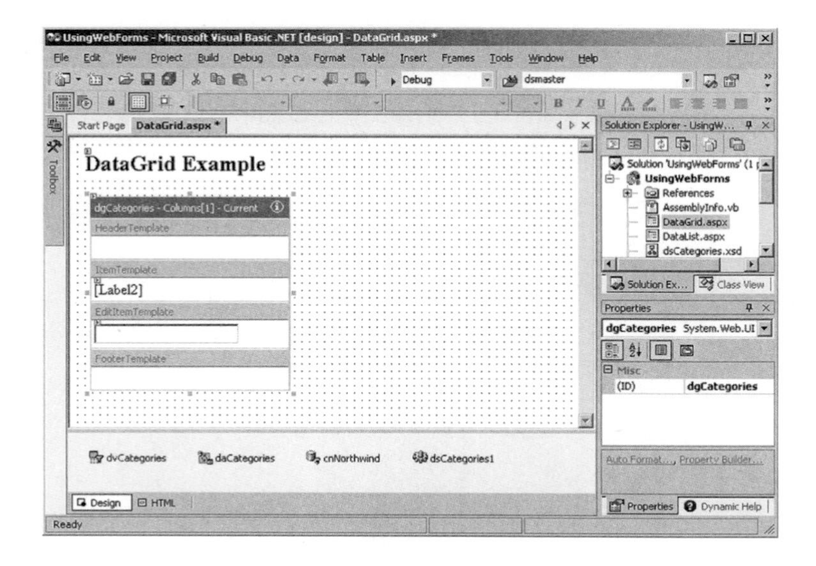

7 Delete the label in the ItemTemplate section, and then drag a CheckBox control from the Web Forms tab of the Toolbox onto the ItemTemplate section.

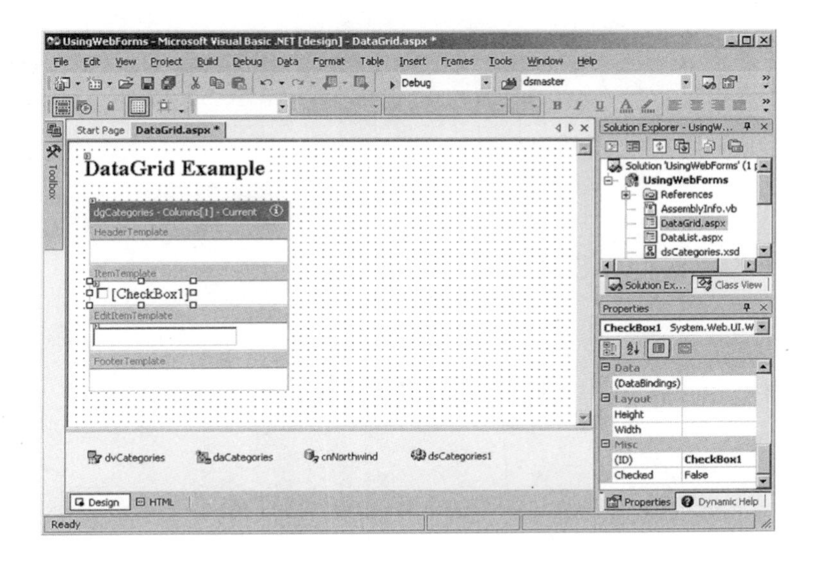

8 Use the same procedure to replace the TextBox control in the EditItem section with a CheckBox control.

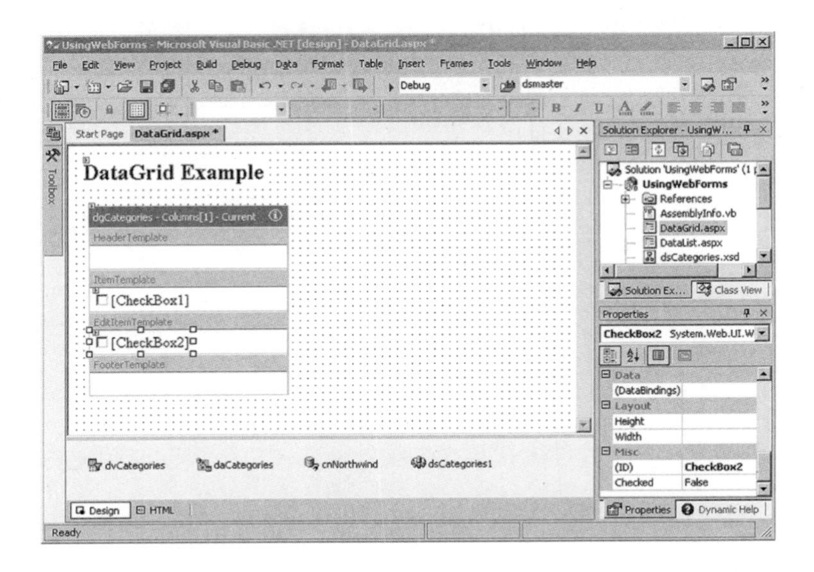

9 Right-click the Template editor, and then choose End Template Editing.

Visual Studio displays the column as a CheckBox in the form designer.

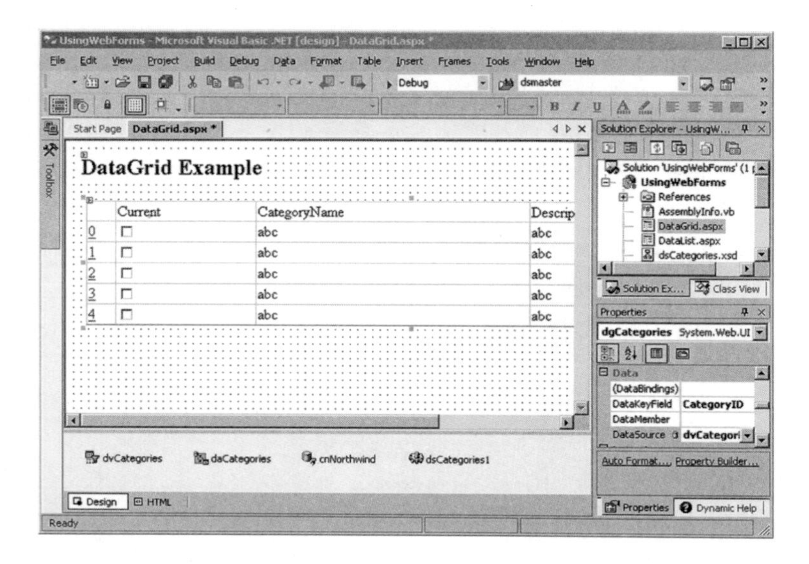

10 Press F5.

Visual Studio displays the page in the default browser.

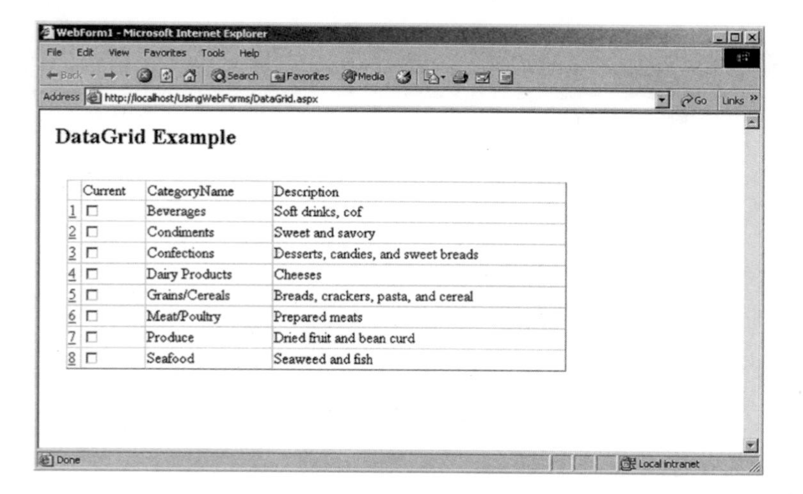

11 Close the browser.

In addition to the ItemCommand event, which is raised by custom buttons (columns of Button type), the DataGrid also exposes the events shown in Table 13-3.

Event	Description
ItemCreated	Occurs when an item in the DataGrid is first created
ItemDataBound	Occurs after the item is bound to a data value
EditCommand	Occurs when the user clicks the intrinsic Edit button
DeleteCommand	Occurs when the user clicks the intrinsic Delete button
UpdateCommand	Occurs when the user clicks the intrinsic Update button
CancelCommand	Occurs when the user clicks the intrinsic Cancel button
SortCommand	Occurs when a column is sorted
PageIndexChanged	Occurs when a page index item is clicked

Table 13-3 DataGrid Events

The ItemCreated and ItemDataBound events occur during the initial layout of the page. They're typically used to format data or other elements on the page. The Edit, Delete, Update, and Cancel commands are triggered by the intrinsic in-place editing buttons.

The SortCommand event occurs when the DataGrid is set to allow sorting and the user clicks a column head in the DataGrid. Finally the PageIndexChanged event occurs as part of the automatic paging of the DataGrid. We'll discuss this event in detail later in this chapter.

note

The use of the intrinsic in-place editing commands is straightforward and well-documented in the Visual Studio online Help. We won't be discussing them in any detail here.

Implement Sorting in a DataGrid

Visual Basic .NET

1. Select the DataGrid in the form designer, and then click Property Builder in the bottom pane of the Properties window.

   Visual Studio displays the Property Builder.
2. On the General tab, select the Allow Sorting check box.

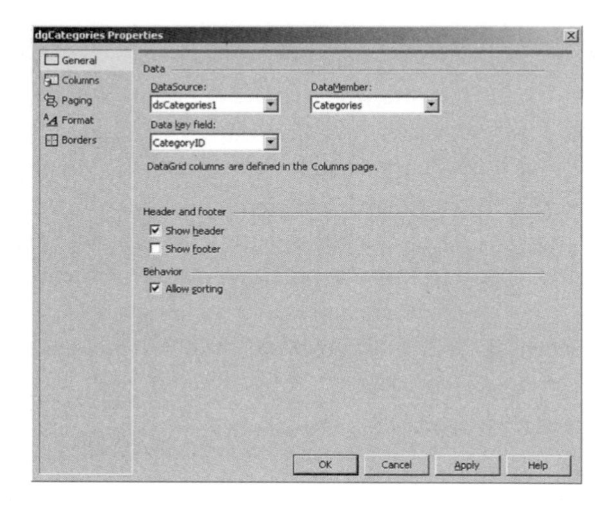

3 Click OK.

Visual Studio displays the column headings as link buttons.

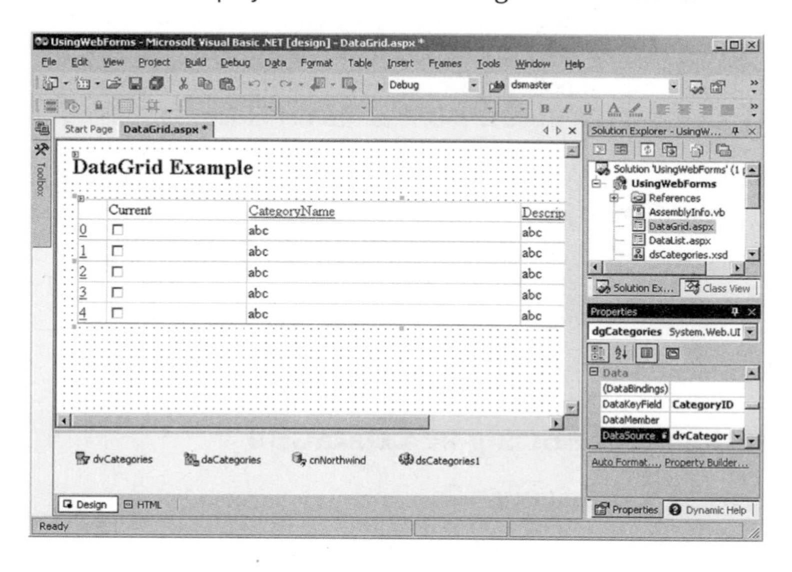

4 Press F7 to open the code editor for the page.

5 Select dgCategories in the Control Name combo box, and then select SortCommand in the Method Name combo box.

Visual Studio adds the event handler to the code.

6 Add the following lines to the event handler:

```
Me.dvCategories.Sort = e.SortExpression
DataBind()
```

7. Press F5 to run the application.

   Visual Studio displays the page in the default browser.

8. Click the Description column heading.

   The page is displayed with the DataGrid sorted by Description.

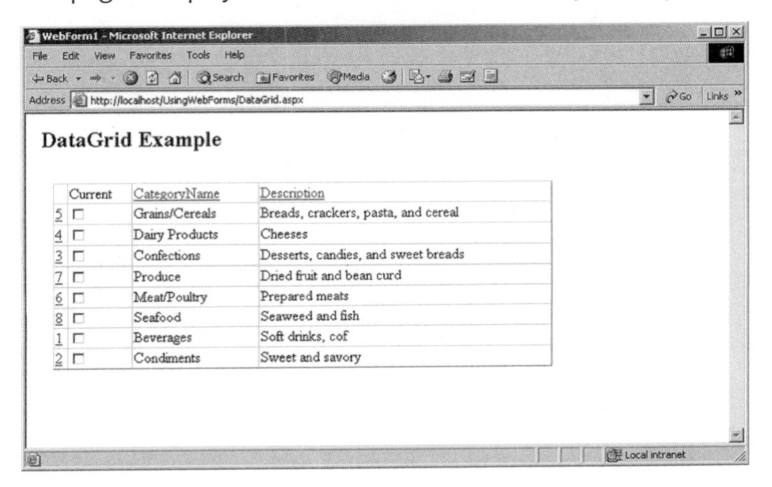

9. Close the browser.

10. Close the code editor and the form designer.

Visual C# .NET

1. Select the DataGrid in the form designer, and then click Property Builder in the bottom pane of the Properties window.

   Visual Studio displays the Property Builder.

2. On the General tab, select the Allow Sorting check box.

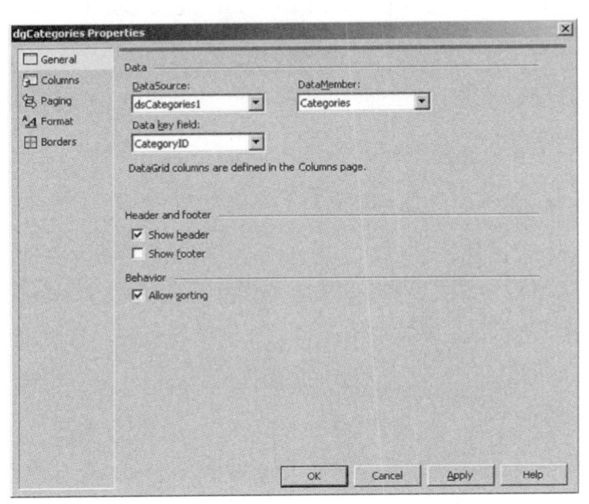

3. Click OK.

   Visual Studio displays the column headings as link buttons.

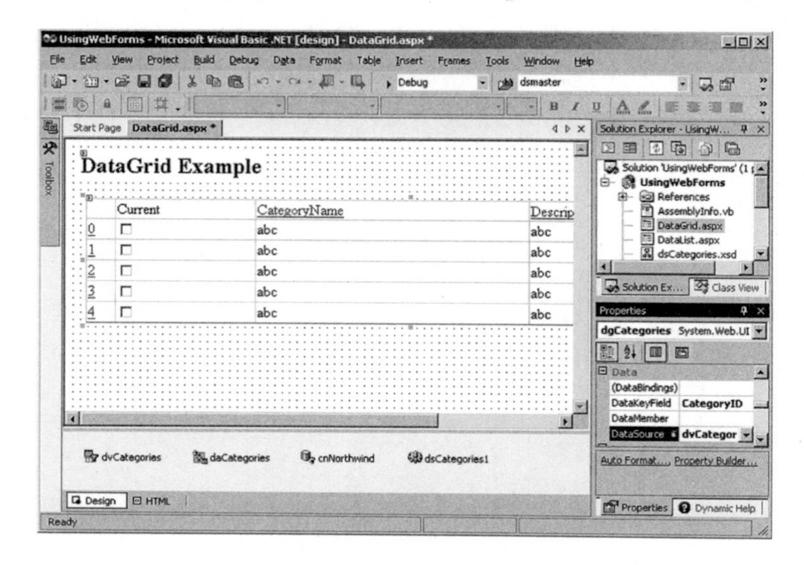

4. Display the DataGrid events in the Properties Window, and double-click the SortCommand property.

   Visual Studio opens the code editor window and adds the event handler to the code.

5. Add the following lines to the event handler:

```
this.dvCategories.Sort = e.SortExpression;
DataBind();
```

6. Press F5 to run the application.

   Visual Studio displays the page in the default browser.

7. Click the Description column heading.

   The page is displayed with the DataGrid sorted by Description.

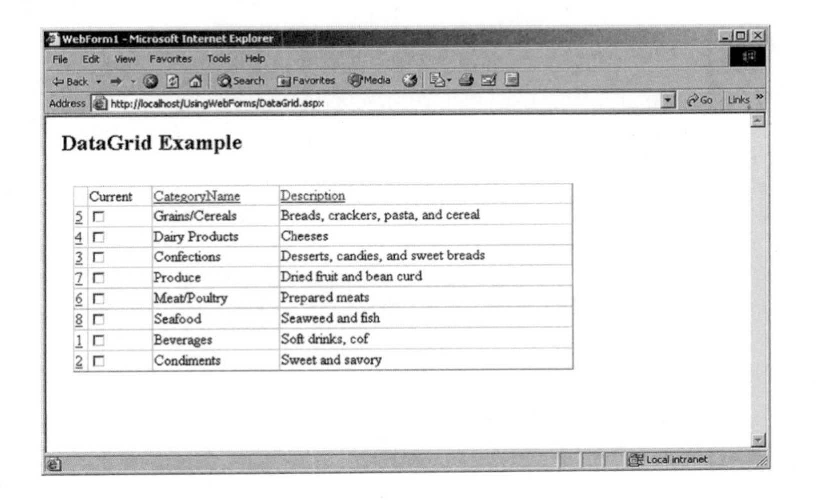

8 Close the browser.

9 Close the code editor and the form designer.

Using the DataList Control

As we've seen, the DataGrid has a default structure. You need to use templates only where your application requires advanced formatting. The DataList doesn't assume any structure and requires that you specify at least the ItemTemplate section before it can display any data.

The DataList control is bound in the same way as the DataGrid control: by setting the DataSource property, the DisplayMember property (if necessary), and, optionally, the DataKeyField property.

The DataList control supports the following templates:

- HeaderTemplate
- FooterTemplate
- ItemTemplate
- AlternatingItemTemplate
- SeparatorTemplate
- SelectedItemTemplate
- EditItemTemplate

The HeaderTemplate and FooterTemplate are identical to the corresponding templates in the DataGrid. Unlike the DataGrid, the four Item templates do not necessarily correspond to a column, only to a single row in the data source. The SeparatorTemplate is used when the contents of the DataList are displayed as flowed text. We'll examine flowed text later in this chapter.

Add a DataList to a Web Form

1. In the Solution Explorer, right-click DataList.aspx, and choose Set as Start Page.
2. Double-click the file.

   Visual Studio displays the Web form in the form designer.

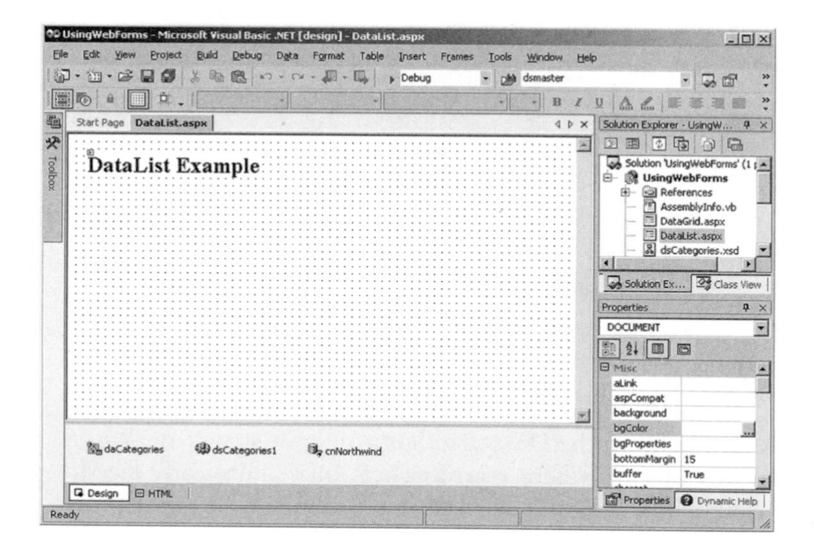

3. Drag a DataList control from the Web Form tab of the Toolbox onto the form designer.

   Visual Studio adds a placeholder for the DataList control.

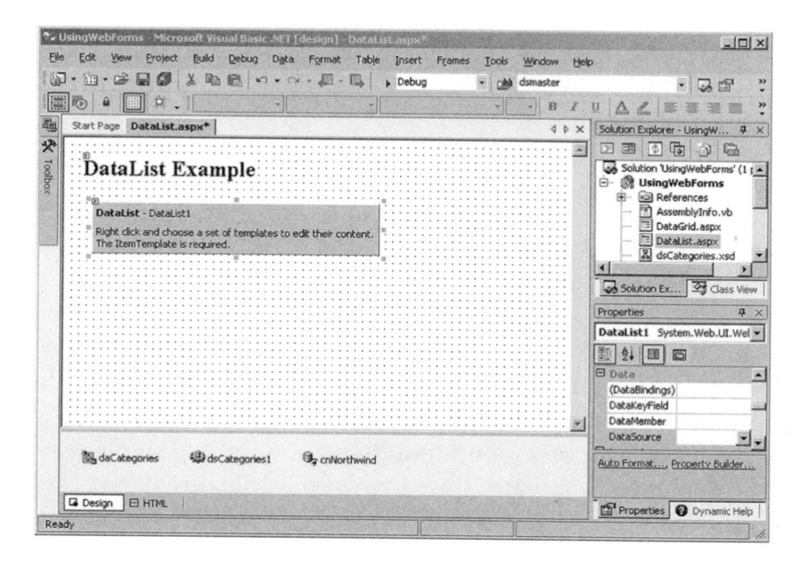

4 In the Properties window, set the DataSource property of the DataList to *dsCategories1*, and then set its DataMember property to *Categories*.

5 Right-click the DataList in the form designer. On the context menu, select Edit Template, and then on the submenu, select Item Templates.

Visual Studio displays the Template editor.

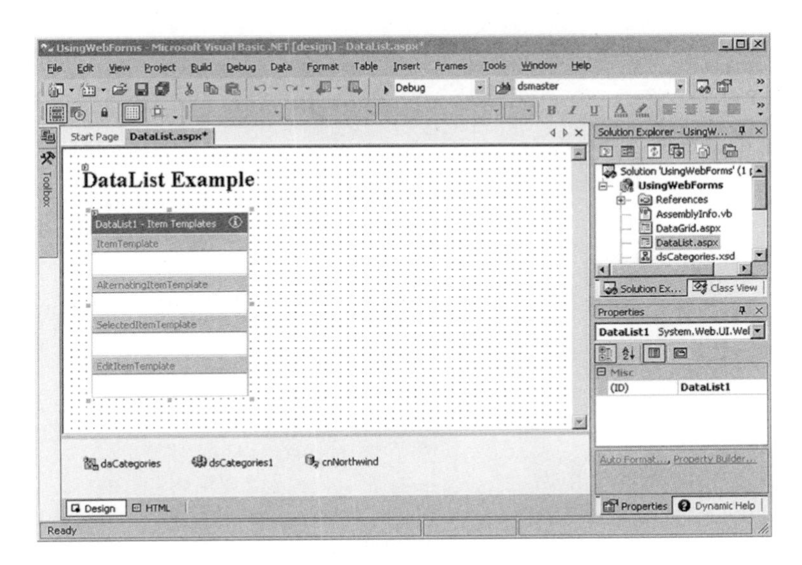

6 Drag a Label control from the Toolbox onto the ItemTemplate section of the Template editor.

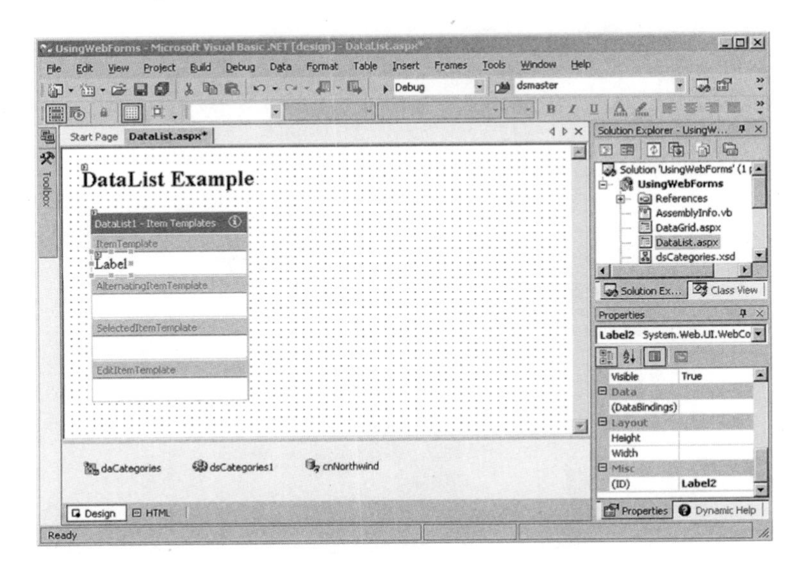

7 In the Properties Window, select the (DataBindings) property and click the Ellipsis button.

Visual Studio opens the DataBindings dialog box.

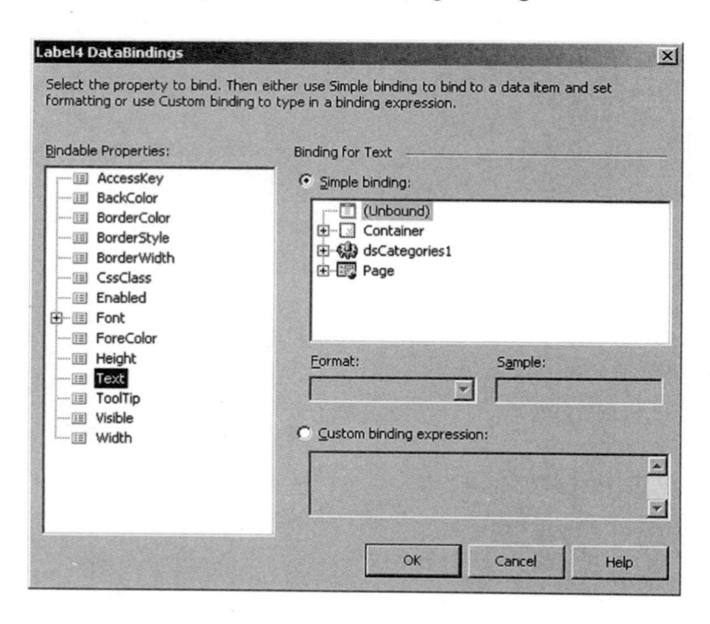

8 Expand the Container node and the DataItem node, and then select CategoryName.

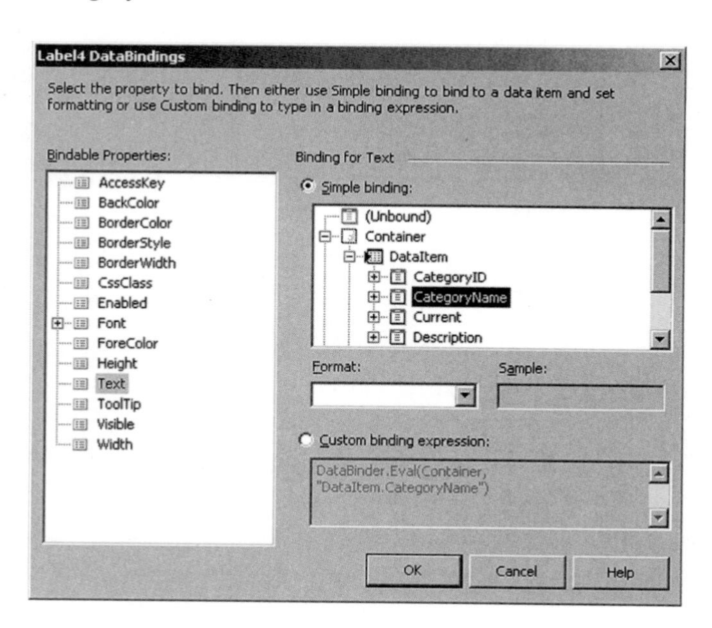

9 Click OK.

10 Right-click the DataList control, and then on the context menu, select End Template Editing.

Visual Studio displays the bound item in the DataList placeholder.

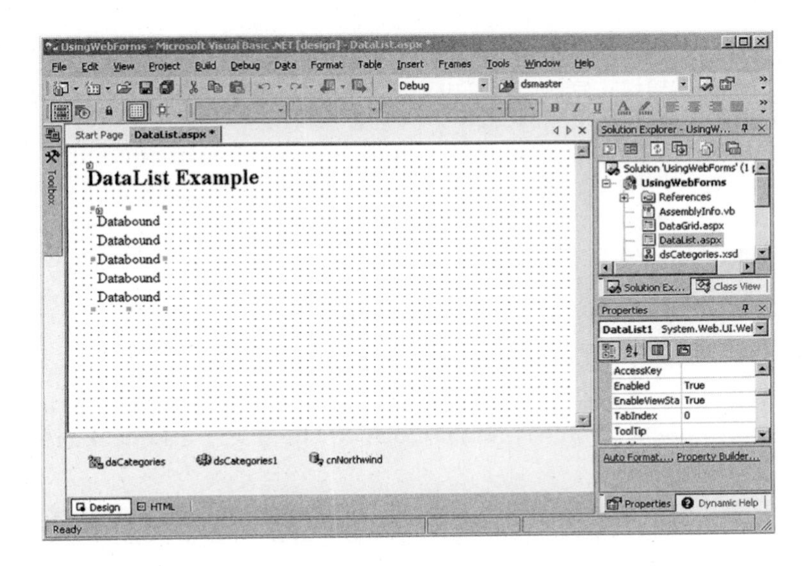

11 Press F5.

Visual Studio displays the page in the default browser.

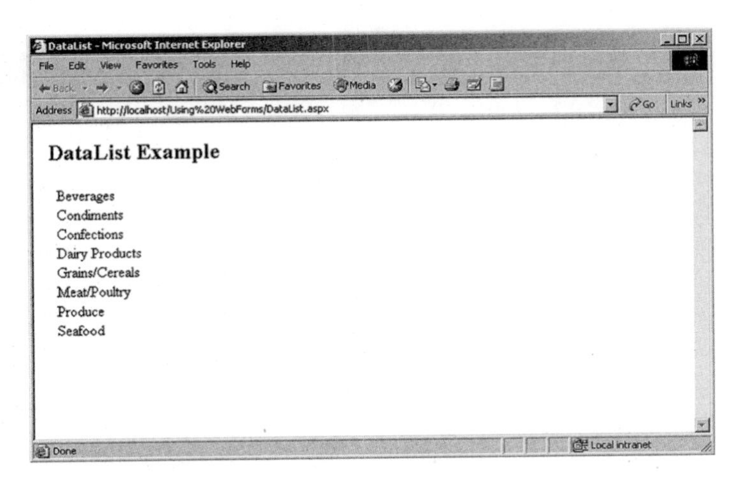

12 Close the browser.

The DataList control doesn't presuppose a table layout, although that is the default layout. There are two options for the layout of the data in the DataList, which is controlled by the RepeatLayout property. If the RepeatLayout property is set to *Table*, the data items are displayed as an HTML table. If the RepeatLayout property is set to *Flow*, the items are included in-line as part of the document's regular flow of text.

If the DataList values are displayed as a table, the RepeatDirection property controls the way in which the table will be filled. A value of *Vertical* fills the table cells from top to bottom, like a newspaper column, while setting the RepeatDirection property to *Horizontal* fills the cells from left to right, like a calendar. The actual number of columns is determined by the RepeatColumns property.

Display a DataList as Flowed Text

1. Select the DataList control in the form designer.
2. In the Properties window, set the RepeatLayout property to *Flow*, set the RepeatColumns property to *3*, and then set the RepeatDirection property to *Vertical*.
3. Right-click the DataList in the form designer, select Edit Template on the context menu, and then on the submenu, select Separator Template.

   Visual Studio displays the Template editor.

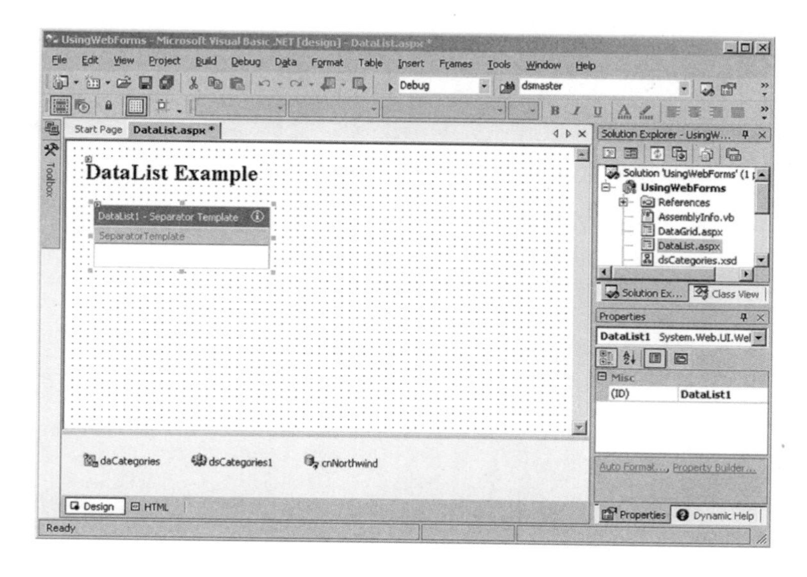

4. Add a comma and a space to the template.

5 Right-click the Template editor, and then on the context menu, select End Template Editing.

Visual Studio displays the data items separated by the comma and a space.

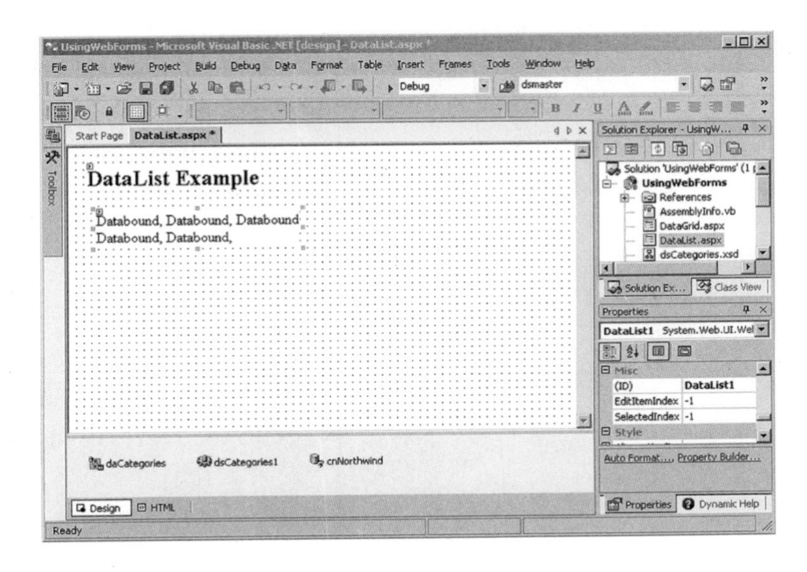

6 Increase the width of the control to about the width of a browser page.

7 Press F5.

Visual Studio displays the page in the default browser.

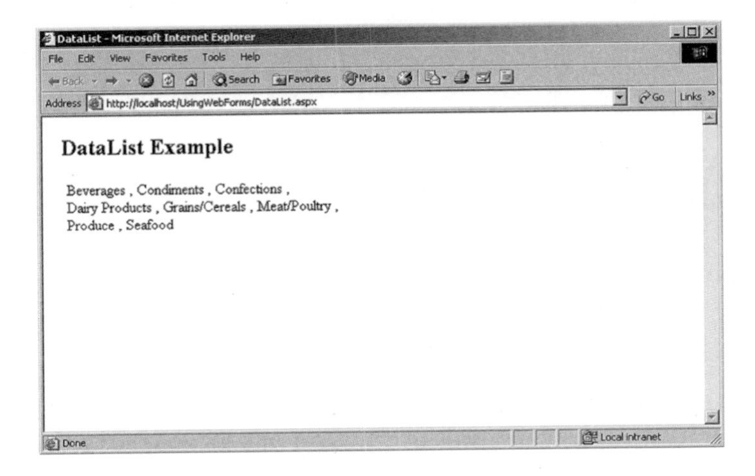

8 Close the browser.

9 Close the form designer.

Moving Through Data

Whenever performance and scalability are issues, it's important to limit the amount of data displayed on a single page. For usability reasons, you should always limit the amount of data that is displayed, no matter what the environment—users don't appreciate having to wade through masses of data to find the single bit of information they require.

One common technique in the Internet environment for limiting the amount of data on a single Web page is to display only a fixed number of rows and allow the user to move forward and backward through the DataSet. This technique is usually referred to as *paging*.

The Web form DataGrid control provides intrinsic support for paging by using the three methods shown in Table 13-4.

Method	Description
Default Paging/Default Navigation	Displays either Next and Previous buttons or page numbers as part of the DataGrid; the CurrentPageIndex property is updated by the DataGrid
Default Paging/Custom Navigation	Navigation buttons are outside the grid, and the CurrentPageIndex property is set manually
Custom Paging	Navigation buttons are outside the grid, and all paging is handled within application code

Table 13-4 DataGrid Paging Methods

The simplest method is, of course, to use the DataGrid control's *Default Paging/Default Navigation* method, but the custom options are only slightly more difficult to implement.

DataGrid paging is controlled by two of its properties. The PageSize property, which defaults to *10*, determines the number of items to display. The CurrentPageIndex property determines the set of rows that will be displayed when the page is rendered.

Though it doesn't control paging, the read-only property PageCount returns the total number of pages of data in the data source.

When the user selects either one of the default navigation buttons, ASP.NET raises a PageIndexChanged event. The event arguments parameter of this event includes a NewPageIndex property. Rendering the new page in the DataGrid is as simple as setting the DataGrid control's CurrentPageIndex property to the value of NewPageIndex and calling the *DataBind* method.

Implement Default Paging in a DataGrid Control

Visual Basic .NET

1. In the Solution Explorer, right-click DataGrid.aspx, and then on the context menu, select Set as Start Page.
2. In the Solution Explorer, double-click DataGrid.aspx.

   Visual Studio displays the page in the form designer.
3. Select the DataGrid, and then click Property Builder in the bottom pane of the Properties window.

   Visual Studio displays the Property Builder.
4. Select Paging in the left pane of the Property Builder.

   Visual Studio displays the Paging properties.

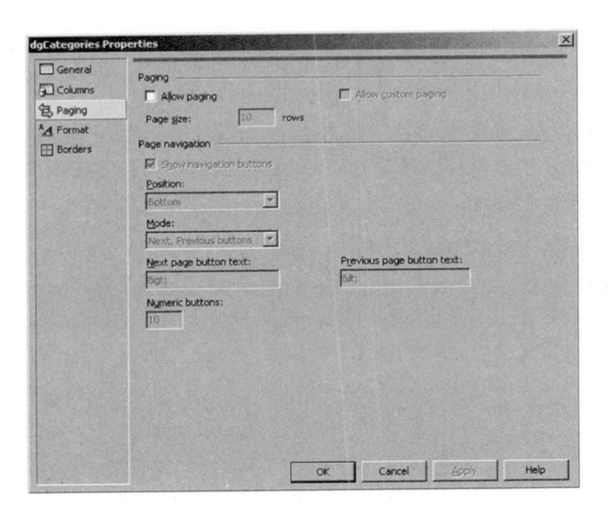

5. Select the Allow Paging check box, and then set the Page Size property to 5 rows.

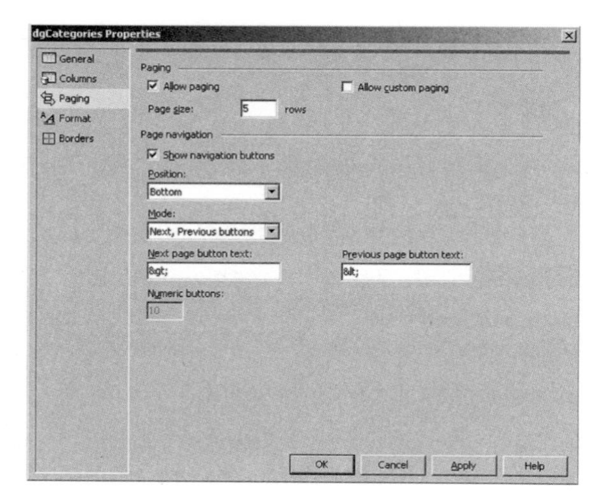

6. Click OK.
7. Press F7 to display the code editor.
8. Select dgCategories in the Control Name combo box, and then select PageIndexChanged in the Method Name combo box.

   Visual Studio adds the event handler to the code.
9. Add the following lines to the procedure:

```
Me.dgCategories.CurrentPageIndex = e.NewPageIndex
DataBind()
```

10. Press F5.

    Visual Studio displays the page in the default browser.
11. Click the Next (">") button.

    Visual Studio displays the remaining 3 rows in the DataGrid.

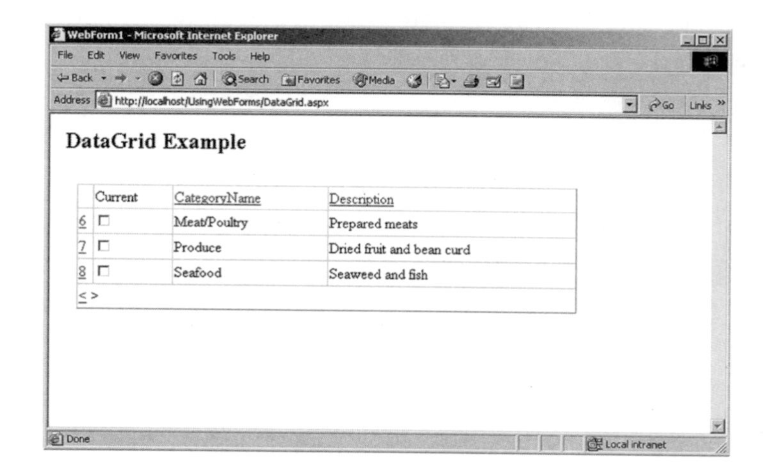

12 Close the browser.

13 Close the code editor and the form designer.

Visual C# .NET

1 In the Solution Explorer, right-click DataGrid.aspx, and then on the context menu, select Set as Start Page.

2 In the Solution Explorer, double-click DataGrid.aspx.

Visual Studio displays the page in the form designer.

3 Select the DataGrid, and then click Property Builder in the bottom pane of the Properties window.

Visual Studio displays the Property Builder.

4 Select Paging in the left pane of the Property Builder.

Visual Studio displays the Paging properties.

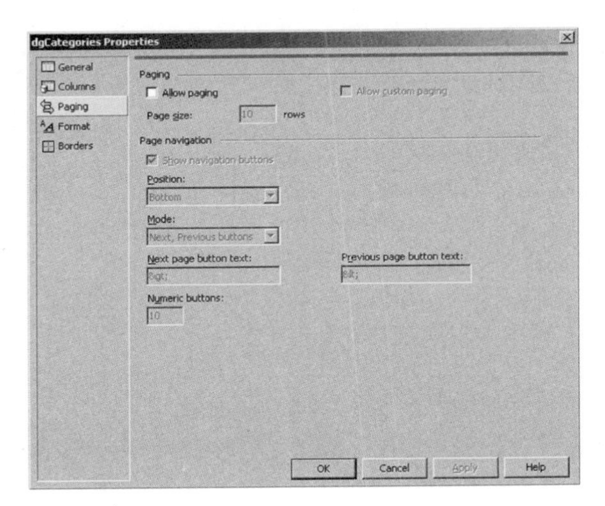

5 Select the Allow Paging check box, and then set the Page Size property to 5 rows.

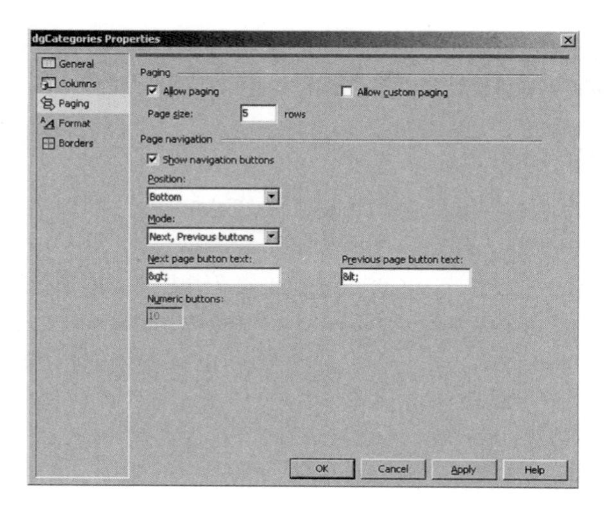

6. Click OK.
7. Display the DataGrid events in the Properties Window, and double-click the PageIndexChanged property.

   Visual Studio opens the code editor window adds the event handler to the code.
8. Add the following lines to the procedure:

```
this.DataGrid1.CurrentPageIndex = e.NewPageIndex;
DataBind();
```

9. Press F5.

   Visual Studio displays the page in the default browser.
10. Click the Next (">") button.

    Visual Studio displays the remaining 3 rows in the DataGrid.

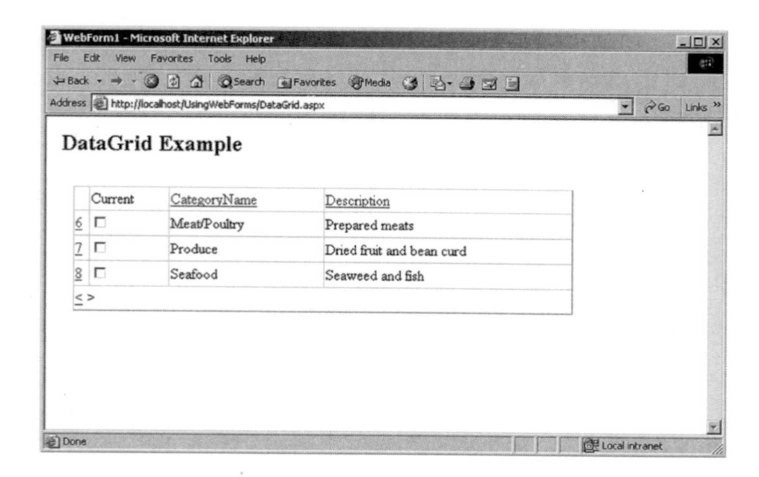

11 Close the browser.

12 Close the code editor and the form designer.

Web forms don't implement a BindingContext property that maintains a reference to a current position in a data source. It's easy enough, however, to maintain a Position property, stored either in the Session state or in the Page object's ViewState, and handle the data manipulation manually.

You might use this technique, for example, if you want to display only a single row on the Web page, but allow the user to navigate through all the rows by using the same navigation buttons that are typically available on a Windows form.

Implement Manual Navigation on a Web Form

Visual Basic .NET

1 In the Solution Explorer, right-click Position.aspx, and then select Set as Start Page.

2 Double-click the file.

Visual Studio displays the page in the form designer.

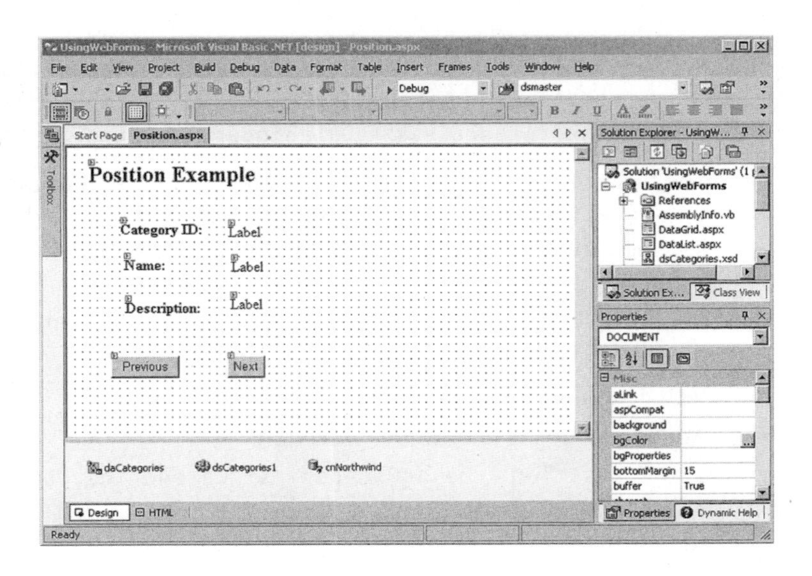

3 Press F7 to display the code editor.

4 Add the following global declaration to the top of the class:

```
Public Position as Integer
```

5 Add the following lines to the Page_Load Sub:

```
If Me.IsPostBack Then
   Me.dsCategories1 = CType(ViewState("dsCategories"), DataSet)
   Me.Position = CType(ViewState("Position"), Integer)
Else
   Me.daCategories.Fill(Me.dsCategories1.Categories)
   ViewState("dsCategories") = Me.dsCategories1
   ViewState("Postion") = 0
End If
Me.DataBind()
```

This code is very similar to the procedure we used in Chapter 12 to store the DataSet with the page, but we're also storing the value of the new variable, Position.

6 Select (Base Class Events) in the Control Name combo box, and then select DataBinding in the Method Name combo box.

Visual Studio adds the event handler to the code.

7 Add the following lines to the procedure:

```
Dim dr As DataRow

dr = Me.dsCategories1.Categories.DefaultView(Position).Row
Me.txtCatID.Text = DataBinder.Eval(dr, "CategoryID")
Me.txtName.Text = DataBinder.Eval(dr, "CategoryName")
Me.txtDescription.Text = DataBinder.Eval(dr, "Description")
```

The first two lines declare a local variable, *dr*, and set it to the row of the Categories table specified by the Position variable. The next three bind the value of columns in the row to the Text properties of the appropriate controls.

8 Select btnNext in the Control Name combo box, and then select Click in the Method Name combo box.

Visual Studio adds the event handler to the code.

9 Add the following lines to the procedure:

```
If Me.Position < Me.dsCategories1.Categories.Count Then
   Me.Position += 1
   ViewState("Position") = Me.Position
   DataBind()
End If
```

The code checks that the current value of Position is less than the number of rows in the Categories table, and if so, it increments the value and stores it to the ViewState.

10 Select btnPrevious in the Control Name combo box, and then select Click in the Method Name combo box.

Visual Studio adds the event handler to the code.

11 Add the following lines to the procedure:

```
If Me.Position > 0 Then
   Me.Position -= 1
   ViewState("Position") = Me.Position
   DataBind()
End If
```

12 Press F5.

Visual Studio displays the page in the default browser.

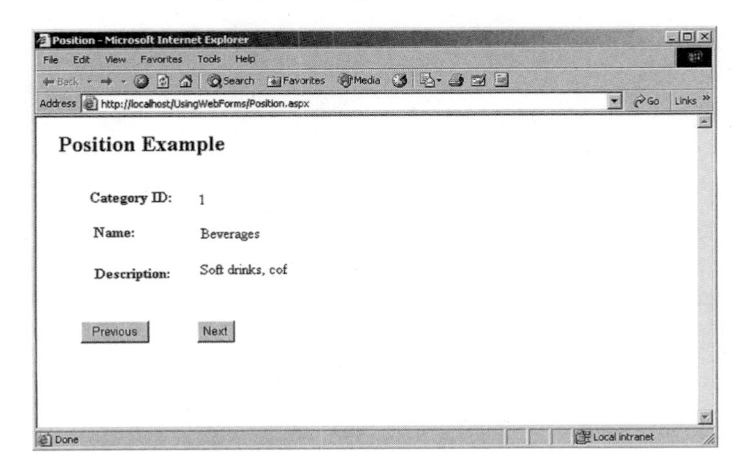

13 Click the Next button.

The page displays the next category.

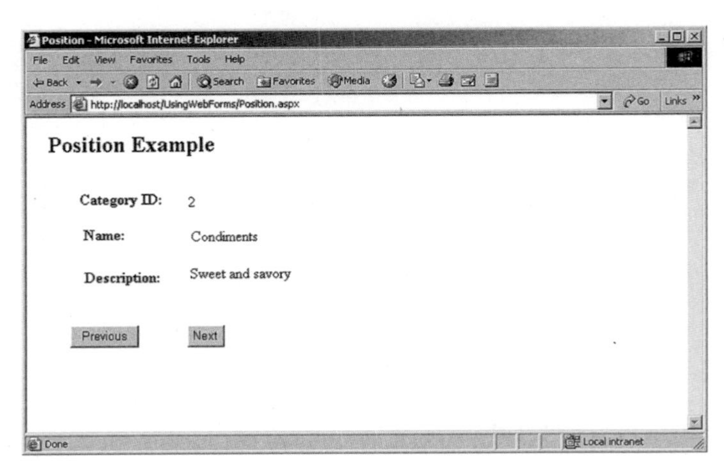

14 Click the Previous button.

The page displays the previous category.

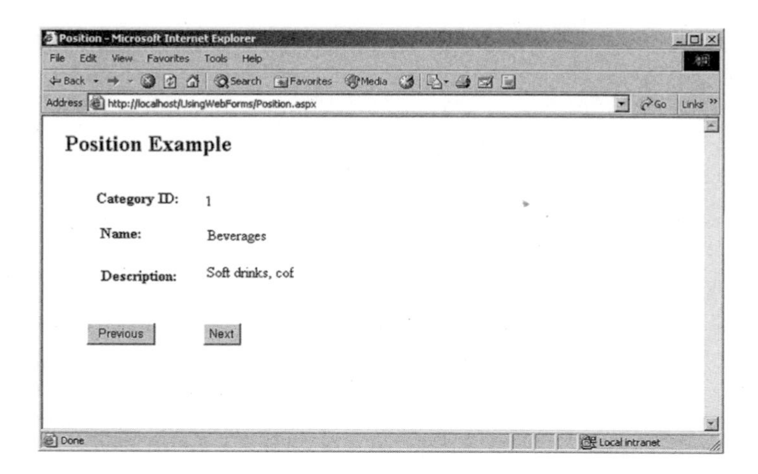

15 Close the browser.

16 Close the code editor and the form designer.

Visual C# .NET

1 In the Solution Explorer, right-click Position.aspx, and then select Set as Start Page.

2 Double-click the file.

Visual Studio displays the page in the form designer.

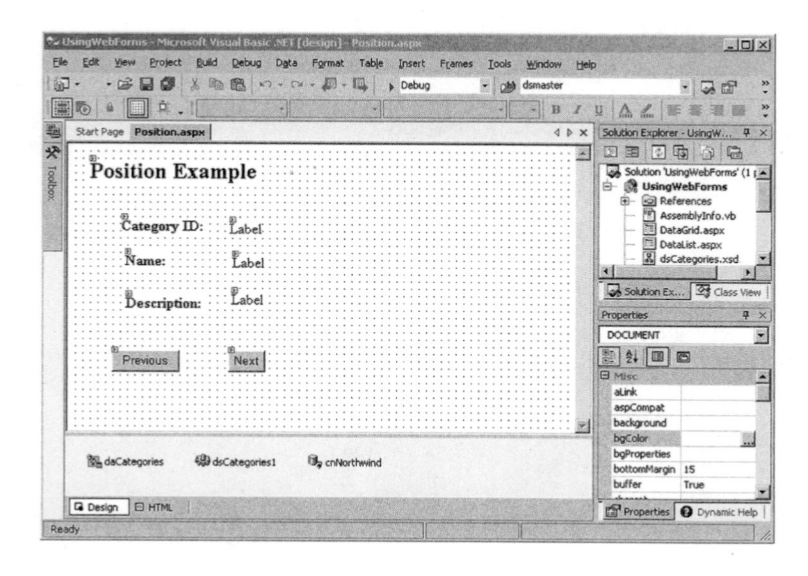

3 Press F7 to display the code editor.

4 Add the following global declaration to the top of the class:

```
public int pagePosition;
```

5 Add the following lines to the *Page_Load* method:

```
if (this.IsPostBack == true)
{
   this.dsCategories1 = (dsCategories) ViewState["dsCategories"];
   this.pagePosition = (int) ViewState["pagePosition"];
}
else
{
    this.daCategories.Fill(this.dsCategories1.Categories);
    ViewState["dsCategories"] = this.dsCategories1;
    ViewState["pagePosition"] = 0;
}
this.DataBind();
```

This code is very similar to the procedure we used in Chapter 12 to store the DataSet with the page, but we're also storing the value of the new variable, pagePosition.

6 In the Properties Window of the form designer, select Position from the controls combo box. Click the Events button, and then double-click the DataBinding event.

Visual Studio adds the event handler to the code.

7 Add the following lines to the *Position_DataBinding* procedure:

```
DataRow dr;

dr = this.dsCategories1.Categories.DefaultView[pagePosition].Row;
this.txtCatID.Text = DataBinder.Eval(dr, "CategoryID").ToString();
this.txtName.Text = (string) DataBinder.Eval(dr, "CategoryName");
this.txtDescription.Text = (string) DataBinder.Eval(dr, "Description");
```

The first two lines declare a local variable, *dr*, and set it to the row of the Categories table specified by the Position variable. The next three bind the value of columns in the row to the Text properties of the appropriate controls.

8 In the form designer, double-click the Next button.

Visual Studio adds the event handler to the code.

9 Add the following lines to the procedure:

```
if (this.pagePosition < this.dsCategories1.Categories.Count)
{
   this.pagePosition++;
   ViewState["pagePosition"] = this.pagePosition;
   DataBind();
}
```

The code checks that the current value of Position is less than the number of rows in the Categories table, and if so, it increments the value and stores it to the ViewState.

10 In the Form Designer, double-click the Previous button.

Visual Studio adds the event handler to the code.

11 Add the following lines to the procedure:

```
if (this.pagePosition > 0)
{
   this.pagePosition--;
   ViewState["pagePosition"] = this.pagePosition;
   DataBind();
}
```

12 Press F5.

Visual Studio displays the page in the default browser.

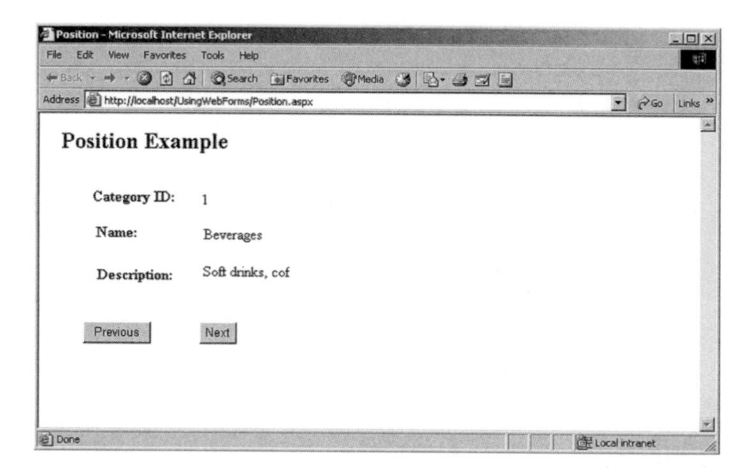

13 Click the Next button.

The page displays the next category.

14 Click the Previous button.

The page displays the previous category.

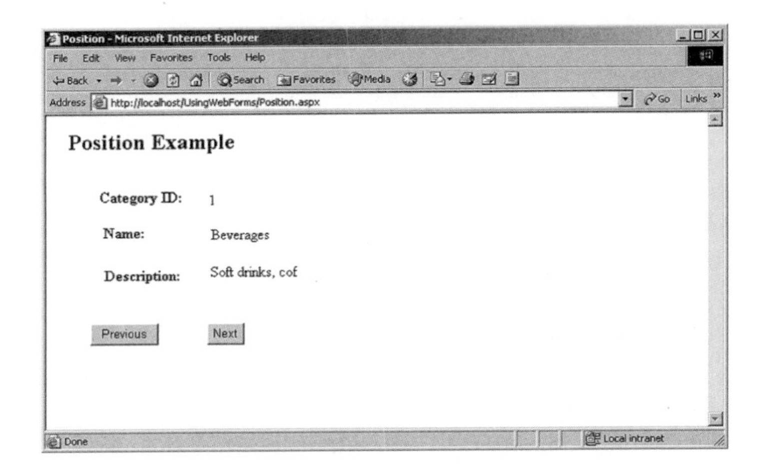

15 Close the browser.

16 Close the code editor and the form designer.

Web Form Validation

The .NET Framework supports a number of validation controls which can be used to validate data. The Web form validation controls, which are shown in Table 13-5, are more sophisticated than the Windows Forms ErrorProvider control, which only displays error messages. The Web form controls perform the validation checks and display any resulting error messages.

Validation Control	Description
RequiredFieldValidator	Ensures that the input control contains a value
CompareValidator	Compares the contents of the input control to a constant value or the contents of another control
RangeValidator	Checks that the contents of the input control are between the specified upper and lower bounds, which may be characters, numbers, or dates
RegularExpressionValidator	Checks that the contents of the input control match the pattern specified by a regular expression
CustomValidator	Checks that the contents of the input control are based on custom logic

Table 13-5 Validation Controls

Each validation control checks for a single condition in a single control on the page, which is known as the *input control*. To check for multiple conditions, multiple validation controls can be assigned to a single input control. This is frequently the case because all of the controls except RequiredFieldValidator consider a blank field to be valid.

The conditions specified by the validation controls assigned to a given input control will be combined with a logical AND—all of the conditions must be met or the control will be considered invalid. If you need to combine validation conditions with a logical OR, you can use a CustomValidator control to manually check the value.

If the browser supports DHTML, validation will first take place on the client, and the form will not be submitted until all conditions are met. Whether or not validation has occurred on the client, validation will always occur on the server when a Click event is processed. Additionally, you can manually call a control's *Validate* method to validate its contents from code.

When the page is validated, the contents of the input control are passed to the validation control (or controls), which tests the contents and sets the control's IsValid property to false. If any control is invalid, the Page object's IsValid property is also set to false. You can check for these conditions in code and take whatever action is required.

Add a RequiredFieldValidator Control to a Form

1. In the Solution Explorer, right-click Validation.aspx, and then on the context menu, select Set as Start Page.
2. In the Solution Explorer, double-click the Validation.aspx.

   Visual Studio displays the page in the form designer.

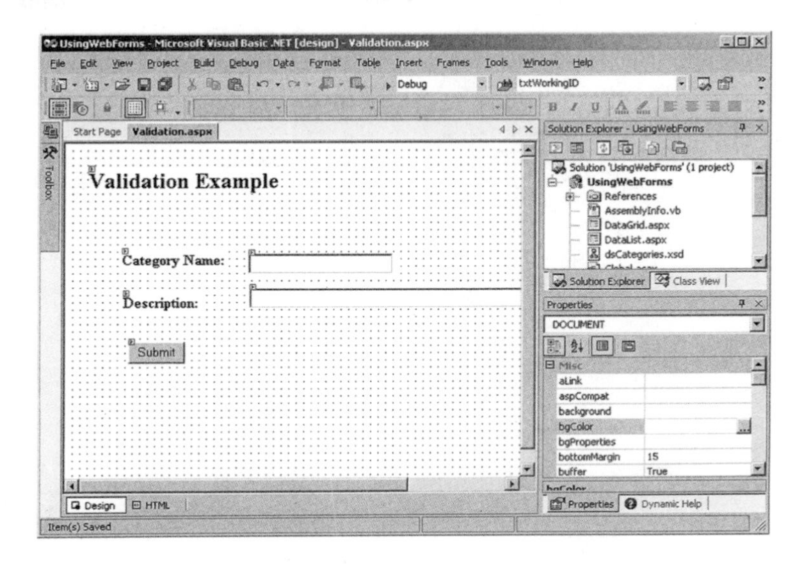

3 Drag a RequiredFieldValidator control from the Web Forms tab of the Toolbox to the right of the CategoryName TextBox control.

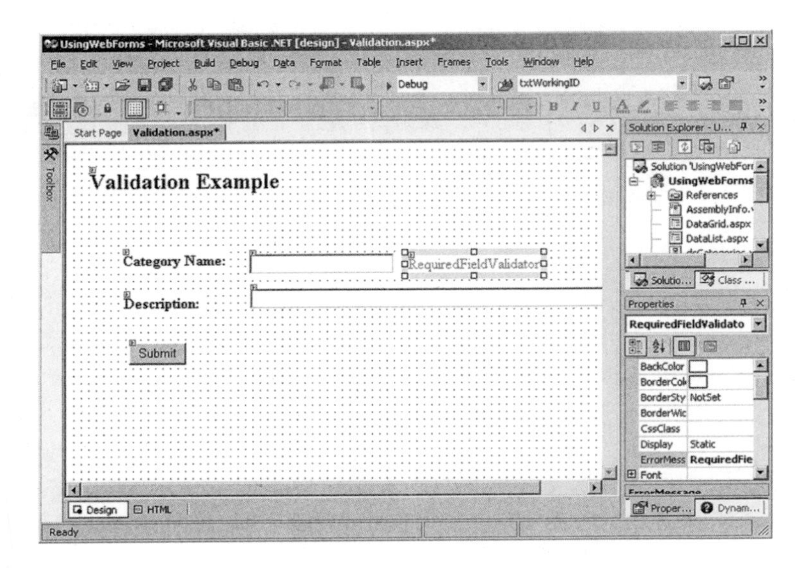

4 In the Properties window, set the RequiredFieldValidator control's ErrorMessage property to *Name cannot be left blank*, and then set its ControlToValidate property to *txtName*.

5 Press F5.

Visual Studio displays the page in the default browser.

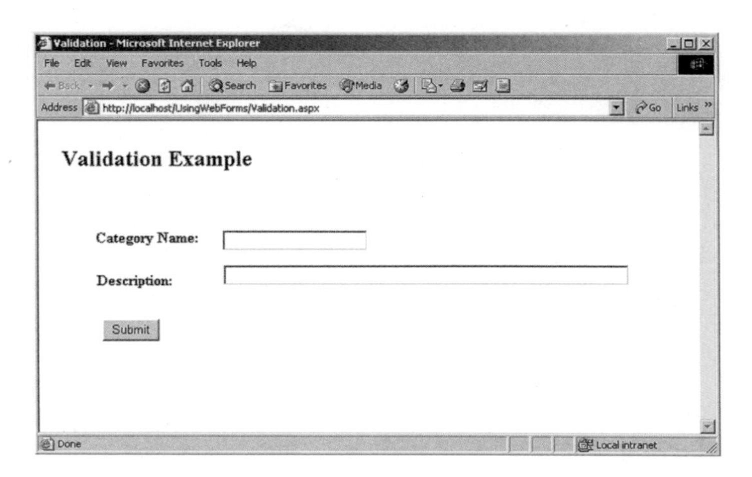

6 Click Submit.

The validation control displays the error message next to the text box.

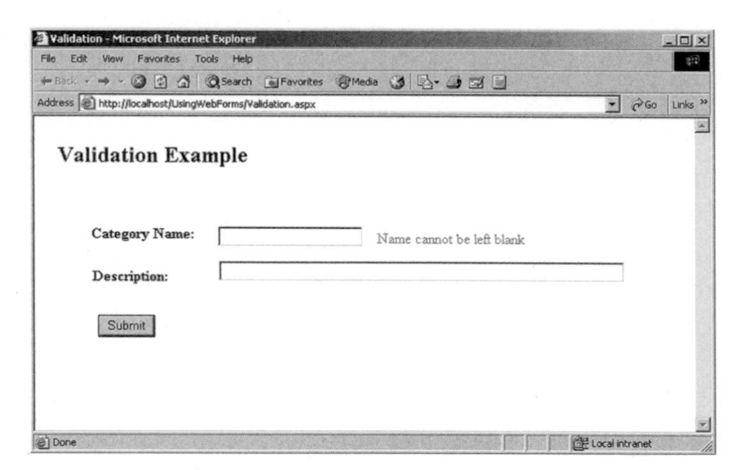

7 Close the browser.

Chapter 13 Quick Reference

To	Do this
Display data in a DataGrid control	Set the DataSource and optionally set the DataKeyField in the Property Builder
Control the Columns displayed in a data-bound DataGrid	In the Columns section of the Property Builder, cancel the selection of Create columns automatically at run time, and then select the columns to be displayed

Implement sorting in a DataGrid control	Bind the DataGrid to a DataView, select Allow Sorting in the Property Builder, and then build an event handler for the SortCommand event:
	`Me.myDataView.Sort = e.SortExpression`
	`DataBind()`

Display data in a DataList control	Set the DataSource and DataMember properties of the DataList, and the specify the data binding for each control in the DataList control's templates
Implement Paging in a DataGrid control	Select a paging option from the Paging pane of the DataGrid control's Property Builder

PART 5

ADO.NET and XML

Using the XML Designer

In this chapter, you'll learn how to:

- ✔ *Create an XML schema*
- ✔ *Create a Typed DataSet*
- ✔ *Generate a Typed DataSet from an XML schema*
- ✔ *Add DataTables to an XML DataSet schema from an existing data source*
- ✔ *Create DataTables in an XML DataSet schema*
- ✔ *Add keys to an XML schema*
- ✔ *Add relations to an XML schema*
- ✔ *Create elements*
- ✔ *Create simple types*
- ✔ *Create complex types*
- ✔ *Create attributes*

In this chapter, we'll look at the XML Designer, the Microsoft Visual Studio .NET tool that supports the creation of XML schemas and Microsoft ADO.NET Typed DataSets.

Understanding the XML Schemas

An XML schema is a document that defines the structure of XML data. Much like a database schema, an XML schema can also be used to validate the contents and structure of an XML file.

An XML schema is defined using the XML Schema Definition language (XSD). XSD is similar in structure to HTML, but whereas HTML defines the layout of a document, XSD defines the structure and content of the data.

note

XML schemas in the Microsoft .NET Framework conform to the World Wide Web Consortium (W3C) recommendation, as defined at *http://www.w3.org/2001/XMLSchema*. Additional schema elements that are used to support .NET Framework objects, such as DataSets and DataRelations, conform to the schema defined at urn:schemas-microsoft-com:xml-msdata. (Such extensions conform to the W3C recommendation and will simply be ignored by XML parsers that do not support them.)

XML schemas are defined in terms of *elements* and *attributes*. Elements and attributes are very similar, and can often be used interchangeably, although there are some distinctions:

- Elements can contain other items; attributes are always atomic.
- Elements can occur multiple times in the data; attributes can occur only once.
- By using the <xs:sequence> tag, a schema can specify that elements must occur in the order they are specified; attributes can occur in any order.
- Only elements can be nested within <xs:choice> tags, which specify mutually exclusive elements (that is, one and only one of the elements can occur).
- Attributes are restricted to built-in data types; elements can be defined using user-defined types.

By convention, elements are used for raw data, while attributes are used for metadata; but you can use whichever best suits your purposes.

Both elements and attributes define items in terms of a *type*, which defines the data that the element or attribute can validly contain. XML schemas support *simple types*, which are atomic values such as string or Boolean, and *complex types*, which are composed of other elements and attributes in any combination. We'll examine types in more detail later in this chapter.

Optionally, elements and attributes can define a name that identifies the element that is being defined. XML element names cannot begin with a number or the letters XML, nor can they contain spaces. Note that XML is case-sensitive, so the names MyName and myName are considered distinct.

XML schemas are stored in text files with an XSD extension (XSD schema files). Visual Studio provides a visual user interface for creating XML schemas, the XML Designer. The XML tab of the XML Designer allows you to examine the contents of the XSD file directly, while the DataSet or Schema tab provides a visual interface. Like the form designer, the XML Designer is closely related to the XSD schema file—changes that you make to one are reflected in the other.

Creating XML Schema and Typed DataSets

Like HTML and other markup languages descended from SGML, XML schema files are created using tags that are delimited by angle brackets:

```
<tag> some text </tag>
```

XML schema files begin with a tag that identifies the version of XML that is being used. .NET Framework XML schema files follow this with an <xs:schema> tag whose targetNamespace attribute defines the namespace of all the components in this schema and any included schemas. The <xs:schema> tag also includes references to two namespaces—the W3C XML schema definition and the Microsoft extensions.

This standard header is created automatically by the XML Designer. If you create an XML schema in a text editor or some other design tool, the heading has the following structure:

```
<?xml version="1.0"encoding="utf-8"?>
<xs:schema targetNamespace="http://tempuri.org/XMLSchema1.xsd "
   xmlns:xs="http://www.w3.org/2001/XMLSchema"
   xmlns:msdata="urn:schemas-microsoft-com:xml-msdata"
>
```

The basic structure of the XML schema file created by the XML Schema Designer is:

```
<?xml version="1.0"encoding="utf-8"?>
<xs:schema id="myDataSet" …>
 <xs:element name="myDataSet" msdata:IsDataSet="true">
        <xs:complexType maxoccurs="unbounded">
               <xs:choice>
               </xs:choice>
        </xs:complexType>
 </xs:element>
</xs:schema>
```

The first two lines are the schema heading. (The xs:schema tag contains attributes that aren't shown.) The next tag, <xs:element>, represents the DataSet itself. It has two attributes: name and msdata:IsDataSet. The first attribute specifies the name of the DataSet; the second is a Microsoft schema extension that identifies the element as a DataSet.

The next set of tags creates a complexType. *ComplexTypes*, which we'll examine in detail in this chapter, are elements that can contain other elements and attributes. Note that this complexType element is not assigned a name—it's used only for structural purposes and not referred to elsewhere in the schema.

The final set of tags creates a choice group. Groups, which we'll also examine later in this chapter, define how individual elements can validly occur in the XML data. The choice group creates a mutually exclusive set. The *maxOccurs="unbounded"* attribute specifies that the data can occur any number of times within the group, but because it is a choice group, all of the data must be the same type.

The DataTables are defined as elements within the choice group. We'll examine their structure later in the chapter.

Visual Studio supports the creation of XML schemas and Typed DataSets interactively. Both types of items use the XML Designer, but an XML schema will output only an XML schema (XSD), while the DataSet will automatically generate both the schema and a class file defining the Typed DataSet.

Creating Schemas

Like any other project component, XML schemas are added to a project by using the Add New Item dialog box.

Add a Schema to the XML Designer

1. In Visual Studio .NET, open the SchemaDesigner project from the Start page or the File menu.
2. On the Project menu, choose Add New Item.

   Visual Studio displays the Add New Item dialog box.

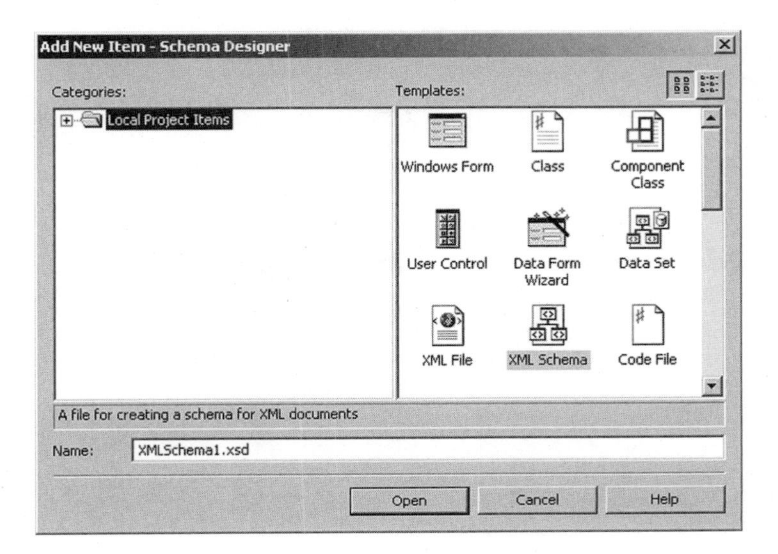

3 Select XML Schema in the Templates pane, and then click Open.

Visual Studio adds an XML schema named XMLSchema1 to the project, and then opens the XML Designer.

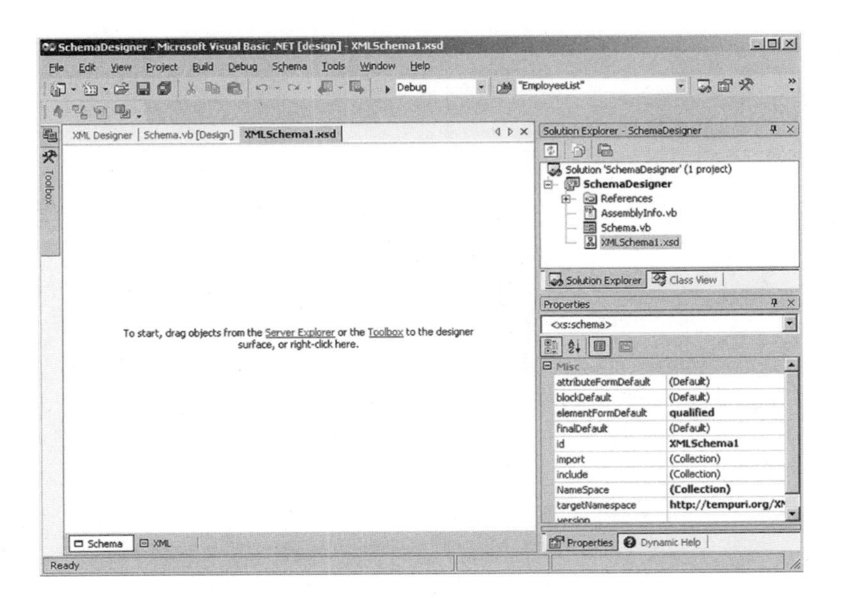

4 Close the XML Designer.

Creating DataSets

In previous chapters, we have seen how to generate a Typed DataSet based on DataAdapters that have been added to the project. It's also possible to add a DataSet to a project and configure it manually, using the same technique we used in the previous exercise to add an XML schema to the project.

Add a DataSet to the XML Designer

1. On the Project menu, choose Add New Item.

   Visual Studio displays the Add New Item dialog box.

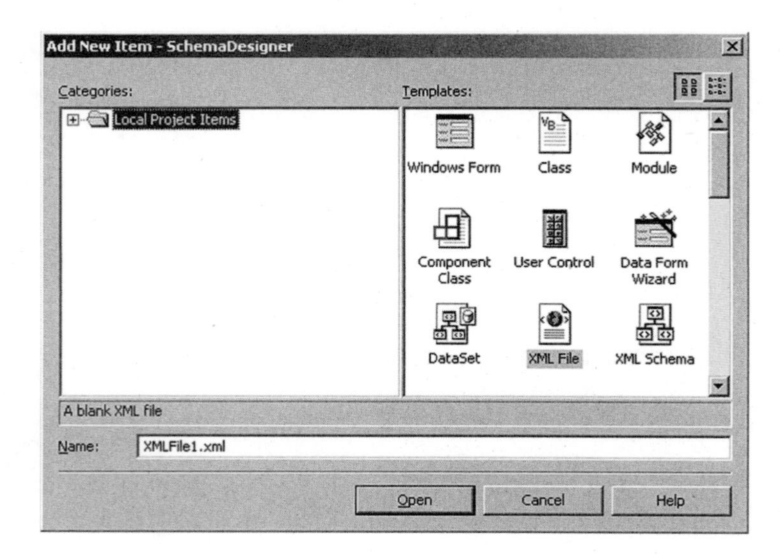

2. Select DataSet in the Templates pane, and then click Open.

   Visual Studio adds a Typed DataSet named Dataset1 to the project, and opens the XML Designer.

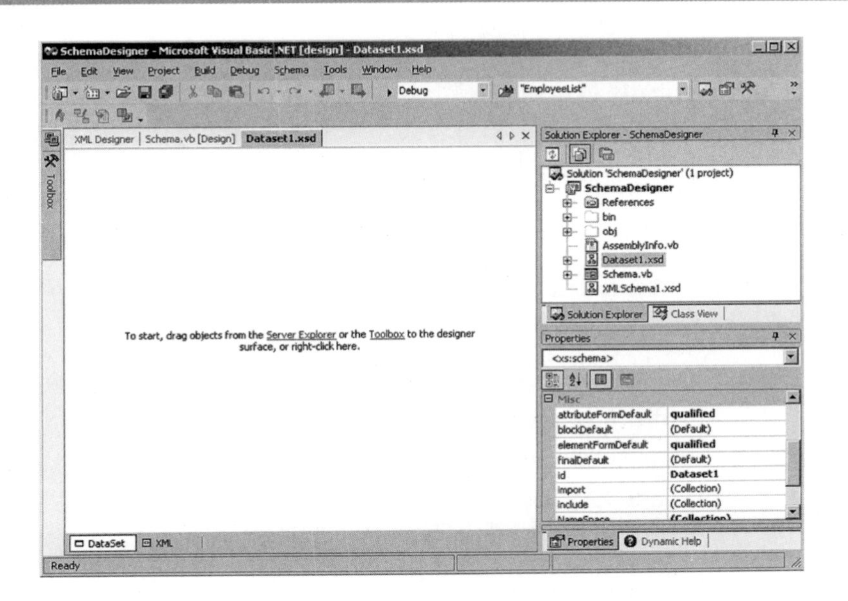

3 Select the XML tab of the XML Designer.

Visual Studio displays the XML schema source code.

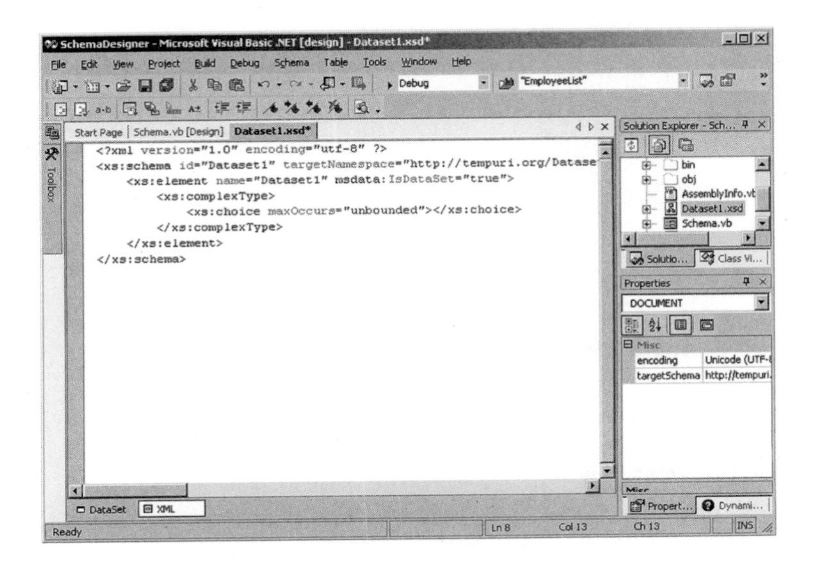

4 Close the XML Designer.

When you specify a DataSet in the Add New Item dialog box, Visual Studio automatically generates a class file from the XML schema to define the DataSet. If you create only an XML schema, or if you import an XML schema from another source, the Typed DataSet won't automatically be added; but you can create it by using the Generate DataSet command on the XML Designer's Schema menu.

Generate a DataSet from a Schema

1. In the Solution Explorer, double-click XMLSchema1.xsd.

   Visual Studio opens the (blank) schema in the XML Designer.

2. On the Schema menu, choose Generate Dataset.

   Visual Studio creates a Typed DataSet class based on the XML schema.

3. Expand XMLSchema1 to display the class file in the Solution Explorer. You may need to click the Show All Files button on the Solution Explorer toolbar.

4. Close the form designer.

Understanding Schema Properties

The XML Designer exposes two sets of properties for schemas: DataSet properties, which are available only for DataSet schemas, and miscellaneous properties that are defined by the W3C recommendation.

The properties exposed by the Microsoft schema extensions are shown in Table 14-1. The IsDataSet property identifies this particular element as the root of the Typed DataSet definition. The XML Designer will generate an error if more than one element has IsDataSet set to true.

The CaseSensitive, dataSetName, and Locale properties map directly to their DataSet counterparts, while the key property is used internally by the .NET Framework.

Property	Description
CaseSensitive	Controls whether the DataSet is case-sensitive. Note that this affects only the DataSet. The XML schema is always case-sensitive
dataSetName	The name of the Typed DataSet based on the XML schema
IsDataSet	Defines the element as the root of a DataSet
key	Set of unique constraints defined on the DataSet
Locale	Locale information used to compare strings in the DataSet

Table 14-1 Microsoft Schema Extension Properties

The Misc section of the Properties window exposes the attributes of the schema element defined by the W3C recommendation, as shown in Table 14-2. The id, targetNamespace, and version properties set the value of these two attributes for the schema, while the remaining properties define the behavior of other schema components.

Property	Description
attributeFormDefault	Determines whether attribute names from the target namespace must be namespace-qualified
blockDefault	Sets the default value for the block attribute of elements and complex types in the schema namespace
elementFormDefault	Determines whether element names from the target namespace must be namespace-qualified
finalDefault	Sets the default value for the final attribute of elements and complex types in the schema namespace
id	The value of the element's ID attribute
import	Collection of imported schemas
include	Collection of included schemas
NameSpace	Collection of namespaces declared in the schema
targetNamespace	The target namespace of the schema
version	The value of the element's version attribute

Table 14-2 XML Schema Properties

The attributeFormDefault and elementFormDefault properties determine whether attribute and element names, respectively, must be preceded with a namespace identifier and a colon (for example, *name="myDS:myName" as opposed to name="myName"*).

The blockDefault and finalDefault properties define the default values for the block and final attributes of elements within the namespace. We'll examine these attributes in the following section.

Finally the import, include, and NameSpace properties contain collections of namespaces that are imported, included, and declared in the schema, respectively.

Examine the Namespaces Declared in an XML Schema

1. In the Solution Explorer, double-click Dataset1.xsd.

   Visual Studio opens the schema in the XML Designer.

2. In the Properties window, select Namespace, and then click the Ellipsis button.

   The XML Designer displays the XMLNamesSpace Collection Editor.

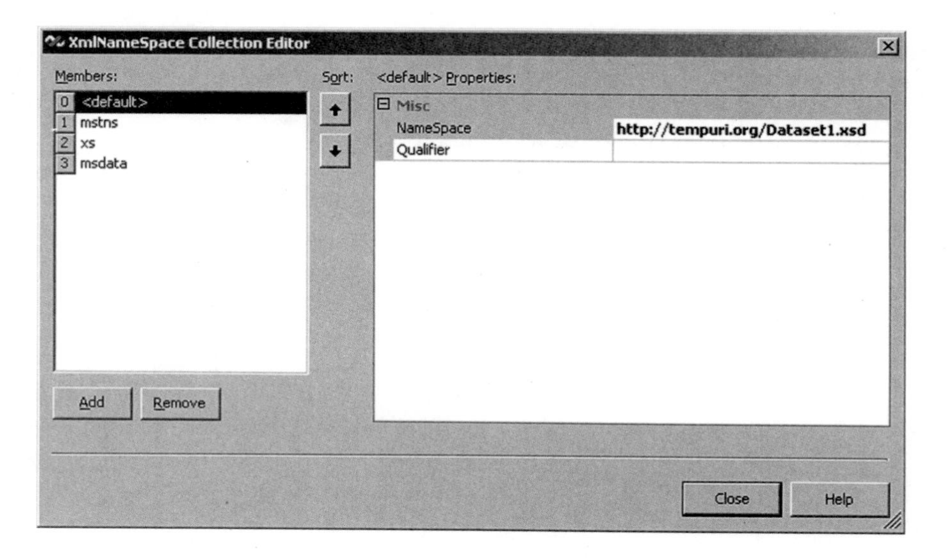

3. In the Members pane, select xs.

   The XMLNamesSpace Collection Editor displays the NameSpace property and qualifier of the W3C XSD recommendation.

Working with DataTables in the XML Designer

In the previous section, we examined the structure of tags within a DataSet schema. Remember that we said that DataTables are defined as elements within a choice group. The DataTable itself has the following nominal structure:

```
<xs:element name="myTable">
 <xs:complexType>
       <xs:sequence>
             <xs:element name:"Column1" type:"xs:string" />
             <xs:element name:"Column2" type:"xs:Boolean" />
       </xs:sequence>
 </xs:complexType>
</xs:element>
```

The structure is similar to the nominal structure of a schema: an element is created and assigned the name of the table. Within the element is an unnamed complex type, and within that is an XML group, and within that are the column elements. The XML group used for a schema is a choice, which makes element types mutually exclusive. The DataTable structure uses a sequence group, which ensures that the nested elements will be in the order specified.

Adding DataTables to the XML Designer

Visual Studio supports a number of methods for creating DataTables in the XML Designer. We've been using one of them, generating a DataSet based on DataAdapters that have been added to a form, for several chapters.

You can also drag an existing table, view, or stored procedure from the Server Explorer to the XML Designer Schema tag, or create a DataTable from scratch. As we'll see in Chapter 15, you can also infer schemas from XML data at run time.

Add a Table or View to a Schema

1. In the XML Designer, open the Dataset1 schema (if necessary), and then select the DataSet tab.
2. In the Server Explorer, expand the connection to the SQL Northwind database, and then expand the Tables node.
3. Select the Categories table, and drag it onto the XML Designer.

   Visual Studio adds the table to the schema.

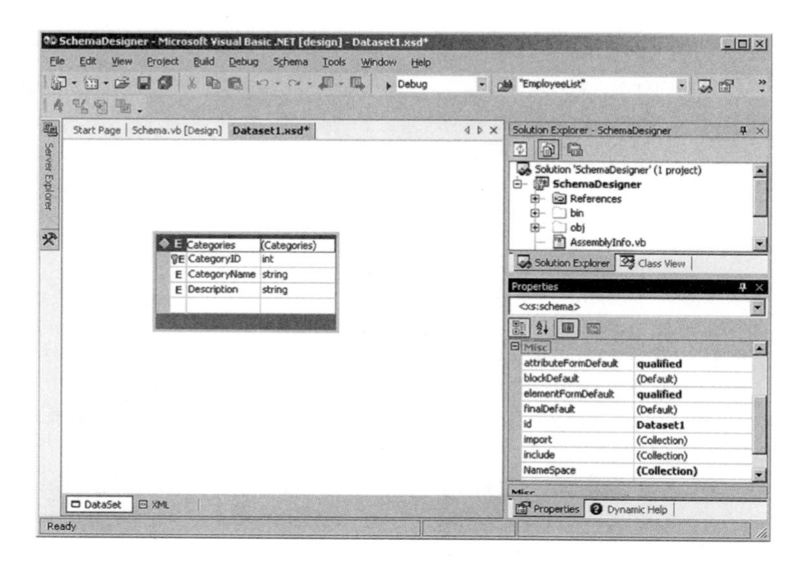

4 Select the XML tag of the XML Designer.

Visual Studio displays the XML schema source code.

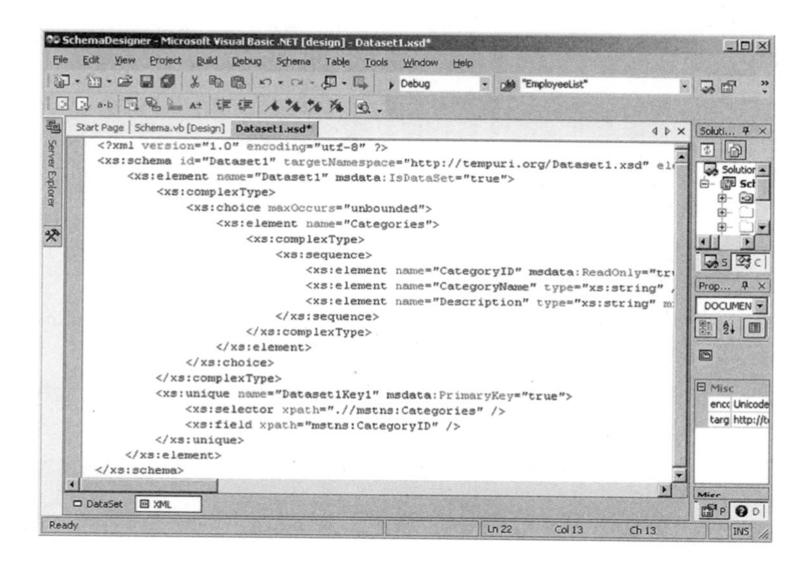

Create a Table from Scratch

1 In the XML Designer, select the DataSet tab.

2 In the XML Schema section of the Toolbox, drag an Element onto the design surface.

Visual Studio adds a new Element to the schema.

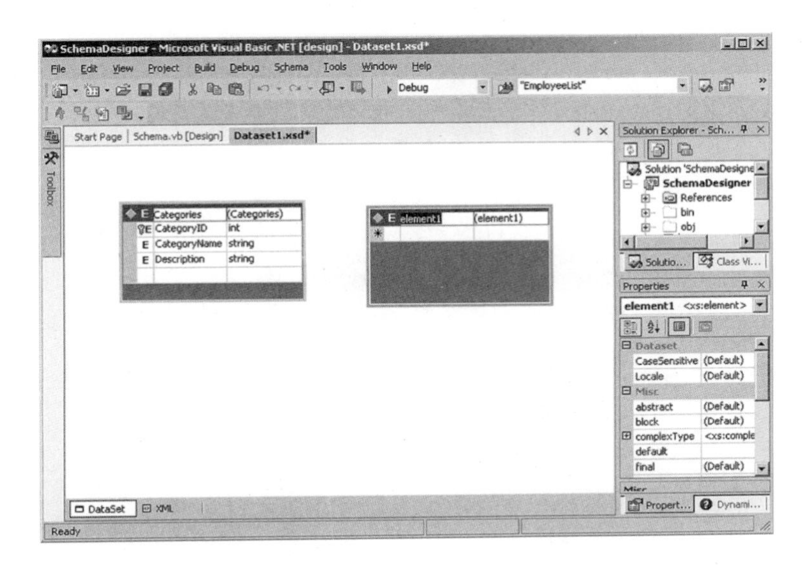

3 The element name, element1, is selected on the design surface. Change it to **Products**.

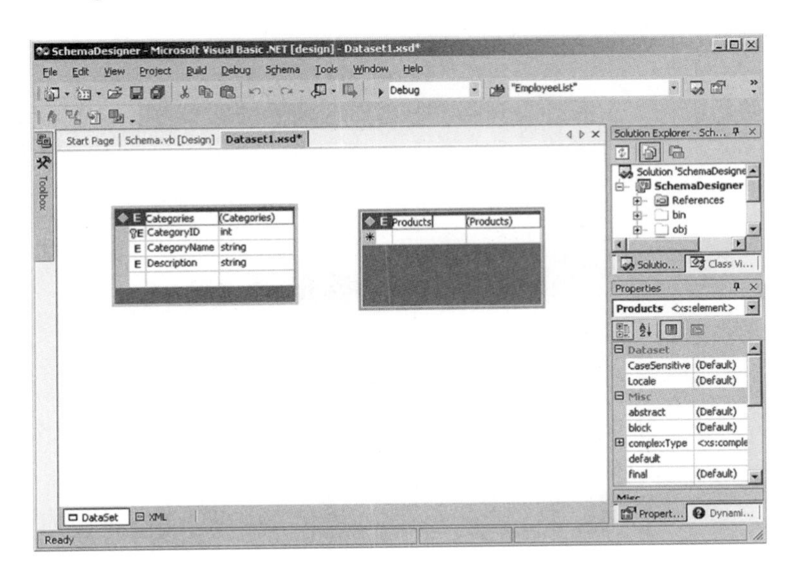

4 Click the first column of the first row of the element, and then expand the drop-down list.

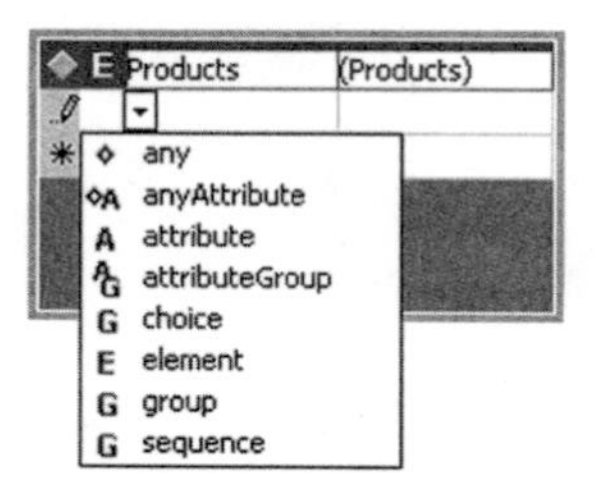

5 Select element from the drop-down list.

The XML Designer adds a nested element to the Products element.

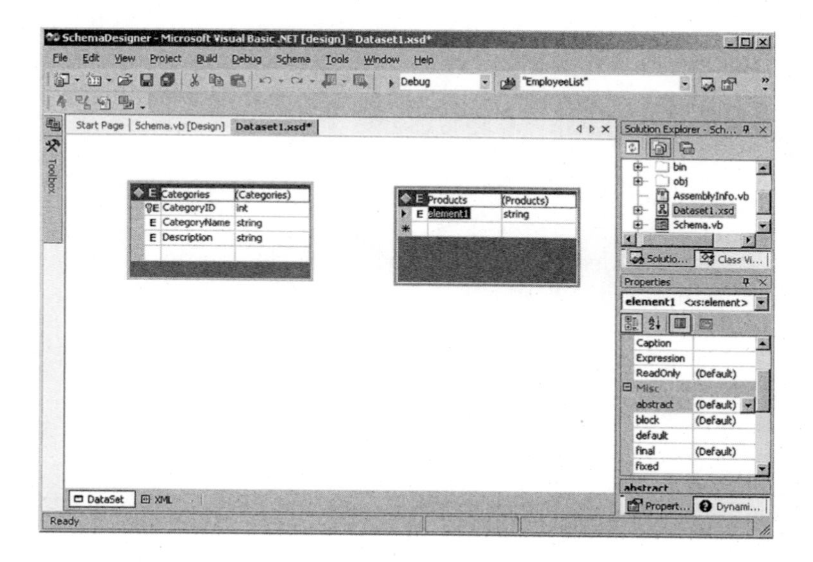

6 Change the element name to ProductID.

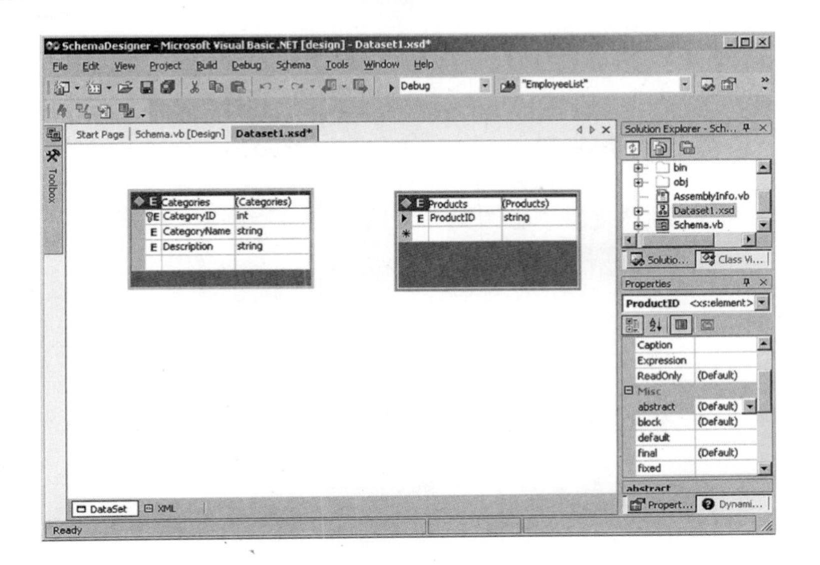

Creating Keys

The XML Designer supports three different tags that pertain to entity and referential integrity: primary keys, keyrefs, and unique keys. Primary keys guarantee uniqueness within a DataSet. A <keyref> tag is essentially a foreign key reference and is used to implement a one-to-many relationship. Unique keys guarantee uniqueness, but they are not typically used for referential integrity.

Creating Primary Keys

The W3C recommendation supports the <key> tag, which specifies that the values of the specified element must be unique, always present, and not null. The Microsoft schema extensions add an attribute to this tag, msdata:PrimaryKey, which identifies the key as being the primary key for the DataTable.

The scope of a key is the scope of the element that contains it. In a .NET Framework DataSet schema, keys are defined at the DataSet level, which means that the key needs to be unique, not just within a DataTable, but within the DataSet as a whole.

Primary keys are added to a DataTable by using the Edit Key dialog box, which is displayed if you drag a key onto an element or choose Add Key from the Schema menu or an element's context menu. The Add Key dialog box allows you to specify multiple fields for a key, if necessary, and also specify whether the key should accept null values or be designated as the primary key for the DataTable.

Add a Primary Key to a DataTable

1. On the Schema menu, point to Add, and then choose New Key.

   Visual Studio displays the Edit Key dialog box.

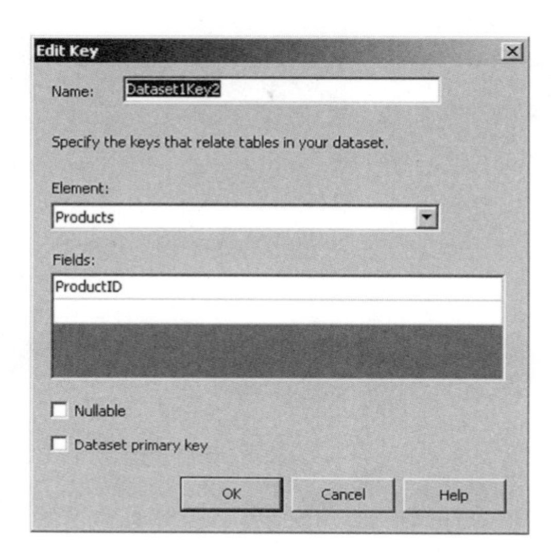

2. Change the name of the key to ProductsPK, and then select the Dataset Primary Key check box.

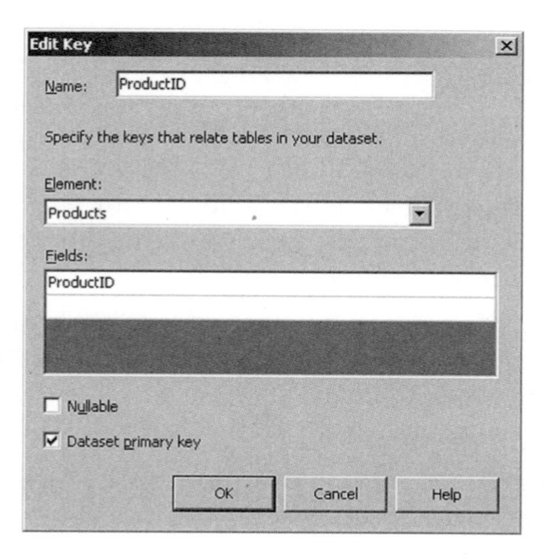

3 Click OK.

The XML Designer adds the primary key to the Products element.

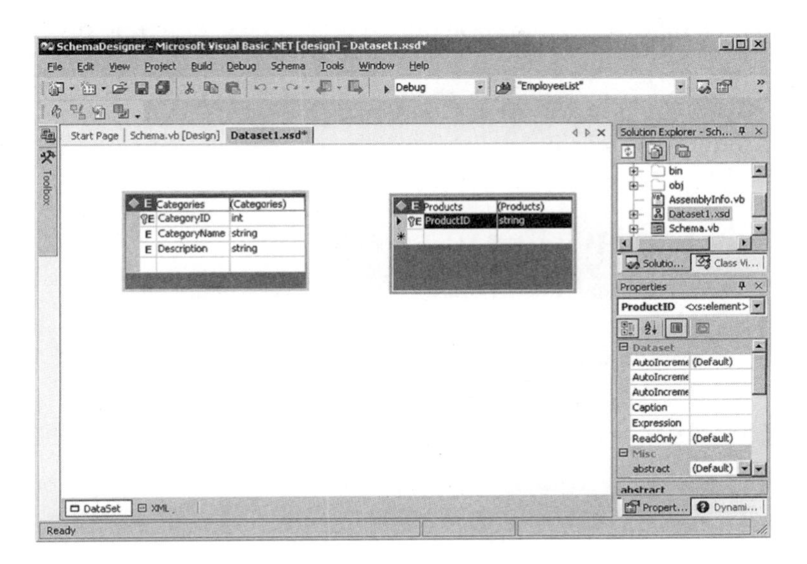

4 Select the XML tab of the XML Designer.

The XML Designer displays the code for the new key.

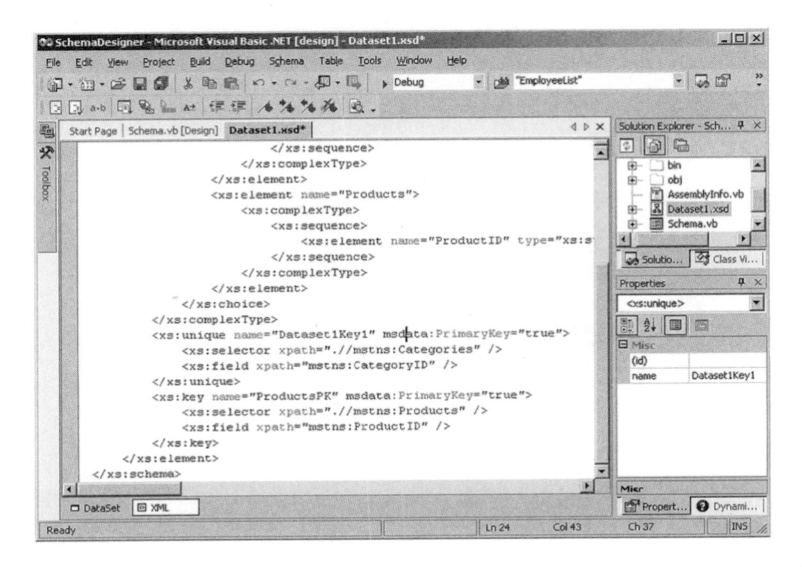

Creating Unique Keys

Primary keys are, as we've seen, required elements that must be unique within the DataSet and cannot be null. There can be only one primary key defined for a DataTable. Unique keys differ from primary keys in that they *can* allow nulls, and you can define multiple unique keys for any given DataTable.

Unique keys are added by using the same Edit Key dialog box that is used to add primary keys.

Add a Unique Key to a DataTable

1. Select the DataSet tab of the XML Designer.
2. Drag a key tag from the XML Schema tab of the Toolbox onto the Categories element.

   The XML Designer displays the Edit Key dialog box.
3. Change the name of the key to CategoryName.
4. Select CategoryID in the Fields pane, expand the drop-down list, and then select the *CategoryName* field.

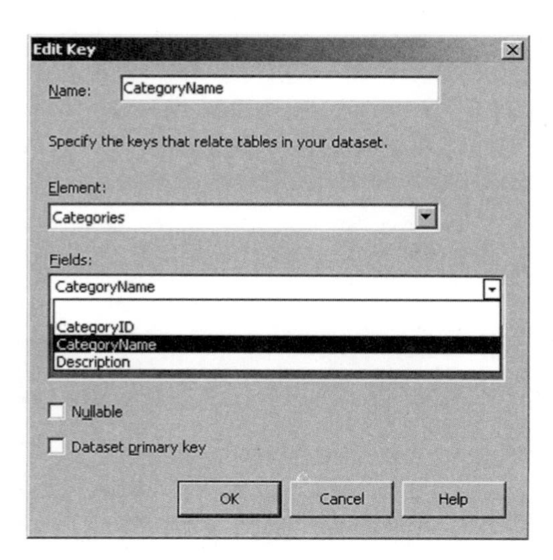

5. Click OK.

   The XML Designer adds the new key to the Categories element.

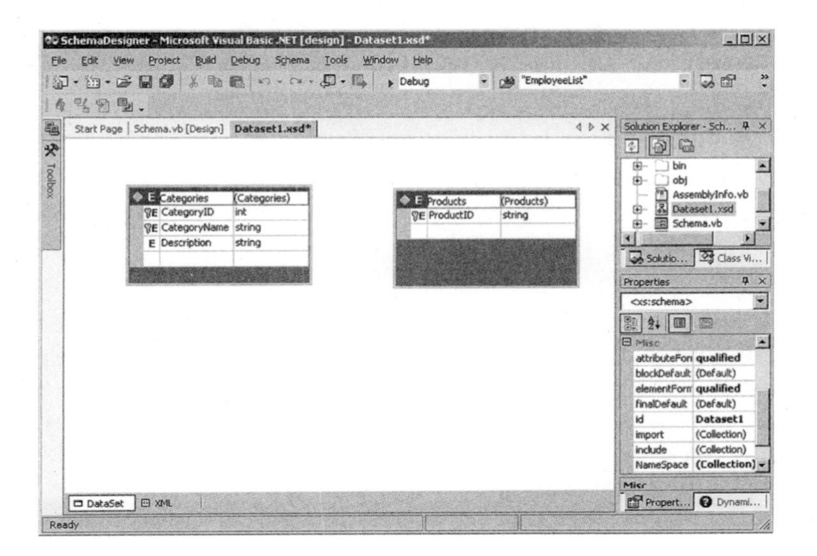

6 Select the XML tab of the XML Designer.

Visual Studio displays the XML schema code.

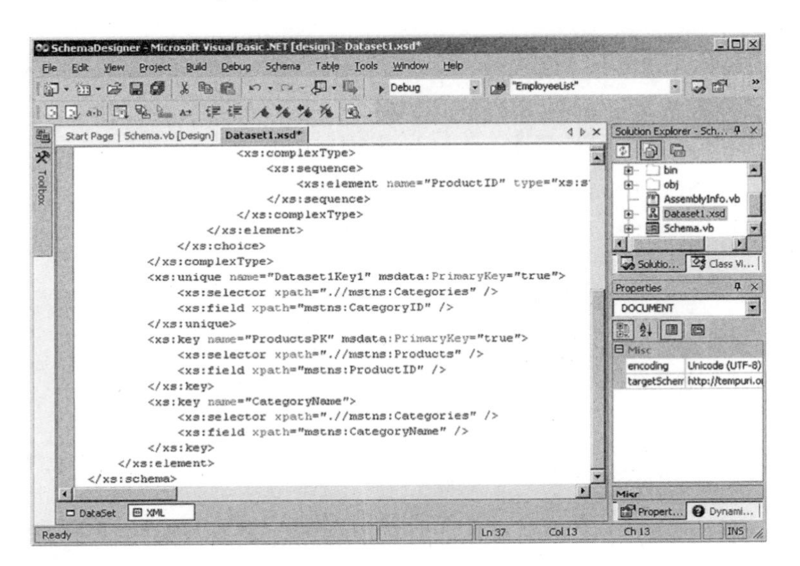

Creating Relations

KeyRefs are implemented as Relations in the XML Designer. A Relation translates directly to a DataRelation within a DataSet. Relations are added to a DataSet by using the Edit Relation dialog box, which, like the Edit Key dialog box, can be displayed by dragging a Relation from the Toolbox or by choosing New Relation on the Schema menu.

In addition to the basic relationship information, the Edit Relation dialog box allows you the option of creating a foreign key constraint only. If you select this option, the DataSet class produced from the XML schema will be slightly more efficient, but you will not be able to use the *GetChildRows* and *GetParentRows* methods to reference related data.

In addition, the Edit Relation dialog box allows you to specify three referential integrity rules: Update, Delete, and Accept/Reject. These rules determine what happens when primary key rows are updated or deleted, or when changes are accepted or rejected. The possible values for these rules are shown in Table 14-3. The Accept/Reject rule supports only Cascade and None.

Rule	Description
Cascade	Deletes or updates related rows
SetNull	Sets the foreign key values in related rows to null
SetDefault	Sets the foreign key values in related rows to their default values
None	Takes no action on related rows

Table 14-3 Referential Integrity Rules

Add a Relation to a DataSet

1 Select the DataSet tab of the XML Designer.

2 Select the Categories element.

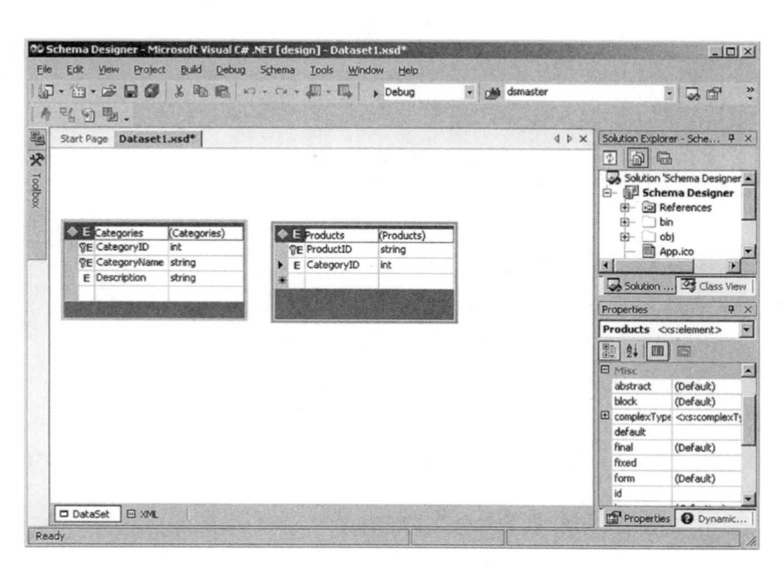

3 The XML Designer displays the Edit Relation dialog box.

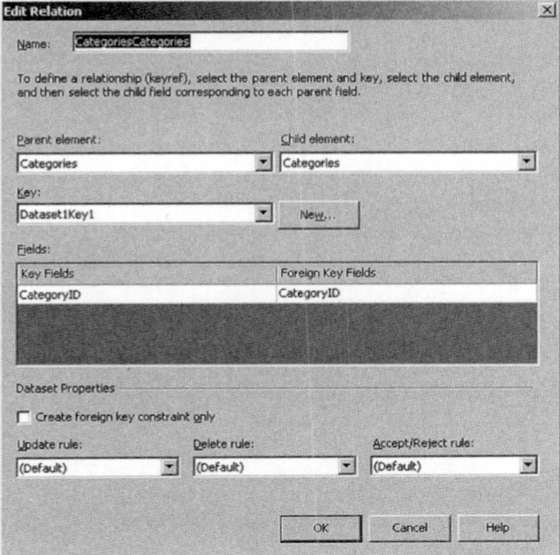

4 Change the Relation name to CategoryProducts.

5 Choose Products in the Child Element combo box.

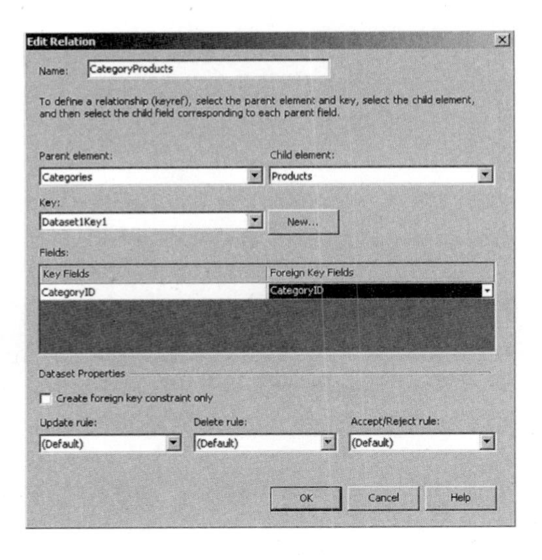

6 Click OK.

Visual Studio adds the Relation to the XML Schema Designer.

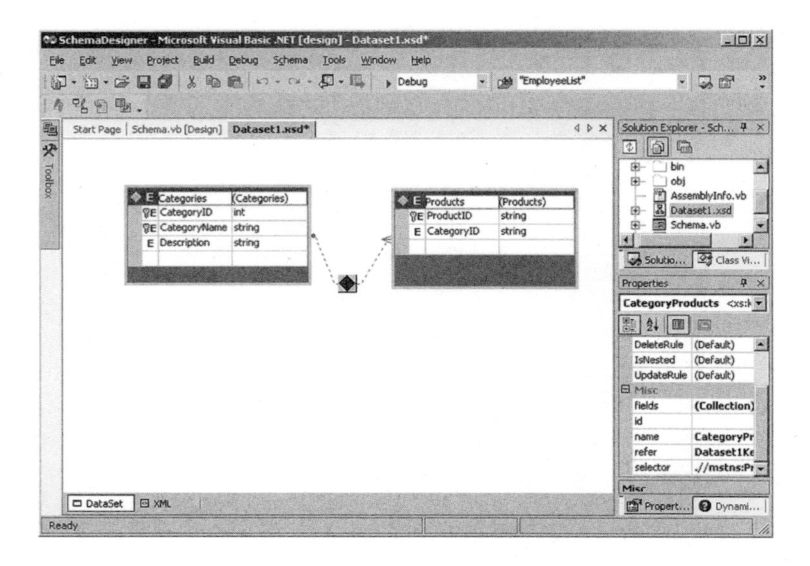

Working with Elements

Throughout this chapter, we've been talking about elements, and even creating them, without examining them in any detail. We'll correct that now. An *element* in a XML schema DataSet is a description of an item of data.

At its simplest, an element consists only of the <xs:element> tag:

```
<xs:element />
```

However, most elements, unless they're being used only as containers, contain a name and type attribute:

```
<xs:element name="productID" type="xs:integer" />
```

Elements may also contain other tags. (Help states that "elements can contain other elements," but that's not strictly true. Specifically, "other elements" doesn't refer to element tags.) The tags that can be nested within an element tag are:

- <xs:annotation>
- <xs:complexType>
- <xs:key>
- <xs:keyref>
- <xs:simpleType>
- <xs:unique>

As we saw in the previous section, the <xs:key>, <xs:keyref>, and <xs:unique> tags are used to define constraints. The <xs:annotation> tag, as might be expected, is used to add information to be used by applications or displayed to users.

The <xs:complexType> type is a container tag, used to group other tags. We've seen it used in the structure of both schemas and DataTables in the XML Designer. The <xs:simpleType> tag defines a data type by specifying valid values, based on other types. We'll examine both of these tags in detail later in this chapter.

Element Properties

As usual, the XML Designer exposes the attributes of the <xs:element> tag as properties. The attributes exposed by the W3C recommendation are shown in Table 14-4.

The abstract, block, final, form, ref, and substitutionGroup properties pertain to the derivation of elements from other elements. Their use is outside the scope of this book, but they are extensively documented in online Help and other XML documentation sources.

The name and id properties are used to identify the element. The ID attribute must be unique within the XML schema. The name property is also shown in the visual representation of the element.

Property	Description
abstract	Indicates whether an instance of the element can appear in a document
block	Prevents elements of the specified type of derivation from being used in place of the element
default	The default value of the element
final	The type of derivation
fixed	The predetermined, unchangeable value of the element
form	The form of the element
id	The ID of the element
key	The collection of unique keys defined for this element
maxOccurs	The maximum number of times the element can occur within the containing element
minOccurs	The minimum number of times the element can occur within the containing element
name	The name of the element

(continued)

(continued)

nillable	Determines whether an explicit nil can be assigned to the element
ref	The name of an element declared in the namespace
substitutionGroup	The name of the element for which this element can be substituted
type	The data type of the element

Table 14-4 XML Schema Element Properties

The remaining properties define the value of the element. Of these, the most important property is type, which defines the data type of the element. The type of an element can be either a built-in XML type or a simple or complex type defined elsewhere in the XML schema. Like the name property, the type property is shown in the visual display of the element.

The default property, not surprisingly, specifies a default value if none is specified, while the fixed property specifies a value that the element must always contain. Both of these properties must be of the data type specified by the type attribute, and they are mutually exclusive. The nillable property indicates whether the value can be set to a null value or omitted.

Finally the maxOccurs and minOccurs properties specify the maximum and minimum number of times the element can occur, respectively. The maxOccurs property can be set to either a non-negative integer or the string "unbounded," which indicates that there is no limit to the number of occurrences.

In addition to the element attributes defined by the W3C recommendation, the Microsoft schema extensions expose the properties shown in Table 14-5. All of these coincide directly to their counterparts in the DataColumn object.

Property	Description
AutoIncrement	Determines whether the value automatically increments when a row is added
AutoIncrementSeed	Sets the starting value for an AutoIncrement element
AutoIncrementStep	Determines the step by which AutoIncrement elements are increased
Caption	Specifies the display name for an element
Expression	A DataColumn expression for the element
ReadOnly	Determines whether element values can be modified after the row has been added to the DataTable

Table 14-5 Microsoft Schema Extension Element Properties

Define the type Property of an Element

1 Select the ProductID nested element in the XML Designer, expand the type drop-down list, and then select int.

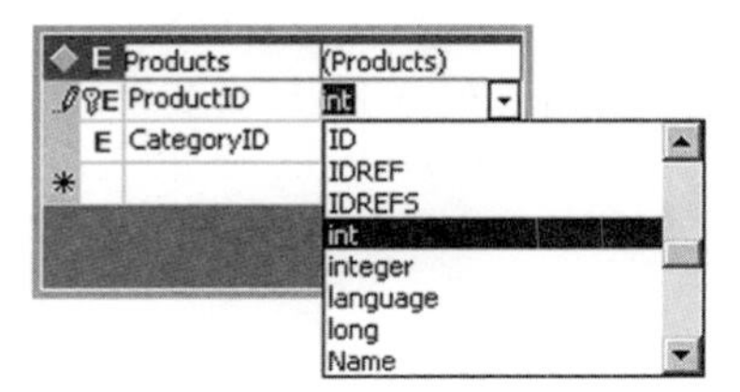

2 In the Properties window, select the AutoIncrement property, expand the drop-down list, and then choose true.

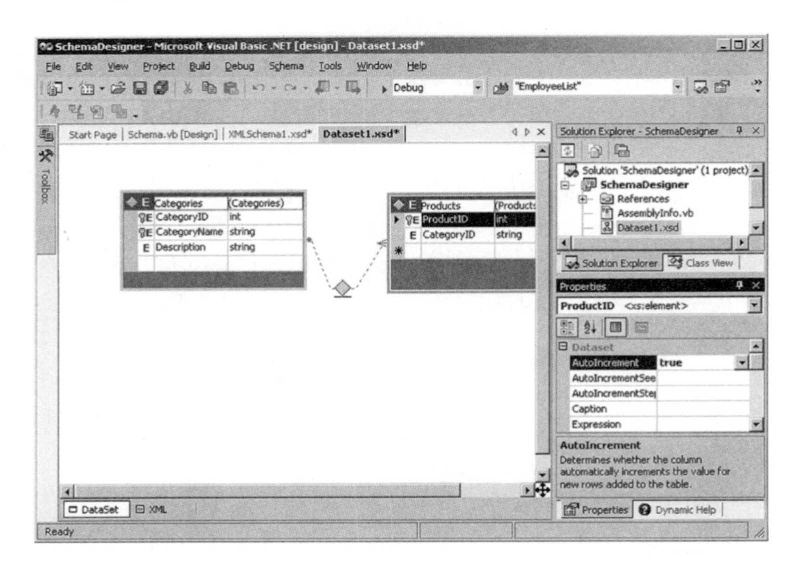

3 Save and close DataSet1.

Working with Types

As we've seen, the type property of an element defines the data type of an element or attribute. XML schemas support two kinds of data types: simple and complex. A simple type resolves to an atomic value, while a complex type contains other complex types, elements, or attributes.

The W3C recommendation allows XML schemas to define user-defined types. As we've seen, the nominal structure of a .NET Framework DataSet XML schema uses user-defined complex types to define the columns of a table.

The XML Designer supports the creation of user-defined types as well. User-defined types are useful for encapsulating business rules. For example, if a ShipMethod element is limited to the values *USPS* or *2nd Day Air*, a user-defined enumeration can be used to restrict the values rather than adding another DataTable to the schema.

Simple Types

The XML schema recommendation supports two different kinds of simple types (primitive and derived) and supports the creation of new, user-defined simple types. Primitive types are the fundamental types. Examples of primitive types include string, float, and Boolean. Derived types are defined by limiting the valid range of values for a primitive type. An example of a built-in derived type is positiveInteger, which is an integer that allows only values greater than zero.

Like derived types, user-defined simple types restrict the values of existing simple types by limiting the valid range of values. User-defined simple types can be derived from base types by using any of the methods shown in Table 14-6.

Method	Description
restriction	Restricts the range of values to a subset of those allowed by the base type
list	Defines a list of values of the base type that are valid for the type
union	Defines a type by combining the values of two or more other simple types

Table 14-6 Simple Type Derivation Methods

Of the available derivation methods, *restriction* is the most common. The valid range of values of a simple type is restricted by applying *facets* to the type. A facet is much like an attribute, but it specifically limits the valid range of values for a user-defined type. Table 14-7 describes the various facets available for restriction of values.

Facet	Description
enumeration	Constrains data to the specified set of values.
fractionDigits	Specifies the maximum number of decimal digits.
length	Specifies the nonNegativeInteger length of the value. The exact meaning is determined by the data type.
maxExclusive	Specifies the exclusive upper-bound value—all values must be less than this value.
maxInclusive	Specifies the inclusive upper-bound value—all values must be equal to or less than this value.
maxLength	Specifies the nonNegativeInteger maximum length of the value. The exact meaning is determined by the data type.
minExclusive	Specifies the exclusive lower-bound value—all values must be greater than this value.
minInclusive	Specifies the inclusive lower-bound value—all values must be equal to or greater than this value.
minLength	Specifies the nonNegativeInteger minimum length of the value. The exact meaning is determined by the data type.
pattern	A regular expression specifying a pattern that the value must match.
totalDigits	Specifies the nonNegativeInteger maximum number of decimal digits for the value.
whiteSpace	Specifies how white space in the value is to be handled.

Table 14-7 Data Type Facets

Create a simpleType Using the length Facet

1. In the Solution Explorer, double-click XMLSchema1.

   Visual Studio opens the schema in the XML Designer.

2. Drag a simpleType control from the XML Schema tab of the Toolbox onto the design surface.

   The XML Designer adds a simple type to the schema.

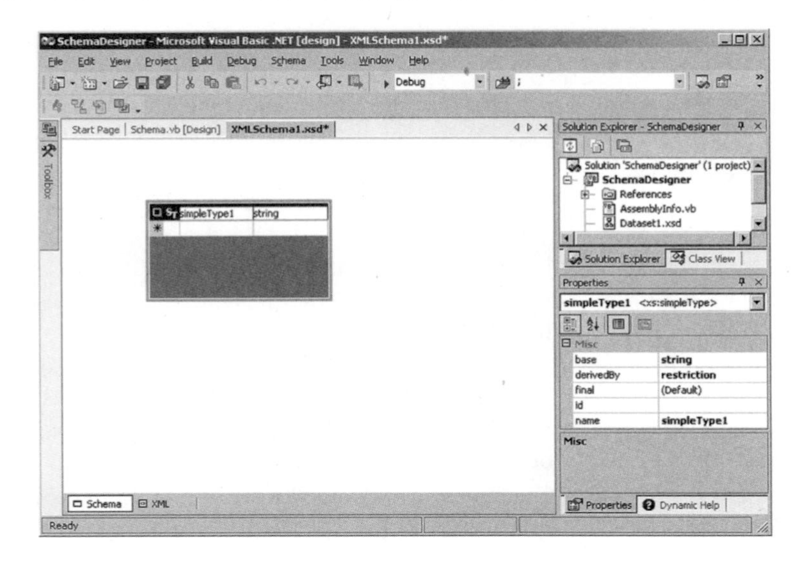

3 Change the name of the type to IDString.

4 Click the first column of the first row of the type, and then expand the drop-down list.

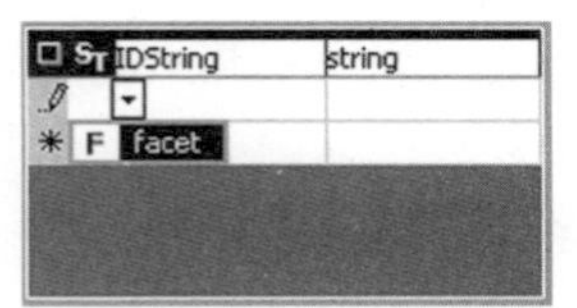

5 From the drop-down list, select facet.

6 From the drop-down list in the second column, select length.

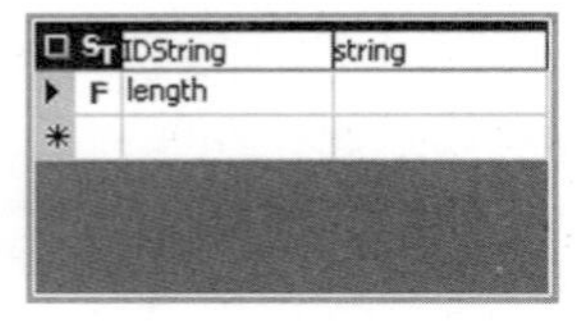

7 In the third column, type **2**.

The XML Designer creates a user-defined simpleType that limits the length of a string to two characters.

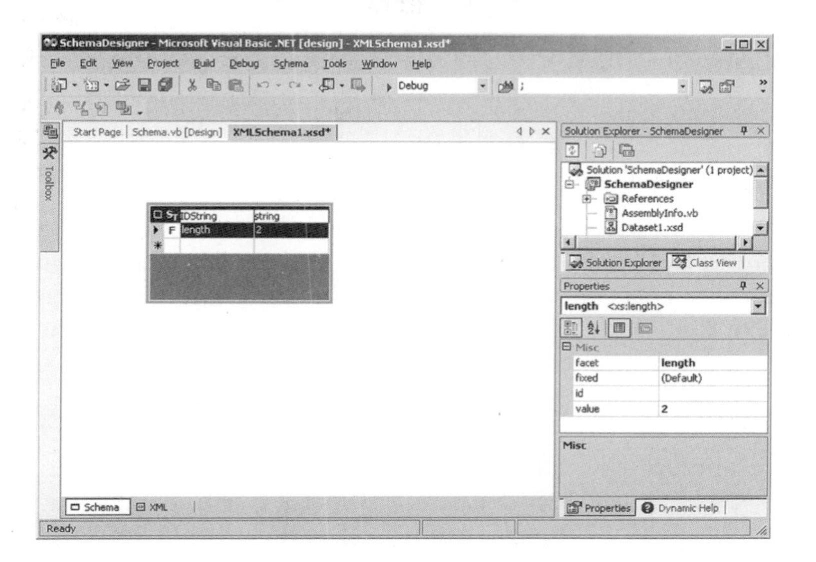

8 Select the XML tab of the XML Designer.

The XML Schema Designer displays the XML code for the simple Type definition.

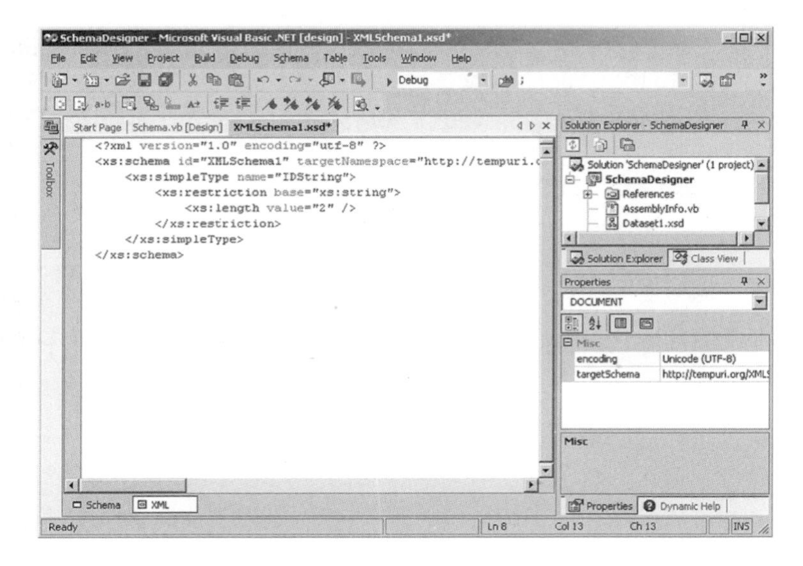

Complex Types

Complex types are user-defined types that contain elements, attributes, and group declarations. The elements of a complex type can be other complex types, allowing infinite nesting.

We've already seen unnamed complex types used to define the columns of an ADO.NET DataTable. A DataTable uses a sequence group to specify that the elements contained within the group must occur in a particular order. The W3C XML schema recommendation supports two other types of element groups, choice and all, as shown in Table 14-8.

Type	Description
sequence	Elements must occur in the order specified
choice	Only one of the elements specified can occur
all	Either all of the elements specified must occur, or none of them can occur

Table 14-8 Element Group Types

Create a complexType Containing a Choice Group

1 Drag a complexType control from the XML Schema tab of the Toolbox onto the design surface.

The XML Designer adds a complex type to the schema.

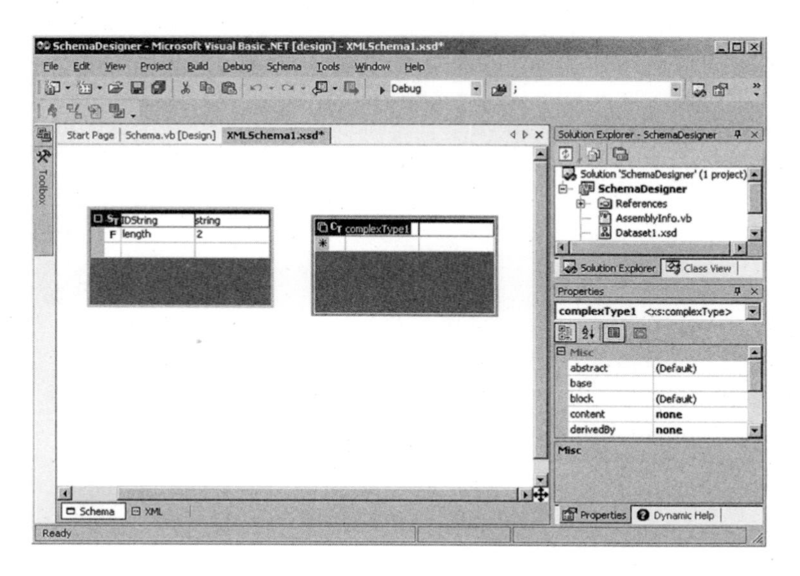

2 Change the name of the type to ChoiceGroup.

3 Click the first column of the first row of the type, and then expand the drop-down list.

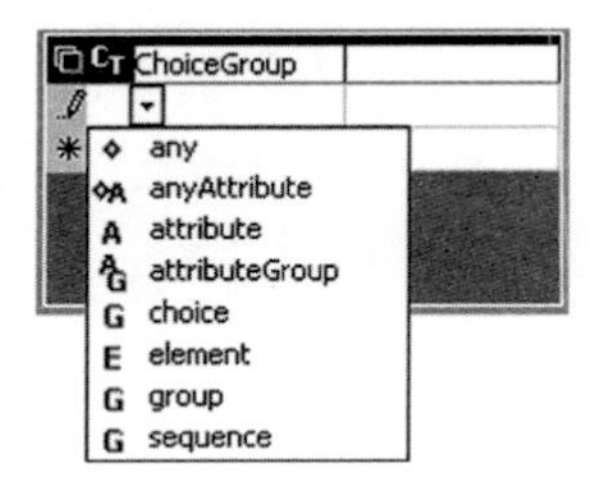

4 Select choice from the drop-down list.

The XML Designer adds a choice group to the type.

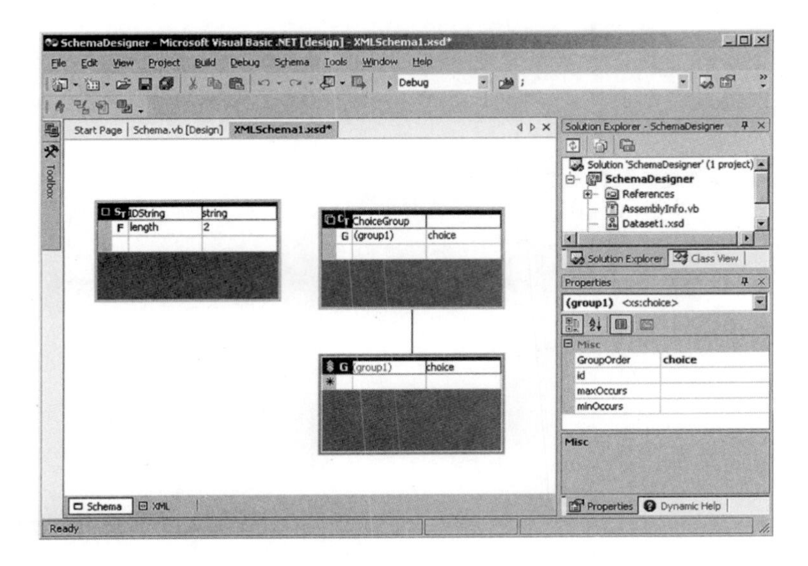

5 Add two elements, Value1 and Value2, to the choice group.

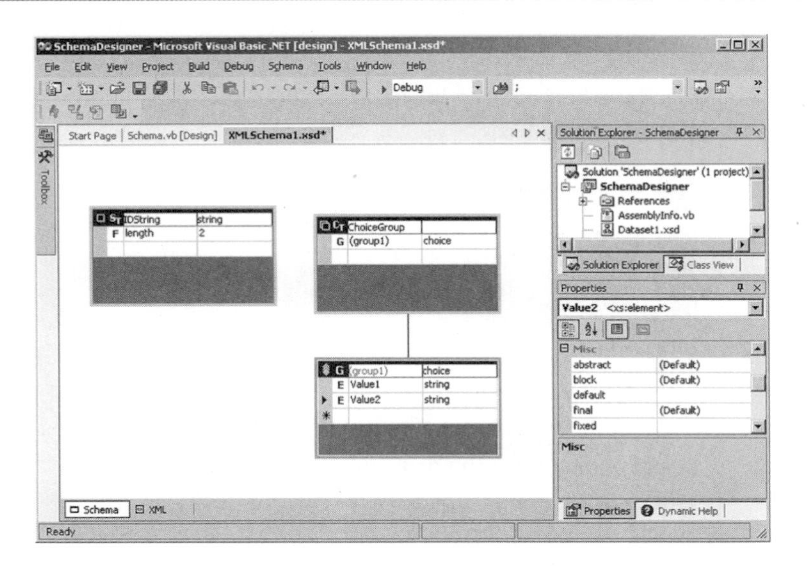

6 Select the XML tab of the XML Designer.

The XML Designer displays the XML code for the complex type.

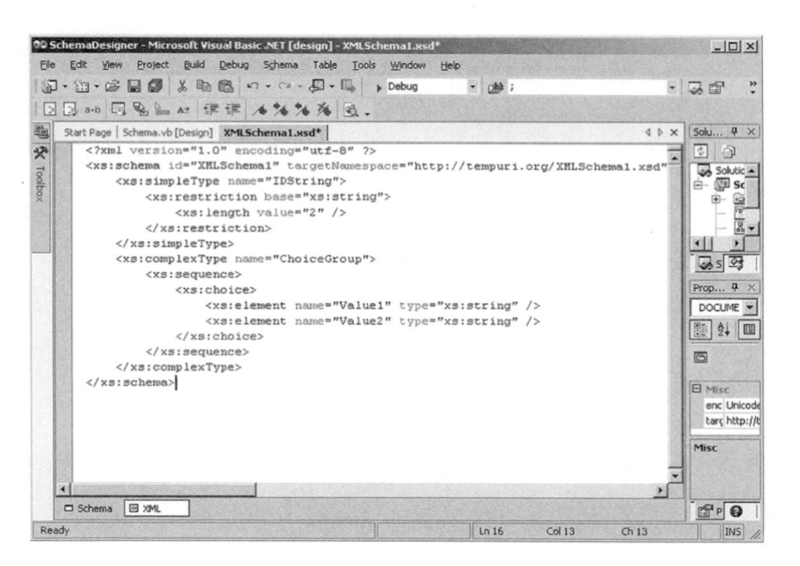

Working with Attributes

Attributes are similar to elements, with some restrictions. Attributes cannot contain other tags, they cannot be used to derive simple types, and they cannot be included in element groups. They do, however, require slightly less storage than elements, and for that reason, they can be useful if you're working outside the context of ADO.NET objects.

Attribute Properties

Attributes expose the same extensions to the W3C recommendation as elements. The W3C properties exposed by attributes are shown in Table 14-9. The attribute property set is a subset of the properties exposed by the element. Because attributes cannot be used to derive types, the properties that control derivation are not exposed.

Property	Description
default	The default value of the element
fixed	The predetermined, unchangeable value of the element
form	The form of the element, either qualified or unqualified
id	The ID of the element; must be unique within the document
Name	The name (NCName) of the element
Ref	The name of an element declared in the namespace
Type	The data type of the element
Use	Specifies how the attribute is used

Table 14-9 Attribute Properties

Attributes expose one property, use, that is not exposed by elements. The use property determines how the attribute can be used when it is included in elements and complex types. The use property can be assigned to one of three values: optional, prohibited, or required.

The meanings of optional and required are self-evident. Prohibited is used to exclude the attribute from user-defined types based on a complex type that includes the attribute.

Create an Attribute

1. Drag an Attribute control from the XML Schema tab of the Toolbox onto the design surface.

   The XML Designer adds an attribute to the schema.

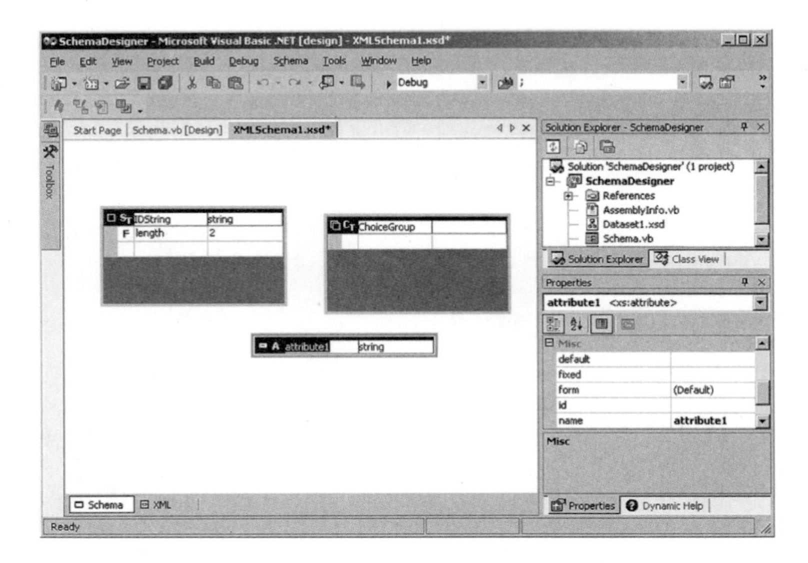

2 Change the name of the attribute to companyName.

3 In the Properties window, set the fixed property to XML, Inc.

The attribute, which will always have the value *XML, Inc.*, is added to the schema.

4 Select the XML tab of the XML Designer.

Visual Studio displays the XML source code for the attribute.

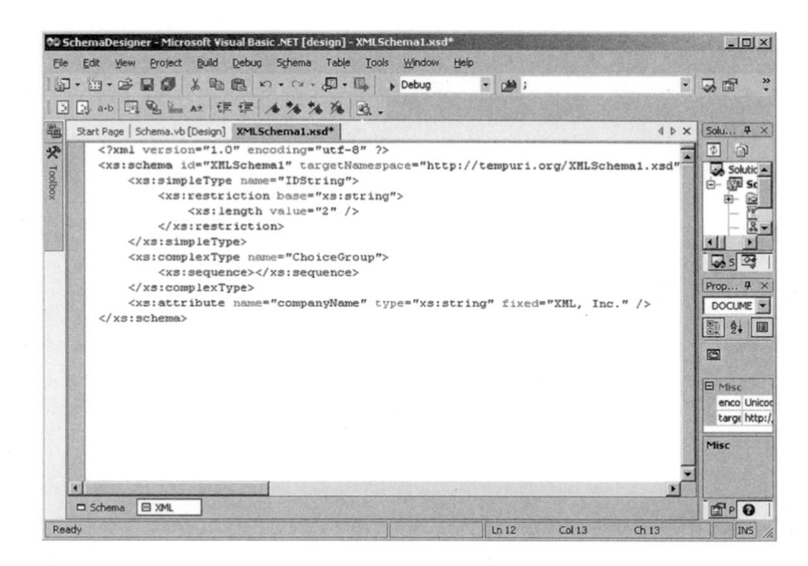

Chapter 14 Quick Reference

To	Do this
Create an XML schema	Choose XML Schema in the Add New Item dialog box
Create a Typed DataSet	Choose DataSet in the Add New Item dialog box
Generate a Typed DataSet from an XML schema	Choose Generate DataSet on the Schema menu of the XML Designer
Add DataTables from an existing data source	Drag the table, view, or stored procedure from the Solution Explorer to the XML Designer
Create DataTables	Add an element to the XML Designer, and create columns as nested elements
Add keys to an XML schema	Select the DataTable and then choose New Key on the Schema menu, or drag a Key control from the XML Schema tab of the Toolbox onto the element
Add relations to an XML schema	Select the DataTable, and then choose New Relation on the Schema menu, or drag a Relation control from the XML Schema tab of the Toolbox onto the element
Create elements	Drag an element control from the XML Schema tab of the Toolbox onto the design surface
Create simple types	Drag a simpleType control from the XML Schema tab of the Toolbox onto the design surface
Create complex types	Drag a complexType control from the XML Schema tab of the Toolbox onto the design surface
Create attributes	Drag an attribute control from the XML Schema tab of the Toolbox onto the design surface

15

Reading and Writing XML

In this chapter, you'll learn how to:

- ✔ *Retrieve an XML Schema from a DataSet*
- ✔ *Create a DataSet Schema using ReadXmlSchema*
- ✔ *Infer the Schema of an XML Document*
- ✔ *Load XML Data using ReadXml*
- ✔ *Create an XML Schema using WriteXmlSchema*
- ✔ *Write Data to an XML Document*
- ✔ *Create a synchronized XML View of a DataSet*

In the previous chapter, we looked at the XML Schema Designer, the Microsoft Visual Studio .NET tool that supports the creation of XML schemas and Typed DataSets. In this chapter, we'll look at the DataSet methods that support reading and writing data from an XML data stream.

The Microsoft .NET Framework provides extensive support for manipulating XML, most of which is outside the scope of this book. In this chapter, we'll examine only the interface between XML and Microsoft ADO.NET DataSets.

Understanding ADO.NET and XML

The .NET Framework provides a complete set of classes for manipulating XML documents and data. The XmlReader and XmlWriter objects, and the classes that descend from them, provide the ability to read and optionally validate XML. The XmlDocument and XmlSchema objects and their related classes represent the XML itself, while the XslTransform and XPathNavigator classes support XSL Transformations (XSLT) and apply XML Path Language (XPath) queries, respectively.

In addition to providing the ability to manipulate XML data, the XML standard is fundamental to data transfer and serialization in the .NET Framework. For the most part, this happens behind the scenes, but we've already seen that ADO.NET Typed DataSets are represented using XML schemas.

Additionally, the ADO.NET DataSet class provides direct support for reading and writing XML data and schemas, and the XmlDataDocument provides the ability to synchronize XML data and a relational ADO.NET DataSet, allowing you to manipulate a single set of data using both XML and relational tools. We'll explore these techniques in this chapter.

Using the DataSet XML Methods

As we've seen, the .NET Framework exposes a set of classes that allow you to manipulate XML data directly. However, if you need to use relational operations such as sorting, filtering, or retrieving related rows, the DataSet provides an easier mechanism. Furthermore, the XML classes don't support data binding, so if you intend to display the data to users, you must use the DataSet XML methods.

Fortunately, the choice between treating any given set of data as an XML hierarchy or relational DataSet isn't mutually exclusive. As we'll see later in this chapter, the XmlDataDocument allows you to manipulate a single set of data by using either or both sets of tools.

The *GetXml* and *GetXmlSchema* Methods

Perhaps the most straightforward of the XML methods supported by the DataSet are *GetXml* and *GetXmlSchema*, which simply return the XML data or XSD schema as a string value.

Retrieve a DataSet Schema Using *GetXmlSchema*

Visual Basic .NET

1 Open the XML project from the Start page or the File menu.

2 In the Solution Explorer, double-click GetXml.vb.

Visual Studio displays the form in the form designer.

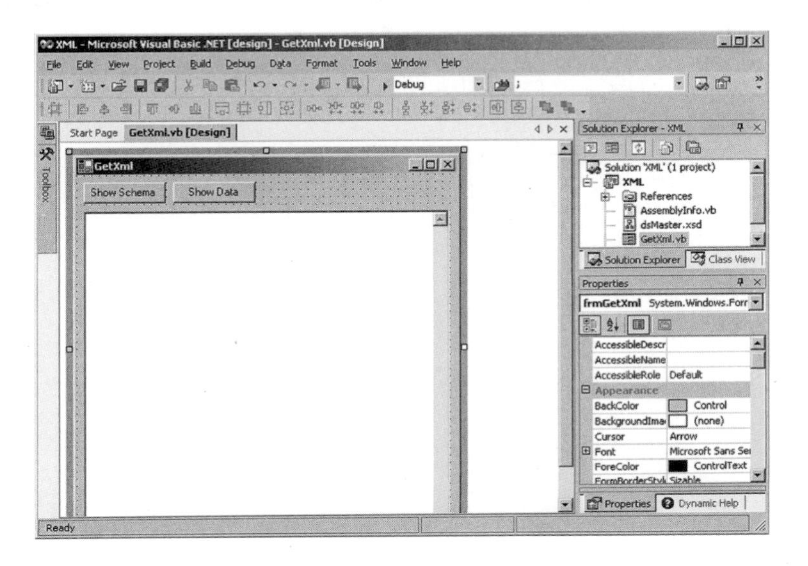

3 Double-click Show Schema.

Visual Studio opens the code editor and adds the Click event handler.

4 Add the following code to the handler:

```
Dim xmlStr As String

xmlStr = Me.dsMaster1.GetXmlSchema()
Me.tbResult.Text = xmlStr
```

5 Press F5 to run the application.

Visual Studio displays the application window.

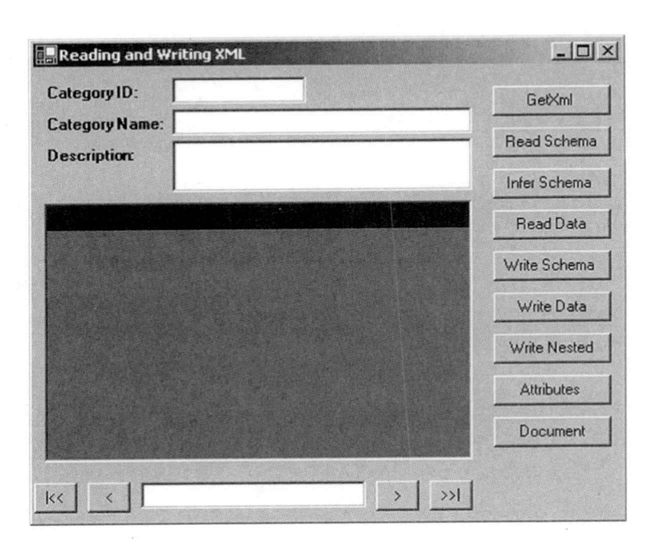

6 Click GetXml.

Visual Studio displays the GetXml form.

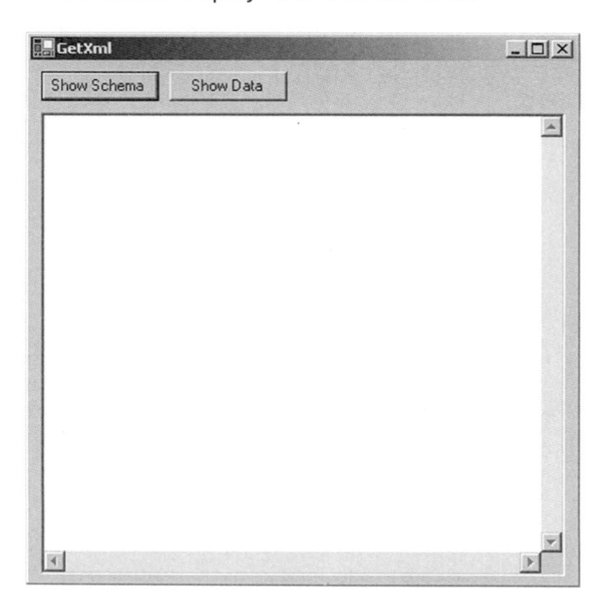

7 Click Show Schema.

The application displays the DataSet schema in the text box.

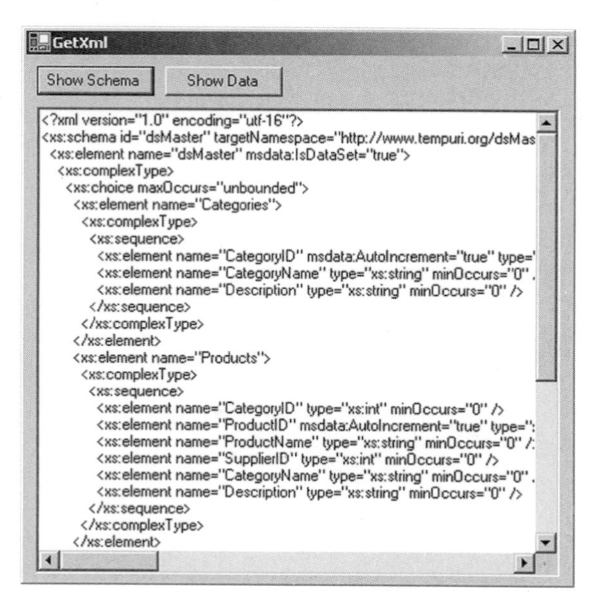

8 Close the GetXml form and the application.

Visual C# .NET

1. Open the XML project from the Start page or the File menu.
2. In the Solution Explorer, double-click GetXml.cs.

   Visual Studio displays the form in the form designer.

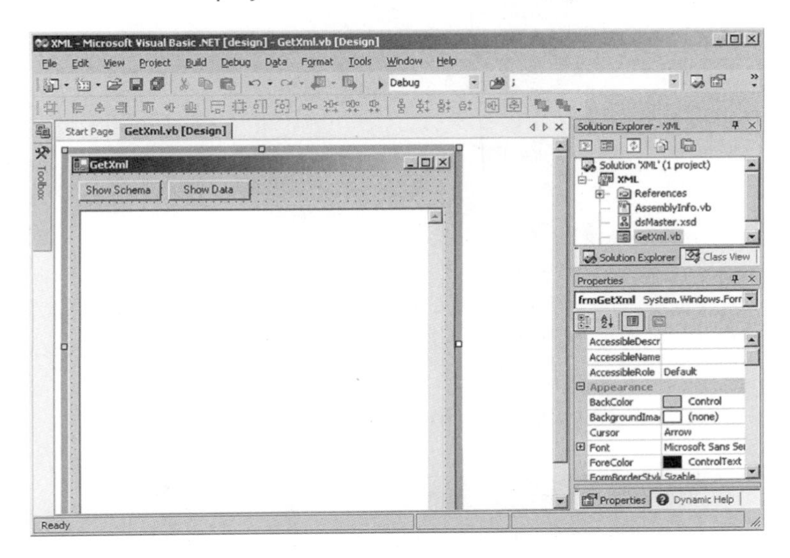

3. Double-click Show Schema.

   Visual Studio opens the code editor and adds the Click event handler.
4. Add the following code to the handler:

```
string xmlStr;

xmlStr = this.dsMaster1.GetXmlSchema();
this.tbResult.Text = xmlStr;
```

5. Press F5 to run the application.

   Visual Studio displays the application window.

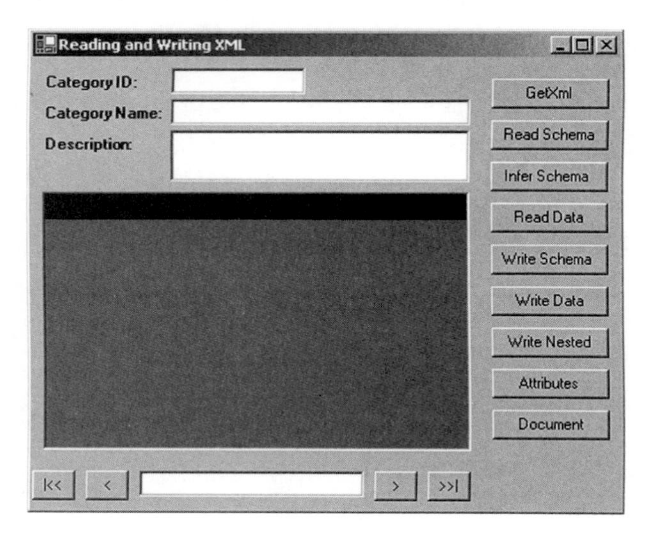

6 Click GetXml.

Visual Studio displays the GetXml form.

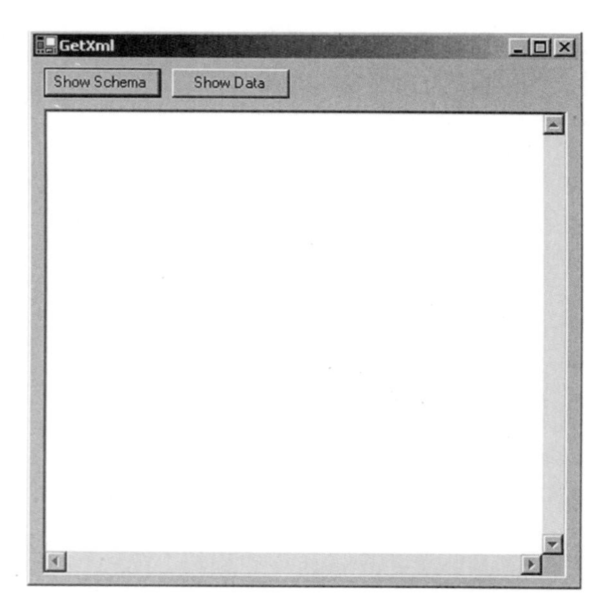

7 Click Show Schema.

The application displays the DataSet schema in the text box.

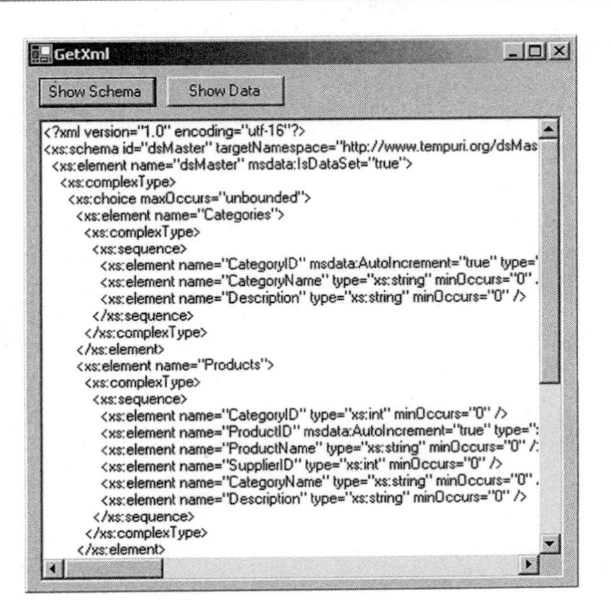

8 Close the GetXml form and the application.

Retrieve a DataSet's Data Using GetXml

Visual Basic .NET

1 In the code editor, select btnData in the Control Name combo box, and then select Click in the Method Name combo box.

Visual Studio adds the Click event handler to the code.

2 Add the following code to the handler:

```
Dim xmlStr As String

xmlStr = Me.dsMaster1.GetXml
Me.tbResult.Text = xmlStr
```

3 Press F5 to run the application.

Visual Studio displays the application window.

4 Click GetXml.

Visual Studio displays the GetXml form.

5 Click Show Data.

Visual Studio displays the XML data in the text box.

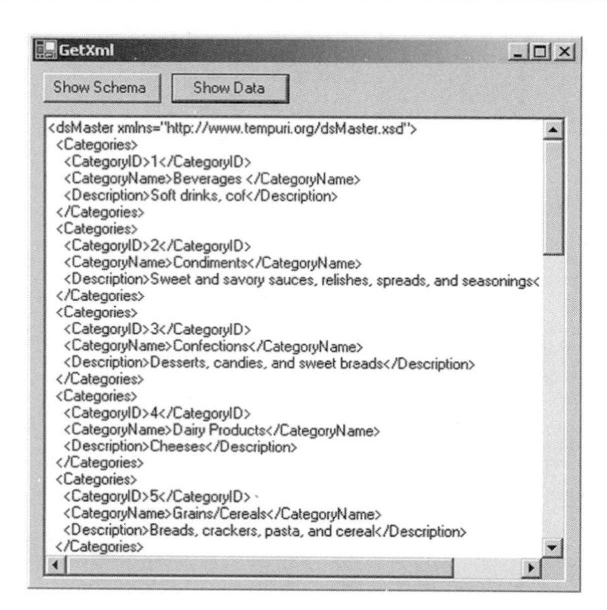

6. Close the GetXml form and the application.
7. Close the GetXml form designer and code editor window.

Visual C# .NET

1. In the form designer, double-click Show Data.

   Visual Studio displays the code editor window and adds the Click event handler to the code.
2. Add the following code to the handler:

```
string xmlStr;

xmlStr = this.dsMaster1.GetXml();
this.tbResult.Text = xmlStr;
```

3. Press F5 to run the application.

   Visual Studio displays the application window.
4. Click GetXml.

   Visual Studio displays the GetXml form.
5. Click Show Data.

   Visual Studio displays the XML data in the text box.

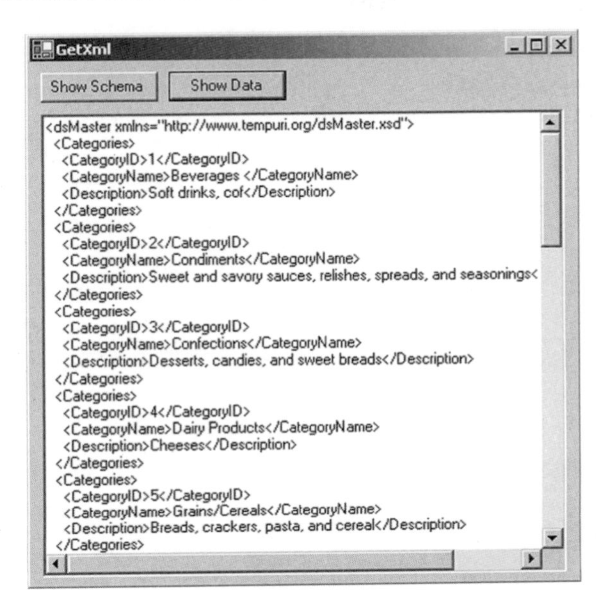

6. Close the GetXml form and the application.
7. Close the GetXml form designer and code editor window.

The *ReadXmlSchema* Method

The DataSet's *ReadXmlSchema* method loads a DataSet schema definition either from the XSD schema definition or from XML. *ReadXmlSchema* supports four versions, as shown in Table 15-1. You can pass the method a stream, a string identifying a file name, a TextReader, or an XmlReader object.

Method	Description
ReadXmlSchema(stream)	Reads an XML schema from the specified *stream*
ReadXmlSchema(string)	Reads an XML schema from the files specified in the *string* parameter
ReadXmlSchema(TextReader)	Reads an XML schema from the specified *TextReader*
ReadXmlSchema(XmlReader)	Reads an XML schema from the specified *XmlReader*

Table 15-1 *ReadXmlSchema* Methods

ReadXmlSchema does not load any data; it loads only tables, columns, and constraints (keys and relations). If the DataSet already contains schema information, new tables, columns, and constraints will be added to the existing schema, as necessary. If an object defined in the schema being read conflicts with the existing DataSet schema, the *ReadXmlSchema* method will throw an exception.

> **note**
> If the *ReadXmlSchema* method is passed XML that does not contain inline schema information, the method will infer the schema according to the rules discussed in the following section.

Create a DataSet Schema Using *ReadXmlSchema*

Visual Basic .NET

1. In the Solution Explorer, double-click XML.vb.

   Visual Studio displays the form in the form designer.

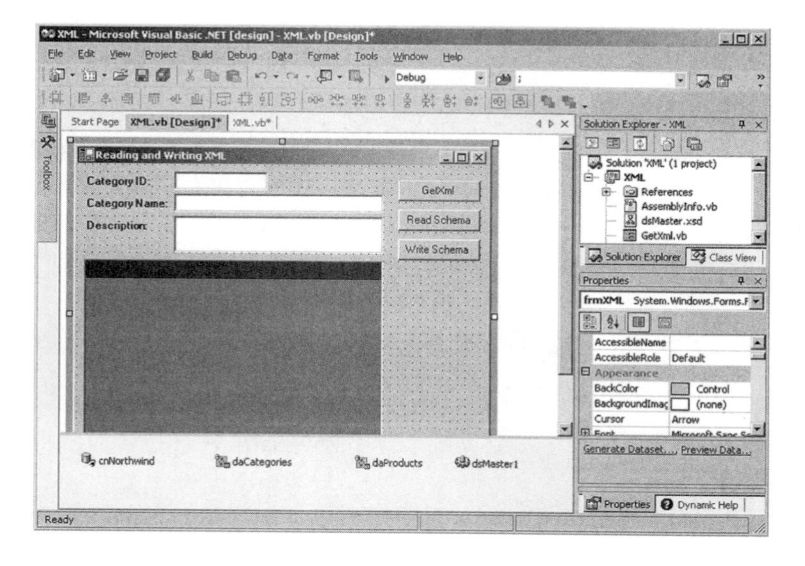

2. Double-click Read Schema.

   Visual Studio opens the code editor and adds a Click event handler.

3. Add the following code to the handler:

```
Dim newDS As New System.Data.DataSet()
newDS.ReadXmlSchema("masterSchema.xsd")
```

```
Me.daCategories.Fill(newDS.Tables("Categories"))
Me.daProducts.Fill(newDS.Tables("Products"))
SetBindings(newDS)
```

The first two lines declare a new DataSet and configure it by using the *ReadXmlSchema* method based on the XSD schema that is defined in the masterSchema.xsd file, which is in the bin folder of the project directory.

The remaining three lines fill the new DataSet and then call the SetBindings function, passing it to the DataSet object. SetBindings, which is in the Utility Functions region of the code editor, binds the controls on the XML form to the DataSet provided.

4 Press F5 to run the application.

5 Click Read Schema.

The application displays the data from the new DataSet in the form's controls. (Note that the navigation buttons will not work because they are specifically bound to the dsMaster1 DataSet.)

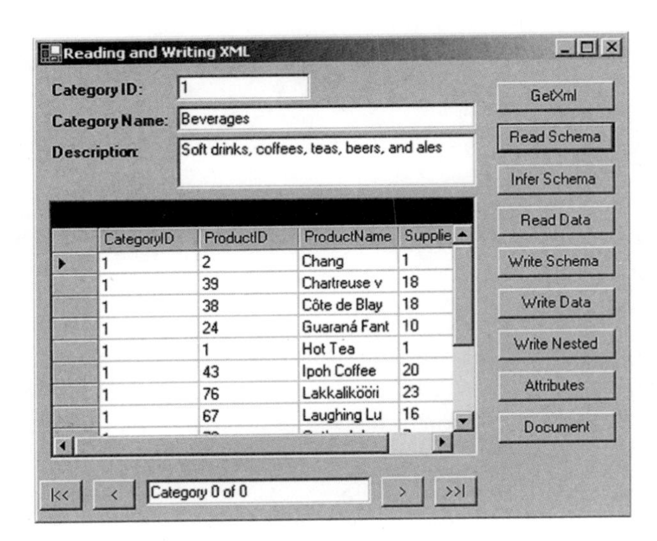

6 Close the application.

Visual C# .NET

1 In the Solution Explorer, double-click XML.cs.

Visual Studio displays the form in the form designer.

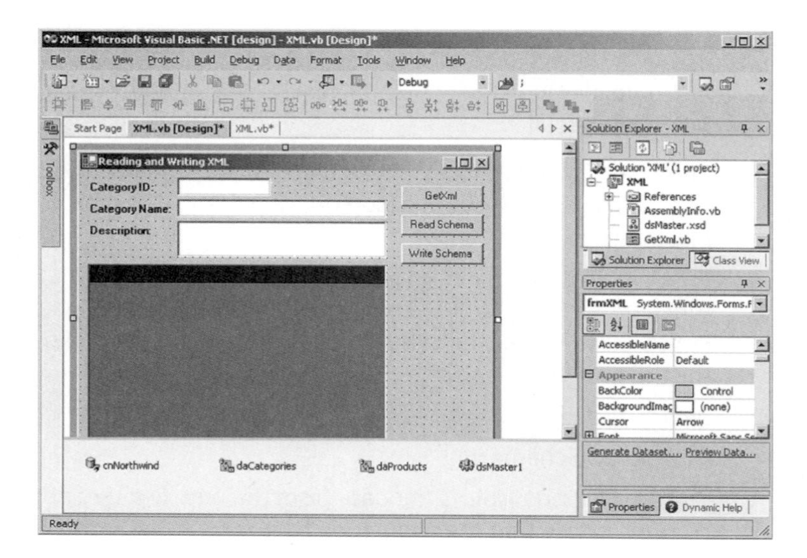

2 Double-click Read Schema.

Visual Studio opens the code editor and adds a Click event handler.

3 Add the following code to the handler:

```
System.Data.DataSet newDS = new System.Data.DataSet();
newDS.ReadXmlSchema("masterSchema.xsd");

this.daCategories.Fill(newDS.Tables["Categories"]);
this.daProducts.Fill(newDS.Tables["Products"]);
SetBindings(newDS);
```

The first two lines declare a new DataSet and configure it by using the *ReadXmlSchema* method based on the XSD schema that is defined in the masterSchema.xsd file, which is in the Debug folder, in the bin folder of the project directory.

The remaining three lines fill the new DataSet and then call the SetBindings function, passing it to the DataSet object. SetBindings, which is in the Utility Functions region of the code editor, binds the controls on the XML form to the DataSet provided.

4 Press F5 to run the application.

5 Click Read Schema.

The application displays the data from the new DataSet in the form's controls. (Note that the navigation buttons will not work because they are specifically bound to the dsMaster1 DataSet.)

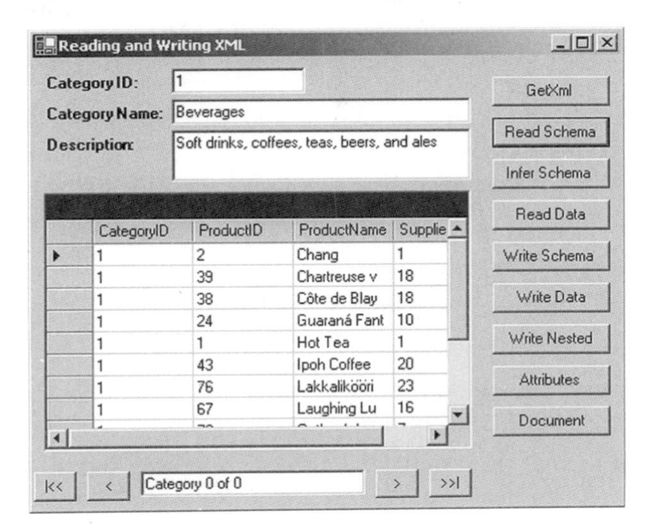

6 Close the application.

The *InferXmlSchema* Method

The DataSet's *InferXmlSchema* method derives a DataSet schema from the structure of the XML data passed to it. As shown in Table 15-2, *InferXmlSchema* has the same input sources as the *ReadXmlSchema* method we examined in the previous section.

Additionally, the *InferXmlSchema* method accepts an array of strings representing the namespaces that should be ignored when generating the DataSet schema.

Method	Description
InferXmlSchema (stream, namespaces())	Reads a schema from the specified *stream*, ignoring the namespaces identified in the *namespaces* string array
InferXmlSchema (file, namespaces())	Reads a schema from the file specified in the *file* parameter, ignoring the namespaces identified in the *namespaces* string array
InferXmlSchema (textReader, namespaces())	Reads a schema from the specified *textReader*, ignoring the namespaces identified in the *namespaces* string array
InferXmlSchema (XmlReader, namespaces())	Reads a schema from the specified *XmlReader*, ignoring the namespaces identified in the *namespaces* string array

Table 15-2 *InferXmlSchema* Methods

InferXmlSchema follows a fixed set of rules when generating a DataSet schema:

- If the root element in the XML has no attributes and no child elements that would otherwise be inferred as columns, it is inferred as a DataSet. Otherwise, the root element is inferred as a table.
- Elements that have attributes are inferred as tables.
- Elements that have child elements are inferred as tables.
- Elements that repeat are inferred as a single table.
- Attributes are inferred as columns.
- Elements that have no attributes or child elements and do not repeat are inferred as columns.
- If elements that are inferred as tables are nested within other elements also inferred as tables, a DataRelation is created between the two tables. A new, primary key column named "TableName_Id" is added to both tables and used by the DataRelation. A ForeignKeyConstraint is created between the two tables by using the "TableName_Id" column as the foreign key.
- If elements that are inferred as tables contain text but have no child elements, a new column named "TableName_Text" is created for the text of each of the elements. If an element is inferred as a table and has text but also has child elements, the text is ignored.

note

Only nested (hierarchical) data will result in the creation of a DataRelation. By default, the XML that is created by the DataSet's *WriteXml* method doesn't create nested data, so a round-trip won't result in the same DataSet schema. As we'll see, however, this can be controlled by setting the Nested property of the DataRelation object.

Infer the Schema of an XML Document

Visual Basic .NET

1. In the code editor, select btnInferSchema in the Control Name combo box, and then select Click in the Method Name combo box.

   Visual Studio adds the event handler to the code.
2. Add the following code to the event handler:

```
Dim newDS As New System.Data.DataSet()
Dim nsStr() As String

newDS.InferXmlSchema("dataOnly.xml", nsStr)

Me.daCategories.Fill(newDS.Tables("Categories"))
Me.daProducts.Fill(newDS.Tables("Products"))
newDS.Relations.Add("CategoriesProducts", _
    newDS.Tables("Categories").Columns("CategoryID"), _
    newDS.Tables("Products").Columns("CategoryID"))
```

The first two lines declare DataSet and String array variables, while the third line passes them to the *InferXmlSchema* method. The remaining code adds a new DataRelation to the new DataSet, fills it, and then calls the SetBindings utility function that binds the XML form controls to the DataSet.

3 Press F5 to run the application.

4 Click Infer Schema.

The application displays the data in the form controls.

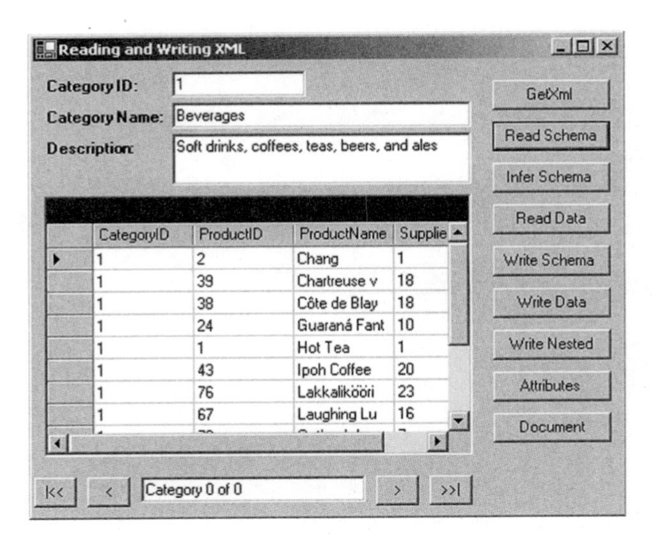

5 Close the application.

Visual C# .NET

1 In the form designer, double-click Infer Schema.

Visual Studio adds the event handler to the code.

2 Add the following code to the event handler:

```
System.Data.DataSet newDS = new System.Data.DataSet();
string[] nsStr = {};

newDS.InferXmlSchema("dataonly.xml", nsStr);

newDS.Relations.Add("CategoriesProducts",
   newDS.Tables["Categories"].Columns["CategoryID"],
   newDS.Tables["Products"].Columns["CategoryID"]);
this.daCategories.Fill(newDS.Tables["Categories"]);
this.daProducts.Fill(newDS.Tables["Products"]);
SetBindings(newDS);
```

The first two lines declare DataSet and String array variables, while the third line passes them to the *InferXmlSchema* method. The remaining code adds a new DataRelation to the new DataSet, fills it, and then calls the SetBindings utility function that binds the XML form controls to the DataSet.

3 Press F5 to run the application.

4 Click Infer Schema.

The application displays the data in the form controls.

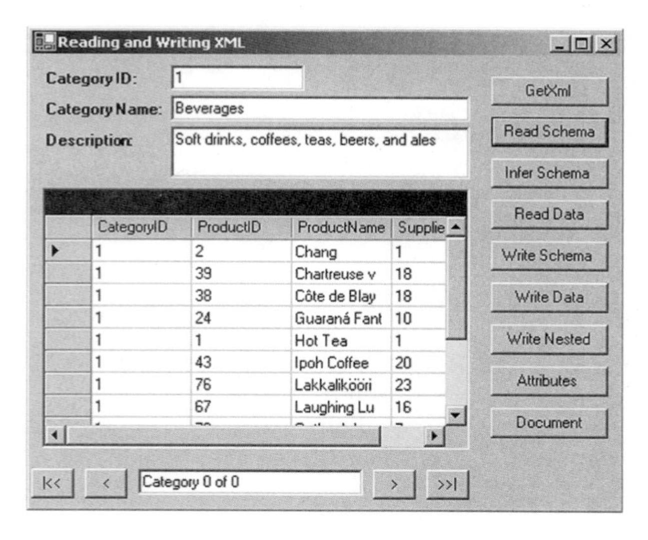

5 Close the application.

The *ReadXml* Method

The DataSet's *ReadXml* method reads XML data into a DataSet. Optionally, it may also create or modify the DataSet schema. As shown in Table 15-3, the *ReadXml* method supports the same input sources as the other DataSet XML methods we've examined.

Method	Description
ReadXml(Stream)	Reads an XML schema and data to the specified *stream*
ReadXml(String)	Reads an XML schema and data to the file specified in the *string* parameter
ReadXml(TextReader)	Reads an XML schema and data to the specified *TextReader*
ReadXml(XmlReader)	Reads an XML schema and data to the specified *XmlReader*
ReadXml(Stream, XmlReadMode)	Reads an XML schema, data, or both to the specified *stream*, as determined by the *XmlReadMode*
ReadXml(String, XmlReadMode)	Reads an XML schema, data, or both to the file specified in the *string* parameter, as determined by the *XmlReadMode*
ReadXml(TextReader, XmlReadMode)	Reads an XML schema, data, or both to the specified *TextReader*, as determined by the *XmlReadMode*
ReadXml(XmlReader, XmlReadMode)	Reads an XML schema, data, or both to the specified *XmlReader*, as determined by the *XmlReadMode*

Table 15-3 *ReadXml* Methods

The *ReadXml* method exposes an optional *XmlReadMode* parameter that determines how the XML is interpreted. The possible values for *XmlReadMode* are shown in Table 15-4.

Value	Description
Auto	Chooses a ReadMode based on the contents of the XML
ReadSchema	Reads an inline schema and then loads the data, adding DataTables as necessary
IgnoreSchema	Loads data into an existing DataSet, ignoring any schema information in the XML
InferSchema	Infers a DataSet schema to the XML, ignoring any inline schema information
DiffGram	Reads DiffGram information into an existing DataSet schema
Fragment	Adds XML fragments that match the existing DataSet schema to the DataSet and ignores those that do not

Table 15-4 ReadXMLMode Values

Unless the *ReadXml* method is passed an *XmlReadMode* parameter of DiffGram, it does not merge the data that it reads with existing rows in the DataSet. If a row is read with the same primary key as an existing row, the method will throw an exception.

A DiffGram is an XML format that encapsulates the current and original versions of an element, along with any DataRow errors. The nominal structure of a DiffGram is shown here:

```
<diffgr:diffgram
       xmlns:msdata="urn:schemas-microsoft-com:xml-msdata"
       xmlns:diffgr="urn:schemas-microsoft-com:xml-diffgram-v1"
       xmlns:xsd="http://www.w3.org/2001/XMLSchema">

   <ElementName>
   </ElementName>

   <diffgr:before>
   </diffgr:before>

   <diffgr:errors>
   </diffgr:errors>
</diffgr:diffgram>
```

In the real DiffGram, the first section (shown as *<ElementName> </ElementName>* in the example) will have the name of the complexType defining the DataRow. The section contains the current version of the contents of the DataRow. The *<diffgr:before>* section contains the original version, while the *<diffgr:errors>* section contains error information for the row.

In order for DiffGram to be passed as the *XmlReadMode* parameter, the data must be in DiffGram format. If you need to merge XML that is written in standard XML format with existing data, create a new DataSet and then call the *DataSet.Merge* method to merge the two sets of data.

Load XML Data Using *ReadXml*

Visual Basic .NET

1. In the code editor, select btnReadData in the Control Name combo box, and then select Click in the Method Name combo box.

   Visual Studio adds the event handler to the code.

2 Add the following code to the event handler:

```
Dim newDS As New System.Data.DataSet()
Dim nsStr() As String

newDS.ReadXml("data.xml", XmlReadMode.ReadSchema)
SetBindings(newDS)
```

The data.xml file contains an inline schema definition, so by passing the ReadSchema *XmlReadMode* parameter to the *ReadXml* method, the code instructs the DataSet to first create the DataSet schema and then load the data.

3 Press F5 to run the application.

4 Click Read Data.

The application displays the data retrieved from the file.

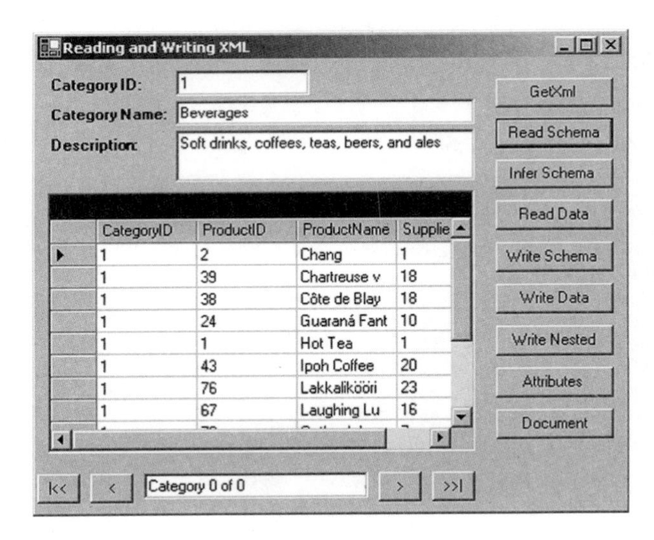

5 Close the application.

Visual C# .NET

1 In the form designer, double-click Read Data.

Visual Studio adds the event handler to the code.

2 Add the following code to the event handler:

```
System.Data.DataSet newDS = new System.Data.DataSet();
string[] nsStr ={};

newDS.ReadXml("data.xml", XmlReadMode.ReadSchema);
SetBindings(newDS);
```

The data.xml file contains an inline schema definition, so by passing the ReadSchema *XmlReadMode* parameter to the *ReadXml* method, the code instructs the DataSet to first create the DataSet schema and then load the data.

3 Press F5 to run the application.

4 Click Read Data.

The application displays the data retrieved from the file.

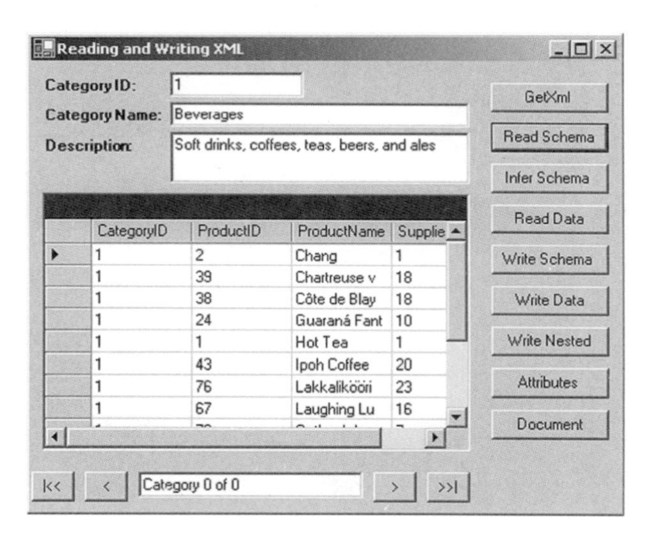

5 Close the application.

The *WriteXmlSchema* Method

As might be expected, the *WriteXmlSchema* method writes the schema of the DataSet, including tables, columns, and constraints, to the specified output. The versions of the method, which accept the same output parameters as the other XML methods, are shown in Table 15-5.

Method	Description
WriteXml(stream)	Writes an XML schema to the specified *stream*
WriteXml(string)	Writes an XML schema to the files specified in the *string* parameter
WriteXml(TextReader)	Writes an XML schema to the specified *TextReader*
WriteXml(XmlReader)	Writes an XML schema to the specified *XmlReader*

Table 15-5 *WriteXmlSchema* Methods

Create an XML Schema Using WriteXmlSchema

Visual Basic .NET

1. In the code editor, select btnWriteSchema in the Control Name combo box, and then select Click in the Method Name combo box.

   Visual Studio adds the event handler to the code.

2. Add the following lines to the event handler:

```
Me.dsMaster1.WriteXmlSchema("testSchema.xsd")
Messagebox.Show("Finished", "WriteXmlSchema")
```

   Because no path is passed to the method, the file will be written to the bin subdirectory of the project directory.

3. Press F5 to run the application.
4. Click Write Schema.

   The application displays a message box after the file has been written.

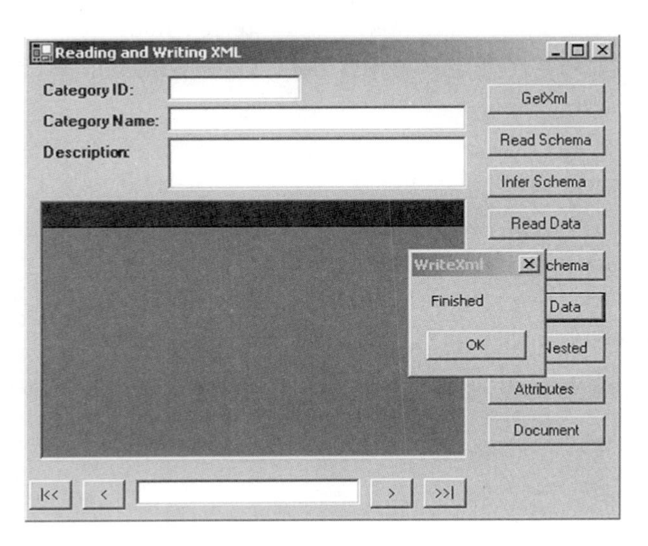

5 Close the message box, and then close the application.

6 Open Microsoft Windows Explorer, navigate to the XML/bin project directory, right-click the testSchema.xsd file, and then select Open with Notepad.

Windows displays the schema file.

testSchema.xsd - Notepad

File Edit Format Help

```
<?xml version="1.0" standalone="yes"?>
<xs:schema id="dsMaster" targetNamespace="http://www.tempuri.org/dsMaster.xsd" xmlns:mstns="
  <xs:element name="dsMaster" msdata:IsDataSet="true">
    <xs:complexType>
      <xs:choice maxOccurs="unbounded">
        <xs:element name="Categories">
          <xs:complexType>
            <xs:sequence>
              <xs:element name="CategoryID" msdata:AutoIncrement="true" type="xs:int" />
              <xs:element name="CategoryName" type="xs:string" minOccurs="0" />
              <xs:element name="Description" type="xs:string" minOccurs="0" />
            </xs:sequence>
          </xs:complexType>
        </xs:element>
        <xs:element name="Products">
          <xs:complexType>
            <xs:sequence>
              <xs:element name="CategoryID" type="xs:int" minOccurs="0" />
              <xs:element name="ProductID" msdata:AutoIncrement="true" type="xs:int" />
              <xs:element name="ProductName" type="xs:string" minOccurs="0" />
              <xs:element name="SupplierID" type="xs:int" minOccurs="0" />
            </xs:sequence>
          </xs:complexType>
        </xs:element>
      </xs:choice>
    </xs:complexType>
    <xs:unique name="Constraint1" msdata:PrimaryKey="true">
      <xs:selector xpath=".//mstns:Categories" />
      <xs:field xpath="mstns:CategoryID" />
    </xs:unique>
    <xs:unique name="Products_Constraint1" msdata:ConstraintName="Constraint1" msdata:Primar
      <xs:selector xpath=".//mstns:Products" />
      <xs:field xpath="mstns:ProductID" />
    </xs:unique>
    <xs:keyref name="CategoriesProducts" refer="Constraint1">
      <xs:selector xpath=".//mstns:Products" />
```

7 Close Microsoft Notepad, and return to Visual Studio.

Visual C# .NET

1 In the form designer, double-click Write Schema.

Visual Studio adds the event handler to the code.

2 Add the following lines to the event handler:

```
this.dsMaster1.WriteXmlSchema("testSchema.xsd");
MessageBox.Show("Finished", "WriteXmlSchema");
```

Because no path is passed to the method, the file will be written to the bin subdirectory of the project directory.

3 Press F5 to run the application.

4 Click Write Schema.

The application displays a message box after the file has been written.

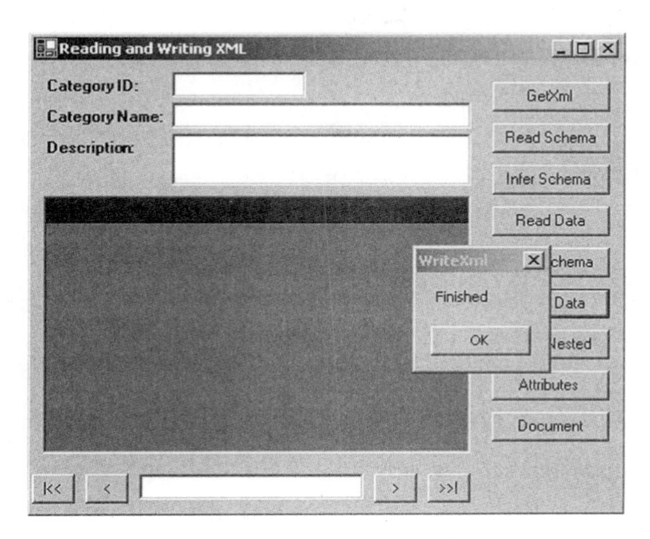

5. Close the message box, and then close the application.
6. Open Microsoft Windows Explorer, navigate to the XML/bin/Debug project directory, right-click the testSchema.xsd file, and then select Open with Notepad.

   Windows displays the schema file.

testSchema.xsd - Notepad

File Edit Format Help

```
<?xml version="1.0" standalone="yes"?>
<xs:schema id="dsMaster" targetNamespace="http://www.tempuri.org/dsMaster.xsd" xmlns:mstns="
  <xs:element name="dsMaster" msdata:IsDataSet="true">
    <xs:complexType>
      <xs:choice maxOccurs="unbounded">
        <xs:element name="Categories">
          <xs:complexType>
            <xs:sequence>
              <xs:element name="CategoryID" msdata:AutoIncrement="true" type="xs:int" />
              <xs:element name="CategoryName" type="xs:string" minOccurs="0" />
              <xs:element name="Description" type="xs:string" minOccurs="0" />
            </xs:sequence>
          </xs:complexType>
        </xs:element>
        <xs:element name="Products">
          <xs:complexType>
            <xs:sequence>
              <xs:element name="CategoryID" type="xs:int" minOccurs="0" />
              <xs:element name="ProductID" msdata:AutoIncrement="true" type="xs:int" />
              <xs:element name="ProductName" type="xs:string" minOccurs="0" />
              <xs:element name="SupplierID" type="xs:int" minOccurs="0" />
            </xs:sequence>
          </xs:complexType>
        </xs:element>
      </xs:choice>
    </xs:complexType>
    <xs:unique name="Constraint1" msdata:PrimaryKey="true">
      <xs:selector xpath=".//mstns:Categories" />
      <xs:field xpath="mstns:CategoryID" />
    </xs:unique>
    <xs:unique name="Products_Constraint1" msdata:ConstraintName="Constraint1" msdata:Primar
      <xs:selector xpath=".//mstns:Products" />
      <xs:field xpath="mstns:ProductID" />
    </xs:unique>
    <xs:keyref name="CategoriesProducts" refer="Constraint1">
      <xs:selector xpath=".//mstns:Products" />
```

7. Close Microsoft Notepad, and return to Visual Studio.

The *WriteXml* Method

Like the *ReadXml* method, the DataSet's *WriteXml* method writes XML data and, optionally, DataSet schema information, to a specified output, as shown in Table 15-6. As we'll see in the following section, the structure of the XML resulting from the *WriteXml* method is controlled by DataSet property settings.

Method	Description
WriteXml(Stream)	Writes an XML schema and data to the specified *stream*
WriteXml(String)	Writes an XML schema and data to the file specified in the *string* parameter
WriteXml(TextReader)	Writes an XML schema and data to the specified *TextReader*
WriteXml(XmlReader)	Writes an XML schema and data to the specified *XmlReader*
WriteXml(Stream, XmlWriteMode)	Writes an XML schema, data, or both to the specified *stream*, as determined by the *XmlWriteMode*
WriteXml(String, XmlWriteMode)	Writes an XML schema, data, or both to the file specified in the *string* parameter, as determined by the *XmlWriteMode*
WriteXml(TextReader, XmlWriteMode)	Writes an XML schema, data, or both to the specified *TextReader*, as determined by the *XmlWriteMode*
WriteXml(XmlReader, XmlWriteMode)	Writes an XML schema, data, or both to the specified *XmlReader*, as determined by the *XmlWriteMode*

Table 15-6 *WriteXml* Methods

The valid *XmlWriteMode* parameters are shown in Table 15-7. The *DiffGram* parameter causes the output to be written in DiffGram format. If no *XmlWriteMode* parameter is specified, WriteSchema is assumed.

Value	Description
IgnoreSchema	Writes the data without a schema
WriteSchema	Writes the data with an inline schema
DiffGram	Writes the entire DataSet in DiffGram format

Table 15-7 WriteXMLMode Values

Write Data to a File in XML Format

Visual Basic .NET

1. In the code editor, select btnWriteData in the Control Name combo box, and then select Click in the Method Name combo box.

   Visual Studio adds the event handler to the code.

2. Add the following lines to the event handler:

```
Me.daCategories.Fill(Me.dsMaster1.Categories)
Me.daProducts.Fill(Me.dsMaster1.Products)

Me.dsMaster1.WriteXml("newData.xml", XmlWriteMode.IgnoreSchema)
MessageBox.Show("Finished", "WriteXml")
```

   Because no path is passed to the method, the file will be written to the bin subdirectory of the project directory.

3. Press F5 to run the application.
4. Click Write Data.

   The application displays a message box after the file has been written.

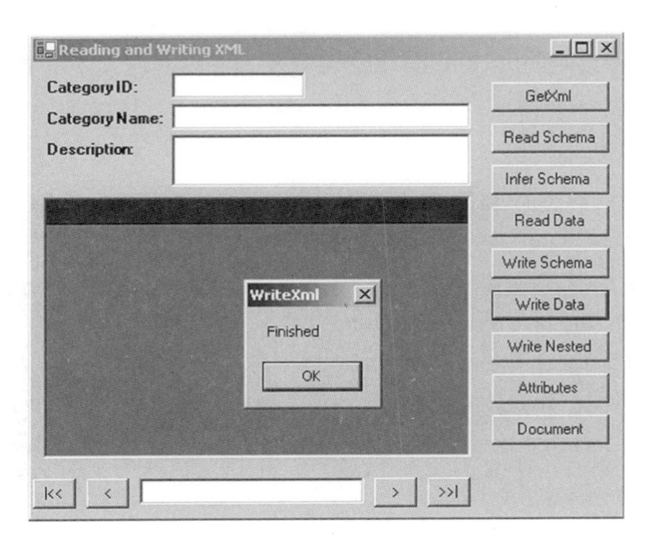

5. Close the message box, and then close the application.
6. Open Windows Explorer, navigate to the XML/bin project directory, and double-click the data.xml file.

   The XML file opens in Microsoft Internet Explorer.

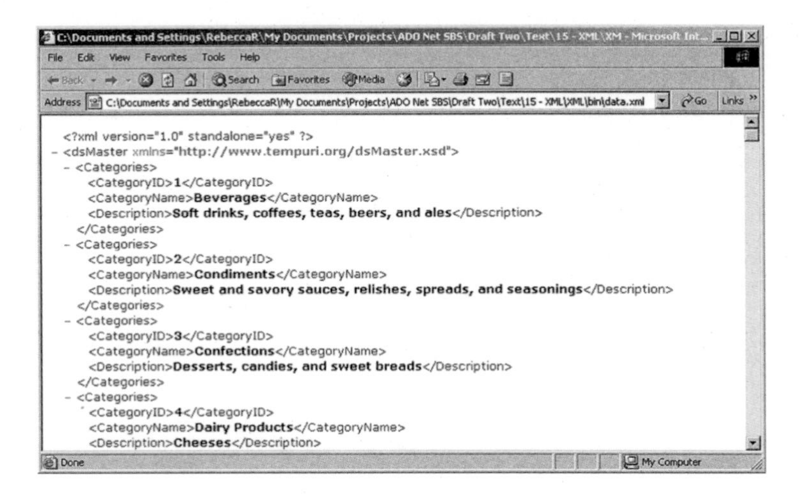

7. Close Internet Explorer, and return to Visual Studio.

Visual C# .NET

1. In the form designer, double-click Write Data.

   Visual Studio adds the event handler to the code.

2. Add the following lines to the event handler:

```
this.daCategories.Fill(this.dsMaster1.Categories);
this.daProducts.Fill(this.dsMaster1.Products);

this.dsMaster1.WriteXml("newData.xml", XmlWriteMode.IgnoreSchema);
MessageBox.Show("Finished", "WriteXml");
```

   Because no path is passed to the method, the file will be written to the bin subdirectory of the project directory.

3. Press F5 to run the application.

4. Click Write Data.

   The application displays a message box after the file has been written.

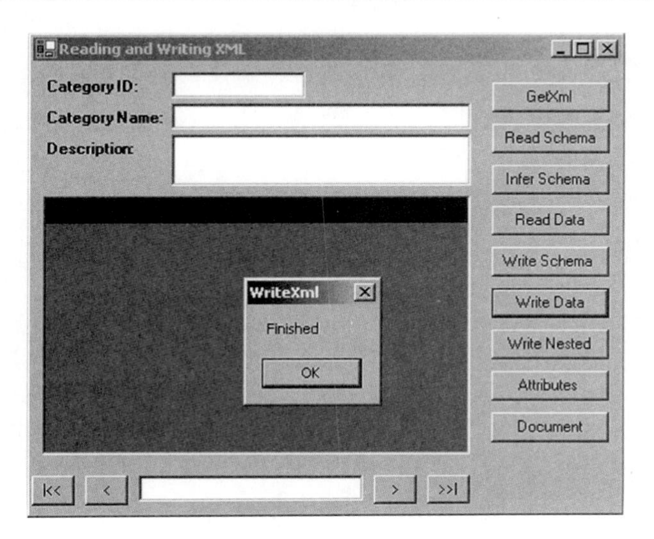

5 Close the message box, and then close the application.

6 Open Windows Explorer, navigate to the XML/bin/Debug project directory, and double-click the data.xml file.

The XML file opens in Microsoft Internet Explorer.

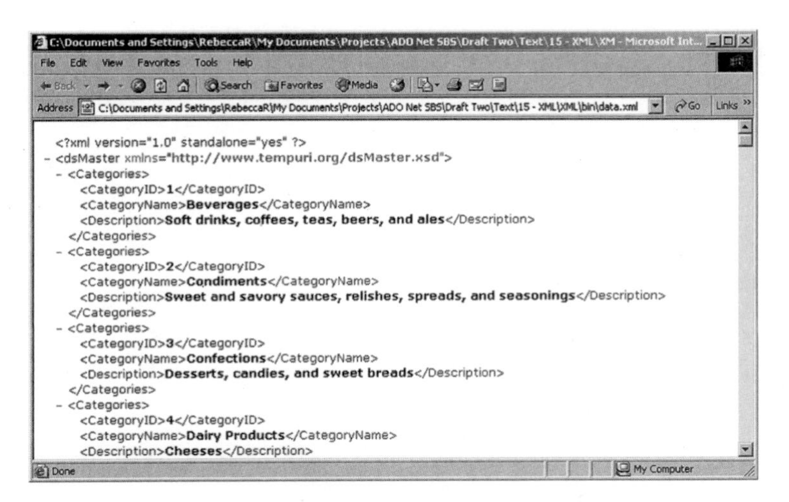

7 Close Internet Explorer, and return to Visual Studio.

Controlling How the XML Is Written

By default, the *WriteXml* method generates XML that is formatted according to the nominal structure we examined in Chapter 14, with DataTables structured as complexTypes and DataColumns as elements within them.

This isn't necessarily what you want the output to be. If, for example, you want to read the data back into a DataSet, ADO.NET won't create relationships correctly unless the schema is present, which is an unnecessary overhead in many situations, or the related data is nested hierarchically in the XML.

In other situations, you may need to control whether individual columns are written as elements, attributes, or simple text, or even prevent some columns from being written at all. This might be the case, for example, if you're interchanging data with another application.

Using the Nested Property of the DataRelation

By convention, XML data is usually represented hierarchically—related rows are nested inside their parent rows.

The Nested property of DataRelation causes the XML to be written so that the child rows are nested within the parent rows.

Write Related Data Hierarchically

Visual Basic .NET

1. In the code editor, select btnWriteNested in the Control Name combo box, and then select Click in the Method Name combo box.

   Visual Studio adds the event handler to the code.
2. Add the following lines to the event handler:

```
Me.daCategories.Fill(Me.dsMaster1.Categories)
Me.daProducts.Fill(Me.dsMaster1.Products)

Me.dsMaster1.Relations("CategoriesProducts").Nested = True
Me.dsMaster1.WriteXml("nestedData.xml", XmlWriteMode.IgnoreSchema)
MessageBox.Show("Finished", "WriteXml Nested")
```

   The code sets the Nested property to *True* before writing it to the nestData.xml file.
3. Press F5 to run the application.
4. Click Write Nested.

   The application displays a message box after the file has been written.

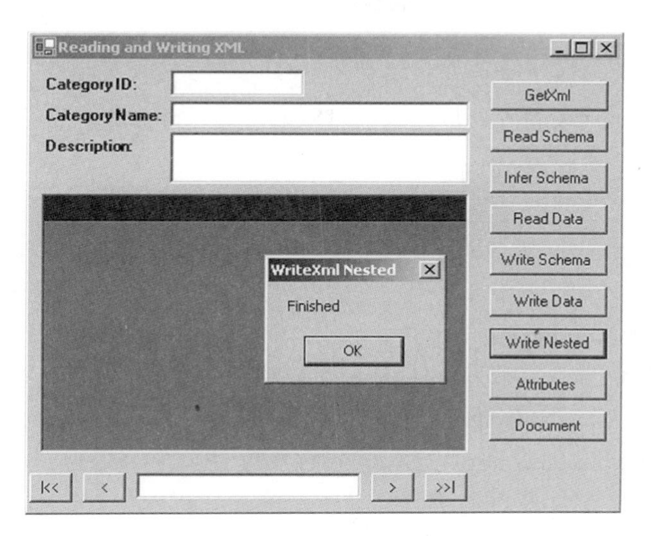

5 Close the message box, and then close the application.

6 Open Windows Explorer, navigate to the XML/bin project directory, and double-click the nestedData.xml file.

The XML file opens in Internet Explorer.

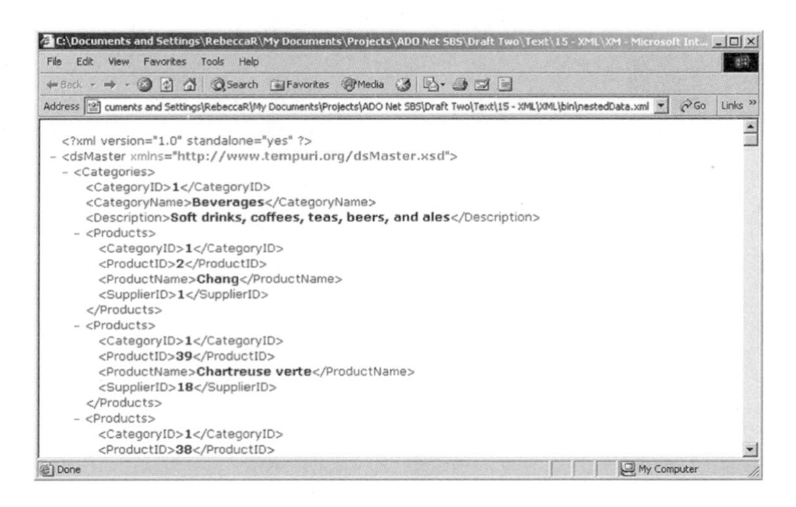

7 Close Internet Explorer, and return to Visual Studio.

Visual C# .NET

1 In the form designer, double-click Write Nested.

Visual Studio adds the event handler to the code.

2 Add the following lines to the event handler:

```
this.daCategories.Fill(this.dsMaster1.Categories);
this.daProducts.Fill(this.dsMaster1.Products);

this.dsMaster1.Relations["CategoriesProducts"].Nested = true;
this.dsMaster1.WriteXml("nestedData.xml", XmlWriteMode.IgnoreSchema);
MessageBox.Show("Finished", "WriteXml Nested");
```

The code sets the Nested property to *true* before writing it to the nestData.xml file.

3 Press F5 to run the application.

4 Click Write Nested.

The application displays a message box after the file has been written.

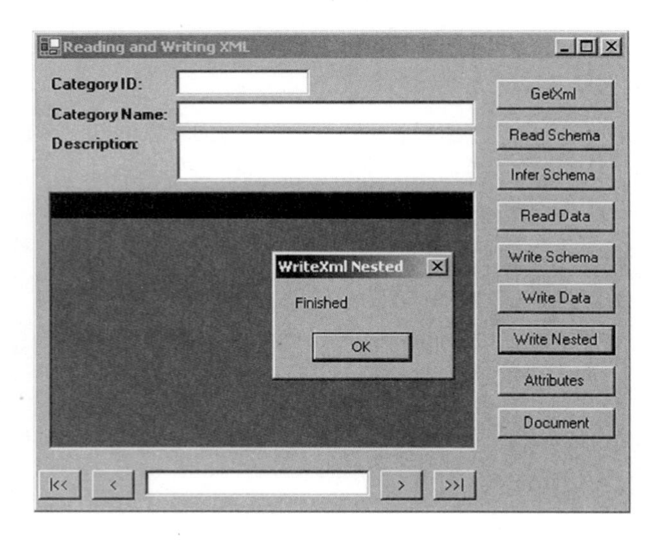

5 Close the message box, and then close the application.

6 Open Windows Explorer, navigate to the XML/bin/Debug project directory, and double-click the nestedData.xml file.

The XML file opens in Internet Explorer.

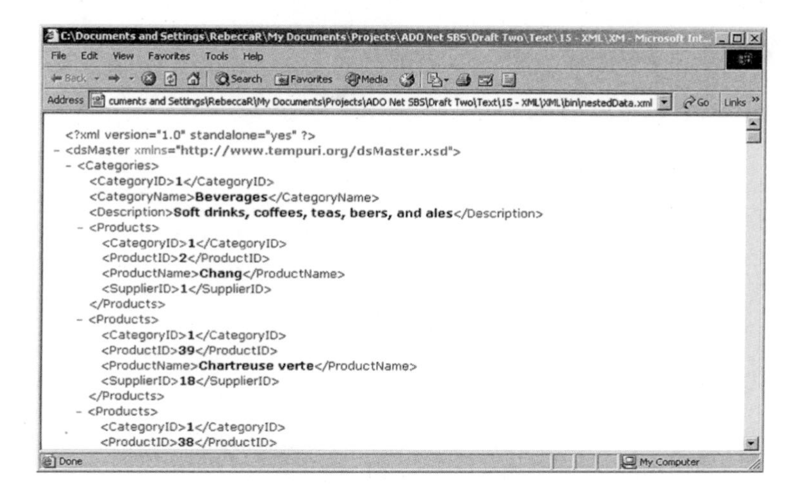

7 Close Internet Explorer, and return to Visual Studio.

Using the ColumnMapping Property of the DataColumn

The DataColumn's ColumnMapping property controls how the column will be written by the *WriteXml* method. The possible values for the ColumnMapping property are shown in Table 15-8.

Element, the default value, writes the column as a nested element within the complexType representing the DataTable, while Attribute writes the column as one of its attributes. These two values can be freely mixed within any given DataTable. The Hidden value prevents the column from being written at all.

SimpleContent, which writes the column as a simple text value, cannot be combined with columns that are written as elements or attributes, nor can it be used if the Nested property of a DataRelation referencing the table has its Nested property set to *true*.

Value	Description
Element	The column is written as an XML element
Attribute	The column is written as an XML attribute
SimpleContent	The contents of the column are written as text
Hidden	The column will not be included in the XML output

Table 15-8 Column MappingType Values

Write Columns as Attributes

Visual Basic .NET

1. In the code editor, select btnAttributes in the Control Name combo box, and then select Click in the Method Name combo box.

   Visual Studio adds the event handler to the code.

2. Add the following lines to the event handler:

```
Me.daCategories.Fill(Me.dsMaster1.Categories)

With Me.dsMaster1.Categories
    .Columns("CategoryID").ColumnMapping = MappingType.Attribute
    .Columns("CategoryName").ColumnMapping = MappingType.Attribute
    .Columns("Description").ColumnMapping = MappingType.Attribute
End With
Me.dsMaster1.WriteXml("attributes.xml", XmlWriteMode.IgnoreSchema)
MessageBox.Show("Finished", "Write Attributes")
```

3. Press F5 to run the application.
4. Click Attributes.

   The application displays a message box after the file has been written.

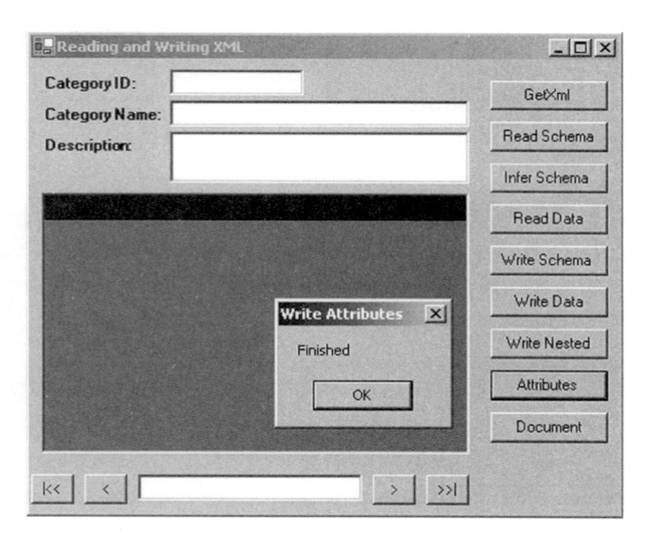

5. Close the message box, and then close the application.

6 Open Windows Explorer, navigate to the XML/bin project directory, and double-click the attributes.xml file.

The XML file opens in Internet Explorer.

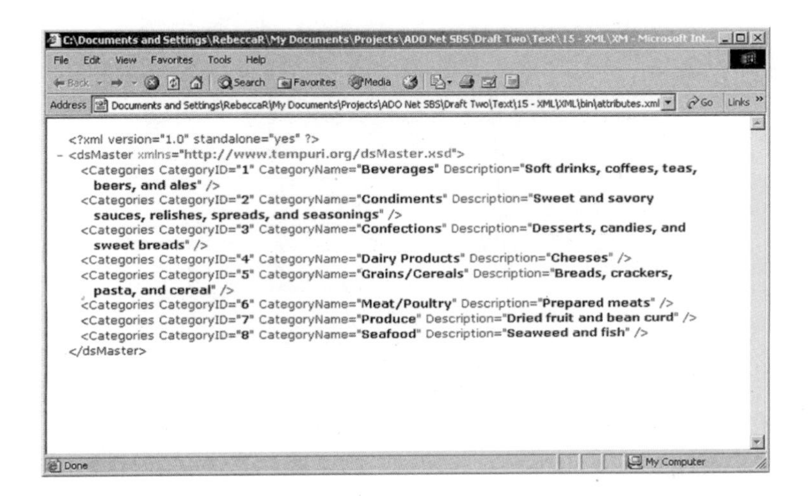

7 Close Internet Explorer, and return to Visual Studio.

Visual C# .NET

1 In the form designer, double-click Attributes.

Visual Studio adds the event handler to the code.

2 Add the following lines to the event handler:

```
System.Data.DataTable cat = this.dsMaster1.Categories;
this.daCategories.Fill(cat);

cat.Columns["CategoryID"].ColumnMapping = MappingType.Attribute;
cat.Columns["CategoryName"].ColumnMapping = MappingType.Attribute;
cat.Columns["Description"].ColumnMapping = MappingType.Attribute;

this.dsMaster1.WriteXml("attributes.xml", XmlWriteMode.IgnoreSchema);
MessageBox.Show("Finished", "Write Attributes");
```

3 Press F5 to run the application.

4 Click Attributes.

The application displays a message box after the file has been written.

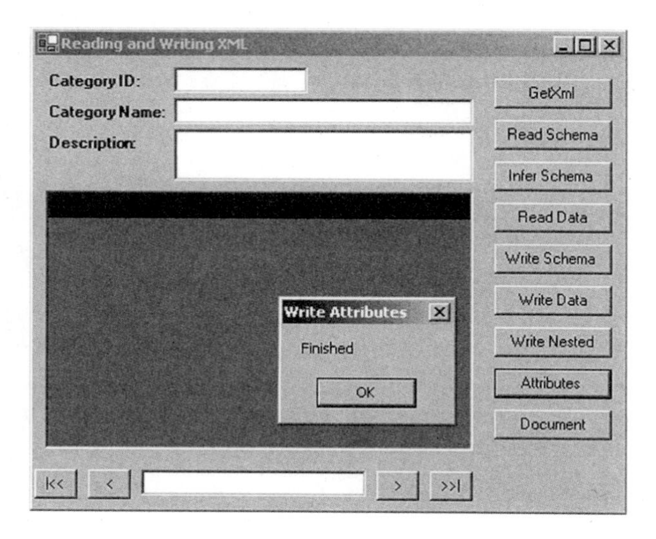

5 Close the message box, and then close the application.

6 Open Windows Explorer, navigate to the XML/bin project directory, and double-click the attributes.xml file.

The XML file opens in Internet Explorer.

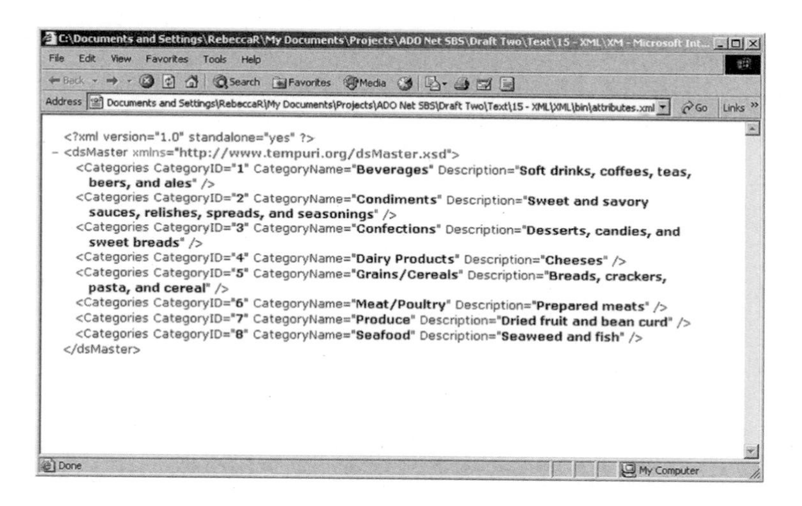

7 Close Internet Explorer, and return to Visual Studio.

The XmlDataDocument Object

Although the relational data model is efficient, there are times when it is convenient to manipulate a set of data by using the tools provided by XML—the Extensible Stylesheet Language (XSL), XSLT, and XPath.

The .NET Framework's XmlDataDocument makes that possible. The XmlDataDocument allows XML-structured data to be manipulated as a DataSet. It doesn't create a new set of data, but rather it creates a DataSet that references all or part of the XML data. Because there's only one set of data, changes made in one view will automatically be reflected in the other view, and of course, memory resources are conserved because only one copy of the data is being maintained.

Depending on the initial source of your data, you can create an XmlDataDocument based on the schema and contents of a DataSet, or you can create a DataSet based on the contents of an XmlDataDocument. In either case, changes made to the data stored in one view will be reflected in the other view.

To create an XmlDataDocument based on an existing DataSet, pass the DataSet to the XmlDataDocument constructor:

```
myXDD = New XmlDataDocument(myDS)
```

If the DataSet schema has not been established prior to creating the XmlDataDocument, both schemas must be established manually—schema changes made to one object will not be propagated to the other object.

Alternatively, to begin with an XML document and create a DataSet, you can use the default XmlDataDocument constructor and then reference its DataSet property:

```
myXDD = New XmlDataDocument()
myDS = myXDD.DataSet
```

If you use this method, you must create the DataSet schema manually by adding objects to the DataSet's Tables collection and the DataTable's Columns collection. In order for the data in the XmlDataDocument to be available through the DataSet, the DataTable and DataColumn names must match those in the XmlDataDocument. The matching is case-sensitive.

The second method, while it requires slightly more code, provides a mechanism for creating a partial relational view of the XML data. There is no requirement to duplicate the entire XML schema in the DataSet. Any DataTables or DataColumns that are not in the DataSet will simply be ignored during DataSet operations.

Data can be loaded into either document at any time, before or after synchronization. Any data changes made to one object, including adding, deleting, or changing values, will automatically be reflected in the other object.

Create a Synchronized XML View of a DataSet

Visual Basic .NET

1. In the code editor, select btnDocument in the Control Name combo box, and then select Click in the Method Name combo box.

   Visual Studio adds the event handler to the code.

2. Add the following lines to the event handler:

```
Dim myXDD As System.Xml.XmlDataDocument

myXDD = New System.Xml.XmlDataDocument(Me.dsMaster1)
myXDD.Load("dataOnly.xml")

SetBindings(Me.dsMaster1)
```

   The first line declares the XmlDataDocument variable, while the second line synchronizes it with the dsMaster1 DataSet. The third line loads data into the XmlDataDocument.

   The final line binds the form controls to dsMaster1. Because the DataSet has been synchronized with the myXDD XmlDataDocument, the data loaded into myXDD will be available in dsMaster1.

3. Press F5 to run the application.

4. Click Documents.

   The application displays the data in the form.

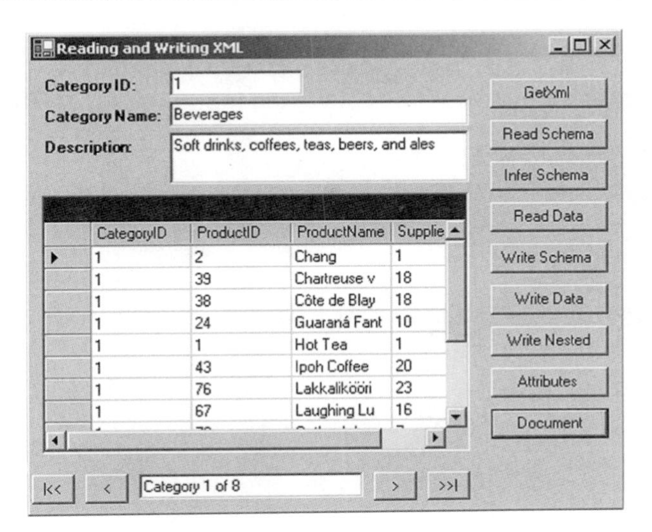

5 Close the application.

Visual C# .NET

1 In the form designer, double-click Document.

Visual Studio adds the event handler to the code.

2 Add the following lines to the event handler:

```
System.Xml.XmlDataDocument myXDD;

myXDD = new System.Xml.XmlDataDocument(this.dsMaster1);
myXDD.Load("dataOnly.xml");

SetBindings(this.dsMaster1);
```

The first line declares the XmlDataDocument variable, while the second line synchronizes it with the dsMaster1 DataSet. The third line loads data into the XmlDataDocument.

The final line binds the form controls to dsMaster1. Because the DataSet has been synchronized with the myXDD XmlDataDocument, the data loaded into myXDD will be available in dsMaster1.

3 Press F5 to run the application.

4 Click Documents.

The application displays the data in the form.

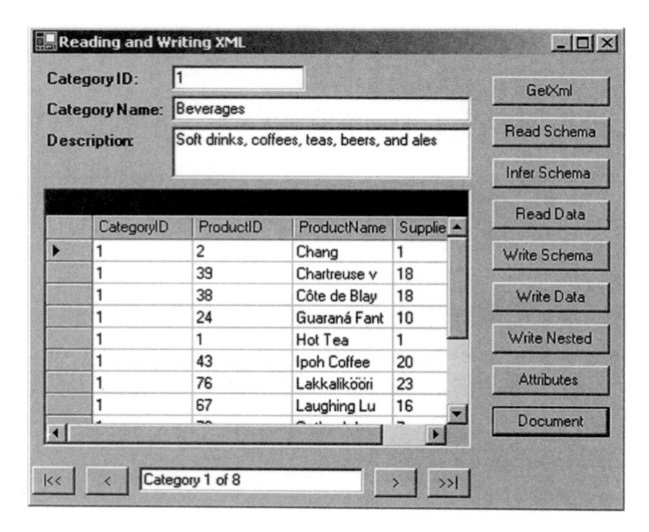

5 Close the application.

Chapter 15 Quick Reference

To	Do this
Retrieve an XML schema from a DataSet	Use the DataSet's *GetXmlSchema* method: `XmlSchemaString = myDataSet.GetXmlSchema()`
Retrieve data from a DataSet in XML format	Use the DataSet's *GetXml* method: `XmlDataString = myDataSet.GetXml()`
Create a DataSet schema from an XML schema	Use the DataSet's *ReadXmlSchema* method: `myDataSet.ReadXmlSchema("schema.xsd")`
Infer the schema of an XML document	Use the DataSet's *InferXmlSchema* method: `myDataSet.InferXmlSchema("data.xml", string[])`
Load XML data into a DataSet	Use the DataSet's *ReadXml* method: `myDataSet.ReadXml("data.xml")`
Create an XML schema from a DataSet	Use the DataSet's *WriteXmlSchema* method: `myDataSet.WriteXmlSchema("schema.xsd")`
Write data to an XML document	Use the DataSet's *WriteXml* method: `myDataSet.WriteXml("data.xml")`

Create a synchronized XML view of a DataSet	Create an instance of an XmlDataDocument that references the DataSet:
	`Dim myXDD As System.Xml.XmlDataDocument`
	`myXDD = New System.Xml.XmlDataDocument(myDataSet)`

CHAPTER

16

Using ADO in the .NET Framework

In this chapter, you'll learn how to:

- ✔ *Establish a reference to the ADO and ADOX COM libraries*
- ✔ *Create an ADO connection*
- ✔ *Retrieve data from an ADO Recordset*
- ✔ *Update an ADO Recordset*
- ✔ *Create a database using ADOX*
- ✔ *Add a table to a database using ADOX*

In the previous two chapters, we examined using XML data with Microsoft ADO.NET objects. In this chapter, we'll look at the interface to another type of data, legacy data objects created by using previous versions of ADO.

We'll also examine the ADOX library, which provides the ability to create database objects under programmatic control. This functionality is not available in ADO.NET, although you can execute DDL statements such as CREATE TABLE on servers that support them.

Understanding COM Interoperability

Maintaining interoperability with COM components was one of the design goals of the Microsoft .NET Framework, and this achievement extends to previous versions of ADO.

By using the COM Interop functions provided by the .NET Framework, you can gain access to all the objects, methods, and events that are exposed by any COM object simply by establishing a reference to it. This includes previous versions of ADO and COM objects that you've developed using them.

After the reference has been established, the COM objects behave just as though they were .NET Framework classes. What happens behind the scenes, of course, is more complicated. When a reference to any COM object, including ADO or ADOX, is declared, the .NET Framework creates an *interop assembly* that handles communication between the .NET Framework and COM.

The interop assembly handles a number of tasks, but the most important is data type marshaling. Table 16-1 shows the type conversion performed by the interop assembly for standard COM value types.

Com Data Type	.NET Framework Type
bool	Int32
char, small	SByte
Short	Int16
long, int	Int32
hyper	Int64
unsigned char, byte	Byte
wchar_t, unsigned short	UInt16
unsigned long, unsigned int	UInt32
unsigned hyper	UInt64
float	Single
double	Double
VARIANT_BOOL	Boolean
void *	IntPtr
HRESULT	Int16 or IntPtr
SCODE	Int32
BSTR	String
LPSTR	String
LPWSTR	String
VARIANT	Object
DECIMAL	Decimal
DATE	DateTime
GUID	Guid
CURRENCY	Decimal

IUnknown *	Object
IDispatch *	Object
SAFEARRAY(*type*)	*type*[]

Table 16-1 COM Data Type Marshaling

Using ADO in the .NET Framework

In addition to the generic COM interoperability and data type marshaling provided by the .NET Framework for all COM objects, the .NET Framework provides specific support for the ADO and ADOX libraries, and COM objects built using them.

This additional support includes data marshaling for core ADO data types. The .NET Framework equivalents for core ADO types are shown in Table 16-2. Of course, after a reference to ADO is established, complex types such as Recordset and ADO Connection become available through the ADO component.

ADO Data Type	.NET Framework Type
adEmpty	null
adBoolean	Int16
adTinyInt	SByte
adSmallInt	Int16
adInteger	Int32
adBigInt	Int64
adUnsignedTinyInt	promoted to Int16
adUnsignedSmallInt	promoted to Int32
adUnsignedInt	promoted to Int64
adUnsignedBigInt	promoted to Decimal
adSingle	Single
adDouble	Double
adCurrency	Decimal
adDecimal	Decimal
adNumeric	Decimal
adDate	DateTime
adDBDate	DateTime
adDBTime	DateTime
adDBTimeStamp	DateTime

(continued)

(continued)

adFileTime	DateTime
adGUID	Guid
adError	ExternalException
adIUnknown	object
adIDispatch	object
adVariant	object
adPropVariant	object
adBinary	byte[]
adChar	string
adWChar	string
adBSTR	string
adChapter	not supported
adUserDefined	not supported
adVarNumeric	not supported

Table 16-2 ADO Data Type Marshaling

Establishing a Reference to ADO

The first step in using a previous version of ADO, or a COM component that references a previous version, is to set a reference to the component. There are several methods for exposing the ADO component, but the most convenient is to simply add the reference within Microsoft Visual Studio .NET.

Add References to the ADO and ADOX Libraries

1. In Visual Studio, open the ADOInterop project from the Start page or the File menu.
2. In the Solution Explorer, double-click ADOInterop.vb (or ADOInterop.cs if you're using C#).

   Visual Studio displays the form in the form designer.

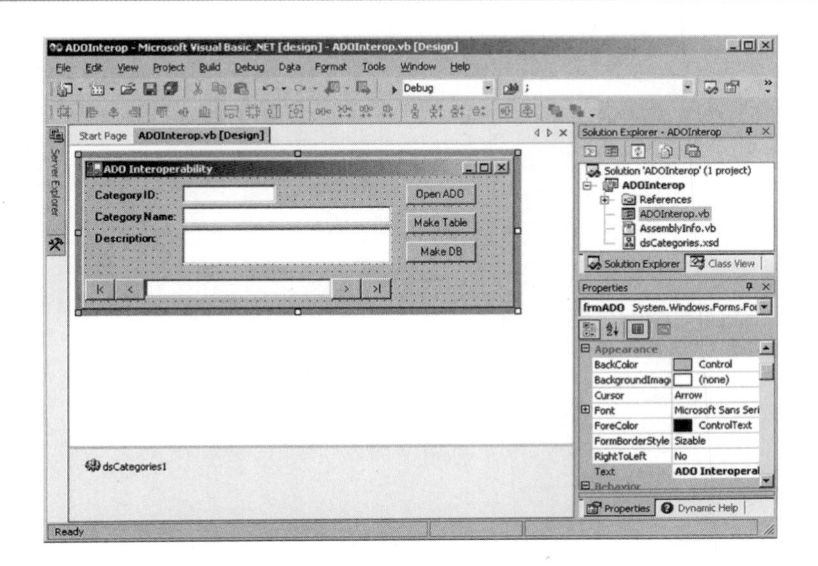

3 On the Project menu, select Add Reference.

Visual Studio opens the Add Reference dialog box.

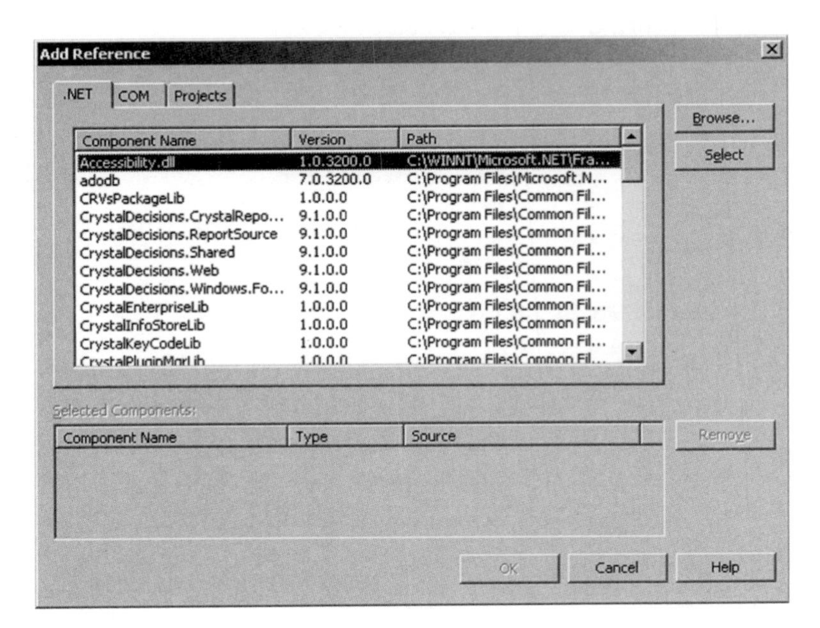

4 On the COM tab, select the component named Microsoft ActiveX Data Objects 2.1 Library, and then click Select.

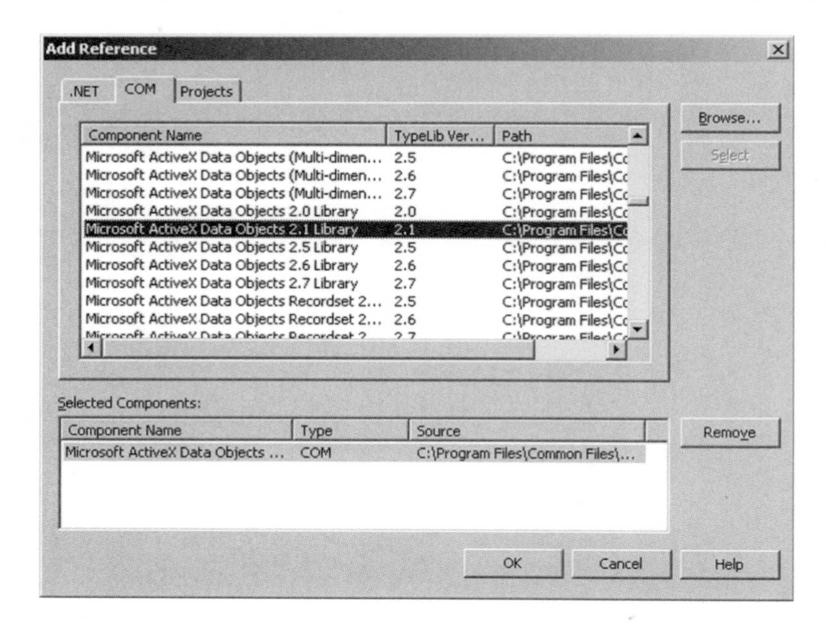

5 Select the component named Microsoft ADO Ext. 2.7 for DDL and Security, and then click Select.

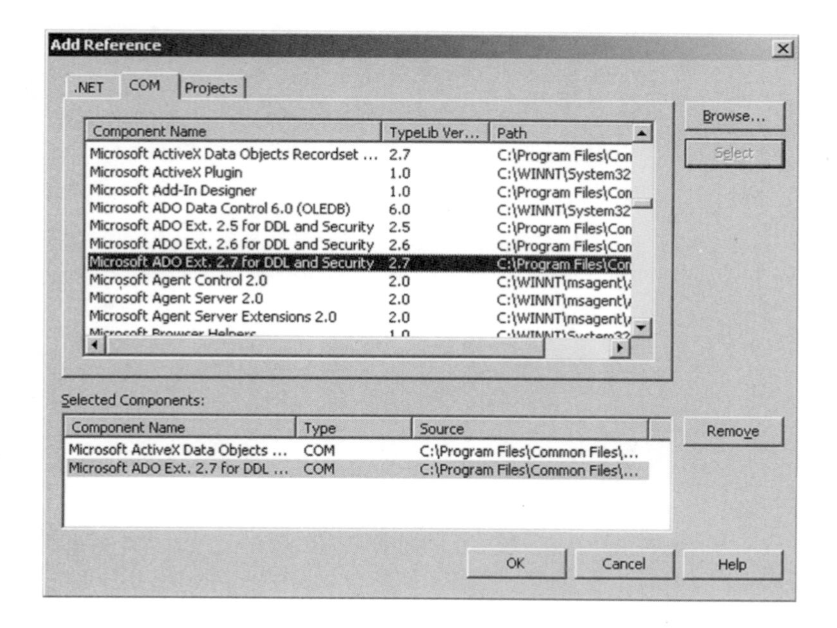

6 Click OK.

Visual Studio closes the dialog box and adds the references to the project.

7 In the Solution Explorer, expand the references node.

Visual Studio displays the new references.

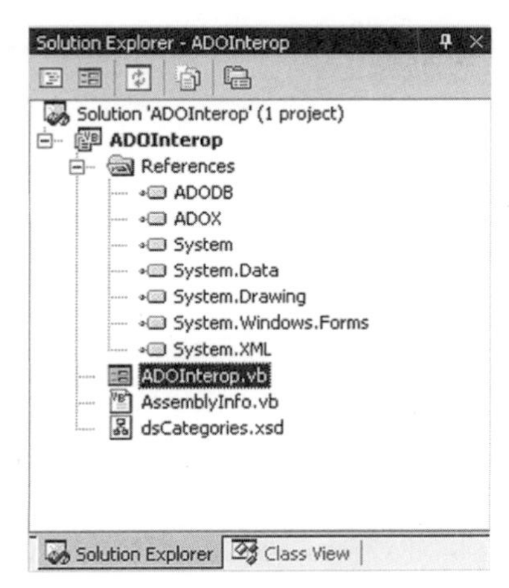

Creating ADO Objects

After the references to the ADO components have been established, ADO objects can be created and their properties set just like any object exposed by the .NET Framework class library.

Like ADO.NET, ADO uses a Connection object to represent a unique session with a data source. The most important property of an ADO connection, just like an ADO.NET connection, is the ConnectionString, which establishes the Data Provider, the database information, and, if appropriate, the user information.

Create an ADO Connection

Visual Basic .NET

1 Press F7 to open the code editor.

2 Add the following procedure, specifying the complete path for the dsStr text value:

```
Private Function create_connection() As ADODB.Connection
    Dim dsStr As String
    Dim dsCn As String
    Dim cn As New ADODB.Connection()
```

(continued)

(continued)

```
        dsStr = "<<Specify the path to the Access nwind sample db here>>"
        dsCn = "Provider=Microsoft.Jet.OLEDB.4.0;Data Source=" & _
           dsStr & ";"
        cn.ConnectionString = dsCn

        Return cn

    End Function
```

Visual C# .NET

1. Press F7 to open the code editor.
2. Add the following procedure, specifying the complete path for the dsStr text value:

```
private ADODB.Connection create_connection()
{
    string dsStr;
    string dsCn;

    ADODB.Connection cn = new ADODB.Connection();
    dsStr = "<<Specify the path to the Access nwind sample db here>>";
    dsCn = "Provider=Microsoft.Jet.OLEDB.4.0;Data Source=" +
       dsStr + ";";
    cn.ConnectionString = dsCn;

    return cn;
}
```

This function simply creates an ADO connection and returns it to the caller. We'll use the function to simplify creating connections in later exercises. (ConnectionStrings can be tedious to type.)

In addition to support for ADO data types, the OleDbDataAdapter provides direct support for ADO Recordsets by exposing the *Fill* method that accepts an ADO Recordset as a parameter. There are two versions of the method, as shown in Table 16-3.

Method	Description
Fill(DataTable, Recordset)	Adds or refreshes rows in the *DataTable* to match those in the *Recordset*
Fill(DataSet, Recordset, DataTable)	Adds or refreshes rows in the *DataTable* in the specified *DataSet* to match those in the *Recordset*

Table 16-3 OleDbDataAdapter *Fill* Methods

If the DataTable passed to the *Fill* method doesn't exist in the DataSet, it is created based on the schema of the ADO Recordset. Unless primary key information exists, the rows in the ADO Recordset will simply be added to the DataTable. If primary key information does exist, matching rows in the ADO Recordset will be merged with those in the DataTable.

Retrieve Data from an ADO Recordset

Visual Basic .NET

1. In the code editor, select btnOpen in the Control Name combo box, and then select Click in the Method Name combo box.

   Visual Studio adds the event handler to the code.

2. Add the following lines to the event handler:

```
Dim rs As New ADODB.Recordset()
Dim cnADO As ADODB.Connection
Dim daTemp As New OleDb.OleDbDataAdapter()

cnADO = create_connection()
cnADO.Open()

rs.Open("Select * From CategoriesByName", cnADO)
daTemp.Fill(Me.dsCategories1.Categories, rs)
cnADO.Close()

SetBindings(Me.dsCategories1)
```

   The first three lines declare an ADO Recordset, an ADO Connection, and an OleDbDataAdapter. The next two lines call the *create_connection* function that we created in the previous exercise to create the ADO Connection object, and then open the connection.

The next three lines open the ADO Recordset, load the rows into the DataAdapter, and then close the ADO Recordset, while the final line calls a function (in the Utility Functions region of the code editor) that binds the form's text boxes to the specified DataSet.

3 Press F5 to run the application.

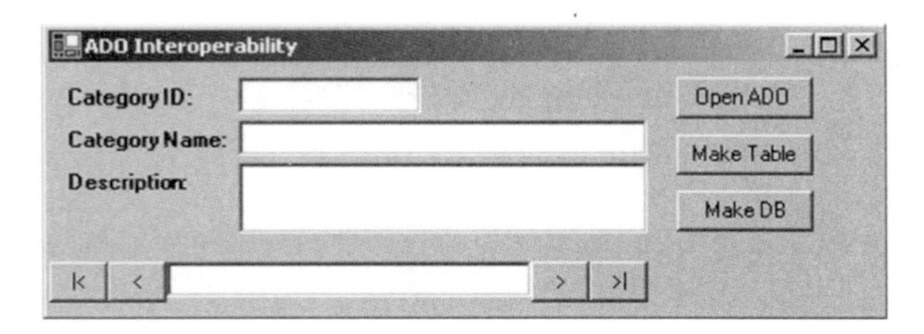

4 Click Open ADO.

The application loads the data from ADO and displays it in the form's text boxes.

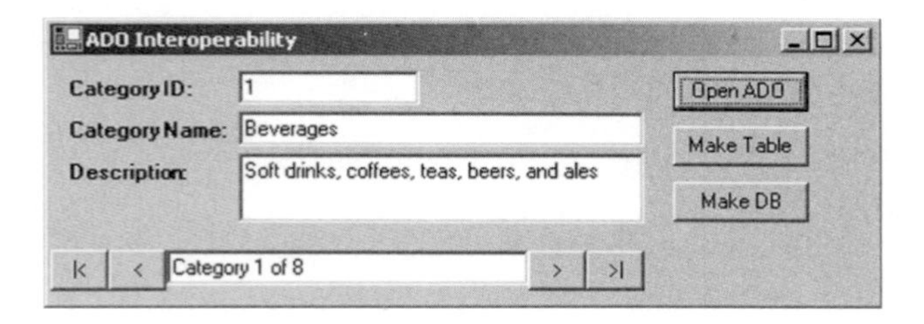

5 Close the application.

Visual C# .NET

1 In the form designer, double-click Open ADO.

Visual Studio adds the event handler to the code.

2 Add the following lines to the event handler:

```
ADODB.Recordset rs = new ADODB.Recordset();
ADODB.Connection cnADO;

System.Data.OleDb.OleDbDataAdapter daTemp =
   new System.Data.OleDb.OleDbDataAdapter();
cnADO = create_connection();
```

```
cnADO.Open(cnADO.ConnectionString, "", "", -1);
rs.Open("Select * From CategoriesByName",
   cnADO, ADODB.CursorTypeEnum.adOpenForwardOnly,
   ADODB.LockTypeEnum.adLockOptimistic, 1);
daTemp.Fill(Me.dsCategories1.Categories, rs);

cnADO.Close();
SetBindings(Me.dsCategories1);
```


The first three lines declare an ADO Recordset, an ADO Connection, and an OleDbDataAdapter. The next two lines call the *create_connection* function that we created in the previous exercise to create the ADO Connection object, and then open the connection.

The next three lines open the ADO Recordset, load the rows into the DataAdapter, and then close the ADO Recordset, while the final line calls a function (in the Utility Functions region of the code editor) that binds the form's text boxes to the specified DataSet.

3 Press F5 to run the application.

4 Click Open ADO.

The application loads the data from ADO and displays it in the form's text boxes.

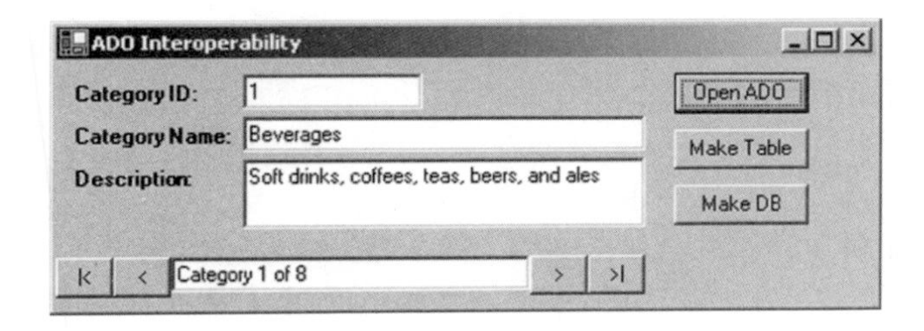

5 Close the application.

The OleDbDataAdapter's *Fill* method provides a convenient mechanism for loading data from an ADO Recordset into a .NET Framework DataTable, but unfortunately, the communication is one-way. The .NET Framework doesn't provide a direct method for updating an ADO Recordset based on ADO.NET data.

Fortunately, it isn't difficult to update an ADO data source from within the .NET Framework—simply copy the data values from the appropriate source and use the intrinsic ADO functions to do the update.

Update an ADO Recordset

Visual Basic .NET

1. In the code editor, select btnUpdate in the Control Name combo box, and then select Click in the Method Name combo box.

   Visual Studio adds the event handler to the code.

2. Add the following lines to the event handler:

```
Dim rsADO As New ADODB.Recordset()
Dim cnADO As ADODB.Connection

cnADO = create_connection()
cnADO.Open()
rsADO.ActiveConnection = cnADO
rsADO.Open("Select * From CategoriesByName", cnADO, _
   ADODB.CursorTypeEnum.adOpenDynamic, _
   ADODB.LockTypeEnum.adLockOptimistic)

rsADO.AddNew()
rsADO.Fields("CategoryName").Value = "Test"
rsADO.Fields("Description").Value = "Description"
rsADO.Update()

rsADO.Close()
cnADO.Close()
MessageBox.Show("Finished", "Update")
```

   As always, the first few lines declare some local values. The next five lines create a connection and an ADO Recordset. The next four lines use ADO's *AddNew* and *Update* methods to create a new row and set its values. Finally, the Recordset and ADO Connection are closed, and a message box is displayed.

3. Press F5 to run the application.

4 Click Update ADO.

The application adds the row to the DataTable, and then displays a message box telling you that the new row has been added.

5 Close the message box.

6 Click Open ADO to load the data into the form, and then click the Last (">|") button to display the last row.

The application displays the new row.

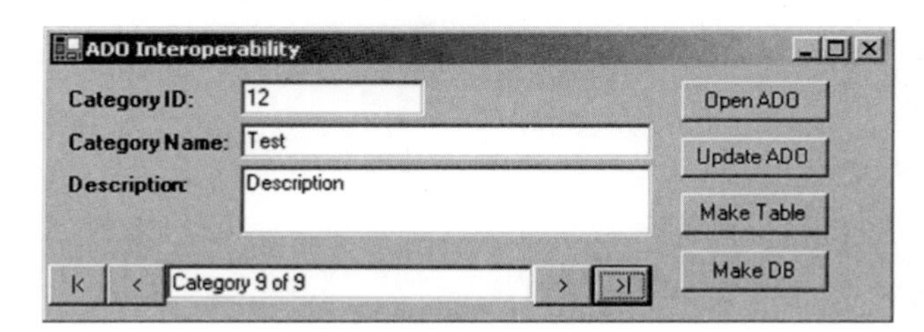

7 Close the application.

8 If you have Microsoft Access, open the nwind database and confirm that the row has been added.

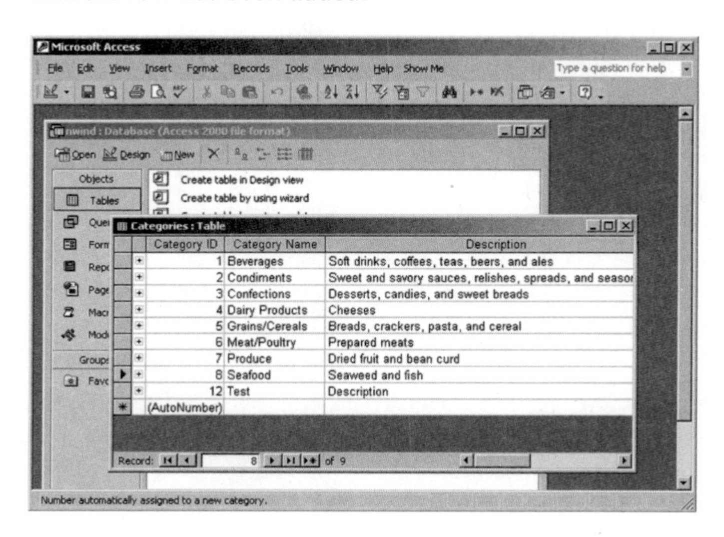

Visual C# .NET

1. In the form designer, double-click Update ADO.

   Visual Studio adds the event handler to the code.

2. Add the following lines to the event handler:

```
ADODB.Recordset rsADO = new ADODB.Recordset();
ADODB.Connection cnADO;

cnADO = create_connection();
cnADO.Open(cnADO.ConnectionString,"","",-1);

rsADO.ActiveConnection = cnADO;
rsADO.Open("Select * From CategoriesByName", cnADO,
   ADODB.CursorTypeEnum.adOpenDynamic,
   ADODB.LockTypeEnum.adLockOptimistic, -1);

rsADO.AddNew(Type.Missing, Type.Missing);
rsADO.Fields[1].Value = "Test";
rsADO.Fields[2].Value = "Description";
rsADO.Update(Type.Missing, Type.Missing);

rsADO.Close();
cnADO.Close();
MessageBox.Show("Finished", "Update");
```

   As always, the first few lines declare some local values. The next five lines create a connection and an ADO recordset. The next four lines use ADO's *AddNew* and *Update* methods to create a new row and set its values. Finally, the recordset and ADO connection are closed, and a message box is displayed.

3. Press F5 to run the application.

4. Click Update ADO.

   The application adds the row to the DataTable, and then displays a message box telling you that the new row has been added.

5. Close the message box.
6. Click Open ADO to load the data into the form, and then click the Last (">I") button to display the last row.

   The application displays the new row.

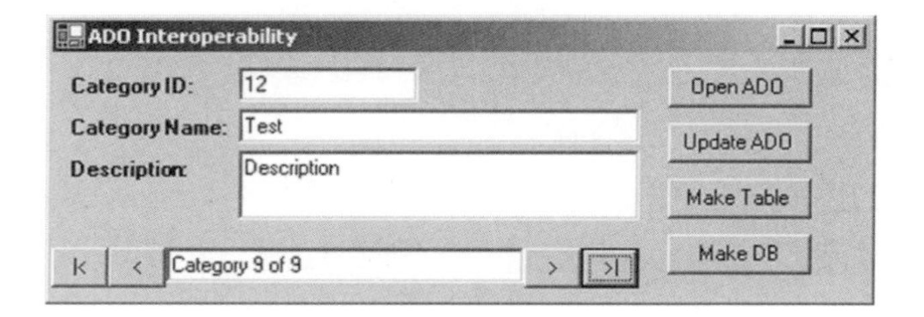

7. Close the application.
8. If you have Access, open the nwind database and confirm that the row has been added.

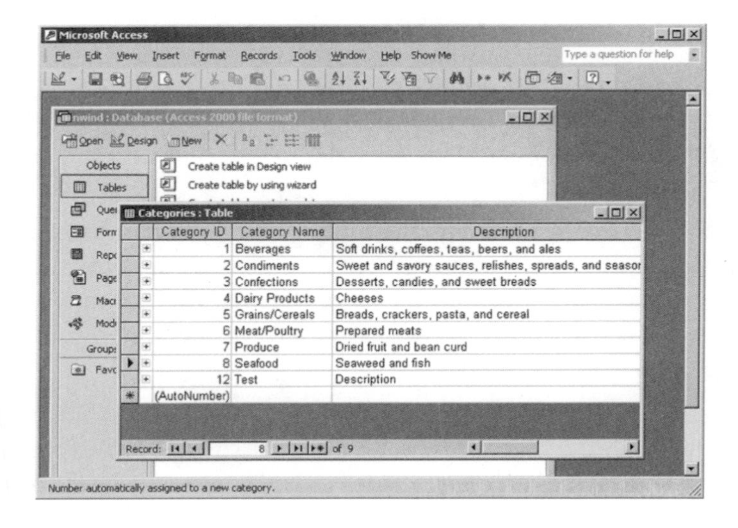

Using ADOX in the .NET Framework

ADOX, more formally the "Microsoft ADO Extensions for DDL and Security," exposes an object model that allows data source objects to be created and manipulated.

The ADOX object model is shown in the following figure. Not all data sources support all of the objects in the model; this is determined by the specific OleDb Data Provider.

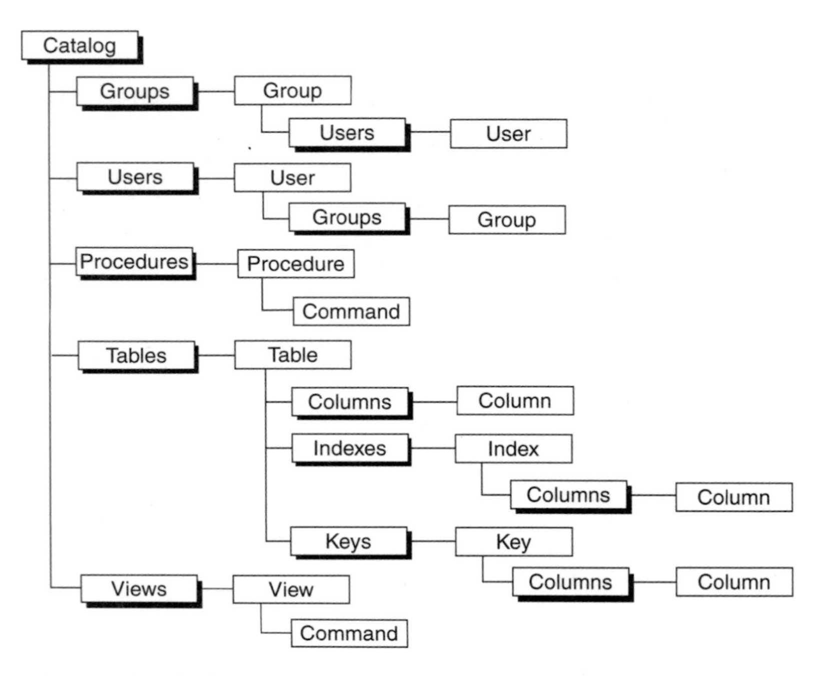

The top-level object, Catalog, equates to a specific data source. This will almost always be a database, but specific OleDb Data Providers might expose different objects. The Groups and Users collections control access security for those data sources that implement it.

The Tables object represents the tables within the database. Each table contains a Columns collection, which represents individual fields in the table; an Indexes collection, which represents physical indexes; and a Keys collection, which is used to define unique, primary, and foreign keys.

The Procedures collection represents stored procedures on the data source, while the Views collection represents Views or Queries. This model doesn't always match the object model of the data source. For example, Microsoft Jet (the underlying data source for Access) represents both Views and Procedures as Query objects. When mapped to an ADOX Catalog, any query that updates or inserts rows, along with any query that contains parameters, is mapped to a Procedure object. Queries that consist solely of SELECT statements are mapped to Views.

Creating Database Objects Using ADOX

As we've seen, ADOX provides a mechanism for creating data source objects programmatically. ADO.NET doesn't support this functionality. You can, of course, execute a CREATE <object> SQL statement using an ADO.NET DataCommand, but data definition syntax varies wildly between data sources, so it will often be more convenient to use ADOX and let the OleDb Data Provider handle the operation.

The Catalog object supports a *Create* method that creates a new database, while the Tables and Columns collections support *Append* methods that are used to create new schema objects.

Create a Database Using ADOX

Visual Basic .NET

1 In the code editor, select btnMakeDB in the Control Name combo box, and then select Click in the Method Name combo box.

  Visual Studio adds the event handler to the code.

2 Add the following lines to the event handler, specifying the path to the Sample DBs directory on your system where indicated:

```
Dim dsStr, dsCN As String
Dim cnADO As New ADODB.Connection()
Dim mdb As New ADOX.Catalog()

dsStr = "<<specify the path to the Sample DBs directory>>" _
   + "\test.mdb"
dsCN = "Provider=Microsoft.Jet.OLEDB.4.0;Data Source=" & dsStr & ";"
cnADO.ConnectionString = dsCN

mdb.Create(dsCN)

mdb.ActiveConnection.Close()
MessageBox.Show("Finished", "Make DB")
```

3 Press F5 to run the application, and then click Make DB.

  The application creates a Jet database named Test in the Sample DBs directory and then displays a finished method.

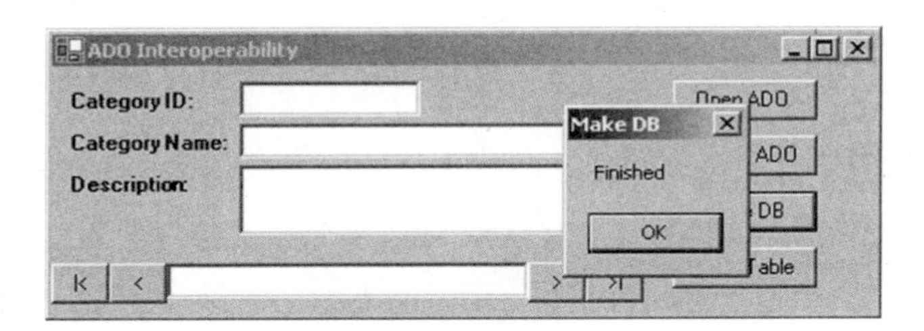

4. Close the dialog box, and then close the application.
5. Verify that the new database has been added using Microsoft Windows Explorer.

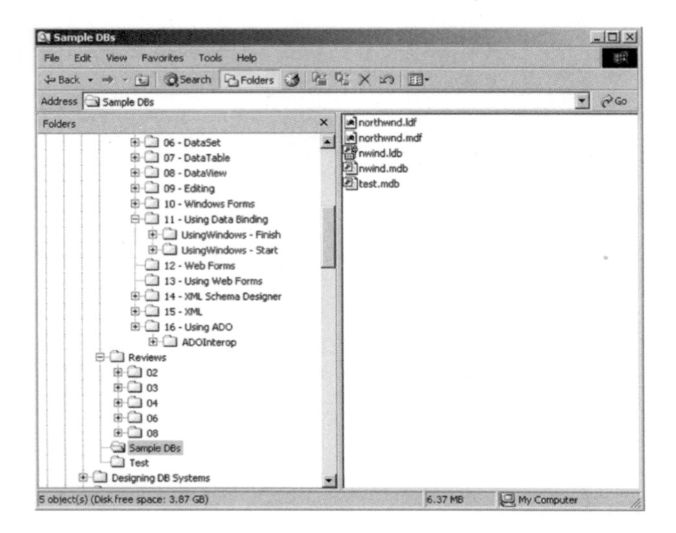

Visual C# .NET

1. In the form designer, double-click Make DB.

   Visual Studio adds the event handler to the code.

2. Add the following lines to the event handler, specifying the path to the Sample DBs directory on your system where indicated:

```
string dsStr, dsCN;
ADODB.Connection cnADO = new ADODB.Connection();
ADOX.Catalog mdb = new ADOX.Catalog();

dsStr = "<<specify the path to the Sample DBs directory>>" _
   + "\\test.mdb";
dsCN = "Provider=Microsoft.Jet.OLEDB.4.0;Data Source=" + dsStr + ";";
cnADO.ConnectionString = dsCN;

mdb.Create(dsCN);

MessageBox.Show("Finished", "Make DB");
```

3 Press F5 to run the application, and then click Make DB.

The application creates a Jet database named Test in the Sample DBs directory and then displays a finished method.

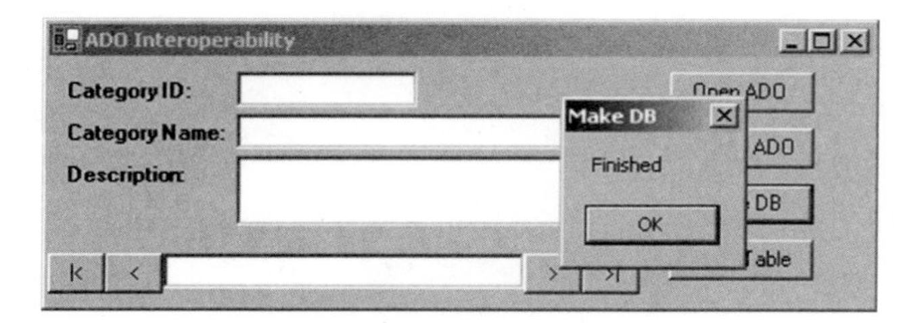

4 Close the dialog box, and then close the application.

5 Verify that the new database has been added using Microsoft Windows Explorer.

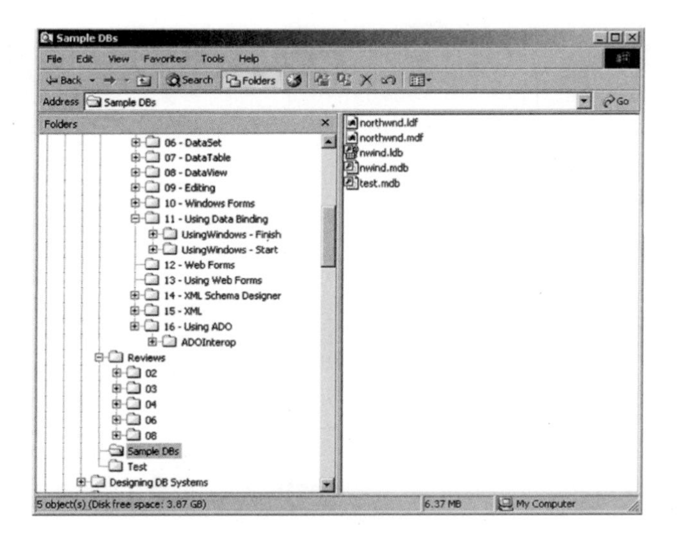

Add a Table to a Database Using ADOX

Visual Basic .NET

1 In the code editor, select btnMakeTable in the Control Name combo box, and then select Click in the Method Name combo box.

Visual Studio adds the event handler to the code.

2 Add the following code to the event handler:

```
Dim cnADO As ADODB.Connection
Dim mdb As New ADOX.Catalog()
Dim dt As New ADOX.Table()

cnADO = create_connection()
cnADO.Open()
mdb.ActiveConnection = cnADO

With dt
    .Name = "New Table"
    .Columns.Append("TableID", ADOX.DataTypeEnum.adWChar, 5)
    .Columns.Append("Value", ADOX.DataTypeEnum.adWChar, 20)
    .Keys.Append("PK_NewTable", ADOX.KeyTypeEnum.adKeyPrimary, _
       "TableID")
End With
mdb.Tables.Append(dt)

mdb.ActiveConnection.Close()
MessageBox.Show("Finished", "Make Table")
```

3 Press F5 to run the application, and then click Make Table.

The application adds the table to the nwind database and displays a message box telling you that the new table has been added.

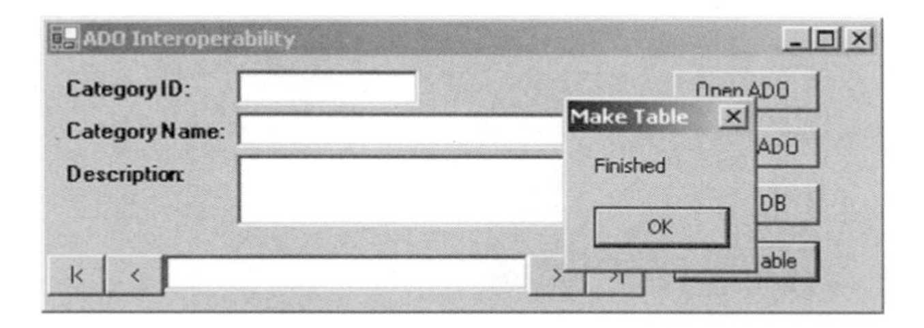

4 Close the message box, and then close the application.

5 If you have Access, open the nwind database and confirm that the new table has been added.

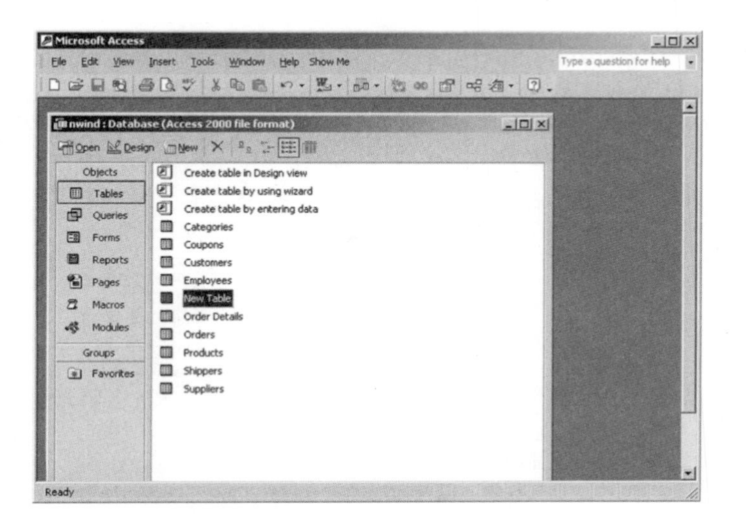

Visual C# .NET

1. In the form designer, double-click Make Table.

   Visual Studio adds the event handler to the code.

2. Add the following code to the event handler:

```
ADODB.Connection cnADO;
ADOX.Catalog mdb = new ADOX.Catalog();
ADOX.Table dt = new ADOX.Table();

cnADO = create_connection();
cnADO.Open(cnADO.ConnectionString, "", "", -1);
mdb.ActiveConnection = cnADO;

dt.Name = "New Table";
dt.Columns.Append("TableID", ADOX.DataTypeEnum.adWChar, 5);
dt.Columns.Append("Value", ADOX.DataTypeEnum.adWChar, 20);
dt.Keys.Append("PK_NewTable", ADOX.KeyTypeEnum.adKeyPrimary, "TableID");
mdb.Tables.Append(dt);

MessageBox.Show("Finished", "Make Table");
```

3 Press F5 to run the application, and then click Make Table.

The application adds the table to the nwind database and displays a message box telling you that the new table has been added.

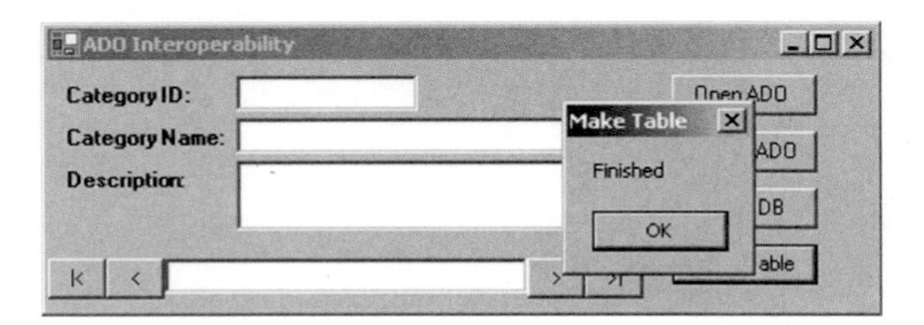

4 Close the message box, and then close the application.

5 If you have Access, open the nwind database and confirm that the new table has been added.

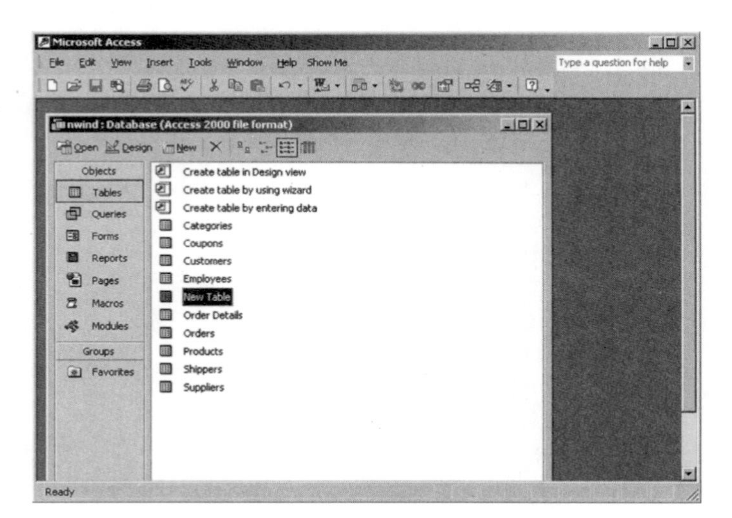

Chapter 16 Quick Reference

To	Do this
Establish a reference to an ADO or ADOX library	On the Projects menu, choose Add Reference, select the library from the COM tab of the Add Reference dialog box, click Select, and then click OK
Create an ADO object	Reference the ADO COM library, and then use the usual .NET Framework object creation commands
Load data from an ADO Recordset to a ADO.NET DataSet	Use the DataAdapter's *Fill* method: `myDataAdapter.Fill(DataTable, ADORecordset)`
Update an ADO Recordset	Open the ADO Connection and ADO Recordset, and then use the *AddNew* or *Update* methods
Create a database using ADOX	Use the ADOX Catalog object's *Create* method: `adoxCatalog.Create`
Add a table to a database using ADOX	Use the *Append* method of the ADO Catalog object's Tables collection: `adoxCatalog.Tables.Append(adoxTable)`

About the Author

Rebecca M. Riordan

With almost 20 years' experience in software design, Rebecca M. Riordan has earned an international reputation as an analyst, systems architect, and designer of database and work-support systems.

She works as an independent consultant, providing systems design and consulting expertise to an international client base. In 1998, she was awarded MVP status by Microsoft in recognition of her work in Internet newsgroups. *Microsoft ADO.NET Step by Step* is her third book for Microsoft Press.

Rebecca currently resides in New Mexico. She can be reached at rebeccar@attglobal.net.

Index

O

P

Q

R

S

T

U

V

Brace Drill and Bit

Brace drills, developed in the Middle Ages, operate on the same principle as levers. A user, placing one hand on the top and the other hand on the grip, operates the drill with a stirring motion. The "cranked" shape provides leverage and increases the turning force. Bits and augers are attached to the brace with the chuck, the metal mechanism at the bottom.*

At Microsoft Press, we use tools to illustrate our books for software developers and IT professionals. Tools are an elegant symbol of human inventiveness and a powerful metaphor for how people can extend their capabilities, precision, and reach. From basic calipers and pliers to digital micrometers and lasers, our stylized illustrations of tools give each book a visual identity and each book series a personality. With tools and knowledge, there are no limits to creativity and innovation. Our tag line says it all: *The tools you need to put technology to work.*

Proof of Purchase

Use this page as proof of purchase if participating in a promotion or rebate offer on this title. Proof of purchase must be used in conjunction with other proof(s) of payment such as your dated sales receipt—see offer details.

Microsoft® ADO.NET Step by Step

0-7356-1236-6

CUSTOMER NAME

Microsoft Press, PO Box 97017, Redmond, WA 98073-9830

MICROSOFT LICENSE AGREEMENT

Book Companion CD

IMPORTANT—READ CAREFULLY: This Microsoft End-User License Agreement ("EULA") is a legal agreement between you (either an individual or an entity) and Microsoft Corporation for the Microsoft product identified above, which includes computer software and may include associated media, printed materials, and "online" or electronic documentation ("SOFTWARE PRODUCT"). Any component included within the SOFTWARE PRODUCT that is accompanied by a separate End-User License Agreement shall be governed by such agreement and not the terms set forth below. By installing, copying, or otherwise using the SOFTWARE PRODUCT, you agree to be bound by the terms of this EULA. If you do not agree to the terms of this EULA, you are not authorized to install, copy, or otherwise use the SOFTWARE PRODUCT; you may, however, return the SOFTWARE PRODUCT, along with all printed materials and other items that form a part of the Microsoft product that includes the SOFTWARE PRODUCT, to the place you obtained them for a full refund.

SOFTWARE PRODUCT LICENSE

The SOFTWARE PRODUCT is protected by United States copyright laws and international copyright treaties, as well as other intellectual property laws and treaties. The SOFTWARE PRODUCT is licensed, not sold.

1. **GRANT OF LICENSE.** This EULA grants you the following rights:
   a. **Software Product.** You may install and use one copy of the SOFTWARE PRODUCT on a single computer. The primary user of the computer on which the SOFTWARE PRODUCT is installed may make a second copy for his or her exclusive use on a portable computer.
   b. **Storage/Network Use.** You may also store or install a copy of the SOFTWARE PRODUCT on a storage device, such as a network server, used only to install or run the SOFTWARE PRODUCT on your other computers over an internal network; however, you must acquire and dedicate a license for each separate computer on which the SOFTWARE PRODUCT is installed or run from the storage device. A license for the SOFTWARE PRODUCT may not be shared or used concurrently on different computers.
   c. **License Pak.** If you have acquired this EULA in a Microsoft License Pak, you may make the number of additional copies of the computer software portion of the SOFTWARE PRODUCT authorized on the printed copy of this EULA, and you may use each copy in the manner specified above. You are also entitled to make a corresponding number of secondary copies for portable computer use as specified above.
   d. **Sample Code.** Solely with respect to portions, if any, of the SOFTWARE PRODUCT that are identified within the SOFTWARE PRODUCT as sample code (the "SAMPLE CODE"):
      i. **Use and Modification.** Microsoft grants you the right to use and modify the source code version of the SAMPLE CODE, *provided* you comply with subsection (d)(iii) below. You may not distribute the SAMPLE CODE, or any modified version of the SAMPLE CODE, in source code form.
      ii. **Redistributable Files.** Provided you comply with subsection (d)(iii) below, Microsoft grants you a nonexclusive, royalty-free right to reproduce and distribute the object code version of the SAMPLE CODE and of any modified SAMPLE CODE, other than SAMPLE CODE, or any modified version thereof, designated as not redistributable in the Readme file that forms a part of the SOFTWARE PRODUCT (the "Non-Redistributable Sample Code"). All SAMPLE CODE other than the Non-Redistributable Sample Code is collectively referred to as the "REDISTRIBUTABLES."
      iii. **Redistribution Requirements.** If you redistribute the REDISTRIBUTABLES, you agree to: (i) distribute the REDISTRIBUTABLES in object code form only in conjunction with and as a part of your software application product; (ii) not use Microsoft's name, logo, or trademarks to market your software application product; (iii) include a valid copyright notice on your software application product; (iv) indemnify, hold harmless, and defend Microsoft from and against any claims or lawsuits, including attorney's fees, that arise or result from the use or distribution of your software application product; and (v) not permit further distribution of the REDISTRIBUTABLES by your end user. Contact Microsoft for the applicable royalties due and other licensing terms for all other uses and/or distribution of the REDISTRIBUTABLES.

2. **DESCRIPTION OF OTHER RIGHTS AND LIMITATIONS.**
   - **Limitations on Reverse Engineering, Decompilation, and Disassembly.** You may not reverse engineer, decompile, or disassemble the SOFTWARE PRODUCT, except and only to the extent that such activity is expressly permitted by applicable law notwithstanding this limitation.
   - **Separation of Components.** The SOFTWARE PRODUCT is licensed as a single product. Its component parts may not be separated for use on more than one computer.
   - **Rental.** You may not rent, lease, or lend the SOFTWARE PRODUCT.
   - **Support Services.** Microsoft may, but is not obligated to, provide you with support services related to the SOFTWARE PRODUCT ("Support Services"). Use of Support Services is governed by the Microsoft policies and programs described in the

user manual, in "online" documentation, and/or in other Microsoft-provided materials. Any supplemental software code provided to you as part of the Support Services shall be considered part of the SOFTWARE PRODUCT and subject to the terms and conditions of this EULA. With respect to technical information you provide to Microsoft as part of the Support Services, Microsoft may use such information for its business purposes, including for product support and development. Microsoft will not utilize such technical information in a form that personally identifies you.

- **Software Transfer.** You may permanently transfer all of your rights under this EULA, provided you retain no copies, you transfer all of the SOFTWARE PRODUCT (including all component parts, the media and printed materials, any upgrades, this EULA, and, if applicable, the Certificate of Authenticity), **and** the recipient agrees to the terms of this EULA.
- **Termination.** Without prejudice to any other rights, Microsoft may terminate this EULA if you fail to comply with the terms and conditions of this EULA. In such event, you must destroy all copies of the SOFTWARE PRODUCT and all of its component parts.

3. **COPYRIGHT.** All title and copyrights in and to the SOFTWARE PRODUCT (including but not limited to any images, photographs, animations, video, audio, music, text, SAMPLE CODE, REDISTRIBUTABLES, and "applets" incorporated into the SOFTWARE PRODUCT) and any copies of the SOFTWARE PRODUCT are owned by Microsoft or its suppliers. The SOFTWARE PRODUCT is protected by copyright laws and international treaty provisions. Therefore, you must treat the SOFTWARE PRODUCT like any other copyrighted material **except** that you may install the SOFTWARE PRODUCT on a single computer provided you keep the original solely for backup or archival purposes. You may not copy the printed materials accompanying the SOFTWARE PRODUCT.

4. **U.S. GOVERNMENT RESTRICTED RIGHTS.** The SOFTWARE PRODUCT and documentation are provided with RESTRICTED RIGHTS. Use, duplication, or disclosure by the Government is subject to restrictions as set forth in subparagraph (c)(1)(ii) of the Rights in Technical Data and Computer Software clause at DFARS 252.227-7013 or subparagraphs (c)(1) and (2) of the Commercial Computer Software—Restricted Rights at 48 CFR 52.227-19, as applicable. Manufacturer is Microsoft Corporation/One Microsoft Way/Redmond, WA 98052-6399.

5. **EXPORT RESTRICTIONS.** You agree that you will not export or re-export the SOFTWARE PRODUCT, any part thereof, or any process or service that is the direct product of the SOFTWARE PRODUCT (the foregoing collectively referred to as the "Restricted Components"), to any country, person, entity, or end user subject to U.S. export restrictions. You specifically agree not to export or re-export any of the Restricted Components (i) to any country to which the U.S. has embargoed or restricted the export of goods or services, which currently include, but are not necessarily limited to, Cuba, Iran, Iraq, Libya, North Korea, Sudan, and Syria, or to any national of any such country, wherever located, who intends to transmit or transport the Restricted Components back to such country; (ii) to any end user who you know or have reason to know will utilize the Restricted Components in the design, development, or production of nuclear, chemical, or biological weapons; or (iii) to any end user who has been prohibited from participating in U.S. export transactions by any federal agency of the U.S. government. You warrant and represent that neither the BXA nor any other U.S. federal agency has suspended, revoked, or denied your export privileges.

DISCLAIMER OF WARRANTY

NO WARRANTIES OR CONDITIONS. MICROSOFT EXPRESSLY DISCLAIMS ANY WARRANTY OR CONDITION FOR THE SOFTWARE PRODUCT. THE SOFTWARE PRODUCT AND ANY RELATED DOCUMENTATION ARE PROVIDED "AS IS" WITHOUT WARRANTY OR CONDITION OF ANY KIND, EITHER EXPRESS OR IMPLIED, INCLUDING, WITHOUT LIMITATION, THE IMPLIED WARRANTIES OF MERCHANTABILITY, FITNESS FOR A PARTICULAR PURPOSE, OR NONINFRINGEMENT. THE ENTIRE RISK ARISING OUT OF USE OR PERFORMANCE OF THE SOFTWARE PRODUCT REMAINS WITH YOU.

LIMITATION OF LIABILITY. TO THE MAXIMUM EXTENT PERMITTED BY APPLICABLE LAW, IN NO EVENT SHALL MICROSOFT OR ITS SUPPLIERS BE LIABLE FOR ANY SPECIAL, INCIDENTAL, INDIRECT, OR CONSEQUENTIAL DAMAGES WHATSOEVER (INCLUDING, WITHOUT LIMITATION, DAMAGES FOR LOSS OF BUSINESS PROFITS, BUSINESS INTERRUPTION, LOSS OF BUSINESS INFORMATION, OR ANY OTHER PECUNIARY LOSS) ARISING OUT OF THE USE OF OR INABILITY TO USE THE SOFTWARE PRODUCT OR THE PROVISION OF OR FAILURE TO PROVIDE SUPPORT SERVICES, EVEN IF MICROSOFT HAS BEEN ADVISED OF THE POSSIBILITY OF SUCH DAMAGES. IN ANY CASE, MICROSOFT'S ENTIRE LIABILITY UNDER ANY PROVISION OF THIS EULA SHALL BE LIMITED TO THE GREATER OF THE AMOUNT ACTUALLY PAID BY YOU FOR THE SOFTWARE PRODUCT OR US$5.00; PROVIDED, HOWEVER, IF YOU HAVE ENTERED INTO A MICROSOFT SUPPORT SERVICES AGREEMENT, MICROSOFT'S ENTIRE LIABILITY REGARDING SUPPORT SERVICES SHALL BE GOVERNED BY THE TERMS OF THAT AGREEMENT. BECAUSE SOME STATES AND JURISDICTIONS DO NOT ALLOW THE EXCLUSION OR LIMITATION OF LIABILITY, THE ABOVE LIMITATION MAY NOT APPLY TO YOU.

MISCELLANEOUS

This EULA is governed by the laws of the State of Washington USA, except and only to the extent that applicable law mandates governing law of a different jurisdiction.

Should you have any questions concerning this EULA, or if you desire to contact Microsoft for any reason, please contact the Microsoft subsidiary serving your country, or write: Microsoft Sales Information Center/One Microsoft Way/Redmond, WA 98052-6399.

PN 097-0002296